ENCYCLOPEDIA OF
STAGE LIGHTING

ENCYCLOPEDIA OF STAGE LIGHTING

Jody Briggs

Foreword by Scott Nolte

McFarland & Company, Inc., Publishers
Jefferson, North Carolina, and London

LIBRARY OF CONGRESS CATALOGUING-IN-PUBLICATION DATA

Briggs, Jody, 1945–
Encyclopedia of stage lighting / Jody Briggs ;
foreword by Scott Nolte.
p.   cm.
Includes bibliographical references.

ISBN 0-7864-1512-6 (illustrated case binding : 50# alkaline paper) ∞

1. Stage lighting — Encyclopedias.   I. Title.
PN2091.E4B66   2003
792'.025 — dc21   2003007619

British Library cataloguing data are available

Cover photograph ©2002 Comstock

Manufactured in the United States of America

*McFarland & Company, Inc., Publishers
Box 611, Jefferson, North Carolina 28640
www.mcfarlandpub.com*

CONTENTS

FOREWORD

When a scenic designer creates a set, the evidence is obvious: there are readable blueprints, remnants of lumber, cloth and steel, and a structure of some sort on the stage. Likewise, a costume designer might leave behind a stack of research into period dress or sketches of dressed characters, yards of fabric, and a rack of costumes and accessories. Even the sound designer leaves behind tapes of live musicians and the creation of sounds from experimentation with physical objects, as well as compact discs or hard drive files. Yet there is barely a trace of the lighting designer except for perhaps a stack of colored gels or a grid of instruments — hardly a hint at the lighting design's many facets or potential. Like an alchemist, the lighting designer blends science and creativity to create something altogether new — coordinated illuminations that evoke emotion, beauty, and surprise along with serving the audience's need to see the action on stage.

Since 1992 Jody Briggs and I have been partners in well over two dozen productions in two very different theatres and the renovation of a theatre facility — myself functioning as artistic director or director of a production and Mr. Briggs as lighting designer. Directors are accustomed to ask-ing for the moon — or light like it — and designers are likely to smile but internally choke. In the case of Mr. Briggs, one is more likely to get a patient "okay," a series of follow-up questions, references to the script (and perhaps to the play's original or significant productions), and options lead-ing toward a design that serves the text and the production's needs.

Whether we were working on a stark white set for *Terra Nova*, where the Antarc-tic setting denied all shadows (the script suggested locales in England too), or for *Wait Until Dark* with a pitch-black scene illuminated by a match or an opened re-frigerator, Mr. Briggs was my ally in cre-ating memorable, even startling images that guided the viewer's perception of the play scene by scene.

The content of this book reflects Mr. Briggs' years of working with numerous directors and hundreds of productions in professional and educational settings and nearly every theatre configuration imagin-able. The breadth of that experience has crafted a reference book that refines our knowledge of theatrical and lighting terms and techniques.

Whether you are a lighting profes-sional, a student or another theatre professional, the encyclopedic format allows for easy referral to specific terms, making it easier to access new information or to quickly review concepts for inclusion in projects.

The legacy of Mr. Briggs' knowledge is in your hands as you use this book as a tool to improve your work.

Scott Nolte
Producing Artistic Director
Taproot Theatre Company
Seattle, Washington

PREFACE

I find myself in the unusual position of not expecting that anyone will read this book — at least not in its entirety — as it is a reference book. Someone whose opinion I have always valued wanted to know whether anyone could actually learn anything about stage lighting from a book like this. Of course they can. Starting at "A" and working your way toward "U" and "V," however, may not be best course of action, as the entire discussion of sightlines (Viewing an Event) and the discussion of the four components of visibility, which are very basic concepts, find themselves at the end of the alphabetic sorting process.

Instead let me suggest that if you are interested in taking this kind of journey, you should start with the Lighting Design Process entry, which is a guide to the articles that follow the design process from the first reading of the script to the lighting designer's duties at the final preview. You should do this in a very leisurely way allowing yourself to be led away on peripheral journeys. Whenever a more detailed discussion of something is to be found elsewhere, take the detour. Search out unfamiliar terms or concepts. Also be sure to read Lighting an Object or Area, The Eye, Lighting Special Problems, and Old Wives'

Tales. Only then would it make sense to read articles from A to Z.

This book is designed for reference use rather than as an instructional manual. The reader will find entries that define terms, discuss equipment and techniques, and provide information on a wide range of topics associated with stage lighting. The entries are designed to be informative and descriptive; they are not meant to guide a lighting designer toward one method or piece of equipment.

For the purposes of this discussion, any event that involves performers and an audience is going to be called a theatrical event, and the buildings constructed to house such events will have two (possibly three) kinds of space within them: the playing area, where the actors perform and its immediate backstage support areas (which include dressing rooms, the greenroom, fly galleries, crew rooms, current prop or scenery storage rooms as well as the control booth and sound and light areas); the audience areas, which include the house where the audience sits (sometimes simply called the audience), their lobbies, their restrooms and their ticket office; and finally, (and optionally) various administration work areas or shops. Such buildings are typically called theatres (sometimes play-houses to distinguish them from movie theatres). Educational institutions sometimes choose to call them auditoriums, but this has a different connotation as it always suggests a proscenium space used mostly for speakers and lecturers and assemblies of various kinds and only occasionally used or equipped for the performing arts. Also, the term auditorium has a second meaning that is synonymous with the house, meaning that part of the theatre complex where the audience sits to watch the performance. Movies are shown in movie houses (movie theaters) and now commonly in a cineplex or multiplex.

Configurations of Theatres

Theatres are not all built from the same model, and as a result their theatrical presentations cannot be lit the same way. It is essential to become familiar with the various configurations of theatres so that what is possible in a proscenium or a modified proscenium theatre does not become confused with what might be possible in, say, a thrust theatre.

For the initial part of this discussion, it is helpful to consider the playing area to be rectangular and assume that the audience will sit on one, two, three or four sides of this playing area. The playing area is often raised up from the level of the audience on some kind of staging, but regardless of whether it is raised or not, it is always referred to as the stage.

If you were watching a staged event from a stationary location, which for convenience we'll call the front, and everyone else was viewing it from the front also, this would be called a proscenium theatre configuration. This is one of several words borrowed from the Greeks, and it literally means "in-front-of" or "before the scene house," and refers to the raised porch area

(what we would now call an apron) where the principal actors in an ancient Greek drama performed, while the chorus sang, danced and made music in a pit area lower down and closer to the audience called the orchestra. In a modern day proscenium theatre, the audience views the stage action from the front only, and the house is separated from the stage by a proscenium arch that usually has a closable curtain right behind it that can hide the stage from view (although this technique has become unfashionable and as a result the curtain, assuming it still exists, is often left open). The performance support areas in such a theatre are commonly called interchangeably either the backstage or offstage areas. "Offstage areas" suggests the wings to the left and right, which is technically more accurate as there is almost never any area directly behind the backwall of the stage proper (cyc or backwall of the theatre) that might qualify as being backstage.

If the audience viewed the event from two sides, the theatre would be either a corner stage configuration (audience on two adjacent sides) or a bowling alley stage (*British:* transverse stage) where the audience sits on two opposite sides. If the audience viewed the event from all four sides, then we would say the theatre was an arena or theatre-in-the-round configuration. If the audience viewed the action from three sides, this would be a thrust configuration. When the corner stage configuration is placed in the center of one of the theatre walls rather than a corner, it is more typically called a modified proscenium. The other way of looking at the modified proscenium configuration is to imagine a thrust theatre where the audience curves around only a quarter of the playing area (i.e. 90 degrees of separation between the end seats in the first row, as explained below).

In the prototype proscenium configuration, the two end seats in the first row point in parallel lines (0 degrees of sepa-

Styles of theater configurations. *Top row, left–right:* proscenium, corner stage, and bowling alley. *Bottom row, left–right:* modified proscenium, thrust theatre, and theatre-in-the-round.

ration between them) toward the stage. In the prototype thrust situation, the end seats are at 180 degrees of separation and face each other. In both the corner stage and the modified proscenium, the end seats are at 90 degrees of separation.

The audience has a never-failing ability to determine where the front is despite anyone's best efforts to conceal it. On a bowling alley stage or a theatre-in-the-round situation, where locating the front is theoretically more difficult, the location of the control booth at the front and the backstage areas toward the back or the orientation of the show's particular set, are usually good indicators of where the front might be. In situations where the audience is allowed to sit where they please (festival seating as opposed to the more common assigned seating with various ticket prices reflecting a hierarchy of good, better, best places to sit), they will rush toward where they perceive the front to be and will sit toward the front of that section or at a point where their eye level will be about as high as that of a seated actor.

Black Box theatres, which get referred to occasionally, are supposed to be capable of assuming any configuration and, as the name suggests, are usually painted a uniformly dark color.

Acting Areas

Imagine that you are an actor standing in the center of the playing area facing toward your front, which in this case means toward the center section of the audience. The name of your location is "center-center." If you moved forward or back, you would be moving either downstage or upstage. These terms date back to the days when the stage floor was slanted (raked) toward the audience to allow them to see better. It worked but it was difficult to stand on or place furniture on, and over time it became simpler to rake the audience seating instead. Your right and left are called stage right and stage left (*British:* opposite prompt and prompt side). If you move directly right, you are in a position called right center. If you move directly left, you are in a position called left center.

If you move up or down stage, you are either up center or down center. If you move diagonally down and to your right, you are down right. The other diagonal locations are up right, up left and down left. This is a standard nine-area proscenium stage, whose eight directions correspond to the 45 degree compass points. In a proscenium house, the first downstage row (or zone) of areas is called in-one, the first two downstage rows are called in-two, and anything using the full stage is usually said to be played in-three — although an unusually deep stage could theoretically have an in-four or possibly an in-five depending on how many wing masking pieces there are. All would typically be backed by a curtain or a drop or scenic piece of some kind, as they not only define portions of the stage that need to be lit, but they specify places in the scenery where the actors can enter and exit. (For example, "You enter from left in-two, but you leave right in-one.")

In a proscenium theatre, the first archway that separates the audience from the stage is called the proscenium arch, and it is usually made of whatever the walls of the building are made of (usually plaster or a plaster-like product). When scenery is placed on the stage, an x-y grid made up of the centerline (left and right) and a setting-line (upstage and downstage) are used to locate the various scenic pieces. The back (upstage side) of the proscenium archway (the plasterline) is traditionally used as the x-axis. Where there is a fire curtain, the setting-line may be designated to be at the back of the metal channel that contains the fire curtain. The fire curtain is often still called the asbestos curtain or the asbestos for short, even though asbestos is no longer used as the fire-resistant material.

Often there are other archways that separate and mask in-two and in-three parts of the stage. They consist of a vertical piece on each side that is usually soft goods (i.e. drapery), and they are called legs regardless of whether they are draperies or a solid material. The top part is called a border drop or border for short, and together with the two legs they make up a portal. The first border that masks the front curtain is called the teaser and the first set of legs is called the tormentors.

Often the floor of the stage may be trapped, which is to say, it has one or more trapdoors in it to allow exits and entries from down below (the trap room). The stage surface is traditionally called the deck and is traditionally made of wood or a wood-like product. The front curtain is sometimes called the main or act curtain or, if it seems ornate enough, the grande drape. Immediately in front of the front curtain is the apron area (if small) or the forestage area (if larger). Unless the forestage is very large, the footlight trough will be right on the edge of the apron. The orchestra pit (if any) will be directly downstage and will typically be sunken into the floor so that sitting or standing musicians or their tallest instruments (such as a double bass or a harp or an upright piano) will not be seen above the level of the stage floor. There will typically be a sound-deadened, half-high wall (pit wall) separating the orchestra pit from the first row of the audience, who are said to be sitting in the orchestra (*British:* stalls). There may or may not be an au-

Proscenium plan view

dience balcony (*British:* dress circle), sometimes called a gallery or tier in older American accounts and often referred to by those in the building trades as a mezzanine, which reflects the fact that it only partially covers the lower audience space. If there is another balcony, it is usually called the second balcony (*British:* upper circle) and so forth.

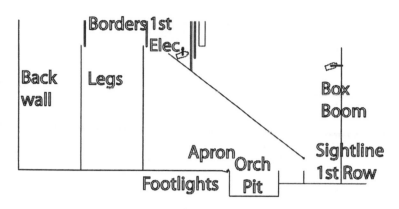

Proscenium cross-sectional view

The balcony fronts are often used as light hanging locations called collectively the balcony rail positions. The instruments are not actually hung on the decorative rail often seen atop such a balcony separation wall but use instead a special light-hanging pipe on the front of the balcony wall, out of sight of most of the audience. As recently as 100 years ago, the sidewalls of the audience were lined with audience boxes, which were luxury seating for small parties of 4–12, a tradition still alive and well in some venues to this day. The boxes are mostly gone now, having been replaced by lighting equipment (box booms). The ceiling above the house is often a false one that is suspended from the actual roof of the building, thus providing an attic space with walkways for houselight maintenance. There are often lighting slots or coves (open gaps in the false ceiling) where stage instruments have a clear light path to the stage but are concealed from the view of the audience. There may also be coves or slots in the audience sidewalls to conceal light hanging positions there.

The rigging of scenery in a late 1800s proscenium house was done following the model of the sailing ships of the time with wooden battens, pulleys, ropes, sandbags as counterweights, and tie off rails that had removable belaying pins and these were called hemp houses to distinguish them from the more modern (mid–1900s) counterweight houses where steel pipes were suspended by wirerope attached to counterweight arbors and operated by a continuous pull rope and a locking rail. In either kind of house, it is not uncommon to have line-sets and battens every foot going upstage. These are traditionally numbered from downstage to upstage, and it is understood that being that close together, some may get blocked by the others.

Stage scenery used to mean painted cloths (canvas or muslin) called drops or backdrops, and there would be a stack of them upstage, but some would also be backing the in-one and in-two locations. Drops would either (1) be attached to wooden battens top and bottom or (2) be tied to a pipe batten at the top with another pipe that would weigh down the lower hem or (3) be framed drops (in which case they would be attached to a frame [usually wood] on all four sides), or (4) have two hemisphere-shaped battens on the bottom sandwiching the cloth and they would be rolled up and down (roll drops). There were often cyc footlights either recessed into the floor directly in front of the drop stack or placed on the floor and concealed from audience view by a short scenery piece called a groundrow. A flat-floor show that played in front of a series of drops was called a wing-and-drop show, and was the norm up until the late 1800s when painted scenery began to fall out of fashion and box sets and hard scenery of all kinds became more popular.

A box set was, by definition, an interior set that had a back wall and two sidewalls. The sidewalls typically trapezoided inward as they went upstage for sightline reasons. The walls commonly had jogs or offsets in them (for both interest and stability), and they were made of flats, which were framed canvas wall units. At the extreme downstage edge, the sidewalls were attached to wing pieces called returns, and the returns were typically kept 3–6 feet upstage of the curtain line so that the downstage areas of the set could be lit from behind the curtain. The area between the curtain and the returns typically concealed lighting positions, both vertical booms and a horizontal pipe position. The light pipe located right behind the front curtain was called the first electric, and it was often a bridge (catwalk) rather than a pipe (*British:* perch or perch position). The second electric, and so forth were further upstage. Instruments placed on the pipes were traditionally numbered from stage left-to-right and front-to-back from the perspective of someone standing on stage looking toward the audience.

If the set had doors and windows (as it usually did), they would have individual backings that would have to be lit and whose purpose was to show what would have been seen outside the window or door when it was open. Especially in the early days of the 20th century, the box set was topped by a ceiling. Over time it became obvious that the ceiling was preventing lighting units from being hung above the playing area, and the ceilings gradually ceased to be used.

The Day the Theatres Changed

Before the 1960s, "theatre" meant a proscenium theatre with a stage at one end and an audience that sat out in front. The stage was usually raised and had a curtain and the machinery for raising and lowering scenery from a high storage location (the flies). This kind of theatre architecture came about in part because of the movement toward realism in the theatre that started around the 1880s.

Part of the attraction of going to the theatre was to see all the impossible things companies tried to portray onstage. They built a ship on stage. They had a real car onstage. It really rained. It looked just like a real sunset. The stage was covered with a huge rock outcropping that they actually climbed and sat on top of. This of course was mostly before motion pictures started photographing real locations.

The motion pictures were able to do realism and special effects of all kinds even better. Movie tickets were cheap, there was often more than one feature, and nationally known stars could be seen. Movies could afford to have casts of thousands because they only paid their actors for the day or days when they were actually being filmed. In a live theatre, the cast actually performed every night, and a large cast meant a large payroll for the entire run of the show. Movie theatres only needed one projectionist and two or three front-of-house staff. Many prints could be made from a single motion picture master so that the movie could be shown in many locations around the country simultaneously. The Broadway musicals, which were the most successful live theatre shows of their time, had huge casts and huge technical budgets. Many people wondered how live theatre could possibly ever compete with the motion pictures, and how it could afford to exist outside of

New York and the major theatre centers along the East Coast.

The Guthrie theatre, built in Minneapolis in the early 1960s, served as an example of how this might be possible. The secret lay in emphasizing what live theatre did best, which was evoking the imagination of the audience, and minimizing what it didn't do well at all, which was special effects and representational scenery of all kinds. The idea was to return to something similar to what Shakespeare had used. Shakespeare had done plays that took place in many different indoor and outdoor places, and he had done it with little or no scenery in a thrust theatre like the Globe. The audience had imagined the locations. Producers liked this idea a lot, and the idea caught on and spread nationwide and became known as the regional theatre movement.

The thrust configuration opened up two additional sides for audience viewing, which either meant the theatre was going to be able to seat more people or it would be able to seat the same number of people, but they would have seats that were closer to the stage, and they would see better and the experience would be more intimate. The Guthrie theatre was a 1400-seat house, which was generally considered a large theatre. It would have been difficult to seat that many people in a conventional proscenium configuration without the seats being objectionably far away.

While this architecture provided more acceptable seats, it completely eliminated the front curtain and all the equipment for flying scenery. The side section audiences were going to see the action against the background of the opposite side section audience. There could be low furniture but no scenery except along the backwall. This greatly reduced the material costs associated with scenery building and storage as well as the substantial labor costs of building and shifting. The day of imagined scenery had arrived again.

Some theatres tried seating the audience on all four sides of the playing area (arena or theatre-in-the-round). Such a system required even less scenery and even more people could be seated close to the action since this configuration provided a whole other side on which to sit. Many theatres were initially built this way, but the idea did not really catch on. While almost any play could be done on a thrust stage because there was still a fourth wall for doors, windows, large furniture items and so forth, in an arena situation, it was not immediately apparent how even a simple piece of business, like having the actor use his house key to enter through the front door could be accomplished. There was no place on the stage itself that a full-height door could be placed without causing sightline problems, and the fire department was not about to allow scenery in the audience egress aisles.

One of the lesser-known facts is that this change in the theatre architecture would not have been as successful (or even possible) without the technological improvements to stage lighting. The invention of the ellipsoidal reflector spotlights made it possible to control where the light went in a way that had not previously been possible. This in turn made it possible to keep spill light out of the audience better than had ever been possible in the past.

Also, with the front curtain gone, it was the lighting that signaled the audience that one scene was over and a new one would be starting as soon as some backstage scene change (now an onstage scene change) had been completed. Now the electrics department had to turn off the lights (blackout) at the end of scenes, provide scene change lights of some kind, and bring the lights up for the next scene.

The regional theatre movement, of course, had no effect on the existing proscenium theatres in New York City or on any of the out-of-town houses that catered to touring shows from New York, as they all continued in the traditional way. It was an entirely new movement (like the little theatre movement of the 1920s and 1930s had been) to create regional theatres that would exist independent of the theatres on the East Coast circuit.

Any lighting book written prior to 1960 will discuss lighting in a proscenium situation because no other configuration existed at that time.

About six sets of abbreviations are used repetitively: Alternating and direct current are commonly referred to as AC and DC. Wire gauge (thickness) is either noted as #14 wire or 14 AWG (American Wire Gauge). An MF is a multiplying factor and a CF is a correction factor (both decimal numbers). Feet and inches are either "ft" and "in" or ' and ". Fifty footcan-

dles of light is written as 50 fc. There are basically three kinds of electrical connectors in common use: Stagepins are abbreviated 2P&G, Parallel Blade Ground are PBG and Twist-Lock Ground are TLG. In reference to pipes, ID refers to the inside diameter and OD refers to the outside diameter. Also, there are three-letter lamp codes, like HPL and FEL, and wire types identified by codes like SPT and THHN. These are not abbreviations for anything, nor do they have any longer, more written-out form.

In the real world, the lighting designer can be of either gender, as can the director, the stage manager and everyone else, and this is the way you find it presented here. In some topics, the lighting designer will be a "she," and in others, a "he."

THE ENCYCLOPEDIA

À VISTA **(scene change)** — A scene change that takes place in plain sight of the audience as opposed to behind a curtain. Although it is sometimes done in the dark (ambient light of the exit signs and aisle lights), it is more common for it to be lit by scene change lights, which attempt to provide light for the actors and technicians while denying it to the audience. See SCENE CHANGE LIGHTS for a more detailed discussion.

ABERRATIONS, CHROMATIC — A rainbow pattern of color rings seen at the edges of a pool of light as it falls on the floor, which is caused by the edges of the lens acting as a prism instead of a lens. This was one of the many problems experienced with the early plano-convex instruments, that was later solved by both the fresnel and ellipsoidal instruments.

ABERRATIONS, SPHERICAL — Stray beams of light caused either by imperfections in the lens or improper alignment of the lamp and the reflector so that the lens does not focus all of the light hitting it to a single focal point.

ABSORPTION — When light hits an opaque object, some of it is reflected and some is absorbed and turned into heat. A surface that reflects 80 percent of the light hitting it absorbs 20 percent. Light colors are more reflective than dark colors. In the context of stage lighting, dark colors in the scenery and costumes are generally preferred because they make a light colored face more visible. See WHITE COLOR PROBLEM and BOUNCE LIGHT PROBLEM for a more detailed discussion.

AC — Abbreviation for ALTERNATING CURRENT.

ACCENT LIGHTS or SPECIALS — See SPECIALS, KINDS OF.

ACCESSORIES (lighting) — Anything that is added to an instrument on an occasional basis is an accessory. With the exception of the gel frames, most of these accessories are relatively heavy and make the front of the instrument heavier, so the yoke locking handles need to be locked down tightly or the whole instrument can tip downward during a performance and, in extreme cases, the barndoor or other accessory can fall out. It is considered good practice to make sure that all heavy accessories are equipped with a dog clip or ring so that they can be clipped to the safety cable on the instrument. Gel frames and other accessories used in a proscenium house where they will be hidden from view are often left as unpainted shiny metal. Accessories intended for use where they can be seen by the audience are typically painted black if they do not already come that way from the factory. Accessories that go in the color frame slot include:

Barndoor: This provides either two or four hinged flippers that work like horse blinders to prevent (in a crude and fuzzy way) light from hitting certain objects in its path. The whole unit can usually be rotated to line up with something but the cut-offs themselves will still be rectangular, rather than trapezoidal as is the case

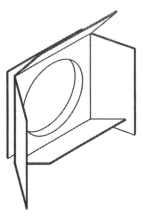

Barndoor

with the framing shutters contained within ellipsoidals. Barndoors are typically only used on fresnels, parcans and photographic floods, and they typically cost anywhere from a quarter to half the cost of the instrument itself.

Color Extender: This is really a short tophat (described below) that has been improved by the addition of a gel slot on its outboard end. When used correctly, it extends the life of color media by keeping it cooler. A gel frame con-

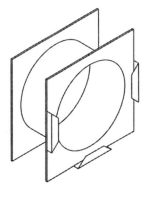

Color Extender

taining a heat shield is put in the first gel slot of the ellipsoidal (the one closest to the lens), the color extender is put in the outermost slot and the actual color is put into the gel slot at the far end of the color extender. These can also be used as if they were tophats. In the motion picture industry, they are called *color stand-offs* and are typically used on 2k and 5k instruments where the heat would otherwise severely shorten the life of the color.

Donut: This is an aperture reducer made out of gel frame material (metal or cardboard) that is designed to go in the gel slot of an ellipsoidal to cut flare and sharpen a gobo pattern. It can be used in a fresnel, parcan or photographic flood as a circular mat but the effect will be fuzzy and soft-edged.

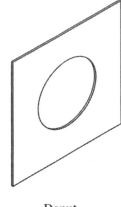

Donut

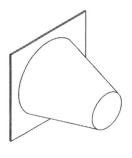

Funnel

Funnel: (1) A true funnel looks like a funnel that is bigger at the gel slot end and smaller in front where the light comes out. This is a vintage item that is not manufactured anymore. A donut and a tophat would achieve the same effect. (2) Funnel was an alternate name for tophats and referred to as such in the 1948 Century Lighting Company catalog.

Gel frame: This is a frame made out of a heat resistant material (metal or cardboard) that opens like a manila folder (with a round hole in it) to sandwich the color media in-between and prevent it from slithering out. They usually come with the instrument at the time of purchase but can get lost or damaged. In those circumstances where the gel has to be changed during the show, it is customary to use split-prong paper

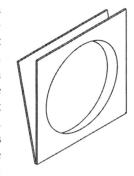

Gel frame

fasteners in the two top holes and to have the 2d gel in a separate frame similarly fastened. The fasteners are usually omitted when the gel is put in once at the beginning of the run of a show and expected to stay in place until closing night or until it fades.

Iris: This is an infinitely variable round aperture accessory that is usually intended to go in the gobo slot of an ellipsoidal to make it work more nearly like a follow-spot. Irises were originally made to go in the gel slot of any lensed instruments, but the iris is a relatively expensive accessory and it works only crudely and fuzzily in the gel slot in a way that could be duplicated by a homemade do-nut, described above. Modern irises that go into the gobo slot produce a sharp, hard-edged light that justifies their considerable expense.

Iris

Louvers: This was a vintage accessory that looked like a gel frame equipped with Venetian blinds that could be set to contain and direct the light either horizontally or vertically depending on how it was inserted into the gel slot.

Mats: This is a generic term that refers to any flat piece of metal or cardboard with an unusual shaped hole in it. This is typically a homemade item, often fashioned out of aluminum foil. Think of it as a donut with an irregular (rather than circular) opening.

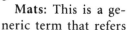
Louver

Spill Rings: As the name suggests, this is a device like a 1–2" tophat that has other smaller cylindrical rings nested inside, and its purpose is to reduce spill to the side. This was a vintage accessory that was out of production and out of fashion

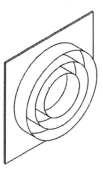
Spill Ring

for a while, but now is back. Built-in spill rings have always been a part of beam projectors.

Tophat: Also called *high hats, snoots* and *funnels.* They slide in the gel slot and add a cylinder of usually 6–8" length to the front of the instrument to cut off stray spill to the sides and in the process create a more nearly round light. They are cheaper but less versatile than barndoors. They are typically used on fresnels and parcans but occasionally get used on an ellipsoidal to cut down flare to the side of the lens or to keep a view of the hotspot out of the eyes of the audience.

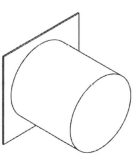
Tophat

Visors: This is a homemade item (made out of flashing or aluminum siding) that works like a barndoor with only one top leaf. It is used primarily on an eyelevel light from the side to keep it out of the eyes of the audience on the far side of a thrust or in-the-round stage. In a proscenium situation could be used on a backlight that threatened to be in the eyes of a front row audience.

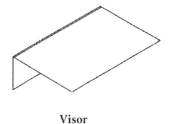
Visor

ACCESSORIZING— The process of adding the gel frame, pattern (if any) and any additional accessory like a barndoor, iris or tophat to the instrument. This is either done when the instrument is hung (during a light hanging session) or as part of the focus. There is usually more time available at the hanging session than at the focusing session, so doing it at the time the instruments are hung and cabled usually makes most sense.

ACHROMATIC— In the context of a lens, it means that it transmits the light without breaking it into colors, which is ideally what all theatre lenses should do. As a purely practical matter, because different colors are different wavelengths, it is not possible for a lens to put all colors in focus equally well. Usually the commercial lenses are made to focus the red-yellow range best on the assumption that light that is blue in color is harder for the eye to perceive as light and will ultimately go unnoticed.

ACL — Abbreviation for AIRCRAFT LANDING LIGHT.

ACTING AREA — (1) The stage portion of theatre as opposed to the audience or backstage spaces. (2) The names of the areas on an empty stage (UL, CC, DL, etc), as presented in the Preface to this book. See AREAS, ACTING, LIGHTING and CONTROL for a more detailed discussion.

ACTION — In the context of a cue sheet, this is a description of what the operators' hands do after the "go" is called. It is often written as a series of fractions with the dimmer number over the level. There will typically be a main action followed by a series of after actions each separated by a "then" to indicate the sequence.

ACTOR LIGHTING — Any lighting that is intended to light the actors as opposed to the cyc or other parts of the set. Usually, it is meant to refer to the arealighting, but it could also include all actor specials and washes.

ADAPTER (also spelled *adaptor*) — Anything that adapts or changes from one kind of electrical connection to another. (1) Lamp socket adapters. There is a full range of screw-type adapters that adapt downward (mogul to medium screw, medium screw to

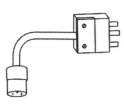

intermediate candelabra, and intermediate to miniature candelabra) and a few that adapt upward (miniature to intermediate, etc). There is a heat sink adapter that allows a GLC lamp to be

Adapter

used in the place of an HPL and there may be others. (2) Extension cords that adapt one connector-type to another, mostly from whatever the theatre uses to PBG. If for example, the theatre typically uses stagepin connectors but needs to use a household table lamp, then there would need to be an adapter to go from the nearest female stagepin outlet to the PBG male of the lamp. These are often only about a foot long, but economically it would make more sense for them to be 5–10' long so that they could not only adapt but could extend to the appropriate outlet and so that they could be combined (with a reverse type) to make up additional extension cords. A 5' PBG male adapter combined with a 5' PBG female adapter could be used to make a 10' extension cord that either had stagepin connectors on the ends and PBG connectors in the middle or PBG connectors on the ends with the stagepins being in the middle. See FLOOR CIRCUITS for a more complete discussion of how to deal with practical lights and electrical appliances used onstage.

ADDED CUES — Cues that have been added since the numbering was assigned. The cues are typically assigned numbers after the lighting designer has met with the director (final lighting meeting), so new cues created after that point are considered added. Let's say there are now two extra cues between cue 8 and cue 9. Before there were computer lightboards, these might typically have been called cues 8a and 8b, but now it would be more common to call them cue 8.1 and 8.3, as this is the way most computer boards handle added cues. Notice that 8.2 was deliberately skipped in case another added cue might be needed.

ADDITIVE COLOR MIXING — The process by which one color of light is superimposed over another on a surface. See COLOR MIXING for a more detailed discussion.

ADJUSTABLE WRENCH (Brit *adjustable spanner*) — A generic term for any adjustable wrench, which could theoretically include such antiquities as the monkey wrench (some-

Adjustable wrench

times called a Ford wrench) or a pipe wrench. In practice, the only kind of adjustable wrench ever used for positioning stage lighting instruments is a crescent wrench. Crescent was originally a tradename but is now in common usage to describe that particular style of wrench, regardless of who the manufacturer might be. See WRENCHES for a more detailed discussion.

ADVANCE— This was whatever the board operator had to do in order to set up for the next cue. This included replugging, resetting presets or whatever else might have been required. With computer lightboards, there typically is no set-up or advance.

AFTER ACTIONS— In the context of manual and preset lightboards, the main action (what happened right after the "go" was called) would involve the master handle coming up to a level or the crossfader creating a transition. After this had occurred, there might be a series of after actions, where dimmers or sliders were adjusted manually ever so gently to avoid the after actions being noticed.

AFTER-IMAGES— An optical illusion where spots of color can be seen. See COLOR ANOMALIES for a more detailed discussion.

AIM-AND-FRAME— Slang for the focusing session, which follows the hanging session (the HANG-AND-GANG).

AIR GAP— The open space between electrical contacts, as in an arc light.

AIRCRAFT LANDING LIGHT (Abbr. ACL)— The most recognizable in a series of sealed beam lamps manufactured for other industrial purposes that have found their way into the theatre. The aircraft landing light usually works on 28 volts, and, therefore, they are customarily hooked up as a

series of four to work on 120 volts. They are typically PAR 36 or PAR 46 lamps, produce a very intense and narrow beam of light, and have a short 10–25 hour lamp life. They are most commonly seen in rock concerts to simulate the effect of a light curtain. There are also 12-volt versions (locomotive lights) that can be hooked together as a series of ten lamps.

AISLE LIGHTS— The running lights, required by building codes everywhere, that are left on during performances to light the audience aisles, which light all the way from row ends to the exits. These are typically built into the side of the last seat of a row or are recessed into stair risers or sidewalls of the house as appropriate to the situation.

AISLES, LIGHTING OF— See LIGHTING SPECIAL PROBLEMS/Aisles and Runways.

A-LADDER— A portable trestle ladder with a huge footprint that looks like an inverted "Y." See HANGING POSITIONS, GETTING TO for a more detailed discussion.

A-Ladder

ALCOVES, LIGHTING OF— See LIGHTING SPECIAL PROBLEMS/Alcoves.

ALIGNING (lamps)— This theoretically refers to the alignment of the lamp with the reflector in all instruments. While early versions of fresnels or plano-convex instruments sometimes had such adjustments on the lamp carriage so that the reflector could move forward or back, this now mainly refers to ellipsoidals where the lamp is centered in the reflector and is run inward or outward until the desired evenness of field is obtained. The older method (no longer commonly in use on new equipment) involved mounting the socket on a triangular metal plate. The metal triangle was then attached to the lamp cap by three bolts. Loosening the bolts allowed the lamp to move inward, and also the balance between these three bolts controlled where the center of the light would be. There was then a fourth bolt that exerted pressure between the triangle and lamp cap to effectively lock the socket into position. The newer method involves one joystick-like knob that centers the lamp and another screw-type knob that screws the lamp inward or outward, which is both faster and simpler.

Lamp alignment was once a problem that might need to be dealt with at each lamp change. Now the lamps are made to more exacting standards, and while alignment has to be checked periodically, in many cases the alignment can be left as it came from the factory.

ALLEN SCREW— A headless bolt with a recessed hexagonal hole in the top, designed to be tightened by hexagonal drivers (Allen wrenches). These are commonly used as setscrews on reflector adjustments, where they exist.

ALLIGATOR CLIP— Once a tradename but now generic, it refers to any electrical connector with two serrated jaws that are spring loaded to clamp onto things. Automotive jumper cables have large alligator clips and

small continuity testers have small ones. Short jumper cords with alligator clips on both ends are used for temporary connections of small bells, buzzers and miniature lights for testing or demonstration purposes. They are mostly used for low voltage battery connections, but can also be used for 120-volt AC testing, and while they grip well enough for testing, they are not secure enough (or safe enough) for use on equipment used in a show.

ALOFT— In-the-air. It refers to instruments that are already hung in position or to the electrician who has climbed up, or has been raised up, to where the instruments are.

ALTERNATING CURRENT (Abbr. AC)— Opposite of direct current. This is electrical current that changes direction (120 times per second, i.e. 60 complete cycles). AC current can travel longer distances using thinner wires without line loss, and its voltage can be transformed up or down. Most of the country was electrified late enough (in the 1920s and 1930s) so that the current was AC. It was really only the big cities on the East coast that had first installed DC current that eventually had to switch to AC. The large East coast theatres in New York, Boston, Philadelphia and Washington DC had no early incentive to switch from the DC current they already had. Stage lights and resistance dimmers worked equally well on AC or DC. Carbon arcs ran exclusively on DC. It wasn't until after the Second World War, when the advantages of the autotransformer dimmers became apparent that there was much of a reason to change. For rental houses that did not actually own any dimmers there was even less incentive.

ALUMINUM REFLECTOR— Reflectors were originally made of mirrored glass, which made them fragile, heavy and expensive. In the mid–1930s, the Alzak process was developed whereby aluminum could be given a durable, virtually maintenance free, mirror-like finish.

ALZAK REFLECTOR— Named after the trademarked process, it was an aluminum reflector as described above.

Alligator Clip

AMBIENT LIGHT— In the context of stage lighting, this is any light that was not deliberately put there. While ambient could be used to describe the reflections off the silver tea service or the bounce light from the white sheets on the bed, it is usually reserved for situations where the source is more mysterious. In a blackout, the aisle and exit lights or orchestra lights are often the source of ambient light. When projections are involved, any unwanted light hitting the projection surface is considered ambient light.

AMERICAN NATIONAL STANDARDS INSTITUTE (Abbr. ANSI)— The organization responsible for three-letter lamp codes like EGE and HPL that completely describe the base, envelope, filament, voltage, color temperature, and so forth of the lamps.

AMERICAN STANDARD CODE FOR INFORMATION INTERCHANGE (Abbr. ASCII)— In terms of computer lightboard technology, a show that can be written as an ASCII file can be read by a number of word processing and spreadsheet programs, thus enhancing the possibility that it can be put into a more readable format.

AMERICAN WIRE GAUGE (Abbr. AWG)— A standard that uses the Brown and Sharp system of wire diameters relative to their current carrying ability. #12 AWG with an ampacity of 20 amps is the most common size used in the theatre. #14 AWG is rated at 15 amps. The higher the gauge number, the lower the capacity of the wire. Orange outdoor extension cords are typically #16 AWG (6–13 amps) and household appliance lamp cord is #18 AWG (3–6 amps). The current carrying capacity of wire is also affected by the material used (copper or aluminum) the length of the run and the ambient temperature, so although the gauge number is a good indicator of the capacity, each type of wire needs to be looked up in the appropriate tables of the code book.

AMPACITY— The current carrying capacity of an electrical device as measured in amps. Amps can be converted to watts by multiplying by voltage. Thus a toaster that draws 10 amps uses 1200 watts of 120-volt power. See ELECTRICITY for a more detailed discussion.

AMPERE (Abbr. AMP)— A measure of the rate of flow of electrical energy named after French physicist André Ampere (1775–1836). Rate of flow of liquids is measured in gallons-per-minute. Rate of flow in electricity is measured in electrons-per-second, and 6.28 billion billion (that's 628 with 16 trailing zeroes) electrons-per-second is equal to an ampere.

ANGLE— One of the eight variables of light. It is used generically to describe the direction from which the light comes. This is usually measured from the point of view of the lit subject where eyelevel front is 0 degree of pan and 0 degree of tilt. It is common to use one of the 26 ideal hanging positions by name or number to describe the angle, i.e. position two, which is front-right on the golden ring. See VARIABLES OF LIGHT and HANGING POSITIONS, IDEAL for a more complete discussion of this subject.

ANGLE OF INCIDENCE— This is the angle between the line formed by a ray of light hitting a point on the surface of an object and a line from that point normal to (perpendicular in all directions to) the surface. Where fronts of faces are the surface, a line normal to the end of the nose runs to the eyelevel front position. If one were interested in the tops of heads, the normal line would run from the end of the nose to the top-dead-center position. In stage lighting work, we are mostly concerned with the fronts of faces and so the angle of incidence is always equal to the throw angle of the instrument.

ANGLE OF REFLECTION— The question at hand is when a ray of light strikes a mirrorlike surface like a watch face, in

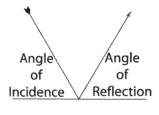

Angle of Incidence   Angle of Reflection

Angle of reflection

what direction will the light be reflected? For flat mirrors, the angle of incidence will equal the angle of reflection, so if a desktop were a mirror surface that was lit from golden ring front, then the reflected light would aim at the golden ring back position. See REFLECTION, LAWS OF for a more detailed discussion.

ANGSTROM— A distance measurement that is a ten billionth of a meter. It is named after Swedish astronomer A. J. Ångström (1814–1874), thus the visible spectrum between 380–780 nanometers could be expressed as 3800–7800 angstroms (or angstrom units).

ANODE— The positive terminal of an electric source like a carbon arc spotlight.

ANSI— Abbreviation for the AMERICAN NATIONAL STANDARDS INSTITUTE, which is the organization responsible for three-letter lamp codes like EGE and HPL.

ANTEPROSCENIUM— This is an archaic and seldom used word for the area in front of the proscenium, and would more commonly be referred to as the front-of-house lighting instruments or positions.

ANTICIPATING A CUE— Taking a cue early to compensate for the slow response time of the lightboard. Anticipating a cue is very dangerous in a live theatre situation. *Taking a lead* achieves the same thing without the same proneness to error.

APERTURE— Any circular opening in the lens system, but most commonly (1) the gate of an ellipsoidal, (2) the opening in an iris or (3) the opening of the lens as stopped down by a donut.

APPEARANCE OF WHITE LIGHT— This is used to describe lights that are ever so slightly tinted with color so that an average audience member will not be aware of the underlying color. While the light appears to be white, the slight differences in colors assist in revealing three-dimensional shapes (faces mostly) and assist in making scenes look different from each other and assist in making colors in the set and costumes more vibrant.

APPIA, ADOLPHE (1862–1928)— A Swiss designer who was mostly interested in Wagnerian operas. He wrote two books: **Staging of Wagnerian Drama** in 1895 and **Music and the Art of the Theatre** in 1899. He believed that the scenery should be three-dimensional and that the light should reveal the three-dimensional shape of both the scenery and the actors. He thought that footlights were a "monstrosity" and should be eliminated. He believed that the light should change like a musical score with the emotions of the actors. There were, he said, two kinds of light: shadowless soft light as from the borderlights or footlights (*verteiltes Licht*) and form-revealing light that casts shadows (*gestaltendes Licht*) that would create the plasticity. It was his idea that the lighting would artistically unify the whole production. Gordan Craig and he are considered the guiding voices of the *new stagecraft* movement of the 1920s that was adopted by American designers such as Lee Simonson and Robert Edmund Jones.

ARC or ARCING— This refers to electricity jumping a gap to create a flash or spark of light. This is the underlying principle of arc welding and arc lighting, as discussed next.

ARC LIGHT— Instruments where the light is created by electricity jumping an air gap between two carbon rods. Although the science dates back to Sir Humphry Davy in 1808, the technology did not find its way into common use in the theatre until well past 1860. In the United States, the earlier limelight technology had barely begun to be used before it was replaced by arc lights, which were less expensive to

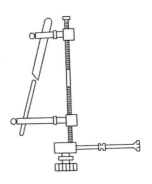

Arc light mechanism

operate. Carbon arc followspots are still in common usage in those places where followspots are still in use. Louis Hartmann circa 1910 talks about the arc lights as being one of the main sources of light from the light bridge where there would be as many operators as there were arc lights.

ARCING PROBLEM— In the context of lamps, when their contact points do not make good electrical contact with their sockets, they become blackened by the arcing. This is typically caused by the springs in the prefocus socket contacts weakening with age. Sometimes the springs can be worked a few times to rejuvenate them. If the sockets contain cup shaped receptacles like those in a TP-22 ellipsoidal socket, then the leaves of the cup can often be bent together to make more positive contact. In the context of connectors, the split pins on stagepin connectors can be spread apart with a knife blade. The prongs on PBG and TLG connectors can be twisted slightly to make better contact with their receptacles. If the problem persists, the socket or connector has to be replaced.

AREA CONTROL— This is the opposite of color control and refers to how the show would be hooked-up if there were not enough dimmers for there to be one for every instrument, which was the case for many years. In a situation where there were six areas being lit by two instruments-per-area but controlled by only six dimmers, area control would assign a dimmer to each area, but color control would assign three dimmers to one color and three dimmers to the other color.

In real life, the problem would be closer to this: "There are 12 autotransformer dimmers of 2.4-kilowatt capacity that can be used for arealighting. There are 3 rows of 3 areas with 4 instruments-per-area for the front 6 areas and 3 per area for the upstage areas. The instruments are 750 watts. Areas 1, 4 & 5, and 7 are used alone. How could this be hooked up?" Each of the 2.4 kw dimmers can handle up to three 750-watt instruments. Thus

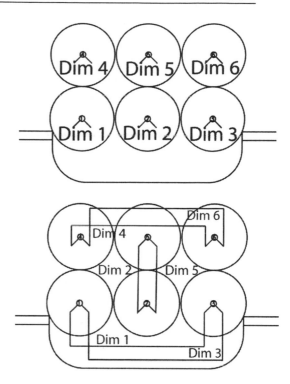

Top: Area control; *bottom:* Color control

areas 7, 8 and 9 can each have their own dimmers. Area 1 (used alone) will need two dimmers and areas 4 and 5 (taken together as a control area) will require three dimmers. This leaves four dimmers to handle areas 2, 3, and 6, and probably the most sensible plan would be to have the backlights for all three areas on one dimmer and the remaining three lights for areas 2, 3, and 6 each on a separate dimmer.

While this used to be a hugely important part of any design plan, it has mostly been made obsolete by the current practice of assigning each circuit its own dimmer. See MATRIX SYSTEM for a more detailed discussion.

AREALIGHTS— The instruments used for arealighting as opposed to those used for specials. Because they are typically used in almost all scenes of the play to light faces, they tend to be tints that are slight variants of white light. Common practice, unless there is a compelling reason to do something else, is to use three instruments-per-area upstage of the proscenium (where a backlight is possible) and four instruments-per-area downstage. This is the modern adaptation of Stanley McCandless' method. Unlike a series of washes, the centers of the areas for all systems are the same, and it is implied that each area can be controlled separately.

When the costumer tells the cast they will all be dressed in leotards but the accessories will be fantastic, it means everyone only gets one costume. When the lighting designer announces that she plans to use arealighting, she is saying that the whole show will be lit with only one set of lights, but the specials will be so fantastic that no one will notice.

Is it ever possible to do a show without any arealights at all? Is it possible to have more than one set of arealights? What (if any) alternate systems might there be?

If the play takes place full stage where there is no need to control parts of the stage separately, then it could be lit by a series of directional washes. Using the guidelines above, there would be three washes upstage of the proscenium and four downstage. The only real difference would be that area centers would not have to line up for all systems, and this might save two or three instruments.

As an alternate plan, if the play consisted of only two scenes, and if there was enough equipment, then each scene might be lit by a separate sub-group of instruments. If both scenes used the full stage, this would probably be the equivalent of having two complete sets of arealights, which is called *double-hanging*. Theoretically, there's also triple-hanging, quadruple-hanging and so forth, but mostly no one has enough instruments for any of that. Most theatres hardly have enough equipment to double-hang on one side only. If anyone actually had enough equipment to light every scene in the show separately, they would find that a great number of the lights were duplicating what other lights were doing, and most of the original looks could be achieved with one set of very neutral arealights with some fantastic specials for each scene.

The reason that the arealighting system has survived so long is because it makes the scenes look different from each other but is very economical on equipment used.

AREAS (Acting, Lighting and Control) — **Acting areas** refer either to the generic UL, CC, DL, etc of the empty stage or to a list of the areas where the director intends to have actors performing. If there is going to be an actor atop the 6' high fence, then this becomes an acting area, which may or may not be able to be lit by the same lights that will light someone on the floor in front of the fence. If the director plans to have any of these acting areas isolated and used alone, they then become individual control areas as will be explained shortly.

Lighting areas refer to how the stage will be broken into smaller pieces for lighting purposes, usually the size of which are determined by the kind of instrument being used. While the play may be set in several locales, the same set of lights (arealights) typically lights all locales, so it is not uncommon for there to be one set of regular areas that most efficiently covers an empty stage and other sets of special areas which are tailored for use only in certain scenes, all areas being the coverage diameter of a single instrument.

Control areas refer to collections of lighting areas that will be controlled together as a unit. If for example the entire playing area were used for each scene of a flat-floor show, then only one control area would be required. If it took nine individual lighting areas to light this space, then the one control area would consist of these nine areas working as one. If the design called for three-instruments-per-area (left-front, right-front and backlight), then there would typically be three submasters on the lightboard (one for each color or direction commonly referred to as a *system*) needed to provide light to this one control area. If the director were to announce twelve acting areas that needed to be individually lit, then there would be twelve control areas and twelve lighting areas (well, at least twelve, assuming that none of the control areas were bigger than what a single lighting area could cover).

AREAS, DIVIDING THE STAGE INTO (regular) — A part of the stage lit and controlled individually, but when used collectively with all the other areas, will light the entire stage.

How big these areas should be is still a hotly debated issue. Although Stanley McCandless was not the first person to discover that it was neither possible nor desirable to light the stage as one big area, lighting in areas is at the core of his method. He favored three areas across the front of the stage and as many rows going back as necessary, which most commonly meant six (possibly nine) areas. It must be remembered that this was in 1932, and theatres meant proscenium theatres, and the instruments he was proposing using were fresnels whose beam size was adjustable.

In more open staging situations (thrust and in-the-round), fresnels have limited uses because their light cannot adequately be controlled. Zoom ellipsoidals are significantly more expensive than their fixed lens counterparts and typically the quality of light, sharpness of the optics and efficiency are not as good either. As the fixed lens models only come in about six sizes, it would not be unusual to have to divide the stage into areas, not based on some ideal concept, but rather based on the beam spread of the available equipment, and this is the more common situation that the designer finds himself in.

In this situation where the instrument defines the size of the area, it becomes a problem of how many circles of this size would it take to fill the entire area of the stage. The circles represent the beam portion of the cone of light (side-to-side) as it hits the nose plane (the portion from center-of-the-beam to the point where the light had decreased to 50 percent). See PHOTOMETRIC DATA for more detail. The beam circles need to touch so that the 50 percent brightness of one circle can touch the 50 percent brightness of its neighbor and return that location to 100 percent brightness. At least that is the theory.

An instrument from a golden ring position does not, of course, produce a circle of light but instead produces a teardrop shaped light on a horizontal surface. The back end of the teardrop is quite dim and difficult to use effectively, so it is common practice to discuss circles of light based on the side-to-side measurement of the beam and to ignore the back tail and the somewhat blunted front, which is not perfectly round.

The circles-in-the-rectangle method is really only a starting point. There are at least a dozen other critical factors that need to be taken into account. Inasmuch as some of them depend on each other, they are usually considered more-or-less in the order presented here:

Staggering: When nine postage stamps are lined up in three rows of three each, the entire rectangular area beneath them is covered. When the stamps are replaced by quarters or some other round object, there will be four interior gaps (where four quarters meet). In lighting terms, these are four areas that are potential dark spots.

If the middle row of areas were pushed a half diameter to the right, this would significantly close up this gap. The middle row would now consist of a half circle on each end and two whole circles in the middle straddling the centerline of the rectangle. The back two rows would also compress forward, reducing the front-to-back coverage.

The question under discussion is whether this is a good idea or not. If it is a good idea, might there ever be a situation where that would not be true?

The fact that it provides better coverage of the potential dark spots is a good thing. The fact that the middle row will end at 100 percent bright and the others at only 50 percent bright is a bad thing. We're ignoring for the moment that putting a shutter cut into the hot center of a beam could potentially burn out a shutter. On a modern instrument adjusted for flat-field, this probably wouldn't be a problem, but the stage usually looks better when the edges are falling away from peak brightness, rather than building toward it. The fact that the middle row does not have a single center area may also prove to be a problem as center stage is a likely acting area. Also the two half circles will each require the same number of instruments as a full circle even though they won't cover as much space, which means instead of nine areas there now would be 10.

On rectangular stages, staggering areas is almost always a bad choice. On trapezoidal stages or curved-front stages, it may be exactly what is needed. In a proscenium theatre, the sidewalls of the set often trapezoid inward as they go upstage, which reflects the diminished sightlines. Forestages often trapezoid inward as they extend out into the house. In either case, a staggered 3–4–5 pyramid-shape of areas might be the only way to end each row at approximately the same brightness, and a special area might need to be added at the CC position to isolate that area. On a curved-front stage, staggering the center column of lights a half diameter downstage, which will compress or reduce the coverage width as the left and right column move inward toward center, may be exactly what is needed to cover the added depth at the center front.

Even or Odd Areas: If the size of the instrument beam is used to determine how many areas each row will contain, then this could be an even or an odd number (usually 3, 4 or 5). Directors typically favor having a column of areas straddling the centerline, so given a choice, odd numbers of areas generally work out better.

Hanging Positions: Up until now the assumption has been that all areas would be lit by the same kind of instrument from an ideal golden ring position, in which case the beam coverage (the circle) would always be the same size. Sometimes different instruments are used for the front-of-house positions or the available hanging positions will deviate from the ideal angle or (even when the angle is the same) the position might be further from the stage. In all of these cases the throw distance will be different, and as a re-

sult, the circle of light coverage will be different also.

Circles vs Partial Circles: Consider a row of three lighting areas. Each area is 100 percent bright at its center and 100 percent (50+50 percent) bright at the point where two areas meet. On the side edge of the stage, however, the brightness will have dropped to 50 percent. On a stage where no one uses the stage all the way to its perimeter edges, this might be exactly what was needed. Where the edges are playing areas of equal importance, then half circles might be exactly what was wanted. We've already mentioned that true half circles don't usually look as good as ⅝–¾ of a circle, where the light is 75–90 percent bright on the edge. In the interests of making that happen, might it be possible to let the beams overlap rather than just touch, which brings us to our next discussion point, *compression.*

Ideal Side-to-Side Overlap: Up until now it has been assumed that the beams would touch. The question now under discussion is whether this is in fact the ideal side-to-side overlap point. When beams are allowed to overlap instead of just touch the areas are said to be compressed.

Imagine a circle divided into thirds by two interior rings. This represents a field of light that is 0 percent bright on its edge, 50 percent bright at its first ring (by definition of flat-field), 75 percent bright (assumed) at its 2d ring and 100 percent bright at its center. Were there two of these circles, the question would be one of how to overlap them so that the light would be most even all the way across. To save you the trouble of working out the math, the brightness will vary within a 25 percent variance from the point where the 50 percent point of one beam edge touches the 50 percent beam edge of the other (100 percent–75 percent, as has been discussed before) and the first beam can continue to overlap the second one up to the point where the 50 percent point of the first beam is at the 75 percent point of the other one (variance between 125 and 100 percent). Where the two beams are further apart or

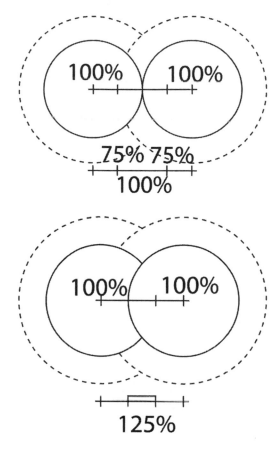

Top: Start of the ideal overlap; *bottom:* End of the ideal overlap.

closer together than this, the variance will be higher (more than 25 percent), so there is an ideal plateau that extends from beams touching to the edge of one beam being halfway to the center of the adjacent beam as illustrated above.

Some people like to talk about instrument overlap in terms of the fields rather than the beams. In that case, the ideal plateau of overlap is between the field edge of one instrument (its 0 percent point) and the 75–100 percent points on the other adjacent field.

Ideal Upstage-Downstage Overlap Point: There is none. Where an instrument lights an area from a golden ring position, it is always brightest on its near side (frontlights brightest on the front edge), dimmest on its far side and not all that different on the left-right edges. The near edge is always brighter than

the center-of-light because the throw distance is shortest. Where areas are laid front-to-back, they are laid like shingles where the 100 percent point of the new area is laid anywhere along the decreasing back tail of the existing area. Wherever the overlap point turns out to be, it will be 100 percent brighter than the place it rests on.

In a thrust or in-the-round situation, these rows of areas that overlap each other as they go upstage will be seen by the side-section audience as sidelights, and as a result the ideal overlap going upstage should duplicate whatever was acceptable from side-to-side across the front, which in most cases is either beams touch or overlapping (up to the point of full compression, i.e. the beam edge of one touches the 75 percent point of its neighbor as described above).

Lighting the Perimeter from the Inside: It's a thrust theatre and an actor is on the SL edge of the stage facing inward. What lights her face for the audience facing her and seated SR? What lights her are what are called perimeter-from-the-inside lights, which do what the name suggests and light actors who are on the very edge (perimeter) of the stage and are facing inward (toward center stage). The problem here is that after the light has hit the actor, it keeps on going and spills out into the audience. To help prevent this, it is not unusual to allow the light to come in from a steeper than normal angle, something closer to 60 degrees than 45 degrees. We're ignoring the fact that if a properly sized light moat had been put in place, this would not be necessary and the lighting would, as a result, have been better.

Perimeter Lighting from the Outside: Up until the present, we have been discussing lighting faces at the nose plane. What then lights the actors' neck-down body for the audience looking at actors who are facing them? To do this the perimeter areas from the house side need to be opened up more, but they are already as wide open as they can be. The easiest method of dealing with this is to assume that the stage area will be larger than it really is, as will be explained shortly as part of the *formula*. This will have the effect of opening up the perimeter areas while keeping all areas the same size.

Control Areas and the Set: It is one thing to decide how to light a flat-floor playing area without considering how dramatically the scenery might affect this. Each distinctive section of the set will usually have to be a lighting control area, and this may add more areas than just the minimum required to cover the whole stage as a unit. In other words, it would be a mistake to finalize the process of breaking the stage into areas until one has seen how the actors move on and otherwise use the set.

Effect of Adding More Areas: Let us take the example of a 24' · 32' playing area divided in 8' areas, which works out perfectly to four rows of three. While the division worked out perfectly to 12 areas (which at four-instruments-per-area would require 48 instruments), had the director demanded full light all the way to the edges of the stage, then an extra area in each direction would have been required. That means that instead of four rows of three, there would now be five rows of four with all rows and columns ending on partial circles with the remaining areas partially compressed. Now the total number of instruments required would almost double, going from 48 to 80.

Areas That Overlap: Take the situation where the in-one areas, i.e. downleft, downright and downcenter, are all used alone at various times and used together at other times. Assume that each area is lit by four instruments. Typically, the sidelights and backlight will be at a 60 degree angle to reduce spill. Both front and backlights will have shutter cuts left and right to prevent spill into the neighboring side areas. This is a very different situation from lighting the in-one area as a unit, in which case, the sidelights would be at golden ring positions, shuttered only on US and DS sides and the frontlights and backlights would be allowed to overlap from side-to-side. Often the best solution is to simply light the whole in-one area from scratch as a *special area*. At the very

least, some kind of additional wash would have to be employed to soften the two places where areas meet.

A Formula: In a situation where arealights are to be compressed, it is often hard to figure out where the centers of the areas will be. There is a formula that will make this easier. Suppose the proscenium opening is 34' and the beam coverage (based on the instrument) has been determined to be 8'. It should be apparent that this will require five areas across and they will have to be compressed somewhat. Five areas uncompressed (beams touch) would cover 40'. Five areas at full compression would cover 75 percent of that or 30'.

First, decide what size of partial circles would be best on the side perimeter. Let's say ¾ circles. This means that each row end will overlap the stage outline by a quarter of a beam diameter (2' on each end equals 4' total).

Second, add the overlap to the stage width (4 + 34=38') and divide by the number of areas to arrive at the size for each area (38' ÷ 5 = 7.6').

Third, the center area will be on the centerline. The next set of areas will be 7.6' to each side and the last set will be an additional 7.6' to the side, which puts their centers 15' from centerline and 2' from the edge of the stage, and the 8' beam will be 6' onstage and overlap by 2' to the sides just as it is supposed to. Since the front is a perimeter and needs to overlap, the center points of all areas will be 2' US from the front of the stage, which puts 6' of beam onstage and leaves 2' of the beam and all of the field to light the neck down portion of the performers' bodies.

AREAS, NUMBERING OF— It is traditional, dating back to when proscenium theatres were the only kind of theatres there were, to number the areas (and everything else onstage) from SL to SR and from downstage to upstage so that for someone with her back against the back wall of the stage could read it like a book (left to right, DS to US). Back then, the lightboards were manual and usually located in the SR wings and the lighting designer often operated the lights. Now the lighting designer spends most of her time seeing the show from the front, and it makes more sense to number areas (and everything else) house left (HL) to house right (HR). Front-of-house positions are still numbered from the proscenium outward so that the 1st cove would be closer to the stage than the 2nd cove, and so forth. Where the theatre is not proscenium, it would be more usual to number from the back of the house (HL to HR) toward upstage, regardless of where the proscenium might be (assuming there is a proscenium as there would be in a thrust situation).

AREAS, SPECIAL— One set of arealights typically covers the whole stage, and the individual areas can be used alone or in various combinations. These are the regular arealights. In situations where these are not adequate (they usually either spill too much into neighboring areas or are not the right size or the right color), it will be necessary to light an area separately as a special area. See the discussion above in AREAS, DIVIDING THE STAGE INTO/Areas that Overlap for an example of how the entire DS area might need to be lit as a separate special area.

ARENA LIGHTING— See LIGHTING, KINDS OF.

ARM— Short for SIDEARM, which is a hardware item that permits instruments to hang sideways from a pipe.

ASBESTOS— A heat insulating material once used in a fabric or paper form as a border drop behind lighting pipes, once used as a fire curtain material, once used to insulate the cords of lighting instruments. Now due to health concerns, it is obsolete, having been replaced by Teflon as a high-heat wire insulation and various fiberglass products for fire curtain and fire cloth uses.

ASCII— Abbreviation for AMERICAN STANDARD CODE FOR INFORMATION INTERCHANGE, which provides a computer format so that plain text can be shared between software programs.

ATMOSPHERE— See MOOD.

AUDIENCE SEPARATION CONVENTION— This is one of several theatrical conventions or traditions. The idea itself dates back to Angelo Ingegneri in the mid–1500s, although it was not possible to fully realize it at that time. It has been traditional, ever since it was possible (from the time of Henry Irving circa 1850 onward), for the audience to be kept in darkness while the stage and the performers were lit. The theory is that the audience would otherwise become distracted by what others of their members were doing. There is some justification for this as audience behavior cannot be predicted, and audience members can forget they are in a public place in more-or-less plain sight. Also at certain points in theatrical history, the audiences brought baskets of fruit or vegetables to either eat during the performance or to hurl at the performers depending on whether they felt they were getting a full measure of entertainment. Now food or drinks are wisely not permitted in the seating areas, and keeping the house dark hopes to suggest to the audience that they are there only to watch but not to interact except at the curtain call. In any event, it is a theatrical/performance art tradition, but is not the tradition at sporting events where it is considered perfectly all right to light up the spectators to the same extent as the performers.

AUDIENCE'S RIGHT TO SEE— When the audience pays for a ticket, they are entering into a contract with the theatre, and they have certain unspoken rights. None of these are written down anywhere but all are generally understood. The one that relates to the lighting and sound is that they have paid for the right to both hear and see the performers regardless of where they sit, and they will be seriously unhappy if this proves not to be true.

AUTOFOLLOW— Also called a *follow* or *follow-on cue*, this refers to a second cue that typically starts to run when the first one finishes. On a computer lightboard this is the most common and most flexible way to do *part cues*. The follow time is typically counted from the button push of the first cue. See LIGHTING CONTROL/Computer Memory Lightboard for a more detailed discussion.

AUTOMATED (fixtures or lights)— Another name for moving lights, usually of the motorized yoke kind rather than moving head intelligent lights.

AUTOTRANSFORMER DIMMER— An outdated (but still used) manual dimming technology that limited voltage to the instruments by means of a continuously variable transformer. See LIGHTING CONTROL, Manual Lightboards for a more detailed discussion.

AWG— Abbreviation for AMERICAN WIRE GAUGE, a system that correlates the diameter of wire to its current carrying capacity.

AXIAL MOUNT— Refers to the lamp in an ellipsoidal instrument being inserted along the centerline of the ellipse. The older style of ellipsoidals (chimney top) was the result of the lamps being so large. Once the lamp technology improved, it was then possible to mount the lamps axially, which created a smaller hole in the reflector and made for a brighter more even field. Once one knows what to look for, it is easy to tell the two styles apart without having to open them up to look inside.

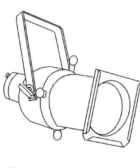
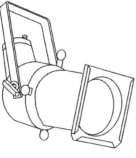

Top: Axial mount ellipsoidal; *bottom:* Chimney top ellipsoidal

AZIMUTH— An artillery term for left/right movement, now more commonly called *pan* in the context of stage lighting.

BABY SPOT— Once a tradename given to a Kliegl Bros product starting in 1906, it came to describe any low wattage (less than 500 watts) plano-convex instrument of a particular shape. They were typically more-or-less cube shaped with a rounded back. The lens could be removed to create a floodlight or could in a later period be replaced by a fresnel lens. They were enormously popular primarily because of their relative compactness.

Baby spot, circa 1936

BACK— Also called a back button, it is a computer lightboard command that returns to the state of lighting of the previous cue in some default time. See LIGHTING CONTROL/Computer Memory Lightboards for a more detailed discussion.

BACK END— In the context of a remote control lighting system, it refers to the dimmers that actually dim the lights and are located at a remote location from the stage (usually the basement).

BACKING LIGHTS— Lighting units made for lighting backings and alcoves. In the old days, short lengths of striplights called *backing striplights* were made for this purpose. Small scoops, cliplights, yardlights or other compact floodlights have all been successfully used since then. See LIGHTING SPECIAL PROBLEMS/Backings for a more detailed discussion.

BACKING STRIP— A small striplight (about 24–36" long, usually uncompartmented

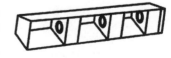

Backing strip

and all on one circuit) intended to be hung over a door or window to light the backing flat.

BACKINGS, LIGHTING OF— See LIGHTING SPECIAL PROBLEMS/Backings and Glows.

BACKLIGHT— In a proscenium theatre, any light that comes from upstage is a backlight. In a thrust theatre or other open staging situation, backlight means the same thing relative to wherever the front is presumed to be, even though it is only a backlight for the center section and is a sidelight for the side sections (and if anyone is sitting on the fourth side as they do in theatre in-the-round, it would be their frontlight).

BAFFLE (light)— In its most generic meaning, anything that prevents light from going where it isn't wanted, but it is usually reserved for metal pieces inside lighting instruments that prevent light leaking out through the vent holes in the housing. In a fresnel, there is a baffle covering the slot that the lamp carriage travels along and there is one covering top vent holes (and the reflector usually masks the back vent holes).

BALCONY RAIL— In the search for hanging positions in the front-of-house in a proscenium theatre, the front edge of the balcony provides a near ideal position. It is parallel to the footlights. It is easily accessible. It is masked from view by its own safety rail (wall). It is true that a pipe has to be secured in place and power has to be run to it, but this is a lot easier than trying to install a cove in the ceiling of the house. The throw angle from this position is very gentle and only slightly steeper than eyelevel (20–35 degrees). While this could cause shadows on the cyc (or whatever the scenic backing might be) if run up too high, it provides a badly needed fill light that can partially get under hat brims and is especially useful downstage of the front curtain.

BALLAST— Arc lights and fluorescent lights have ballasts, which are resistances in series with the light-producing source to prevent a short circuit occurring (as when carbon rods touch).

BALLYHOO— A followspot swings figure eight patterns around the stage, around the orchestra pit or around the audience. Where this occurs, it is usually at the end of a performance as part of the curtain call or as a post-curtain call celebration. It would be more usual to encounter this at an ice show or the end of the high school play rather than at the opera.

BANKS OF LIGHTS (or dimmers)— When used in the context of manual dimmers, it often refers to a row of manual dimmers that have a mechanical interlock. In the context of preset lightboards or computer memory lightboards, the sliders are often spaced in groups of six or ten or whatever to make it easier to guide the hand to the one that is needed. Where this hasn't been done, it is common for the board operator to use colored tape to create such a separation. A bank of lights can either be in a line like a striplight or in a rectangular group. Aircraft landing lights or similar low voltage sealed beam units are hooked in series and arranged in banks. Each bank usually operates as one unit. Cyc lights are also arranged in banks, but are more commonly referred to as *cells* that make up a complete unit.

BARE CONDUCTOR— A bare conductor is a wire that has no insulation. It almost always refers to a green wire (ground wire) that either has no insulation or has green insulation and is connected to the metal housing of lighting instruments. In old time flash pots, a very thin bare conductor was attached between the two contacts, and when current was applied it "blew" like a fuse causing a spark that set off the flash powder.

BARNDOOR— A device that fits in the gel slot of an instrument and has either two or four flippers that control where the light will go. See ACCESSORIES for a more detailed discussion.

BASES, BOOM— Any base that secures a vertical lighting pipe (boom) to the floor. To secure a top-heavy structure like a boom, the base either has to be extraordinarily heavy or has to have a big footprint. The commercially made bases are typically about 18–24" in diameter and are made out of cast iron (heavy), and they are intended to be screwed or bolted to the floor. If the boom can be secured from above to a fly floor, sidewall of the stage or to the grid, then the base could be reduced to a 6" diameter floor flange. In touring situations, it is not uncommon to mount a metal boom base to a half sheet of ¾" plywood, thus giving it a big enough footprint so that it wouldn't need to be bolted to the floor. Booms are almost never stable enough to lean a ladder against, but like the mast of a ship they deflect when things bump into them or are leaned against them.

BASES, LAMP— Most theatre supply catalogs will usually reprint the lamp manufacturers' drawings of the different kinds of lamp bases and shapes of lamps, but these are no longer as critically important as they once were. In the old days when one went shopping for lamps, it was necessary to know what kind of base, what shape of bulb, what filament configuration, burn-base-up or not, and it was still possible to return with a lamp that had a different LCL (length-to-center-of-light). However, since the advent of the three-letter ANSI lamp codes, one merely has to ask for "one of these" or quote the three-letter code. See LAMPS for a more detailed discussion.

BASIC LIGHTING PLOT— (1) Also called a *rep plot*, this is whatever is typically provided to visiting groups by way of lighting. It usually provides arealighting only, but may include a blue wash and the provision for a few specials. The rental contract will specify how much time the group gets onstage, which effectively limits how much lighting work can be done and still get in some rehearsal time before it becomes show time. The *light-the-set* method of lighting is used, which is explained in more detail separately. (2) A style

of drawing the Light Plot that includes only the instrument symbol and an identifying number. See LIGHT PLOT for a more detailed discussion.

BATTEN TAPE— In its most generic meaning, it refers to any markings on the light battens that assist in the placing of instruments. Sometimes it involves a light colored cloth tape stretched along the entire length of the pipe with 1' or 4' markings. More commonly it is simply ¾" wide tape wrapped around the pipe at four foot intervals from center and marked with a felt tip marker. For touring, it is often a grommeted piece of webbing that is tied to the pipe and marked with the actual instrument locations. On a pipe grid where there are cross pipes at 3–5 foot intervals, it is usually not necessary to have any further marking. In situations where there is a plugging channel immediately above the light pipe, the instruments are often located by their position relative to the numbered circuits above them and no batten tape is necessary.

BATTENS— Although battens can be used to describe either wooden or pipe battens, the term is most commonly used in American terminology for the wood kind, with the pipe kind just being called *pipes*.

BATTERY (of lights)— See BANKS OF LIGHT.

BAY— Where a lighting grid is in use, the length between two cross pipes is a bay. It is easier for the ladder assistant to say, "In this next bay, the instrument (that was just sent up) goes halfway across (to the next cross pipe)" rather than naming the pipes involved.

BCP— Abbreviation for BEAM CANDLE-POWER, which is a measure of the *intensity* of an instrument.

BEAM— A beam is generally taken to mean any cone of light, but it has a specific scientific meaning, which is that portion of the cone of light where the intensity goes from center-of-beam, assumed to be 100 percent, to a point where it has dropped to 50 percent. This should not to be confused with the *field*, which represents the point at which the light has dropped to 0–10 percent. See PHOTO-METRIC DATA for a more detailed discussion.

BEAM ANGLE— The angle of the beam portion of a cone of light, as described above.

BEAM CANDLEPOWER— Also called *peak candlepower*, it is the most commonly understood word for what the scientists call *intensity* and it is measured in candlepower, which are now called *candelas* in scientific circles.

BEAM DIAMETER —The side-to-side diameter of the beam portion of a cone of light as it hits the nose plane.

BEAM POSITION— See COVE POSITION.

BEAM PROJECTOR— This is a long throw, lenseless instrument similar to a searchlight. See INSTRUMENTS, KINDS OF/Lenseless Instruments for a more detailed discussion.

BEAM REDUCER— Any device that reduces the width of a beam. This is a generic term that includes gate reducers that are installed in the gobo slot of an ellipsoidal and any of a number of tophat-like devices that would install in one of the color slots. It would be more common to mention the device by name.

BEAM SHAPING— This is a generic term referring to any method of shaping the light and includes the framing shutters on ellipsoidals or an iris or a pattern as well as barndoors and other accessories that typically are installed in one of the color slots or in some cases are taped to the front of the instrument.

BELASCO, DAVID (1859–1931)— An American stage director credited with demanding a natural acting style, absolute authenticity in his stage settings and demonstrating the potential of stage lighting to enhance the play. He is probably best remembered for his production of **Girl of the Golden West** in 1905, which began with a spectacular sunset that lasted for five minutes before the dialogue started. His productions were an inspiration to several generations of theatre lighting practitioners. Although David Belasco envisioned the effects, supplied the research and development money, and built the workshop/laboratory, and allowed time in his rehearsals to integrate the lighting into the show, he was not the person who actually created the effects. Louis Hartmann, his lighting assistant (designer) for 28 years was the one who actually devised the effects, but it is impossible to talk about the one without mentioning the other because they worked as a team. See HARTMANN, LOUIS for more detail.

BELLS, BUZZERS and MISC LOW VOLTAGE DEVICES— Everyone knows that a bell or a buzzer is not a lighting effect. In the absence of anyone else to rig these, the electrics crew may be called upon to at least provide the wiring and the expertise. Where this is the case, the stage manager is provided with a push-button switch and a transformer plugged into power and a signal is sent to the stage (often on speaker lines) to a place where the bell is plugged in. Most bells or buzzers typically work on low voltage (6–10 volts). A phone bell has its own special ringer but can often be made to produce a credible ring on 120 volts.

BENCH FOCUSING— This is usually part of a once yearly (or some other periodically scheduled) maintenance routine that can include cleaning the instruments and checking for loose and missing parts, etc. The actual bench focusing part involves aiming the instrument at a wall a fixed distance from the hanging position (usually 15–20' away) and aligning the lamps in relation to the reflectors so that they are centered and so that the field is as even or uneven as desired. Each instrument of any type should be adjusted so that it is approximately as bright and as even as all the rest, so that all instruments of that type can be used interchangeably. A light meter is typically used at the center of the area on the wall since the eye is a poor judge of brightness differences. Ideally, the light meter can be read from the hanging position. Otherwise an assistant may have to read the meter. See ALIGNING for a more detailed discussion.

BIFOCAL (shutters)— Some profile spots made by Strand Lighting have a second set of shutters that are out-of-focus and somewhat indistinct because they are not located exactly at the gate.

BLACK FOIL— The generic name for Black Wrap™, which is a heavyweight of black aluminum foil, described below.

BLACK LIGHT— See ULTRAVIOLET LIGHT.

BLACK LINE— This refers to a photocopy process that duplicates Light Plots or other plans so that the drawings have lines that are black in color and can be photocopied again. This is the opposite of a blue line (blueprint), which in contrast cannot be copied on a photocopier but is typically less expensive to produce.

BLACK POINT— The illumination level at which the eye registers an absence of light and vision. As the eye adjusts to increased light levels, the black point rises. In the context of getting light into eye sockets, as the general scene level rises, the eye sockets become increasingly hard to see into until the level of illumination there finds itself below the black point of the surrounding light and effectively the eyes inside the sockets cease to be visible anymore.

BLACK WIRE— A normal female connector has three slots or holes, each connected to a different color of wire. Theoretically, you could safely stick a nail file or your tongue into two of these holes without getting a shock, but this assumes that whoever wired the connector followed the electric code rules, which is yet another reason why one should always use an electrical tester and assume that all wires are electrically hot. In any event, the hole connected to the black wire is the hot wire, the one that can produce a potentially life-ending shock. The manufacturers try to help make it possible to figure out which is which by a visual inspection of the connector (assuming it has been wired correctly). In terms of stagepin connectors, the black wire will be one furthest away from the center prong. In terms of either parallel-blade-ground or twist lock, when looking at the male with the grounding prong on the bottom, it will be the one on the left (the one on the right for the female). Often they will make this even easier by making the male prong gold-colored (rather than silver) and often the black prong (or slot) is narrower.

BLACK WRAP™— This is a heavyweight black aluminum foil used to block light leaks and do primitive beam shaping where no other method exists, sometimes called *wrap* for short.

BLACKOUT— As a verb it originally referred to a *switch out*. Today to make the meaning clear, one would have to say an "instantaneous" or "zero-count" blackout.

As a noun describing the state of lighting where there are no lights on, it is the only word there is to describe this.

Having said that, there, of course, is no such thing as a genuine blackout in the theatre and never has been. It would be illegal to have one, but even if that could be overcome, no one would actually want one.

As to the legality, most building/fire codes require that exit signs and aisle lights remain lit during the performance. In theatres under about 500 seats this means that even with the stage lights off, some of the audience will still be able to see the actors and stagehands moving around in a blackout (nominal blackout).

If an audience member were asked what happened in a blackout, she would likely say that the actors moved to the positions where they needed to be for the next scene and the set or props were modified in some way. The actors and technicians could see where they were going. The audience, at least those who were close-by, could see as well, even though there often is only a tiny fraction of a footcandle of light present, which is often the result of the exit and aisle lights alone.

The point of a blackout is to provide light for the actors to see while at the same time denying visibility to the audience. Unfortunately, that isn't always possible. How well this works depends on how far away an audience member is. The further away, the better it will appear to work. Even if it were possible to achieve a total blackout, it would then be necessary to have some light added back in for the actors and technicians to see by.

A blackout is, of course, a theatrical convention, and the audience understands that whatever they get to see was something they were not intended to see.

BLANK CUES— On a computer lightboard, these are empty cues (no channel levels set) that have been created ahead of time in order to save time at the level-setting session. They typically are labeled and have time, link, and follow information attached. See FORMATTING A DISK for a more detailed discussion.

BLANK DISK— This is a show disk, which when read into the internal memories of a computer lightboard will have the effect of clearing out the old show in preparation for loading the new show while at the same time preserving the houselight, worklight, running light patches, the macros and other venue-specific configurations. There will also frequently be 100 or so blank 5 count cues included, which when loaded can quickly be labeled and have their times corrected to correspond to the new show. Extra cues that won't be needed can also usually be deleted in one operation. See LIGHTING CONTROL/Computer Memory Lightboards and FORMATTING A DISK for a more detailed discussion.

BLANK LIGHT PLOT— A plan view showing the hanging positions and circuit plug-in points but without instruments. See LIGHT PLOT, BLANK

BLEED—(1) When used in the context of a gauze or scrim, it refers to bringing up light behind the scrim and thus revealing the scene set up behind. (2) In the context of supposedly solid scenery, it refers to backing lights or offstage lights showing through a fabric drop or fabric covered scenery piece. In this case, the bleeding is unwanted and the fabric needs to be back-painted or needs to have a black masking cloth hung behind. (3) If a lightboard controller is not adjusted properly, it is possible that there will still be a slight glow onstage even when the control handle is all the way down. This most commonly would be referred to as *ghosting*, but it could also be called *bleeding* and everyone would know what was meant.

BLENDING— Although the stage or a portion of the stage is lit by many instruments, the intent is usually to create a seamlessly even light over the whole control area. This used to be achieved by bringing up the borderlights to a low level. Now it is more commonly achieved by more careful focusing and the use of various frost gels (diffusion media). Once the evenness has been achieved, it is usually then made uneven in a deliberately controlled way.

BLIND DISPLAY MODE— Sometimes called *previewing*. On a computer lightboard, the monitor screen is set to display and modify any cue, group or submaster in the show without affecting the cue onstage. See LIGHTING CONTROL/Computer Memory Lightboards for a more detailed discussion.

BLINDERS—(1) The black disc in the center of a beam projector that prevents direct light from going out the front. (2) Lights mounted on the front of the proscenium and aimed into the house designed to prevent the audience from seeing something. Audiences typically hate this, remember it forever, and write rude letters to the management about it. On the whole, audiences are prepared to pretend that they don't see anything that they aren't supposed to see, which mostly includes anything lit with blue light, so there is really no reason to try to blind them. During a daytime performance outdoors where blue light is not an option, a set of low wattage blinders (that wouldn't cause any eye discomfort) could be used on the front of the proscenium arch to symbolically tell the audience that a scene change was in progress. They would probably know this anyway, but it would not cause a problem to use them.

BLOCKER or BLOCKING CUE— See NO-TRACK BLOCKER CUE.

BLOOM— This is a colloquialism, which refers to a mirror-like reflection coming from the set, costumes or props. Silver trays, watch faces or anything shiny can cause this. Typical solutions involve tipping mirrors forward or back, dulling spray (either the commercial kind or a soap solution), or replacing the object.

BLOW— This is what fuses do when they are overloaded. When circuit breakers replaced fuses, it was common to refer to having blown the circuit breaker when in fact it had only been *tripped* and could be *reset*. Occasionally someone may refer to a lamp as having blown, but with lamps it is more common to call them *burnouts* or say that they are burned out unless they have somehow actually exploded in a spectacular way.

BLUE LINE— This refers to the blueprinting process that involves a master on tracing paper being combined with a specially treated piece of bond paper and being fed through a machine that smells heavily of ammonia. The result is a blueprint that cannot be photocopied. This is the opposite of a black line, which in contrast can be copied on a photocopier and is typically more expensive to produce.

BLUE-OUT— A near blackout. Something that simulates a blackout without actually taking all the lights out, usually used during an early technical rehearsal or rehearsal-with-light to make sure that no one gets hurt.

BOARD or CONTROL BOARD— In a lighting context it refers to the *lightboard*, which might just be called the *board* for short. In a broader context it could be used to refer to a control panel or board for sound or slide projections or some other purpose. See LIGHTING CONTROL for a more detailed discussion.

BOARD (dimmer)— See DIMMER BOARD.

BOARD, PIANO— See PIANO BOARD.

BOARD, SWITCH— See SWITCHBOARD.

BOOK— Usually referred to as The Book, it is the stage manager's copy of the script that includes all the staging and cues for the show. It is typically contained in a three-ring binder where the smaller script pages show through windows cut in letter-sized card stock, thus providing wide margins for notes. The stage manager uses it during rehearsals as an archival record of where all the actors are at every moment of the play (staging) and uses it during performance to call the cues.

BOOM— A vertical pipe used as a hanging position for lights and typically located in the wings or out in the house in a proscenium theatre. The boom is usually tall (21' or so) secured by a heavy iron base that is firmly attached to the floor and attached by one or more guy wires at the top. It sometimes will have one or more crosspieces along its height, which would technically make it a *light tree* even though it would commonly still be called a boom. Short booms (10 feet or less) would more commonly be called *light stands* and if they had casters, *rolling light stands* (or *rovers*).

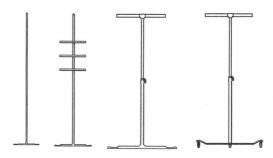

Left to right: Boom, light tree, light stand, and rover.

BOOMERANG (Brit *color magazine*)— This is a color-changing mechanism usually found on a followspot. See COLOR CHANGING, METHODS OF for a more detailed discussion.

BOOTH (Light, Control or Projection)— Usually the stage manager, the lightboard operator and the soundboard operator all sit in the same room where they can all have an adequate view of the stage and can communicate without the need for headsets. There may also be followspots in this booth. The booth is usually at the back of the house although sometimes due to the architecture, it will be on one of the sides instead. In older proscenium houses, the lighting position may be in one of the wings (usually stage right where the stage manager at one time was expected to be). If for some reason there are separate booths, they would be separately named, i.e. sound booth, projection booth and so forth.

BOOTH LIGHTS— There will be two kinds of booth lights: dim running lights for use during a performance and bright worklights, usually coming from overhead, for vacuuming the floor. The most common kind of running lights are swing-arm drafting lights with dim (15 watt or less) lamps and possibly with gels covering or partially covering the light opening. This is to prevent light leaving the booth and also to prevent the audience from being distracted by movement inside the booth. The booth window is often partially obscured either by pieces of poster board or by some kind of gel or mirror film to achieve the same thing. This is more important where there is seated audience immediately on the other side of the window and considerably less important the further the booth is removed from proximity to the audience.

BORDERLIGHTS— A generic term for trough lights of all kinds hung overhead whether they are of the open trough variety or the compartmented kind. Borderlights were originally used to light the painted bor-

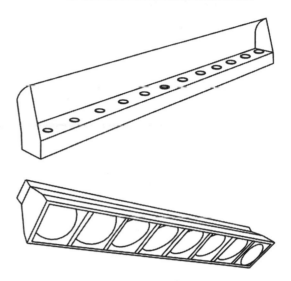

Top: Trough-type borderlight; *bottom:* Compartmented borderlight

ders but over time came to be used as acting area downlights over the stage. They are typically wired in three circuits (sometimes four). If they are broken into 6–8' sections, then they could be referred to as *striplights*, but it would be more correct to say "striplights being used as borderlights." The continuous troughs that once covered the width of the stage were usually suspended from their support pipe by chain.

BORDERLIGHTS, THREE-CIRCUIT (Brit *magazine batten*)— These were said to have been the idea of Munroe R. Pevear, a Boston architect and manufacturer of gelatine color in the early 1900s. His idea was based on the tri-chromatic color theory and was supposed to produce either all other colors of light or almost all other colors of light. This three-circuit wiring was immensely popular and was extended to footlights and striplights and cyc lighting and exists to this day.

In practice, it was never possible to create all colors or even very many colors at all, but this was alternately explained away on the grounds that the individual light sources were not bright enough to produce saturated colors or that the colors themselves were not pure enough. A four-circuit version appeared that added uncolored white light to the mix, but in most venues the green circuit had already been replaced with either amber or no-color as green was a particularly unflattering facial color. Over time many other colors have been tried in the available circuits, but none have ever produced anything approaching all colors. Louis Hartmann complained at length about the "veeing" problem caused by the lamps being too far apart and said this was one reason why he refused to use the four-circuit version, preferring to stay with the three-circuit version. See VEEING PROBLEM for a more detailed discussion.

BOSUN'S CHAIR— This is a vintage method of going aloft, only used in a fly house, and not used there much anymore, that involves flying the electrician to a position behind the light pipe. See HANGING POSITIONS, GETTING TO for a more complete discussion of this subject.

BOTTLES— A colloquial term for the facets of a PAR-type lamp that create an oval rather than a circle of light depending on which way they are oriented. Most parcan instruments allow the sealed beam unit to be rotated so that the "bottles" can be aligned with something on the set.

BOTTOM-DOWN-UNDER— The lighting position on a hypothetical glass sphere that lights from below as if through a glass floor. This is the traditional campfire position. In actual practice the light typically comes through either a transparent (plexi-glass) floor or through some kind of grating. See HANGING POSITIONS, IDEAL for a more detailed discussion.

BOUNCE— In the context of a computer lightboard, this refers to a chase sequence in which the steps run first in forward order (1, 2, 3) and then in reverse order (3, 2, 1).

BOUNCE LIGHT— Diffusely reflected light, resulting from light hitting an object and then being diverted from its original path. On an overcast day, most of the light present will be bounce light, and, in real life, bounce light provides a shadowless fill light that softens hard shadows and helps promote visibility. Whenever indirect light is mentioned, this is light that has been directed at an unseen surface and then some of it has bounced onto the surface that is lit. Indirect lighting is often used to light window and door backings and the inside of light boxes of all kinds. In the theatre, light pointed at the actors from above will go on to hit the floor, and while light bounces off of everything and everyone onstage, it is the floor that has the largest area most nearly perpendicular to the light paths and is responsible for the greatest quantity of bounce.

Lighting designers are rarely neutral about bounce light. They either want to promote it or eliminate it. In a proscenium situation, it is not unusual to want to have as much bounce as possible because it will get light under hat brims and into eye sockets. In this situation, the fact that the bounce is uncontrollable makes no difference because the stage is typically lined with a light absorbing material like black velour and any light that might bounce toward the audience would fall harmlessly into the orchestra pit. In a thrust theatre, however, where the first row of audience is right up against the stage, the bounce light will bounce out into the house and ruin the audience separation, and so attempts will be made to lessen the bounce.

While the direction of the bounce cannot be controlled, whether there will be bounce or not can be partially promoted or discourage by the use of color and brightness. Stated simply, light colors are better reflectors and therefore bounce more light, and higher light levels make more light available to be bounced. If light levels onstage were allowed to spiral upward, the bounce light into the house would eventually reach a point where the house was lit almost as well as the stage.

The easiest way to visualize bounce light is to imagine that you are washing a car with a garden hose. At the moment, only a small trickle of water is hitting the surface and running down onto the ground. Were you to open the hose nozzle all the way, the water would splash in all directions and you and whoever was behind you would get wet. There is a certain water pressure at which you will get wet but not the person behind you. Similarly with light, at very low levels most of the light is absorbed by the objects being hit, but there is a certain brightness of light at which the actors on the stage will be splashed by reflected light and a certain brightness at which the audience will begin to be splashed also. Call this the *threshold of bounce*. If it is possible to hold light levels below this threshold, bounce into the house will be less. Often several sources at low readings appear to bounce less light than a single much brighter source. Dark colors are capable of absorbing more light before they begin reflecting it, and rough surfaces absorbs more than smooth surfaces.

Lighting designers tend to think in terms of white and black floors, but if the stage floor is visible to the audience or a portion of the audience (as it usually is), it will be considered a scenic element and its color and pattern will ultimately be determined by what is appropriate to the rest of the set. Although by mentioning the effect it will have upon the lights, it can often be made lighter or darker than it would otherwise have been. Floors that are white (or any color that is lighter than an actor's face) are going to cause a different problem altogether if the face will be seen against the background of the floor, as is the case where the audience in the balcony looks down upon the action (White Color Problem).

The easiest way to actually see the effect of bounce light is to put a candle a foot away from a whiteboard or other reflective surface, making sure the candle is shielded so that its light does not directly fall on you. At a foot away from the whiteboard, your hand will be lit (by reflected bounce light). As you move away, the light on your hand will decrease with the square of the distance. See INVERSE SQUARE LAW for a more detailed discussion.

BOUNCE LIGHT PROBLEM— The problem with bounce light in the theatre is that it cannot be controlled well and as a result it bounces out into the house and lights up masking and stage machinery that everyone would rather keep in the dark. As a result, an attempt is often made to eliminate it as described above by the use of dark colors and subdued light levels, but this creates a whole series of new problems.

There is now no shadowless, general illumination to fill in the harsh shadows of the face and other objects. This can be solved in part by borrowing a technique from the painters and using a different color to indicate the presence of shade. In real life there is direct light and lots of reflected bounce light, which is dimmer. In the theatre there is direct light representing the source (called *key light*) and then there is direct light representing the effect of the shadowless bounce light (called *fill light*), which cannot be allowed to be present because it cannot be controlled. The level on the shade side could be lower than the source side (as it is in life), but it is more common to let the color indicate the presence of the shade and keep the brightness about the same. This is because the audience as a general rule does not like to sit on the shady or dim side of the action. See SUNNYSIDE CONVENTION for a more detailed discussion.

On the whole, the direct light that simulates the bounce light works well except that it is not shadowless and it came from the wrong direction. Bounce light should have come from the floor rather than from above, and now there is no light capable of getting under the hats and softening the harsh facial shadows. Direct light from the footlights (where they still exist) would help with this problem but the board operator would probably have to ride the levels up and down as the actors got closer or moved further away to control the Distance Problem that the footlights have. Assuming there weren't any footlights (as there often aren't these days) then a low angle wash (as from a balcony rail) would help, but the levels would have to be kept low enough to prevent there being shadows of the actors projected on the back wall. Again someone might have to ride the levels on these controls. In most theatres, despite the best efforts of everyone involved, getting light under the hats is a continuing problem that never gets completely solved.

BOWLING ALLEY STAGE LIGHTING— See LIGHTING, KINDS OF.

BOX BOOM— The boxes refer to the tiers of private rooms along the sidewalls of the house for the first 15–20' into the house where it was customary to have VIP seating. Abraham Lincoln was sitting in a box at Ford's theatre, and John Wilkes Booth jumped from the box to the stage to escape. Where no longer used as VIP seating, vertical pipes are often installed to create front-of-house sidelighting positions. Even where the boxes don't exist anymore, the box boom position refers to where they would have been if they still existed and the booms are simply installed at various points along the sidewalls of the house (sometimes in recessed coves in the wall).

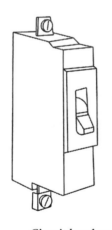

Circuit breaker

BREAKER (circuit)— An overcurrent protection device (like a fuse) where an overload causes the circuit breaker switch to *trip*, which breaks the circuit. Circuit breakers that have tripped can be *reset*, and the switch can be used to turn off power to any given circuit. For most purposes, circuit breakers have replaced fuses in the theatre because of the ease with which they can be reset.

BRIDGE or LIGHT BRIDGE— A temporary catwalk that provides both hanging positions and a means of getting to the instruments hung upon it. See HANGING POSITIONS, GETTING TO for a more complete discussion of this subject.

BRIGHTNESS (apparent)— This is a layperson's word to describe the quantity of light present. The human eye is poor at remembering light levels from the past, so it is a relative word that would be more correct if it were always referred to as *apparent brightness*. A single spotlight on a dark stage may appear to be bright, but when that same spotlight is seen in the context of the rest of the scene lights it may appear to be dim. It is, however, the word most commonly used by lighting designers, technicians, directors and other theatre workers, and it is usually used in a comparative sense as in, "This scene needs to be brighter or dimmer." It is commonly recorded into cues based on the level of the dimmers (or channels) on a scale of 1–100, which more-or-less represents percentages of full brightness of the instrument or instruments. Scientists on the other hand use words like *luminous flux*, which is measured in lumens, *intensity*, which is measured in candelas (formerly candlepower) or *illumination*, which is measured in footcandles in the Imperial measuring system and luxes in the metric measuring system.

Twice as much light does not make something look twice as bright but only about 26 percent brighter. This is according to G. Ekman's power formula ($I_p = 3\ I_m$) where the perceived brightness is equal to the cube root of the measured brightness. Stated simply, if you want to double the perceived amount of light, you have to provide eight times as much actual light ($2^3 = 8$). This particular field of science where subjective responses to different physical stimuli are measured is called psychophysics, which has been pioneered by Professor Stevens of Harvard among others. It is a formula without an application in the theatre as all light cues are visually evaluated. See LIGHT, QUANTITY OF for more complete discussion of this subject.

BRIGHTNESS ADAPTATION LEVEL— The eye adjusts to various brightness levels and accepts them as normal. When one steps outside and sees the first snow of the season covering everything, there may well be the sensation of glare and the pupil in the eye will probably close down. After some time has elapsed, however, the eye registers this level as the new "normal" and the rods and cones adjust their sensitivity and the pupil opens back up to its more normal position. In a theatrical context, the first impression of a scene is always the most significant. If the scene is to appear very dark, it will often begin darker than playing level and then the level can be brought up to a more acceptable level as part of a second delayed cue. The eyes of the audience, of course, are adjusting to the reduced light levels, and as a result they can't tell that additional light is also being brought up to assist in this process. If on the other hand the effect of a very bright scene is wanted, it might also be done with two cues for a slightly different reason. The first cue would be the transition from the blackout and would bring the lights up to a somewhat reduced level, which will seem bright by comparison but will not be hard for the eyes to adjust to. It will then be followed by a second cue that will bring the lights up to playing level and in the process will continue the impression of brightness over a longer period of time until the eye eventually adapts to the final brightness level and accepts it as normal.

BROKEN COLOR— This refers to gels taped together in a pattern of some kind like a stained-glass window. See COLOR MODIFICATIONS for a more detailed discussion.

BRUSH— Also called a *shoe*, this is the sliding contact on a resistance dimmer board, usually made of brass.

BULB— The glass portion (sometimes called the *envelope* or *glass envelope*) of a lamp. Also, it is sometimes used to refer to the entire lamp, but this is considered the mark of an amateur who doesn't know any better or it is done as a joke. Light "bulbs" is also used to refer to household light bulbs, which have no other name, and even in a theatrical situation would not be called household lamps.

BUMP— On a zero count. Once called a *bang up* or a *slam up*, these terms are all

falling into disuse because there are no handles to slam or bang or bump anymore.

BUNCHLIGHTS— Vintage floodlights (modeled after the gas bunchlights) consisting of a metal dishpan-like reflector sometimes round and sometimes rectangular with many standard light bulb sockets mounted inside. The earliest light bulbs were only about 16 candlepower bright (which is about half as bright as what is commonly inside a microwave oven). To get any punch, they had to be clustered together in a bunchlight. These instruments were replaced by olivettes and later scoops that only required one, much larger, lamp.

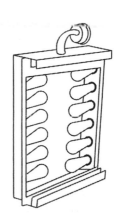

Bunchlight, circa 1900

BUNDLES (of cable)— Where loose cables are tied to a light pipe, they are typically tied together with a clove hitch and then the bundle (being 3" or less in diameter) is tied with a shoelace knot to the pipe. Sometimes the bundle is held against the pipe and a couple of wraps of tie line are taken around the whole thing, and it is finished off with a shoelace knot. Where this is done out of sight of the audience, the cables may only be tied every 4 or 5 feet, which creates great swags of cable. Where it is done in a place that the audience can see, the bundles are usually tied every foot or so in very neat bundles and the tie line will be a dark color. This tying up of cable is often left to the end of the light hanging process as it is time consuming, and one doesn't want to tie up a 30' bundle only to discover that one or two additional cables now have to be added. A well-designed system of plugging channels is supposed to drastically reduce the need for loose cable and thus all but eliminate the need to tie any of it up.

BURNDY— This is a tradename for a solderless lug connection for large feeder cables, usually for connection to a company switch or other source of power.

BURN-OUT— When used as a noun, it refers to a lamp that has ceased to produce light. It is also common to say that gels have "burned out" when, in fact, what is actually meant is that they have faded to the point where they no longer faithfully represent their color and can no longer be used alongside other cuts of the same color.

BUS BAR— A heavy (usually copper) bar used in place of a wire as an electrical conductor in a breaker box or other electrical service box. The bar often has tapped holes in it for attaching lots of smaller individual wires. Where all circuits from the grid circuits terminate in a dimmer rack, it is not unusual for the white wires of every circuit to attach to the same neutral bus bar with individual screws and terminals.

CABLE— Cables have an outer sleeve (often rubber) that contains several individually insulated conductors and some packing material to keep the shape round. For theatre use, the cables by code have to be type S (or an S variant like SO), have two current carrying conductors and a ground wire, and they are usually 12 gauge (20 amp) wire. All this is commonly referred to as *12/3 type S*. Sometimes the borderlights may have a multi-conductor cable (borderlight cable) running to it, which for a three-circuit strip, would have 6 current carrying conductors and one common green ground wire. Feeder wires for temporary lightboard hookups usually have only one conductor in a heavy-duty rubber outer insulation, but four or five of them will be run together. Individually insulated wires that are run through some kind of flexible or rigid conduit are simply referred to as *wires* or *conductors* but they have a code-approved

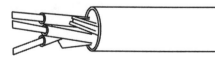

Type S cable

wire type like THHN printed on the wire insulation along with their gauge number. Practical lights and appliances are allowed to have lamp cord or other light duty electrical cords but these are supposed to be adapted to stage cable as soon as they are out of sight of the audience. In practice, light duty extension cords type SJ (and variants) are often used and fire department inspectors tend to be more tolerant of the green and black colored cords than the orange ones, which because of their color demand to be noticed and written up.

CABLE BOX— This generally refers to a rolling wooden road box that is used to store spare cabling and supplies.

CABLE COVERS— Where cables are run across a walkway, something has to be done to prevent people from tripping over them. Sometimes the cables are taped down, but if more than one cable is involved, this becomes both expensive and labor intensive. There are commercially made molded plastic thresholds made for exactly this purpose, and while they can be useful for sound and other low voltage cables, they are rarely large enough to accommodate stage cables. A very serviceable unit can be made from 1 · 1's with a ⅜ ply top. Sometimes a piece of scrap carpet can be taped or stapled down, but the cables usually have to be taped down in parallel lines first at intervals of perhaps a foot apart.

CABLE CRADLE— See CRADLE.

CABLE HOOK— This is a u-shaped hook attached to a lighting stand so that excess cable can be coiled and hung on the hook. Often it is something homemade that has been fabricated out of stiff wire.

CABLE PIPE— In a proscenium house, this refers to a lighting pipe that is used to carry cable from the dimmer board side of the stage to the other side, and it may or may not have any actual instruments on it. It may also be called a *crossover* pipe.

CABLE TIES— These are devices to either bundle cables together in permanent installations or they are used to keep coiled cables from twisting and kinking. The permanent kind is typically made of plastic and there is a ratcheting mechanism that cinches them up tight, at which point the excess tail can be cut off. For keeping coiled cables together, either webbing with Velcro or tie line secured to the female end is most commonly used. The tie line would typically be clove hitched to the end of the cable and then a shoelace knot would hold the coil together. When cable is run to an instrument, whatever slack there might be will be needed at the instrument (female) end, so the same tie line could then be used to tie up the excess.

CAD— Abbreviation for COMPUTER ASSISTED DESIGN.

CALCIUM LIGHT— See LIMELIGHT.

CALIBAN FLOODS— Said to have been named for a production of *Caliban* in New York in 1916. They were lenseless floodlights with parabolic reflectors that used the newly invented 1000-watt lamp. They worked the same as *gallery reflectors* except they used an incandescent lamp rather than an arc light mechanism and as such were an early precursor of beam projectors.

CALIBRATE— On older dimming systems the dimming curve depended on a calibration adjustment on the dimmer or slider. Now the dimming curve is set electronically as a menu choice and is more commonly referred to as a dimmer *profile*.

CAMPFIRE RING (positions)— All light hanging positions that are at a 45 degree angle below the nose plane. Since hanging positions are usually discussed as being at 45 degree increments from each other, there would be eight positions: front, back, left and right and the intermediate positions of left and right front and left and right back. The instruments would typically be mounted on wood or metal floor plates attached to the deck, or they might be c-clamped to the bottom part of a vertical boom. Footlights would be at the campfire front position. Shinbusters, used mostly when lighting dancers, typically come from below knee height on the sides or diagonal sides. See HANGING POSITIONS, IDEAL for more detail.

CANDELA— This is a measure of *intensity* or as the common person might say the brightness or strength of a source. The old name, found in books pre 1948 and still in use by some, was *candlepower*, which compared the brightness of unknown sources to the brightness of an international candle. Once the intensity of a source is known, then the amount of illumination that will be produced at any distance can be calculated using the inverse square law.

CANDLE, INTERNATIONAL— A candle that would produce a footcandle of light on the surface of a sphere that was a foot away. Strength of unknown light sources could then be compared to this standard candle much as an automobile engine is compared to the strength of a single horse. The international candle has been replaced by a definition that involves a hypothetical black body radiator and the solidification temperature of platinum, but a footcandle of illumination is still approximately what would be produced by a candle that was a foot away.

CANDLE EFFECT— See EFFECTS, KINDS OF.

CANDLEPOWER— The old name for *candelas*. For the most part its use has been purged from scientific papers, but it is still used in sales literature and in common conversation as it evokes a much clearer image of how bright something is.

CAP— A building trades' term for a connector, usually PBG and usually male as the female would more commonly be called a *receptacle* or *outlet*.

CAPACITY, CURRENT CARRYING— See AMPACITY.

CAPTURED CHANNELS— A computer lightboard term that refers to channels put onscreen by means of the keypad. They are captured in the sense that they are a pile-on, and they will remain at their settings through successive cues until manually released.

CARBON ARC— See ARC LIGHT.

CARDS (number)— These could be ordinary playing cards, but they are often simply cards of that size with a felt-tip numbers or letters on them. The lighting designer drops these on the floor at the beginning of the focusing session to mark the locations of areas and specials. The measurements would have been done previously, and the lighting designer would line the card up with something. It is however a lightning fast way to mark the floor and get underway, and whoever is modeling can simply be told to stand on number "4." If the cards get jostled by ladder movement, the designer can simply line them back up again. At the end of the session they can be picked up and put back in the deck for next time.

CARTRIDGE FUSE— A cylindrical fuse with electrical contacts at both ends, it usually pushes into place in a spring-loaded holder.

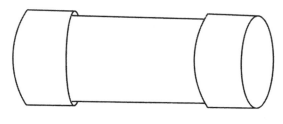

Cartridge fuse

CATHODE— The negative terminal (in a DC circuit) and often used in the context of an arc light.

CATHODE RAY TUBE (Abbr. CRT)— Once the only technology for TV-type monitor screens and, as a result, used generically to mean the display screen, more commonly now simply called the *monitor*.

CATWALK— This is a permanent walkway (platform) rigidly suspended below the ceiling or roof structure that allows access to the various instruments hung on it. See HANGING POSITIONS, GETTING TO for a more complete discussion of this subject.

C-CLAMP (BRITISH: *hook clamp*)— An adjustable c-shaped hook that connects a lighting instrument to a support pipe (usually up to about 2" in diameter). There are three bolts involved. The smallest is the square-headed *shaft set screw* bolt. Its primary purpose is to allow the shaft to be removed entirely in order to create a sidearm. If it is enthusiastically tightened down, it will never need to be dealt with again as there is an alternate and better way to adjust the pan of the instrument, which is the hex-head *yoke-attaching bolt* at the bottom of the shaft. It has a wide washer that adds friction and can be tightened down to a point where most pan adjustments can then be made by twisting the yoke by hand. At least one manufacturer (Colortran) started putting a handle on the shaft set screw, which then encouraged its use to set the pan of the instrument. On instruments so equipped, it makes more sense to enthusiastically tighten down the yoke-attaching bolt and use the handle provided to set the pan even though the shaft is typically wobbly and harder to position exactly. The third bolt is the square-headed *pipe-attaching bolt*, which is the one that will have to be

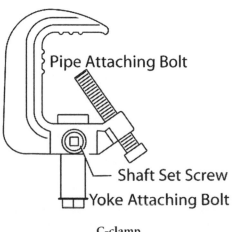

C-clamp

loosened or tightened every time to attach the instrument to its pipe.

It should be apparent that the c-clamp should be attached from far-to-near so that the pipe-attaching bolt faces the electrician (rather than being on the opposite side of the pipe). This can usually be done one-handed by using the thumb and index finger to hand-tighten the bolt while the longer fingers are pulling the clamp firmly against the pipe. Once the c-clamp is finger tight it cannot then slip off the pipe and a wrench can be used to tighten it the rest of the way. Once this has been done, the forward and back movement of the instrument has been locked, and the instrument can only be moved in pan and tilt. See YOKING for a more detailed discussion.

CEILING SLOT— See COVE POSITION.

CELL— Where a bank of lights is created from individual units (as with a cyc light), each unit or compartment is commonly called a *cell.*

CELLOPHANE TAPE— Commonly called Scotch™ tape. See TAPES, KINDS OF.

CENTERBEAM— This refers to the ray of light that passes through the center of the lens and whose aimpoint is on the nose plane at the center of the lighting area.

CENTURY LIGHTING COMPANY— Along with Kliegl Bros, it was one of the two giants of early American lighting manufacturers dominating the market in the early and mid–20th century. The Leko and Lekolite were their tradenames for ellipsoidal instruments. Wizard and Wizardlite were their names for scoops. The company was bought by Strand lighting and although it was called Century Strand for a while, it became just Strand lighting in the 1980s.

CF— Abbreviation for *correction factor,* which when applied to a lamp that is brighter or dimmer than the test lamp, will indicate by how much the illumination will have changed. See PHOTOMETRIC DATA for a more detailed discussion.

CHAIN HANGING— This is a vintage method (pre–1920) for hanging lighting equipment, which has all but vanished since the advent of yokes and c-clamps. Striplights and olivettes were at one time commonly chain hung. The chain was usually about the weight and style of dog tie-out chain. By taking at least one full turn around the support pipe, enough friction was created that the position of the equipment was held in place unless it was bumped.

CHAIN HOIST or MOTOR— An electrically powered hoist (similar to a block-and-tackle except that chain and chain gears are used in place of the pulleys and rope) used for raising really heavy equipment like light trusses or speaker towers in a big venue. See HOISTS, KINDS OF for a more detailed discussion.

CHANGEOVER PERIOD— This is the name given to the strike of the old show and set-in of the new show when they occur as one operation. As it relates to lighting, there is clearly no point in striking all the lights only to have to put them back in approximately the same place just a few hours later.

What would typically be done would be called a *missing-instrument rehang* where the ladder moved from instrument-to-instrument along the pipes. If an old-show instrument was encountered that was not to be used at that location in the new show, it would be struck and lowered to the floor (or kept in the lift basket as appropriate). If the instrument were to remain in place (or within arm's reach of the correct place), it would be re-circuited (if necessary), re-accessorized with gel, pattern and/or accessories and aimed in the new correct direction. If an empty space were encountered, where a new-show instrument needed to be, it would be hauled up from the floor if one were available or a yellow ribbon or other marker would be hung to mark the place of the missing instrument. By carefully planning the ladder route, it is possible to greatly reduce the number of instruments that will be missing because they haven't been struck from their previous location yet.

The other parts of the set-in (the focus and integration of the lighting into the show) proceed in the usual way. See LOAD-IN and SET-IN for a more detailed discussion. There are compelling reasons for the rehang to occur not on closing night, as is the tradition, but on the morning after. See STRIKE THE LIGHTS, WHEN TO and STRIKES, KINDS OF for a more detailed discussion.

Mon 28th Final Dress		Up	Dow n	Follow	Link	Wait	1	2	3	4	5	6	7	8	9	10	11	12	13	14	15	16	21	22	23
Cue	Label																								
1	Preset I	5	5								60		50	50											
2	House to half	5	5										50	50											
3	Hse & Pre out	5	5																						
4	Lts up desk	8	8				FL	60FL		40						21	21	21					19	19	19
5	Doorbell-OH on						FL	60FL		40	3	4				45	40	60	2	2	2		45	37	37
6	Hall on						FL	60FL	60	40	3	4				45	40	60	2	2	2		45	37	37
6.3	Hall off						FL	60FL		40	3	4				45	40	60	2	2	2		45	37	37
7	An tak clo up on						FL	60FL		40	25	80FL		27		45	40	60	16	16	18		45	37	37
8	An bk up off						FL	60FL		40	3	4				45	40	60	2	2	2		37	37	37
9	Mi EXT OH off						FL	60FL		40		1				20	20	20					19	19	19
10	BR on						FL	60FL		40				80		20	20	20					19	19	19
11	BR off						FL	60FL		40						20	20	20					19	19	19
12	Little light OH						FL	60FL		40						45	40	60					45	37	37

Channel reading by cue

CHANNEL— Often thought of as a one-to-one alias for a dimmer, they can be used in other ways and can address other equipment. A channel is a signal path from a computer lightboard to a device or group of devices that it is controlling.

A lightboard with 100 channels can address 100 devices or groups of devices. Think of the lightboard as a telephone switchboard with 100 telephone lines. The line that serves your house makes all the phones work. They all ring together and if one is busy, they all are busy, which is to say they work together as a single group. Each signal path (channel) from the lightboard is connected to a dimmer or group of dimmers or some other device, like a fog machine or an intelligent light. Channel numbers could be set identical to dimmer numbers, but it is more usual to take advantage of the opportunity to assign more logical numbering to the dimmers.

CHANNEL READING BY CUE (BRITISH: State of the Board Plot)— This is a spreadsheet where channels are listed across the top and cues down the side and the body of the table shows the levels of all channels in that cue. It is used to compare the levels between different cues, making sure *looks* that are repeated are actually the same, and making sure that filaments are warmed a cue ahead of time. At one time it was called a *tracksheet*, but that term is now used to trace the use of one channel through each cue of the show. The Channel Reading by Cue can also be used to document the show, but the show disk or a collection of pages where each page shows the readings of one cue in the show would work as well for this purpose. See HARDCOPY PRINTOUT for a more detailed discussion.

CHANNEL SCHEDULE— See HOOKUP SHEET.

CHASE EFFECT or CHASE LOOP— This is a series of cues that follow each other automatically and the last cue of the series is linked back to the first creating an effect that continues until it is interrupted in some other way. There have to be separate circuits. Think of a theatre marquee where the lights may be wired in three circuits. Where that is the case, a *positive chase* would bring up circuit one, replaced by circuit two, replaced by circuit three, and then the pattern would repeat. In a *building chase,* circuit one would be followed by adding circuit two and then adding circuit three, and then the pattern would start over again. In a *dark (negative) chase*, all circuits are on except one, except two, except three, at which point the pattern would repeat. A *forward chase* does the steps in numerical order. A *reverse chase* does the steps in reverse numerical order and a *bounce chase* would alternate between the two. Positive and negative chases can often be made to alternate, and sometimes the steps can be done in random order, which usually works well for fire and lightning effects.

CHEAT— This is usually used in the context of moving an instrument slightly so that it can light something else that also needs to be lit.

CHEAT SHEET— This is a memory aid for the lighting designer to remind herself what the various channels control. See PAPER-WORK for a more detailed discussion.

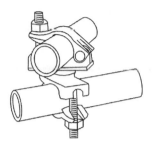

CHEESEBORO— A brand name for a device that will lock two pipes together at a 90 degree angle (or any other angle for that matter) as on a grid or as a crossarm on a boom.

Cheeseboro

CHERRY PICKER— A portable and manually operated telescoping ladder that is placed and then climbed. See HANGING POSITIONS, GETTING TO for a more complete discussion of this subject.

CHIAROSCURO— See PLUCKING SCENES OUT OF DARKNESS.

CHILDREN'S THEATRE LIGHTING— See LIGHTING, KINDS OF.

CHIMNEY TOP ELLIPSOIDALS— Named for the chimney-like protrusion from top back, these were the old style of instrument (T type lamps that burned base up). The development of smaller lamps that could burn in any position and were then axially mounted in a way that made them brighter and more even, made these ellipsoidals obsolete.

Chimney top ellipsoidal

CHINA MARKER— An alternate name for a *grease pencil*, it is used to write gel numbers on gels. The best colors for dark gels are white or yellow and black or dark blue for light colors.

CHOPPER— Also called a *douser* or a *cut-off*, this is a part of a followspot that allows the operator to cut off the light. It typically works like two sliding doors on a freight elevator that come together from top and bottom.

CHRISTMAS TREE LIGHTS— There are basically three kinds: C9, C7 and miniature. The C9 kind are wired in parallel (if one burns out, the rest continue to work) and use a 7/16" screw base (sometimes called *intermediate candelabra*) and can be viewed as a series of 25, 50 or 100 prewired sockets. They can be used for chase lights, for providing a glow behind a sign or under a platform and for any other purpose where a lot of small lights are better than one large one. The C7 size are also wired in parallel and use a 3/8" screw base (sometimes called *mini candelabra* size) and are smaller and less bright but can be used in similar ways. The miniature size is wired in series and the lamps have two wires that make contact with the sides of their sockets as they are pushed into place. They are used mostly for stars or indicator lights on electrified props. They are very delicate and if one stops working, they all stop working. They can also be used for their intended purpose as Christmas decorations on the set or out in the lobby.

CHRISTMAS TREE LIGHTS, MAINTAINING— This refers to the miniature kind that are wired in series. Hours are often lost as all the lamps are changed to no effect. It makes no difference how many times all the lamps are changed since it is just as easy to introduce new problems as it is to fix old ones and there may be more than one lamp that isn't working right. Here's a five-step method that has yet to fail:

Step one is laying them out flat on a couch or other soft surface and checking that each lamp is seated properly. This involves wiggling each lamp in its socket with the power on to make sure it is firmly seated. This often is all that is needed to get them working again.

Failing that, set a multimeter for resistance measurements and remove the first lamp after the plug. Unplug the unit and touch the near contact (one closest to the plug) in the socket and there should be continuity with one of the two prongs on the connector. Mark whichever prong this is with an alligator clip or in some other way because it represents the plug-side contacts of every socket on the string.

Replace its lamp, and now remove a lamp at the middle of the string. If there is a resistance reading between its nearside contact in the socket and the marked prong, then this first half of the string is okay and the problem is in the other half.

Once one finds the half that has the problem, one can keep halving the remaining (non-working) part to try to isolate the bad light or lights. When one gets to the far end of the string, the last lamp should have continuity between its far-side contact and the unmarked prong on the connector, so one could work from either end depending on where the problem was.

Once the string is working again, change any burned out lamps. Depending on how a lamp burns out, it is possible for it to still pass current (the rest of the string still works) even though it does not itself light.

If you happen to be the one who actually purchases the Christmas tree lights, 20–35 light strings that can be connected together are infinitely easier to check than 100–300 light strings. This is true for home-use as well. When you think about what you're paying an electrician by the hour or what your own time may be worth, it's easy to see that paying $2 instead of $5 for a string of Christmas lights is not much of a bargain unless you are getting the best, most reliable, and easiest-to-fix product that money can ever buy.

CHROMA— One of the three perceivable properties of color. It refers to the amount of pure color in the mix. It is sometimes referred to as *purity* or *saturation*. See COLOR for a more detailed discussion.

CHROMATIC ABERRATIONS— These are uneven color rings around the pool of light. See ABERRATIONS, CHROMATIC.

CID— Abbreviation for COMPACT IO-DIDE DAYLIGHT, which is one of several kinds of discharge lamps.

CIE— Abbreviation for *COMMISSION INTERNATIONAL de l'ECLAIRAGE*, which is the international organization that regulates lighting standards. Among other things they have developed a chromaticity diagram (similar in concept to the Munsell color solid) that catalogs color by dominant wavelength and purity.

CIRCUIT— In its most generic meaning, this refers to a completed electrical path through a load. In practice, the electrical path is completed when an instrument or device is plugged in, so the circuits then refer to the female outlets. Each circuit is wired to a dimmer either in a flexible (patch panel) way or a permanent (hardwired) way.

CIRCUIT BREAKER— An overcurrent device that can be reset. See BREAKER.

CIRCUITING— In many venues the lighting designer is considered incapable of being able to figure out the complexity of the house circuiting. As a result, she is asked to submit her Light Plot without assigning circuits. This is usually based on one or more past bad experiences with previous lighting designers.

Even where the lighting designer is expected to assign the circuiting, the master electrician is supposed to check the designs for accuracy, and if he were to encounter weird or incorrect circuiting, he is usually empowered to correct it on the spot.

Having said all this, if there are to be 20 instruments at a position to which only 15 circuits are run, it is only the lighting designer who knows which (if any) of the 20 instruments could be combined together on the same circuits.

While there are clearly differing opinions on this, most lighting designers consider the circuiting to be part of their job and take the initial run at it. They are however thrilled (or ought to pretend they are thrilled) when someone else can come up with an even more efficient way to do the same thing.

CLAIR OBSCURE— There isn't really a comparable English word for this. Well there is (chiaroscuro), but it is hard to pronounce and spell and, as a consequence, will never be in common usage. It is usually explained as a light and shade drawing, which rather misses the point because the drawings are mostly shade with very little light. In a theatrical context, it refers to the ability to isolate a scene in light while keeping the rest of the surroundings in relative darkness. Someone called this "plucking the scenes out of darkness," which is a very visually accurate description of the process. Henry Irving is said to have been a master at this using gaslight and to have passed the technique along to his son-in-law, Gordan Craig. Both Craig and Appia did most of their theatrical sketches this way, as did Robert Edmund Jones in this country. It should be noted that it is considerably easier to sketch than it is to actually do with real lighting instruments.

CLAMP— This is a generic term covering a number of things that might be clamped together. In the context of stage lighting there are four general categories of hardware involved. First (and most obviously), it refers to attaching an instrument to a light pipe. Although in the early days there was a two-piece clamp (*yoke clamp* described separately), the *c-clamp* is now the most universally used method because the weight of the instrument is transferred to the pipe as soon as the instrument is hooked on. Where the instruments are being attached to a square channel like Unistrut™ or where they are being mounted on angle-iron-like wall brackets, then other special fasteners or clamps are used. Second, clamps refer to a group of cable or conduit clamps that attach the cables, wires or conduit to the sides of wooden members (beams) that are part of the building. Third, clamps refer to things that attach to ropes or wireropes. Sandbags attach to rope sets by means of trim clamps. Wireropes are attached back to themselves by means of Nicopress sleeves or wirerope clamps. Wirerope often attaches to a pipe by

means of two-piece pipe clamps that locks around a pipe with a bolt top and bottom and provides one or more holes on top for attaching a shackle. Fourth, clamps refer to crosspipe connectors of which Rota-locks and Cheeseboros are but two of many different brands and styles.

CLEAR— This is a computer lightboard term that usually means deleting the contents of something without deleting the container. Keyboard entries can be cleared. Channels can be cleared which sets them at off but typically displays blank on the screen rather than at 00. Faders can be cleared. Various parts of the old show (cues, patch, group assignments, submaster assignment, macros, etc) can be cleared.

CLEAR GEL— A clear color media that transmits almost all visible light. It is used primarily as a transparent base for broken color or painted on dyes.

CLEARING THE BOARD— This dates back to preset lightboards where it referred to taking all the sliders in a given preset to zero in preparation for resetting the next cue.

CLIP TERMINAL— See ALLIGATOR CLIP.

CLIPLIGHT— This is a commercially available product that has a semi-circular shade/reflector attached to a clip mechanism and takes ordinary light bulbs. Normally, it is used as a temporary shop light in the garage and around the home. In the theatre, it is sometimes used behind backings and in hallways or alcoves to make them look lit.

Cliplight

CLOTH FOCUS— See FOCUS, KINDS OF.

CLOUD EFFECT— See EFFECTS, KINDS OF.

CODE— The National Electrical Code has been adopted at the state and city level by law, often with some special modifications at the local level. Where only one code is referred to, it is usually the NEC.

CODES, COLOR— (1) Electric wires meant for high voltage are color coded as described below. (2) For low voltage direct current (battery) connections, the red wire is typically positive and the black wire is negative (common). (3) Color monitors on computer lightboards commonly display the channels in different colors to distinguish channels set by a fader pair from channels set by a submaster, from channels set by the keyboard, and so forth. (4) In its most generic usage, it refers to the color-coding of anything that looks identical but is in fact different, such as lengths of loose cables or instruments with different lamps (or different features).

The color-coding is usually done by means of colored tape or Avery labels or spray paint, and it usually needs to be readable from up close as well as from the deck. Bands of tape around the two ends of loose cables or bands of tape on the yokes of instruments are the most common methods. Light colored tape shows up best on black cable and dark colored instrument yokes. While the color-coding of cable lengths is not uncommon, cables are more commonly labeled with a unique number that is something like "xx-y" where "xx" represents the cable length and "y" is a unique 1,2,3,4 identifier. The reason for this is because it is often necessary to run several cables at the same time and there needs to be some way to determine which cable goes to which instrument on the other end.

CODES, COLOR (wire)— This is specified in the electrical code and has been adopted everywhere. Green means ground (sometimes called case ground), which connects the metal housing or "case" of instruments and other electrical apparatus to a metal rod driven into the ground. White means neutral which is also by a separate route connected to the same or a similar metal rod driven into the ground. Any other color is a hot wire connected to the electrical power. In 120-volt

circuits, this usually means black. In 240-volt circuits where there is no neutral, the two hot colors are usually red and black. In three phase services, the hot wires are usually black, red and blue. In conduits and electrical gutters where there are numerous conductors, it is not unusual to have many other colors and to have colors that have stripes of other colors. In the UK, green with yellow means ground, brown is hot and blue is neutral and the voltage is typically 240/415 rather than 120/208.

CODES, DATE or SHOW— As the lighting designer sits in the house looking at the display monitor waiting for the preview performance to start, it would not be uncommon to wonder if the corrected version of the show has been loaded onto the machine. She could use her headset and call and ask, but this is a lot like checking up on someone who one doesn't think is entirely trustworthy. It is far easier to simply imbed a code in the preset cue. Pick a channel that isn't used in the show (a phantom channel) and set it at a 1–31 level, which represents days of the month. Use other channels if needed to specify which show this is or what act this is as appropriate, but often the day of the month in the preset cue is all that is needed.

COLD— Disconnected from the electrical power, as in a "cold grid" where no power runs to the circuits.

COLOR— One of the eight variables of light caused by differing wavelengths within the visible range. Colors can essentially be different from each other in one of three ways. They can be a different *hue*, in which case they will be bluer or greener or redder than something else. They can be different in *value*, in which case they will be lighter or darker than a test gray scale. They can be different in *chroma* (also called *purity* or *saturation*), which means that on a scale between this color and a gray of equal value, a pure color has little or no gray. Scientists believe we can distinguish between 100–200 hues. We can distinguish between about 100 shades of gray and about 100 steps of saturation, which means we can see (distinguish) thousands of individual colors. In light, hues are equated to their dominant wavelength. Since black as a color of light does not exist, it is not immediately apparent how darker values of a color could be achieved, and without black to mix with white it is not immediately apparent how colors could be grayed down. In a very clever way the scientists have equated the brightness of the light to lightness or darkness, and have equated the amount of monochromatic color in the mix to purity.

Unfortunately, the human eye perceives brightness of the light distinct from its color qualities. A light blue gel dimmed down does not appear to be a darker blue but merely a dimmed down version of light blue. While it is true that a dark value of gel can be lightened by the addition of white light and made to appear a lighter color, there is no way to darken a light color without using a different gel. Grayed down colors can be created by adding complementary colors into the same gel frame (subtractive mixing) much in the same way that paint colors could be grayed down by the addition of the complementary color. For darker values of a color, a darker gel is required or double (triple) thicknesses of the same color. See VARIABLES OF LIGHT and also COLOR SPECTRUM and also COLOR MIXING for a more complete discussion of this subject.

COLOR ANOMALIES— Color perception phenomenon that do not follow Selective Absorption rules and that science cannot fully account for and explain.

After-images: If one were to stare intently at a green dot and then look away at a white wall, a reddish-orange dot might seem to appear on the wall, but it wouldn't really be there. If one stares into the faces of lighting instruments without proper eye protection, then one might well see dots of color, where there weren't any, for several days to come. If this were to occur during the load-in (which, of course, is exactly when it would

happen), it could prevent you from seeing the colors in any of your cues and would rapidly become a source of grave concern. This is why lighting designers wear glacier glasses or something similar. It is also possible (but rare) for an audience to see an afterimage during a blackout following an intensely bright scene

Color Constancy: The human eye has the ability to compensate for changes in illumination and viewing conditions that affect the color of an object. When we step outdoors, our clothes do not appear to change color even though the color temperature of the light has changed. The eye of a camera is not so forgiving and needs filters or color correction for the colors to appear to remain the same on the finished film. When you put on a cheap pair of sunglasses, the objects around you change color and become the color the glasses are, but the brain knows what the true colors are and so it compensates for whatever difference there may be. A series of color swatches lit by highly saturated colored light (deep red or deep something) will still look like their true colors. The red in a union jack should theoretically under blue light turn purplish, the blue should become a more intense blue and the white should turn blue. Thanks to color constancy a union jack looks red-white-blue whether it is lit by blue light or green light or any other color light. It may look somewhat different under different colors of light but it always looks like the true object color being lit by a strongly colored light. As a result true color distortion is a relatively rare occurrence. For the same reason, a white cyc looks like a white cloth lit by blue light rather than a homogenous blue surface.

Color Distortion: When a yellow book is lit with a blue light, it is supposed to turn green. It usually doesn't but merely looks like a yellow object lit by blue light, thanks to color constancy described above. On the rare occasion when it actually does make the object appear to change color, then it is called color distortion. It was the fashion for quite some time for lighting books to include a chart of what happened when green light interacted with a yellow surface color. Generations of costume designers and set designers worried about how the lighting would distort their work. Where true color distortion is most likely to occur (when it occurs at all) is with black because the color or dye may not be a true black but a very dark blue or dark maroon or dark something else. A saturated light like a dark blue scene change light can suddenly make a black sweatshirts look maroon, and the distortion is so complete that one has to walk onstage with a flashlight to see that the object itself is really not the maroon color it appears to be.

Color Neutralization: When one first looks at a blue-period Picasso, it may look awfully blue, but after having looked at it for a while, one gets past the blueness and starts to see the picture. The scientists have a name for this. They call it *color neutralization* and it relies on the fact that there is nothing real or absolute to compare the perceived color with. This is the active ingredient in putting color filters on cameras. If everything shifts, the eye adjusts and resets what it considers normal to be.

Incandescent Color Change: This is not really an anomaly at all, but it does result in the color appearing different. When stage lights are dimmed (whether incandescent or halogen), they change color (their Kelvin temperature changes) and as a result the gel colors look different. This is most noticeable when the lights are dimmed way down as is the case in extremely short throw situations. The colors become highly desaturated (not brilliant) and appear as a grayish version of what one thinks of as the "real" color. To some extent the eye compensates for the color shift by expecting white light to be redder when dim (Kriuthof Effect). There are also several other color changing effects caused by brightness changes. Something known as the Berzold-Brucke Effect notes that at brighter levels the two ends of the spectrum appear to move inward making the reds more yellow and the violets appear bluer. The Purkinje Phenomenon notes that in the low light conditions of twilight the red

flowers of the scientist's garden lost their color before the green ones. In terms of stage lighting, it is easiest to assume that incandescent color shift is responsible for all color changes related to brightness level. Since these changes cannot be successfully anticipated or counteracted in advance, the folk wisdom on the subject is that colors that sometimes look perfect at home look different when used onstage and have to be changed.

Simultaneous Contrast: This is an odd name for a vastly important concept, but it is intended to distinguish it from something called "successive contrast." If you were to see a blue-green light and then a blue light, successively (one after the other) the blue-green would appear to be much greener and the blue would appear to be much redder. In other words the contrast between the two colors would appear to be greater. This is called *successive contrast*, which we are not interested in because it has no real application in terms of stage lighting.

However, if you were to look at two colors side-by-side, they would appear to be more widely separated than they really were. In other words, the contrast between them would appear greater. This is called *simultaneous contrast* and is the basis of having arealight colors only moderately separated from each other (rather than absolute complements) and is the basis for our amazing ability to see microscopic color differences between two samples when viewed side-by-side, as when sorting through a box of mystery gels.

Overtones of Color & Complementary Shadowy Things: The scientists consider this all part of simultaneous contrast, explained above, but it is different enough that it needs to be discussed separately. Were you to shine a red, green and blue light at something, the results would be whitish but would not match the original white light because the shadows (from the multiple lights) would appear to have color overtones, which appear to be the complementary colors of the lights themselves. When a blue-green light strikes an object, its shadow will appear to be magenta-ish, and when a magenta light strikes the same object, its shadow appears to be blue-greenish. Whether these are the true complements or not is still being debated and it depends in part upon which color theory one subscribes to. Certainly the contrast between the original light color and the shadow has widened, and in that sense it is an example of simultaneous contrast.

COLOR CAPS— A vintage method of coloring an ordinary light bulb that involved putting colored glass globes about the size and shape of a jelly jar over them. It was primarily used with the footlights and to a lesser extent with the borderlights.

COLOR CHANGING, METHODS OF— This refers to changing colors in instruments while the performance is in progress. They fall into two general categories depending on whether they are done manually or by remote control.

Boomerang: These are either independent add-on devices or part of a followspot where colors are either put into the light path or removed from the light path. This can be done manually with each color having its own handle that tips the color into or out of position (as on a followspot) or it can be done electrically from a remote location.

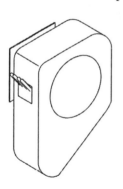
Color boomerang

Changing the Gel Frame: This is used on floor instruments and during intermission on easily accessible instruments, and it simply involves removing the old gel frame and inserting a new one. Often both are secured by safety lines to the instrument or support pipe. It is standard practice to use paper fasteners (or some other means) to secure the gels into the frames so that they cannot flutter out as they are being changed.

Color Wheel: This is an add-on accessory for a spotlight that fits in the gel frame slot.

A large wheel (18– 24" diameter) with 5–7 lens diameter sized holes spaced around its perimeter is affixed so that each one can be rotated in front of the lens. There often are no positive stops and the operator simply holds the wheel in place with one hand.

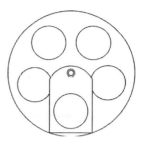
Color wheel

When the openings were stopped down to eye-shaped openings and the colors removed, a crude blinking or strobe effect could be created by spinning the wheel. This was called a *lobsterscope*, and it served much the same purpose as a current-day strobe light. Both color wheels and lobsterscopes could be motorized and controlled remotely.

Dichroic Filters: These are specially coated mirrors that only reflect certain wavelengths of light, making them work like color media except the color produced is purer and the transmission higher than that typical for ordinary plastic color media. They are presently used in intelligent lights for seamless color transitions. Their continued high cost, however, stands in the way of a more general use in the theatre.

Scroller: Color media is taped or glued together into a long roll that is rolled onto an empty roller on the other side of the instrument. Louis Hartmann describes using a manual version of this made of colored silk to create the famous three minute transition to dawn scene in the Belasco 1900 production of *Madam Butterfly*. Modern color scrollers can be remotely controlled and can

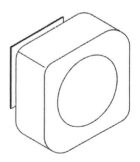
Color scroller

randomly select any frame of color, which is usually done while the instrument is off.

COLOR CODING OF WIRE— See CODES, COLOR (wire).

COLOR CONSTANCY— The human eye adjusts its color perception to take into account differences in the light color and sees the true color of objects. See COLOR ANOMALIES for a more detailed discussion.

COLOR CONTROL— This is the opposite of area control and refers to how the show would be hooked-up to the dimmers if there were not enough for there to be one for every instrument. In a situation where there were six areas being lit by two instruments-per-area but controlled by only six dimmers, area control would assign a dimmer to each area but color control would assign three dimmers to one color and three dimmers to the other color.

While this used to be a hugely important part of a design plan, it has mostly been made obsolete by the current practice of assigning each circuit its own dimmer. See AREA CONTROL and also MATRIX SYSTEM for a more detailed discussion.

COLOR CORRECTION— These are color media designed to make the color temperature of one source match the color of another source so that they will register the same on film or TV. The most common kinds of sources are tungsten, daylight and fluorescent but there are others including HMI and CID. In theatrical usage they are used like any other color, and it is not uncommon for the manufacturer to invent a new color name for them and put them in the gel sample books twice, once as a color correction filter and once as a stage color.

COLOR DISTORTION— A color phenomenon where the color of the light affects the perceived color of the object. See COLOR ANOMALIES for a more detailed discussion.

COLOR EXTENDER— A device that adds 3–6" to the front of a lighting instrument to protect saturated colors of gel from fading. See ACCESSORIES for a more detailed discussion.

COLOR FAMILIES— While the human eye can distinguish between thousands of colors, we tend the think in terms of color families. Thus red, orange, yellow, green, blue-green, blue, purple, magenta, brown, gray are all families of colors. Is yellow-green a family of color? Is violet part of the purple family or a family of its own? There is no definitive answer to these questions because individuals see colors differently, but most people think there are 10–15 color families and recognize that while peach, tangerine and cantaloupe may all be individual color names, they are all part of the orange family of color. When asked about favorite colors, most people pick a family of color like blue rather than a specific color like cobalt. When Sir Isaac Newton used a prism to separate white light into its component colors, he said he saw seven colors (representatives from seven families of color): red, orange, yellow, green, blue, indigo, violet. Indigo is usually dropped from the list these days, presumably because the scientists think Sir Isaac got it wrong.

Most people, if given a set of color chips, can arrange them in a circular way. In other words they think that orange looks like a combination of red and yellow and as a consequence should go between them, and when this is set up in a circular way it makes a *color wheel.*

COLOR FILTERS or MEDIA— The color of theatrical lights is changed by filtering out unwanted wavelengths of light by means of a filter. The filter can be either glass or plastic or gelatine (an animal product).

True gelatine has all but vanished from current usage. It dissolved when wet, became brittle when dry and faded almost instantly, so nobody misses it all that much. Its name, however, lingers on. While color filters and color media are the names that will be found in catalogs, in practice they are called either the *color* or the *gels* and when the color is put into the instruments, they are said to be gelled.

Glass was the first kind of color filter and was used as *rondels* for striplights. Traditionally its color selection has been limited, but the color never fades and the transmission percentages are acceptable. It is however expensive and fragile, but it is not nearly as fragile as one might expect, being about as difficult to break as a glass ashtray.

The plastics (of various kinds) hold up for a long time before they fade and are relatively inexpensive and come in a dizzying array of colors.

COLOR FRAME— A frame, usually metal but sometimes a heat resistant cardboard, that holds the color media in place in the front gel slot of the instrument. See ACCESSORIES for a more detailed discussion.

COLOR INTERACTION— This is a generic term that refers to colors looking different when seen in different contexts. See COLOR ANOMALIES for a more detailed discussion.

COLOR MIXING— For centuries graphic artists have been mixing pigments to produce paint colors. This is considered a subtractive process even though the paints are added to each other because it is thought the pigments absorb (which is to say subtract and filter out) some wavelengths and reflect the rest. See SELECTIVE ABSORPTION, THEORY OF for a more detailed discussion. When two colors adjacent to each other on the color wheel are mixed, a predictable intermediate color is produced, which will be slightly less pure than the purest of the parent colors. Yellow and orange for example will produce a yellow-orange. Mixing exact opposites will result in a color so desaturated that it will be virtually devoid of any color at all (grayish), and this is one of the most common ways that painters create muted colors. The other method involves mixing the pure color with a gray of equal lightness/darkness value. The mixing of not exactly opposite but widely separated colors will produce predictable intermediate colors with an intermediate value but a highly desaturated purity. The mixing of yellow and blue (widely separated by not opposite in most systems) produces an unsaturated greenish color.

There is an empirical principle at work here: *the mixing of two pure colors always results in a less pure color and the more widely separated the two parent colors are, the more impure the resulting color will be.* For a painter who has experience mixing color, it would be unthinkable to suggest that a pure green could result from a mixture of blue and yellow, so most painters do not believe that all colors can be created from any three or five basic colors.

In terms of light, the intermixing of two or more gels in one frame is a *subtractive mixing* process and follows the rules outlined above, including blue and yellow making a desaturated greenish color. Subtractive mixing is an excellent way to produce a desaturated color from a purer one, as most colors in a typical gel swatch book will be relatively pure or as pure as they can make them. Having two gels in the frame will also cut transmission significantly so less light will hit the stage than if a single gel of the correct color could have been found in the gel book.

In the mixing of paint, there is really no such thing as additive mixing. What comes closest is *mosaic fusion*, which involves tiny dots of color placed close together like a Scurat painting that the eye (when too far away to distinguish the dots from each other) interprets in terms of an intermediate color. Tiny dots of color is the principle behind color television screens, color photography and color printing.

Light is additively mixed together when two or more different colored lights hit a surface like a cyc. Adjacent colors can be mixed together to produce a predictable intermediate color of slightly less purity than the purest parent in the mix. The mixing of exact opposites will produce a whitish light, but the mixing is much less homogenized than either the mixing of pigments or the subtractive mixing of gels. It is as if each component color passes through each other, and the whitish color produced has color overtones of the two parent colors. On a colorimeter with two test screens, the white produced by the mixture of two opposite colors cannot be matched to a single source of white light. Widely separated colors produce for the most part predictable but highly desaturated intermediate colors. Thus red and blue will produce a highly subdued magenta. Blue and green will produce a desaturated blue-green, and red and green will produce a whitish color that some people interpret as being a representative of the yellow family. Sir Isaac Newton, who had no preconceived notions of how many primaries there ought to be, said categorically that the combination of red and green did not create yellow. This unfortunately has also been the theatrical experience of using three-color striplights or borderlights or any red, blue and green instruments used together. Mixing these three colors to produce white light produces a whitish light with objectionable color overtones that is not very bright. Any mix that involves green light produces green overtones that are particularly annoying as neither faces nor scenery nor costumes seem to look particularly good in green light, as it is not a naturally occurring light color. As a result, the green color is often removed and either left as white light or an amber is put in.

The additive color mixing process is often described as a way to produce almost any color that can be imagined. Certainly when Munroe R. Pevear introduced the three-circuit borderlight, this is what he hoped would result. In practice, however, amazingly few colors from a gel swatch book can be color matched by the mixing of any two other colors whether they are red, green, blue or some other combination closer to the color one is trying to match. Much in the same way that artists' colors are in their purest state as they come out of the tube, so lighting colors are often in their purest state as they come out of the gel book as it is the attempt of the manufacturer to produce brilliantly pure colors by dyeing plastics with the purest dyes that can be produced.

Color mixing is often a hotly contested issue, especially among those who have never actually tried it. I don't ask the reader to take my word or Sir Isaac's word or anyone's word for what color might be produced by the mixing of any two parent colors. Instead, I suggest the reader try this out independently with actual lights and gels. The information in the topic entitled COLORIMETER includes enough information to build such a device in an afternoon. Color mixing on a computer is done by mosaic fusion. A computer programmer decides what color is created when two other colors are supposedly mixed and then makes it so. Thus, in many color simulation programs the combination of red and green light will be seen to produce an intense yellow light because this is what the tri-chromatic theory suggests is what ought to happen. Lighting designers and students of lighting design, of course, need to look at what actually happens in the context of the colors and instrument sources they will be actually using.

COLOR MODIFICATIONS— Refers to modifications made to color media that either adds something else to the original color or cuts away parts of the original gel.

Broken Gel: This involves scotch taping gel scraps together into a collage. When used in a fresnel, an intermediate color often with slight color overtones is usually produced. When used it an ellipsoidal, an extremely soft-focus and very vague projection of the pattern will be produced. Intricate detail will not read onstage, but something simpler like blue on top and green below will.

Double Gelling: Also triple gelling and so forth creates darker versions of the same color. Each successive layer is less effective than the previous layer. If the initial gel cut white light by 90 percent, then the second layers cuts 90 percent of the remaining 10 percent and the third layer cuts 90 percent of the remaining 1 percent and so forth.

Frost Gel: Adding a frost gel has long been the answer to softening hard shutter lines and spreading the light further than it would otherwise want to go. There are a dizzying array of toughspuns, silks and frosts, all with very specific uses and properties. These are all *diffusion media* and commonly called *frosts* or *frost gels*.

Holes in the Gel: Where paper punch sized holes are put in the gel, it will have the effect of adding white light to the mix and lightening the color produced. The white light added in this way is usually a more homogenized mixture than can be achieved with additive mixing from a second instrument, and assuming that a lighter color could not be found in the gel box, this is an acceptable field expedient to produce one. The usual method involves folding the gel into quarters and cutting off the central tip with a pair of scissors, thus creating an irregular 1" or so hole in the middle of the gel. This hole-in-the-center method appears to work best with fresnels. For ellipsoidals, multiple use of a paper punch on a folded up gel seems to work better.

Multiple Gels: This was discussed as part of the subtractive color mixing process. Two colors are combined in a gel frame to produce a muted intermediate color that usually also has a low transmission percentage.

Strainer: This is usually a homemade device that looks like a sink strainer or a piece of a colander. It is made of a non-combustible material (metal or foil) with a lot of holes punched in it that is put in the gel frame with the gel or in the second gel slot (assuming there is one). It reduces the amount of light passing through and is used as a counter-measure to incandescent color shift. Let's say there is a bright blue gel in the instrument. Bringing down the dimmer is going to gray it down and make it less brilliant whereas the use of a strainer will allow the dimmer to remain at full, which will result in a somewhat more brilliant color onstage. Sometimes neutral density gray gel is used for the same purpose, but it does not appear to work quite as well.

Tracing Wheel: A tracing wheel is a sewing tool that has a circular wheel made up of needle-like points that is mostly used to trace a pattern onto fabric. The same tool in a scenic painter's toolbox is called a pounce wheel and is used to transfer a stencil to a

Tracing wheel

wall or other solid surface. Whatever name it is called by, when it is run across a piece of gel, it creates lines of tiny holes that are supposed to allow heat to escape and thus slow down the fading process (at least that is the theory). It used to be quite the fashion to do this to all dark colored gels, but the practice seems to have all but died out now. Whether it actually worked or not is still being debated but it certainly did no harm, as the holes were so small that they could not possibly have affected the color produced.

COLOR NEUTRALIZATION— A color perception phenomenon whereby the eye becomes accustomed to a color and no longer sees it as a strong color. See COLOR ANOMALIES for a more detailed discussion.

COLOR ORGAN (BRITISH: *sound-to-light*)— An electronic device that flashes circuits to the beat of the music. They are most common in a disco setting. Usually there are at least three circuits that respond to high, low and medium pitches. There is usually a slider to control the brightness of each circuit. As the name suggests they can often be played manually like a keyboard instrument. This is not to be confused with the color organs of the 1900s which were really a dimmer board designed to be operated by hands and feet like an organ console and were commonly called *lighting consoles* to distinguish them from other more conventional dimmer boards. Stanley McCandless in 1930 designed one for the Severance Hall in Cleveland, Ohio.

COLOR OVERTONES— Color rings at the edge of the cast shadow and also around white light created by widely separated colors being focused at the same spot. See COLOR ANOMALIES for a more detailed discussion.

COLOR PERCEPTION— The ability of the eye to distinguish colors. There are various kinds of color blindness, which prevent people from seeing colors normally. Color perception requires light levels higher than about 1 fc. In low-light conditions, all colors turn varying shades of gray. See EYE for a more detailed discussion.

COLOR SCROLLER— See SCROLLER.

COLOR SLOT— The groove at the front of the instrument that holds the color frame or some other accessory. On modern instruments there are often two color slots.

COLOR SOLID— A visual representation of color that extends the color wheel into three dimensions. It looks like a pyramid-shaped cone that has an identical cone upside down beneath it forming a diamond shaped solid. The round, fat center is a color wheel and the most pure colors are on the perimeter. The up-down centerline represents the white-black scale. Colors can occur anywhere in the solid. Colors get lighter as they move upward (*tints*) or darker as they move downward (*shades*), and get less pure as they move inwards (*tones*). Where the colors are

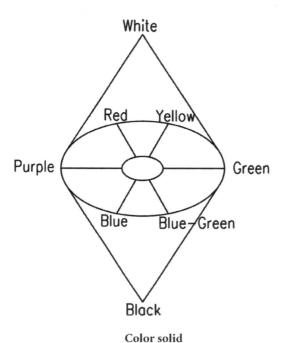

Color solid

chemical colors or mined colors, they will be of varying levels of purity. In purely practical terms, it will not be possible to find colors of equal purity to be on the outside of the circle, so the circle would look more like an irregularly shaped island, but it is otherwise an excellent visual aid and said to be the invention of Albert H. Munsell.

COLOR SPECTRUM— Light is electromagnetic energy that can be visually evaluated, which as it happens is a wavelength range from 380 to 780 nanometers, divided into seven color bands (of uneven width) which are the seven colors seen by Sir Isaac Newton (the colors of the rainbow). "ROY G BIV" is the acronym for remembering them in long-to-short wavelength order: red, orange, yellow, green, blue, indigo, violet. Indigo is often dropped from the list these days and sometimes replaced with blue-green. In gel sample books, it is common to provide a graph for each gel color showing what percent of which spectral colors it contains.

COLOR STANDOFF— The motion picture industry's name for a *color extender*. See ACCESSORIES.

COLOR SUBSTITUTION— The color for a show is typically decided upon at about the same time as the Light Plot is drawn. Depending upon where in the country one might be, the colors might or might not be in stock at the local theatrical supplier. As a result it is common practice for the lighting designer to either shop for the gels himself or to provide a list of alternate colors for each color listed. The manufacturers of the color usually provide color comparison charts on their web sites. However, these do not agree with each other. Most lighting designers do their own cross-comparisons, and although these have to be periodically revised as new colors are produced, they are also often included in lighting books.

COLOR SYMBOLISM— This dates back to the ideas of Adolphe Appia who envisioned light being like a musical score constantly changing with the emotions of the presentation (Wagnerian operas), and it is mostly expounded upon in older books. We have idioms in the language that relate colors to emotions: "His wife had left him, so he felt blue, and although he was green with envy, he was too yellow to do anything about it."

The problem with trying to use this in a theatrical way is that each color has multiple meanings, and when unnatural colors of light are used onstage, the audience tends to become confused and think they are missing something or worse they feel they have been deliberately kept out of some secret.

Color symbolism can work in a simplistic way in situations where the audience has come to understand what each color is supposed to represent. Let's assume that there is some story-theatre narration, "...and she walked through the woods (color one) until she burst forth into a rainy clearing (color two) and after walking many miles, finally the rain stopped and the sun burst through the clouds (color three)." At this point, those three light cues can be used symbolically to represent the woods, the rainy clearing, and the sunny clearing. It should be evident, however, that this kind of symbolism has the subtlety of a crayon drawing. It may be acceptable in a children's show or an opera, but most designers would find it too heavy-handed for a realistic play.

It was commonly believed around the turn of the century that science was getting very close to establishing a scientific base for the meanings of colors, but another century has turned, and we are no closer to having any conclusive evidence on this subject.

On the other hand, over the years the audience has come to understand that light that is blue in color is light provided so that they (the audience) can see but that the actors are not supposed to see. This is commonly called the *Night Vision Blue Convention*. Night scenes are typically lit this way, as are most scene changes. It has been going on since the time of Louis Hartmann and has now been borrowed by the cinema and television and is now more-or-less universally understood, and it is an example of a symbolic use of col-

ored light (as there is no naturally occurring source of blue light anywhere outdoors at night), but it may be the only one.

COLOR TEMPERATURE– The color of the light produced by a lamp will vary depending on what temperature the filament is heated to. When a blacksmith puts a piece of metal on the fire, it will first turn red and eventually become white hot. The Kelvin scale sets absolute zero (–273.15 degrees C) at 0 K. Visible light begins about 600 K and most theatre spotlights are in the 2700–3400 K range. Kelvin temperature makes a huge difference to the eye of the camera and various methods of color correcting need to be applied. In a live theatre situation, the human eye is much more flexible and tends to even out the differences. Still, the higher the Kelvin temperature at which a lamp burns, the whiter its light will appear to be, and it is hard to blend two instruments with the same gel color when their Kelvin temperatures are different.

COLOR TESTING— Most designers simply hold a gel sample up to a light source to evaluate its color. In most cases this is more-or-less accurate, but there are colors like x59 that appear to be one color when held up to a light source (purple) and appear to be another color when hitting a neutral surface (magenta). The safest method is to always test a color by putting it in an actual light and aiming it at a surface. Looking at objects through the gel, which is a third method that is sometimes mentioned, is an extremely poor way to judge the effect of a color as it will always appear more deeply colored than it will when put into an instrument and focused on the object.

COLOR THEORIES— Color theories are based on how many primary colors one thinks there are and how many steps one thinks there are around a color wheel. Sir Isaac Newton who invented the concept of primaries and secondaries said that when he divided white light into its component colors that he saw seven colors and five of them were primaries. This is not repeated much anymore because it conflicts with the currently held tri-chromatic theory, which is usually attributed to the work of English physicist Thomas Young and German physicist Hermann Ludwig Ferdinand von Helmholz in which the primary colors of light are said to be red, green and blue, and this is supposed to correspond to red, green and blue receptors in the human eye. The tri-chromatic theory however fails to explain how it might be possible to have a certain form of color blindness in which yellow can be seen but not red, and yet that form of color blindness is documented and exists.

In the early days of stage lighting in this country (1910 and earlier) the tri-color theory was embraced by Munroe R. Pevear and in addition to manufacturing a line of gelatine colors of exceptional purity, he is credited with producing the first three-circuit borderlights in order to take advantage of color mixing. Three-circuit borderlights were amazingly popular and are still available in striplights today, despite the fact that they have never been able to produce all colors, certainly never a usable yellow or even very many different colors at all. The continental Europeans of the time had their own tri-color system for theatrical use that favored red and green with either white or yellow. See COLOR MIXING/Additive Mixing for a more detailed discussion.

For paint mixing purposes the primaries are considered to be red, yellow, and blue, and this works out about as poorly except that paint tends to mix more completely than light. Red and blue can produce purplish colors. Yellow and blue can produce greenish colors. The colors produced are never pure, saturated colors but tend instead to be highly grayed down, unsaturated colors. Graphic artists use color that is in its purest state as it comes out of the tube. Intermixing two pure colors always results in a less pure color. Graphic artists typically have hundreds of colors at hand. If they could mix all these from any three other colors, they would certainly be doing so.

Why should painters have one set of primaries and lighting designers another set? This is particularly baffling because according to the currently accepted color perception theory (the theory of selective absorption) objects aren't supposed to have any color. A red car looks red because its paint coating absorbs all wavelengths of light (colors) except red and as a result the car appears to be red. So if objects (which includes paint) don't really have color, then they couldn't have primaries or secondaries or any other kind of color. Harold Ridge among others has suggested that the graphic artists might have been a bit confused on their color names and what they were calling blue was really more of a cyan and their red more of a magenta, so according to this line of thinking the painter's primaries would then be the same as the secondary light colors (CMY) which would then restore some semblance of symmetry, but most painters are not confused and know the difference between blue and cyan.

Out of frustrations such as this, other color theories have come into being. In the opponent-color theory of Ewald Hering, the differences between having one set of primaries for surface colors and another for light are resolved because yellow is added as a primary color.

A Boston painter and art teacher, Albert H. Munsell, developed a five primary system that included purple, that some would say was really intended to be a 10 primary system as there are 10 principle colors with 10 even steps between them and thus 100 hue steps around a color wheel.

There is also a six-color theory that adds blue-green.

For color cataloguing purposes, the tri-chromatic theory is adequate but only by using the concept of negative mixing. A brilliant yellow could be color matched to a percentage of red and green and negative blue. In terms of a colorimeter with two test screens, the brilliant yellow would be so grayed down by the addition of blue that it would at some point match a mixture of the red and green. Obviously, this has no application for stage lighting where the only question is what colors when mixed together will produce which other colors.

COLOR TRIANGLE— A variation of the color wheel that only applies to a three primary system. It is a way to visually represent the relationship of primary to secondary colors, and like the color wheel, which is discussed next, opposite colors are presumed to be complementary colors.

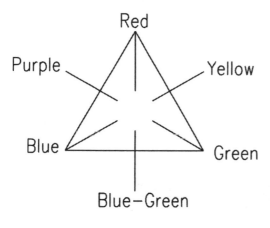

Color triangle

COLOR WHEEL, ACCESSORY— See COLOR CHANGING, METHODS OF.

COLOR WHEEL, PHYSICS— Families of color are organized into a circular pattern, which is the way most people think color

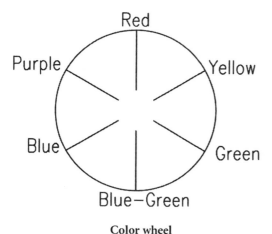

Color wheel

families relate to each other. Theoretically, each color is supposed to be opposite its complementary color. In a three or six primary system (as it relates to light rather than paint) the complement of red will be blue-green, but not so in a four primary system such as the opponent-color theory of Ewald Hering. The color wheel then is a visual representation of a particular color theory. See COLOR SOLID and COLOR THEORIES for a more detailed discussion.

COLORED LIGHT— Colored light is rare in nature. Sunlight is by definition white light. Moonlight as a reflection of sunlight is also white. While the sun at sunset or sunrise can produce spectacular sky colors, the color of the light hitting a white piece of paper would appear colorless or a very pale tint.

In the absence of real shade and shadows, colored light (different colors) are used in a theatrical situation to make the hills and valleys of three-dimensional objects (like actors' faces) look different, thus making the objects visible (plasticity). The bounds of naturalism are often stretched and light at dawn can be a good deal pinker onstage than it ever is in real life. Afternoon light can be much more amber-colored than it would ever be in real life. To a certain extent the audience expects that the lighting in the theatre will be somewhat romanticized. It is all too easy however to let the color become so exaggerated and unrealistic that the audience doesn't know what is being suggested anymore.

The truth of the matter is that at the time it became possible to use colored lights, the theatre was badly in need of a way to separate one scene from another visually. The only existing method at the time had been to make the lighting brighter or dimmer. With the advent of easy to install color, it became possible to make scenes a slightly different color, and this was such a powerful tool that no one much cared if it made naturalistic sense or not.

There have been over time people who have complained about the use of color in the lights in theatre. Bertolt Brecht was certainly one of these and Tyrone Guthrie was, perhaps, another because in a celebrated quote he complained that the stage always appearing to be "a weak solution of apricot jam," but perhaps he was just trying to be humorous. Where the use of color is not permitted, the amount of differentiation possible between scenes is disappointing. Since the lighting designer's two principle tools are brightness and color, ripping one away from her seems a pointless injustice. It does however point to a very real problem, which is that beginning lighting designers tend to use way too much color because they find white light boring and don't see how their designs will get noticed unless they are somehow shockingly different. It is a common and predictable mistake, but it leads to overreactions by directors and producers. When color is used delicately, the scenes can be made to look different while no one is particularly aware that color is being used at all, which is commonly referred to as having the *appearance of white light.*

COLORIMETER— This is a device with a divided screen where there are typically three lights aimed at each screen. In its scientific use, a test color can be placed on one screen and by the use of negative mixing it can be color matched to a RGB combination on the other screen. In the theatre, since negative mixing has no application, the colorimeter then acts as a test screen to see what colors can be produced by additively mixing RGB or any other combination, and then these colors can be compared to commercially available colors. Disappointingly few gel colors can actually be produced from intermixing RGB or any other three-color combination for that matter. The product of a mix of two pure colors is usually a middle color that has been so grayed down that the color is often unrecognizable.

A good classroom demonstration unit can be made with drafting paper screens and bedroom pin-up lights of about 60 watts each plugged into household dimmers. A good personal unit can be made with C7 Christmas tree lights, PVC plumbing tees and household dimmers that is so compact that it can use the gel samples in the gel book without having to remove them.

When people talk about experimenting with color mixing, this is usually the device they envision using.

COLORINE— See LAMP DIP.

COLORS, PRIMARY— A unique color that cannot be created by the mixture of any two or more other colors. Primary colors by definition can be combined with other primaries to produce secondary colors and tertiary colors and all other colors, but not visa-versa (intermixing secondaries will not produce the primaries, at least that's the theory). Lest there be any confusion, if there is even one color sample produced that cannot be duplicated by the intermixing of the primary colors, then those colors were not really the primaries. The idea of primaries and secondaries dates back to Sir Isaac Newton who first discovered or was the first person able to prove that white light was made of component colors (he saw seven). In the course of experimenting with these colors, he decided that indigo and orange could be created by the intermixing of blue with violet and red with yellow. The other five colors he considered primaries. The question of how many primaries there are is a hotly contested issue, but it has little actual effect on the theatrical lighting designer except as it relates to color mixing. See COLOR THEORIES and COLOR MIXING for a more detailed discussion.

COLORS, SECONDARY— The intermediate colors created by mixing two primary colors.

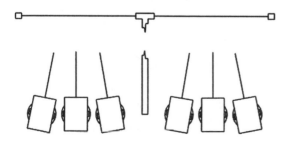

Colorimeter

COLORS, TERTIARY— A color derived from mixing three primary colors. In the tricolor system orange and yellow-green would both be considered tertiary colors as yellow is the secondary color that they lie on either side of, and they are a mixture of the secondary and a primary (i.e. three primaries).

COLUMNS— In the context of dividing the stage into areas, there are rows of areas that extend left and right and columns that extend downstage and upstage.

COMMISSION INTERNATIONAL de l'ECLAIRAGE (Abbr. CIE)— This is the organization that regulates international lighting standards. Among other things they have developed a chromaticity diagram that catalogs color by dominant wavelength and purity.

COMMON— In reference to DC current, it refers to the negative pole and is typically color-coded black.

COMPACT IODIDE DAYLIGHT (Abbr. CID)— One of several kinds of gaseous discharge lamps that approximates daylight lighting at 5600 K.

COMPANY SWITCH— A fused electrical box including a disconnect handle that is provided for hooking up auxiliary dimmers. In a rental house, it is common to have a house board that controls the houselights and worklights and a few stage pockets and a company switch that handles the road boards brought in by the production company. The company switch is often one or more three phase, four-wire services with legs of 400 amps or more.

COMPARTMENTED— Divided into compartments to keep the colors from mixing together. It has been used on borderlights, footlights, cyc lights etc since about 1903 onward, although the older trough kind of borderlights were still being listed in catalogs well into the 1960s.

COMPLEMENTARY COLORS— Colors that are opposite on a color wheel, and which when mixed together, will theoretically produce a white light.

COMPONENT DIAGRAM— One of two ways to draw an electrical circuit diagram that shows the components located where they will be. See WIRING DIAGRAM.

COMPRESSION (of areas)— Placing lighting areas closer to each than beams touching so that their beams actually overlap slightly. See AREAS, DIVIDING The STAGE INTO for a more detailed discussion.

COMPUTER LIGHTBOARD (operation)— They all come with an instruction manual that often runs to 1000 pages or more. Often these manuals can be downloaded from the manufacturer's site on the Internet. One should, of course, read the one that pertains to one's particular lightboard. Having said that, they are well on their way to having standard features that work more-or-less the same way. See LIGHTING CONTROL/ Computer Memory Lightboards.

COMPUTER-ASSISTED DESIGN— While this has broad applications for the many drawings done by the scenic designer, it is mostly limited to a Light Plot drawing program in the context of lighting design as this is often the only "drawing" as opposed to a list or other form of paperwork. .See LIGHT PLOT, CAD for a more detailed discussion.

CONCAVE— Like a cave, it goes inward. This is a term used to describe the shape of lenses and reflectors. Reflectors are for the most part concave and lenses tend to be convex and hump outward.

CONCEPT, LIGHTING— This is a lighting idea that needs to be explained in order to be understood. It usually is used to explain why the lighting is going to do something different from what is called for in the script or different from what a reasonable person would consider logical in the context of time, place and situation. A director once told me that the scenes where the characters lied to each other should be dark and the scenes where they were being truthful should be brightly lit, to which I wisely said, "Uh huh." This is clearly a lighting idea that needs to be explained to be understood. Unhappily, the idea never made it to production because the director subsequently decided that since it was a comedy, all the scenes should be brightly lit, so there couldn't be any dark scenes. There is nothing wrong with a symbolic use of lighting as long as the audience knows the code. However, the introduction of an unmotivated and unexplained weird color or brightness level of light is more likely going to confuse an audience. It is quite possible to design the lighting for a show and to have no concept whatsoever except that the audience should be able to see the actors perform.

CONCEPT, PRODUCTION— Where it exists, it is a statement by the director usually related to what this play is about or what its importance is supposed to be. In the commercial (as opposed to academic) theatre, most directors usually say they expect comedies to be funny and serious plays to be interesting and leave it at that. Where there is an announced concept, it usually involves some scheme to make a vintage play more accessible to a modern audience by setting it in a different historical time period or something similar. The concept can embody a production style that will affect the lights.

CONCERT BORDER— Although the term is not universally understood to mean the same thing, it is said to date back to a time when a concert often followed a dramatic production and the front set of borderlights (usually the best set) would be used to illuminate this. Thus, it is commonly used to refer to the borderlights on the first electric.

CONCERT LIGHTING— See LIGHTING, KINDS OF.

CONDENSER LENS— This refers to lenses that consolidate the available light into a tighter more compact angle. Often more than one lens is involved. All ellipsoidals have condenser lens systems.

CONDUCTOR— Anything that conducts electricity is a conductor. Some materials like gold, copper and aluminum are better than say steel, water or tin, which is not to say that one couldn't get a shock from any of the latter materials. Electric cattle fences, for example, typically use steel wire.

CONDUCTOR'S LIGHT— This is the light or lights that illuminate the musical conductor both during the curtain call and during the performance so that the singers and musicians can see her. See ORCHESTRA LIGHTS for a more detailed discussion.

CONDUIT— This refers to a metal or plastic pipe in which individual electrical conductors run as part of a permanent wiring system. The most common kind of conduit is called EMT (thin wall conduit), which stands for electrical metallic tubing, which is too thin to be threaded like water pipe.

CONNECTION, MAKING ONE— The electric code requires that these be made inside an electrical box or device. The secret of doing this successfully is making sure that the electrical cable is firmly gripped by the device so that there is no strain on the connections themselves. This is commonly called *strain relief* and it is especially important on electrical connectors. Once strain relief is provided, the actual connection can be made by means of a crimp on lug (notorious for not holding very well), or by bending the wire to the right around the connecting screw. Another method, called a *pressure connection*, (which was used before the concept of strain relief had been fully visualized) can be used inside connectors and it involves dividing the wire strands in half, capturing the connecting screw in the middle and then joining all the strands back into one wire before bending to the right around the screw. It provides an extremely secure connection that is unlikely to pull loose. Two or more loose wires are usually connected together by wirenuts, which rely on friction.

CONNECTORS, KINDS OF— There are three kinds in common usage in the theatre.

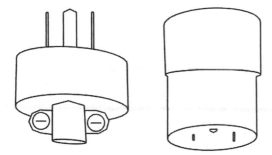
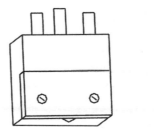
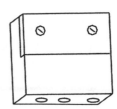

Stagepin connectors

Parallel-blade grounded connectors

Parallel-blade Connectors (Abbr. PB): These are household connectors except that household connectors mostly have a 15-amp capacity and the code requires that connectors used as permanent wiring in the theatre be 20-amp capacity. The 15-amp version has two parallel blades that do not stay connected very well. The 20-amp version has two blades at 90 degrees to each other, which also don't stay connected very well. They are designed so that 15 amp males can be plugged into 20 amp females but 20 amp males can only be plugged into 20 amp females. The prongs can be twisted slightly to increase friction and improve electrical contact but they usually need to be taped or tied together. The two blades used to be identical in shape but now the neutral is wider. When there is a third grounding prong, which is round or half-round, the connector is called *parallel-blade-grounded* or *PBG* for short. In stage usage, they are mostly encountered on practical lights or small appliances used onstage. While the 20-amp size could be used on stage lights, they do not stand up as well to long-term usage as the stagepin connectors (prongs bend and plastic housing breaks).

Stagepin Connectors (Abbr. 2P&G): These are the most widely used because they are both inexpensive and extremely durable. They have ¼" split-pins that provide excellent electrical contact. When the pins begin to loosen up, the split-pin can be spread apart. They often have see-through covers so that the inner connections can be plainly seen. Since they rely on friction to keep them connected, they are often gaffer taped or tied

together in a situation where they might pull apart of their own weight.

Twist-lock-ground Connectors (Abbr. TLG): These have blades that slide together and because they can be twisted to lock them together, they are supposed to stay together better. Unfortunately, they do not twist more than about an eighth of an inch and the slightest movement can unlock them, and in that respect they are no better, but are significantly more costly, than either stagepins or parallel-blade-ground connectors, which they are supposed to replace. They are also not very forgiving of being dropped, and not only can their prongs be bent but the plastic housings on the connectors can be cracked and broken.

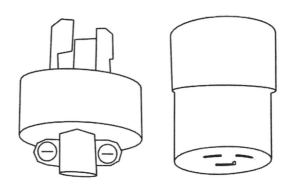

Twist-lock ground connectors

CONNECTORS, SOLDERLESS or WIRE— See WIRENUTS.

CONSOLE— Another name for a LIGHT-BOARD, which suggests an organ-like desk of some kind that is not portable.

CONTACTOR— Another name for a RELAY.

CONTINUITY— This refers to electricity being able to follow an uninterrupted path around a circuit. Where continuity does not exist, the circuit is broken, as with a burned out lamp.

CONTINUITY TESTER— See ELECTRICAL TESTERS.

CONTROL BOARD or CONTROL HEAD— See LIGHTBOARD.

CONTROL BOOTH— See BOOTH.

CONTROLLER— This refers to a control handle on a preset or computer memory lightboard, where the controller is a potentiometer that sends a low voltage signal to a dimmer or other control.

CONVENIENCE OUTLET— Electrical outlets (PBG females, usually duplexes) that are provided at 12' or less intervals for the plugging in of miscellaneous unspecified electrical loads. Both residences and theatre workspaces have places where appliances or portable lights can be plugged in, and these are all commonly called convenience outlets. The opposite of a convenience outlet is a *dedicated* outlet, which is an outlet provided for a specific appliance or tool and is usually on its own circuit.

CONVENTIONAL (lights)— Instruments that don't move. Where this term is used, it would be used to differentiate moving lights from stationary lights.

CONVENTIONS— See THEATRICAL CONVENTIONS.

CONVEX— This is the opposite of concave and refers mainly to lenses that are flat on one side and humped out (convex) on the other side.

COOKIE— Short for CUCALORUS, which was the vintage name for a *gobo* pattern.

COOL COLORS— Warm colors are those found in flames or embers. The cool colors are the opposite and include greens and blues and some violets. When a green color becomes too yellow, it becomes a warm color. The same thing happens when a violet color gets enough red in it to look like magenta. Whether a color is warm or cool is to some degree a matter of personal judgment and what other colors the test color is seen in proximity to. Surprise Pink is usually used as an example of a color that can be either warm or cool depending on its context.

CORD— (1) This is what comes on electrical appliances and table lamps. It may or may not be lamp cord, but it is usually a smaller gauge than stage cable and typically has a lighter duty outer sheathing and is very flexible. (2) Cordage like Venetian blind cord used for tie lines.

CORD TIES— See CABLE TIES.

CORE— The soft iron core in the center of an autotransformer dimmer.

CORNER STAGE LIGHTING— See LIGHTING, KINDS OF.

CORRECTION FACTOR (Abbr. CF)— This is a number which when multiplied by some other number corrects for a different circumstance. Lamp correction factors when multiplied by the illumination levels found will correct for the use of a less bright lamp.

COSINE DISTRIBUTION— Also called *flat-field distribution*, it refers to adjusting the position of the lamp in an ellipsoidal relative to the reflector so that there is no center hot spot and the whole area appears evenly lit. Technically the beam angle will be set to 2/3 of the field angle.

COSTUME DESIGNER, MEETING WITH— It is traditional for the lighting designer to look at the costumes prior to their appearance onstage. There is no corresponding duty to look at the set in the set designer's presence.

Whether this viewing of the costumes makes any difference whatsoever in how the lighting plan is worked out can be a hotly contested issue. On the one hand, the lighting designer is supposed to make the costumes look as good as possible. How is that going to be possible if she hasn't even bothered to look at them? On the other hand, the lighting designer's first duty is to make the actors' faces look good, and it is unclear how one might go about lighting the faces trapped within the clothes in one way and light the clothes themselves some other way. None the less, if this is expected and a tradition, there is no reason to snub the costumer.

Where this is regarded as an unpleasant necessity by the costumer, it can be eliminated by mutual consent. As mentioned elsewhere in the context of the agenda at production meetings, the lighting designer is mostly concerned about big hats and vast expanses of white around the faces and the costumer is mostly concerned that the lighting colors might somehow distort the costume colors. If these things can be laid to rest, there is really no point in having an inspection.

Costumers don't like to be told they can't use hats because they consider them a hugely valuable tool in revealing character and differentiating one character from another. It is the director who ultimately must decide which way to go on this issue.

If the lighting designer were to conduct an inspection of the costumes and came upon things she didn't like, what would she then do about it? Having a fight with the costume designer would be pointless and would be remembered forever. She could take her concerns to the director who would then either do something or not. All costumes are accepted by the director on the condition that if they don't work out, they can be cut. Lighting cues are also treated in a similar way. It is usually easier to wait until the hat or other costume piece appears onstage so that everyone can clearly see what the problems with it (if any) are, and the director can then either cut it or not.

COSTUME PARADE— A time when the director looks at all the costumes (sometimes also the make-up and hair) under stage light.

This is often scheduled just prior to the first technical rehearsal that will involve costumes. Often it is omitted and the costumes are merely seen in the context of the first runthru in which they appear. While the costumes are seen under stage light, they are not necessarily seen in the same light they will be seen in during the show. The lighting designer usually provides a generic, white light for the occasion. Any time a single element of the show is singled out like this for a detailed inspection, the more likely it becomes that there will be things found wrong, which is why most costumers are under-enthused about the event.

COUNT— There were no clocks or electronic timers on manual lightboards, so the operator or board captain counted off seconds, "one-thousand and one," and so forth. Cues are usually still described in terms of counts where it is understood that they correspond to seconds.

COVE POSITION— Used interchangeably with *beam position* to refer to any front-of-house position on or near the ceiling of the house. A cove is always a concealed-from-view slot in the ceiling that goes in like a cove. Sometimes slots in the audience sidewalls are also called *coves* or *wall coves*. While it is a relatively simple matter to design a cove that will conceal lighting instruments from view of the audience, it is considerably harder to do that in a way that also allows the light to travel to the stage without hitting anything along the way. If the coves are too deep or their openings too small, the light will hit the inside of the opening on the way out and possibly cast a shadow on the stage below. If they are not sufficiently below the ceiling or away from the sidewalls of the house, they are likely to *flash and burn* on these surfaces, which at the very least is distracting and unattractive.

CP— Abbreviation for CANDLEPOWER. Early light bulbs were rated by their candlepower rather than their wattage or lumen output.

CRADLE (cable)— Where light pipes raise and lower, there has to be enough slack in the cable bundle so that the pipe can be lowered in to chest height. When it is taken out to working height, then the slack is taken up in a loop and a cable cradle is used (like a wirerope thimble) to make sure the bend in the cable bundle is gradual over a crescent shaped surface. The cable cradle usually has high sides or clamps of some kind to contain the bundle and is taken up on a spot line.

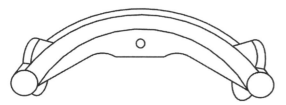

Cable cradle

CRAIG, EDWARD GORDON (1872–1966)— An English actor, son of Ellen Terry, who played leading roles for his father-in-law Sir Henry Irving on the London stage before becoming a producer and establishing a theatre and school in Florence Italy. He wrote two books that related to scenery and lighting: **Art of the Theatre** in 1905 and **Towards a New Theatre** in 1913. He thought that the scenery should be three-dimensional and simple, and he believed in the importance of light and shade in setting the scene. In 1912, he designed a production of **Hamlet** at the Moscow Arts Theatre for Russian director Konstantin Stanislavski, and his books are filled with sketches of moments from famous Shakespearean plays. He is best remembered for his *Übermarionette* theory, which depending on how one looks at it, suggested either that live actors be replaced by puppets or suggested that they should act more like puppets and do only what their puppet master told them to do. He and Adophe Appia are considered the prophets of the *new stagecraft* movement of the 1920s adopted by American designers such as Lee Simonson and Robert Edmund Jones.

CRESCENT WRENCH— Once a tradename, it is now used universally to describe an adjustable open-end wrench of a particular style. It is the most commonly used lighting tool because it will fit all common sizes of bolt heads, but there are other kinds of wrenches specifically made for stage lighting purposes. See WRENCHES for a more detailed discussion.

CRESSET— A torch-like object that involves a container on a pole in which oil, pine knots, pitch or resin soaked rope is burned. Its use as a source of stage lighting is said to date back to the 1300s. Candles eventually replaced cressets, and primitive oil lamps as they provided a more smoke-free light.

CRIMPING TOOL— This refers to one of two tools used by electricians. The most commonly seen tool in the theatre is the one that applies crimp-on terminals to the ends of 12 gauge wires. It looks like a pair of pliers and usually has built-in wire-stripper slots. The second tool (not pictured) is used by professional electricians to connect bare grounding wires together into a bundle as in a circuit breaker box, which is not something that lighting designers or technicians are likely to have occasion to do.

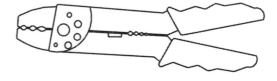

Crimper

CROSSARMS— In the context of a lighting boom, this refers to pipes that are attached horizontally to provide hanging positions, which technically turns the boom into a lighting tree even though it would not be uncommon for it to still be referred to as a boom.

Right: Crossarms on a lighting boom.

CROSSFADE— See FADES, KINDS OF.

CROSSFADER— Also called a *split-cross-fader* or a *fader pair*. It is a pair of handles on a remote control lightboard (either preset lightboard or computer memory lightboard) that work together to transition from one cue setting to another. See LIGHTING CONTROL/Computer Memory Lightboards for a more detailed discussion.

CROSS-LIGHTING— Originally one of three competing methods of lighting the stage, it referred to lighting the stage with two washes, one coming from the right side of a pipe on a proscenium stage and the other from the left side of the pipe. Stanley McCandless popularized this method as being the minimum required, and he declared the best angle of separation between left and right instruments to be 90 degrees. Depending on the location of the light pipes, this sometimes resulted in the far right stage area being lit from some place to the right of the centerline of the pipe. As time went on, cross-lighting came to be synonymous with two instruments-per-area regardless of the exact angle of separation and regardless of which half of the pipe the instrument was on.

CROSSOVER PIPE— See CABLE PIPE.

CROSSPIPE CONNECTORS— A hardware piece that holds two pipes together where they cross each other. There are several different styles and brands (*Rota-lock* and *Cheeseboro*) that differ from each other in terms of ease of installation and number of bolts that need to be tightened. Some involve sliding the second pipe through an opening in the hardware piece and some are composed of two halves bolted together.

CROSS-SECTIONAL— Called a *sectional* for short. It is a drawing showing a vertical slice of the stage area usually taken at the centerline. The instruments appear in side view. It is most commonly produced as a working drawing and not meant to be shared or distributed. Its primary use is to make sure that

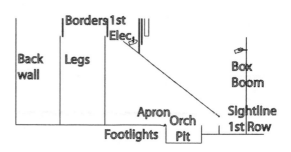

Cross-sectional drawing

rows or zones of lights adequately cover the stage from front to back and, in proscenium theatres, are adequately masked from view. A second, less frequently needed, cross-sectional would show a left/right slice and would be used to show the way the sidelights crossed the stage.

CRT— Short for *cathode ray tube*. It was once the only technology for monitor screens and as a result used generically to mean the display screen, more commonly now just called the *monitor*.

CTB or CTO— Color correction filters that correct-to-blue (daylight) or correct-to-orange (tungsten). Typically, the correction is done by eighths or sixth's, so there would be colors with names like half-blue and quarter-blue and one-third-blue and so forth.

CUBE TAP— This is a common household electrical device that allows three appliances to be plugged into one outlet. It is used for the same purpose in the theatre. A plugging strip achieves the same result and is marginally safer because it has a built-in circuit breaker, but the fire department inspectors do not like to see either one in plain sight.

CUCALORUS— From the Greek meaning the breaking up of light. They were called *cookies* for short, but neither term is used anymore, although either might be encountered in a vintage book. Now they are called *gobo* patterns. *Gobo* originally referred to an opaque mask (whatever preceded black foil) at the front of the instrument to control the light.

CUE— A very overused word that has at least three different meanings, and it is always essential to hear it in its context. (1) The event that triggers the change in the lighting, usually an actor's movement or a cue line (2) The actual lighting transition (the part of the cue where the lights are changing) (3) The state of the lighting at the end of the transition. Here's an example in context "What's the cue (trigger) for cue 56, and could you put us in the cue (state of lighting) before that so that we can see it (the transition) run?"

CUE SETTINGS— This refers to a completed state of lighting, which is commonly called a *look*. See LIGHTING IDEAS for a more detailed discussion.

CUE SHEET (BRITISH: *Board Running Plot*)— Once the most valuable lighting document there was, now it has been reduced to an area on the display screen that displays the cue number, the time, and optionally a short description.

For a manual board, there would typically have been three columns of information. On the left, there would have been the cue line, the cue description, the cue number, and the timing. The middle column would have described the *action*, i.e. what the operator's two hands were supposed to do. This was often written as fractions (dimmers on top, levels below them) with a "then" written between steps in the process. The last column was the *advance* column, i.e. what needed to be done to prepare to do the next cue. This usually meant replugs. Most designers and electricians made up their own blank forms for this. The one below is typical of the information contained.

When preset boards came in, the cue sheet remained essentially the same but now there were no longer sequential things that had to be done by both hands during the actual cue. Now essentially the split crossfader (XA and XB) moved between up and down positions. The advance column not only included replugs but also included notes about when to reset the presets. It was easier and less con-

Manual Board Theatre Company		Artichoke 2/12/01		Lighting Cue Sheet Page 4
Description			Action	Advance
"Have mercy…EXT Gib			8-12	
12	5 ct	Dn on Kit	0	
			1-4	
13	5 ct	Up on J&A #2	8	
"days have elapsed…advisable			1-4	
14	5 ct	Dn on J&A	0	
			8-12 20 then 8,10	
15	5 ct	Up on Kit, late aft	7 5 8	
"leave my hair on your pillow…embrace			8-12	Replug to 9A
16	5 ct	Dn on Kit	0	
			1-4	
17	5 ct	Up on J&A #3, morn	8	
"makes the tea taste funny			1-4	
18	5 ct	Dn on J&A	0	
…			8-12 20 then 8,10	
19	5 ct	Up on Kit, morn	7 5 8	

Cue sheet, manual board

fusing to actually have the resets on a separate sheet and identify them as either A1,B1, A2,B2 or Ia,IIa, Ib,IIb, etc depending on if one called the up position A and the down position B, or if it was a multi-preset board and there were 5 or more presets, which might be numbered I thru V. Presets were either adjusted as-noted-but-otherwise-left-alone (*readjusted*) or they were cleared and *reset*. The form below is a combination form that could be used both as the Cue Sheet form and as a Reset Sheet. If the show were uncomplicated, it would be possible to put the resets on the same sheet as the cues, but if a cue didn't look right, the operator would have to page backward to the point where the reset had been done, and this had to be clearly marked because if a mistake had been made, it had to be found and fixed fast.

Note that the reset that occurs after cue 15 is an adjustment and only the three dimmers noted change. This is the preset for cue 17. When one gets to cue 17, if it looks wrong, then it would be necessary to page back to here to see what went wrong.

If one were to write a cue sheet for a computer board, it would look a lot like the second one on page 67.

This is about the same as what is typically presented onscreen.

Preset Board
Theatre Company — Artichoke — 2/12/01 — Lighting Cue Sheet — Page 4

Description	Action	Advance
"Have mercy….EXT Gib	XB	
12	5 ct	Dn on Kit	Up to bo	
	XA	
13	5 ct	Up on J&A #2	Up to A3	
"days have elapsed…advisable	XA	
14	5 ct	Dn on J&A	Dn to bo	
	XB	Adj Sc A for 17
15	5 ct	Up on Kit, late aft	Dn to B4	
"leave my hair on your pillow…embrace	XB	Replug to 9A
16	5 ct	Dn on Kit	Up to bo	
	XA	Adj Sc B for 19
17	5 ct	Up on J&A #3, morn	Up to A3	
"makes the tea taste funny	XA	
18	5 ct	Dn on J&A	Dn to bo	
…	XB	
19	5 ct	Up on Kit, morn	Dn to B4	

Computer Board
Theatre Company — Artichoke — 2/12/01 — Lighting Cue Sheet — Page 4

Description	Action	Advance
"Have mercy….EXT Gib	GO	
12	5 ct	Dn on Kit		
	GO	
13	5 ct	Up on J&A #2		
"days have elapsed…advisable	GO	
14	5 ct	Dn on J&A		
	GO	
15	5 ct	Up on Kit, late aft		
"leave my hair on your pillow…embrace	GO	
16	5 ct	Dn on Kit		
	GO	
17	5 ct	Up on J&A #3, morn		
"makes the tea taste funny	GO	
18	5 ct	Dn on J&A		
…	GO	
19	5 ct	Up on Kit, morn		

Top: Cue sheet, preset board; *bottom:* Cue sheet, computer board.

CUE SHEET MODE— This refers to a display setting on a computer lightboard that allows editing of the time, rate, label information of the cue sheet that displays onscreen.

CUE SYNOPSIS— The most readable of all lighting documents in terms of understand-

Adolphe Appia
Theatre Company — CUE SYNOPSIS — 11/3/01 — App Christmas Homecoming — 3

CUE	PAGE	COUNT	CUE	DESCRIPTION
51	5		"Sorry to bother you…To X	Add other half of bnch
52	8		"The Old man got	Add DS, bnch, barn and sub narr
53	15		They move to barn	Iso barn and warmer w/ bnch
54	5		"All went to bed …Ry X to stool	Add sto
54.1	15		Immediate follow	Iso to stool
55	3		"Old man woke up	Dn lt barn + bnch at glow
56	3		"Ran out into cold..They X to barn	Subt bnch
57	1		"Threw open the door	Barn bright w/ dn light
58	5		"afraid to approach the strangers	Subt sto
59	10		For Oh Holy Night (17)	Add blue in barn
60	10		End Oh Holy Night…"Come on Lynn	Restore but later w/ porch

Cue synopsis

ing what is being planned. It typically includes the cue number, the page number, the speed in counts, a description of what triggers the cue and a description of what in a general way occurs that is different.

Cue Number: If there are to be draft copies, it is easier to let the computer autonumber the cues up until the final copy, at which point the numbering can become final and any additional cues after that point can be point cues like 21.1, 21.2 etc.

Page: This is self-explanatory as it is simply an indication of what page in the script the cue line (trigger) is on and is provided so that everyone can locate the cue.

Count: How long does it take to get from the previous cue to the completion of this one? If there were separate up/down times, they would be entered as "xx/yy." For reasons explained in the topic FADES, KINDS OF, one will usually want ups and downs to be separate cues; so every cue done will be either a crossfade, a fade out, a fade up or an effect and will have a single duration time (thus uptime and downtime will most likely always be the same).

Cue Trigger: What triggers the occurrence of this cue? Wherever possible this is taken on the movement of an actor because actors' movements always cover (prevents the audience from being aware of) lighting movement. One usually doesn't want the audience to be aware that the lights are changing because it draws their attention away from the play. When actors move, they look different as they move through the various lights that illuminate their path. The audience cannot tell that the changes they are witnessing are a result of the actor walking in-and-out-of different lights or because the lighting is changing. Stage managers usually don't like this because the actor doesn't always move at the same place in the script at every performance, and yet they need to write the cue in their book based on what line of text precedes it. The reason why the lighting designer wants the cue taken on the movement is because she knows it will occur at different lines on different nights. Other triggers include on the music or sound effects. Cues that don't have to be placed exactly (beginning of a long sunset cue) can be triggered by cue lines. The lighting designer often provides a cue line that preceded the movement or business when she saw it during the runthru but makes it clear that it is to occur on the business.

Description of What Changes: There are really three parts to this: the kind of cue (i.e. its purpose), where in the play it occurs, and what is going to be different. There are some catch phrases to describe the kind of cue. The three basic kinds of cues are: The lights go out (*fade out*), the lights come up (*lights up on sc xx*) or the lights change (*xfade to xxxx*). Others include *fade to special, isolate to center, fade to scene change lights*, and *turns on practical light*, etc.

When lights come up on a new scene, one needs to describe the time of day or what it looks like (Lights up Sc 11, Beach, Bright day, cheerful). Sometimes all that is needed is a phrase like "gets darker" "becomes foreboding," whatever seems to work. This is both a reminder to the lighting designer as to what is trying to be achieved and a note to the director to explain why the lights are changing. It is not unusual for a transition to require a series of cues to achieve what may be viewed as a single lighting change. It is common to describe the entire effect and include just the number of the starting cue with a note that there may in fact be follow cues in the sequence and that the machine has already been coached on how to do this.

It is always easier to cut cues than it is to add them later. Most designers tend to leave

places for cues that they think might occur. After their meeting with the director (final meeting) and after the runthru, if these cues have not been used, then they can either be deleted entirely or the number can be left without any other descriptive data (the number is in effect skipped), before a clean copy is printed for the stage manager and director.

In American practice, the Cue Synopsis is often considered an optional document. Certainly the lighting designer needs a draft copy of this information either written out separately or written into her script. The advantages of giving the director a written copy of this information to confirm what she has been told orally is discussed in DIRECTOR, FINAL MEETING WITH. The advantage of giving a copy to the stage manager is that it often avoids having to have a separate meeting (paper tech) where the stage manager, awash in rulers, templates and sticky notes, enters the cues with painful slowness into the book as the lighting designer watches.

CUELIGHTS— Theoretically a vintage method for the stage manager to give cues to remote locations. The cuelight was typically turned on as an indication that it was time to stand by on a cue, and the light going off meant to take the cue.

Headsets and intercom systems have presumably made this system obsolete, but this isn't necessarily so. Most people don't like wearing a headset. Certainly an actor waiting for a signal to enter can't wear one and enter at the same time.

If the only message being sent is "stand by on the next cue" and "go on the next cue," then cuelights will work as well as any headset.

Cuelights can become quite elaborate. There can be a green light for get ready and a red light for go. If so, the red light goes on at the standby and when it goes off, it means "go." The green light is often omitted. There can be different colors of lights at the same remote location. When the blue one goes off, so-and-so enters, and when the red one goes off, everyone else enters.

In the old days, people worried about providing a way for the remote location to signal back. This was typically to acknowledge that they were looking at the cuelight and had seen the stand-by. This is still usually possible, but if a remote location has a problem, they will more typically pick up the headset and explain it.

CUES, CALLING OF— While there is a certain allowance for personal preferences, the calling of cues (both light cues and other cues) follows a ready-set-go pattern or to be more precise a *warning-standby-go* pattern. The warning traditionally comes about a half page before the actual cue and is supposedly the time when the operator re-reads her notes to make sure she recalls what she is about to do. The standby usually comes 10–20 seconds before the go and is the time when the operator would put her hands on the dimmers, and the go, of course, triggers the start of the cue. Most cues on a computer lightboard can be run by pushing the go button, so most of this preparation is a matter of historical tradition and not necessary to actual modern practice.

From the stage manager's point-of-view, the hard part is getting all the words out. Ends of scenes are always busy times, so it would not be uncommon for there to be a "Warning on light cues 17, 18 and 19, sound cues 14 through 20 and the scene change." This in due course would be followed by a "Stand by on light cues 17, 18 and 19, sound cues 14 through 20 and the scene change." This would be followed by something like "Lights 17 and sound 14, lights first … go and sound go. Lights 18 go. Scene change and sound 15 go" and so forth. It's not unusual for there to be a longish pause between the cue number and the go. It is not unusual for the stage manager to lose track of the numbers altogether and say something like "next sound cue go." The operators (sound and lights anyway) are usually sitting on either side of the stage manager and can see the stage and also know where their cues are supposed to come, and if something were to

happen to the stage manager could probably run their part of the show by themselves if only they were permitted to do so, but they seldom are.

CUES, KINDS OF— See FADES, KINDS OF.

CUE-SETTING SESSION —A time when the cues for the show are roughed-in. See LEVEL-SETTING SESSION.

CUE-TO-CUE TECHNICAL REHEARS- ALS— Each technical cue is done in order. Sometimes this is limited to sound and light cues, and sometimes it involves entrances, exits, costume and scene changes and the handling of difficult props. When each cue has been approved, then the stage is set for the next cue.

This kind of rehearsal dates back to the days of manual lightboards when it simply was not possible for the lighting crew to do cues on the fly. Since the cues were not going to get smoother until their basic operation had been decided upon, the director decided to give up an entire rehearsal to this process, after which everything was expected to work as it would in performance. Suppose that in a transition, three dimmers have to come up to half and two others to 25 percent. The lighting operator has been running them all up to half and then sneaking the two down, but the director doesn't like how that looks. She now tries running the three up on the master handle and dealing with the other two manually, but this kind of one-handed operation is too uncontrolled and jerky. Next she tries running them all on master up to 25 percent, clicking the two off master and sneaking the other three (on master) up to half. The director likes this best, so everyone takes a break while the lighting operator writes it down so that she can remember to do it that way from now on.

The actors are typically told not to bother acting. They merely go through the motions, and everyone waits while one person writes something down at a furious pace. At the end of the evening the lighting operator or operators are sweating and stressed out but everyone else is bored beyond belief.

A modern computer board can operate an almost unlimited number of channels at the same time, and it never needs to write anything down. It does not need to stop after every cue. It only needs to stop if the cue didn't look right and that kind of rehearsal is called a *stop-and-go* rehearsal and is discussed separately.

In the days of manual boards, once the lighting for a scene had been approved, they could skip ahead to the next scene transition, thus saving time, which is one of the alleged purposes of the cue-to-cue tech. In a modern play where there may be an average of a cue per page, it may often save no time at all to stop after every cue. By the time the props have been rearranged for the next cue, it would often have been easier to simply have allowed the scene to run.

What is particularly annoying for the lighting designer is that all she gets to see of her cues is their timing as they run in at the top of cues. What she often badly needs to see at this point is how they look when the actors walk around in them and this doesn't happen because the scenes are stopped too soon.

The actors do not really benefit from this kind of rehearsal either. They are asked to deal with the play out of sequence, from such-and-such a cue line. They are bombarded with completely new information: "Grab the doorknob with your upstage hand, your special is down here, remember don't say your line until you hear the sound cue, and this light is really steep so keep your head up." Because it comes to them out of context, they remember very little of it by the next rehearsal. In contrast, if the actors have had a couple of rehearsals-with-light, they will have already gotten used to scene transitions and figured out by themselves that they need to stand where their light is, and this in turn reduces the number of times the rehearsal has to be stopped so that they can be given notes, which means more time is spent actually rehearsing.

CURRENT— A flow of electrons measured in *amperes* or amps for short where each amp represents a rate of flow of $6.28 \cdot 10^{18}$ electrons per second.

CURTAIN LIGHTING or CURTAIN WARMERS— Any front-of-house lighting that hits the front curtain to illuminate it prior to the show and during intermissions. The footlights are commonly used for this, but there are also often frontlights dedicated to this purpose. The arealights for the first row of areas is usually too uneven to be used.

CUT—(1) When used as a verb, it means to eliminate as in, "Cut cue 54." (2) In reference to color it means a piece of color media that has been cut to size, so a cut list is a list of colors that need to be cut to the sizes listed.

CUT LIST— A list of colors that need to be cut (or pulled from stock) in the sizes indicated. In an informal setting, it might be hand written on scratch paper and the lighting designer might actually be the one who did the picking.

Cut List		Inspector Calls		
	4"	6.25"	7.5"	
X60	18	20		
X80		1		
G107				
G840		12		
G885	36			
L202		6	12	

Cut list

CUT-OFF— Also called a *douser* or a *chopper*, this is a part of a followspot that allows the operator to cut off the light. It typically works like two sliding doors on a freight elevator that come together from top and bottom.

C-WRENCH— Short for a *crescent wrench*. See WRENCHES for a more detailed discussion.

CYC— Short for *cyclorama*, it was originally meant to describe a surface that partially enclosed the back of the stage in a cylindrical way and extended in some cases all the way around to the proscenium arch. Cyc is used generically now to refer to any sky-type background whether it is cloth, plaster or some other hard surface, usually located on the back wall of the theatre or a measured distance in front of this if there is a provision to backlight the cyc or provide a crossover behind it.

While the question of how to light a cyc is discussed in LIGHTING SPECIAL PROBLEMS/Cycs and Drops, one of the major factors (if not the major factor) in how sky-like it will look depends on the surface and its treatment. A cloth, no matter how well laced to a support frame will usually show wrinkles if lit along its surface and will ripple in the backstage air currents. Solid materials don't have wrinkles and they don't ripple, but they can't be backlit and often they cannot be flown. Plaster is a wonderful textured surface, but it is hard to maintain and where it exists, it is usually built in place onto the back wall of the stage thus assuring no passage behind. A lot of hard products either have a grain or have a smooth surface like Masonite that does not have enough tooth to hold the paint well. Muslin over a hard sheet product is still however a superb painting surface.

Where the intention is to suggest the sky, the surface should be painted to represent the sky. Paints and dyes can create color washes, gradations of color and clouds in a way that the lighting can't. Due to color constancy, using blue light on a white surface is unlikely to make the surface look any color other than white. Colored light on a uniformly aqua dyed commercial cloth is most likely to be perceived as an aqua cloth lit by whatever colors the lights are. For contrast reasons, there should be an interest in keeping the actual lights on the cyc at low levels relative to the acting areas. This is most possible in situations where the paint treatment has done most of the work of creating the look of the sky. In the early 1900s most theatre companies owned both a day sky and a night sky.

CYC FOOTS or CYC FOOTLIGHTS— Lights at the base of the cyc or drop stack. Sometimes they are recessed in the floor and sometimes they are temporarily installed on top of the floor and then usually masked by a groundrow (a low vertical scenery piece usually depicting distant mountains or whatever is supposed to be in the middle distance).

CYC LIGHT— Any lighting instrument designed to light the cyc or sky-cloth or a drop, usually a floodlight of some kind, often a composite instrument with separate circuits or compartments (cells) for separate colors. See INSTRUMENTS/Floodlights for a more detailed discussion.

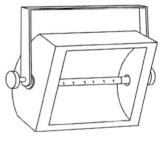

Cyc Light

CYCLE— In the context of electrical current, it refers to alternating current that reverses direction 120 times per second or completes 60 complete cycles in a second. In Europe, Australia and the UK, it is more commonly 50 cycles per second.

CYCS, BACKLIGHTING OF— See LIGHTING SPECIAL PROBLEMS/Backlighting Cycs and Drops.

DAISY-CHAIN STYLE— This mostly relates to how two-fers and three-fers are made up, but it could also refer to the way the wiring inside a light box is done. When electrical devices are hooked together in a daisy-chain style, the power for the second device is drawn from the first device; the power for the third device is drawn from the second, and so forth. This is the way a set of C7 or C9 Christmas tree lights is hooked up. The opposite of this is *spoke style* (often seen in two-fers) where each female connector draws it power from a single male, and so the pigtails radiate outward like spokes on a wheel. See TWO-FERS for a more detailed discussion.

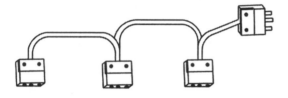

Daisy-chain style three-fer

DANCE LIGHTING— See LIGHTING, KINDS OF.

DAVIS, ARIEL— The owner of the Ariel Davis Manufacturing Company that produced lightboards, patch panels, and instruments in the 1940s, 1950s and 1960s. He either invented or popularized the disc-lock method of securing the yoke of an instrument in place, and he devised instruments with fins (like a heat sink) that did not require vent holes (and so did not leak light). He was also responsible for having Louis Hartmann's 1930 book reprinted in 1970.

DC— Abbreviation for DIRECT CURRENT.

DEAD—(1) Disconnected from electricity as in dead front equipment or a dead circuit (also called a *cold* circuit) (2) Unlit as in a dead spot or dead area on the stage.

DEAD FOCUS (BRITISH: *bouncing bars*)— The opposite of a *live focus*, this is a trial-and-error method of focusing that is some- times used as a field expedient. See FOCUS, KINDS OF.

DEFYING THE GRID— The question at hand is whether the lights should come from a diagonal position or not when the stage is either thrust or in-the-round. This can be a hotly debated issue. Where the audience is equally distributed around the playing area, half of them see it one way and the other half sees it the other way. Only where more than half the audience sees it one way or another does it ever become an issue.

The grid of course will align with the stage so that its pipes run, right/left and up/down. When the lights are aligned in this way, the frontlights will be on one pipe, the backlights on another and both sidelights on a third pipe, and the shutter cuts will be easy to make.

When the lights are not aligned, then the front-left and front-right lights will be on one pipe and the back-left and back-right lights will be on another pipe. Even where the grid has been designed with movable pipes to accommodate this, this puts what would otherwise have been distributed onto three pipes onto only two pipes. In this way, it is much more demanding of circuiting on the grid. Also, if the barrels on the ellipsoidals are not the rotating kind, then it is almost impossible to get the correct shutter cuts on the diagonal. On a six area (two rows of three) thrust instead of having only seven instruments pointed into the audience from the inside perimeter, there will be twice as many (14), and as a result there is likely to be more spill.

DEGREES OF SEPARATION— This is a term used with both audience seating and light placement. In the case of seats, the end seats of a row usually point toward the center of the stage. The angle between their lines-of-sight is the angle of separation. In a thrust theatre, the two end seats face each other and are said to be at 180 degrees of separation. In a proscenium theatre, the two end seats could theoretically both point straight ahead (0 degrees of separation) but more commonly are tilted slightly toward center at about 10 degrees of separation as they typically curve around the front of the stage.

DELAYS— Also called *waits*. In the context of computer lightboards, it refers to a delay before the next part or next cue is automatically taken. The time is usually counted from the button push (start of the first cue).

DELETE— This is a computer lightboard command and often the name of a button. It is used to delete cues mostly, but submasters and groups and macros can also be deleted. Once deleted, they are usually gone forever.

DELTA CONNECTION— This is a connection method for a three-phase, four-wire system used for an electrical service that provides 240 volts between any two hot legs and produces 120 volts between two of the hot legs and neutral and produces 180–190 between the third hot leg and neutral. The more common connection is called a *wye connection* in which the voltage is 208 between any two of the hot legs and 120 between any hot leg and neutral.

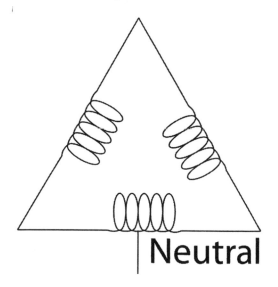

Delta connection

DEMONSTRATIONS— Called *demos* for short. They are an enormously valuable tool

for the lighting designer because they show (rather than tell) how something will appear. Wherever there is uncertainty as to how something will look, it is always less work to arrange for a demonstration of the color or effect in advance to show to the director rather than actually hanging the lights and finding out they are wrong later. The list of things that could be demonstrated is endless, but includes the lighting designer's ability to get light under hats, how a flown object will cause shadows on the set, how a steep angle will fail to adequately light a face, how three colors of light on the cyc will fail to produce a nighttime sky. In most cases, the lighting designer knows in advance what the demo will show. It is the director who may be surprised by the outcome. In those situations where the director has come to trust her lighting designer and believes what she has been told by her, then demos are for the most part unnecessary.

DESIGN BRIGHTNESS— The minimum brightness that any instrument needs to be before it is pronounced too dim to be in this show. This is a contested issue. Many designers, however, would typically expect each instrument to produce at least 100 fc of light before the color was added. See LIGHT, QUANTITY OF and INVERSE SQUARE LAW for a more detailed discussion.

DESIGNER'S PACT— Lighting designers often have been actors or directors or set designers before and therefore know, or think they know, a lot about the other artistic disciplines in the theatre. The same is true of the other designers and the director and many of the actors for that matter. In order to all work together in relative harmony, it is tacitly understood that everyone will concentrate on their small cog of the great wheel and will not volunteer or otherwise butt into someone else's area of concern unless it either directly relates to them in some way or unless they are invited to do so. One soon acquires a sense for who might be open to suggestions, but even the most open minded of designers will want to hear any "suggestions" in private and outside of a public gathering like a production meeting.

It is not unusual for the management of the theatre (sensing that this might become a problem) to remind everyone that they each have been chosen because they are uniquely qualified to do their particular part of the production and that everyone should respect this. As a general rule, no one likes being told how to do their job by someone else. While this may have to be tolerated when it comes from the director, it can precipitate a feud if it comes from another designer because it will be interpreted as the criticism, which it is.

DESIGNER'S RUN or RUNTHRU— An early runthru (usually the first). It is provided specifically for the lighting designer, but the other designers are usually invited to attend. Who attends depends in part on the complexity of the running part of the show, i.e. fast costume or set changes between or during scenes. The artistic director of the theatre (if she is not also the show's director) or some other representative from management may show up. Sometimes department heads or running crew attend. The lighting designer uses it to determine where cues need to be and to guess at how fast these cues should be.

DIAZO— Blueprinting process whereby a tracing paper original together with a photosensitive sheet of blueprint paper are fed through a special machine where ultraviolet light and ammonia fumes transfers the image to the special paper.

DICHROIC FILTER— Coated mirrors that reflect only certain wavelengths of light and in this way color the light. They are capable of purer colors and higher transmissions than ordinary color media, but they continue to be expensive. They are used in projectors and high-end intelligent lights.

DIELECTRIC— A non-conductor of electricity like plastic electrical tape.

DIFFUSE LIGHT— Light that has been bounced off a diffuse reflector and is now shadowless (almost shadowless) and is spread over a wide area. Light from borderlights, footlights and floods where there is no reflector and the inside is simply painted white are all considered sources of diffuse light.

DIFFUSE REFLECTION— All objects reflect light to some degree (ignore the hypothetical black body radiators that don't actually exist). The reflection is either specular (mirror-like) or diffuse, so diffuse reflection encompasses all non-specular reflection. Light colors reflect better than dark colors. Smooth surfaces reflect better than rough ones. See REFLECTION AND ABSORPTION for a more detailed discussion.

DIFFUSION FILTER or MEDIA— These are manufacturers' catalog terms for what are commonly called *frost* or frost gel. They soften hard edges and spread light to cover more area. They also cause a diffused spill on everything around them, which is sometimes enough of a problem that it limits their use. There is however a dizzying array of products so the degrees of possible diffusion are more-or-less controlled. See COLOR MODIFICATIONS for a more detailed discussion.

DILUTE PRIMARIES— Assuming that the primaries were red, green and blue, the dilute primaries would then be light red, light green and light blue. The theory is that much more white light will get through and a range of tints can be created. These are mostly put into borderlights or footlights, which for blending purposes usually have the appearance of white light. They are also useful for toning assuming that pink and light blue are colors that one would want to tone with. Most designers will not find the light green a very useful color. It does not produce light yellow when mixed with light red, so light yellow or pale amber might be more useful. See COLOR MIXING for a more detailed discussion.

DIMMER— An electrical device for reducing the brightness of lights. In the early days of DC current this was achieved by increasing the resistance in the circuit usually by wire coils embedded in some kind of ceramic material. These were called *resistance dimmers*. It was common to put 12–14 of these and their accompanying switches in a road box for touring, as this was about all one operator could be expected to control, and these were called *piano boards* because they were the approximate size, shape and weight of an upright piano. The *salt-water dimmers* were an early resistance-type dimmer where the amount of salt in the water controlled how well the solution would carry current. Another vintage system was the *reactance dimmers* that require both AC and DC current. When AC current became firmly established, *autotransformer dimmers* became the most common dimming system, and they worked as infinitely variable transformers that regulated the voltage.

In the 1960s these began to be replaced by various electronic solutions. The most successful was the *silicon-controlled-rectifiers* or SCR's for short, which is still the most popular (but not the only) current technology. See LIGHTING CONTROL for a more detailed discussion.

DIMMER BOARD— Where this term is used, it refers to the one-hand-operates-one-dimmer manual system where the technician manipulates actual dimmer handles. The dimmers referred to are usually either resistance dimmers or autotransformers. It replaces the older term *switchboard*, which reflected an earlier time when there were often more switches than dimmers on the panel. Now operators sit at lightboards, which is the control portion (front end) of an electronic system.

DIMMER CURVE or PROFILE— On a manual lightboard, while the slider or dimmer handle might move perfectly smoothly from 0 to 10 on a 10 count, the effect onstage might be that nothing happened for the first four counts, and then the lights flashed up and finished fast. On a modern computer lightboard, the lights are supposed to come up in a way that the calibrations represent percentages of brightness. This is usually called the IES square law curve, and it is slightly faster at the low end and slightly slower at the top end. If this does not look good, the dimmer curve can typically be custom set by the user to one of several other preset dimmer curves with names like *fast bottom*, *fast top* etc. Also dimmers can be set to operate like a switch. This is usually called *full at 1 percent* and is very useful for mirror ball motors or fan motors or anything else that shouldn't dim. Most designers, however, do not change the default settings unless something looks wrong.

DIMMER LEVELS— These are calibration numbers usually ranging between 1 and 10 or between 1 and 100 that are used to record the brightness of various dimmers or channels in cues. Although the calibration of how they work can be altered, they normally are set in such a way that they more-or-less represent percentages of apparent brightnesses, so that a channel set a 47 would appear to be about 47 percent of its full brightness.

DIMMER PER CIRCUIT— It was Stanley McCandless' dream that one day it would be possible for each light to have its own dimmer. Thanks to SCR dimmers and computers to control them, the dream has become a reality in most venues and having a dimmer for each circuit is now standard practice.

DIMMER RACK— See RACK.

DIMMER READING BY CUE SHEET— A vintage document usually handwritten on graph paper in a spreadsheet format that listed dimmers across the top and cues down the sides and the levels in the body of the table. In the days of manual boards, it was kept up-to-date by the lighting designer or more commonly by a lighting assistant based on what she heard the lighting designer asking for over the headset. In the absence of an assistant, lighting designers sometimes tape-recorded themselves talking on the headset, but this then required that they listen to the tape sometime after rehearsal. It was a vitally important document for reading back cues to the operator to check that they were correct (when they looked wrong). There was, of course, no monitor screen, so this was the only way the designer had of "seeing" what the levels of the dimmers were.

In the days of preset lightboards, a copy of the reset sheet usually served the purpose and the Dimmer Reading By Cue Sheet fell out of regular use.

When computer memory lightboards appeared, the show was in fact being saved on disk, so often a copy of the disk was kept as a backup record of the show even if it wasn't readable unless inserted back into the machine. If the lightboard could print, often a hardcopy printout could be made of the cues and a marked up version of this could be kept up to date. See HARDCOPY PRINT-OUT for a more detailed discussion.

DIMMER ROOM or VAULT— The room where the dimmers are located. This is usually also the place where the electricity from the street enters the building and where the main disconnect and other electrical equipment is located.

DIMMER SCHEDULE— This is usually a re-sort of the instrument data in dimmer order. It is used as an aid in hard patching circuits to dimmers where these are not the same. It is not necessary where circuits are hardwired to their dimmers and both share the same number.

DIMMING, PROPORTIONAL— See PRO-PORTIONAL DIMMING.

DIODE— An electrical device that when used on DC current allows it to flow only in one direction. When used on AC current, it allows only half of the current to pass and has the effect of dimming lights to half brightness.

DIP—(1) A lacquer color used to dye low wattage light bulbs. See LAMP DIP (2) A drop in illumination in the lit portion of the stage (3) A crossfade that does not smoothly transition but appears to get dimmer around the midpoint.

DIPLESS— Refers to crossfades between cues and is mostly used to describe a fader pair operated together, which is supposed to eliminate any dips in intensity.

DIPLOMACY— This is sometimes called *manners* or *getting along with your fellow designers*, but really it goes way beyond that and extends into a method of getting your own way without hurting anyone else's feelings. Asking nicely is part of it; so is knowing whom to ask and when to ask. Husbands and wives usually have a keen understanding of how to ask in a way that is sure to cause an argument or asking in a way that is more likely to be looked on favorably. When asking for favors from other designers, wouldn't it make most sense to ask in a way most likely to succeed?

The giving of advice is a particularly sensitive area where big egos are concerned because there is always implied criticism, and while everyone has an opinion about almost any subject and a bursting urge to express that opinion, not everyone enjoys hearing (especially at a public gathering) how someone else could do their job better, which is often what it sounds like. On the other hand, when someone asks someone else for advice, it is hard to then reject that advice and do something completely different without there being hurt feelings and a sense of implied criticism that their advice wasn't good enough.

Most lighting designers, realizing that they are at the bottom of the production team pecking order, are usually quite good at doing this. See ORCHESTRA LIGHT PROBLEM for an example of how this might be achieved.

DIRECT CURRENT (Abbr. DC)— This mostly refers to electrical current that comes from batteries, as DC current is not in common household or theatrical use at the moment. There are two poles. The positive is the pole to which the electrons flow and is typically color-coded red. The negative is the pole from which the electrons come and is typically color-coded black and is called the *common*.

DIRECT LIGHT — Light from a source that has not been reflected or bounced yet. Almost all stage lighting is direct lighting. It does, of course, bounce after it has hit the object (actor) it is aimed at. Direct light can be controlled by shutter cuts and barndoors. Indirect bounce light goes where it will and cannot be controlled very well at all.

DIRECTIONAL LIGHT — The sun rises in the east and sets in the west. Up until the 1970s or so, it was considered very important to decide how the set related to the sun's position because it would not do to have morning sun stream in the same windows that afternoon sun streamed in. If this was outside light that was supposed to be illuminating this room, then it was coming from a direction and that direction was expected to be both brighter and a different color. The light coming from its supposed source is called *key* light. The concept of directional light works best in a proscenium situation where the audience always sits out front, and it is a question of key light coming from either the left or right. On a thrust stage, this would put some of the audience on a shady side, where no one ever wants to be, so the whole idea is considerably softened in a situation like that so that the stark contrasts are eliminated, and while there may be directional lighting, there is also an almost equal amount of fill light from the other directions, but it is a different color. See SUNNYSIDE CONVENTION for a more detailed discussion.

DIRECTOR, FINAL MEETING WITH — This usually is the next event following the *designer's runthru*. If there is the time, it typically occurs on the next day, thus giving the lighting designer a chance to review the notes made during the runthru. If the schedule is tight, the lighting meeting may follow the runthru by a matter of minutes.

The lighting designer usually sets the pace and the agenda for the meeting. If the show is uncomplicated and limited to the lights coming up at the beginnings of scenes and going out at the ends (lights-up-lights-down show), then she may prepare the Cue Synopsis in advance and use it as the discussion document for the meeting. If the show is at all complicated, the designer will probably transfer her cues into the script and use the script as the discussion document. While the lighting designer can quote almost any line from the play and the director will remember when it occurs, the reverse is not true. If the director quotes a line and says he wants a cue there, it will send the designer scurrying for her script. If they are both paging through their scripts together, this won't be a problem.

How the designer actually organizes the meeting will depend in large part upon how much detail she thinks the director really wants. Some directors want to know before the meeting begins how many areas there are going to be and how many systems are being used and what kind of control there is over them and where the specials are. Sometimes it is a good idea for the lighting designer to give the director a plan of the stage (on letter-sized paper) with areas and specials marked, so that they can be referred to during the body of the meeting (Director's Key Sheet).

Usually the cues are not already numbered and transitions may be left somewhat vague. Speed of cues is rarely mentioned unless something unexpected is being proposed. The lighting designer usually starts a descriptive narrative that begins with the houselights fading out. That usually signals either a crossfade into lights-up on scene one or the actors getting into place first and then the lights fading up. The lighting designer will usually describe the time of day and the weather if appropriate, something like "sunny morning," "evening," etc. The next cue comes at such-and-such a point and the designer describes what will now be different. Sometimes a different part of the stage is lit, sometimes it becomes darker or brighter, and sometimes it just looks different. The director is often asked if he knows of any intervening cues that the lighting designer might have missed. Sometimes the lighting designer has two possible ways to handle something or has no idea what the director is envisioning and a short discussion ensues.

It is not unusual to get through a 100-cue show in about an hour if the lighting designer is well prepared and the director trusts her designer's descriptions. If the director trusts that if it looks like *romantic moonlight* to his designer then it will probably look the same to him, then things can progress quite quickly. If the director wants to see gel samples, then this will take longer. Directors almost never want to see the Light Plot (assuming it existed at this point, which it usually doesn't), they rarely want to see color samples, and are usually content with whatever level of description they are given as long as they understand the purpose of why the lights are going to change and understand in a general way what will happen.

If there are going to be areas on the stage that will be hard to light, now is the time to discuss them because the designer is in effect asking that the director not use these areas very much since they can't be lit very well. This is really the last chance to change the proposed plan before the crew starts hanging the lights. If there are any issues that the director seems unsure about, the designer will typically arrange to do a demonstration of some kind. No one wants to hang all the lights only to discover that their angle is too steep. If the director is concerned, it is always best to do a demo in advance.

Having the lightboard out in the house for the tech period greatly simplifies the entire process of integrating the cues into the show. If the master electrician or the board operator seem less than enthusiastic about this, it may be worthwhile for the lighting designer to explain the advantages to the director. See TABLE for a more detailed discussion.

Having several rehearsal-with-light prior to the official technical rehearsals can greatly simplify the dry tech and the first tech. See REHEARSALS-WITH-LIGHT for a more detailed discussion.

Cue-to-cue technical rehearsals are a particularly odious waste of almost everyone's time and a traditional hand-me-down from the days of manual lightboards that has not been entirely stamped out yet. See CUE-TO-CUE TECHNICAL REHEARSALS for a more detailed discussion.

The designer may discuss any or all these issues with the director in the hopes of enlisting his aid if it does not look as if these things can be achieved without his help.

It is not universally agreed that the director should be given a Cue Synopsis, and certainly for many years it was traditional not to give him one. The director got the nice little talk, and that was as detailed as it got. The advantage of giving him the Cue Synopsis as a confirmation document is that there is much less chance of a technical rehearsal coming a halt because the director did not know there was going to be a cue here or did not know it was going to look like this. While it is true that directors rarely do anything with their copy of the synopsis except put in their show file, they implicitly become responsible for its contents and so there can be no dispute about what was supposedly decided upon at the meeting. In addition, it can be given to the stage manager so that he or she can put cues in the book and it can be given to the master electrician or board operator so that one of them can *format the disk* if they are the ones who are going to do this.

Occasionally, the stage manager wants to attend the light meeting and, sometimes, the master electrician does too. One of the reasons for eliminating the cue numbers from the light meeting discussion has traditionally been to discourage attendance by anyone else. Lighting designers typically understand that their meeting will go best when conducted in private. This is true not only of the lighting designer but really of all the designers. Designers will rarely want anyone else present. Directors are free to invite whomever they please, and there is little the individual designer can do about it. Any additional participants usually slow down the process and add their opinions to the mix.

DIRECTOR, FIRST MEETING WITH—
This is a meeting that the lighting designer typically asks for at the first production meeting. The purpose of this meeting is threefold. First, the designer needs to find out what if anything the director knows or thinks he knows about lighting because this will affect the way he will have to be dealt with. Second, the lighting designer needs to determine if the director is going to let his designers design or if he plans to be the puppet master and tell them how he wants everything done. If he is going to leave the design up to the individual designers, how supportive is he likely to be, i.e. how strong does he appear to be? Third, the lighting designer is going to spend 8–12 weeks in production meetings where she will have nothing very remarkable to say because she won't have seen a runthru yet and as a result won't have done a design yet. The director needs to leave this meeting confident that his lighting designer is superbly gifted and highly competent.

It is customary at this meeting to ask the director if he knows of any specials or effects that he's going to want. In other words, does he have any lighting ideas at this point?

Directors who believe they know something about lighting usually have thought about the lighting ahead of time and will have a list of ideas and will be anxious to talk about them. These ideas are usually not open for discussion and are not very likely to change.

What is more likely to happen is that the director will explain that the show is not entirely cast yet, and he just approved the set yesterday, and he hasn't thought about the lighting much at all. Most directors don't know all that much about the lighting anyway, but instead rely mostly on their designers, which is usually just the way the lighting designer hopes it will be. It is often said that the only note a lighting designer ever wants to get is, "The lights were great."

Lighting designers usually have a standard list of things that they discuss with directors that they have not worked with before. There are three things that usually find their way on this list. First, one needs to discuss hats with big brims, sometimes even hats with little brims and sometimes all it takes is a hairstyle that puffs out on the forehead enough to shade the face. Is there any way to get light in under the brim of hats (like footlights)? Usually there isn't. In a proscenium house it may be possible to paint the floor a light color so that light from the cove positions will bounce light onto the faces to some extent. If there is a balcony that can see the floor, then this will create another problem in that the faces will appear dimly lit in comparison to the floor because the floor will be more reflective and will appear to be more brightly lit, so the idea of painting the floor white wouldn't work. The reason for telling the director all this is because he's the one who ultimately will have to decide whether he would rather see faces or tops of hats. If the show that is currently running has hats in it, the director can take a look at the problem without having to take someone else's word for what the results are. The lighting designer may offer to do a demonstration where some arealights are turned on and some actors try on some hats.

Costumers tend to consider hats a very important part of the overall picture and aren't anxious to be denied the use of this tool just because the lighting designer can't figure out how to get light under their brims. They usually argue that if their hats become a problem, they can always be cut from the show later, and directors usually agree to this.

Item two on the list has to do with making faces visible. Faces (Caucasian faces) are most effectively seen against a dark background. Black faces need to be seen against a contrasting background, which of necessity needs to be lighter but hopefully won't be white or any variant of white because that would reflect too much light and would make any color face even harder to see. This is discussed separately in SKIN TONES, LIGHTING OF. Anything lighter than a Caucasian face is going to reflect more light and, thus, make the face harder to see. In terms of costuming this means no light colors around the face and it terms of the set and floor it means no huge expanses of really light colors that will cause the pupils in the eye to close down. It is the director's job to police the set and costume designs and concern himself with this issue or not as he sees fit, and to take the responsibility for any bad effects caused by his ignoring the good advice he has been given by his lighting designer.

The third item on the list involves the evil effects to having scenery objects like chandeliers and false beams and posts that wind up in the light path because they will cause objectionable shadows.

If there are things about the costumes and sets that the lighting designer thinks will interfere with the lighting, then she will typically discuss these with the director, explaining what she's concerned about, and if it seems appropriate what she thinks the solution should be. If the director cannot be gotten to go along with whatever it is that the lighting designer wants done, then the idea is effectively dead and off the table.

If all goes well, the entire meeting will have lasted half an hour and the director will be thrilled that his lighting designer is so on top of the problems. At the very least the lighting designer will come away from this meeting with a sense of what the director knows (or thinks he knows) about lighting and how involved in the details he intends to become, and how supporting/trusting he is going to be, and for this reason, the meeting will always be worthwhile even though there is really nothing tangible yet to discuss. This is, in fact, a dry run to see how it is going to go in the future at the next (and usually only other) light meeting.

Directors, especially young or otherwise inexperienced directors, often may feel the urge to somehow let their designers know that they are not going to be allowed do their own thing, unsupervised. When directors have this need to show that they are the boss, they can say some incredibly stupid things that they will later be too proud to retract. If

one can accord them a certain measure of respect (that they have not had the opportunity to earn yet), it may be possible to head this off before it occurs. They need to be reassured that they are going to get to see every light cue in the show and have the opportunity to approve it, and that nothing final will happen with the lighting design, which won't begin to become final before there has been a runthru, without there being a discussion with them. Their lighting designer is their trusted ally not an adversary or a threat. Her purpose in life is to make the director's show look good.

At this first meeting, the lighting designer won't have a design (or even any ideas for a design) yet, but she still needs to create an impression of overall competence. The other designers will never know what went on in this meeting. As a result, they are most likely to take their cues from the director. If he seems satisfied and is not demanding that the lighting designer explain how she is intending to handle this or that lighting situation, then they won't want to rock the boat and they won't want to demand answers either, and all of that is good, because lighting designers don't really have very many answers until they have see a runthru.

At the same time that the lighting designer is evaluating what kind of a person the director is, the director is becoming acquainted with what kind of a lighting designer the theatre has given him this time. Is it someone who will have to be coached and prodded and will only do cues that the director has thought of first or will it be someone who is likely to come forth with a proposal for how the show should be lit? When a director goes to a meeting like this, he is usually prepared with about a paragraph's worth of platitudes about lighting in general or the lighting for this particular play, which he can unleash if compelled to. He usually likes to avoid this because it typically will reveal how little he actually knows about lighting. In situations where the lighting designer talks to him as an equal in lighting knowledge, accords him respect in advance, and merely reminds him of things that, of course, he already knows, a much better working relationship can be established that will carry all the way through the rehearsal period.

DIRECTOR'S KEY SHEET— See KEY SHEET.

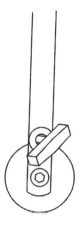

DISC LOCK— This is a method of locking the yoke in position either invented by or popularized by Ariel Davis, as it was certainly part of his company's instrument design. A circle of metal is attached to the instrument housing with its center at one of the yoke bolts. Higher up the yoke there is another knob that locks the edge of the disk to the yoke at that position. The added leverage helps prevent slipping, and the disc lock has a hand operated handle whereas the yoke bolt may simply be a bolt head.

Disk lock

DISCHARGE LAMPS— There are a number of these including florescent, neon, sodium, mercury, xenon, CID and HMI. They typically involve a warm-up period, the color of the light is often not quite white and they can't be dimmed (at least not all the way out). HMI produces the most acceptable color and is used in followspots where it competes with carbon arc lights, which also cannot be dimmed. Some of the others find their way onstage as practicals of one kind or another. Others may hold promise for the future.

DISCO EFFECTS— There is a dizzying array of lighting effect machines created to provide moving lights around a dance floor. Some are not much more complex than a mirror ball, but many of them have built-in color organs or can be hooked up to a separate color organ that will activate the lights to the beat and pitch of the music. Some of these find their way into the theatre as special effects.

DISCONNECT— To unplug or otherwise disconnect from electrical power. When used as a noun, it refers to a main switch or company switch that disconnects the dimmers (or other apparatus from power).

DISKS and DISK MANAGEMENT— Disks refer to the storage media, which are most commonly 3.5" floppy disks. In a few years time it may well be something else, but the principles of managing them will still be the same. Every rehearsal from level-setting onward is saved to disk, often in multiple copies. The question is how can these be kept in a way that they cannot become mixed up, and how long does one need to keep the disk from some past rehearsal and how many copies does one need to make?

This is one of those subjects that can provoke a heated argument and a description of that time in the car when all the disks fell in a pile at an unexpected stop. Most designers keep their own set of disks (separate from the set kept by the theatre), so that they do not have to concern themselves with how the board operator is or isn't planning to do this. Most designers want at least two copies at the end of each rehearsal. In addition, it is common practice to save at least one copy from the previous (yesterday's) rehearsal. This is a minimum of three disks. Keeping them straight could involve labeling each one, but most people would color-code odd or even numbered rehearsals (which at one rehearsal per day is the same as odd/even days of the month). In addition, the protective sleeve might say either "yesterday" or "today." The protective sleeve alone won't help if you have to stop the car suddenly and all the disks wind up in a pile, whereas the color-coding will.

Inasmuch as it is now possible to take disks home and work on them on a home computer, this somewhat complicates the problem. Let's say that last night's rehearsal is on green disks. When loaded on the computer at home and modified, they are saved onto blue disks. Tonight the modified show (from the blue disks) will be loaded onto the lightboard at the start of rehearsal. At the end, the show will be saved onto red disks, which may then be modified at home tomorrow and recorded on orange disks.

The lighting designer and the master electrician or board operator all get to make up a system that makes sense to them. It is also possible to take an unused channel and record it at a level between 1 and 31 (days of the month) thus providing a time-stamp in the preset cue. This is particularly useful, when the designer is not present to see which disk is used to load the show at the top of the rehearsal.

DISPERSION— This is the scientific word to describe a prism's ability to separate white light into its component colors.

DISPLAY or DISPLAY SCREEN— More commonly called the *monitor*, it is the visual interface for a computer lightboard. If there are more than one display, one usually displays the cue that is live onstage and the other displays the cue sheet or a blind view of another cue, etc. In a very large venue with more than 100 active channels, it may take two screens to view all the channels.

DISPLAY MODES— In the context of a computer lightboard, it refers to what is being displayed on the monitor. The default is usually the cue that is up on stage, which is called either *live* mode or *stage* mode, but there are at least 20 other display modes that could be looked at or edited (like *patch* or *park*). See LIGHTING CONTROL/Computer Memory Lightboards for a more detailed discussion.

DISTANCE, AS A VARIABLE OF LIGHT— Stated simply, light that comes from more than 20 feet away is much more even and looks different from light from the same angle that comes from close-by. This is a direct result of the inverse square law in action where the illumination diminishes with the square of the distance. When one is only a foot from the light source, moving a foot backward will diminish the light by a factor of four ($1^2 = 1$ and $2^2 = 4$). At 20 feet away,

moving a foot backwards is hardly noticeable ($20^2 = 400$ and $21^2 = 441$). Sources placed too close to the things they will light are said to have a *Distance Problem*. See VARIABLES OF LIGHT for a more complete discussion of this subject.

DISTANCE, HORIZONTAL— The distance on a plan view between the light source and the aim point.

DISTANCE, THROW— The straight-line distance between the actor's nose and the source of light. It is usually calculated as the hypotenuse of a right triangle in which the legs are the vertical elevation and the horizontal distance.

DISTANCE, VERTICAL— The distance between the nose plane and the source of light, and it would be more common to call it *vertical elevation*.

DISTANCE PROBLEM— When actors walk around in the lit area, their throw distance to the source of light changes depending upon whether they are in the exact center of the lit area or not. When the lights are more than about 20 feet away, each additional foot of throw distance causes less that a 10 percent difference in illumination. However, when the lights are closer than that, the actors get visibly brighter as they approach the center of the light and dimmer as they move away.

This was a huge problem for Louis Hartmann in the early 1900s. He was trying to light actors from the tormentor positions and every time the actors walked toward that position he had to have his operators reduce the light to make them appear to be evenly lit (ride the levels). He complained about this and recognized that it would have been solved if he had been able to have his operators further away in better positions, but, of course, at that time there were no better positions.

In most cases, this continues to be a problem that has to be solved by the architect during the planning stages of the building as it unfixable once the lighting positions have been decided upon. Not only is it necessary to plan for shows that will be done on flat floor, but one has to provide a means to light double-decker sets and high platforms as well.

Clearly the instruments need to be relatively far away from the stage so that their distribution of light will appear even. If, however, they are placed too far away, they become too dim and more instruments will be needed. I think 20 feet is a minimum distance, but I think all would-be lighting experts should do their own tests to see if they concur or not.

DISTRIBUTION OF LIGHT— When used in the context of the variables of light, it refers to *size, shape, texture* and *edge quality* as a group. When used in its more common meaning, it is a study of the size and shape of the beam of light on the nose plane showing where it is brightest. Usually, a few typical examples tell the whole story.

The shape part is relatively uncomplicated. The light coming out the front of the instrument is cone-shaped. Toplights point straight down on their aim point and produce a circle of light on the nose plane and a somewhat larger circle on the floor below. Eyelevel lights produce a circle of light on a vertical backing wall. Golden ring positions produce an egg shape where the centerline of the light runs forward and back and the pointy end of the egg is further away. This can be estab-

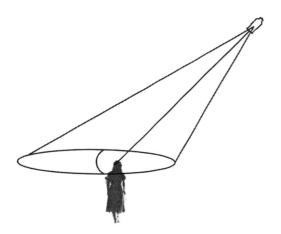

Distribution of light

lished by turning on the actual lights and looking at the pattern created on the floor or it can be worked out mathematically or can be demonstrated by cutting apart a Styrofoam cone. While the pattern on the floor is the same shape as the one on the nose plane, it is, of course, larger on the floor and is located further from the instrument.

Since it is not possible to see the pattern of light on the nose plane, it is common to talk about the *walkpath* of the light. In other words, where would the actor's feet need to be to keep her face in the light? For the toplight, one would need to stay about 18" inside the circle on the floor. For a golden ring front light, one could be outside the egg on the near side (downstage), but would have to stay about 18" inside at the two side points and would have to be 4–6' inside at the back. The center of the light (centerbeam) is always about a third of the way back (based on the pattern on the floor). This is a somewhat simplified explanation based on golden ring positions and a 20' throw distance that will vary somewhat from venue to venue.

Now we turn to the question of how bright it will be, and this is considerably harder because there are three factors, and they don't work together. The first factor has to do with the lens system. As a general rule, optical systems are brightest right around the center where the light hits the flat side of the lens at a perpendicular. This is offset somewhat by adjusting the focus for flat field, because that tends to create a slight dip at the center, which is what it is supposed to do.

The second factor is related directly to the inverse square law. In the case of a toplight, the light that goes through the center of the lens has less distance to travel and is consequently brighter than the sides or back or front. In the case of a golden ring light, the near side will always be brightest because its light travels the least distance.

The third factor has to do with the angle from which the ray of light hits the object. This is the Cos part of the inverse square law so do read that topic before continuing onward.

In the case of a golden ring light, the near side always has the shortest throw distance, which makes it brighter, but it also hits the face at the steepest angle, which makes its Cos low and reduces its apparent brightness. This tends to create a bright evenly lit oval at the base of the pool of light bounded by the near point, centerbeam point and two side points that are equal in brightness to the centerbeam.

Let's take the case of a golden ring frontlight hung on a 16' grid whose E is 32,000 cd. We would be interested in the centerbeam point, the two side points and the front and back points. Assuming that the instrument is underhung and its aim point is on the nose plane, then its vertical elevation would be 9.5 ($16 - 1 - 5.5 = 9.5$). Since it is a golden ring position, its horizontal distance has to be 9.5 also. Using $a^2 + b^2 = c^2$ where a = horizontal distance and b = vertical elevation as explained in the topic on LIGHTING CALCULATIONS, then c, which represents the throw distance will equal 13.44. At this point, we could use the inverse square law and divide the square of 13.44 into 32000, which would give us a footcandle reading of 177 at centerbeam. The throw distances for the two side points (14.05) and the back point (20.24) are longer but the front point (10.76) is shorter. We'd have to calculate all these distances first and then calculate the illumination levels, which would turn out to be 276 in front, 78 in back and 162 fc to the side. Notice that there is a 198 fc different between the high in front and the low in back, but this is only based on distance without taking the effect of Cos into account.

When the effect of the angle of incidence is taken into account, the centerbeam reading becomes 125 at Cos 45 degrees, the front becomes 130 at Cos 62 degrees, the back becomes 69 at Cos 28 degrees and the sides become 118 at Cos 43 degrees. Because none of the instruments are coming from eyelevel, all of their levels are reduced by their Cos , but the light at the back has the best angle and the light at the front has the worse angle, which tends to even out the front-to-back

differences. Now there is only 61 fc separating the brightest and dimmest reading, which means the lighting is much more even.

When the effect of the optical train is taken into account, it makes the centerbeam 118 instead of 125 and thus closer to the readings on the sides, which are 117.

If an actor were to start at a side position and walk along the edge of the light toward the most downstage (near side) position, then she would get increasingly brighter. After only a step at most she would be 118 fc bright (same as centerbeam). These two new sidepoints plus the centerbeam point and the downstage point would constitute the boundaries of the *hot oval* mentioned earlier. So, although the egg shape perhaps suggests that the instrument lights a narrow width but extends more deeply upstage, it is really only the downstage (near-side) third of the egg that is very useful at all.

DISTRIBUTION SYSTEM— This refers to the way the instruments are connected to the dimmers. While this could be just bundles of loose cables, it is more commonly a commercially made electrical gutter about $4 \cdot 6$ in cross-section that either has surface mounted receptacles or receptacles on pigtails, and the whole thing is commonly called a *plugging channel*. It often has a short length of multi-conductor flexible cable that then connects to standard electrical conduit, which then runs to the dimmers. Short versions of this are commonly called *drop boxes* and may be $6 \cdot 6$ or $10 \cdot 10$ electrical boxes rather than the raceway material. These boxes can be dropped in on spot lines or permanently attached to a grid or pipe.

Older systems that employed the one-hand-operates-one-dimmer system often had a patch panel on the load side of the dimmers to allow for replugging. When the electronic dimmers came along, the dimmers were left in a remote electric room in the basement somewhere and only the control portion went into the booth or position from which the lights were to be run. At that point, it would have required a second person to do the replugging. Since that was not going to happen, replugging ceased to exist and there was no longer a need for a patch panel. The load circuits could simply be permanently wired to their dimmers, as had been the original circa 1910 custom.

Whoever designs the distribution system effectively controls how much labor it will take each-and-every time instruments are connected to circuits. It should be obvious that the objective should be to have a plugging point anywhere along the grid where one is likely to plug in an instrument so that no additional loose cabling is required. To do this, the system designer needs to understand how the shows will most likely be lit by a lighting designer. Here are some of the considerations that should affect the final design. Some are so simple that they would not ordinarily be mentioned except that there are plenty of examples where they have been ignored.

- There should be **as many circuits as there are dimmers.**

- **Dimmers should not be used for things** like worklights **that do not need to dim.**

- The circuits, that are placed where the arealights will be, only need **one drop point** because they will be used every time (almost every time). Circuits that serve washes can have **several drop points** so that the wash can be ganged at the pipes and thus use as few circuits as possible. The rest of the circuits are for specials of some kind or another. They need to have three or four drop points each to insure that each dimmer gets used in every show. This is especially true of weird locations that may be used only once every five years. Of course a receptacle has to be put in the weird places like the trap room and the lobby, but that circuit should have additional drop points in other locations as well. It is common practice to put three or four drop points in the booth for followspots or movie projectors or whatever. Those circuits should have other drop points out on the main grid in more commonly used positions.

- Plugging channel is typically priced by the foot with a surcharge per circuit and per drop point. On the extreme ends, **it may be more cost effective to simply sprout 6–8' pigtails rather than carry the gutters to the extreme edges** of the area that needs circuits.

- The extreme edges are usually the golden ring positions that will cover the perimeter of the stage. There is **no practical reason to cover the entire area above the audience** with a pipe grid and circuits if it extends well beyond the golden ring positions outward.

- **Pigtails are always better than the flush mount receptacles** because they require fewer jumper cables to get the instruments to reach the plug-in point.

- The plugging channels traditionally are above the instruments and the pigtails hang down to just above instrument height. On grids that are tight against a ceiling or mechanical ducting, it often makes more sense for the **pigtail to sprout upward** (or sideways) so that they do not hang below the grid when not in use.

- Floor pockets are expensive and likely to be covered with platforming. Running cables from circuits in the wings or wing-walls is both more practical and less expensive. **Floor circuits** tend to be used for practicals and small cliplights and floods that all have PBG plugs, so it usually makes more sense to have these receptacles **be PBG** and adapt them to stagepin when and if the need arises.

DOG CLIPS— Also called *snap hooks*, these are what are found at the end of dog leashes. There are several different styles and many different strengths. They all work approximately the same way. By pushing against something that is spring loaded, the hook opens. When the pressure is removed, the hook closes. All lighting safety cables use these. Lighting wrenches are commonly attached to the electrician by means of a spiral phone cord with dog clips at each end. Light-

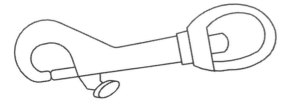

Dog clip

ing accessories and buckets of tools and supplies are sent aloft by clipping the bucket to the hauling rope. These should not be confused with Bull Dog clips, which is a tradename for an office supply product that works like a clipboard or clothes pin. Bull Dog clips are also used in the theatre to temporarily pleat curtains and to attach a tape measure to a piece of soft goods aloft.

DONUT— A gel frame sized piece of fire resistant material with a smaller than gel frame sized hole in its center, one of several aperture reducing lighting accessories. See ACCESSORIES for a more detailed discussion.

DOOR BACKINGS, LIGHTING OF— See LIGHTING SPECIAL PROBLEMS/Door Backings.

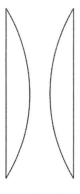

Double Plano-convex

DOUBLE PLANO-CONVEX— A lens system made up of two plano-convex lenses, with convex faces pointed toward each other, that reduces the focal length of the composite to about half where trying to use one lens would make the lens too thick and make it prone to cracking and other problems. Two 6 · 9 lenses put together have a composite focal length of about 4.5. See FORMULAS/Lens Maker Equation for the method of calculation.

DOUBLE POLE or DOUBLE THROW SWITCHES— See SWITCHES, KINDS OF.

DOUBLE-DECKER SET— A set that has two levels where the second level is high enough (usually around +7') so that actors can walk under the top level. This often places the actors on the upper level very close to the lights, which results in coverage being small, the channel levels being very low, and it brings with it all the difficulties of the Distance Problem.

DOUBLE-HANGING or DOUBLING— The practice of hanging two instruments in approximately the same place, used most commonly in order to effect a color change. This is done for whole systems of lights, like all the arealights or a whole perimeter wash. The same effect could be accomplished with one set of lights if they were equipped with color scrollers or some other remote color changing mechanism. In a proscenium situation it is common, when using Stanley McCandless' method, to double-hang on one side and single-hang on the other side. The theory is that the single-hung Surprise Pink gel color can be used with either the double-hung pink or the blue (or whatever the actual colors are). Washes especially can be triple-hung and quadruple-hung and so forth to provide a change of color.

DOUSER (sometimes spelled dowser)— Also called a *chopper* or a *cut-off*, this is a part of a followspot that allows the operator to cut off the light. It typically works like two sliding doors on a freight elevator that come together from top and bottom.

DOWNLIGHT— Also called a *toplight*, this refers to any light that comes from above, the top-dead-center position.

DOWNTIME— This is a computer lightboard term that refers to the time it takes those channels that are decreasing in a transition to reach their new lower levels. In most cues, uptime and downtime will be the same, but they don't have to be.

DRAMATIC INTEREST— It is one of about four criteria of excellence in lighting design, and it is usually characterized by the deliberate and artful unevenness of light distributed over the scene as a whole. See LIGHTING, FUNCTION OF and LIGHTING, ART OF for a more detailed discussion.

DRAWING EXCHANGE FORMAT (Abbr DXF)— A computer file format similar in concept to ASCII text files (plain text) designed so that CAD programs can share information with each other.

DRAWINGS— There are typically only two lighting documents that could be called drawings. The plan view is called the *Light Plot* and one or more section views are called *Lighting Sectionals* or *Cross-sectionals*. See PAPERWORK for a more detailed discussion. There are four questions that have to be answered before any drawings are undertaken or even contemplated: (1) What will the scale of the drawing be, (2) How big will the drawing be, (3) How will the original be drawn, and (4) How will the copies be produced?

There are four standard paper sizes: A-sized paper is 8.5 · 11(also called letter sized), B-sized paper is 11 · 17 (also called ledger sized), C-sized paper is 17 · 22 and D-sized paper is 22 · 34. The common scales are ¼, ⅜ and ½. There are two methods of doing the original drawing: manual drafting or the use of a CAD program like Autocad, in which case the original would be printed on a computer printer or plotter. The copies will be either blueprinted or photocopied or printed/plotted like the original.

If the drawings have to be manually drawn, then their scale will be limited to what sizes the lighting templates are made in, which is usually only ¼ and ½ scale. If that is so, then the size of the theatre space determines what size paper would be needed to encompass the whole area. Having said that, most theatres have copy machines capable of copying B-sized paper, so if there is any possibility that the drawing could be made to fit on one or more B-sized sheets it is often considered advantageous to do it that way.

Usually the master electrician will make it clear what size and scale drawings she expects to get and how many copies and on what kind of paper. She will customarily give a new designer a blank plot that shows the theatre's outline and the lighting and circuit positions. What she gives the lighting designer is usually a good indicator of what she expects to get back in return. If she includes an instrument count on the blank plot, it usually means that she expects to get an instrument count on the final plot. She also may have strong feelings about how much information ought to be included on the plot in addition to just the instrument symbol. See MASTER ELECTRICIAN, MEETING WITH and LIGHT PLOT, DRAWING ONE for a more detailed discussion.

DRESS PARADE— See COSTUME PARADE.

DRESS REHEARSALS— These are technical rehearsals that include costumes and usually make-up and hair. The costumes by tradition are the last technical element integrated into the show. Difficult costume changes are often worked out and practiced as part of the first technical rehearsals and often costume elements like hats are introduced early, but the general uncomplicated wearing of the costumes is delayed until the chances of soiling, spilling and generally destroying them has significantly diminished.

DROP BOX— An electrical distribution box with usually 4–6 circuits that is permanently wired but has enough cable so that it can be dropped in where needed. In a proscenium situation, these would typically be in the wings at the ends of the pipes and would be used to add circuits to a heavily loaded pipe. In a theatre with a permanent grid, they may

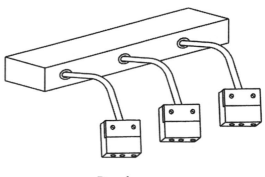

Drop box

be permanently located. It is unclear whether their name originally derived from the fact that they could be dropped into place on a spot line or because the box itself contained circuit drop points. In any event, whether movable or fixed in place, they would be considered a drop box. If however they were recessed in the floor or wall, they would be referred to as a wall pocket or floor pocket.

DROP LIGHTING— See LIGHTING SPECIAL PROBLEMS/Cyc and Drops.

DROP POINTS— The number of receptacles or plug-in points on a single circuit. A dimmer connected to a floor pocket will have other drop points around the theatre to ensure that it (the dimmer) gets used more frequently that just when that particular floor pocket is used (which could be once every four or five seasons). Convenience outlets are wired using this principle of having lots of plug-in points. While the prop room may have eight convenience outlets at intervals along the walls, they will typically all be on the same circuit.

DRY TECH— A lighting rehearsal without the actors. In addition to the lighting designer, it frequently includes the board operator, the stage manager and the director. If the sets are to be moved around, then it may also involve a running crew and perhaps the set designer. It also typically involves the sound designer and the sound operator. If it is done as the next call after the lights have been focused, it can take 8–10 hours or several days to complete. If the lighting designer is given an opportunity to work by herself at a level-setting session and to work during a couple of rehearsals-with-light, then it can take less than an hour.

Dry techs are notorious for not starting on time and for bogging down partway through, but that need not be the case. Where the lighting designer is showing the director cues that she already knows she likes, then the speed of the process is almost wholly dependent on how long the director needs to look at each cue. The stage manager should al-

ready have put the cues in the book, so the session should not be held up by this. Sometimes walkers are brought in to stand where needed, but there is not universal agreement as to how useful this is as they do not have the same facial coloring as the actors, are not the same height, do not stand in the same places, are not wearing costumes, and there are rarely enough of them to populate the whole stage. As a result, they make the dry tech last considerably longer as they are moved from place to place, but there is often little evidence to suggest that they are doing anything that is useful. This is especially true if there have already been rehearsals-with-light where the real actors have already served as the models.

Sometimes there will be the suggestion that the sound tech be handled at a separate session, but usually sound and light cues come at the same general place and have to work together and so it is usually helpful to have everyone there together. See INTEGRATING THE LIGHTS for a more detailed discussion.

DULLING SPRAY— This is a commercially made artist's material in an aerosol can that cuts the shine on shiny objects. It is used to dull down silver trays and the glass in picture frames and anything else that might be causing a problem onstage. It should not be confused with *frosting spray* that makes transparent objects translucent.

DUPLEX RECEPTACLE— Two side-by-side female receptacles designed to be installed in an electrical box, most commonly parallel-blade or twist lock. The parallel-blade kind is universally used for convenience outlets.

DUTCHMAN— In the context of stage lighting, it refers to a vintage objective optical train designed to turn a spotlight into a projector, such as a *sciopticon*.

DWELL TIME— This is a computer lightboard term that refers to how long a *step* remains up as part of the in time/dwell time/out time/step time effect process.

DXF—Abbreviation for DRAWING EXCHANGE FORMAT, which is a computer file format similar in concept to ASCII text files (plain text) designed so that CAD programs can share information with each other.

EDGE-QUALITY—One of the eight variables of light. It refers to whether the pool of light appears to have a sharply defined edge (hard edge) or whether it gradually tapers away to nothing (soft edge). Fresnels and floodlights of all kinds are soft edged. Ellipsoidals can be either, but their soft edge is in many cases not as smooth or gradual as that of a true soft-edged instrument. Frosts of various kinds can make hard edges soft or at least softer, but at present very little can be done to make soft edges hard. See VARIABLES OF LIGHT for a more detailed discussion.

EDISON CONNECTORS—Another name for *parallel-blade* or *parallel-blade-grounded* connectors. See CONNECTORS, KINDS OF for a more detailed discussion.

EDISON LAMP BASE—The medium screw base normally used in residences and everywhere else. See LAMPS for a more detailed discussion.

EFFECT CUES—These are computer lightboard cues that involve flickering lights, i.e. lights that have a high/low setting. See LIGHTING CONTROL, Computer Memory Lightboards for a more detailed discussion.

EFFECTS HEAD—Sometimes an effects machine is built as a two-part unit where there is a light source and then various interchangeable effects heads that attach in front and provide various kinds of motion.

EFFECTS, KINDS OF—There essentially are three different classes or groups of effects: static, flickering and moving:

Static Effects

Celestial Bodies: Sun, moon, stars, clouds. All of them can be projected by a gobo pattern onto something. Clouds probably work the best but at extremely subtle levels onto a lit cyc. Stars can also be produced by tiny individual lights either hanging down in front of the cyc on tiny wires or behind the cyc showing through tiny holes in the cloth or surface. Miniature Christmas tree lamps would typically be used for this either run low voltage or run on standard AC with a balancing resistor. The behind the cloth method dates back to Louis Hartmann and is highly labor-intensive but is said to look quite impressive. The in-front-of-the-cloth method either needs the audience to be far away or it needs a scrim to prevent the wires being visible. Sun and Moon can be projected but are usually most effectively done with a light box, often called a sun box or a moon box. See LIGHT BOXES for a more detailed discussion.

Glowing coals: This is a static fire effect that involves reddish and yellowish-orange lamps concealed from view but shining through a translucent mound of what looks like coals (usually a fiberglass sculpture). Static candle or lamplight effects can be created in a similar way by using amber lamp dip as a paint on a tiny light (often battery operated) in a candle or lamp unit.

Pyrotechnics: Flash pots are most common but they are silent. When something with more of a bang is needed, i.e. a controlled explosion, then it has to be suitably enclosed so that it cannot create a fire hazard, and in most localities either a permit or license is required, sometimes both. For the occasional user, there are manufacturers that specialize in pre-packaging these effects with controlled times, controlled colors and controlled levels of bang and smoke, which is considerably safer than kitchen table experiments with what amounts to bomb-making materials.

Shafts of Light: Usually these are shafts of sunlight or moonlight, but they could be shafts from a lighthouse or other artificial source. Beam projectors are the only stage instruments that can produce the parallel beams of light needed. Where a beam projector cannot be procured, an ellipsoidal would be typically used from as far away as possible. When it is not the surface being lit that is important but the actual "shafts" then some kind of smog has to be introduced into the air. Any smoke or fog will work, but where this effect is used, it is more common to use a hazer, which as the name implies creates something much more subtle and usually less offensive to the audience.

Flickering Effects

Chase Lights: Any kind of chase pattern can be treated as a series of effects cues. See LIGHTING CONTROL, Computer Memory Lightboards and CHASE EFFECT for a more detailed discussion.

Fires, Candles and Lamplight: Modern computer lightboards are superbly good at creating precisely timed and randomly executed flickering light effects. Anything like a fire where several circuits of red and orange colors can be hooked up to the lightboard will work well. This technique is equally good for stationary (non portable) candles or lamplight. The secret (if there is a secret) is being able to wash out the blinking effect part in an infinitely variable way as flickering lights become old news after the first few seconds and need to be subdued for the remainder of a scene so that they won't draw focus. There are several commercially made portable candles and lamps but they often don't have a way that the flickering can be reduced or balanced. Real candles and real lamps (where they are permitted, often look the best). Rotating cylinders both horizontal and vertical have been used for a fire effect, as has a fan with strips of silk, as has light bouncing off crushed glass on a turntable, as has light released into a cylinder with a fan on top that will be operated by the hot air like a Christmas angel display.

Lightning: Louis Hartmann describes a girl on a stepladder with a magnesium gun. I'm not quite sure what a magnesium gun is or was, but I'm pretty sure it's not legal to use one anymore. Scratching a carbon electrode against a metal file is another old time method described by Theodore Fuchs and also entirely illegal these days. Lightning bolts can be projected or lights can be flashed, but both of these methods suffer from the fact that incandescent lamps cool down slowly. A carbon arc spotlight, however, will work quite well as will a strobe light, as both have a fast cool-down period. There are a number of small strobes made for disco use that can produce flashes bright enough to be mistaken for lightning in the proper circumstances.

Slow Motion or At the Movies: One way to do this is with flickering lights from the lightboard. Another method involves moving effects and will be described next.

Moving Effects

Moving effects usually involve a projection loop. Sometimes the projection is constant and a wheel or film loop or gobo rotator creates the movement. Whatever the method it is critical that the looping, the point where the loop joins back on itself, remain undetected.

Clouds: These were one of the first moving effects ever tried and they relied on a projector with a circular wheel, but their progress across the cyc, unless very slow, was detectable as circular. For the most part, no one expects clouds to move anymore. It is true that they move in real life, but everyone understands they are at a theatrical performance and if the clouds don't move, no one usually cares. The reverse is actually true, and clouds that do move (unless it is artfully done) risk calling attention to themselves and away from the action of the play.

Water, rain and snow: The traditional way to create the sense of light being reflected off of water was to shine the light on a shallow pan of water and let this reflect onto the scene. The space necessary to set up such an effect is not always available. Sometimes a flickering light will work. Sometimes a film loop is employed. Sometimes a rotating wheel either in the gel slot or the gobo slot can be employed.

According to Louis Hartmann, the secret to creating effects is that the mechanism of how they were created has to be kept a secret from the audience. Although he may have been the first one to say this in print, several other lighting designers have said it more eloquently since. The effect has to be complex enough, the patterns have to be out-of-focus enough and the time the audience has to study them has to be seriously limited. Only then will any effect truly succeed, at least that is the folk wisdom on the subject.

EFFECTS MACHINE— A device for producing moving lights. It can either be a self-contained unit or it can be something that attaches to a spotlight of some kind. *Gobo rotators*, for example, slide in the gobo slot of a standard ellipsoidal spotlight.

EFFICACY and EFFICIENCY— These are scientific words that are easily confused. Efficacy describes how much of the electrical power consumed by a lamp got turned into light. Efficiency is a measure of how much light came out the front of the instrument relative to how much the lamp produced.

ELECTRICAL METALLIC TUBING (Abbr. EMT)— Thin-walled conduit that is commonly called "conduit" but always referred to as EMT in the electrical code, as real conduit is threaded and looks a lot like water pipe.

ELECTRICAL SERVICES— This is the way electricity from the generating plant is brought into the building.

Two-Wire, Single Phase: There may be a few barns or outbuildings still wired this way, but it is all but obsolete today and purely of historical interest. This involved one hot wire and one neutral wire and provided 120 volts of power. This was standard practice for residences up until perhaps the Second World War when it was replaced by what will be described next.

Three-Wire, Single Phase: In this configuration there are two hot wires (called *legs*) and an unfused neutral. Voltage between the two hot legs is 240 volts and 120 volts between either hot leg and the neutral, thus allowing both 240-volt appliances like

water heaters and electric stoves to be installed as well as providing 120 volts for everything else. In a small summer stock theatre, this might still be the kind of electrical service in use.

Four-Wire, Three-phase: This however is what would more likely be encountered. There will be three hot legs and a common neutral. Any connection between any two hot legs will usually be 208 volts and any connection between one hot leg and the common neutral will be 120 volts. Depending on whether it is a *wye* connection or a *delta* connection, this could vary, so it is always necessary to double-check each leg with a tester.

ELECTRICAL TAPE— A plastic tape that does not conduct electricity (dielectric), usually black, usually ¾" wide. See TAPES, KINDS OF for a more detailed discussion.

ELECTRICAL TESTERS— Basically there are two kinds depending on whether one is testing for high voltage current (120 volts or higher) or checking for an unbroken current path. A serviceable version of each can be had for well under $5.

To check to see that there are no breaks in the wires and that the connections at the lamp and connector are good, a **continuity tester** is needed. It is in essence a penlight

Continuity tester

where the circuit is closed when the two test leads touch something that conducts electricity. With an instrument sitting on the deck, touching the black and white prongs of the connector with the continuity tester should make the test light work because the battery power travels up one prong and through the lamp and back to the other prong. Extension cords are often checked by touching each color prong at each end to see if there is continuity in the wire. A horn or buzzer is sometimes substituted for the light so that one can keep one's eyes on the two electrical contacts and simply listen for the sound.

The **neon tester** has two neon lights hooked in series and two test leads. When connected to the hot and neutral of a 120-volt line, they will glow. When connected to 240 volts, they will brightly shine and when connected to 208 volts, they will shine but not quite so brightly. A homemade version of this (commonly called a *double pigtail tester*)

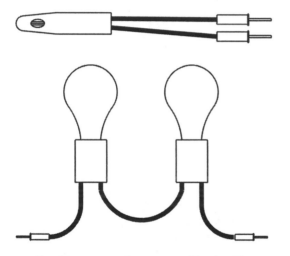

Top: Neon tester; *bottom:* Double pigtail tester.

that uses two outdoor type sockets and ordinary light bulbs can be made for about six times the price with 80 percent more bulk, plus it will be fragile because of the glass light bulbs. It is mentioned in older books and was used before other kinds of testers became hardware store items and stocking stuffers, which is why it is referenced here.

Multimeter

Electronics supply stores sell **multimeters** (sometimes called *VOMs*), which can measure AC and DC current and also check continuity and measure resistance. Small models can be had for $5–10, and $30 will purchase a meter with more accuracy than a stage lighting person is ever likely to need. If repairing Christmas tree lights is a possibility, then a meter will be needed. Some lighting manufacturers sell their own testing units that plug in, but while being marginally easier to read, they do nothing that the multimeter doesn't do for a fraction of the price.

ELECTRICIAN— Any one working on the electrics crew but usually not someone who has another title, like board operator or ladder electrician.

ELECTRICIAN'S PLOT— A simplified plot. See LIGHT PLOT, ELECTRICIAN'S.

ELECTRICITY— Like light, it is a form of electromagnetic energy. It is usually described as a flow of electrons in a conductor. The rate of flow is measured in electrons per second past a fixed point (amperes of current flow). The pressure necessary to make that happen is called the *electromotive force* (EMF) and is measured in volts. The resistance of the wire to the flow of current is called *resistance* and is measured in Ohms. These are related by Ohm's law: $E = I/R$ where E = electromotive force in volts, I = current flow in amps and R = resistance in ohms. The ability of electricity to do work like running a motor or operating a light is a product of the current flow and the electromotive force, and this is called *power*, and it is measured in either horsepower (for motors) or watts (for lights). One horsepower is equal to 745.7 watts. This is called the *power formula*, and it is usually expressed as $P = IE$ (power = current flow * electromotive force) by scientists and as $W = VA$ (watts = volts * amps) by stage technicians. The power formula is sometimes referred to as either the *PIE formula* or the *West Virginia formula* as a memory aid. The power formula is widely used in the theatre because dimmers and wire are usually rated in amps but instruments and dimmers are rated in watts, and it is often necessary to figure out how many 500 watt instruments could be safely put on a 20 amp cable (unknown wattage capacity of wire = 120 volts * 20 amps = 2400 watts, and thus four instruments at 500 watts apiece could be used).

ELECTRICS— Sometimes used as the name for the crew or department, but when numbered (first electric, second electric, etc) it refers to the pipes in a fly house devoted to lighting equipment. It is not unusual for them to have some kind of permanent plugging channel mounted above the pipe itself on which the lights hang. The first electric by tradition is located right behind the front curtain and often is the most useful and most heavily loaded of the electric pipes. The first electric is sometimes a light bridge that can be walked across or manned during a performance.

ELECTRODE— The pole or terminal in an electrical device, usually used in the context of a battery.

ELECTROMAGNETIC ENERGY (Abbr. EME)— Radiant energy from outer space, mostly from our sun, in diverse wavelengths. Aside from electricity and sound and light, it also includes heat, gamma rays, x-rays, microwaves, radio waves, ultraviolet light and more.

ELECTROMOTIVE FORCE (Abbr. EMF)— The pressure needed to cause a flow of electrons. A flashlight battery starts out with 1.5 volts of pressure, which is enough to make the light work. After the light has been on for a few hours, the chemicals in the battery become depleted and the voltage has dropped to 0.8 volts of pressure and the flashlight no longer is bright enough to use and its battery is pronounced dead. EMF is sometimes in scientific circles referred to as a *potential difference*.

ELEVATION— An artillery term for up/down movement, now more commonly referred to as *tilt* in the context of stage lighting.

ELLIPSOIDAL REFLECTOR— One of three common reflector shapes. See REFLECTION, LAWS OF.

ELLIPSOIDAL RE-FLECTOR SPOT-LIGHT (Abbr. ERS)— But commonly called an ellipsoidal by almost everyone. It is named after the shape of its reflector and is now the pre-eminent of all theatre spotlights. It produces a light that has a uniform beam that can be soft or hard-edged, can be pattern modified and has shutters to cut it off objects that shouldn't be lit. See LIGHTING INSTRUMENTS/Lensed Instruments for a more detailed discussion.

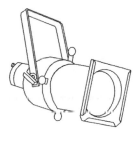

Ellipsoidal

ELLIPSOIDALS, SIZES OF— Ellipsoidals come in sizes based on how large an area they will cover at a given distance. The three most common sizes are smalls, mediums and larges that roughly correspond to 30 degree, 40 degree, and 50 degree field angles. There are also three smaller sizes of 5 degrees, 10 degrees, and 20 degrees that are customarily only needed for really long throw distances. A 50 degree instrument has a wide-angle lens, the lens itself will be thick and have a short focal length, and because it covers so wide an area it will be used at close distances. In contrast, an instrument with a smaller field angle (say a 30 degree instrument) will have a flatter lens that has a longer focal length, and the instrument will be used at longer throw distances because the light will travel a long way before it opens up to cover an 8–10' area. If the 30 degree instrument is used at very close range, its coverage area will be very small, sometimes only one or two feet across.

EME— Abbreviation for ELECTROMAGNETIC ENERGY.

EMERGENCY LIGHTING— Specifically the battery powered back-up lights that will come on if the power fails. Emergency lighting is extended to mean everything electrical related to emergency planning, which would include the exit signs, the aisle lighting, fire and smoke alarms, etc.

EMF— Abbreviation for ELECTROMOTIVE FORCE.

EMPHASIS SPECIAL— See SPECIALS, KINDS OF.

EMT— Abbreviation for ELECTRICAL METALLIC TUBING.

ENCAPSULATED ARC LAMP— Describes a whole series of gaseous discharge lamps including CID, HMI and xenon where electricity arcs between two contacts within the glass envelope of the lamp. They cannot be dimmed by standard theatrical dimmers, and as a result are used at present in followspots only.

END-OF-SCENE CONVENTION — There are really two slightly different conventions depending on whether a front curtain is being used or not. Where the curtain closes at the ends of scenes, the lights typically fade out at the same speed. Where the intention is to close the curtain as fast as possible, the lights usually go out on a zero count as soon as the curtain starts moving. When the curtain opens on a new scene, the lights (at least those in front of the curtain) mimic the curtain speed. In the absence of the curtain, the lights fade out (or almost out) at the ends of scenes and fade up at the beginnings of scenes and there may or may not be scene change lights used between scenes depending on the complexity of the scenery and property changes.

ENVELOPE— Sometimes called the glass envelope, it is more commonly just called the *bulb* portion of the lamp.

EQUITY LIGHTS— Named after the actors' union that first required them as a safety measure. See RUNNING LIGHTS.

ERS— Abbreviation for ELLIPSOIDAL REFLECTOR SPOT.

ESTIMATING TIME— How long will it take to hang the instruments? How long will it

take to focus them? This is often considered a subject so difficult that no one could possibly figure it out. If that were the case, who then would be left to plan the schedule? Someone figures it out. What method do they use? The very best method is to know how much time it took last time and assume that (in the absence of any special circumstances) it will take as long this time. Where the master electrician is the one who estimates the time, this is most often the system that is used.

When a lighting designer looks at a schedule and sees that four hours have been allotted to a focusing call, she needs to know if that is a reasonable amount of time or not. That will depend on how many instruments there are and how hard they are to get to and how fast and experienced the crew is and so forth, which is, of course, what makes it hard to estimate.

How long does it take to hang an instrument? If you don't know, you should time yourself and see how long it takes you. Most people can do this in well under two minutes. The bigger problem is how long it will take to set up a ladder (or do whatever has to be done) to get to the instruments.

I have a formula. I don't claim that it is original, but I do, however, say that it works. First, one establishes how long it takes to gain access to all of the hanging positions. While it may only take a minute to get to a catwalk position, it may take 20 minutes to set up a ladder at a box boom position out in the house. If one ladder position services 10 instruments, then the time can be apportioned among them. Once there is a list of positions and times it takes to get to them, it is merely a matter of deciding how many instruments fall into which category and multiplying by the access time. It takes approximately as much time to hang an instrument as it takes to focus an instrument.

The lighting designer is mostly concerned with how long the focus will take because she is in charge of that. The amount of time it took to do the hang is a good indicator of how long it will take to do the focus (assuming there are as many ladder crews and other factors are equal). While the savvy lighting designer does her own time estimates of everything, she also likes to have the master electrician agree that xx number of hours is the usual time for a focus session, which then makes her in part responsible if it turns out not to be true.

In terms of getting another job at this theatre (often at any other theatre too), a lighting designer does not want it said that she couldn't focus the lights in the time allotted. If she thought the time was inadequate, then she should have said something in advance. Indeed she should have and this implies that she was capable of estimating time, which she should have been capable of. See HANGING AN INSTRUMENT for a more detailed discussion.

EXCEPT— This is a computer lightboard *number-stringing* term and frequently the name of a button whose purpose is to exclude certain numbers from a previously established list. "Channels 1 thru 18 except 2" would exclude 2 from the 1–18 group.

EXECUTE— Used in reference to cues meaning to *take* or *do* the cue.

EXIT LIGHTS— Lighted signs that say "exit" in green letters and usually have an arrow pointing in a direction. These are typically at the ends of aisles and above all door and doorways that lead to outside the building. They are required by building and fire codes and are one of a group of safety-oriented lights that stay on during the performance. There are usually two lights in every sign thus increasing the chances that the sign will stay lit.

EXTENDED APRON— In a proscenium theatre, this refers to a larger than usual apron or forestage in front of the main curtain, often created by covering over an orchestra pit. Audiences do not typically sit on the sides of anything referred to as an *apron*.

EXTENSION LADDERS— A telescoping ladder that has to lean against a wall or a rigidly attached grid pipe. See HANGING POSITIONS, GETTING TO for a more detailed discussion.

EYE (human)— The human eye is the part of the body that is normally associated with sight. Scientists have dissected and studied the eye and exhaustively named its various pieces and components. Light enters the eye through the pupil, which is the central hole in the center of the iris. The size of the pupil changes to admit more or less light depending on the amount of illumination present. The light then passes through the lens, which focuses it on the rods and cones, which are the receptors or sensors on the sensitive inner surface (retina) of the eye. While most people have heard this at some point in their life, they usually have no idea how many receptors are actually present. There are 115 million rods and 7 million cones in each eye, give or take a few millions. Theoretically, their vast number and smallness of size is taken to explain why the apparent brightness of objects remains the same regardless of the eye's distance from an object. Cones are interspersed with rods, but there is a central area (fovea) that is almost entirely made up of cones, and this is where distinct focused vision occurs. It covers only about a 1 degree field of view, which explains why our eyes are almost constantly scanning back and forth as we look at things.

The cones see in color but don't operate in light levels below about a footcandle. The rods see in black-and-white but are much more sensitive to motion and can operate in much lower light levels by increasing their sensitivity. When people talk about night vision, they are talking about rod vision where the eyes have to adjust to the dark (which can take 20–30 minutes), and objects can then be seen best by not looking directly at them, as this would merely focus their image on the central area where all the sleeping cones are.

Light entering the eye causes some kind of chemical reaction in the receptors. Among other things a substance called *visual purple* is bleached yellow, and the individual nerves send an electrical impulse to that eye's optic nerve which sends it to the optic lobes at the back of the brain. Impulses from the right eye are processed by the left side of the brain, and visa-versa. This is the point at which no one seems to understand exactly what happens next or how. It is clear that the brain forms a mental image of what was seen, but how it does this remains both a mystery and a miracle. The brain maintains a database of other past mental images that help it evaluate what it is seeing now.

It should be pointed out that even as we sleep, our sensation of sight, the brain function part of it, continues and we see things in our dreams even though our eyes are closed and the presence of light on the retina is not a factor.

Our eyes are extremely good comparative instruments. Show us two lights side-by-side, and we can see minute brightness differences. Show us two colors side-by-side, and we can detect minute color differences. When seen sequentially, however, our eyes are very poor at remembering either some previous brightness level or a previous color. Everyone is familiar with Coca-Cola red and Makita blue, but given a sample of 10 reds or 10 blue-greens, few people can pick out the right colors from memory.

We can actually make out 100–200 different hues and thousands of tints, shades and tones, which is a huge miracle when one considers how infinitesimally small the wavelength differences are.

We respond better to light that is in the yellow-green range (we see it better), which explains why yellow light appears to cut through all other colors of stage light and why a little of it goes such a long way.

Our eyes being situated on the front of our faces as they are, we see in only two dimensions, and we estimate and guess at depths. We are really extremely good at this. The two best indicators are (1) shade and shadow and (2) perspective. When direct light hits an object, it makes the side on the sunnyside brightly lit and the sides in the shade lit only by reflected bounce light (and therefore dimmer) and it casts a shadow (absence of light) on the surroundings. Perspective is also called convergence. Think of two railway tracks vanishing "down the line." The two tracks appear to converge as they recede into the distance. They are also getting smaller, but all this is easier to see on the telephone poles that are usually beside the railway tracks.

In the absence of other clues, there also are six other indicators used by our eyes to help in estimating depth and size:

Brightness: Objects more brightly lit are usually assumed to be closer than those more dimly lit.

Distinctness: Objects that are clear and distinct are usually assumed to be closer than hazy, fuzzy objects.

Elevation: Objects located higher in our view are assumed to be further away. This is especially true in outdoor scenes where a horizon line can be seen.

Known size: One knows how high telephone poles are supposed to be. One knows how big the front door of a house is. One can use this knowledge to estimate the size and distance of nearby objects.

Overlap: Objects that appear to partially obscure other objects are assumed to be in front. This becomes particularly clear where movement is involved because the moving object obscures the background and is obscured by the foreground.

Stereopticon vision: Two eyes are better than one. Each eye sees a slightly different view of the same thing. We see depth better with both eyes open.

Graphic artists (painters) have understood all this since the time that paintings came off the walls of caves and started being put on cloth and paper. Paintings are 2-dimensional representations, but they hope to suggest to the eye that it is seeing a three-dimensional image. It obviously works or we wouldn't have TV or photography, and the only kind of painting would be house painting.

When people talk about painters, they often talk about their sense of light. The paintings themselves are most often viewed by being uniformly lit from the front; so what, one might wonder, are they talking about exactly? They are talking about the artist having used different colors of paint to differentiate between the sides of an object that face the light and those that are in shade. In any irregular 3-dimensional object (like an outcropping of rock), our eyes determine the shape of the object by the shade and shadow. In a painting of an outcropping of rock, the three-dimensional qualities are represented by different colors.

The theory of sight starts with light hitting an object. Part of the light is absorbed by the object and part is reflected. If the object were a perfect blackbody radiator (assuming such a thing existed, which it doesn't), then it would absorb all the light, reflect none and as a result couldn't be seen. According to the theory, some of the reflected light hits the eye and thus causes sight, in a way that is not fully understood yet. The light that is reflected to the eye does not behave as other light because it does not appear to decrease in strength over distance according to the inverse square law. Let's suppose you are standing a foot away from an eyechart with one inch print and there is a candle also a foot away from the print in some kind of shielded box, so that you can't see the candle itself. If you were to look at your hands, they would appear to be lit because they are being lit by reflected (bounce) light from the eyechart. Were you to step back a foot, there would only be a quarter as much bounce light hitting both your hands and your eyes. Your hands will look noticeably dimmer, but the eyechart will look as bright as ever. No matter how far away you were to move, the energy radiating from the object to your eye would not appear to decrease in strength at all. Mountains that are forty miles away appear as brightly lit as they would at a mile away. In theatrical terms, the scene will look as brightly lit from the first row as from the last. The scientists explain this by saying that when one is close, the light from the object is spread over a larger area in the retina, but when one is far away the same amount of light is concentrated on a much smaller area in the retina thus making it appear as bright as before because the same quantity of light is present. In any event, it is clear that the eye adjusts to maintain the apparent brightness of objects.

We see sources of light (self-luminous objects) better than ordinary objects. Imagine that there are two objects in shielded containers at the end of a vast parking lot. One is a lit candle and the other is a white piece of cardboard that has been lit until it was equally bright. If you were to hold up your hands and look at them as you walked away, you would see that both samples are following the inverse square law because your hands are getting noticeably dimmer. You will still see the candlelight at 50'. Even when you reach a distance where you can no longer make out the white card or the easel it is on, you will still see the candlelight. Galileo once did an experiment where he had an assistant with a covered lantern on a hill that was exactly a mile away. The idea was that the assistant would uncover his lantern as soon as he saw light. The point of the experiment was to measure the speed of light. It failed because human reaction time was too slow at only a mile away, but the important part of the experiment from a lighting point-of-view was that no one had the slightest problem seeing a lantern being uncovered from a mile away, even if they couldn't see either the lantern or the man holding it. In fact the light from the lantern would probably still have been visible at more than 15 miles away.

Here are the things that it is important to know about the human eye. Some of these are discussed in more detail in VISIBILITY.

First and foremost, you should have a sense of wonder and the belief that sight is a miraculous gift beyond compare.

Second, visual acuity decreases with distance, even though apparent brightness of the object does not.

Third, there needs to be enough light hitting the object to see by. Once the threshold is crossed (at a fraction of a footcandle), there is a small period of time when visual acuity increases as the illumination increases After that, the iris in our eye progressively closes down to limit incoming light and visibility remains more-or-less constant throughout our visible range. At high light levels, we are forced to squint or to limit incoming light with sunglasses or some other means. We can however see in conditions as bright as 10,000 fc or in conditions as low as 1/10,000 fc.

Fourth, we can only see a tiny portion of our total range at any one time (limited to contrasts of about 20-to-1) without our eye readjusting. Our entire concept of brightness is based on contrast or what we might call *apparent brightness*. An actor being spot lit on a dark stage may appear bright. When the background behind her is brought up, she may appear grossly underlit.

Coming out of blackouts to full scene level needs to be done gradually enough so that the audience's eyes have time to adjust. Strobe lights are particularly annoying because they don't do this, and audience members often shade their eyes with their program to avoid them, much as anyone would look away from someone who was arc welding. These are all results of what happens when the 20:1 contrast limits are violated.

Fifth, compared to animals like the family dog, we don't really see all that well. This is actually a good thing. If we saw better, we'd see flashing dots of light when we turned on the TV and 24 frames a second when we went to a movie. If we could remember light levels better, we'd realize that what is typically passed off in the theatre as a daytime scene was seriously underlit by several thousand footcandles. We see in two-dimensions. In order to see three-dimensional shapes, they have to be lit so that there is a contrast between their hills and valleys that makes them look different (plasticity). Occasionally our bad eyesight gets us in trouble, and we see things like mirages or steam coming off the roads, but for the most part in the theatre it allows the use of broad suggestion to stimulate the imagination of the audience, which is a good thing.

Sixth, the eye has a very narrow field of view (about 1 degree), which means that when one reads a pocket book, it takes 3 shifts of focus to read a line. When a more complex scene on stage is evaluated, it is viewed one-segment-at-a-time and the brain puts the whole picture together. During a stage play, the audience has to continually move their eyes to take in the whole stage. When they fail to do this, one might suspect (usually correctly) that they are asleep.

The easiest way to become aware of this is to watch a videotape taken at a rehearsal. Assuming the camera was set up where an audience member would normally have been sitting, one might think it would be an accurate representation of how the audience would see the show, but, of course, it's not. The camera has been set up with its widest field of view so it provides a continuous view of the whole stage. Actors' faces appear on screen about the size of pencil erasers. There will be a voice inside you screaming at you to please zoom in on something so you can actually see something, anything. If you were actually watching the play, you would scan across it looking for the most interesting thing to watch. Then your eyes would zoom in on something and watch it for a while, usually until you were distracted by movement somewhere else.

Seventh, the human eye sees colors in the yellow-green range better than other colors and sees self-luminous objects better than ordinary objects.

EYELEVEL RING (positions) — All light hanging positions that are at the eyelevel of a standing actor. Since hanging positions are usually discussed as being at 45 degree increments from each other, there would be eight positions: front, back, left and right and the intermediate positions of left and right front and left and right back. See HANGING POSITIONS, IDEAL for more detail.

EYE-PROTECTION — Looking into the bright faces of stage lighting instruments can certainly cause temporary eye damage and perhaps permanent damage as well. Eye-protection can take the form of holding up piece of dark blue gel, but this is purely a field expedient. If the room is noisy, the designer may be forced to use hand signals to communicate with the ladder electricians who are focusing. Even if this is not the case, it is tiring to have to hold up anything for more than just a few seconds. Ordinary sunglasses are typically not dark enough. Glacier glasses, which are part of mountain climbing gear, are just about the ideal darkness.

EYE-TEST— A test to determine the position of the back row of the house and to determine how normal the lighting designer's eyesight is. See OPERA GLASSES TEST and VISIBILITY.

FADE UP or DOWN, IN or OUT— See FADES, KINDS OF.

FADER or FADER PAIR— See CROSS-FADER.

FADER MODE— In the context of computer lightboards, this would be a display screen that revealed what the contribution of one or both fader pair was to the overall cue onstage. This would be an aid to figuring out pile-ons as it is often hard to figure out what contributes what to the overall effect.

FADES, KINDS OF— When a light cue is taken, the stage either looks brighter, dimmer or different. A number of descriptive names have been made up to describe to the stage manager, board operator and director what they should expect to see happening. These fall into three general groups.

First, there are cues that interact with the audience and separate the play or event from its various time-outs. There is usually a preset that "warms the curtain" or in the absence of a curtain warms the set (*preset I cue*). Then the house goes to half as a sign that the play is about to start (*house to half cue*). Then the house and preset go out (*house and preset out cue*), actors take their places and the lights come up on the first

scene (*lights-up scene X*). This repeats at intermission. At the end of the performance, after the *final fade-out* the actors come back on stage to take a curtain call (*calls or bows up*) and the houselights come up as they exit (*house up cue*) followed by a crossfade to a *postshow cue* that warms the stage as the audience leaves. This typically involves 16 cues more-or-less depending on how they are counted and assuming there is only one intermission. Where a curtain is involved, there is usually an additional cue that brings up light from the front-of-house as the curtain opens and to remove it as the curtain closes and these are commonly referred to as *fronts up* and *fronts out*.

Second, there is the scene separation category of cues. Books are divided into chapters. Plays are divided into scenes. Scenes are expected to look different from each other or be separated from each other by light cues. In the old days the curtain was used for this. It would come in, the scenery and props would get moved around as appropriate, and the curtain would be opened to reveal the new scene (usually lit the same way as the old scene). Curtains have gone out of fashion along with the proscenium arch behind which they hid.

Curtains were really good at preventing the audience from seeing what changes were being made. If the set was lavish enough, one could get a gasp or a round of applause from the audience when it was revealed for the first time. Without the curtain, the audience has way too long to get used to the set. The problem with the curtain was that it was a slow-mover and took about 5 seconds to either open or close, the up-and-down curtains being better at this than the side-to-side ones.

If a scene ended on a joke or a punch line, then 5 seconds could seem like an awfully long time. The usual solution was to have the actors freeze in place after the punch line. This was a way of signaling to the audience that they had stopped acting and the scene was over (a theatrical convention). When it became possible to dim the lights, then the lights mimicked the curtain. If the curtain were opening on a 10 count, then the lights would dim up on a 10 count. The lights behind the curtain would most commonly have been already on, but the lights from the house typically did not look good when they hit the curtain so these were brought up with the curtain opening. If the scene needed to end on a punch line, then the actors could freeze in place and the lights could go out instantaneously as the curtain was closing. Once the curtain was closed, worklights were turned on backstage to facilitate the scene change. If a change was merely representing the passage of time (later that night) and no actual scenery was going to get moved, then often the curtain was omitted and the lights would go off and then come back on.

When the proscenium theatres became thrust theatres and the curtains went away, then it was the lights alone that had to separate the scenes from each other. On the plus side, most of the scenery changing went away too. This meant that a simple lights down, followed by a lights up, could and did signify a new scene. If scenery or props actually did change significantly, then it might become necessary to have scene change lights between scenes. These were typically very dim giving the scene changers just enough light (worklight) to see the marks on the floor. The important thing was that the audience was expected to know that what they were seeing was not really part of the play (it was in effect another form of time-out, a theatrical convention).

Movies and TV don't have to bother with any of this because they can stop the camera to change scenery any time they want, and since they always photograph something real, it is obvious when the scene has shifted to a new location. In the theatre there tend to be "sitting places" that are sometimes the bench in the railway station and at other times an outcropping of rock on the hill that overlooks the valley. There desperately needs to be something to tell the audience that they are now in a new place. Sometimes the playwright has some text that tells the audience

where they are. Shakespeare always remembered to do this. Not everyone since has copied his methods. Sometimes it is left up to the lighting to make the place seem different.

When the theatres changed in the 1960s, the playwriting did too. Now there are plays that flow from scene-to-scene much more smoothly, in a stream-of-consciousness style, and there are fewer scenes that end in a blackout followed by lights-up on the next scene.

Transitions from scene to scene basically fall into three groups depending on how many cues it takes to complete the transition:

One-Cue Transitions: these are commonly called *crossfades*. Some lights go down and others come up. Sometimes this means that one area of the stage goes down and another area comes up, and sometimes it just means that the same part of the stage just changes and looks different.

During the days of preset lightboards, any cue transition that anyone could imagine from a lights out, followed by a lights-up (100 percent lag) to piling on the lights for the new scene and then subtracting the old scene lights (100 percent lead) was possible. Separating uptime from downtime on a computer lightboard was supposed to provide for leads and lags, but unfortunately the lags work somewhat differently. Having the downtime occur first does not create the hoped for fade out. It simply removes all lights that were to go out in the new scene, readjusts downward those channels going down somewhat and leaves on lights that are at the same level in the next scene.

As a result, a one-cue transition only makes sense where it is clearly agreed upon that the transition will either be a straight crossfade or a lead. Where the nature of the transition is in doubt, it is always more prudent to create a blackout followed by a lights-up. If the follow time is zero, the effect will be of a crossfade. If the follow time is positive, it will be a lag. If the follow time is zero but there is a downtime wait on the first cue, this will have the effect of a lead, as will be explained next.

Two-Cue Transition: While this is most commonly thought of as a *lights down* followed by a *lights-up*, it is a very flexible method to transition from one look to another when one is not entirely sure how that will work once the actors are present. It can be broken into two separately called cues when necessary, or it can be left as one cue that autofollows the other. The first is a blackout cue, except that it warms the filaments of the next cue. The second cue, which is typically a point cue (meaning if the first cue is numbered 15, the second one will be 15.1), autofollows the blackout by a certain follow time and is the lights-up cue. Follow time is set as an attribute of the first cue and usually starts counting at the first cue's go. If the first cue is a 5 ct and one sets the follow time at 0, then it becomes a straight cross-fade. Set the follow time at 2.5 and it becomes a 50 percent lag. Set the follow time at 5 or more and it becomes a blackout followed by lights-up. The old method of calling a blackout and waiting to see when the change was complete before calling lights up was often way too slow because of human reaction time. Letting the machine have a follow time, often produces the best results. When actors come to realize that the length of the blackout is being timed by a machine that does it the same way every night, they often learn how to do what they have to do to make that work. It certainly eliminates the lag between the stage manager seeing something and the machine responding to a button push. In most situations the stage manager is too far away to see well (if at all) and consequently waits overly long to call the cue to avoid catching anyone in the light.

The Other Kind of Two Cue Transition: This is mainly (if not entirely) a way to transition from the existing lights to something else (travel or time-lapse cue) and then to return to the original cue, thus signaling either a change of location or a change of time. Let's say that the play has scenes that take place in various parts of a jungle, where the

jungle will always use the full stage, and the lighting will always be pretty much the same. In order to indicate that one was moving to a new place, a *transition cue* would be needed. If there is a passage of time that occurs between two scenes, then the lights would typically be brought down to a low level and then restored, thereby using two cues to achieve the transition but always returning to the original cue.

Four Cue Transition: This is almost always a scene change scenario. The stage lights *fade out*, the actors clear and then the *scene change lights come on*. When the change is complete or almost complete, the *scene change lights go out*, the actors for the new scene take their places and the *lights come up* on them.

The third category of types of cues encompasses the ones that are internal to the scenes. These include (1) *Isolation specials* where one of the characters has a monologue, aside, flashback or spoken thought that is not really part of the existing scene (2) Anything involved with *practical lights,* i.e. turning them on or off, opening the shades on the window, etc. (3) *Effect cues* like lightning or a distant fire (4) General *eyestrain relief,* which basically means reducing parts of the stage where no one is standing to make the scene look different or simply changing the stage picture for no reason at all except to make sure everyone stays awake.

In the transition category are *fade ups,* which means something gets brighter. Occasionally someone will call them a *fade in,* which suggests a fade from black but this is seldom heard unless one is talking about a movie scene. A slow fade up might be called a *sneak up.*

When things get dimmer, it is typically called a *fade down,* a *fade to a special,* or a *fade out.* Fade outs clearly end in darkness and are sometimes called *blackouts* or a *fades-to-black.* A slow fade out or down might be called a *sneak down* or a *sneak out.*

When the stage simply gets different, it is commonly just called a *crossfade,* which for clarity is sometimes called a straight crossfade to distinguish it from a *lead* or a *lag*, but they are all crossfades.

A *restore* returns the stage to a previous look.

The reason there are more cues these days is mostly because the plays have more scenes, because areas can now be controlled more precisely which makes it possible to have more internal cues, and because the light-boards can remember an unlimited number of cues, which means no one cares how many cues there are anymore

FAMILIARIZATION SESSION— This is a euphemism for a session where the lighting designer who is new to the theatre will measure the space and count the inventory and generally snoop around. See MEASURING THE SPACE.

FEEDER or FEEDER CABLE— This is a large conductor designed to supply power to an entire dimmer package. Where it is run along the floor, there will typically be four or five of them because the wire size will be so large that it would create a very fat, very hard to deal with cable if combined.

FELT TIP MARKERS— These are used as they are everywhere for labeling things and creating signs. The permanent black kind can be successfully used to put color numbers on light colors of gel, but they really have to be permanent for this to work. The so-called highlighting colors (yellow, orange, pink, light blue and light green) are often used on the plot itself to highlight important information that might otherwise be overlooked. This includes non-standard lamps, weird yoking, the presence of gobo patterns or other accessories, and so forth. The hanging crew often use a highlighting color of their own to put a check mark on instruments that are done.

FEMALE CONNECTORS or RECEPTACLES— These are the ones with holes as opposed to prongs. They are also on the *line* side as opposed to *load* side of the electrical current. A male connector plugs into the dimmer or source of power. A female con-

nector (like on a plugging channel) is what the instrument gets plugs into. Female connectors are almost always electrically hot. Males never are because of the danger posed by the exposed prongs.

FIBER OPTICS— Transparent glass fibers that have the ability to transmit light, even around corners, it is a technology that is mostly used at present for data and voice transmission, but there are fiber optic lamps that can be used as special effects.

FIELD— That portion of the cone of light coming from an instrument that goes from 100 percent bright at the center to 10 percent bright on the edge. When an ellipsoidal in hard focus is turned on, what is seen projected on the floor is the field of the instrument. The actual plane of interest for the lighting designer would be whatever is happening at nose height. See PHOTOMETRIC DATA for a more detailed discussion.

FIELD ANGLE— The angle of the field portion of the cone of light as it leaves the instrument.

FIELD DIAMETER— The side-to-side diameter of the field portion of the cone of light as it hits the nose plane.

FILAMENT— The part of the lamp that incandesces when heated. Attempts have been made and continue to be made to make this as small as possible so that the light source is closer to a point source.

FILAMENT IMAGE— This was a huge problem with plano-convex instruments because it was possible to slide the lamp carriage into a position that put the lamp filament in focus in relation to the lens. This is not a problem with a modern fresnel or ellipsoidal spotlight, where the source of light is forward of the focal point.

FILL LIGHT— Any light that is not a *key* light is considered to be a fill light. In real life, fill light is created by reflected light (bounce), but in a theatrical situation both key and fill are created directly. The fill is usually a different color and sometimes less bright and lights the side of objects supposed to be in the shade.

FILLER (cable)— This refers to the string-like material or twisted brown-paper-like material often found in electrical cables to preserve their round shape.

FILTERS, COLOR— See COLOR FILTER or MEDIA.

FINDING THE LIGHT— This is something that actors are typically told to do when they are standing somewhere other than where their light is. For the most part, they are standing where the director told them to stand, but the light is somewhere else where the director agreed it would be but never got around to telling the actors. As a result the actors are too scared to change their blocking until specifically given permission to do so.

FIRE CODES— Laws have been passed on the state and local level to protect audience members when they go to "places of public assembly" regardless of whether it is a union hall or a church or a theatre. Mostly the provisions of the National Electrical Code (NEC) have been accepted as a whole, as have been the recommendations of the National Underwriters Code. There may also be local codes. In any event, the local enforcement authority is the local fire department, which visits theatres on a regular basis. They expect to see an abundant supply of properly charged fire extinguishers present. They expect to see a building-wide profusion of sprinkler heads or smoke alarms. They expect to see clearly marked, lighted exit signs for every audience egress with no curtains or anything else that might block the exit. They expect that flammables will be locked away in metal cabinets. They expect trash cans to be covered, fire doors to be shut rather than propped open, they expect electrical boxes to all be closed over. They do not like electrical cables looped around sprinkler pipes, they do not like instruments hung on sprinkler pipes, they do not like orange ex-

tension cords because it reminds them that they are not type S. They do not like to see wirenuted electrical connections made outside of an electrical box, and they do not like to see lamp cord in any context other than wiring up speakers. They also wear uniforms that have to be dry-cleaned, and they tend to ignore anything that isn't in plain sight.

FIRE EFFECT— See EFFECTS, KINDS OF.

FIRST ELECTRIC— This is the first lighting pipe, counting from the proscenium going upstage. It is usually right behind (upstage of) the front curtain, and it is typically the most important lighting position and will be heavily loaded and may encompass more than just one pipe. It may in fact be a light bridge that can be walked across.

FISH TAPE— This is an electrician's tool made for pulling wire through conduit. It consists of a 50 or 100-foot reel of flexible spring steel about a quarter of an inch wide. It is fed through the conduit from the pulling end, the wires are attached at the other end, and then usually one electrician pulls while another feed in the wires from the opposite end. In the theatre, it is used for running cables under platforms that are already in place or through *rat holes* in the set.

FIXTURES (lighting)— An architect or building-trades word to describe electrical devices that create light, which would include recessed ceiling lighting, lighting around make-up mirrors, aisle lighting, etc. It would not be unusual to find stage instruments on an architect's list of other fixtures required in the stage and auditorium areas.

FLAG—(1) As a verb it refers to waving something in front of the instrument (usually a hand) to try to draw attention to where the cone of light is hitting onstage (2) In reference to tape ends, it means folding over a tape corner back onto itself so that it can be easily removed later. (3) As a noun it is a vintage name for a mask placed in front of the light that would prevent the light from going where it was not wanted. The term is still used in this way in the motion picture business.

FLARE— Scientifically referred to as *halation*, it is an unwanted ring of light at the edge of the beam that is usually muddying a gobo pattern. A donut or other aperture-reducing device is usually used to counteract it.

FLASH— This is a computer lightboard command and also frequently the name of a button that will make a channel (that isn't on) bump to full or a channel (that is on at more than 50 percent) bump out. The purpose is usually to locate or show someone where a particular channel is casting its light.

FLASH AND BURN— A colloquial expression to describe instruments that are placed so close to scenery pieces that some of the light hits the scenery, thus making the scenery very bright and a visual distraction. It can also be seen on ceilings in front of ceiling coves and on audience walls where there are wall coves.

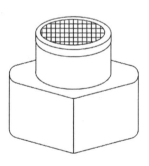

Flash pot

FLASH POT (sometimes Flash Box)— This is a metal container that encloses the source of the spark and provides a receptacle for the flash powder itself. The flash is almost always set off electrically either with an *igniter* or a very thin piece of fuse wire that melts.

FLASH POWDER— This is the pyrotechnic powder that produces a flash when a spark is provided. It is typically set off electrically in a flash pot, which is designed to reduce the danger of fire. Depending on the blend of the powder, the flash can be colored or accompanied by noise or smoke.

FLAT-FIELD DISTRIBUTION— Also called *cosine distribution*, it refers to adjusting the position of the lamp in an ellipsoidal relative to the reflector so that there is no center hot

spot and the whole area appears evenly lit. Technically the beam angle will be set to be ⅔ of the field angle.

FLATTED REFLECTOR— This is a faceted reflector rather than one with smooth curves. It was originally made to smooth out the light from large filament lamps, but has mostly disappeared now as the filaments have become smaller.

FLIPPERS— The most commonly used name for the leaves or flaps of a barndoor.

FLOODLIGHT— A lenseless lighting instrument intended to provide a diffuse general illumination. See INSTRUMENTS, Lenseless Instruments for a more detailed discussion.

FLOOR CARDS— Cue sheets for floor electricians for instruments that change color or focus during the performance.

FLOOR CIRCUITS— What is under discussion here is how best to get power to the various practicals located on the set. These are for the most part lights but could be anything that requires electricity. In this regard, it is not unusual to install flush mount electrical boxes in the walls of the set and then plug appliances into them such as coffeepots and toasters and electric shavers, whatever. It is also not unusual for the cords from these appliances simply to vanish under a rug or behind a piece of furniture and the audience never to see how they were connected to power.

Most electrical devices that appear onstage will have PB or PBG connectors. As a result, it makes sense that the onstage circuits should also have PBG receptacles to plug into. These could be in floor pockets, but floor pockets often get buried under the platforms or floor treatment. It is far easier to run an extension cord after the fact than it is to get into a floor pocket covered over by a platform. This is why it is often preferable to have wall pockets in the wings in locations where they are unlikely to be blocked.

If these are recessed into the walls, their

plugs cannot be knocked out accidentally and a cover can be installed over them that will be flush with the wall surface, which will hide the electrical connections, and plugging strips, and so forth from plain sight.

FLOOR LIGHTS— This usually refers to any instruments that can be reached for focusing purposes from the floor or from a stepladder on the floor. This would include the footlights and cyc footlights, anything on a floor mount stand (rolling or not) and the lower lights on any booms. Practical lights on the set might also be included in this even if they are often viewed as electrified props.

FLOOR PLUG— A very sturdy, very high capacity, very ancient (and now completely illegal) plug that fits in a special recessed receptacle in the wall or floor. It had exposed copper contacts on its two sides and no provision for grounding. It also had a large handle part to grab onto, but it was possible to touch the exposed contacts by accident. These were also called *stage plugs*, although that would typically be taken to mean

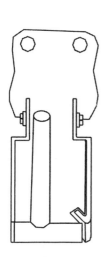

Floor plug, circa 1936

stagepin connectors today. They also came in a *half plug* version, that was only half as thick and so two could fit in the same receptacle. Except for the built-in ceramic receptacles there never was a female version of this for extension cord use. In situations where an extension cord was needed, a distribution box (fused metal box with ceramic receptacles) was plugged into the floor pocket, which amounted to the insides of a floor pocket mounted in a movable box.

FLOOR POCKET (BRITISH: *dip*)— An electrical box containing receptacles and recessed is such a way that only the cable

emerges from the trapdoor-like cover. At one time these would have been floor plug receptacles but today they are more likely to be stagepin receptacles, but they could also be twist lock or parallel blade.

Floor pocket

FLOOR STRIP— This would refer to a set of striplights temporarily set up on the floor and usually aimed at the cyc or drop stack. If the theatre had permanent cyc footlights that were recessed into the floor like the footlights, they would more commonly be referred to as *cyc foots* or *cyc footlights*.

FLOPPY DISK— In the context of a computer lightboard, this refers to the storage media, which are most commonly 3.5" floppy disks.

FLUORESCENT— Anything that becomes visible under ultraviolet light, usually a paint or dye but it could refer to a tape or a fabric. Fluorescent lights use a mercury arc to create a visible light that is rich in the ultraviolet range. A blacklight fluorescent is a fluorescent where most of the visible light has been filtered out so that it can be used as a ultraviolet source.

FLUX, LUMINOUS— Lamp output in all directions measured in lumens. Lighting designers are more interested in how much of this comes out the front end of an instrument, which is called *intensity* and is measured in candelas.

FLUX, SOLDERING— A Vaseline-like substance that prevents oxidation and assists in making the solder flow. A rosin core is used in electronics work, which is the most common theatrical use.

f-NUMBER— The ratio between the diameter and focal length of a lens. Mostly used in photography and almost totally ignored in stage lighting instruments except in regard to slide projector lenses.

FOCAL LENGTH— The distance between the center of the lens and its focal point, usually measured in inches. The longer the focal length, the narrower the beam angle. Older ellipsoidals used to be referred to by two numbers, where the first was the lens diameter and the second was the focal length of the lenses. So a 6 · 12 was an instrument that had lenses with a focal length of 12", and this kind of instrument had a narrower beam than a 6 · 9, which had lenses with a focal length of 9".

FOCAL PLANE— The place where an image would be in sharp focus. When a magnifying glass is used, a virtual and enlarged image of the object is created. The glass is moved forward or back from the object until the focal plane of the image is brought to the eye.

FOCAL POINT— This is the point at which light passing through the lens would converge. The distance from this point to the center of the lens is the focal length.

FOCUS—(1) In its most narrow meaning it refers to adjusting the size of the beam on a fresnel (or the hardness or softness of the focus on an ellipsoidal). (2) In its more common general meaning, it refers to any adjustments made to the instrument so that it is ready to be used in this particular show. This includes (in addition to the focusing adjustment mentioned above) putting its center at an aimpoint, locking the instrument in position, setting any framing shutters or barndoors and adding color or accessories.

FOCUS, KINDS OF— The normal kind of focus (**live focus**) involves the lights being at working height and an electrician adjusting them as they hit their aimpoints just as they will in the show. Even if the scenery is missing, it is still a live focus. A **dead focus** involves bringing the light pipe into chest height and aiming the light at the floor and taking it out to working height to see how it looks. This is a trial-and-error method that is used as an expedient when there is no convenient way to get to the lighting position anymore, and it is as you might expect slow.

A **cloth focus** is similar in the sense that the light pipe is brought into chest height and the lights are aimed at the floor, but they are aimed at a specially marked focusing cloth on the floor. This is used in touring shows or situations where the show has been done before, and it is a very fast method. Often the original cloth is prepared by focusing the equipment live and then bringing the pipe in to chest height to mark the cloth. Instead of there being a cloth, sometimes the aimpoints are listed as x, y coordinates relative to the centerline and setting line, but this requires marking out the stage every time and is nowhere near as fast and it doesn't include shutter cuts.

FOCUS-AS-YOU-GO METHOD— This is an expedient method for hanging and focusing the lights when all other assistants or help have vanished, leaving one technician alone by himself. The lightboard needs to be onstage on a table that has a worklight, and there needs to be some kind of glow up in the grid so that the plot can be read and the instruments hung. The ladder needs to be carefully placed so that it can reach as many instruments as possible at each move. There would also need to be several hoisting ropes.

The technician would start at the center of a position and works outward. If there were scenery that needed to be moved around, one would start with the first stage setting. The idea would be to do a missing instrument rehang. Let's suppose the ladder is in the middle of a four-foot area in which five instruments will eventually be placed. Assuming that one of those instruments is already hanging in approximately the right place, the four other instruments (fully accessorized) would be on four separate hauling ropes and all circuits would be turned on. The technician would turn out the main worklights and ascend the ladder and focus the instrument that is already there. Then it would be unplugged, and the next instrument would be hauled up and focused. At the end, just before coming down, all instruments would be reconnected to power.

At that point the ladder could be moved, and another set of instruments could be prepared and focused. Any instruments already in the air that were not needed would be lowered on one of the hauling ropes once it became available.

FOCUS CHARTS — These are pictures of the beam of light as seen from the back of the instrument with shutter cuts marked and a note as to hardness or softness of the beam and the aimpoint. These are most useful when they are simply penned onto a copy of the plot. They are often not bothered with when the run is brief and the designer could be called on the phone. Instead of a picture, the shutter cuts might be described.

FOCUSING ATTENTION — Once thought by some to be a function of stage lighting, its role in "controlling" where the audience will look has changed in terms of modern practice. The primary mechanism for making this work was the followspot. Live theatre discontinued using followspots because it was thought to be boring and repetitive and because the motion pictures did this all the time (pointed the camera at what they wanted their audience to see) of necessity. The live theatre reconsidered their position on this subject, and decided that it was more democratic and more interesting to present a panorama to the audience and let them decide for themselves where they would like to look.

There was some hope however that the lighting could still achieve the same ends subliminally by accenting some places on the stage more than others. The audience, however, tends to look at the speaking actor or the actor being spoken to or the actor or thing being talked about or anything that is moving and only then will they be affected (if at all) by what is the brightest lit object in their field of view. See LIGHTING, FUNCTIONS OF for a more detailed discussion.

FOCUSING CLOTH — A specially marked ground cloth showing the aimpoints of all the instruments when the light pipe is at chest height. See FOCUS, KINDS OF for a more detailed discussion.

FOCUSING CUES — If it is known in advance the order in which the lights will be focused, which typically has the most to do with making ladder movements logical and efficient, then writing simple focusing cues in advance will save time during the actual focusing session. No one will have to call forth from memory, or from the paperwork, which channel will be next. The designer merely needs to call for the "next" focusing cue. If it is essential to see a particular channel along with one previously focused to match shutter cuts or whatever, this can be made part of the focusing cue.

FOCUSING SESSION — This is the crew call at which the lighting instruments are focused. The lighting designer typically asks in advance that it be both dark and quiet. In the early stages of production, usually everyone agrees that this is reasonable. On the actual night, it often turns out that the carpenters are behind schedule and the sound designer is also and that both expect to share the focusing session, thus making it anything but dark or quiet.

While the lighting designer could wake up the producer to complain, she will probably not get the kind of satisfaction she thinks she deserves, and she will have wasted some of her already diminishing time. It is often better to simply press onward and discuss the blame later. Unlike the hanging session that can expand into other load-in time, the focusing session is usually just prior to the first scheduled rehearsal onstage.

The guiding principle of the focus is that the lighting designer is nominally in charge, and whatever else happens she needs to finish in the allotted time. She has had plenty of time to petition for more time if she felt she needed it. If she has gotten this far, then it is because she tacitly accepted the amount of time she has been assigned.

Usually she only has to manage one ladder crew although it is possible to manage more than one, as will be discussed later. While she does not control how much time it takes to move the ladder from one position to another, she does control the ladder path and she does control how much time is spent on each instrument. If scenery has to be moved around, the session may be organized around getting that done first (so that those stagehands can be released) regardless of how much ladder movement it requires. While it requires less ladder movement to start at the ends of pipes and work across them, it is more common to start in the center and work toward one side and then toward the other, as this allows the spacing between aimpoints to be adjusted if there are coverage problems.

If it has not been possible to have the gels and accessories put into the instruments as part of the hang, then this will consume some of the precious focusing time. Even if the gels are laid out in some kind of logical order on a table and can just be handed to the ladder assistant, there may be upside-down instruments (hitherto undiscovered) that will have to be turned around, and without the color it makes the instruments harder to identify when they are first turned on. If no focusing cues have been set up in advance, this will also add time to the process.

There is a four-part litany involved in focusing a light. The designer is supposed to stand at its center (although she will often arrange to have someone else stand in her place).

She asks that the hot spot (center) be put on her.

She will then call for spot/flood settings on fresnels or in-focus/out-of-focus settings on ellipsoidals.

Then barndoor cuts or framing shutter cuts can be made.

She will then ask that the color be put in (where tints are involved they can stay in from the beginning of the process).

Sometimes the shutter cuts will be set first and then the instrument taken out of focus, but this most often results in the shutter cuts having to be redone. When it is done in the order described above, nothing usually has to be done over.

The designer is typically obsessively mindful of the time. As each hour is struck (dinged on her watch) she probably knows where she should be in the process. She will skip instruments that refuse to light or where there are problems that may take a long time to fix. She may also skip instruments if their focus points are not yet complete on the set. She may have a special for the portrait, but without the portrait being there she must decide between skipping it or roughing it in. When time is short, skipping it is probably the most practical solution.

If there are to be multiple ladder crews, one would have been asked about this in advance and would have had to agree to it. There are at least three ways to deal with this. Regardless of which method is used, care has to be taken that the beams of light being focused at the same time do not interfere with each other, which involves careful planning.

Probably the best system is to allow the most competent ladder crew to work independently (or with a designer's assistant) focusing one or more washes or something else that is repetitive. They will have to call for their own channels and provide someone to stand in the center of the areas, and they will have to work around whatever the main ladder crew is doing, but they will have had the shutter cuts and the sharpness of focus and whatever else explained to them in advance at the start of the session, and washes tend to be repetitive in the sense that the same thing is done to every instrument and they are often focused on the floor rather than on a face.

Another system that sometimes works involves alternating between ladder crews, focusing one crew's instruments while the other crew is setting up their ladder. This often involves quite a lot of waiting for the crews, as the ladder will usually already be in place and ready to go long before the other crew has finished focusing. It works best where the ladder moving is slow and complicated.

Another system involves two crews working concurrently from one set of instructions. As the main ladder crew does *wing entry* lighting on SL, the other crew mirrors what they're doing on SR.

If the designer has an assistant capable of directing a ladder crew, and if the assistant knows exactly what is wanted for each light (sometimes even the designer doesn't know until she's seen the instrument turned on for the first time), then miscellaneous specials can be left to the assistant to do as the opportunity presents itself.

FOG EFFECT— See EFFECTS, KINDS OF.

FOH— Abbreviation for FRONT-OF-HOUSE.

FOLLOW or FOLLOW-ON CUE— Sometimes called an *autofollow cue*, this is a computer lightboard term for a cue that automatically follows another with only one push of the go button. Its follow time is usually set relative to the button push. See LIGHTING CONTROL, Computer Memory Lightboards for a more detailed discussion.

FOLLOWSPOT— A high-powered spotlight usually located at the extreme back of the house (often in the light booth or in a projection booth of its own). It has an operator and it follows designated performers around the stage. The first followspots were limelight spotlights, and they were in common usage by 1860 in Great Britain, somewhat later in the USA. This was superseded in the 1880s by carbon arc lights, which were enormously popular. Louis Hartmann talks about having 20 operators on the light bridge and

Followspot

in the tormentor positions. It has been a dream that one day there would be an incandescent (or at least dimmable) followspot bright enough to carry from the back of the house. For small theatres, there are such sources, but it is rarely the small theatres that really need the followspots. Al-

though HMI technology has been added to carbon arc lights, modern big followspots are not dimmable except in the crudest way by means of a douser or other louver-type attachment, and dimmable (incandescent) followspots are only bright enough for small venues. See INSTRUMENTS, KINDS OF for a more detailed discussion.

FOLLOWSPOT CUE SHEET— A cue sheet for the followspot operator. Where there are several operators working different lights, they either will each have a separate cue sheet or they will all have a common cue sheet where they each do one small part of what is listed. Main pickup cues are often given by the stage manager but the operator usually takes the smaller cues and does the following without further supervision. The operator may write her own cue sheet and simply deliver an archive copy to the stage manager.

FOLLOWSPOT CUES— Lightboard cues start in one static moment and over a period of time transition to another static moment or until they are interrupted by another cue. Followspot cues have a "do until" format where a body-sized spot of a certain color is to follow a certain character until he or she exits. This is in effect a static moment because even though the light is moving, its aimpoint is constant, and it is the movement of the actor that precipitates the movement. Every time the spot shifts from one person to another or fades out constitutes a major cue. Within any one major cue sequence, there may be several steps or subcues. While following a character, the followspot may spot down to a headshot or change colors. This is a step or subcue within the major cue. Much of what the followspot operator does is learned through practice and simply remembered. Followspots often have a warm-up period and as a result are turned on at the beginning and left on for the duration of the act.

FOOTCANDLE— This is a measurement of what scientists call *illumination*, which is a measure of how much light is coming from a certain direction. It is generally calculated using the inverse square law. Its metric equivalent is *lux*. If lux is known, footcandles can be calculated by multiplying by 0.0929. Conversely, if footcandles are known, lux can be calculated by multiplying by 10.7643. Obviously, a square meter is a much bigger area than a square foot (about 10 times bigger). As a field expedient, it is common practice to move the decimal point one place to the right to convert to lux and to the left to convert to footcandles, so 4 fc is approximately equal to 40 lux.

FOOTLAMBERT— When light hits an object, a portion of that light is reflected making the object a kind of sub-source or self-luminous source that bounces light to other locations. $L = RE$ where R = reflectance of the surface as a decimal (or percent) and E = illumination in footcandles. Unless the surface diffuses light evenly in all directions, then the luminance would also vary with the viewing direction. In the context of stage lighting, the luminance is only taken into consideration in the sense that light-colored objects are known to reflect more light than dark-colored objects.

FOOTLIGHTS— Lenseless instruments similar to striplights located at the front edge of a proscenium stage, often recessed into the floor in such a way that they could be covered over when not in use. See INSTRUMENTS, KINDS OF/Lenseless Instruments for a more detailed discussion.

FOOTSPOT— A spotlight put in the footlight trough. At the time this was mostly done (pre 1940), a baby spot would have been used. Today it would be more common to use a 3" fresnel or a PAR or R40-type lamp or a miniature flood.

FORMATTING THE DISK— This refers to the process of entering as much as is known of the current show's information onto the disk (or storage media) in advance of any level-setting session and usually prior to a focusing session also, since part of the set-up includes the softpatch and the focusing cues

(if any). Typically *blank* (and *no-track blocker*) cues are recorded for all cues in the show that include the preliminary time and label information but no levels. Groups and submasters or other building blocks are often roughed-in also. The guiding principle is that stage time is precious, so it is desirable to do everything that can be done in advance. Opponents of this system point to the fact that cues have to be recorded twice, which takes more time overall. There is no question, however, that the softpatch has to be done ahead of time, and little disagreement that where focusing cues exist, they save time during the focusing session. The old show will have been cleared off the machine prior to this. If this has been done by means of a *blank disk,* then a series of blank cues will already have been recorded. They merely have to be re-labeled, have their times adjusted from whatever the default is, and have new *point cues* added (if any) and all excess cues can then be deleted. This is much faster than creating the individual cues one-at-a-time from scratch.

The monitor can only display about 100 channels on each screen. If the lightboard has more channels than that, an extraordinary effort will be made to consolidate the channels in a way that only a screenful are used, as having to look at two pages of levels will almost double the time required to set each cue. Sometimes there is a feature that allows one to use any channel numbers from 1 to 999 but only displays the ones have been used. Where this is the case, one could have channels 120, 181, and 219 but still have them displayed on one screen.

The building block cues will be constructed to reduce the number of control channels, so that all 100 channels do not have to be set to a level for each cue. Let's suppose that the stage is lit in six areas and that the frontlights are channels 11–16, the SL sidelights 21–26, the backlights 31–36 and the SR sidelights 41–46. Since many of the scenes will typically involve the full stage, these will mostly work together as systems, so it would not be uncommon to assign frontlights to sub 1, SL to sub 2, back to sub 3 and SR to sub 4, which would also be recorded as groups 1–4.

Let's further suppose that there is a platform upstage supporting the three upstage areas, so even though their throw angle will be the same, their throw distance will be shorter, and as a result they will not need to be as bright. This will typically be calculated so that while channels 11–13 are at 60, channels 14–16 will be at say 53. It would then be common to select all the channels and use the *wheel* or *touch screen* to roll them upward until something (11–13 in this case) touched 100 percent. This is now the brightest possible version of the frontlights, and it can now be re-recorded as sub 1 and group 1, even though no one thinks it is likely to run higher than 60. This same procedure could be done for sidelights and backlights. When done, it would not be unusual to use these systems to rough in the first look of the show. The four control subs (or groups) would be set at differing levels (calculated mathematically ahead of time but checked visually at level-setting) and the whole thing rolled upward using the wheel until something touched full and the whole thing could then be recorded as say sub (and group) 21.

This was just an example. In this case *systems* and *looks* were recorded as building blocks, but this is not the only way to create building blocks. It is important to remember, however that each layer of control adds another layer of control numbers that have to be memorized or otherwise called forth. Each building block (whose levels were set mathematically) would need to be looked at during the beginning part of the level-setting session and the levels readjusted as necessary until it looked right visually. Having roughed them in ahead of time, however, saves valuable stage time, which is the purpose.

Houselights and worklights (if applicable) are typically assigned to submasters so that in an emergency during the rehearsal process either one or both can be brought up quickly.

In the rare instance where either the time is so limited that the designer will not be permitted to have a level-setting session or where the show has been done before and the cues have been set already, then the cues may be roughed in ahead of time based on math and guesswork.

FORMULA LIGHTING— This refers to the base lighting (arealighting) for the stage, and the term "formula lighting" has a negative connotation that suggests that while this might be all right for a "high school production," it is hardly custom-designed lighting and is therefore somehow inferior and perhaps even someone else's idea or formula to begin with.

After 100 years of stage lighting using electricity, it is very hard to come up with an idea that no one else has thought of before, and why would anyone want to invent a different method of doing something if they were convinced that the method they had been using was still the best one?

Each designer will over time develop a system that she feels works best in any particular situation (proscenium, thrust, arena, whatever). She may have discovered it independently or read about it in a book. It becomes her formula, which is to say her best solution to a specific problem.

It will involve six areas of concern: area control, number of instruments-per-area, angle of horizontal separation, throw angle, color use, and amount of duplication. The easiest way to understand this is to answer a series of questions:

1. Do you need to have area control? If the stage is always used as one playing area, you probably don't and would do as well with a series of system washes from various directions.
2. Do you believe that the ideal angle of horizontal separation is 90 degrees? If you do, then this translates to three instruments-per-area behind the proscenium and four in front. Some people think that there should be five instruments-per-area downstage of the proscenium. Some people think that three instruments-per-area

are sufficient for thrust or in-the-round situations.

3. Do you believe the ideal throw angle is 45 degrees? Some people think the throw angle should be closer to 60 degrees.

4. How many instruments-per-area does that work out to by your calculations? This will vary depending on the configuration of the house, but usually a certain number US of the proscenium and another number DS of the proscenium covers it.

5. Will all the components of a system be the same color (all frontlights one color and sidelights another color, and so forth)? If so will the colors of alternating systems be widely separated, slightly separated or not separated at all (i.e. the same color, usually white)?

6. How many duplications do you need? In other words should the show be double-hung or triple-hung?

In terms of Stanley McCandless' method as it relates to these areas of concern. He felt strongly that area control was necessary. He favored 90 degrees of separation and a throw angle of 45 degrees and he thought 2 instruments-per-area with a wide separation of color was sufficient on a proscenium stage (and he did not comment on other configurations), and he didn't mention any possibility of duplication.

Most designers today would most likely agree that Stanley got it right based on the situation he knew of at the time. They support area control, 90 degrees/45 degrees placement, three instruments-per-area upstage of the proscenium and 4 instruments-per-area downstage with each system having its own color, and duplications and amount of color separation as required by the show. Call this *modified Stanley* because it is his method as it is most usually extended to apply to thrust and in-the-round situations.

Are there other formulas? Yes an almost infinite number if one were to count every tiny difference. However, since most designers will agree with Stanley McCandless on at least four out of the six areas of concern, then it is probably reasonable to say that their formula is really a variant of his method. There are not a profusion of radically different formulas for lighting the stage, and most of the formulas that one may hear about will be very similar to the Stanley McCandless method. So called "jewel lighting" involves high levels of side and backlighting and relatively dim frontlighting and is mostly found in Broadway theatres that don't have front-lighting cove positions. The stage is still divided into areas, 90 degrees/45 degrees placement is used, and components of a system have the same color. Really the only significant difference is that instead of having three instruments-per-area, there are either four or five depending on whether the frontlight comes from a balcony rail (or first electric) or from booms on the two sidewalls of the house.

FORMULAS— These fall into five general categories or groups: electricity, trigonometry, light, reflectors/optics and projection.

Electricity

1. Ohm's Law, used for figuring out electronic circuits: $E = IR$ where E = electromotive force in volts, I = current flow in amps and R = resistance in ohms.

2. In a series circuit:
$$R_T = R_1 + R_2....$$
$$I_T = I_1 = I_2...$$
$$E_T = E_1 + E_2....$$
In a parallel circuit:
$$1/R_T = 1/R_1 + 1/R_2....$$
$$I_T = I_1 + I_2....$$
$$E_T = E_1 = E_2...$$

3. Power Formula (also called the PIE or West Virginia formula), used for converting watts to amps: $W = VA$ where W = watts, V = volts and A = amps.

Trigonometry

4. Pythagorean Theorem, used to solve right triangle problems where the length of any two sides are known: $a^2 + b^2 = c^2$,

where a and b are the legs and c is the hypotenuse.

5. Sin = opposite/hypotenuse, where opposite is the leg opposite the angle .
6. Cos = adjacent/hypotenuse, where adjacent is the leg adjacent to the angle .
7. Tan = opposite/adjacent.

Light

8. Inverse Square Law, used to determine brightness when the distance from the source is known: $E = I/d^2 * Cos$, where E = illumination in footcandles, I = Intensity of the source in candelas, d = the throw distance and = the angle of incidence (throw angle).
9. Luminance, used to describe light that has been bounced off an object: $L = RE$, where R = reflectance of the surface as a decimal, E = illumination in footcandles and L = luminance in footlamberts.
10. Psychophysical power law (generally not calculated) relates apparent brightness to actual brightness by $I_p = {}^3\sqrt{}\ I_m$ where I_p = perceived intensity and I_m = measured intensity. Stated more simply, it takes eight times as much light to double the apparent brightness ($2^3 = 8$).

Reflectors and Optics

11. Reflection from a flat surface: Angle of incidence is equal to the angle of reflection.
12. Reflection from a spherical surface: When a point source (light source) is placed at the focal point (which is the center of the sphere), then all light hitting the reflector will be reflected back along the same path.
13. Reflection from a ellipsoidal surface: When a point source (light source) is placed at the near focal point, then all light hitting the reflector will be reflected through the far focal point (the gate).
14. Reflection from a parabolic surface: When a point source (light source) is placed at the focal point, then all light hitting the reflector will be reflected back in parallel lines relative to the centerbeam.

Projection

15. Lens Maker's Equation, used to calculate the focal length of two lenses used together: $f = f_1 * f_2/f_1 + f_2 - d$, where f = the combined focal length and f_1, f_2 = focal lengths of lens nr 1, nr 2, and d = the distance between the lenses.
16. Projection Equation, used to determine image size and projector position: $1/f = 1/p + 1/q$, where f = focal length of the projector lens, p = object distance (slide to lens) in inches and = image distance (lens to screen image) in inches.
17. $P/p = Q/q$, where P = object height (or width or diagonal) and Q = image height (or width or diagonal). Magnification is defined as either $M = Q/P$ or $M = q/p$.

• There is also the arealighting formula: $w + 2*v/n = d$, where w = the stage width in feet, v = the amount of overlap desired in feet (usually a quarter of the beam diameter), n = number of areas, and d = diameter of each area in feet. Where there are an odd number of areas, one will be centered on the centerline. Where there is an even number of areas, two areas will meet at the centerline.

FOURSQUARE BOX— A very common size of electrical box that is 4 inches square and 1.5" or more deep (there are several depths). It typically houses two duplex PBG receptacles or two light switches.

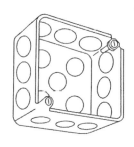

Foursquare box

FRAME, COLOR— See ACCESSORIES.

FRAMING SHUTTER— These are the four beam shaping cut-offs that are part of an ellipsoidal. They slide in-and-out at the gate of the instrument and can be twisted into trapezoidal shapes.

FRENCH SCENES— The entrance or exit of a character typically triggers a new French scene, but inasmuch as this is a technique for breaking long scenes into more manageable parts for rehearsal purposes, common sense has to be applied. The non-speaking servant coming in to set up the table for dinner would not precipitate a new French scene because it would not be rehearsed separately and does not in any way interrupt or change the scene already in progress.

FREQUENCY— When used in the context of AC current, it refers to the number of cycles per second (60).

FRESNEL LENS— In 1822, a French physicist, Augustin-Jean Fresnel, invented a lens for use in lighthouses, in which the thickness of the glass was reduced by the use of concentric curved rings. See LENSES, KINDS OF for a more detailed discussion.

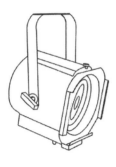
Fresnel

FRESNELS— The theatre spotlights named after the man who invented the lens, they produce a soft-edged light that blends well and whose size is adjustable, but their light cannot be controlled very well. See INSTRUMENTS/Lensed Instruments for a more detailed discussion.

FRICTION TAPE— See TAPES, KINDS OF.

FRONT END— In the context of the remote control lightboards, this refers to the keyboard or keyboard/monitor package that is viewed and manipulated by the operator and that sends a signal to the dimmers and any other devices controlled by the board. See LIGHTING CONTROL/Computer Memory Lightboards for a more detailed discussion.

FRONTLIGHT— (1) Any light coming from the front direction regardless of where the hanging position might be (including positions behind the curtain). (2) Any light coming from the front-of-house. (3) All followspots are commonly called *frontlights* whether they actually come from the front or from off to the side.

FRONT-OF-HOUSE (Abbr. FOH)— The audience areas of the theatre, which includes the auditorium, lobby, box office and audience restrooms.

FROST— A technician's term for any diffusion media whether it is a frost, silk, tough spun or whatever.

FROSTING SPRAY— This is a commercially made product that frosts over glass or other transparent materials to make them translucent. Sometimes it can be obtained the year-round, but it is most commonly available around Christmas for display purposes.

FUCHS, THEODORE— A consulting illuminating engineer, who wrote the first American textbook on stage lighting in 1929 (**Stage Lighting**). It was mentioned by both Louis Hartmann and Stanley McCandless, and it remained the only comprehensive and authoritative book on the subject well into the 1950s. Stanley McCandless refers to it repeatedly in his 1953 book **Syllabus of Stage Lighting.** It was a huge volume running to almost 500 pages. It covered the physics of light, optics, reflectors, and electricity in detail and had an extensive 60-page chapter on home-built equipment. While it described the equipment in detail, it had a disappointing 40-page chapter on "methods and practice" that somehow failed to make it clear how one might go about actually lighting a play.

FULL— In the context of dimmers, it refers to maximum brightness (100 percent). On a computer screen where only two digits have been allotted to depicting the level, this is often represented as "FF" or "FL."

FULL REHANG— One of four methods of changing the lights from one show to the next. See STRIKES, KINDS OF for a more detailed discussion.

FUNCTIONS OF LIGHTING— See LIGHTING, FUNCTIONS OF.

FUNNEL— One of several lighting add-on accessories. See ACCESSORIES for a more detailed discussion.

FUSE— An electrical device that melts apart during an overcurrent situation and then has to be replaced. Fuses on the dimmers (and practically everything else) have been replaced by circuit breakers, which can be reset. Fuses are still used on main disconnects and company switches because they are never expected to blow. They may also be used on effect boxes and low voltage lines to protect the transformers and other electronics.

FUSE HOLDER— Whatever holds the fuse in place.

FUSE PLUG— Another name for a screw-in type fuse.

FUSES, KINDS OF— There are three basic types of fuses in use today. Cartridge fuses often with knife blade-like protrusions at each end are used in the main disconnect box (electric room) or company switches (backstage). Screw-in type fuses are not used anymore except as a prop in the play although they might be encountered at a summer stock theatre somewhere. Automotive type glass fuses are used on small electronic controls like cuelight boxes or bell ringers.

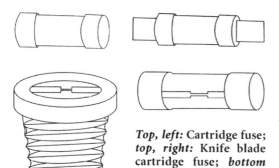

Top, left: Cartridge fuse; *top, right:* Knife blade cartridge fuse; *bottom left:* Screw-in fuse; *bottom above:* Glass fuse

GAFF, GAFFER and GAFFING— His tape has survived modern usage but the verb and the noun have for the most part disappeared except in the motion picture business. A gaffer is anyone who plans the job or is in charge of the job, which in the case of the lighting usually means the master electrician or some other crew chief.

GAFFER'S TAPE— See TAPES, KINDS OF.

GALLERY REFLECTOR— An old time beam projector with a carbon arc light source used as a general floodlight circa 1906. Louis Hartmann talks about these, as does Theodore Fuchs. They were said to have been an improvement over the earlier olivettes that had no reflector.

Gallery reflector

GANGING— Hooking together in parallel, usually two or more instruments on one circuit by means of a two-fer or three-fer or simply by plugging them into two different drop points on the same circuit.

GAP— This refers to the space between the two carbon arcs in an arc spotlight. When the spotlight is in running mode, a motor often controls this for optimum light.

GATE— The aperture in an ellipsoidal where the framing shutters are located and where the gobo slot is, which is located at the far focal point of the ellipsoidal reflector.

GATE REDUCER— This is a gobo pattern that has a round hole in it that is smaller than the gate of the instrument. Since gobo patterns are relatively expensive, it is common practice to make up a set of these in a metal shop using standard electrical punches (a Greenlee™ set or anything similar, as used for putting holes in electrical boxes where no knock-outs exist). For smaller holes, drilled holes are sometimes used, but they tend not be perfectly round, and this shows up under magnification. Electrical reducing washers can also be used by taping them together with photographic slide mount tape (or some other heat resistant tape) to a backing of black foil or roof flashing cut to the size needed by the gobo holder.

GAUGE (wire)— A method of relating the wire diameter to current carrying capacity. See AMERICAN WIRE GAUGE for a more detailed discussion.

GEL BOOKS— These are samples about 1 · 4" in size in all the colors in a manufacturer's line of color filters, which is typically about 100 colors. They are used by designers to compare and pick the colors for the show, and they usually specify a transmission percentage and have a graph showing what wavelengths of light are passed in what approximate quantities.

GEL FRAME— One of several lighting accessories. See ACCESSORIES for a more detailed discussion.

GEL FRAME LOCK— This is the wire clip or spring-loaded hook that holds a gel frame in position even if the instrument is turned upside down. The wire clip kind can usually be disengaged and pushed up out of the way and some of the spring loaded ones may be locked in a disengaged position also. Those that can't be disengaged have to be manipulated at the same time that the gel frame is being inserted. This requires two hands where two hands are not always available. In a proscenium situation where there is a chance that either flown scenery or tall rolling wagons could collide with a light pipe, then this provides an extra measure of safety. In a situation where nothing is likely to impact against the lights, then it is simply another added and unnecessary step that adds time to the job. The instruments need to be hung right side up, so that the gobo pattern, which doesn't have any such "safety" feature, won't fall out.

GEL MODIFICATIONS— See COLOR MODIFICATIONS.

GELATINE or GEL FOR SHORT—(1) It refers to use of gelatine (an animal product) as one of the earliest forms of color media. Actual gelatine colors were extremely inexpensive and came in a wider selection of colors than did the colored glass rondels (which for the longest time were the only other competing color media). The gel faded quickly and had to be replaced often (sometimes after every performance). They were very sensitive to moisture and dissolved if they got wet and became brittle if they became too dry. (2) In its generic sense, gel refers to any color media. It would sound academic and pompous to ask that the crew put the *color media* in the instruments. Technicians typically talk about either putting the *color* in or putting the *gels in*.

GENERAL ILLUMINATION— This usually refers to the light created by striplights and footlights, which used to be used to blend and tone the acting areas. While the term may still be used in older books, it is not in common usage anymore having gone out of fashion along with the striplights and footlights. Any non-descript general lighting onstage is usually a result of the arealighting and would commonly be referred to as such.

GHOST DESIGNING— This is where the person who takes the credit for the design is not in fact the same person who did the actual work. In educational circles, this is usually considered a form of "cheating" similar to putting your name on someone else's term paper. It makes no difference if this is a set designer who has hired someone to do a lighting design for her or a teacher/mentor who is trying to give a special student a leg up in the profession, while it may have been (certainly was) a common practice, it is no longer a common practice, as it is now considered completely unethical and dishonest.

GHOST LIGHT— This refers to a nightlight left onstage so that anyone walking in the darkened theatre will be able to see well enough to find their way. It is often a single 40–100 watt light bulb on a floor stand. It could also be a socket on the ceiling above the grid. It is common to use something like a fluorescent or a compact fluorescent for this as absolutely no one cares about the quality or color of the light.

GHOST LOADS or GHOSTING— Also called a *phantom load*. Some older and now obsolete dimmer systems (most notably resistance dimmers and to some extent autotransformer dimmers) would not dim out all the way unless they were loaded either to capacity or in the case of the autotransformers to a point where the dimmer would recognize that there was in fact a load. The most common solution was to add a "ghost load," which was one or more floodlights in a hallway, workroom or other location where they would not be seen onstage. Ghosting is used to refer to the lights on stage that have not entirely gone out yet, as if they needed a larger ghost load. In current practice, the filaments are often kept warm during blackouts to improve response time going into the next scene, and this can cause the appearance of ghosting.

GLACIER GLASSES— These are half way between sunglasses and the goggles used for gas welding in terms of the amount of light they transmit. They can be bought in outdoor equipment stores where mountain climbing equipment is sold. These are perfect for looking through a lens at the lamp, being dark enough to provide adequate eye-protection while still providing enough light to see by.

GLARE— Glare is the sensation of it being too bright. The human eye can see in conditions thousands of times brighter than the light of single candle, but in order to do that the pupil in the eye needs to close down to limit the amount of light entering. At any given pupil setting, the eye can only see contrasts on the order of 20:1. When one meets an oncoming car at night, it is common to experience the sensation of glare because the headlights, although only about 70 watts bright, are so much brighter than what the eye has adjusted for. Were one to meet that same car in the daytime, the light would be as bright and aimed the same way, but because the eyes would now be adjusted for daytime light, the headlights might not even be noticed.

GLARE PROBLEM— In the theatre (as in life) the audience finds glare annoying. Strobe lights are particularly annoying and where they are used, it is not uncommon to see audience members shading their eyes

from the effect. It is also considered polite to warn the audience of strobe effects by means of a lobby sign or program note or both. Coming from a blackout or a very dim scene into very bright light has to be done slowly or as a several part cue to avoid glare. Obviously where the light levels can be kept low, there will be less glare problems and lights can be snapped on or off at will without causing eyestrain of any kind.

The eye sockets of the face are notoriously hard to light because the stage light comes from above and they are recessed inward. In most theatres they will be in almost complete shadow. Yet this is the part of the face that the audience is most interested in seeing. The brighter the lighting gets on the rest of the face, the harder it is to concentrate on seeing into these dark caves, and the darker they will appear to get. From a visibility standpoint, the face will be most visible if the contrasts do not exceed 20:1. Adding more light will increase glare and decrease rather than increase visibility. See VISIBILITY for a more detailed discussion.

GLASS ENVELOPE— Sometimes called the envelope for short, it is more commonly just called the *bulb* portion of the lamp.

GLASS RONDEL (sometimes spelled roundel)— Glass color media mostly used in striplights. See RONDEL.

GLASS SPHERE— See HANGING POSITIONS, IDEAL.

GLOWS, LIGHTING OF— See LIGHTING SPECIAL PROBLEMS/Glows and Indirect Light.

GO— This is the command to execute the cue now. It follows a *warning* and a *stand-by*. See CUES, CALLING OF for a more detailed discussion.

GO BUTTON— On a computer lightboard, this is the button that makes a cue load and execute. There is usually one button for each fader pair, in which case they would typically be referred to as AB-GO and CD-GO. Where only GO is mentioned, it refers to the active or default fader pair, which is usually the AB pair.

GOBO or GOBO PATTERN— A metal (usually stainless steel) or heat resistant glass insert that is placed at the gate of an ellipsoidal to project a light/shade image on the floor or walls or in the case of glass patterns, a color image. Modern ellipsoidals have a slot just forward of the framing shutters to accept a *gobo holder*, which in turn holds the pattern. Gobo is said to have originally referred to an opaque shadow mask at the front of the instrument (alternately called a *flag* or *French flag*, and still called a *flag* in the motion picture business), and this older usage may be found in vintage books, but not in spoken conversation. The derivation of the word is somewhat cloudy, but the most plausible explanation is that it originated in the early days of the American motion picture industry when the director of photography would say, "Go Blackout," at which point members of the shooting crew would put black material between the sun and the set. "Gobo" is still used as a verb in the film industry as in, "Gobo off that light so that the camera won't see it," meaning to put something opaque between the light and the object being lit. A gobo pattern goes between the light and object being lit and is a contraction of "Go Blackout."

GOBO HOLDER— A metal frame with a hole that is the approximate size of the gate

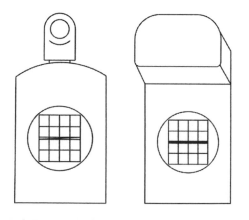

Left: Pattern and holder; *right:* Gobo rotator

that sandwiches in the gobo pattern and prevents it rotating or falling out of position. It also has a heat resistant knob as both holders and patterns can get very hot, very fast.

GOBO ROTATOR— An electrical device that holds one (or sometimes two) gobo patterns and rotates them, usually in opposite directions. On the most expensive models, both the speed and direction of rotation can be remotely controlled (usually by 4 otherwise unused channels on the lightboard).

GOBO SLOT— The opening in an ellipsoidal's housing at the far focal point (gate) where the gobo holder is supposed to go.

GOLDEN RING (positions)— The 45 degree above positions, usually thought of as being eight positions at 45 degrees of separation starting at the front, although clearly an infinitely variable number of slightly different positions are possible. See HANGING POSITIONS, IDEAL for a more detailed discussion.

GOLDEN TIME— Union slang for double-overtime. It usually is triggered when the crew is already in an overtime situation and the clock touches midnight, which puts everyone at double the prevailing rate (i.e. quadruple time).

GRADUAL METHOD (of integrating the lights)— A method of integrating the light cues into the show without stopping every time something is not as it should be. See INTEGRATING THE LIGHTS for a more detailed discussion.

GRANDMASTER— This refers to a handle that can dim out all the dimmers. On manual boards, it was critically important and was used for every blackout and every lights-up and was most frequently a mechanical grandmaster, which when fully loaded could take several people to operate. On remote control lightboards, the dimming is proportional and done electronically, and the handle or slider itself is typically used only in an emergency where there are mystery lights on that need to go out immediately as all other blackouts are typically assigned cues numbers and set into the normal sequence of cues.

GRAPHIC STANDARDS— These are mostly graphic standards under continuing debate by the USITT. Most designers adhere to these in an approximate way. The use of CAD programs, however, has led to more deviance now than there had been in the past. Many lighting books include these standards and symbols (**Photometrics Handbook** by Robert C. Mumm), and they are available on-line from Altman Stage Lighting (www. altstg.com).

GREASE PENCIL— Also called a *china marker*, it is used to write gel numbers on gels. The best colors for dark gels are white or yellow and black or dark blue for light colors.

GREEN WIRE— A normal female connector has three slots or holes, each connected to a different color of wire. The hole connected to the green wire is the grounding wire, which is connected to a metal rod driven into the ground. The manufacturers try to help make it possible to figure out which is which by looking at the connector (assuming it was wired correctly). In terms of stagepin connectors, it will be the middle hole or prong and the prong will be longer than the other two. In terms of parallel-blade-ground, it will be the roundish one. In terms of twist locks, it will be the one with a 90 degree bend in it.

GRID or GRIDIRON— This refers, in a proscenium house, to the structure that supports all the pulleys or sheaves over the stage house. It will mostly be made of steel these days. In thrust or open staging situations, it refers to pipes that are supported from the ceiling or roof of the space. Pipes running 90 degrees to this will typically be supported by the first set of pipes and will either be under-hung-from or resting-on top-of the supporting set. On rare occasions the cross pipes of the grid are welded together or connected together with pipe fittings. Any light hanging positions that are created by pipes that are pipe fitted together need to be enthusiastically tightened down to a point where the individual pipes won't rotate when force in the form of several overhung instruments is applied. The pipes themselves are most commonly 1.5" ID, which is approximately 2" OD, schedule 40 black pipe. See NEW THEATRE LIGHTING for a more detailed discussion.

GROUNDING (BRITISH: *earthing*)— Attaching the metal housing of all equipment by means of a green wire to a metal rod driven in the ground. It is a safety precaution that provides a second path for the current to travel in the event that the electrician somehow becomes the primary path.

GROUP— This is a computer lightboard term that refers to one or more channels at varying levels (a cue, in other words) being recorded as a building block entity. Unlike a cue, several groups can be brought up to different levels at the same time on the same fader. It is common to have both subs and groups for all systems (frontlights, backlights, etc) in the show to make cue setting easier. Groups work on the *last-takes-precedence* principle and thus can either raise or lower current readings onstage. Subs can only raise the levels onstage. See FORMATTING THE DISK for a more detailed discussion.

GUTTER (electrical)— Another name for a WIREWAY.

GUY WIRE— This is a wirerope from the top of a boom to secure it horizontally to the theatre walls. To be entirely effective three or four guy wires are needed, and this is rarely possible, but even a single guy wire from directly above will prevent a boom from falling over even if it were to become detached from the floor.

HALATION— A ring of light around the apparent beam, more often referred to as *flare*. A donut would typically be used to stop down the lens aperture.

HALF PLUG— This refers to a half-thick floor plug, which is now obsolete along with its fully thick counterpart.

HANDY BOX— An electrical box, half the size of a foursquare box, made for surface mounting that is sized to contain a single switch or duplex outlet. In the theatre, it would typically be used as a small junction box to provide a place to wirenut wires together or to mount a practical like a yardlight or security light so that it could be wall-mounted or pipe-hung. If the bolts on the blank cover and on the strain-relieving clamp are replaced with thumbscrews that can be finger-tightened instead of screwdriver-tightened, then they can be made more useful for the extremely temporary wiring encountered in the theatre.

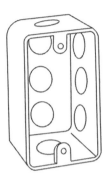

Handy box

HANG-AND-GANG— A colloquial expression for the hanging session and reasonably descriptive of what usually occurs.

HANGING AN INSTRUMENT— Let's assume that the instrument is on a haul rope within reach of the ladder electrician, and that it has a safety cable attached to the yoke of the instrument.

We are ignoring the fact that a 20 lb instrument isn't going to cause a 600 lb-test c-clamp to fail in an earthquake and thus we by-pass the discussion of whether there needs to be a safety cable at all. Legislatures across the country have voted on this and it's the "law of the land." It provides additional work for stagehands and provides an extra add-on sale to every instrument for manufacturers and distributors, so who could be against anything that had "safety" in its title?

The time when an instrument is most vulnerable to falling (i.e. being dropped) is when it is being attached or detached from the pipe and not during an earthquake, civil disturbance or nuclear war. Since the safety cables have been mandated into law in most places, the following method of using them will actually make the hanging and striking process safer.

The ladder electrician would first attach the safety cable around the pipe, clipping it back to itself. At that point the hauling rope could be slipped off, as the safety cable would now be supporting the weight of the instrument (and all its accessories). The instrument c-clamp could now be hooked around the pipe and locked in place. The instrument could be pointed in the correct general direction and could be checked to make sure its shutters had been opened all the way (so that they would not burn out when the instrument was first turned on). The safety cable could now be opened and the electrical cable and other accessories removed. The safety cable would then usually be wrapped around the pipe twice and clipped back to its fixed loop (which is typically attached permanently to the yoke of the instrument). The instrument could now be electrically cabled to the correct circuit and its iris or other accessories added. The gel and pattern will usually have already been installed by the ladder assistant before the instrument was hauled up. The instrument is most vulnerable to being dropped between the time it is taken off the hauling rope and the time its c-clamp is attached to the pipe. By hanging the instrument in the sequence just described, the safety cable will support the instrument at this critical time.

If the electrician is on a catwalk or on the stage floor working on a pipe that is at chest height, then the instrument c-clamp can simply be attached to the pipe first and the safety cable attached last. The instrument can be accessorized with gel, pattern and other accessories from a box on the floor. Striking the instrument simply reverses the process.

HANGING CREW— Anyone involved in the session at which the lights are hung in position. A select number of these technicians may be later used to focus the lights, which typically requires fewer people.

HANGING POSITIONS— Any place a lighting instrument can be located. Although most instruments hang from a pipe, the term hanging position is used generically whether the instrument sits on a floor stand or is attached to a rover or boom or catwalk or lighting pipe, etc. See HANGING POSITIONS, IDEAL for a more detailed discussion.

HANGING POSITIONS, GETTING TO— Whenever hanging positions for instruments are contemplated, some thought has to be given to how a technician will later be able to get up to them to hang, focus, and maintain the lights. There are at least seven factors that must be taken into consideration: (1) grid height because above a certain height, it is no longer practical to have the electrician climb down after every ladder move. (2) Footprint size of the ladder or structure. (3) Weight of the ladder or structure (4) Amount of assembly or set-up time required. (5) Storage space required. (6) Speed with which the electrician can be gotten from one location to another. (7) Expense both initial cost and maintenance and continuing stagehand labor expense.

There are three general methods. Either the electrician climbs something, or she is raised up from below or she is hauled up from above.

Structures Climbed After Every Move

A-ladders: Also called trestle ladders, essentially these are wooden stepladders with a big footprint (more than 4 · 8) that have a raiseable-and-lowerable vertical center fly section, commonly called a *stick*, capable of reaching heights 20–40'. It is a vintage method most commonly used on older proscenium stages, but the ladders are still being

A-ladder

made in a limited number of sizes by Louisville Ladder and perhaps by others as well. While it is possible for one man to drag it to position, it is typically carried and steadied by four stagehands while a 5th ascends. Whoever climbs it customarily straddles, and appears to be sitting on, the stick (throws one leg over and hooks it under a rung) and leans in one direction or the other and typically comes down when the ladder is to be moved. In this configuration, being little more than a big stepladder, it is both slow (having to come down after every placement) and highly labor intensive (needing four stagehands to steady it) and no competition for the more efficient cherry pickers or rolling scaffolding. It is one of the least expensive (in initial cost) of the high grid solutions, and it folds flat for storage.

Extension Ladders: These typically are made for heights under 40' and consist of two straight ladders that telescope to approximately double their height and need to rest against something stable at the top (a grid or wall rather than a flown pipe). They are typically made of wood, aluminum or fiberglass. In low locations, where weight is not a problem, wood is less expensive and fiberglass is more electrically safe (as it does not conduct electricity). In situations where someone is going to have to carry the ladder around for 6–8 hours, which is the most common situation, aluminum is the only viable choice because it is lighter and nothing else matters. In heights above 20', the deflection becomes more pronounced, and the fact that they have to be dismounted and remounted after every move slows down their effectiveness as a method of getting to the lights. They are, however, low in initial cost, require only one assistant to steady them, have a very small footprint so they can be placed on uneven sets, and take up very little room in storage. They are most commonly used where there is a fixed grid that is 20' or less in height.

Stepladders: They fold flat for storage, but when swung open in the shape of an "A," they have a medium-sized footprint. They are made in wood, aluminum and fiberglass. Weight is seldom a problem in the most common 6, 8 and 10' sizes. They are useful for reaching things mounted on the set or in the wings on booms or on the walls. They require flat floor or nearly flat floor, but are ideal for low positions.

Climbed Once but Requiring Flat Floor

Cherry Picker: The term is usually used to describe a portable and manually operated 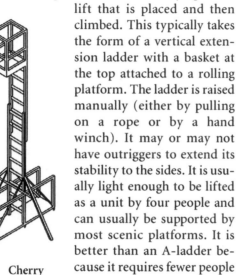 lift that is placed and then climbed. This typically takes the form of a vertical extension ladder with a basket at the top attached to a rolling platform. The ladder is raised manually (either by pulling on a rope or by a hand winch). It may or may not have outriggers to extend its stability to the sides. It is usually light enough to be lifted as a unit by four people and can usually be supported by most scenic platforms. It is better than an A-ladder because it requires fewer people steadying it, it has a basket that is more stable and allows storage of items and it can be rolled with an electrician aloft. It usually folds down for storage and can be rolled or carried through doorways.

Cherry picker

Rolling Ladder: Usually a 12–14' stepladder (or rarely a small A-ladder) mounted on a rolling platform that allows it to move on flat floor with an electrician aloft. These are typically used on grids or light pipes at an elevation of 20' or less. A-ladders are generally not good candidates because they are already prone to swaying and putting wheels on them makes this worst. Any kind of stepladder, however, can be used because weight is not a problem as the whole unit rolls. The base of the platform is useful for accessories, cables and supplies. The ladder is typically attached to the platform with loose-pin hinges to allow the ladder to be removed and folded flat for storage. The assembled unit usually won't fit through doorways unless the ladder is detached from its base, which is often 3 · 6 or thereabouts. It is a very fast low grid solution when there is flat floor.

Scaffolding: This is either a high or low grid solution to getting to the lights. It is assembled piece-by-piece and height-layer by height-layer, typically for the duration of the changeover period and disassembled and stored as opening night approaches. It has a huge footprint and won't go through doorways, but it provides a very stable and large platform for several people to work from. The electricians can remain aloft as four floor assistants carefully roll it from place-to-place.

Climbed Once not Requiring Flat Floor

Catwalks: This is a walkway (platform) rigidly suspended below the ceiling or roof structure that allows access to the various instruments. It is typically about 2–2.5' wide. Its light hanging location is usually at +1–2' above the level of walkway and sometimes "outboard," i.e. in front of (or back of) the catwalk itself. This is particularly true for sidelights where the catwalk is positioned left-to-right and the sidelights are positioned in front of (or behind) this is to prevent them hitting the catwalk itself. It is usually suspended at least 7' below the closest vertical obstruction so that a person can walk upright along its length. In some circumstances, it allows a person to crawl or walk hunched-over along its length. It is a highly efficient. In fact in is the best method of gaining access to the instruments, being both fast and safe. Inasmuch as the lights are mostly mounted low, the walking surface should be soft enough to be knelt on. Usually a modest number of instruments and cables can be temporarily stored along its length.

Rolling Catwalks: The only instance I know of this having been done is at the University of Washington in Seattle, but it may have been done elsewhere as well. It is not as fast as permanent catwalks, and only one crew can work in the air at the same time, and it was expensive to build, but the crew can work on instruments that are at chest height, or a bit higher, rather than on their hands and knees on the floor, and the structure of the catwalk (while it may be in the way during focusing) will be out of the way during performances. While it may not be a universal solution, it is certainly worth considering in situations where permanent catwalks would block balcony sightlines or cause some other problem.

Vertical Ladders: These are permanent ladders, mostly steel (except in some very old buildings) attached to the wall and held about 6" away from it. They may or may not have a safety cage around them. This is often the only way to get to a fly-floor or catwalk position.

Raised Up from Below

Powered Lifts: In their lowered-down state, these can usually be rolled through doorways. They are typically very heavy, often more than 1000 lbs. They are usually self-propelled, steerable and have a generous basket (usually 24 · 48" or thereabouts) that can be operated by electrical or electro-hydraulic means from within the basket. Scissor lifts are probably the most common design. Their biggest disadvantage, aside from their high initial cost, is that they require flat floor that can support their weight and they take up more storage space than other options. They also have batteries that have to be kept charged and have to be regularly replaced, and they have lots of moving parts that have to be maintained.

Hauled Up from Above

Bosun's Chair: This is a vintage method of going aloft, only used in a fly house and not used there all that much anymore, presumably for safety reasons. The chair itself is typically simply a piece of 2 · 6. It is rigged like a sling or child's swing and hoisted aloft. In the theatre, it would typically be attached to an empty pipe and flown and counterweighted in the usual way as opposed to the block-and-tackle or winch methods more common aboard a sailing ship. There is usu-

ally a chest strap or something similar to tie the electrician in, and tools and supplies are often attached to the chair itself. It is a secure, reasonably safe way to a put an electrician in-the-air, especially in a place where the deck is uneven and a ladder cannot be used. Unlike other methods, the electrician does not need to hold on in any way and can use both hands.

When the electrician is finished in one location, the chair is typically lowered back to the deck and moved to its next location on the same pipe or some other pipe. In rare situations there may be a method of moving the chair left and right while remaining aloft. While an ordinary theatrical curtain track is usually not strong enough to support this kind of spot loading, there are I-beam carriers that are industrially used to raise engines out of vehicles and move them laterally that could be used.

The principal problem with the bosun's chair is that there will rarely be that many free line-sets that don't already have scenery on them. Theoretically a block-and-tackle could be rigged in spot locations on the grid but this would be hugely labor intensive.

Light Bridge: A narrow (about 20"), usually temporary, usually raiseable and lowerable catwalk that provides both hanging positions and a means of getting to them. There can be more than one bridge, but where there is only one, it is by tradition right behind the front curtain (British: *perch position* or *perches*). It is customarily the most heavily loaded and most useful behind-the-curtain lighting position. It can be manned during a performance and some of its instruments used as followspots. Light bridges are typically suspended on wire rope. They are much less rigid than permanent catwalks, and while they can be manned during a performance, the crew cannot walk around or shift their weight without causing the whole position and all its lights to move. A better solution where a manned position is envisioned involves having the hanging positions suspended independently on a line-set slightly upstage of the manned bridge.

While theoretically a manned bridge could be moved from place to place to provide a way to focus the lights, there will rarely be enough line-sets in the places needed to suspend a bridge from.

Analysis

Of all the desirable qualities, *speed* is probably the most important because time is short and labor is expensive and reoccurring. Imagine that there are 10 instruments in 10 different locations on a 20' grid. Let's say that it will take about 15 seconds to climb to the first light. Let's say that getting to the second and subsequent lights will only take a second if the electrician can walk or be rolled there and 40 seconds if she has to come down while the structure is moved. In this situation, it is easy to see that ladders of any kind and bosun's chairs and movable bridges are the slow methods. This leaves cherry pickers, scaffolding, rolling ladders, powered lifts and catwalks as the fast methods. Where there is a set with levels onstage, none of the four rolling methods will work, and this leaves only the catwalks as a fast method. Once the architecture of the building has been decided upon, catwalks may no longer be an option, and there may not be an ideal way to get the job done.

There are also two focusing methods that don't involve actually getting to the instruments, although neither one of them is particularly fast. First, there are the intelligent lights that are manipulated from the lightboard. Second, there is dead focusing, which is a trial-and-error method for fly houses that involves focusing the pipes when they are at chest height by pointing them at spots on the floor.

HANGING POSITIONS, IDEAL— Imagine that you are standing in the center of a huge glass sphere. The question is how many possible places would there be on the surface of the sphere to hang instruments directed toward you. Even on a not-so-huge sphere, this would be thousands of instrument locations. For discussion purposes, it is easier to talk about hanging positions that are separated by 45 angular degrees from each other in all directions. That would be a total of 26. At the 45 degree above positions (golden ring) there would be eight positions, often numbered clockwise from 1–8 starting at the front (alternately referred to as golden ring front, front-right, right, back-right, back, back-left, left, and front-left. At the 0 degrees of elevation position (eyelevel ring) there would be another eight, numbered 9–16 and named as before. At the 45 degree below position (campfire ring) there would be another eight positions (17–24). Position 25 is top-dead-center and position 26 is bottom-down-under.

In a real theatre, it is not always possible to find a hanging position located in the places one thinks they should be, and it is necessary to use the closest (to ideal) position that can be found. This used to be a lot harder than it is now.

The most useful positions are the eight golden ring positions plus top-dead-center because there are usually hanging places in those locations, the light path is usually unobstructed and the shadows will primarily be on the floor. Light from the eyelevel positions all cast life-sized shadows against the background or shine in the eyes of the audience

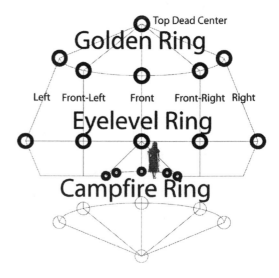

Ideal positions

if the audience is in the background (as in a thrust or other open stage theatre). This is the traditional balcony rail position, but in theatres lacking a balcony there may be seated audience at the ideal eyelevel hanging position. Eyelevel lights from the side in a proscenium house may be (usually are) blocked by scenery or masking. The campfire ring and bottom-down-under positions are most useful for fire effects. They cast giant shadows against their background, they need to have their light sources masked (which means concealing them inside a prop or under a special platform with a Plexiglas or a metal-grating top), and they are going to have the same Distance Problem that footlights have, which is to say anyone who walks toward or away from them will get noticeable brighter or dimmer.

Stanley McCandless was certainly the first American to write about and popularize the use of the 45 degree above positions (specifically front-left and front-right for a proscenium house). While the 45 degree above and 90 degrees of separation remains the most commonly taught way to arealight a playing area, there has been over time some honest disagreement as to which angles are the best. Pan angles tend to vary between 60 degrees and 120 degrees of separation and tilt angles tend to vary between about 30 degrees and 60 degrees.

All potential lighting designers need to do tests of their own and decide for themselves what they think works best. In most cases, it is a balance between how well the light get into the eye socket versus where the shadow falls.

HANGING SESSION (British: *fit-up*) — This refers to the crew call at which the instruments are hung in place and usually accessorized and tested. The master electrician usually organizes this. It typically occurs either on strike night or the first day of the load-in. It usually involves one or more ladder crews who share the space with other crews.

It is usually organized so that it minimizes the amount of ladder movement, but in the event that it doesn't get finished in the allotted time, there is usually plenty of other time that it could extend into since it usually takes two to three times longer to install the set than it does to install the lights.

In some venues, the accessories are added as part of the focus session. In some venues, there is a troubleshooting call that involves only one or two electricians prior to the focusing session to make sure that all the lights are working and plugged (or soft patched) correctly.

The role of the lighting designer during these sessions is mainly that of observer and fount of knowledge. She may be allowed to pick gel from the theatre's stocks and put them in frames, she may be allowed to sort old gel, she may be allowed to format the disk, she may be allowed to set up her tech table or she may be allowed to do none of these things, in which case she will still typically be present to answer question.

Usually both the lighting designer and the master electrician have estimated the time that it would take to do the job, and both usually know (as each hour strikes) what the progress should be. The lighting designer has to be particularly interested in this because at the focus session, similar paths of travel for the ladders will be used, but she will be in charge and there is usually no time to expand into if the focus does not finish on time.

There frequently comes a time toward the end of the hanging session when everyone seems to have run out of things to do, but there are either still instruments on the floor (but no one knows where they should go) or there are empty places in-the-air (but there don't appear to be any left over instruments). In either case, the master electrician needs to sense this time coming on and needs to study the plot to either locate the missing instruments (usually they have not been struck yet) or the missing locations. If the lighting designer is standing around with nothing much to do, she may undertake to figure this out as she is usually more familiar with the plot.

See STRIKE THE LIGHTS, WHEN TO

and also LADDER CREW for a more detailed discussion.

HARD FOCUS or HARD EDGE— Focusing adjustments on an ellipsoidal are set in such a way that the outline of the light is clearly visible and in sharp focus on the floor. This is the opposite of a *soft focus* or *soft edge.*

HARD PATCH— A patch system in which circuits are physically plugged into dimmers either by having loose cords that plug into the backs of dimmers or through a more sophisticated patch panel with telephone switchboard-type cords (or bus bar sliders).

HARDCOPY PRINTOUT— Theoretically, this could be a printout of anything, but in the context of computer lightboards it is almost always a printout of the cues showing the level of each channel in each cue. Many lightboards still print this out as a cue per page, which means that if there are 100 cues in the show, then there will be 100 sheets of paper. If the purpose of the printout were merely to document the cues in a non-electronic way, then this would be acceptable although obviously not very compact.

More commonly what is wanted is a way in which cues can be cross-compared with each other. Are all the cues that take place in the doctor's office exactly the same, as they should be? Are all the filaments that will play in the next cue being kept warm? When the desk light is used, does it always play at a level of 30? The kind of document that best answers these question is what used to be called *Dimmer Readings by Cue* (now a *Channel Reading by Cue*), which is a spreadsheet with dimmers (channels) across the top and cues down the side, so that the whole show can be contained on one B or C-sized sheet of paper.

Some lightboards can write in an ASCII format that can be further manipulated by a spreadsheet program like Excel to produce such a spreadsheet. Where that isn't possible, cues that print in a vertical column can be cut apart and pasted next to each other. In the absence of any of the methods mentioned, it may have to be created and kept up-to-date manually. There is no question that it is immensely useful. When a cue is "lost," which is to say deleted by accident, it is the lighting designer who has to recreate it. While theoretically it could be retrieved from a previous rehearsal disk, that is a method that is very prone to error, as will be explained shortly. The safest and easiest method is for the lighting designer to read it back from the hardcopy. See RETRIEVING LOST CUES for a more detailed discussion.

HARDWIRE— As a verb, it refers to the load being permanently wired to the dimmer. This was the custom when electricity first came into the theatre. It was replaced in the late twenties when patch panels were developed. When the price of dimmers dropped in the 1980s, the patch panels and their attendant wiring and connectors became more expensive than having more dimmers and having them hardwired. This is commonly referred to as a *dimmer-per-circuit* system these days, and it is often meant to mean a dimmer-per-instrument.

HARTMANN, LOUIS— David Belasco's right-hand-man in all matters related to electricity and one of America's first lighting designers long before America had any lighting designers at all. He worked for David Belasco for 28 years, producing all his electrical effects, and eventually in 1930 wrote a book, **Theatre Lighting: A Manual of the Stage Switchboard**, which was reprinted again in 1970. He devoted his entire life to stage lighting and had many thoughts about the nature of lighting that are as true today as they were then. His best-lit cyc was one where he managed to keep all light away from it. He understood the Distance Problem and declared it to be one of his biggest problems. He warned against having too much light before most theatres had realized they now had enough. What David Belasco and he achieved with the antiquated equipment of the time served as a visual inspiration to several generations of future lighting designers. He designed and invented and built lighting instruments long before any commercial company could be induced to do so.

HAULING ROPE— Any rope used to haul up an instrument or accessories, tools or spare lamps to an electrician in-the-air. See HAULING UP AN INSTRUMENT below.

HAULING UP AN INSTRUMENT— Instruments get from the deck to the place where they are going to be hung either by being carried up by the ladder electrician (something that most electricians cannot sustain for hours at a time) or the ladder assistant hauls them up by means of a rope.

The haul rope has to be hemp or some other non-slippery material. It will have a non-slip loop in one end. See KNOTS/Bowline. The rope is either run through a pulley (that is attached to the pipe or ladder) or more commonly is simply thrown over a ladder rung or the pipe itself.

The non-slip loop is typically run under the yoke and over the c-clamp. This hauls the instrument up in a nearly vertical position and can be slipped off (without any untying) once it is aloft. Often an accessory or a bucket containing accessories, tools or spare parts can be clipped to the bowline and hauled up in the same manner. It is the ladder assistant who is most commonly expected to do the hauling. The use of the pulley will not only make this easier, but it will save chafing on the rope, and the non-slip loop will act as a stopper knot to prevent the rope from running out of the pulley and falling to the deck by accident.

HAZE EFFECT— See EFFECTS, KINDS OF.

HEADSPOT— A spotlight (usually a followspot) irised down to about a 2–3' diameter and focused on the head of an actor. Anything smaller than this would be called a *pinspot* and would be relatively rare.

HEAT SHIELD— A colorless media that absorbs infrared heat while passing most visible light. It is usually less rigid than regular color media having the consistency of transparent kitchen wrap. To get it to work as effectively as possible, it needs to be separated by an air space from both the gel color and the lens. Often this means the two slots usually present at the front of the instrument, but it can mean the two sides of a color extender, where its effectiveness will be even more pronounced.

HEAT SINK— Anything that by its design aids in the dissipation of heat. This usually means that whatever it is will have metal fins. Automobile radiators are a good example of a heat sink. For many years, Ariel Davis Manufacturing made instruments that had aluminum fin bodies that dissipated heat, thus eliminating the need for any ventilation holes.

HEAVY SHOW— One that requires a lot of instruments, but not necessarily a lot of cues, i.e. the light pipes will weigh a lot.

HIGH HAT— Another name for a *tophat*, which is one of several lighting add-on accessories. See ACCESSORIES for a more detailed discussion.

HIGH PLATFORM, LIGHTING OF— See LIGHTING SPECIAL PROBLEMS/High Platforms.

HIGH VOLTAGE— In theatrical usage anything that will break skin contact and produce an electrical shock that can be felt (anything above about 30 volts, which is a typical headset voltage) is usually thought of as high voltage, and there is traditionally no lighting or communication gear that runs on anything in the 31–109-volt range. 120 volts, 208 (three phase) volts and 240 volts (single phase) are the most common high voltages.

HIGHEST-TAKES-PRECEDENCE (Abbr. HTP)— This is a computer lightboard term where in a pile-on situation, the highest reading is the one used. The opposite of this is LTP (last action takes precedence). Subs work on the HTP principle. Groups typically work on the LTP principle.

HIGHLIGHTING (monitor)— In the days of monochrome monitors, this meant double bright and was a way to boldface onto a monochrome screen. This function is now usually handled by a designated color on color-screen-monitors.

HISTORY OF LIGHTING— From the first appearance of indoor theatres in the early 1400s until quite recently, stage lighting meant candles or some other combustible material (torch, cresset or crude oil lamp). These were typically installed above the stage in chandeliers or in long troughs, and there was a row along the front edge of the stage in the footlight position. It was both a badly flawed system and the best system that could be devised given the technology of the time.

The candles above the stage tended to light the underside of the roof or ceiling better than the stage floor below. This was a result of the fact that they had to burn base down and could not be aimed in any way. To overcome this, some kind of metal shield was often installed to both block the light from spilling into the audience and to attempt to reflect it downward toward the stage. While this helped to light the background setting, it did little to light the actors directly below as it mostly lit the tops of their heads rather than the fronts of their faces. What was desperately needed was some kind of frontlight, something that would come from the same direction as the line-of-sight of the audience, but there was nothing and there continued to be nothing for several hundred years.

What came closest were the footlights, and they proved to be the most useful of the available positions for lighting faces. Footlights were much closer to the actors than the lights from above, and their light was direct rather than reflected. Unhappily, it also came from a somewhat unnatural angle (much like the effect of a flashlight held beneath the chin), and it was only marginally possible to overcome this facial distortion with makeup. The footlights also caused giant shadows of the actors on the background, and this could neither be helped nor overcome.

It was not uncommon for the footlights to be recessed into the floor. When it became common to have a stack of painted drops at the back of the stage, it then became common to have a row of candles recessed in the floor back there, also (cyc foots). If the floor lights were not recessed in the floor, then there would have been a metal hood or groundrow to block light from going out into the house (or, to be more specific, to block the audience's view of the actual flames).

Added to all this was the constant potential for fire. The troughs typically were filled with sand or water so that if a candle fell out of its holder it would extinguish. It was also common to install a low railing on the onstage side of the footlights to keep trailing costumes from sweeping across the open flames. Even so, candles did misbehave and costumes did catch fire, and it was often necessary to send the snuff-boy out on stage during the performance to deal with these problems.

In terms of light cues, most shows were of the two-cue variety: the candles were lit at the top of the show and snuffed-out at the end. The actual mechanics of this would have involved lowering in all the troughs and chandeliers before the house opened and putting in all new candles, lighting them and then raising them into position for the show. The curtain (if there was one) was brought in and the audience took its place. When the audience had left at the end, the troughs and chandeliers would be lowered back in, all the candles snuffed and removed and taken to the candle maker to be traded for new candles.

The chandeliers that lit the house customarily remained on during the performance, as there was generally no convenient way to do anything else. If the theatre was exceptionally fancy, there might be a hole in the ceiling above the house, opening into an attic space. If this were the case, the house chandeliers could be hoisted out through this hole in the ceiling where all but a few of the candles could be extinguished until it was time to relight them and lower them in again at the end of the show.

Shakespeare and most of his contemporaries favored the outdoor theatres of the day and allowed themselves to be driven indoors only during the severest winter months. Dry cleaning, of course, had not been invented yet. Bathing on a daily, weekly or even monthly basis had not caught on yet, neither amongst actors nor the audience. The indoor theatres that smelled bad already were made worse by the combustion gases and smoke caused by the candles or whatever was burned to produce the murky lighting. The outdoor theatres, in contrast, were better lit and better ventilated.

This was the way stage lighting began, and it remained virtually unchanged for almost 400 years. For a while it becomes troughs of oil lamps, whose wicks need to be trimmed between shows. Then gas jets replaced both candles and oil lamps. One of the advantages of gas jets, aside from the fact that there was nothing to trim, change or replace between shows, was that they could more-or-less be dimmed. Any trough of stage lights could be set by adjusting the gas flow from glow to full. Since this was done by eye, the common levels were half, three-quarters and full. The house chandeliers could also be dimmed in the same way.

When electricity came along, light bulbs replaced gas jets but the system of lighting the stage remained unchanged, which is to say the troughs of light were still the prevailing system. Light bulbs were at least 16 times brighter than the candles they replaced (16 candlepower), they could be dimmed completely, did not flicker all that much, did not produce any combustion gases, were less yellow and were cool enough so that they could be dipped in a transparent dye to color them (red, blue, green, yellow being the most common colors). They burned base down or base horizontal so the light could actually for the first time be more effectively tipped downward. Despite all these advantages, the stage was still murky and dim and lacking in light coming from the audience's viewing direction (i.e. the front).

Things might have gone on in this leisurely manner had it not been for three technological advances of such immense proportions that they significantly changed the course of stage lighting forever. The first of these took place in the mid–1800s, but the other two have occurred much more recently.

Limelight: This was in essence a non-electric follow spot. It's essential components were oxygen, hydrogen, a piece of limestone and a fireproof place to stand. The limestone was heated to incandescence and a lens tube captured and directed a portion of the light produced. It needed a full-time operator, but it was exceptionally bright. It was a very white light, and it could travel a long distance. It was the first time anyone had been able to light from the front. Followspots are to this day called "frontlights" even though there are now lots of other kinds of lights that also come essentially from the front.

When electricity came along, carbon arc technology replaced limelight because the cost of electricity was low compared to the cost of bottled gases. Carbon arcs are still in use today despite the immergence of metal halide and several other competing technologies.

This started a 50 year tradition of having the same dim stage lights but following the speaking actors around the stage with followspots, which is a tradition still alive and well today in the opera, some Broadway musicals, and any performance that takes place on ice.

Although limelight is now completely obsolete, its name lingers on. Celebrities or public figures are said to be "in the limelight" when they are publicly noticed.

Spotlights: From the day that theatres had first switched over to electricity, the dream was that one day there would be theatre spotlights that would, on a smaller scale and without the operator, be able to do what followspots did, which is to say project light over long distances from the front.

Such an instrument would have to involve a bright light source that would project the light in all directions, a housing to prevent the light from going where it wasn't wanted, a lens system that would bend the light into a narrow cone, and a reflector that would help capture some of the wasted light and send it back through the lens system.

There were, however, a number of seemingly insurmountable problems. Both the lenses and reflectors captured only the tiniest portion of the total light output. The rest hit the housing and was transformed into heat. Bright light sources were also hot sources, and this shortened lamp life and cracked lenses. There was also a problem getting the lenses to not act as prisms. While rainbow rings of color (known as *chromatic aberrations*) might be acceptable for a followspot, it was going to be too distracting for a stage spotlight. The early spotlights were called *plano-convex* instruments or PCs for short. Probably the most famous of these was the Baby Spot from Kliegl Bros first introduced in 1906. It typically had a 250–500 watt screw-type lamp in a fixed relationship to the reflector on a sliding lamp carriage. The PC lens could be removed to create a floodlight or it could be used as a lensed spotlight. Bigger versions of PC lights were called *hoods* and typically were modeled after the small arc lights they replaced. The housing was called the *hood*, and they had either a large side access door to get at the lamp mechanism or their top hinged to get to the lamp. The ones with a side door were typically hung by a single sidearm attached to the side without the door.

The invention of theatre spotlights then was the second major technological advance, and it did not happen all at once but evolved over a 50-year period and may still be evolving. In the interests of keeping this history brief, *fresnels* and *ellipsoidals* were the stars of the show. The fresnels, using lens technology originally created for lighthouses, found their way into the theatre in the late 1920s. They were compact, inexpensive and produced a soft-edged light that had no color rings and had solved the lens-cracking problem by cleverly reducing the thickness of the glass. The lamp and reflector moved as a unit

in relationship to the lens to make the light bigger or smaller. Ellipsoidals were developed in the 1930s (but did not become popular until the late '40s when the size of the instrument became more compact). Although the size of the light was not controllable (except by changing the lens tube assembly), they could produce a hard or softish-edged light whose beam shape could be controlled by the use of 4 framing shutters. They could also accept a heat resistant metal pattern (gobo) that could produce a light/shade slide projection.

Prior to the invention of spotlights, followspots had been lighting the actors and the trough lights had been providing the general illumination and color toning. By this point, trough lights were not simply empty troughs with light bulb sockets and lamps colored by lamp dip. They were now striplights that came in modular lengths of 6–8' and were divided into compartments that had reflectors and they were circuited so that lamps 1, 2, 3 were all on different circuits, which repeated along the length of the trough. This allowed the use and control of three colors of light. These were typically red, blue and green, but the green often was changed to an amber or no-color. Sometimes, especially when there was a double-row of compartments, they were wired in four circuits, which was intended to provide a no-color circuit. Each circuit of each trough was hard wired to the dimmer that controlled it. The dimmers were of the one-hand-operates-one-dimmer type, which encouraged the use of large capacity dimmers to reduce the number of hands required to run any given show.

It was possible to operate several with a forearm or a short stick if they were side-by-side. Also, a mechanical mastering system often existed for selected groups of 6–14 dimmers. Then these submasters could often be controlled by one big grandmaster handle. The master handles had to be first preset in either an up or down position. Then individual dimmers could be clicked on or off the mastering system. As the submaster handle moved, it picked up dimmers along the way and brought them all either up or down to the level of the master (or submaster) handle. This allowed one operator to manipulate perhaps as many as twenty dimmers. If this were the start of a scene, typically everything would be brought up to some general playing level, then the individual dimmers would be clicked off the master and slowly adjusted up or down from there. Each cue consisted of a main action and a lot of after actions that sneaked dimmers up or down from their starting level.

At first the spotlights, were used as specials to highlight certain parts of the stage and separate them by brightness or color from the general murk produced by the striplights. By the time fresnels had arrived, they were being used as general illumination and a system of using them, pioneered by Stanley McCandless, evolved. They were soft-edged so they blended well. They provided front light, they revealed three-dimensional shape better because of their angle, and they could be made to spill less on the scenery. The development of ellipsoidals made it possible to consider getting rid of the front curtain and having thrust theatres or extended apron proscenium theatres because the light could now be controlled well enough to keep it out of the house.

By the 1960s, the striplights had been relegated to the relatively minor role of downlight toning and drop lighting, and the fresnels and ellipsoidals were doing most of the stage lighting work. The much-maligned footlights were not being used much, and the followspots were only brought out on special occasions or for musical numbers.

It now became necessary to consider cabling and repatch systems. The striplights had been hardwired to the dimmers shortly after their purchase, and no one had thought about them since. It became obvious that the spotlights were not going to stay in one place but were going to move around from show to show. Also, very often a special might only be used in Act I, and it would be nice if its dimmer could be used for something differ-

ent in Act II. What evolved then was a "distribution system" which in the beginning consisted of bundled extension cords from the lighting positions to the dimmers with connectors on each end. This meant the extension cords from the lights had to have male connectors, and the dimmers had to have female connectors. Repatching became a simple matter of unplugging one circuit and plugging in another. As time went by, the distribution system became an electrical raceway with pigtails or flush mounted plug-in receptacles and permanent conduit wiring going through some kind of telephone switchboard-type patch panel and from there on to the dimmers. This is what we would now call a *hard patch*, but at the time it was the only kind of patch there was.

Computer Lightboard: The third major technological advancement was the computer lightboard that could, from a remote location, record both the levels of all the dimmers and the timing of the cues in a way that it could be set once and then recalled from some kind of memory storage system and played back at will. This process started in about 1960 and continues to the present. There have been three general levels of advancement along the way. First, there was the separation of the dimmers from their control mechanism (like the Century Edkotron's of the mid–'60s). This produced miniature controls that took less upper body strength to manipulate and made it possible to manipulate more of them at once. The second advancement was the preset boards, where an entire setting or cue could be proportionally brought up or crossfaded with another entire setting. Two-scene presets were the most popular because they were the least expensive, but there were 5-scene presets, and some boards had as many as 50 or 100 presets. The third level of advancement has been the memory board that actually stored the show and recalled it from memory. These started out recording only to the internal memories of the machine, but then began recording to removable disks or tapes that no other machine could read, and have now become recordings to disks that can be read and manipulated by ordinary personal computers.

First, the separation of the dimmers that did the work from the control mechanism that sent the signal changed the whole concept of replugging. The dimmers could now be located in an electrical room closest to where power from the street entered the building. This saved money on wiring. One could still theoretically do replugs, but it would involve a separate person (not the board operator) working by headset alone here in this remote electric room. It soon became apparent that when one took into account the price of the patch panel and its numerous interconnecting cables and connectors, it became more cost efficient to spend the available money on more dimmers and to hard wire each circuit to its own dimmer with the much cheaper conduit wire. The dimmers themselves had dropped in price and there was now virtually no limit to how many dimmers one could have as the computer could control all of them.

Second, there were now virtually no limits on how many cues could occur in rapid succession so it now became possible to record an opening sequence as 5 or 6 cues that all followed each other in succession. The machine remembered the cues perfectly and could perform them the same way every time.

Third, up until now (prior to the memory boards) most of the lighting notes on any given production related to the speed with which a cue was performed. What the lighting designer thought of as a 5 count, the board operator might do as a 3 count; so it got changed to an 8 count in the hope that this would make it look more like a "real" 5 count. With practice, the cues got smoother and more refined as opening night approached. Also up until this time, each cue had to be set anew each night. Just because the lights had worked perfectly the night before was not a guarantee that they would be the same tonight. The memory computer changed all this. Five counts always lasted 5 seconds and cue timings were exactly the same from night-to-night, and assuming one pushed the right buttons, the cue was always the same, too. It was now possible to set the correct timings the first time the cue was looked at and to have them remain that way for the entire run.

Fourth, not only did it take fewer hands to make all the dimmers work, it did not require as skilled and dexterous an operator. The board operator now mostly only needed to know how to push the go button because it was possible to program in all the hard stuff ahead of time.

HISTORY TIMELINE— A list of dates and events related to stage lighting:

1545 Sabastiano Serlio, an Italian architect, publishes book II of his **Architecttura**, wherein he suggests producing colored light in the theatre by letting it shine through bottles of colored liquids, like wine, aqua vita, vernis, saffron and sulfuric acid. He had built a theatre in Vicenza in the 1530s, and presumably it is this experience that he draws upon in his book where he presents plan and sectional views of an amphitheatre with an acting area about 58' long by 10' deep in front of a raked perspective stage (picture stage) that was an additional 12' deep. He presents woodcuts for three sets: one for comedy, one for tragedy and one for satirical plays. He describes in some detail how all of this is to be illuminated, but he also covers the three signature marks of the Italian renaissance which were (1) the stage was to be brighter than the house (2) the lighting was for the most part to be out of the direct sight of the audience (3) much of the light was to be reflected off of colored silks or shone through colored glass or chemical liquids.

1550 circa Leone di Somi in the **Means of Theatrical Representation** describes a tragedy that began brilliantly illuminated but when the first unhappy event occurred, he had the stage light that was not used for lighting the perspective backing, shaded at the same time. This created an impression of horror, he said, that was widely praised. This idea has since been taken to mean that comedies should be bright and tragedies should be dark. He also mentions keeping the back of the hall darker than the stage, keeping the torches and candles out of sight and using reflectors and other indirect means to put shadowless bounce light on the playing area.

1507–73 Giacomo da Vignola presents the idea that the best angle to view an object is along the diagonal of a cube.

1598 Angelo Ingegneri publishes **Il discorso della poesia rappresentativa e del mode di rappresentare le favole sceniche** in which he talks about his production of Oedipus Rex at the Teatro Olimpico in 1585. He says he favors a darkened house, concealed lighting and reflected light. He discusses how best to light the facial expressions of the performers, and he describes mounting a row of lamps high on the backside of the proscenium arch with reflective material behind. He, also, describes a frightening effect involving the appearance of ghostly apparitions by using a black veil stretched across the back of the perspective stage, dimly lit, where the "ghost" appears huge in comparison to the surrounding buildings and appears cloaked in black with no arms or legs showing and glides as if on wheels back-and-forth and then vanishes suddenly.

1605 Inigo Jones is appointed as a theatrical designer for James I. He subsequently introduces the proscenium arch, the raked stage, concealed wing lights and shielded footlights to the English stage, presumably based on an Italian model seen during his trip to Italy sometime between 1600 and 1603.

1610 Samual Pepys writes about an evening performance lit by candlelight alone.

1628 Joseph Fürtenbach, a German architect, in his **Sciena di Comoedia**, describes a stage he has seen where the stage was raked, there was an orchestra pit that masked the musicians from view and borderlights, footlights and wing lights were used. He spent 10 years in Italy and was the town architect in Ulm, where among other things he built a comedy playhouse for the grammar school.

1638 Nicola Sabbatini in his **Manual for Theatrical Scenes and Machinery** presents a design for dimming candles by means of opaque cylinders being lowered over them. His book contains numerous sketches showing methods of concealment, methods of creating reflection and methods used to insure that the front of the stage was the most brightly lit.

1672 In the front piece to **The Wits**, a collection of short comedies performed in private halls during the Puritan ban, two-branched chandeliers can be seen along with a row of six footlights.

1673 In an engraving of the Red Bull, footlights can be seen.

1674 In an account of the production of the **Tempest** at the Dorset Garden Theatre, as the ship sank the houselights were raised up (dimmed) and the footlights were lowered and the wing lighting was shielded to make it darker.

1773 David Garrick, who had taken over the second Drury Lane Theatre in 1747, hires Philip de Loutherbourg, a French designer, who is said to have made many improvement to the lighting which are thought to have included borderlights, wing lights and footlights.

1781 Aimé Argand, a Swiss scientist, invents the Argand lamp that uses a circular wick and a glass chimney.

1791 William Murdock, a Scottish engineer, develops a process to manufacture illuminating gas from coal.

1800s early The Haymarket Theatre is described as using oil lamps with white or green glass cylinders that could be raised into place to color the lights.

1803 Frederick Albert Winsor installs gas in the Lyceum Theatre, London.

1808 Sir Humphry Davy demonstrates carbon arc light at the Royal Institution in London. It will take another 30 years before it is first used in the theatre.

1816 (1) Gas is installed at the Chestnut Street Opera House in Philadelphia. (2) Thomas Drummond, an Englishman invents limelight, but it will take another 40 years before it will be in common use in English theatres.

1817   Gas is installed at the Drury Lane and Covent Garden theatres, London.

1822   (1) Augustin Jean Fresnel invents a lens for use in lighthouses. It will take 100 years for it to find its way into the theatre. (2) Gas is installed at the new Opera in Paris.

1830 circa   A carbon arc light makes a brief appearance at the Covent Garden but is deemed too expensive to operate.

1837   William Macready first uses limelight in a pantomime, *Peeping Tom of Coventry* at the Covent Garden, London.

1843   Gas is installed at the Comedie Francaise, Paris.

1846   An electric arc light is used at the Paris Opera to simulate sunlight in a production of the *Prophet*.

1849   By this time, it has become possible to dim the houselights as Charles Kean on the London stage is said to have done so in a contemporary account.

1850   The fishtail gas burner is invented that creates fewer fumes.

1860   (1) By this time, gas is being lit by a spark instead of a torch, and the gas jets now have chimneys. (2) An electric arc spotlight is used in a production of Rossini's *Moses* at the Paris Opera.

1875   Two Canadians, Mathew Evans and Henry Woodward of Toronto patent an electric light bulb. Lacking the funds to commercialize their invention, they sell their patent to Thomas Alva Edison, who then alters and refines it.

1878   (1) Charles Francis Brush produces the first commercially successful arc light. (2) Sir Henry Irving takes over the management of the Lyceum theatre and is to make many improvements to the gas lighting, which are believed to include splitting the borderlights and footlights into smaller units, masking the lighting from the view of the audience, and having lighting rehearsals. He is said to have produced effects with gaslight that were never equaled by electric light.

1879   Thomas Alva Edison invents the incandescent lamp in America using carbonized bamboo fibers for the filament. At about the same time, Sir Joseph Swan invents an incandescent lamp in England.

1880   The Paris Opera is electrified.

1881   (1) Richard D'Oyly Carte at the Savoy theatre in London lights the production of Gilbert and Sullivan's *Patience* exclusively with electric light. Six dimmers are used and the electricity is generated on-site. (2) Edmund Audran's musical *Olivette* is done at the Bijou theatre in Boston, and presumably the carbon arc olivette instruments were named for this production in which they first appeared.

1882   The Munich Exposition has a theatre lit by incandescent light. A number of other theatres are said to have converted to electricity in that year, including the Bijou in Boston, the People's Theatre in New York, the Halsted Street Academy of Music in Chicago, and the Baldwin Theatre in San Francisco.

1885   Carl Freiher Auer von Welsbach of Vienna invents an incandescent mantle for use with gaslight that increases the light output about five times as compared to the standard slitburner of the time. It is named after him and called either the Welsbach mantle or the Auer burner.

1892   Altmeyer's Theatre in McKeesport, PA, installs Vitrohm resistance dimmers manufactured by Ward Leonard.

1896   Earl's Court Exhibition Theatre, London installs reactance dimmers.

1897   August D. Curtis is said to have introduced the X-ray borderlight with the mirrored glass reflectors invented by Everly Haines in 1896.

1900   David Belasco produces *Madam Butterfly*, which includes the famous transition to dawn cue that is slightly less than three minutes long.

1902   Mariano Fortuny in Germany invents the cyclorama and an indirect method of lighting the stage (*Fortuny method*) that involves directly lighting colored silks and letting the reflected light illuminate the stage. The results are said to have simulated natural lighting.

1903   The Metropolitan Opera Co in New York is equipped with new lights and a new switchboard.

1905   (1) David Belasco's produces *Girl of the Golden West* that opens with a five-minute sunset cue. (2) Metalized carbon filaments are developed to make lamps brighter and more durable. (3) Around this time, the first gallery reflector that used a parabolic reflector and an arc light are invented.

1906   (1) Tantalum filaments are developed. (2) The Illuminating Society is founded. (3) Kleigl Bros. introduces the first Baby Spot. It uses a 100 cp Edison base lamp and has a 5" diameter lens but does not yet have the small compact shape associated with later versions. (4) David Belasco produces *Rose of the Rancho* that used four olivettes to light the cyc. Presumably these were of the open box arc type because they were located behind a high garden fence (to conceal the operators) and Louis Hartmann talks about taking 20 operators to the Boston try-out.

1907   (1) Tungsten filaments are used for the first time in pressed form, but the process will not really be perfected until 1911.

1911   (1) William David Coolidge, an American engineer at the GE Research Lab produces drawn tungsten filaments. (2) David Belasco produces the *Return of Peter Grimm* that involved personal followspots for everyone onstage.

1913   (1) First 750 and 1000 watt lamps are said to have been produced. (2) First gas filled lamps are developed. (3) First disappearing footlights are offered for sale.

1914   Strand Electric and Engineering Ltd. is established in London.

1916   (1) The Caliban floodlight is developed and named after a production of *Caliban* staged by Percy MacKaye at the stadium, College of the City of New York. It is in essence a gallery reflector in which the arc mechanism has been replaced by the new 1000-watt lamp. This is supposed to be the first time the 1000-watt lamp has been used, but according to Louis Hartmann, this lamp was specially made for David Belasco, who is

supposed to have had exclusive use of it for two years (presumably 1914–15). (2) Adolphe Linnebach, the technical director of the Munich Opera, invents the Linnebach projector but it will take six years for it to get to America.

1918   Reference is made to the use of motorized wheel color changers.

1919   The 100 watt T20 lamp is developed.

1922   Klieg Bros. offers the Linnebach projector in America for the first time.

1925   The 500 watt T20 lamp is developed.

1926   Yale University builds their new theatre with switchboard and other lighting enhancements (like the footlights that could be either direct or indirect) designed by Stanley McCandless.

1929   (1) Theodore Fuchs publishes the first American lighting textbook **Stage Lighting**. (2) It is at about this time that the fresnel lens is first used in the theatre, but it take almost 5 years for them to become popular. Neither Theodore Fuchs nor Hunton D. Sellman mentions such a lens or instrument.

1930   (1) The bi-plane filament is developed. (2) The bi-post lamp base is invented. (3) Stanley McCandless designs an organ-type console for the Severance Hall in Cleveland. (4) Hunton D. Sellman publishes the second American lighting textbook as part of **Stage Scenery and Lighting**. (5) Louis Hartmann publishes **Theatre Lighting**, which recounts anecdotes from his 28 years with David Belasco.

1932   (1) The first ellipsoidal reflector instrument is used at the Center Theatre as a pinhole downlight in the auditorium. It uses a 250 or 400 watt G type lamp. (2) Klieg Bros. completes the lighting for the Radio City and Rockefeller Center theatres. (3) Stanley McCandless publishes **A Method of Lighting the Stage**.

1933   (1) 1000, 1500 and 2000 watt lamps that burn base up are developed for use in ellipsoidals, and the first Klieglight (an ellipsoidal) is said to have been used at a production of *Romance of the People* at the Polo

Grounds in New York. (2) 100 watt single contact bayonet lamp is invented. (3) The first autotransformer dimmer is invented by the General Radio Company, but it will take until the 1950s before they are in common use. They are not listed in the Century Lighting catalog of 1948.

1935   (1) The 500 watt T10 lamp is invented. (2) The Alzak process for aluminum reflectors is invented.

1936   There is a full range of fresnels from 250 to 5000 watts for sale.

1938   Fluorescent light is debuted at the Exposition in New York, but it is based on a mercury-vapor lamp developed by Peter Cooper Hewitt in 1901 and a subsequent patent by Thomas Edison.

1940   PAR lamps appear for the first time on 1940 model cars. Daniel K. Wright is the patent holder.

1947   The Izenour dimmer is produced commercially by Century Lighting Co.

1948   Sometime prior to 1948 actually, Edward Kook and Joseph Levy of the Century Lighting Co. invent a compact ellipsoidal spotlight that becomes enormously popular. They name it after themselves, calling it a Leko or a Lekolight, and it appears prominently in their 1948 catalog.

1956   Klieg Bros. introduces an oval beam fresnel.

1958   The General Electric Company invents the silicon-controlled rectifier, but it will take more than five years for it to find its way into stage lighting control devices.

1960   USITT is founded.

1965 circa   (1) Century Lighting Co introduces the Edkotron dimmers, one of the first remotely controlled SCR-type dimmers. (2) The first light-emitting diodes are developed.

1971 circa   (1) Kliegl produces small 3.5" ellipsoidals that use a double-ended tube lamp. (2) Dyna-light produces the Moto-Light, which is one of the first moving yoke lights.

1975 circa   AMX-192 multiplexing protocol is introduced, which allows up to 192 dimmers to be addressed by single pair of wires.

1981   (1) Vari*Lite introduces the Model 1 automated moving head light for the Genesis Tour. (2) An Oleson catalog shows several small ellipsoidals including the Berkey-Colortran Mini-Ellipses, full-sized axially mounted ellipsoidals, and both a Kliegl and a Colortran computer memory lightboard. The former uses a tape back-up and the latter uses a 5.5" floppy disk.

1983   Electronic Theatre Controls (ETC) introduces their Concept computer memory lightboard.

1983   Lighting and Electronics (L&E) introduces a compact striplight (Mini-Strip) that uses MR-16 lamps.

1986   USITT DMX512 multiplexing protocol replaces AMX-192 and can address up to 512 dimmers on a 5-wire signal cable.

1992   Electronic Theatre Controls introduces the Source Four series of ellipsoidals, which use the new 575W HPL lamps, use joystick lamp centering, and have rotating barrels.

1993   Around this time, Rosco Laboratories offers a line of gobo rotators, which can inexpensively produce moving effects previously only possible with more expensive dedicated effects projectors.

2001   Rosco Laboratories invents the ImagePro, which is a device that slides into the gobo slot of a conventional ellipsoidal and turns it into a color slide projector. The slide has to be specially made up, but the original can be a computer enhanced digital image. It is *Lighting Dimensions*' product of the year in the scenic effects category.

HMI — Abbreviation for *hydrargyrum-medium iodide*, where hydrargyrum is Latin for mercury. A tungsten short-arc encapsulated lamp that produces the full daylight spectrum (5600 K), typically used in followspots that cannot be dimmed out all the way although it can be dimmed to about 40 percent. It is the most useful so far of the gaseous discharge family of lamps.

HOISTS, KINDS OF — This is a generic term that covers various kinds of leverage methods used to raise really heavy loads where hauling it up by rope is not an option.

Block-and-Tackle: This involves rope and a number of pulleys. With one pulley, it takes 100 lbs of pull to raise a 100 lb load. With two pulleys, it only takes 50 lbs and so forth, but 6' of rope has to be pulled to raise the load 3'. The capacities of rope are measures in the hundreds of pounds.

Cable Puller: This is a wirerope method that involves pulleys and a ratcheting handle mechanism and is typically used for a short haul (20' or less) where the expectation is that when the item is in position it will be dead hung and the come-along will be detached and used for the next item.

Winches: These can be motorized or manual and involve wirerope and gears and have capacities in the thousands of pounds.

Chain hoist: This is usually motor-driven although it could be manual and it involves welded link proof chain and its capacities are usually measured in tons. When fully loaded trusses are hoisted into position, these are usually the means by which this is accomplished.

HOLD— Also *halt* or *stop*. This is computer lightboard term and frequently a button name that refers to stopping a fade in progress. There is usually one hold button for each fader pair.

HOLD-FOR-GO— This is a computer lightboard term that refers to interrupting a timed sequence of cues by remaining in the last cue or step of the sequence and waiting until a new cue is launched from the keyboard.

HOLOGRAM— An apparent three-dimensional image that is a virtual image but can be viewed from several angles. While possible in the context of magic shows and museum showcases, it has not quite developed to the point where it is possible onstage.

HOOD—(1) A vintage term for the housing of a spotlight that usually had an access door to get at the lamp. (2) A vintage term for a lensed instrument that was brighter than

Hood, circa 1920

about 500 watts. A similar instrument under 500 watts was typically called a *baby spot*. Hoods could be as big as 1500 or 2000 watts.

HOOK, CABLE— See CABLE HOOK.

HOOKUP— Connecting circuits to dimmers or dimmers to channels or both.

HOOKUP SHEET— Also called a *Hookup & Softpatch Sheet*, a *Channel Schedule* or the *Instrument Check List*, this is a table containing all the known information about each instrument arranged in channel number order. If the *Light Plot* was done in a CAD program like AutoCad, then typically the information will have been extracted from the drawing as a comma-delimited list and then converted into a text-table by a word processing program like MS Word. It is used by the electrician to patch circuits to dimmers or where these are hardwired (as is current practice) then to soft patch dimmers to channels. It is used by the designer as a reminder list of what each channel controls. It is used by the board operator or master electrician to perform an instrument check before each performance to see that all instruments are working.

Chn	Cct/ Di m	Use	Inst nr	Instrument	Watt	Color	Access	Notes
1	10	ROF	F1	SOURCE 4/50	575 GLC	x68	brk	-
2	15	FOL	31	SOURCE 4/50	575 GLC	x67	fol	-
3	38	GRE	D4	SOURCE 4/36	575 HPL	x91	-	-
4	20	NAR	D1	SOURCE 4/36	575 HPL	g107	-	-
5	31	Orange		SOURCE 4/50		x321	-	-
6	32	BR	C2	SOURCE 4/36	575 HPL	g885	-	-
7	85	BLKLT		Practical			uv	
8	43	YEL	101	SOURCE 4/50	575 GLC	X4530	-	-
9	46	DN	B19	SOURCE 4/36	575 HPL	g685	-	-
10	37	BL	F14	SOURCE 4/36	575 HPL	g885	-	-
11	12	A1F	21	SOURCE 4/50	575 GLC	X53	-	-
12	7	A2F	25	SOURCE 4/50	575 GLC	X53	-	-

Adophe Appia Theatre Company — PLUGGING & softpatch CHART 11/6/01 — App Christmas Homecoming

Unused Circuits: 51-53, 75 onward exc 85
X385 + x93—may substitute x83 for x385

Hook-up sheet

HORIZONTAL ANGLE— The angle between straight ahead from the aimpoint (in plan view) and straight to the instrument location (in plan view). In practice, this is seldom needed.

HORIZONTAL DISTANCE— The distance on a plan view between the light source and the aim point (actor's nose).

HOT—(1) Electrically hot (the opposite of cold). A hot grid is one where there is power running to some or all of the circuits. (2) Footcandles of light hot, i.e. bright (the opposite of dim).

HOT OVAL— In the context of a golden ring light, this refers to the near-side third of the egg shaped distribution bounded by the centerbeam point and the near point and two points along the sides of the light where the brightness is equal to the centerbeam (usually 1–2' nearer than the centerbeam point). See DISTRIBUTION OF LIGHT for a more detailed discussion.

HOT PATCH— To plug a light into an electrically hot outlet or cable. The more common procedure is to plug the lights in cold and then run up the dimmer or channel, which is easier on the lamps and safer for the electrician. As an alternative, the hot plug can be on a dimmer that is not run all the way up.

HOT SPOT— Where only one instrument is involved, it refers to the brightest part of the light beam (usually center). This can be adjusted on ellipsoidals up to a point, and it is common to try to produce an even field that won't have any hot spots. When a whole system of instruments is involved, then it refers to an area that appears to be brighter than the surrounding ones.

HOTLY CONTESTED ISSUES— From time to time mention is made in the course of this book when there is not universal agreement about methods, procedures or concepts. These include:

1. How to arealight the stage, which includes the six areas of concern discussed in FORMULA LIGHTING and LIGHTING AN OBJECT OR AREA.

2. COLOR THEORIES and COLORS, PRIMARY as they relate to COLOR MIXING.

3. Meeting with the COSTUME DESIGNER to view the costumes and what should be discussed or whether there should even be a meeting?

4. Lighting Paperwork and how much of it should be produced. In particular, should the lighting designer give a CUE SYNOPSIS to the director and/or stage manager? Does anyone other than the master electrician need to see the plot? How necessary is the hardcopy of the CHANNEL READINGS BY CUE? How should the disks be managed? (DISK MANAGEMENT)

5. Is 100 fc an acceptable DESIGN BRIGHTNESS? Is Stanley McCandless' 5–50 fc range for theatre scenes still accurate? How far back from the action can the audience sit and still see acceptably well (OPERA GLASSES TEST).

6. How many times should the lighting designer read the script and how many rehearsals or runthrus should she go to? (LIGHTING IDEAS) Who should she have to explain her design to and how should she have to do this? (DIRECTOR, FINAL MEETING WITH)

7. How should the lighting be INTEGRATED into the show, which includes whether the lightboard should be out in the house during the tech period and whether there should be REHEARSALS-WITH-LIGHT and so forth?

HOUSE— The auditorium or audience part of the theatre.

HOUSE BOARD or HOUSE ELECTRICIAN— The lightboard and electrician that are provided free with the rental of the theatre. The houseboard is usually used for the houselights, and the house electrician is often the one who runs it.

HOUSELIGHTS— The lights above the auditorium part of the theatre that allow the audience to read their programs before the show starts and during intermission.

HOUSING— This refers to the housing on the instruments, which prevents the light from going where it is not wanted.

HTP— See HIGHEST-TAKES-PRECE-DENCE.

HUE— In the context of a color wheel it refers to a family of color like red, orange or green. See COLOR for a more detailed discussion.

ICE SHOW LIGHTING— See LIGHTING, KINDS OF.

ID— Abbreviation for INSIDE DIAMETER of a pipe or tube.

IES— Abbreviation for ILLUMINATING ENGINEERING SOCIETY.

IGBT— Abbreviation for INSULATED GATE BIPOLAR TRANSISTOR DIMMERS. A modern electronic dimmer technology based on the gating principle that is different from (and competes with) SCR technology. See LIGHTING CONTROL for a more detailed discussion.

IGNITER— An electrically operated remote-control match used to set off a pyrotechnic device, sometimes called a *squid* with *squib* being a brand name, sometimes also called an *electronic match*.

ILLUMINATING ENGINEERING SOCI-ETY (Abbr. IES)— Although there are regional chapters, their scope is North American. They were founded in 1906. They publish a handbook and other literature of interest to the scientific and engineering community. Louis Hartmann presented a paper to them entitled **Lighting Effects on the Stage** on January 11th 1923, which is reprinted in its entirety as an appendix to Theodore Fuch's book.

ILLUMINATION— This is a scientific word that represents the quantity of light hitting a surface (and coming from a direction called an angle of incidence). It can be measured by a photometer, commonly called a *light meter*, in footcandles of light or metrically in luxes (quantity of light in lumens on a square meter area as opposed to on a square foot). It can be calculated by using the inverse square law.

IN TIME— This is a computer lightboard term that refers to how long it takes a step to dim up all the way as part of the in time/dwell time/out time/step time process. This is not to be confused with the adverb *in-time*, which refers to the previously programmed speed of a light cue, as in, "Let's see that cue run in-time."

INCANDESCENT COLOR SHIFT— When incandescent lights are at full, they are as pure a white color as they will ever be. As they are dimmed the color becomes more reddish, and this often affects the apparent color of the gelled light. Also, all colors are most brilliant when at full and more grayed down at lower levels. This is often attributed to the incandescent color shift, although this may not be the only factor. See COLOR ANOMALIES for a more detailed discussion)

INCANDESCENT LIGHT— A generic term used for all situations where a wire filament of some kind has been heated to the point of producing light. Thomas Edison first used carbonized bamboo fibers and later a carbon wire. Current practice is to use a tungsten wire and put a gas from the halogen family in the glass bulb of the lamp. Most references to incandescent light will be to its most modern incarnation as *tungsten-halogen* light.

INDEPENDENT— This is a lightboard term that refers to making an individual dimmer (or channel) independent of some kind of mastering system. It was most significant when preset lightboards were used as it made dimmers independent of the crossfaders and scene masters (if any). Independent dimmers often had one or more master handles of their own. In computer lightboard terminology, it can refer to setting a *channel attribute* to independent, in which case its readings will display and the levels will be recorded in all cues or it can refer to *parking* the dimmers or channels, which makes them immune to all board operations except the blackout button or grandmaster and the levels are typically not seen onscreen or recorded into cues.

INDICATOR LIGHTS— See PANEL LIGHTS.

INDIRECT LIGHT— This is a diffuse, shadowless light produced by a light source hitting an unseen surface and being diffusely reflected. There are three essential components to making this work. First, the source has to be hidden from view. Second, the surface that it is reflected off of has to also be hidden. Third, the resulting light has to be contained and encouraged to bounce in the correct direction. It is used as a method of lighting backing areas, for light boxes, and for backlighting drops or anything requiring a glow of any kind. The point is to get the shadowless, evenly distributed light even if the amount gotten is disappointingly small. See LIGHTING SPECIAL PROBLEMS/ Backings or Light Boxes for a more detailed discussion.

INFINITE PRESETS— Where the term is used, it applies to a system of key punched cards or something similar that provided an unlimited number of preset possibilities for a preset lightboard. Most modern computer boards now provide this automatically, and while the number of cues per disk may be limited, the user can usually change disks mid-show if that were to become necessary.

INFRA-RED LIGHT— This is not really light at all but heat. It is not visible in normal circumstances but feels warm to the touch.

INHIBITIVE— This is a computer lightboard term that reverses the way submasters work, so instead of piling their channels onto the existing stage picture, they work like master dimmers and subtract their channels from the existing cue onstage. When they are used in this way, their handles are typically left in the up (full on) position. Usually, only certain submasters can be made inhibitive

and they are typically identified as being inhibitive by a color-coded LED or panel light.

Inky Fresnel

INKY or INKY FRESNEL— Vintage jargon for a 3" fresnel, whose entire existence is now for the most part obsolete, having been replaced by other small sources of light like the Stik-up™ light and other small floodlights.

INSIDE DIAMETER (Abbr ID)— In the context of pipes, it refers to the diameter of the open area between the two opposite pipe walls. When a pipe is referred to as being a 1.5" pipe or a 0.5" pipe or whatever, it is the interior diameter that is most commonly being referred to, even though it is the outside diameter that the c-clamp of the instruments must fit around. This is often a subject of confusion and more than one theatre has wound up with 2" ID pipes when it was 2" OD (1.5" ID) that they really wanted.

INSTANTANEOUS— See ZERO COUNT.

INSTRUMENT CHECK— A check performed prior to each performance to make sure that all the instruments are working. It used to involve an assistant bringing up the dimmers one-at-a-time as the board operator watched from onstage to insure that they were all working. Now, the board operator still watches, but it is more common to program the lightboard to run a sequence of time-delayed cues.

INSTRUMENT CHECKLIST— See HOOKUP SHEET.

INSTRUMENT SCHEDULE— A vintage list in instrument number order that was used in conjunction with the Light Plot to read out all the details about each instrument. Now this information is usually contained on the plot.

INSTRUMENTS (British: *lanterns*)— A light-producing device used to light the stage as either an arealight or a special.

All instruments consist of up to four principle parts: the housing, the lamp assembly, the reflector, and the lens system. The housing protects the delicate lamp from impact, prevents light spilling onto surrounding areas, and provides a means to mount the instrument on a pipe and aim it in the correct direction. It may also have shutters or barndoor-type flippers to keep light off things that no one wants to see lit or these may be one or more add-on accessories. The lamp assembly consists of a socket, cord and connector and, of course, the lamp. The reflector captures light spilling backward that would otherwise be absorbed by the housing and transformed into heat, and it reflects that light out the front. The lens system (where one exists) is designed to bend the light and concentrate it into a smaller area, thereby lighting less area but lighting it more brightly.

Instruments fall more-or-less into two general classes depending on whether they have a lens system or not. Sealed beam units where the lens is part of the lamp fall into a gray area somewhere in between. The parcans tend to be considered as lensed instruments and striplights using sealed beam lights are usually considered in the lens-less category.

Lensed Instruments

Louis Hartmann simply called them *lenses*, but they are most often referred to as *theatre spotlights*. In today's inventory, the stars of the show are the fresnels and ellipsoidals, but we'll start with their predecessor, the plano-convex spotlights.

Plano-convex Instruments: The big ones were called *hoods* (named after the housing which was called the hood portion of the instrument) and the little ones (usually less than 500 watts) were called *baby spots*. Lensed instruments had not existed in the era of gaslight. They

came into being with the development of carbon arc technology, first used at the Paris Opera in 1846 but not used again there (or elsewhere) until 1860 and not in common usage until at least 1880. Since they required an operator, they are mostly thought of as followspots and will be discussed later. Once the arc light mechanism was removed and replaced by an incandescent lamp, they became plano-convex instruments. Thomas Edison invented the first incandescent lamp in 1879 using carbonized bamboo fibers for the filament. It wasn't until 1905 that metallized filaments were developed that enabled the light to be brighter and the lamp to be more durable. The first baby spot was introduced by Kliegl Bros in 1906. It had a 100 cp screw-in lamp and a 5" lens and was at least as large as a modern ellipsoidal. It had a spherical reflector attached to the back of the lamp carriage and the whole carriage moved to and from the lens. When it was at the focal length of the lens, an image of the lamp filament was projected onto the stage and the rays of light were most nearly parallel. As the lamp carriage was slid closer to the lens, the area of coverage increased and the image of the filament became fuzzier. The lens could also be removed to create a lenseless floodlight. These instruments had three basic problems that limited their usefulness.

First, they badly needed to be brighter but brighter lamps created more heat and this shortened lamp life and cracked lenses. Second, there was the problem of the filament image, and it was not immediately obvious how this could ever be overcome. Third, the rays of light that passed through the center

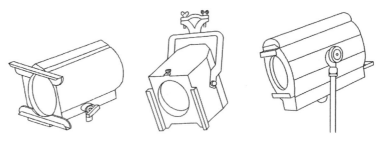

Left: **Baby Spot 1906;** *middle:* **Baby spot 1936;** *right:* **Hood 1920**

of the lens did not get bent at all but they were bent increasingly as they approached the edge of the lens, and at the very edge they bent the light so much that the various wavelengths of light bent differently as occurs with a prism. This resulted in uneven color rings at the outside of the light beam (chromatic aberrations) and it was unclear what could be done about this. Tungsten filaments were first used in pressed form in 1907 and this made it possible to produce lamps up to 500 watts. In 1911 tungsten filaments drawn out like a wire were developed and by 1913 the first 750 and 1000-watt lamps were made. The hoods became larger to accommodate the larger lamps, but none of the essential problems had been solved nor would they be solved for almost another 20 years.

Fresnels: The fresnels are usually described as baby spots that have been given a new lens, and up to a point this is accurate except that two other improvements were made at about the same time, which became incorporated into them. In 1930 the first bi-plane lamp was invented along with the first bi-post lamp base to keep it aligned properly with the reflector. The medium pre-focus base soon followed. Also in 1935 the Alzak process was invented for aluminum that made it shiny and suitable for reflectors. Although fresnel-type lenses were used as early as the late 1920s, it wasn't until 1936 that a full range of fresnels in wattages from 250 to 5000 watts became available.

Fresnel

The fresnel lens itself had been developed in 1822 for use in lighthouses and had been named after its inventor, Augustin Jean Fresnel. The fresnel lens took advantage of the principle that it was the curve of the glass rather than its thickness that controlled how much the light would bend. This allowed the lenses to be thinner and to have rings of the correct curvature and to be cast rather than

ground. The thinner lenses solved the lens cracking problem, and since the lamp was located forward of the focal point of the lens, there was no problem with an image of the filament of the lamp being projected onto the stage or of there being color rings. Fresnels have spherical reflectors mounted at the back of the lamp carriage and the lamp carriage moves forward and back from the fixed lens position to increase or decrease the size of the beam within a range of about 10–60 degrees. They produce a soft-edged light that blends well. To further control the light, add-on accessories like a barndoor or tophat can be put in the gel slot.

Beam Projectors (British: *pageant lanterns* or *beam lights*): They don't have a lens anymore but at one time they did have a very small central lens (now typically replaced by a blinder or small spherical reflector). They were the first long range lighting instrument and as such were a forerunner of the ellipsoidal, which will be discussed next. The beam projectors have spill rings rather than a lens, and they block (either by means of the black disk mentioned above or more commonly by a small spherical reflector) any direct light from the light source so that all the light pro-

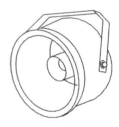

Beam projector

duced is reflected from the parabolic reflector itself, which when the lamp is at the focal point produces parallel (nearly parallel) rays of light. They are used today for the huge searchlights that can be seen at fairs or public events lighting up the sky, but they have fallen out of favor in the theatre for reasons that will be described next.

They date back to 1906 when they contained an arc light mechanism and were called *gallery reflectors*, and as the name implies they were operated from the balcony. In 1916, they were converted for the first time to use the new 1000-watt lamp and were called *Caliban floods* (named after the show in which they first appeared which was a production of *Caliban* at the stadium of the College of the City of New York). It is unclear at what point they began to be called beam projectors, but they are listed as such in the 1948 Century Lighting Co catalog. Theodore Fuchs in 1929 describes the way the reflectors work and says that this kind of reflector is used in searchlights and floods that need to be projected from a long distance like at an "outdoor pageant" and Hunton D. Sellman in 1930 refers to them as *parabolic floods*. They typically have an adjustment that moves the lamp carriage with blinder and spill rings into or out of focus in relation to the parabolic reflector, which has the effect of making the light diverge slightly and appear fuzzier and more uneven in texture. They produce nearly parallel beams of light (as if from the sun or moon) in a way that no other instrument can duplicate. They also are extraordinarily bright partially because the beam is so narrow and partially because there are no losses from a lens system. At one time they were used from the front-of-house to light the front of the stage, but they fell out of favor after ellipsoidals came into common usage because the ellipsoidals, which cost only slightly more, could cover any given area more evenly and with fewer instruments, did not require as large a gel (they typically have 10–20" faces), and were more versatile, so for the most part they have now been dropped from the lighting catalogs.

Ellipsoidals (British: *profile spots*): These more-or-less date back to 1932 when a pinhole downlight with a G-type 400 watt lamp was used as a houselight at the Center The-

atre, and around this time a similar fixture was manufactured in Europe by A.E.G. Electric Co. Ltd. as an acting area downlight. The advantages of the ellipsoidal reflector were that when the source of light was placed at the near focus point, then all the light hitting the reflector was redirected through the far focus point, and the far focus point (the *gate*) acted as the source of light. The added distance meant that the heat could be dispersed better as it kept the lamp further from the lenses. Since it was the gate that was at the focal point of the lens, there would be no filament image and the gate itself effectively kept light away from the edges of the lens where color rings could be produced. There were two problems, however, involved in producing a theatre spotlight based on this principle. First, it needed a smaller diameter lamp, because a fat lamp could not be placed at the near focal point without its glass envelope hitting the reflector unless the reflector was really large, which explains the huge size of the early instruments. Second, the fresnel had dissipated heat by providing vent holes in the top and back behind the reflector, but the ellipsoidal reflector completely encircled the lamp (except at the front) so some kind of chimney would have to be cut at the top back (since heat rises) to vent the instrument. It made sense then to use this same chimney hole as the way to insert the lamp inside the reflector, but this would require a lamp that could burn base up, and neither a thin lamp nor a burn base up lamp had as yet been invented. By the following year, however, 1000, 1500 and 2000-watt burn base up lamps had been developed specifically for use in ellipsoidal instruments. A narrow tubular 500-watt T20 lamp had been developed in 1925, but it was still 2.5" wide. In 1935 a 500 T10 lamp was invented, which was only 1.25" wide. The early ellipsoidals were huge instruments (as big if not bigger than a modern day followspot) and they were typically equipped with a step lens, and it was unclear where to put them or what specifically to use them for.

Sometime in the 1940s Edward Kook and

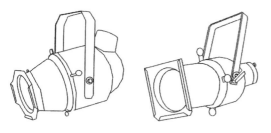

Left: Ellipsoidal, circa 1940; **right:** Ellipsoidal, circa 1970

Joseph Levy of the Century Lighting Co developed the first truly compact version of the ellipsoidal, which they named after themselves and called the *lekolight* or *leko* for short, and these instruments became enormously popular. The 1948 Century Lighting Co catalog listed a traditional model that was 32" long, 19" wide with either an 8 · 7.5 fresnel lens or an 8 · 10 PC lens that took a 1000 T24 or 1500 T24 or 2000 T30 burn base up lamp. In addition there were three more compact models:

8" model that was 27" long and 12" wide with lenses as above that used a 100 T10 or a 250 T12 or a 500 T12 lamp

6" model that was 16" long and 9.5" wide with two 6 · 9 lenses and used the same lamps as mentioned above, i.e. 100, 250 and 500.

4.5" model that was 14" long and 10" wide with two 4.5 · 6.5 lenses (or a fresnel lens) and used the same lamps as the above.

Most of these models could be purchased with one of three accessory packages, either with (1) just the four framing shutters and three separate gate reducers or (2) with "vertical and horizontal shutters individually operated with a swivel device for oblique shaping" or (3) with an iris and follow handle. Gobo slots did not come into common usage until the 1960s.

In the 1970s, the development of really small diameter lamps with compact spiral filaments made it possible to axially mount the lamps (push them in from the center back). This resulted in a much smaller hole in the reflector and a brighter, more even light. It became possible at this point to make even smaller ellipsoidal instruments in the 300, 400, 500, 650 watt and under 10 lb category with typically a 3.5" lens, but they were for the most part disappointingly dim, producing only about half the light of their larger counterparts with the same wattage lamp. In the 1980s Berkey Colortran invented the Mini-ellipse, and it was a small instrument that produced a big light. It had a rectangular body and weighed in at just under 9 lbs. It used an axially mounted mini-

can screw base lamp whose socket is one of the most maintenance-free of all time. It provided joystick lamp centering and an easy way to run the lamp inward and outward in relation to the reflector, and it had two lenses of unequal focal lengths (4.5 · 9 and 4.5 · 6.5). The fat lens was closest to the gate. The thinner lens had three preset slots it could fit into making the field angle of the instrument 50, 40, or 30 degrees and by putting the thin lens in its 30 degree position and removing the fat lens, an approximately 20 degree instrument could be created. While the instrument was only rated for a 250, 400, or 500-watt lamp, there was a 750-watt lamp that was often used without a problem. It was an enormously popular instrument because it was light to move around and a lot of them could be put in a crowded space. In the 1990s the 575-watt lamps like the HPL and FLK were developed and they produced a whiter light than that produced by the Minis. Rotating barrels were also developed that allowed the shutters to be better aligned with the set, which was particularly important when the light was coming in from a diagonal, and joystick lamp-centering became standard and the gobo slots became wider to accommodate drop-in accessories like irises or gobo rotators.

Zoom Ellipsoidals: These have been available since the 1970s and are based on changing the distance between the lenses of the objective system. While different field angles can be obtained by dropping the lenses in different slots as has been described relative to the Mini-ellipse, a true zoom does this in an infinitely variable way using two sliding carriage mechanisms that changes the positions of both lenses. Zoom instruments have always been substantially more expensive. Typically five fixed lens instruments can be bought for the price of three zooms. Also the optics at any given size never seem as bright or sharp as those of their fixed lens counterparts. As a result, they are not as common as one might suppose that they ought to be.

Followspots: Limelight and carbon arc technology preceded the invention of the incandescent light, so followspots have been in common use since about 1860 in Great Britain and somewhat later here in America. Since they required an operator, they were used to follow the speaking actors around the stage, and this continued in some places well in the 1930s.

Followspot

When fresnels came into common usage in the early 1930s, they could light the stage well enough so that the followspots were not needed for illumination, and as a result they fell out of favor. While in a proscenium theatre they are typically operated from a ceiling cove or booth at the back of the house, there is often no place provided for them in a thrust or arena house. This is further complicated by the fact that while a single followspot will work where the audience views only one side of the action, two or three would be required in a thrust or arena situation, and they would have to be positioned so that their light did not fall into the audience section on the opposite side. While it is quite possible to do this at the time the theatre is first designed, it is frequently not possible to provide for it later.

Followspots are still used in musicals and opera and dance and shows on ice. Incandescent technology for the most part has been unable to produce an adequately bright light, so while there are some incandescent followspots for small venues, some kind of arc or encapsulated arc technology still has to be used for large venues. There are many different designs and several kinds of light sources although carbon arc and HMI are probably the most common. They all involve a reflector and a two or three element optical train that zooms and can be put into hard or soft focus. In addition, there is typically a cooling fan, a douser, an iris, and a color boomerang, and the whole thing is mounted on a rolling stand. Even the incandescent

units are generally not rigged to dim, although by putting the fan on a non-dim circuit, they usually can be made to dim. They are all expensive (the non-incandescent ones are exceptionally expensive), and in a small venue where they are not used all that often, an iris and a followspot handle added to a large ellipsoidal is commonly used in their place. When a followspot with a long throw is needed, however, there is no substitute for the real thing, and it simply will not matter that it costs several thousands of dollars.

Parcans: These were based on homemade instruments that were called either *coffee can lights* or *stovepipe lights.* Louis Hartmann certainly made many of the lighting instruments he used. Theodore Fuchs has a long chapter explaining how to make borderlights and olivettes out of wooden boxes lined with metal, and there were other books and articles on the subject in the 1920s and 1930s as part of the Little Theatre movement. With the advent of R type and PAR type lamps in the 1950s, it became even easier to do. The R type lamp was in effect a reflector, lens and filament all combined into one unit with a screw base. It was in effect a spotlight that just needed a way to be aimed. A socket could be mounted in the back of a 3 lb coffee can, a yoke made out of strap iron. Drill a few vent holes, add a cord and plug, and find a pipe clamping device and the job was done. The gel could be taped to the front of the opening. Also one could buy a store display fixture that had a universal joint and could be clamped onto a pipe and already had a cord and plug attached, and these could be purchased with an add-on color assembly

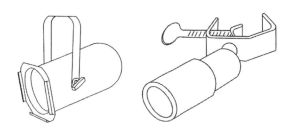

Left: Parcan; *right:* PAR display clamp

that clipped onto the front of a PAR lamp and worked like a mason jar lid in the sense that a threaded ring screwed onto the clip-on accessory trapping the gel in-between.

It was at about this time that local ordinances started requiring that all electrical devices used on stage be UL approved, so Ariel Davis Manufacturing and others began making UL approved coffee can lights. Although it was just an Edison socket (medium screw) at the back of a cylindrical housing, it had the familiar yoke and c-clamp and it came with a gel frame and a gel slot and was legal. Both the PAR 20s and PAR 38s have a medium screw base and could fit in these units. In addition, there are at least three other sizes of PAR lamps (PAR 46, 56, 64) for which parcans have since been made. The parcans are inexpensive, and they don't require any fancy focusing. They typically produce an oval light, so once they are pointed in the right direction, the lamps are rotated so that the oval is twisted until it looks right, and that's as hard as it gets. They have traditionally been more popular with musicians and rock bands than with live theatre technicians because their light quality is uneven and makes the scene look as if it is being lit by automobile headlights, which in a sense it is because automobile headlights are simply a 12 volt version of PAR lights. Parcans were in the past mostly used in the theatre by groups that could not afford anything better, and while the parcan is still less expensive to purchase and operate, the cost difference between it and an inexpensive fresnel is considerably less than it once was, and the fresnel has a significantly better permanent lens and an adjustable beam. Parcans are now being made that don't use PAR lamps at all but instead have a separate reflector and lens and a separate lamp that simulates the effect of the PAR light. There is also at least one brand of retrofit kit (Raylights™) that will do something similar for existing parcan units, the advantage being that one doesn't throw the reflector away at every lamp change.

Lenseless Instruments

Borderlights: When the incandescent lamp was first invented (1879), the first commercially produced lamps were screw-in type, 16 cp lamps. These were placed in the long troughs above the stage where the gas jets (and candles before that) had been. Within a few years a 32 cp lamp had been developed. The lamps could be colored with lamp dip, which was really the first time that the light source had been cool enough to color without using mica or some other high heat material. This open trough style of borderlight was still being sold well into the 1960s and may even still be available today as a special order item.

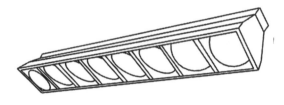

Borderlight

There were however four improvements that occurred in the early 1900s. First, reflectors were put behind the lamps and this may have occurred as early as 1897 with the introduction of the X-ray units. They were at some early point divided into compartments. This would have come about as a result of lamps brighter than 32 cp that burned off the lamp dip and so had to be put in compartments with gel used in slots in front. There was certainly a 100 cp lamp by 1906, so this probably occurred around the same time or a bit earlier. Then around 1911 or perhaps earlier, Munro R. Pevear introduced the three-circuit wiring pattern. Also around that time, the long continuous units started being broken into 6–8' units (striplights) that could be used as borderlights or cyclights or cyc foots as required. There were also short sections 2–3' long called *backing strips* that were intended to be hung over a door or window to light the backing scenery.

Footlights: Everything said of borderlights applies equally to the footlights, which operated on the same principle. Borderlights, however, usually point either straight down or down and slightly toward upstage at perhaps a 60 degree angle. Footlights are intended to point upward at about a 45 degree angle, but should the tops of the light bulbs point upward or should it be the side of the lamp that points upward? There are more than a dozen photographs of vintage footlights and borderlights in Theodore Fuch's book, and it was tried every way it could be tried including having the lamps point toward the audience and being intercepted by a curved diffuse reflector that threw the light indirectly back onto the stage. There were double rowed footlights (and borderlights). There were various designs of footlights that either pivoted back into a closed position or could be removed and the floor closed-over flat behind them. There is a picture of a removable unit borderlight where each compartment could be removed and used separately as a floodlight. David Belasco is known to have intensely disliked borderlights of all kinds, and although there are footlights indicated on Louis Hartmann's Light Plot for the 1906 production of *Rose of the Ranchero*, there are no borderlights.

Once they were the primary location for getting light on the actors' faces, but they have now fallen into disuse since the advent of theatre spotlights like the fresnels and ellipsoidals. They still remain the only viable way to get light in under wide hat brims and into the actors' eye-sockets to counter the effect of raccoon eyes.

It should be said in their defense that they were never placed in their ideal location. They should have been mounted inside and at the top of the wall that separates the first row of the audience from the musicians' orchestra pit (pit wall). Had that been done, the light could have traveled over the heads of the musicians to the stage some 8–12 feet away.

The actors then could have moved all the way to the edge of the stage without their ankles being brightly lit, which was the first

(and least fixable) of five complaints that had to do with the footlights.

Second, it was said that they came from an unnatural angle (like holding a flashlight under your chin). This was not entirely true. They came from the direction of bounce light that is encountered in everyday life. The unnatural look was caused by them being too bright relative to the lights coming from above.

Third, it was said they created giant shadows of the actors on whatever scenery was behind them. Again, they only did this when they were too bright. At low levels they provide a wonderfully low-level of fill light.

Fourth, it was said that they stuck up above the floor and were ugly to look at. Many of them did stick up about 3", but whether this should be objectionable or not is debatable. In any event for those offended by this, there were plenty of brands or styles that were totally recessed.

Fifth, they were wired in three circuits and there was, of course, objectionable veeing caused by the use of red, green and blue lamps. Had the lamps all been some variant of white, this would not have been a problem.

None of this matters anymore because footlights are simply not being installed in new theatres. It is not immediately apparent how they could be used in thrust and other non-proscenium theatres because there is the fear that they would shine in the eyes of audience members who sat on the sides.

Both Louis Hartmann and Stanley McCandless eloquently defended them and said that any system of lighting that did not include them would be less effective and less versatile, but Adolphe Appia had declared them a monstrosity, and so having (or using) footlights became a kind of litmus test for how modern and up-to-date one was, much as Light Plots drawn in CAD are now a litmus test for the same thing.

Floodlights: It is easiest to think of these as one compartment of a borderlight that is used alone. The earliest kind of floodlight was probably the open box arc, which as the

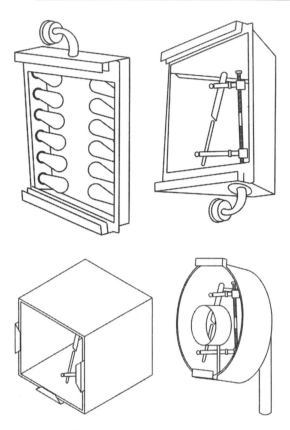

Top, left: Bunchlight; *top, right:* Olivette 1900; *bottom, left:* Open box arc; *bottom right:* Gallery reflector

simply replaced by one big light bulb. 500-watt light lamps were available by 1907, and 750 and 1000-watt lamps became generally available in 1916.

Floods had originally been used to light the cyc or a drop and on stands backstage to provide light that could come in through door and window openings. With the advent of the fresnels that were more compact and could be controlled better, the floods began to be used almost exclusively for drop and cyc lighting. They were particularly useful for lighting a curved cyc, as striplights did not turn corners well. By 1948 Century Lighting Co was manufacturing a line of scoops with spun aluminum ellipsoidal (or parabolic) reflectors called Wizardlites in three sizes handling lamps from 75–1500 watts. Scoops are still in use today, but they require a large piece of gel. Thanks to improved double-ended lamp technology, it is possible to approximate their coverage with more compact units that are about a quarter to an eighth the size. Yardlights are available at home improvement stores for less than $10 apiece in wattages from 150 to 500 and are now used extensively in the theatre as work-

name implies was a metal box painted white with an arc light mechanism inside that required an operator. The early olivettes (1881) were a distinctive trapezoidal shape of open box arc and Louis Hartmann used four of them in the 1906 production of **Rose of the Ranchero**. The *gallery reflectors*, described earlier, were essentially an open box arc with a parabolic reflector, but because of their narrow beam they behaved more like a lensed instrument than a floodlight, which we tend to expect to spread out and flood an area with light.

The first floodlight that did not require an operator was the bunchlight. This was based on a gas jet version of the bunchlight but can be thought of an open box arc where the arc light mechanism has been replaced by lots of light bulbs. When lamp technology provided larger lamps, the many small light bulbs were

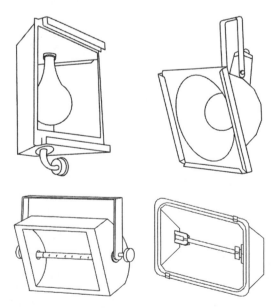

Top, left: Olivette 1000 w lamp; *top, right:* Scoop 1950; *bottom, left:* Cyclight 1980; *bottom right:* Yardlight

lights and small floodlights for backings and enclosed alcoves that are hard to get conventional lights into. In addition, there are now many theatrical versions in wattages from 100 to 2000 and these units are often sold as single units or cells that are intended to be combined into 2, 3 or 4-celled units.

INSTRUMENTS-PER-AREA— Once an area size has been determined, the question becomes one of how many instruments it will take to light it, based on how many sides the area will be viewed from. The rule of thumb is that areas behind the proscenium line need to be lit by three instruments per area coming from 45 degrees left and 45 degrees right and from the direct back (180 degrees) on the golden ring. Where a backlight is not possible, this means just the two lights from the front sides. Areas downstage of the proscenium will need to be lit by four instruments per area. This whole subject of how many instruments-per-area are needed is a hotly disputed issue, so each individual designer needs to decide for himself how best to light something. See LIGHTING AN OBJECT OR AREA for a more detailed discussion.

INSULATED GATE BIPOLAR TRANSISTOR DIMMERS (Abbr. IGBT)— A modern electronic dimmer technology based on the gating principle that is different from (and competes with) SCR technology. See LIGHTING CONTROL for a more detailed discussion.

INSULATOR— A non-conducting (dielectric) material like rubber that insulates rather than conducts electricity.

INTEGRATING THE LIGHTS (into the show)— The question is, once the lights have been focused, how are the cues created and worked into the run of the show?

In the old days, back before there were paper techs or dry techs when 24 dimmers were considered more than adequate, the director started rehearsing on stage as soon as the set was in place and the lights had been focused, and yes, time was in very short sup-

ply then as well. The lighting person (there were no designers back then) brought up the arealights to some general level and adjusted it from there and wrote down what she'd done as the scene progressed. At the end of each scene, the stage manager would announce that the lights were going down; so the lighting person would take them down and bring them back up to a general level for the next scene and would adjust them as she had done before and continue in this way to write cues on the fly. If the director didn't like what she saw, she'd either yell over the sound of the ongoing rehearsal or would make a note.

It was often difficult, however, for the director to tell if what she was seeing on stage was a finished cue or a work in progress and even harder to determine what percentage of the show might have been finalized (was never going to get better) by the end of any rehearsal. Often when lights changed, it was not clear whether this was a deliberate cue or just the lighting designer doing a level adjustment to the previous cue.

A dry tech was invented so that the light cues could be roughed-in ahead of time and approved by the director before being put into the show. Typically the cues would already have been numbered and located in the stage manager's book, and the speed of the cue would have been decided upon, and it would be generally known what the cue was supposed to do. Everyone understood that getting two hands to operate 20 or more dimmer handles involved complicated manual maneuvers that only got better with practice; so the timings were discussed but were not part of the dry tech. The primary purpose of the dry tech was to view the completed cues. With only 20 or so dimmers, it was possible to create most cues in under a minute. Since each cue had to be manually set, it was common to skip cues that were repeats of something that had already been seen and approved. The whole thing was only expected to take an hour, two at most (certainly less than the running time of the complete show). Everyone understood that levels set on an empty stage would have to be adjusted once they were tried out with the real actors, but it was thought that roughing them in ahead of time would save valuable stage time later, and it usually did.

The invention of the computer lightboard changed much of this. It could operate hundreds of dimmers or channels at once and did not need to practice in order to get better. No presets had to be manually reset anymore; so it could do sequences of cues in rapid succession. The speed of cues could be programmed once and they would remain the same until deliberately changed. Cues that repeated could be copied and given a new cue number. Much of the "writing down" of the cues had been eliminated because the board recorded cues at the push of a button.

Dry techs, however, despite the elimination of much of the scribe work, now no longer worked out as well as they had before because the director was having to wait while the lighting designer manipulated 100 or more channels. Instead of just seeing the main cues, the director now wanted to see the whole show from beginning to end including the blackouts and all the repeats, and she wanted to see all the cues run at the speed they would run in the show. From the point of view of the lighting designer, there were now many more cues, many more channels that had to be set, all the timings had to be set, and the director wanted to see everything. It was no longer possible to set cues while she waited unless she was prepared to wait a good long time. Cues could take several minutes to set, and complicated sequences or effects could often take more than an hour to work through. Timings had to be tried over and over again before they began to look right.

From the director's point of view, she had arrived on time ready to see some cues, but instead the lighting designer seemed lost in her paperwork and did not appear to know where anything was, and it took forever to arrive at the first cue setting; and even though the director approved it instantly, it still took forever to get to the second cue. So some four to six hours later the director and stage manager, and whoever else happened to have been there, would leave the theatre frustrated and unhappy. The lighting designer would also leave frustrated and unhappy because she had been forced to try to improvise cues on the spur of the moment without having had a chance to try out any other possibilities because she had felt rushed by everyone else being there.

It became increasingly apparent that the lighting designer needed to have a separate cue-setting session all by herself (or alone with the board operator). Then the dry tech, as a separate session, could start at the top of the show and the director could view the cues in sequence and run at their programmed time. The dry tech could theoretically occur during the last hour or so of this cue-setting session, but as this was likely to be at some unpredictable late hour of the night, it often made more sense to schedule the dry tech for another time, like the next day.

Although the dry tech is often still scheduled as the next work session after the cue-setting session, there are good reasons for scheduling it even later than this. The dry tech is really the only session at which the lighting designer and the director will get to discuss the way the cues look and neither one will yet have seen the cues played back on the faces of the actors.

Much of what typically goes on in a dry tech (when it comes directly after the cue-setting session) is a complete waste of time because everyone is looking at the cues as they hit the floor, and watching the timings as they imagine what the actors might be doing at that point. Most of these cues are going to change dramatically once the actors get on stage. Sometimes production assistants are brought in to walk around (*walkers*), but this just makes the whole process take all that much longer and the walkers are not the same height as the actors, do not have the same skin coloration, are not in costume, and do not stand in the same places on stage as the actors will.

When the furniture is placed for the first time on stage, do they lay down the final show spikes for it on the floor? No, of course not because they know that in the rehearsal process the furniture is likely to get moved around as different placements are experimented with. Are the light cues any more likely to be perfect when they are tried out for the first time or do they also need to be experimented with?

What has often been found to work the best is to let the director begin rehearsing as soon as the level-setting session is complete. This is what is commonly called a *rehearsal-with-light* and there will usually be two of these, for reasons that will be explained shortly. The actors rehearse on stage using the set and props and whatever costume pieces are available, and the lighting designer provides stage light instead of worklight. The cast is assured that the light that is being provided is not necessarily what the cue for that particular scene will actually be, so they (the actors) should ignore the lights and do whatever they have been rehearsed to do and the lighting designer will try to catch up as best she can. Everyone is assured that for safety reasons there will be no blackouts. What will be done instead is either temporarily set the blackouts to *blue-outs* or a submaster will be brought up at the same time as the blackout so that it doesn't really go dark.

The lighting designer has already roughed-in the cues. All she needs to do is play them back and adjust them as the scene progresses. Every time they repeat a scene, she gets to try out the timings again. If someone is standing in the dark, it will be obvious, and she will either bring up more light or make a note (to be discussed with the director) that the actor should stand where the light is. It is a nearly perfect situation. The cast gets to rehearse the entire time without ever stopping for lights. The lighting designer gets to work the entire time using the actual actors as the models as she builds and refines the cues.

At the end of the rehearsal, she will have a long list of ladder work that needs to be done

before the next rehearsal. This typically involves focus adjustments and color changes and can involve whole systems of light being dedicated to a new purpose. All of this is going to change the cues. Some of the changes can be roughed-in blind but some will have to be done as she sees each scene again. This is why a 2nd rehearsal-with-light is needed. The lighting designer needs to see the effect of the major changes she has made and needs to further refine the cues before they are ready to be shown to the director.

Now (after the second rehearsal-with-lights) is an optimum time to have the dry tech because both the lighting designer and the director have already seen all these cues in the actual context of the scenes. Even if the director were not paying any attention to the lights, she would have remembered if they had been totally wrong, as sometimes they are. The lighting designer can talk intelligently about which specials may need to be moved and those places where the actors and the lights are in different places and whether timings need to be changed. Seeing the cues in sequence reminds everyone of what it looked like before in the previous rehearsal. The lighting designer will already have seen the various problems and had an opportunity to try various solutions. She may have discovered that there is just no way to get light into some particularly dark corner of the stage without creating a worse problem somewhere else. She's tried several solutions but they have not resolved the problem. Now she can discuss what other alternatives may exist.

On level-setting night, the lighting designer had not worked with the design before. She did not know which channel was responsible for that light over there. Now some two days later, she knows exactly what the design will do and what its limitations are and what every channel's contribution is. Now is the time that a discussion with the director will be most productive and move the process ahead the fastest.

Integrating the lights into the show is but a small part of integrating all the technical elements into the show. There are two general methods of doing this: the *zero tolerance method* and the *gradual method*.

The actors will have been rehearsing in a rehearsal room with rehearsal props and rehearsal furniture and a make-believe set. There are typically five technical elements that need to be introduced: set, props, lights, sound and costumes (which is taken to include make-up and wigs, etc). While the actors actually touch and work with the sets, props and costumes, the lights and sound are generally timed to what they are doing. The number of light or sound cues that require some kind of interaction from the actors (like turning on a light switch or playing a phonograph record) are few and far between. So while there is sometimes talk about introducing the technical elements gradually, it is unclear how that could be accomplished. It would be strange to attempt to separate the use of the set from the use of the props since the props are usually on (or right behind) the set. The costumes are by tradition already separated so that they are added last when most of the good opportunities to dirty and destroy them have passed. The lights and sound, as just pointed out, can pretty much be integrated independently at any time.

In the *zero tolerance method*, which is historically the older and more traditional method, the rehearsal is stopped every time something does not work as it should. It can take 8–10 hours to work through a single act in this way. The next time this act is rehearsed, which may be two days later, the expectation is that it will be perfect. It hardly ever is, and as a result that rehearsal will typically be stopped because "some people" didn't remember what had been done two days ago.

In the *gradual method*, the actors work on the set and with the props (with or without lights or sound cues happening around them) at a speed that essentially they set for themselves. If they do something wrong, they are allowed to back up a few lines and try it over again. If they forget to pick up their prop or can't find it, they usually say some-

thing like, "Couldn't find the prop" and keep on going. The guiding principle here is to keep on going wherever possible, take notes wherever possible and to not overload the actors with all the information at this one session. The director still stops to correct major problems, but usually the whole show can be gotten through in a four or five hour session. There is also usually no sense that anyone has let anyone else down, and more time is spent actually rehearsing and less time waiting while a prop is retrieved from the wings.

INTELLIGENT LIGHTS— Sometimes colloquially called *wigglies* or *wiggly mirror lights*. These are remotely controlled instruments that typically work off a DMX signal and are controlled by eight (give or take) channels on the lightboard where their movement can be pre-recorded and played back. These instruments usually shine their light onto an external mirror whose pan and tilt and focus can then be controlled. Color can often be controlled by means of either a scroller or boomerang mechanism or by means of dichroic filters. Pattern and pattern rotation can often be controlled too, but not the actual instrument location. They are heavily used in rock concerts where initial costs are not a problem and where batteries of lights need to move and be synchronized to the music. As yet, they have not found much of a foothold in live theatre presentations because it is still considerably less expensive and more flexible to buy several manual instruments rather than to invest in one intelligent light. In a rock concert however, it effectively eliminates 20 or more followspot operators, who would otherwise have to have been rehearsed and paid by the hour and who as a group might never achieve the precision of the machine. Also these lights can be placed in locations that couldn't accommodate operators. Once the lights have been timed to the music, then the performers and the music (when done live) are timed to the lights. They are also sometimes called *moving lights* or *automated fixtures*, but both these terms were used to refer to the older motorized yoke instruments, and this new generation of equipment needs a name of its own.

INTENSITY— One of the eight variables of light, it refers to the apparent brightness of a source, and in stage lighting work it is most commonly associated with the 0–100-calibration scale of the channels as controlled by the lightboard. It does however have a specific scientific meaning, which is the light-producing power of a source. It is abbreviated in formulas as "I" and is measured in *candelas* these days.

The intensity of a stage instrument is a product of the lumen output of its lamp combined with the efficiency of the instrument design (i.e. the lens and reflector system). It is measured at an independent lab and is a true measure of how much light came out the front end of the instrument, which is really the only thing that most lighting designers need be concerned with. Using the inverse square law, the illumination at any distance can then be calculated, which determines if the instrument will be bright enough if placed at that distance (design brightness). See VARIABLES OF LIGHT for a more complete discussion of this subject.

INTERACTION OF COLOR— This is another name for *simultaneous contrast*, which is discussed in more detail in COLOR ANOMALIES.

INTERLOCK— (1) This refers to a mechanical interlock between manual dimmers that mechanically masters them. (2) On main disconnects and company switches it refers to a system by which the cover of the electrical box can only be opened when the switch handle is turned off and no electricity flows to the load side.

INTERMEDIATE CANDELABRA— A screw lamp base that is ⅞" in diameter. See *LAMPS* for a more detailed discussion.

IN-THE-AIR— This refers to instruments that are hung in the light hanging positions, usually in the places where they are to be for the current show. The opposite of this is in-storage and not presently being used.

IN-THE-ROUND LIGHTING— See LIGHTING, KINDS OF.

IN-TIME— This is an adverb used in the context of a light cue to mean that it is being run at its programmed speed as had been previously set, not to be confused with *in time*, which is a noun and relates to the uptime of a step.

INTUITIVE METHOD (of Lighting Design)— This is a method for locating instruments on the plot that involves no math or calculations of any kind. It does not even require that one know how high the grid might be. All that is needed is a blank ground plan showing the light hanging positions and a Short Plot or list that assigns a use to each of the available instruments.

Before we continue, be sure you have read AREAS, DIVIDING THE STAGE INTO because it explains why most designers agonize over whether they should have 2 rows of 3 or 3 rows of 4 areas. Should the areas be compressed? Should they end on full circles or half circles? By doing it one way or the other, two or three instruments could be saved for some other purpose. Where more specials are needed, they almost always come from a clever consolidation of the arealighting.

Those who practice the intuitive method will not be bothered by such seemingly trivial problems because they will take a look at the stage and pick a number that they think represents how many areas it would take to cover it, and that will be as hard as that part of it ever gets.

It should be pointed out that those who practice the intuitive method typically do not know how to do lighting calculations, they also are usually not interested in learning how, nor are they interested in learning how to program a computer to do the math for them, and they do not want to buy someone else's computer program that would do it for them. In fact, they don't think any calculations are necessary, or at least not necessary for them. They are artists who have talent, not some kind of bean-counting technocrat who has to do scale drawings and calculations on a pocket calculator.

They have worked in a lot of different theatres before (probably true), and they've used most of the instruments that this theatre owns at one time or another (which also may be true), and they have developed a sense of how they will work in different situations (yet to be demonstrated).

In any event, having decided how many areas there will be, they stand on the stage and look up at the hanging positions with a blank light plot in their hands. They imagine what the set will look like around them as they stand in area "1" and point to the place where they want the frontlight to come from. They mark this on the blank ground plan. Now they point to the sidelights and the backlight, and note it all down. Then they move on to area 2, and so forth. They do all the area systems this way and then their washes and then their specials. They take this marked-up ground plan home, recopy it neatly and assign colors, circuits and the rest of the usual information for the Light Plot, and they are done. They did not need to know how high the grid was because they pointed to the golden ring positions (held their arm up at 45 degrees in one or more directions).

To a certain extent all lighting designers use the intuitive method on shows done in familiar circumstances. They know where they put the arealights last time. Within broad limits that's where they plan to put the arealights this time. Since it worked out well, there's no point in refiguring it all since the instruments being used will be the same and the throw distances will be the same even if the exact positions and angles may be slightly different.

The real test is whether one can visualize all that familiar equipment being used in someone else's theatre. Few people can, but it is quite easy to devise a test to see who is amongst the chosen few and who is not. This is a hugely important issue because most of the lighting literature written post-Stanley McCandless has suggested that math or calculations were not necessary, and in this regard they have not done a service to their readers because the intuitive method works for most people about as well as putting the textbook under the pillow on the night before the big test.

To understand this better, let's consider it from a different point-of-view. Let's imagine that you have used the intuitive method and here we all are on focusing night. You've focused all the instruments and now we've turned on the arealights and someone is walking around from area to area, and it is rapidly becoming apparent that you have a problem because they (the walkers) are bright at the center of the areas but dim inbetween areas. You have clearly placed the instruments too far apart from each other, and this is a very serious and labor-intensive error to fix (usually unfixable due to time constraints).

You only get one chance to light the show. If you guess wrong, the show won't look the way you intended, and even if you knew what you did wrong, there won't be enough time to correct it, certainly not enough time to rehang 50 or 60 arealights.

They are counting on you having the technical know-how to produce the effects you have described. Do they expect you to be able to predict how this or that instrument will perform when placed in a certain location? Indeed they do; in fact it is your job or at least part of your job. You say you can light the entire front of the stage with 4 instruments. Is that a mere guess? Or is that a statement of fact? See LIGHTING CALCULATIONS for the method that works every time and does not rely on intuitive powers that not everyone has.

INVENTORY—This typically is prepared by the master electrician and lists the lighting equipment that the theatre owns. It always includes lighting instruments, but often includes cables, adapters, barndoors and accessories, and gobo patterns. It usually explains the logic of where the circuits are located and may include information about the lightboard. It is intended to contain all the information that a new lighting designer would want to ask and to prevent the new lighting designer from using submaster nrs 9 and 10 for some other purpose if they are always by tradition used as the houselight faders.

INVERSE SQUARE LAW — There is both the simplified formula and the more complete version (Lambert's cosine law). The simple one is $E = I/d^2$ where E = illumination in footcandles, where I = the intensity of the source in candelas and where d = the throw distance in feet. Let's say one has a 50 degree Source Four ellipsoidal. When its intensity (sometimes called *peak candlepower*) is looked up, it is found to be 32,000. The question is at a throw distance of 20', how much illumination will be produced (32,000/20 * 20 = 80 fc), which most designers would consider too dim as 100 fc is usually taken to be the minimum *design brightness* necessary since it is going to be reduced about 50 percent by a gel and an additional 30 percent based on its angle of incidence, which will be explained next.

The inverse square law ($E = I/d^2$) was conceived with the notion that the point source of light was at the center of a sphere and the E (fc) measurements were being taken on the surface of the sphere so each ray of light hit the sphere at an angle perpendicular to that point on the sphere (perpendicular to a plane tangent at that point to be more exact) and the distance was always constant (radius of the sphere). When we discuss light hitting flat surfaces, we are obliged to take into consideration the increased distance due to the fact that the surface is not curved.

Imagine that there is an actor onstage and her head is cube-shaped. With the light coming directly from above, we would say the top of her head was getting all the light and the front of her face was getting none. If we were to slowly rotate the lighting instrument position out toward the front eyelevel posi-

tion, the top of her head would get less light and the front of her face would get more until the instrument was at eyelevel front, at which point the face has all the light and the top has none. The light is always brightest when it hits a surface at the perpendicular (normal).

Still using the downlight as an example, when the actor moves to the back edge of the lit area, the light is hitting at a slight angle (called the angle of incidence) and this is providing better light on her face but less on the top of her head. E measurements are made in reference to light coming from a particular direction and the complete formula (seldom given) is $E = I/d^2 * \text{Cos}$ where is the angle of incidence (pick a point on the lit surface and run a line normal to the surface and one to the light from that point and the angle between these two lines is the angle of incidence).

In the theatre we deal with vertical surfaces; so the angle of incidence is always the throw angle. The Cos varies between 0 and 1. When the light is perpendicular to the front of faces (eyelevel), the angle is 0 and its Cos is 1. At any other angle, it is less than 1 until at 90 degrees (top-dead-center) it has diminished to 0. So when an actor stands on the edge of a down lit area, the top of her head is always getting less than full light and the near side of her head (face) is always marginally better lit. For a more complete understanding of what the cosine of a number is, read the topic on LIGHTING CALCULATIONS, but for our purposes here all one needs to know is that if you punch in "45" on a scientific pocket calculator and then hit the "Cos" key that the machine will produce a result of 0.7071, which means that from a golden ring position the face is getting about 70 percent of the light.

With this in mind let's return to the previous example of a 32,000 cd instrument at a throw distance of 20' that produced 80 fc of light, but it only produces that if the light is normal to the front of the face, i.e. coming from eyelevel front. At a golden ring front position, the light on the front of the face would be reduced to 57 fc (80 fc * 0.7071 = 56.57), and this has as yet not taken any color into account.

The most common theatrical use for the inverse square law is to determine if a particular instrument will produce enough light at a certain hanging position. First, the throw distance has to be calculated using methods described in LIGHTING CALCULATIONS. Then typically the simplified inverse square law is used to see if the instrument meets some minimum design brightness like 100 fc. If it does, it can be used. If not, another instrument or a brighter lamp or a different location needs to be found.

It is not necessary to do a calculation for every instrument in the show. Usually, a typical frontlight, sidelight, backlight and a representative from whatever other systems there may be are selected. Eight or ten calculations are usually more than enough, less when the instruments tend to be all the same brand with the same lamp, as is often the case.

IRIS— An add-on device that can reduce the circle of light down to a *pinspot*. See AC-CESSORIES for a more detailed discussion.

ISINGLASS— A silicate mineral used to make color media for open flames. See MICA.

ISOLATE TO— See FADES, KINDS OF.

ISOLATION SPECIALS— See SPECIALS, KINDS OF.

IZENOUR DIMMER— Named after George Izenour of Yale University who in the 1940s did the research for this thyratron tube dimmer. See LIGHTING CONTROL, Computer Memory Lightboards for a more detailed discussion.

JACK— This is the female receptacle of a sound or other low voltage line, and although it would have made more gender sense to call it a "jill," that wasn't the way things worked out. The jack is the female and the male is generally called a *plug*.

J-BOX— This is short for *junction box* and can refer to any electrical box in which wires pass whether they are spliced or not. When it refers to boxes that have female pigtails, a *drop box* would be the more common description.

JOYSTICK— A controller that works in two dimensions. In the context of stage lighting, the mechanism that centers the lamp in the reflector usually works on the joystick model. Also, the touch screen on a computer lightboard can work like a joystick to control intelligent lights.

JUICE or JUICER— Slang for electricity or someone on the electrics crew.

JUMPER— A short extension cord where the connectors are usually of the same type. All patch cords are usually called jumpers. All extension cords whether short or long are usually considered to be adapters rather than jumpers, if their connectors are of different types.

JUMP-TO-CUE— This is a computer lightboard term that refers to ending an automatic sequence of cues by loading and going on a designated cue.

JUNCTION BOX— This can refer to any electrical box in which wires pass. When it refers to boxes that have female connectors, a *drop box* would be the more common description.

KELVIN TEMPERATURE— See COLOR TEMPERATURE.

KEY— In the context of a Light Plot, it refers to the *legend* that translates what the symbols mean and usually counts the number of instruments used. This is often done as "4 of 8" to indicate there are 8 in the inventory and 4 are being used in this show. The locations of other information about the instruments are also decoded in the key so that it is clear that a number in front of the lens is a color number and so forth according to the system being used.

KEY LIGHT— This is the light that comes from the presumed source and is directional in nature. Where the audience sits on several sides of the action, the actual directional quality of the light is minimized so that the entire audience thinks they are sitting on a side that isn't in the shade.

KEY SHEET— A plan view drawing of the stage (usually on letter-sized paper) that shows the focus points of the various are-alights and/or the isolation specials. There are usually two versions. The **designer's version** usually includes color numbers and direction arrows along with group or submaster or channel numbers and is used as a memory aid for the designer to remind her of what channels hit what areas from what locations. The **director's version** is simplified and typically includes only the center-point of arealights or specials and includes color names only when they are distinctive and not just some variant of white light.

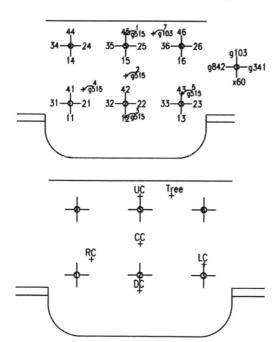

Top: **Designer's keysheet**; *bottom:* **Director's keysheet**

KEYPAD— In the context of a computer keyboard, this refers to the number keys, which are oriented like the numbers on a touch-tone telephone.

KEYSTONING— Another name for TRAPE-ZOIDING.

KICKERS— Scc SHINBUSTERS.

KILL— To turn off.

KILOWATT—1000 watts.

KILOWATT-HOUR—1000 watts per hour. Often this is the standard used to determine an electric bill where it is said that the electricity used was the equivalent of so many hours at 1000 watts/per hour.

KLIEG LIGHT— Although the original Klieg light was an ellipsoidal, the klieg light that made it into the dictionary is a carbon arc searchlight.

KLIEGL BROS.— Established in 1896, it was the earliest American stage lighting manufacturer, serving the needs of such early customers as David Belasco and Flo Ziegfeld. It was founded by Anton and John Kliegl as the Universal Stage Lighting Company but the name was changed to Kliegl Bros. in 1931, and that is the name that for simplicity has been used throughout this book. So when you read that they introduced the first Linnebach projector in 1922 and the first baby spot in 1906, you will understand that it was their company even if the company name at the time was different.

KNIFE BLADE FUSE— A cartridge fuse with flat blades projecting out of both top and bottom, used primarily for high amperage.

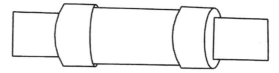

Knife blade cartridge fuse

KNIFE SWITCH—An exposed contact switch that pivoted downward like a paper cutter blade to make contact. They are no longer legal because of the exposed contacts but were once common on old time lightboards to create blackouts of both individual dimmers and the whole board. When the term *switchboard* is used, these are the switches that would have been on it.

KNIGHTS OF THE ROUNDTABLE MODEL— Production meetings are typically based on one of two models, either the *military briefing model* or the *knights of the roundtable model*. See PRODUCTION MEETING for a more detailed discussion.

KNOTS (essential lighting)— A theatre electrician has to tie tools to her body, tie up loose cabling, haul things up-and-down by rope and in some cases suspend trapezes or lighting equipment or add new temporary pipes and lash them into place. All this involves knots, which are listed below in the order of their frequency-of-use. This is by no means a comprehensive list of all the knots that one might encounter in the theatre, but these are the most common, and they all are essential in the sense that they each have a unique purpose.

Working with rope involves its own terminology, which to avoid personal humiliation one needs to learn to use. Most rope is made up of three strands that are twisted spirally around each other in an apparently clockwise direction. This is commonly called either *right-hand laid* rope or *plain-laid* rope, and it is what is typically used in the same way that we expect that turning a bolt or screw to the right will tighten rather than loosen. Plain-laid rope is coiled clockwise and uncoiled counter-clockwise to avoid kinks. The end of the rope that is already attached to something is called the *standing part*. The part that is being worked with is called the *working part*. The middle is called the *bight*. When ropes are tied together to make a longer rope, they are said to be *bent* to each other and a special kind of knot called a *bend* is used. A *hitch* ties a rope to an object like a ring or a batten. To prevent the ends of the rope from unraveling, the ends are *whipped*. Wire or light cordage can be used for this purpose, but the most common method these days is some kind of plastic

(electrical) tape or in some cases a stopper knot. Some knots need to be *worked*, which is to say snugged up carefully or the knot will collapse into some other less desirable knot. The square knot is like that and can collapse into a couple of half hitches. As a result it is not on the list below although it is very common and almost everyone already knows how to tie it (or knows how to tie a granny knot, which is shockingly similar but does not hold quite as well).

The criteria for a good knot used to be that it would be easy to tie and untie and that it needed to be strong. Inasmuch as knots are seriously under-appreciated and under-taught these days, I'm prepared to accept that no one will find any of them easy-to-tie even though I have chosen ones that are. Knots that are hard to untie are however easy to identify because they require an ice-pick-like object called a *fid* to pick them apart. A common overhand knot made with the bight of a rope creates a non-slip loop that is quite strong, but it tightens up in a way that makes it very hard to pick apart.

Knots are confusing because the same knot may have several names and several methods of tying it, and this may not be immediately apparent. In all matters dealing with ropes and knots, I defer to Clifford Ashley's **The Ashley Book of Knots**, which catalogs close to 4000 knots in its 600 pages. Many of these knots have different names. I've used the names most commonly used in theatre. They are in the order that makes them easiest to learn with the simplest and most common knots listed first.

Shoelace Knot (Ashley Nr 1214, 4, 8): There are really three knots here, all based on an *overhand knot*: a *stopper knot*, a *slip loop* and a *bend*. The traditional shoelace knot is a bend as there are two working parts of what amounts to two separate cords (even if they are both part one lace). What is tied first is called an overhand knot. Then a second overhand knot is tied on top of this using the bights rather than the ends of the cords. This results in the bow tie that most of us have on our shoes that have laces on them, and I'm

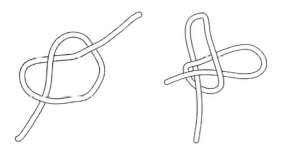

Left: Overhand stopper; *right:* Overhand slip-loop (noose)

Bowline

going to assume that everyone knows how to tie their shoes. This is the knot most commonly used to tie-up loose cabling to the pipes using light cordage called *tie line*, which is often either a braided Venetian blind cord or a three-strand tarred *seining line*. Three strand polypropylene seining line is an amazingly useful product that, when tarred, comes in a black color already and comes in a number of sizes from thin trick line to a medium weight tie line to something about a quarter of an inch thick for suspending equipment. When an overhand knot is tied in the end of a cord, it becomes a stopper knot. On light cordage, a stopper knot is sometimes used in place of whipping the ends. Whenever pulleys of any kind are used, a stopper knot prevents the working end of the rope from running out of the pulley. If a bulkier knot is needed, a **figure-eight knot** (discussed below) can be used. Third, a slip noose can be made by making an overhand stopper-knot that uses the bight rather than the end of the rope or cord. This is used as part of the **trucker's hitch**, which is also described below.

Bowline (Ashley Nr 39): This is a non-slip loop. It is typically what is used on the equipment end of the hauling rope. I first learned how to tie it with the help of a story about a rabbit and a tree. To tie the knot, make a small counter-clockwise coil with the running part (the end closest to you) on top of the standing part. Grab the point at which the ropes cross and twist this a quarter turn away from you (like a wheel rolling away). This makes the first small coil (now hori-

zontal), the "rabbit hole." "The rabbit (running part) came out of her hole and ran around the tree (standing part) and went back down her hole." By grabbing the two trips the rabbit made with one hand and the tree with the other, the knot can be snugged up without collapsing. It may have to be worked a bit to get its size just right. The rabbit traditionally runs around the tree counter-clockwise (making an *inside bowline*), which the **Riggers Handbook** says is marginally stronger than an outside bowline, but both knots will work. The reason it is such a hugely popular knot lies in its strength and in the ease with which it can be untied. It is typically used aloft on rings or around pipes that are so long that it can't slip off their end.

Clove Hitch (Ashley Nr 53): This is a friction knot that tightens as more weight is applied and does not slip. It is typically used on all battens (wood or pipe), and on trapezes of all kinds. It is tied by taking a turn around the pipe by going clockwise (as

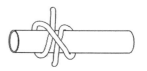

Clove hitch

seen from your right) making sure that the running part crosses the standing part. Take another turn and pass the running end under the standing part of this second turn. The clove hitch is always finished off with two half hitches even though they are not part of the knot itself. If one of the ropes on a trapeze were to break, the free end would then swing downward to point at the floor, but the remaining clove hitch would in most cases apply enough friction to the pipe that it is unlikely that the pipe would slide through the knot to fall to the deck.

Trucker's Hitch (Ashley Nr 4 for the loop, Ashley 2124 for the concept and Ashley 2138 for the tie-off): This is a load-binding knot used to secure equipment inside trucks or to

Trucker's hitch

tie down a load. Basically what is done is a loop is put in the bight of the rope and then the running part is passed around a pipe or ring and passed back through the loop and the slack is adjusted until there is enough tension and two half hitches then lock down the running end on the loop. The loop could have been a bowline tied in the bight or an artilleryman's loop and the knot would work as well, but in this case a simple overhand slip loop is used (be sure it is formed using the bight of the *running* end so that by pulling the running end the knot will collapse as doing it with the bight of the standing part will not keep the loop open).

Double-Sheet Bend (Ashley Nr 1434): This is used to bend two ropes together whether they are the same diameter or not. To tie it, fold the bigger rope back on itself forming a loop, bend this horizontally to form a rabbit hole. Bring the second working end out of the hole, go around the tree twice starting high and tuck the running end low under the part that came out of the rabbit hole. The knot is then carefully worked snug.

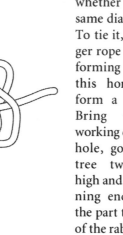

Double-sheet bend

Tie-Off Knot (Ashley Nr 1611, 1614): This is used to tie-off to a belaying pin on a pinrail. The rope comes from above and is wrapped clockwise around the lower pin and counter-clockwise around the upper pin,

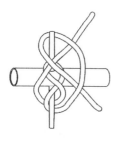

Tie-off knot

then clockwise around the lower pin again and then a loop in created in the running part such that the running part is behind the standing part, and this loop is passed over the top pin and snugged down. The remaining rope is neatly coiled in a clockwise direction and laid over the top pin. If there is too much extra rope for this, then an alternative is to reach through the coils and grabs the standing part of the rope (between the tie-off knot and the coils and to pull it under the coils and over the pin). Where a pinrail does not exist, a trucker's hitch can be used around a pipe or an audience seat in the house or anything else that is securely fastened down.

Sunday Knot (Ashley Nr 1412): Sundays are rope loops usually about 8–10 inches in diameter used to temporarily attach a dog-clip to something like the handle of a pail or to attach the hauling rope pulley to the grid or a ladder rung. When you pass a rope loop through the ring on the end of a pulley and then pass the other end of the sunday through this loop, the result is called a **ring hitch** (Ashley Nr 310). The whole pulley can then be passed through another bight of the sunday after it has passed around a pipe or ladder rung (forming another ring hitch). The sunday knot is the knot that joins the two ends of the rope into the loop. It is common practice to simply have a small collection of sundays made-up in advance that never get untied, which is fortunate because they snug up very tightly and are hard to untie. They also have to be worked more than most knots to make them look right. From a strength point-of-view a double-sheet bend would work as well but one of its ends sticks out at 90 degrees whereas with

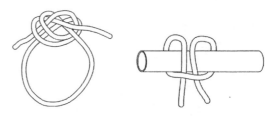

Left: Sunday knot; ***right:*** Ring hitch

the sunday knot, both ends lie right against the sides of the loop. To tie one, tie an overhand stopper knot in one working end leaving it very loose. With the other working end simply trace the path of the first knot from working end back to its standing part. Work it tight making sure the two ends stay about the same length (1").

Rolling Hitch (Ashley Nr 503): This is a knot for tying one rope to the bight of another rope. In a

counter-weight house where a line-set (as for an electrics pipe) is temporarily unweighted, it is common to attach a safety line so that if someone were to release the locking rail, nothing bad would happen. A short length of rope is

Rolling hitch

first attached to the locking rail with a bowline or clove hitch and then the other end is attached to the appropriate pull rope with a rolling hitch. It is in essence a clove hitch with one or more extra initial turns being taken before the running part crosses the standing part. It is important that the load pull against the part with the extra turns rather than against the single half hitch. There are many other very similar crossing knots that are also called rolling hitches, so it would not be unusual to have learned a slightly different variant of this.

Figure Eight Knot (Ashley Nr 2083): This is a packaging knot that is used to bundle together small pipes or wooden pieces that make up the tech table or whatever. When

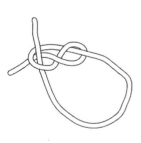

tied at both ends of the bundle, it leaves a loop that serves as a carrying handle. Let's suppose there is a collection of 3–6 foot pipes that need to be bundled together for transport. Take a 6–8 foot

Figure eight knot

length of tie-line cordage and take a turn around one end of the bundle, take the running end around the standing part and form a figure-eight shape using the turn around the standing part as the first loop, pull the running end back through that first loop and snug up the knot on the end of the bundle. Tie a second knot with the other working end of cordage at the other end of the bundle. When you are done, the interconnected bight of the rope serves as the handle.

Fisherman's Bend (Ashley's Nr 24, 25 or 26): This is really an optional knot for attaching cordage to dog-clips or rings. A bowline or clove hitch although bulkier and less attractive would do the

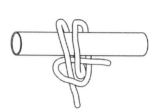

Fisherman's bend

job as well. To tie it, take a turn and half around the ring and tuck the running end under the turns and snug it up.

Rafting Knot (Ashley Nr 2114): This is used to lash two pipes together at a 90 degree angle as when an added pipe is stretched between two catwalk rails and lashed down so it won't slide. While this won't prevent the added pipe from rotating, it will prevent it from moving along its support pipes. It is assumed that the added pipe rests on

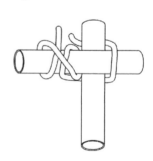

First turn rafting knot

top of the support pipes. Tie a clove hitch on the added pipe and go under and around the support pipe, over the added pipe, and under and around the other side of the support pipe so that the working end is back where it started. Do this 3 or 4 times (or until the length of rope is within 24" of being used up), then take 3 or 4 turns horizontally around the point where the two pipes touch to apply tension (like a belt squeezing a waist) and finish off with a shoelace knot using the two working ends.

Artilleryman's Loop (Ashley's Nr 153): This is used to tie a loop in the bight of a

Left: **Start artilleryman's loop;** *right:* **End artilleryman's loop**

rope to provide a handhold. When heavy equipment is moved (like a piano board), often several people are needed to get it up a steep incline like from a truck to the loading door. Being able to have handhold loops often helps. A bowline could be tied in the bight, but the artilleryman's loop is faster. To tie it, create a counter-clockwise coil with the running part behind the standing part and then lay the running part across the center of the coil. Grab the top loop and pull it over the running part and under the bottom loop and snug it up.

Scaffold Hitch (Ashley Nr 200): The scaffold hitch attaches rope to each side of a

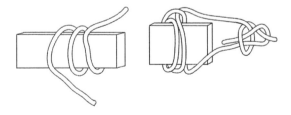

Left: **Start scaffold hitch;** *right:* **End scaffold hitch**

bosun's chair or swing. Take three turns around the plank so that both parts of the rope are falling below the plank. Take the most inboard turn and carry it around the end and under the plank. Raise the two ends and tie a bowline at about chest height. Do the same with the second rope on the other side of the plank. The safety harness can be clove hitched just above the two bowlines and tied in front with a loop of some kind and a couple of half hitches.

There are two other knots that sound as if they ought to be electrical knots but have been deliberately excluded from the list. The first is the **electrician's knot**, which is a simple overhand knot, presumably tied where extension cords join to prevent them from pulling apart. It works but it puts a strain on the wires bending them into a tight 180 degree turn. Current practice would be to gaffer's tape the connectors together or to tie them together with a piece of tie line, which would be easier on the electrical connection. The second knot is the **underwriter's knot**, which is a bulky stopper knot used originally as a strain relief by being bigger than the hole that the wire passed through. The code no longer accepts this kind of strain relief because it bends the wires too much.

KW or KWH— Abbreviations for KILOWATT or KILOWATT-HOUR.

LABEL— This is a computer lightboard term referring to giving names to things like the show, the dimmers or the cues. It is common to label the cues with either their cue line or a short description of what they do like "calls, house & preset up, lights-up Sc x, etc" because it makes the onscreen cue sheet more readable.

LADDER (lighting)— A suspended hanging position for lighting instruments similar in function to a trapeze or inverted tree, but it has two side rails and as the name suggests it looks like a ladder that has been suspended downward.

LADDER CLIMBING— Can it be learned and is there such a thing as fear of heights? In the same way that skydiving and bungee jumping can be learned, so ladder climbing can for the most part be learned. The fear of heights (at least those associ-

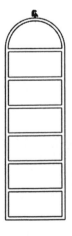

Light ladder

ated with ladders in the theatre) can usually be overcome by practice at progressively higher heights.

If a 2 · 6 plank were laid across two cinder blocks, no one would have any difficulty treating the plank as a bridge and walking across it, but when the same plank is laid across the tops of two firmly supported stepladders, it becomes a whole different problem. In the first instance, one's brain knows that nothing bad would happen if it were necessary to step off. In the second instance, it is now a much greater distance, and it is perfectly natural to be afraid of falling. The balance problem has not gotten harder, but the fear now has to be overcome. One has to reassure the brain that although it may look dangerous, it is really relatively safe. The problem with climbing ladders usually has to do with their sway and deflection. This is never a problem at a low height, but one has to get used to it at higher heights. Compared to the sway of a mast on a sailing ship, the sway of a ladder is completely insignificant. The use of a climbing harness and safety line can go a long way to easing the fear while learning. Vertical ladders are probably the easiest to start with because they are securely fastened to the wall and don't sway at all. Extension ladders and stepladders sway a little bit, but they are at a gentler (not vertical) angle. It is the stick of the A-ladder and the basket of the cherry picker that provides the real adrenaline rush.

The larger question is whether a lighting designer really needs to be able to climb ladders at all. The simple answer is that lighting designers don't; lighting technicians do, and most lighting designers start their careers as lighting technicians.

Many of us look forward to a day when the lighting instruments everywhere will be gotten to by walking along a catwalk. However, old methods and traditions, especially in the theatre and especially when they cost money, change slowly, and some theatres are still providing frontlight from booms along the sidewalls of the house instead of having a ceiling cove, so it is most likely to continue the way it is for a good long time.

LADDER CREW— A relatively generic term relating to the crew of any device that sends an electrician aloft whether that be a stepladder or an extension ladder or an A-ladder or a cherry-picker or an electric lift of some kind or a bosun's chair or some other device or method.

The *ladder electrician* is the one who goes aloft, and those who are assisting or steadying or standing around close to his ladder are the *ladder assistants*. The ladder assistant or assistants usually haul up the supplies, roll the ladder (assuming that it rolls), keep track of the paperwork and specifically tell the electrician in-the-air what needs to be done, where the instrument should be aimed, what circuit it gets plugged into and everything else. The ladder assistants are also often the fresh horses that will go aloft later in the session.

LADDERS— There are four kinds of ladders in common use in theatres: stepladders, A-ladders, extension ladders and vertical ladders. See HANGING POSITIONS, GETTING TO for a more complete discussion of this subject.

LADDERS, PLATFORM— This is a special kind of stepladder where the paint shelf has been replaced by a solid platform on which to stand that is about 24" lower than the actual top height of the ladder, although it is the highest that one can climb.

LADDERS, ROLLING— This refers to a stepladder that has been mounted on a rolling platform, so that an electrician can be rolled around from lighting position to lighting position. Often this is used in combination with a platform ladder, described above.

LAG—(1) When used to describe a lighting transition, a lag refers to the fact that the lights coming in for the new scene are lagging behind the old lights going out, and the effect onstage is of it getting darker before it gets brighter again. (2) When used in reference to a computer lightboard, it most commonly refers to the follow time between the start time of one cue and the start time of its linked follow cue. (3) The time it takes a lamp's filaments to warm up and for the light to become apparent onstage but this would more commonly be referred to as *response time*.

LAMP— See LAMPS.

LAMP ALIGNMENT— See ALIGNING.

LAMP CARRIAGE— This is a piece of metal that has the lamp socket and reflector mounted on it, usually in a fixed relationship, that slides to and from the lens system in a fresnel or plano-convex instrument.

LAMP CORD— This is the kind of electrical cord that is most commonly found on

Lamp cord

household appliances and commonly referred to as *zip cord* presumably because of its resemblance to a zipper. In the theatre it is commonly used for low voltage cuelights or as speaker wire. It is a flat cord consisting of two side-by-side plastic insulated conductors, referred to in the code as type SPT or some variant thereof. The 18 gauge cord is the most common, but the 16 gauge works well for strings of light sockets of the kind seen at used car lots, carnivals or construction sites, where the top of the socket screws down hard onto two conductors sitting on nail-like prongs, thus connecting the socket to the wires to create a string of lights. In real life, special outdoor wire has to be used, but the lamp cord works for an indoor theatrical simulation.

LAMP CORRECTION FACTOR— Photometric data is usually produced using the brightest available lamp. There will then be a list of correction factors for other lamps that are not as bright. If the brightest lamp produces 160,000 cd, then a lower wattage or

long-life lamp might have a correction factor of 0.75, which when multiplied by the intensity of the light would indicate that it produced 120,000 cd with the alternate lamp. Alternately if the instrument produces 100 fc of light with the bright lamp, it will produce 75 fc with the dimmer lamp.

LAMP DIP— A transparent dye-like substance, usually a lacquer, into which small wattage (usually 40 watts or below) light bulbs can be dipped to color them. In the early days of light bulbs when they were still of small capacity, it was common practice to dip footlight and borderlight and bunchlight bulbs. Higher wattage lamps tend to burn off the coating too quickly. It is also used to paint glass (or clear plastic) slides for a Linnebach projector. Lamp dip is still available today, but is more commonly used for prop purposes as a glass paint than for dipping light bulbs. Running lights (most commonly blue) are sometimes dipped as a money-saving measure. Lamps that have been dipped are not as uniformly coated with color as commercially made colored lamps and always have a homemade look, which is sometimes exactly what one is looking for. It is traditional to dip them while they are lit so that the heat from the lamp will help dry the lacquer.

LAMP FILAMENT— This is the part of a lamp that incandesces when electricity is applied. There are many shapes of filaments, but the emphasis has been on making them as small as possible (most like a point source).

LAMP HOLDER— The entire assembly, including the socket, which holds the lamp, sometimes including provisions for adjusting the actual position of the lamp. In many cases, however, the socket alone is the lamp holder. On an ellipsoidal the entire lamp cap with its mechanism for adjusting the position of the lamp would be considered to be the lamp holder.

LAMP LIFE— You have no doubt accidentally bumped against a light bulb and seen it get brighter. Lamp life and lamp longevity are directly related, as is the Kelvin temperature. A lamp that was accidentally bumped tends to be brighter (and have a higher Kelvin temperature) but have a shorter life. Many manufacturers offer both a standard life and a long life version of a lamp. In situations where the extra brightness is not needed, the long-life version often makes more sense, but lamps fail due to impact more often than they do because of old age, so this whole question has to be evaluated in the context of each venue. Long life lamps make most sense in places where the instruments are not moved often and increasingly less sense in places where they will be moved frequently.

LAMP LIGHT EFFECT — See EFFECTS, KINDS OF.

LAMPS — Light bulbs used in theatrical instruments are called *lamps* and are identified by a three-letter (ANSI) code that defines the base, the bulb shape, the voltage, the wattage, the length to the center of light and the overall length and several other things like life expectancy and lumen output.

Thomas Edison started with a screw base that still bears his name, which is also now called a *medium screw base* ($1\frac{1}{32}$") as there is one larger size, *mogul screw* ($1\frac{1}{32}$") and two smaller sizes, *intermediate candelabra* ($\frac{7}{16}$" = C9) and *miniature candelabra* ($\frac{3}{8}$" = C7). When the bi-plane filaments were invented, it was necessary to invent a new lamp base that would insure that the planes aligned with the reflectors. *Medium prefocus* and *medium bi-post* were invented along with *mogul prefocus* and *mogul bi-post* to provide better contact for larger wattage lamps. After tungsten-halogen lamps were invented and the lamps became smaller, then another smaller two-pin base was developed called *medium two-pin*, which is currently used in most ellipsoidals. There are many, many more types of bases. Consult any theatre supply catalog that sells lamps and a dizzying array of styles will be graphically presented.

Thomas Edison's first light bulb had a teardrop-shaped envelope that we would now call an "A" shape like a modern sign light. Household light bulbs are pear shaped (PS). Fat Albert, make-up mirror light bulbs are globular (G) as were a number of the early theatrical light bulbs. T-type or tubular light bulbs were invented in 1933 to go inside ellipsoidal reflector spotlights. The other common shapes are R-type lamps and PAR type lamps which are both mushroom shaped. Where a number follows a type letter (like PAR 36), it describes the diameter of the bulb in 8ths of an inch, which indicates that the PAR 36 is 4.5" in diameter.

When the technician installs a new lamp, not only does the base have to be right, but the bulb shape and the filament and the length to the center of light have to be right, too. The three-letter ANSI codes were specifically invented to simplify what one needed to know.

LASERS — Lasers stands for *light amplification by simulated emission of radiation.* Only laser beams less than 0.5 watts are usually permitted in the theatre, and they produce a visible ray of light (usually red) traveling through the air like a pointer. They are used for special effects.

LAST-TAKES-PRECEDENCE (Abbr. LTP) — This is a computer lightboard term that describes a pile-on situation where the most recent reading is the one used. The opposite of this is HTP (highest takes precedence). Subs work on the HTP principle. Groups typically work on the LTP principle.

LAW OF MAGNETISM — Opposite charges attract each other. Like charges repel each other. This is the principle that makes motors rotate.

LAW OF SQUARES — See INVERSE SQUARE LAW or DIMMER CURVE.

LCL — Abbreviation for LENGTH-TO-CENTER-OF-LIGHT, which is a measurement from a point on the lamp base to the center of the filament.

LD— Abbreviation for the LIGHTING DE-SIGNER, used mostly by crewmembers among themselves.

LEAD—(1) When used to describe a lighting transition, a lead (pronounced to rhyme with "reed") refers to the fact that the lights coming in for the new scene are coming up before (leading) the old lights going out, and the purpose is usually to make the transition look smooth and dipless. (2) When used in reference to a computer lightboard, it most commonly refers to the follow time between the start time of one cue and the start time of its linked cue.

LED— Abbreviation for LIGHT EMITTING DIODE.

LEG— In the context of electrical services, the hot wires are called legs and a connection between any one of them and the neutral will in most systems produce a voltage of 120 volts. This should not to be confused with scenery legs, which are described in the Preface to this book.

LEG WASHES— See LIGHTING SPECIAL PROBLEMS/Wing Washes.

LEGEND— Also called a *key*, this is the part of the Light Plot where the symbols and notations are defined and where the instruments that are being used are counted.

LEKO or LEKOLITE— A tradename for a compact ellipsoidal reflector spotlight developed in the 1940s by Edward Kook and Joseph Levy of the Century Lighting Company and named after themselves.

LENGTH-TO-CENTER-LIGHT   (Abbr. LCL)— A measurement from a point on the lamp base to the center of the filament.

LENSES, KINDS OF— Lenses bend light. When the ray of light goes from one medium (like air) to another medium (like glass) it bends once as it enters and again as it leaves. The amount of bending depends on the curve of the entrance and exit surfaces, and does not have anything to do with the actual thickness of the glass.

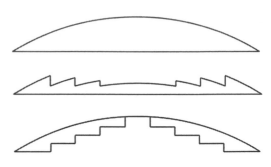

Top: Plano-convex lens; *middle:* Fresnel lens; *bottom:* Step lens.

There are three types of lenses in common usage in theatrical instruments: plano-convex, fresnel, and step lenses.

LENSLESS INSTRUMENTS— See INSTRUMENTS, KINDS OF.

LEVEL— This is a computer lightboard term and frequently the name of a button and it refers to setting a channel at a default brightness level. Unlike the *full* or *half* button, the brightness of the *level* button can be set as desired.

LEVEL-SETTING SESSION— Also called a *cue-setting session*, this is a time when the lighting designer works on the empty stage setting preliminary channel levels for the cues in the show. It usually involves either the designer alone or the designer and the board operator. On a complicated show it can often take four or five hours.

If the director and stage manager were present, it would typically be called a *dry tech* and would take 8–10 hours. Level-setting sessions were invented because the dry techs were taking too long. It was thought that if the lighting designer had some time alone to work out cues by himself, then time would be saved at the dry tech. That's still the prevailing theory. It often occurs in a time block that no one else wants. On a show that is behind schedule it may be difficult to find such a time block. Like the focusing session, it is a period of time on stage that almost no one else can share.

Detractors of this system often refer to it as a time when the lighting designer "plays around with his lights" and they consider it a waste of precious stage time. If it can reduce the dry tech to a one-hour session, as it often can, then it is hard to characterize it as waste of time. The sound designer is often allowed to "play around with the sound cues" at the same time, which somewhat mitigates the time expended because it can be shared between the two departments.

In contrast to a dry tech, the lighting designer will hardly ever start at the beginning of the play and work toward the end. Instead he usually begins with building block cues. These are usually *groups* or *subs* recorded in advance that are now looked at live onstage and adjusted until they look right. Once these building blocks are in place, the designer works on the first major *look* and creates all its repeats and variants and moves from look to look in this way. When all the looks (and variants thereof) have been done, the show is theoretically complete since all the cues were originally recorded as blackouts, so all blackout cues are automatically done without ever having had to set them.

At this point, it would be typical for the lighting designer to work through the timings of all cues. The timings will have been set at some default time, but now that the cues have been set, they need to be seen run *in-time* to see if their speed matches what the designer remembers from the runthru. It often takes numerous tries before something acceptable can be achieved.

When the timings have all been set (or reset), then often the warming of the filaments is dealt with and every cue that involves a crossfade (which is often 90 percent of all cues in the show) are re-recorded to include just the faintest readings (often 01 or 02) from the next cue.

Having done this, it is not unusual if time is still available for the designer to watch his whole show again from start to finish, watching every cue played back in-time. This often takes 15 or 20 minutes and is a fairly accurate indication of how the cues will be presented to the director at a dry tech or the way they will be played back on the actors at a rehearsal-with-light.

LIFTS, MANUAL— A telescoping ladder mounted on a stable platform that is raised and lowered by hand and then climbed and commonly called a *cherry picker*. Where the floor is flat, it can often be rolled with an electrician aloft. See HANGING POSITIONS, GETTING TO for a more detailed discussion.

LIFTS, POWERED— A means of raising an electrician up to where the instruments are hung by means of a hydraulic and/or electric powered basket or platform. See HANGING POSITIONS, GETTING TO for a more detailed discussion.

LIGHT, NATURE OF— Light is a form of electromagnetic energy. The earth is the continual recipient of radiation of various kinds, primarily from our own sun. Some of this energy is in the form of beta or gamma waves, which is the kind of radiation that a Geiger counter measures. X-rays, electrical energy, sound waves and light and heat and microwaves are other forms (wavelengths) of EME. Scientists define light in terms of the wavelengths of EME that we can see, which is 380–780 nanometers. This is a very tiny band of wavelengths. The differences in these wavelengths are perceived as colors by the human eye. See EYE for a more detailed discussion.

LIGHT, QUANTITY OF— The quantity of light present is perceived by the eye as brightness. Theatre people, regardless of whether they are designers, technicians or directors or stage managers or anyone else, seldom use any other word other than *brightness* to describe this, and it is mostly used in a comparative sense as in, "I want it brighter or dimmer than this." When it is recorded into cues, the dimmer or channel levels are used as the gauge of how dim or bright any given light might be.

In the planning process, one often wonders how bright this particular light would be if placed in that particular location and run at full power. The scientific name for this is *illumination* and it is measured in foot-candles of light, at least in America it is, and is measured in luxes in countries that use the metric system. In order to calculate it, one needs to know the *intensity* (still called *candlepower* by some) of the lighting instrument, which is measured in candelas.

When a footcandle of light hits black velour, almost all of it gets absorbed and almost none is available to be reflected elsewhere. When light hits the stage floor, some of it is absorbed and some is reflected based mostly on how dark and rough the surface of the floor was. If anyone really cared in a scientific way how much got reflected, one could look-up the reflectance of the surface and multiply by the amount of light hitting the surface and come up with something called the *luminance* of the surface, which would be measured in footlamberts. This is seldom measured or calculated in the theatre because it is the apparent luminance as judged by the eyes that is important.

As pointed out earlier brightness is a relative concept. While the headlights on an oncoming car might seem bright at night, they may seem insignificant during the daytime. When measured absolutely they consume about 70 watts of power, which makes them about as bright as a light over a kitchen counter.

In any event, returning to the problem of how bright this particular light would be if placed in that particular location and run at full power, one would look-up the instrument and its lamp and apply the inverse square law, which would result in a footcandle reading at the centerbeam of let's say 30 fc.

Is that a lot of light or just a little? Is it enough? In order to be able to make any sense out of absolute illumination levels, one needs to know how bright things are on average. Below are a number of sample brightnesses:

10,000 fc: The equator at noon on the brightest day of the year.

5000 fc: A bright sunny day.

3000 fc: An overcast day.

100 fc: The common minimum design standard for any instrument used in the theatre. After the angle of incidence is taken into account and after the transmission of the color media is factored in, this usually results in an actual fc reading of significantly less than 50 fc of light. There may be some honest disagreement on where this minimum design brightness should be (50–200 fc). Bear in mind that too much light causes way more problems than too little.

5–50 fc: Stanley McCandless said this was the range of onstage levels for an average play.

10–20 fc: Average indoor residential lighting.

5 fc: The amount of light typically provided by the houselights.

1 fc: The light of a single candle and about the point at which color perception is lost.

2/100 fc: Moonlight on a bright moonlit night.

1/10,000 fc: The limit of human perception. No motion will be detected at levels dimmer than this.

Lest anyone forget, General George Washington moved an entire army across the Delaware River by starlight, undetected by the British sentries who were expecting just such a thing to occur. Starlight is what we commonly call a moonless night, and it is so dark that it almost defies measurement. One could literally walk into trees in light this dim.

Quantity of light is one of three components that contribute to visibility. The other two are *contrast* and *plasticity*. While it is theoretically possible for visibility to fail because there is too little light, quantity of light is seldom the problem. Both of the other two components are much more likely to be the cause of visibility problems. See VISIBILITY for a more complete discussion of this subject.

Architects and illuminating engineers tend to measure the light on horizontal surfaces, but lighting designers are more interested in the fronts of faces (vertical surfaces).

LIGHT ACCESSORIES— See ACCESSORIES.

LIGHT AREAS— See AREAS.

LIGHT BATTENS— More commonly called *light pipes*. See PIPES.

LIGHT BOARD— See LIGHTBOARD.

LIGHT BOOTH— See BOOTH.

LIGHT BOXES— As the name implies these are boxes lit on the inside with at least one translucent face. They can provide lit signs that say something like "On the Air" or "Hotel Paradiso" or they can simply be a sun or moon box or a traffic light. They don't have to use indirect lighting methods, but they almost always do because otherwise the light sources will be visible through the translucent material, and that is usually not the effect wanted. They are typically black on the outside (to hide the box itself) and white or silver on the inside (to promote reflection). Lots of little light bulbs usually produce a better result than a few larger ones, no matter how well the larger ones are concealed. C7 or more commonly C9 Christmas tree lights are often used for this. The translucent material is often some kind of frost gel but it can be tracing paper or bond paper or muslin or white plastic grocery bags or whatever can be found that will diffuse the light. The whole box may then be placed behind a drop or several layers of black scrim to help conceal it from view. See INDIRECT LIGHT and LIGHTING SPECIAL PROBLEMS/Backing and Glows for a more detailed discussion.

LIGHT BRIDGE— See BRIDGE.

LIGHT CUE— See CUE.

LIGHT CURTAIN— A lot of narrow sources (usually aircraft landing lights or some sealed-beam variant) in a row pointing straight down. This works best when there is some kind of particulate matter or haze in the air and significantly less well when it is not present. This effect is most commonly used in rock concerts or musicals.

LIGHT DISTRIBUTION— See DISTRIBUTION OF LIGHT.

LIGHT EMITTING DIODE (Abbr LED)— An electronic device that is extremely efficient at transforming electricity into light but only at low levels, as for panel lights.

LIGHT MEETING— This usually refers to the meeting with the director after the lighting designer has seen the runthru where they discuss how best to light the show. See DIRECTOR, FINAL MEETING WITH.

LIGHT METER— Its real name is a *photometer*, but everyone just calls it a light meter. Photographers use a version of this that relates the available light to f-stops on a camera lens. The architect's or lighting engineer's version of this will measure illumination in footcandles or its metric counterpart, lux. Anyone in the building trade is customarily interested in light on horizontal surfaces, while in the theatre it is faces that need to be lit. As a result, although the same meter is used by everyone, lighting designers hold it differently to get a reading.

LIGHT MOAT— The walkway between the stage and the first row of audience designed to provide a place where spill light can fall harmlessly without spilling out into the house.

LIGHT PIPES— See PIPES.

LIGHT PLOT (BRITISH: *lighting plan* or *layout*)— This is a plan view drawing of the stage showing the location of the light hanging positions with symbols for all the lighting instruments placed at those positions. It is usually either on a B or C-sized piece of paper and the scale is usually either ¼ or ½. See DRAWINGS for a more detailed discussion. If it is manually drafted, the instrument symbols are traced using a plastic stencil called a *template* of the correct scale. If a

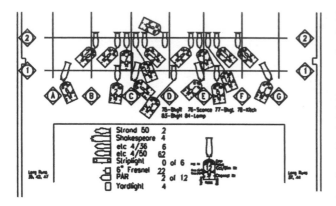

Light plot

CAD program is used, the instrument symbols are often scale drawings of the instruments themselves, often provided free by the manufacturer on their web site.

There are at least three different styles of plots depending on how much information is included and where it is placed, but there would also be many individualized variants of these.

The *basic plot* includes the hanging positions and the symbols with no information or data about the instruments except an identifying number, which often is coded to describe the location (as in FOH-4 for front-of-house number 4 or A-3 for pipe A, number 3, etc). The rest of the data would be on the *Instrument Schedule* in instrument number order. The reason this system fell out of favor is that it took longer to get the job done because after the instrument had been placed according to the Plot, it then had to be

looked up in the Schedule to find out where it plugged in and what color it should be and so forth.

The *standard plot* is based upon the *USITT* model and includes most, if not all, the information that would have been on the Instrument Schedule, which includes an instrument id number, color number, focus point (which describes the use or purpose of the instrument), circuit number, dimmer number, channel number, pattern or accessory and yoking information. It may include wattage or lamp information. It may include ganging or twoferring information. All of this data about each instrument is going to be repeated on the HookUp Sheet, so any of it that is not essential to the hanging or focusing process is usually omitted from the plot to make the plot more readable. For example, if all the fresnels use a 500-watt BTL lamp, then this information is typically included on the HookUp but omitted from the plot (in a CAD program the text is set to have an "invisible" attribute). If the instruments are placed every foot along a pipe as they often are, this does not leave a lot of room to write in all the other information even in a greatly abbreviated form.

The *tagged plot* is a CAD method and includes all the data about each instrument as described above but puts it on what looks like a baggage tag, which is attached to the instrument. The advantage of this system is that the baggage tag as a unit can be moved and/or rotated taking all of its text with it. While most CAD programs can duplicate the look of the standard plot, the attributes (color number and so forth) have to be placed in a standardized location in relationship to the instrument symbol they relate to. In the course of drawing the plot, this information often gets in the way of other

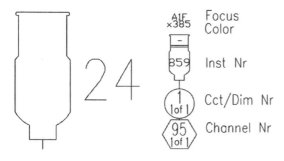

Left: Basic plot notation; *right:* Standard plot notation

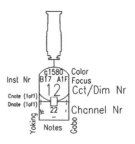

Tagged plot notation

instruments. Moving and rotating the attributes out of the way is usually a slow, painstaking, tedious job that has to be done one attribute at a time. Hence, there was the need for a simpler and more flexible system.

The primary function of the Light Plot drawing is to assist the light hanging crew for the four, eight or twelve hours that it takes to hang the instruments. Each ladder crew will have either a copy of the whole plot or that portion of the whole plot that relates to their location. The stage manager may also keep an archive copy to document the show. The master electrician keeps a copy but rarely needs to look at it again. If a lamp or color media burns out, the electrician usually replaces it with whatever burned out without needing to reference the original plot. The lighting designer or one of his assistants may or may not refer to the plot during the focusing session.

The plot (either standard or tagged) is often simplified for the hang crew to include only the information needed to hang the instruments (electrician's plot). In that event, the designer may add pen-and-ink notations of the focus point, channel number and other information needed for focusing and copy this for the stage manager's archive copy and the master electrician's reference copy.

LIGHT PLOT, BLANK— This is usually something drawn by the master electrician or technical director. It shows the stage with its hanging positions and indicates the location of the permanent circuits, and it is given to new lighting designers along with an inventory of equipment to serve as a model for their Light Plots. It can be copied and used for a draft plot. For manual plots, it can be traced to provide the theatre and stage outline. In some instances, it can be doctored with whiteout to remove the circuit locations and other helpful notes so that it can serve as the base for the final version. This depends on the size of the drawing and the method used to make copies. If it is available on disk, it can simply be imported as a block into the

lighting designer's CAD program, thus saving hours of work. It, of course, has to be verified by an actual inspection of the space. See MEASURING THE SPACE for a more detailed discussion.

Once the lighting designer has worked in that space, he will already have a blank plot of his own that he trusts and can use both for a sketched draft plot and as the basis for the final plot.

LIGHT PLOT, CAD— In the context of a Light Plot, a computer-assisted-design program is a symbol insertion program. Each lighting instrument symbol is saved as a reusable block that can be inserted over and over again in different locations and at different rotation angles. Each insertion can often have attributes such as color, id number, circuit number and so forth. A dedicated lighting program can make this process relatively painless. Doing it in the context of a generic program will take somewhat longer as the rotation angle of each unit and the placement of text may have to be set separately, and the information about the instrument (its attributes) can often block the position of other instruments and will then have to be moved out of the way (often in a one-at-a-time manner). On a crowded plot, this may take up considerable time as everything gets moved around so that everything else can be seen.

On the plus side, the attributes typically can be extracted to a word processing program and, as a result, this will prevent there being any variance between what is drawn on the plot and what the attendant paperwork indicates.

The Light Plot is typically done from a base document that shows the empty hanging positions. If the set design was also done on a CAD program, as will usually have been the case, it is possible that the set design can be obtained on disk (emailed to your computer), in which case it will only be necessary to insert the set portion of it into the already created base drawing. While it is handy to be able to see the set during the process when instruments are inserted, it would be confusing to have the set on the final drawing so the set would typically be on its own layer so that it could be turned on or off as appropriate. The same would be true of the locations of the permanent circuits. While they need to be seen at the time the instruments are placed, they may or may not need to be on the finished drawing. If their positions are used to locate instruments, then this would be an example of a situation where circuit locations would need to remain on the finished drawing.

Once the system is learned, CAD drawings can be done very fast as they can be built off of previous drawings.

LIGHT PLOT, DRAFT— In the interests of speed and efficiency, one only wants to draw the Light Plot once, and it will go fastest when it is done at a single sitting while all the information is fresh in one's mind. For those of you who can still remember back to "typewriters," it was easiest to write a term paper long hand, make corrections in the margins, and then when the revisions were complete, to then type the final version. This was because making a typing mistake often meant retyping the entire page. In a similar way, the most efficient way to draw a Light Plot is to work from a sketch drawn on a blank plot, so that all the circuiting and numbering is figured out first and it is merely being recopied. A draft plot typically uses hand drawn symbols and includes at least the instrument number and the circuit number. The channel assignment may be on a separate Number Sheet or other work sheets. The colors, yoking, and function of each instrument are usually just remembered but could be penciled in or could be on a separate Short Plot. When the final Light Plot has been printed, the draft copy and the notes related to its creation can be folded in half and put at the back of the show file, never to be looked at again (at least one hopes they won't be needed again).

LIGHT PLOT, DRAWING ONE— There are two approaches depending on whether the Plot is going to be done manually or by using a CAD program. There has been a rush to embrace the new CAD technology, and rightly or wrongly it has become something of a litmus test for lighting designers. There is nothing inherently wrong with a manual Light Plot. It is often faster for everyone except expert users of CAD, and it requires considerably less equipment and expense, and it is accurate enough for theatrical purposes. It is however now considered old-fashioned.

Doing it manually suggests that the designer is not fully committed to doing this as a profession or is intractable and not willing to change with the times. The people charged with hiring lighting designers typically know next to nothing about stage lighting. They often have not seen any show or shows the lighting designer may have designed, and even if they had, they might not remember the lighting part of them and even if they did remember it, they might not know whether it was any good or not. They are looking for an excuse to eliminate someone (perhaps you) from consideration. Manual drafting or handwritten paperwork often gives them just the excuse they were hoping to find.

Both the manual and CAD systems are based on the concept of there being layers of drawings. In the manual system, the layers are layers of tracing paper on top of a bond paper original. In a CAD system the layers are color-coded and can be turned on or off at will. See LIGHT PLOTS, CAD or LIGHT PLOTS, MANUAL for a more detailed discussion.

LIGHT PLOT, ELECTRICIAN'S— A simplified light plot that only has the information needed by the hanging crew. If the instruments are not to be accessorized during the hanging session, then color numbers and accessory designations are not needed, which leaves only yoking information, circuit information and possibly channel information if the lights are to be tested. The theory is that including all the other information (useful to the designer on focusing night) simply gets in the way on hanging night and makes the plot confusing and hard to read for the crew, but most crews are smart enough to be able to ignore the notes that don't concern them. What is more likely to happen is that the print on the plot (because it has so much information) will be small and hard to read and the master electrician may ask that a larger scale be provided for his crew. This is no problem for a CAD program, and a manual drawing can usually be enlarged on a copy machine (but cannot be enlarged as a blueprint). This makes the plots easier to read, and while they are still technically in-scale, they are no longer in a commonly recognized scale, which means that one can no longer measure distances on them with a scale ruler, but this is usually not a problem.

LIGHT PLOT, MANUAL— The set designer's ground plan (or a copy of this) is often used as the base drawing to which hanging positions and instruments are added. Then a final tracing is made, all text added, and the result is copied by blue line or black line and distributed. The final version can always be done fastest from a hand drawn draft copy that includes a draft Hookup Sheet, which is later revised and printed in final form. Even if the Light Plot is manual, the attendant paperwork is often done on a computer and the same table of data can be resorted to become a Dimmer Schedule, Instrument Schedule or Cut List (assuming there is a need to produce any of these) depending on which column it is sorted by.

LIGHT PLOT, PRELIMINARY— Sometimes because of the scheduling, it is necessary to hang some of the instruments before the lighting designer has had a chance to see a runthru. A preliminary plot is an incomplete or partial plot. It may be made up ahead of time and have pen-and-ink changes based on the run-through or it may simply be hung as if it were the final plot with a small collection of instruments being added later. In a situation where there is a prelimi-

nary plot, there typically won't be a final plot except in the sense of there being pen-and-ink changes made on the preliminary plot that make it final. If a final plot does happen to be made, it will be done as an archive copy or reference copy since the lights for the most part will already have been hung.

LIGHT REFLECTION—See REFLECTION AND ABSORPTION.

LIGHT SHIELD— See SHIELD.

LIGHT SHOW—(1) A show whose light pipes will be light in weight and therefore an easy show requiring few instruments. (2) A performance art situation (like the "color music" exhibitions of the 1920s) in which the lights play a principle part usually in conjunction with music.

LIGHT SOURCES— See SOURCES OF LIGHT.

LIGHT SPILL— See SPILL.

LIGHT STAND— A short boom (vertical pipe), usually with at least one crosspiece across the top, usually 10 feet or less in height with a heavy iron base, often screwed to the floor. Occasionally, the stand telescopes. Occasionally, it has casters, in which case it would more commonly be called a *rover* or *rolling light stand* (or *rolling pipe stand*). It is rarely high enough to require securing at the top.

Light stand

LIGHT VARIABLES— See VARIABLES OF LIGHT.

LIGHTBOARD— Also less frequently called the *light console, control head, memory head* or *front end*. This is the part of light controlling system that the operator manipulates and that sends signals to the actual dimmers that do the work. See LIGHTING CONTROL, OPERATIONS/Computer Memory Lightboards for a more detailed discussion.

LIGHTING, ART OF — It does not require very much skill to throw enough light at the stage to cross the threshold of visibility, but it requires something close to genius to render the things visible that need to be visible while at the same time keeping those things in darkness like the other audience members and the backstage machinery that should remain unseen.

A long time ago on the occasion of my first show, the director took me aside and told me he didn't care what I did artistically with the lights as long as the actors were lit up so the audience could see them.

Stanley McCandless said essentially the same thing when he said that once the stage had been lit in a flexible way, then the lighting could do a number of other things.

In the desire to make some artistic statement with the lighting, it is sometimes forgotten that its prime function is that of visibility, and it must provide this before it seeks other things to do. So what are these other things that lighting might do?

Students especially want to know how they are going to be graded and what they would have to do to get an A. The best answer for this echoes back to what Stanley McCandless said on this subject. A quarter of the grade would be for lighting the things that needed to be seen (visibility). Another quarter would be for keeping in darkness the things that no one wanted seen (composition). A third quarter was for how consistent the lighting was with the time, place, situation and style (naturalism), and the last quarter was for how dramatically interesting the lighting was.

Is that it? Is that the extent of artistry in lighting? Those are merely the four items that are universally agreement upon. Can the lighting express or reinforce the theme of the play? Can the lighting express the character's inner emotions? Can the lighting make the set look taller than it really is or at a further distant or whatever? Most people don't

believe that it can, but just because you or I aren't able to do something doesn't mean it can't be done by someone else. There are two books in the bibliography (one by Willard F. Bellman and the other by Richard H. Palmer) that I invite you read to learn more about this.

All potential lighting designers need to have a standard by which they judge their own work and the work of others. Many of the criteria for this will come from the list of other functions discussed in LIGHTING, FUNCTION OF.

LIGHTING, BUSINESS OF — Lighting design is fee-based and does not pay by the hour. Clearly from a business standpoint, the objective has to be to do the job in the most time efficient manner possible, but it is not immediately apparent how that might be possible as much of the lighting designer's time is planned out for him in advance. He is expected to attend weekly production meetings, over which he has little if any control. He has to be present at the hanging session and the focusing session and every subsequent rehearsal that involves the lighting, which in most schedules is somewhere in the 40–80 hour range.

The designer has to remind himself that he is responsible for the way the show looks on a moment-to-moment basis on opening night. Anything that does not directly contribute to that end is in essence wasted and unpaid time. This is particularly true of most paperwork and meetings, which take up a disproportionate amount of the available time for very little tangible result.

The meetings that the designer has one-on-one with the director are an exception to this and are usually entirely worthwhile. Since the designer controls the agenda, he effectively controls the length of the meetings. The general production meetings, however, that involve all the designers and often many of the support personnel can often be long and unproductive. This is partially because while they are supposed to stick to the subjects of concern to everyone, like the schedule and use of the theatre space, they easily can degenerate into a lengthy discussion of stage blood or the relative merits of using rubber soles on the shoes. The problem is compounded by the number of people who have opinions on all those subjects and feel they ought to be heard.

The situation with paperwork is somewhat more controllable. The lighting designer will have to produce any document specifically asked for by the director, stage manager or master electrician, but since they rarely ask for anything until they see what the designer is planning to provide, this leaves it up to the designer to produce only the documents he specifically needs. These will probably include, at the very least, the Light Plot and the Hookup Sheet, but what is needed in addition to these is a question that has to be evaluated in the context of who might use them and for what purpose. In addition to cutting down on additional documents produced, it is also considered wise to wait until the last minute to produce them and then to limit their distribution to just the concerned parties. If the Light Plot is created a week early and given to eight people, then when it is later revised in some way, each of the original eight would expect to get the revised version, and one would further want to make sure that all the old and now obsolete versions were gotten rid of. All this would take time but wouldn't be contributing to the finished project.

Another area of concern from the standpoint of time required is the presentation of the design (usually to the director alone). While a simple description of what the cues would look like may take under an hour, a set of sketches or storyboards or a computer simulation could require days if not weeks to prepare, and the designer must decide if he is getting paid enough to spend his time in this way or to phrase it another way: might his time be better spent working on the design?

The lighting designer also controls how often he reads the script and how often he attends rehearsals. Also to some degree he can minimize through careful planning the number of mistakes that are made in locating instruments that later have to be redone and can attempt to place the instruments in places where they can be easily accessed.

This is not to say that the designer cannot make a gift of his time in the interests of doing the best possible job and spend whatever time he wants doing something he enjoys doing.

LIGHTING, FUNCTIONS OF— This has been the source of some confusion over the years where the function of stage lighting and the criteria for evaluating whether any given lighting design was good or not became entangled, and a kind of competition developed to see who could come up with the greatest number of functions. Theodore Fuchs who wrote the first American textbook on lighting listed five functions. Stanley McCandless, whose book was published a mere two years later, is usually credited with mentioning four. Other writers, designers and teachers have named numerous additional functions although they don't all use the same exact terminology.

If I were to ask you what the job of a carpenter was, I would expect you to say that it referred to someone who built things out of wood or something to that effect. Many years ago at Thanksgiving, I built a table out of a sheet of plywood and used a bed sheet as the tablecloth. Did this then make me a carpenter? It did, but it did not make me an especially gifted one. Whether someone is a good carpenter or not is a separate issue.

If I were to ask you what the purpose was of lighting the inside of your home, you would unfailing say something to the effect that it was so that you could see at night and see better during the day in areas where windows or natural openings to the outside were limited. The purpose of artificial light in the theatre is no different. The actors need to be lit so that the audience can see them. Does this mean that if we were to light the stage with a single metal halide placed top-dead-center, that we would then have fulfilled the function of a lighting designer? It does, but it would not necessarily make us gifted lighting designers.

In order to be gifted designers, most designers would expect us to do three other things:

Selective Visibility

Stated simply, we are not interested in seeing the whole stage picture at optimum visibility all the time. The lighting designer lights the scene the way he wants the audience to see it and as a result some things will be fully visible, some will be partially visible and others won't be visible at all.

Audience Separation: It is traditional (or has been from about 1850) for the stage to be lit and the audience to be kept in darkness because it is felt that it will be too distracting for the audience members to see each other. The audience also for the most part doesn't like being lit, as it makes them feel uncomfortable, and they sometimes think their right to remain a spectator is about to be violated. Sometimes this is mentioned as a separate function of lighting. We certainly expect the lighting to do this. This could be stated separately, but is simply an example of selective visibility.

Plasticity: Although this is sometimes separated out as a separate function or subfunction of lighting, it is part of selective visibility. Clearly we expect stage lighting to reveal the three-dimensional shape of objects. We couldn't see the objects if it didn't. See VISIBILITY for a more detailed discussion.

Theatre Masking: In a proscenium theatre, it is also traditional to keep light off the masking borders and legs and to allow the top of the set to "vanish into darkness." We certainly expect the lighting to do this, and it is usually understood to be included in what is meant by selective visibility.

Time, Place, Situation and Style

Almost everyone agrees that the lighting should establish where the sun or moon or other light sources enter the scene and should approximate the brightness of the time of day and so forth. Situation refers primarily to weather but would include a forest fire on the far ridge or anything else mentioned in the script that would affect the lighting. This is commonly called either *naturalism* or *realism*. Theodore Fuchs called it *hour, season and weather*. Stanley McCandless called it *time and locality*. The lighting is rarely expected by itself to establish the time, place and situation, but rather it is expected to be consistent with an already explicit time, place and situation. In other words, no one expects the audience to look at a light cue and know that it is supposed to be March 8th at 3 P.M., but knowing the date and time in advance, the lighting is then expected to be consistent with an early afternoon in the spring.

Both realism and naturalism are theatrical styles, and time, place and situation lose much of their meaning when the production is of another style. The style will become apparent from a reading of the script and from seeing a runthru and will have an effect on the subtlety or lack of subtlety in the lighting. In a presentational style, lighting a narrator with a followspot might be exactly the right thing to do, even though followspots are otherwise usually considered out of place in a dramatic play.

Dramatic Interest

There is great pressure on the lighting designer to fill the play with memorable moments, which are like snapshots in time and are commonly referred to as *looks*. The more of these memorable looks one has, the better, so in the same way that an actor often counts how many lines he has to determine how good his part might be, a lighting designer may count the number of distinctive moments called for by the script to determine how good a lighting play this will be. While the number of moments is mostly controlled by the script, it can be expanded upon by the director and by the imagination of the lighting designer. A solitary light cue that does not change, no matter how good it may be, is often considered boring. This is very apparent in rock concerts where movement by the performers is often limited by their instruments (most notably drums and keyboards) being rooted in place. The lights then are depended upon to be in constant movement to provide excitement and dramatic interest. To a lesser extent, this is true of plays too where any excuse to change the light setting onstage is often considered good. There are two guiding principles here: *change is more interesting* and *things seen less well leave more to the imagination* (and thus are more interesting). The following five are sometimes listed separately, but they all relate to dramatic interest.

Composition: This is a very confusing word that has most often been used to explain that parts of the stage picture are going to be lit more brightly than others. Wherever that is done, the reason is to make the stage picture look either different or more interesting, which is why it is being mentioned here. Stanley McCandless was mostly concerned that the scenery not be lit as brightly as the actors. The lighting instruments that do this are often called either *accent* or *emphasis* specials.

Light as Scenery: Some like to claim that when photographic projections are used or even when a gobo pattern projects light and shade patterns that the lighting is functioning as scenery. While we all understand what they mean, the light never functions as scenery. It may replace paint on the scenery, but the light itself is invisible until it hits a surface. The surface is the scenery whether it is painted upon or decorated or not. Even when the light is projected on dust or haze or fog in the air, it is the particles that are the actual scenery. The light is making the scenery look interesting or, at least, more interesting.

Making the Set Look Good: Many have remarked that the set as seen under worklights often looks ugly but looks magical under stage lights and have thus concluded that it is a function of stage lighting to do this. The lighting designer also tries to make

the costumes, the props, the actors — the whole production — look as interesting as possible.

Reducing the Light in Unused Areas: The reason for doing this is often misunderstood. It is usually done simply to change the stage picture and create another lighting moment. The audience, of course, is savvy enough to know that nothing of interest will ever take place in an unlit part of the stage, so it serves as a clue to them that they need not look there anymore, but that is not usually the intent of doing it.

Relieving Eyestrain: This is a light change designed to make the stage look different in some way, whose only purpose is to keep the audience interested and awake.

Other Things

Some people think that the lighting can routinely control where the audience will look and can create a mood. Both are contested issues.

Directing the Eye of the Audience: Also sometimes called *focus*, the theory is that the eye is drawn to the brightest object in the field of view. This is only true, however, in an absolutely static situation like a painting. In a theatrical scene, the eye is first drawn by movement of any kind. Any one who has ever tried to play a scene downstage while a scene change was going on behind them knows that the audience is much more likely to watch the scene change. Second, if there is no movement, the audience tends to watch the speaking actor. Failing that, they'll watch the actor who is reacting. Failing that, they will look at an object like the painting above the fireplace if it is the subject of the conversation. Only then will their eye be drawn to the brightest object. This does not mean however that the lighting cannot show the audience where it expects them to look, but it takes the equivalent of a followspot and an otherwise darkened stage to make this happen.

While followspots were once used in this way, the intent was not to direct where the audience would look as much as it was to recognize who was speaking and to put the only adequate light source available in that place. We no longer do this except as a special effect. It is thought to be undemocratic these days. Since it is something the movie camera does, live theatre likes to do something different and likes to imply that the audience is free to look where they wish, just like in real life, rather than being shown where to look at every moment (as is the case in a movie).

While the audience is in fact free to look where they will, this does not mean that the director and lighting designer don't know where they would like them to be looking at any given moment of the play. It is the director, who, by using movement or the lack of movement, controls the audience focus most directly. The lighting designer, however, traditionally reduces light in areas not presently being used, but this is not really a technique related to focusing where the audience will look as much as it is a method of making the stage look different.

Mood: Almost everyone has mentioned mood or atmosphere. This was originally an idea borrowed from Adolphe Appia that lighting like music could, when it was done just right, create a mood and evoke an emotional response from the audience. There is no question that a theatrical moment can evoke an emotional response from certain members of the audience. The problem is that not everyone will get the same response and some may not get any at all. Even if they did, there is no way to exit poll the audience's subconscious feelings. Further, no one has the slightest idea how to manipulate the variables of light to achieve an emotional response, which makes it totally unteachable as a lighting technique.

For a while back in the 1920s, there was great interest in something we now call the *psychology of color*, where red means war and yellow means cowardice and so forth. Stanley McCandless believed that this kind of color symbolism might someday become part of plays. It is now more than 80 years later, and we are no closer to having any sci-

entific evidence that seeing any of these colors will evoke any of the listed feelings. Some people think of grass and serenity when they see the color green. It reminds other people of life forms from outer space. It's also supposed to be the color of jealousy. For a number of years, it was common for books about lighting to contain a list of what each color was supposed to mean. The lists have for the most part disappeared, and I think it's probably time we removed *mood* from the list of things we expected a lighting designer to achieve until someone can explain it better and demonstrate in a tangible way what role stage lighting has in its creation.

LIGHTING, KINDS OF — The question is how to light a number of performance-oriented events, of which live theatre is but one of many. There are really six factors: (1) what it is that specifically needs to be seen, (2) the size of the venue, (3) the attitude toward scenery, (4) the attitude toward followspots, (5) what motivates the cues, and (6) other traditions of the event.

Live Theatre (non-musical)

In live theatre, it is the facial features that are supposed to be important, particularly the eyes. This is true regardless of the size of the venue, but clearly in large venues only the audience sitting close to the stage actually gets to see the eyes of the performers, and the rest of the audience understands they are paying less but also getting less. The most commonly used lighting method for all live theatre presentations (mentioned several times in this book) is to light from golden ring positions where possible with three instruments-per-area upstage of the proscenium and four instruments-per-area downstage of the proscenium. This is more-or-less true regardless of whether the audience sits on one, two, three or four sides of the action. Although realism is not the only possible style for live theatre presentations, it is the dominant one and it requires that light cues be motivated in the context of realistic lighting and that the overall looks be consistent with the supposed time, place and situation of the scenes. The two most common configurations are proscenium and thrust, so it probably makes most sense to discuss them first, as they serve as a basis for lighting in the other situations

Proscenium Configuration: Proscenium lighting is probably the most difficult because it is hard to find good places to put the instruments. There are actually three factors at work here. First, many of the proscenium theatres are either genuinely ancient or have been restored to look ancient, but in either case inadequate front-of-house lighting locations have been provided. Second, places that otherwise might serve as light hanging locations aren't being used at all because the lighting instruments couldn't be masked from view by the audience, which is a proscenium theatre tradition that seriously hampers the placing of instruments. Third, the fly houses are often only high enough so that full height scenery can be flown out of view behind a border, but they would need to be at least 6–8 feet higher than that to provide instrument backlight locations so that these instruments wouldn't hit scenery on their way to the stage. The three most prominent problems involve lighting the apron, sidelighting and backlighting. Frontlighting is generally well provided for in all places except on the apron and in box sets that have a ceiling.

Using the apron as an acting area is a relatively recent practice. In the old days, the actors used to know that there was no light out there and that they needed to stay 6–8 feet upstage of the curtain to get into the light produced by the first electric (and footlights) and the sets were set back that far from the front curtain specifically for that reason. In theory, there is no particular problem in lighting the apron, but it needs to have been provided for by locating coves in the ceiling of the house. The fact that these often don't exist is the problem. The alternative is to locate vertical booms along the sidewalls of the house. This provides miserably inadequate lighting for reasons discussed in LIGHTING SPECIAL PROBLEMS/ Tormentor Lighting.

The sidelighting problem is at its worst when there is a box set with a ceiling because then sidelighting can only be done through slots in sidewalls of the set. Even then it would be a near, middle and far tormentor-kind of lighting that would have a huge Distance Problem on its near side. The removal of the ceiling would help because the instruments could at least be at golden ring positions from a horizontal pipe running across (and above) the set, but the near side area could still not be lit successfully from such a pipe but instead would either have to be omitted or would have to be done through a slot in the sidewall of the set as just described, even though this wouldn't provide very good lighting. Often there is no "extra" pipe available for just 6 or 8 sidelighting instruments. If there are customarily three or four electrics pipes, there is sometimes the attitude that this has always been enough in the past and the rest are all "scenery" pipes, so an extra lighting pipe would have to mean one less scenery pipe.

The backlighting problem is somewhat similar to the problem of sidelighting. First, it is simply not possible to backlight the extreme upstage row of areas because there will be a cyc or a drop or the backwall of the set in the way. Even if this weren't true, the theatre building is usually not deep enough, and there can't be a slot in the backwall because it would be seen by the audience. Second, unlike frontlights that are masked by a border immediately downstage of them, backlights are sometimes 8–10 feet upstage and correspondingly higher than the border that masks them, and if the scenery in storage cannot be hauled any further out, there may be no place for them at all.

Since the audience sits on one side of the action only, it is traditional to allow more directional light and more actual shade on the sides than would be permitted if an audience had to watch from those side positions, so some of the photographs of dramatically shadowy lighting only looked good from one viewing angle.

Thrust Configuration: Instruments are

typically not masked in thrust theatres. Where they are masked, they pose the same difficulties as encountered in a proscenium situation. Thrust theatres can't have flown scenery downstage of the proscenium, which is where the majority of the playing area is, because it would interfere with audience sightlines. The playing area is usually topped then by a lighting grid with pipes at approximately four-foot intervals in both directions. A less dense grid could be used at grid heights greater than 20' and a more dense grid would be needed at significantly lower heights. Finding golden ring hanging positions either at the cardinal points of the compass or at the diagonals is seldom a problem. The biggest problem is keeping light out of the house. This does not even begin to become possible until the fresnels and borderlights have been replaced by ellipsoidals. This is best handled by the use of a light moat and by understanding the physics of sightlines vis-à-vis how high the eyelevel of the audience should be in relationship to a standing actor. See VIEWING AN EVENT for a more detailed discussion.

Where the architect has not solved the problem, the ellipsoidals from the center aimed at the actors on the perimeter may need to be at a steeper angle, which will not light them as well but will keep more light out of the house. More attention is paid in a thrust theatre to bounce light and the color of the floor as these are contributing factors to light finding its way into the house, but this will also make it more difficult to get light in under hat brims, which is a continuing problem that won't be solved until some kind of footlights are put back in the theatre. The frontlights are often allowed to come in at a lower than usual angle, which improves the light under the hats problem and causes no harm because the lengthened shadows that it also creates fall onto the set (rather than into an audience section) and can be partially washed out by other lights.

Arena Configuration: Arena lighting is identical to thrust lighting following the rule of four instruments-per-area except that the frontlighting cannot be allowed to come in at a low angle because of the audience sitting on the far side. The aisles are used extensively as acting areas and are customarily lit by two-point lighting along the line-of-travel. It is not unheard of to have an acting scene take place at the head of an aisle (the end furthest away from the stage). This won't be visible to the quarter of the audience that has their backs to it (unless they were to turn their heads, which they usually won't do) but it will be visible to everyone else. This might be lit by two instruments from front-left and front-right (from the point-of-view of the actors, i.e. to their front).

Bowling Alley Configuration (British: *transverse*): These have audience seated along their long edges and scenery and entrances at both ends. While in a thrust situation it would be more usual to orient the four instruments-per-area to the audience sections and to the cardinal points of the compass, i.e. front, the two sides and back, it is more common in the bowling alley configuration to light from the diagonals, i.e. left and right from the front and left and right from the back, with the understanding that "from the back" is "from the front" to the audience who is sitting on that other side.

Corner Stage Configuration: These typically have generous forestages and cramped spaces behind the proscenium that taper to a point, and there is usually no other room or space behind the stage or it would not have needed to have been designed as a corner stage in the first place. In any event the audience sits on two adjacent sides of the action. The rule of thumb would require four instruments-per-area on the forestage, but to most designers this would seem like one too many for an audience that has not made it even halfway around yet. Three instruments-per-area are often used here instead, either as a front with two sidelights at 90 degrees of separation or as a front-left and front-right at 90 degrees of separation with a backlight at 135 degrees of separation.

Modified Proscenium Configuration: This is lit the same way as the corner stage because it in effect seats audience on two adjacent sides of the playing area. Since modified prosceniums are not in the corner of the building, however, their stage is not necessarily cramped, and it will certainly not taper to a point. The area behind the proscenium may share some of the problems of the proscenium house except that clearly lighting its apron won't be one of them.

Performances with Live Musicians

One of the shared concerns is where to put the musicians and how much a part of the performance they are to be. In a rock concert, the musicians are the show, but in a Broadway musical they have a necessary but supporting role. In a dance performance, they may not be live at all but may be on tape. A second shared concern is that unlike the straight drama where there aren't any small parts (just actors who don't have very many lines), there are now principals and a chorus or corps de ballet, and while the principals must be lit, this is not always true of the chorus. Less emphasis is generally placed on realistic lighting, and in many cases the lighting cues are motivated by the changes in the music.

Children's Theatre: While usually not musical, as a genre it has more in common with opera (in terms of lighting) than it does with other forms of live theatre. It typically has lots of cues, locales are symbolically represented by distinctive lighting, colors are wildly exaggerated and the cues often are presented to the audience from the point-of-view of one of the main characters. The story-theatre style of narration, in particular, requires that the lighting follow along and create some kind of recognizable lighting for the places being described.

Dance: Dancers don't speak, their faces are often deliberately blank, and they are not trying to "act" within the usual meaning of the word. It is their bodies that tell the story or express the emotions. Because they are moving, they need height and they need distance on a flat floor. The performances mostly take place on large proscenium stages and are mostly of the wing-and-drop style because it leaves the floor clear and yet provides a minimal scenic background. The lighting does not need to be realistic and usually isn't, but the dancers do need to be able to see where they are going, so the light changes have to either be done gradually or they have to be done while the dancers are on solid ground and not in the middle of a difficult sequence, and the timing needs to be very precise. There sometimes needs to be a spotting light of a distinctive color out front that the dancers can sight on during turns. Since seeing the bodies is all-important, the wings typically bristle with sidelights at all heights. Shinbusters are dance lights seldom used in other kinds of performances. Since the faces are unimportant, there is more use of toplighting, and it actually shades the face, which discourages the audience from trying to look at faces, when they should be seeing bodies. It is also commonly believed by dancers that toplight makes them look fat because it accents their horizontal surfaces, so in some venues this will become a factor in their use even though the eye compensates and can tell how tall everyone is. Followspots are sometimes used depending on the style of the individual piece, but dancers are much harder to follow than actors in a musical show because they move faster and further. Where possible, the followspots will do a better job of keeping the light out of the dancers' eyes if they are placed at a steeper angle, while still fulfilling their purpose of isolating the principal dancers from everyone else.

Ice Shows: Ice shows are essentially dance shows that take place on ice instead of flat floor. The venues are huge, often the size of a hockey rink (80 · 200'). The orchestra is typically at one end, so they are usually seen from three sides only. The audience separation convention does not really apply, and the audience is often lit almost as well as the rink, but there is often a black light number that will require more subdued lighting everywhere in order for its effect to read. Followspots are used extensively. They are of necessity the biggest and best that technology can provide, and there will typically be a lot of them. There is no scenery, often not even a show-specific background.

Musical Comedy: Musicals have been done successfully in all configurations of live theatres, but they are mostly associated with big casts, big sets, lavish costumes and big proscenium houses that have orchestra pits and lots of flying space. The orchestra is traditionally not lit but can be seen in the glow of their music stand lights. The conductor is lit, at least from the stage side so that the singers can see him. He may or may not be lit from the house side at a reduced level. This depends in part upon how energetic (and consequently distracting) his conducting style is. Musicals typically have about a dozen songs per act, and there will typically be a cue at the beginning and end of each one and sometimes several internal cues. This separates visually the dialogue scenes from the musical numbers. If the musical numbers are ballads, the rest of the stage is usually dimmed and the performer or performers highlighted either with stage lights or more commonly with one or more followspots. If the musical numbers involve dance (commonly called *production numbers*), then the lights might bump up at the end to start the applause, and there would be more use of sidelight to reveal the movement of the bodies. At one time it was fair to say that musicals had more cues than straight dramatic pieces but that is no longer so.

Musical Concerts: We're talking about classical music where the musicians sit in chairs for the most part, and there is often a conductor. It could also be chamber music where there is no conductor. There might be one or more singers as for the *Messiah*. The audience has come to hear the music. They also get to watch the musicians at the same time because there is nothing else to watch, but no attempt is made to make what the musicians are doing seem more interesting. The lighting tries very hard to light the musicians so that they can be seen without putting bright lights in their eyes, and the lighting is not expected to change in any noticeable

way. The most important thing is that the musicians see their music, and they must be able to see the conductor if there is a conductor. There may be a musical shell of some kind behind the performers but there is no stage set or scenery in the usual sense, and a followspot would only be used for a curtain call and perhaps not even then.

Operas: There are not a lot of new operas being written, and from all the operas that have ever been written, there are only a few that are done all the time. The audience for the most part is familiar with both the music and the story before they take their seat and have come to see a particular opera star perform the leading role. Not only are the operas themselves steeped in hundreds of years of traditions, but the opera stars have enormous influence on all aspects of the production and have typically done their role many times before. The scenery is often kept in storage from year-to-year. The lighting is often expected to duplicate what was done previously, or to be the way the star wants it to be, and there is little room for any new ideas.

In some ways it is best to think of operas as dance pieces or mimes done to music, which is to say without words. The words are unintelligible (even when the opera is either one of the few that was actually written in English or one that is being done in English) and more a part of the music than something to be listened to and understood. Where there are subtitles (which is not a practice that is universally encouraged), fifteen minutes of action may be reduced to "She is thinking of leaving him." The plots are often fantastical or at least highly romanticized, there is little attempt to achieve a naturalistic acting style, and as a result the lighting tends to be bold and colorful and in many ways free to follow its own course. It is certainly not necessary to have visibility in the conventional sense that the eyes or faces of the performers would need to be clearly seen. It is important that the look of the stage changes when the music and action changes. The director will usually have assisted with this, and vast numbers of extras will move from one side of the stage to another. The star or stars are what it is important to see. While there may be a large crowd onstage, they must always be separated from the crowd and never lost in it. Followspots are used extensively to achieve this.

Rock Concerts: Any kind of popular music presents the same problems as the symphony orchestra but the traditions of the event are significantly different. Most of the musicians also sing. Everyone who can both move and play at the same time usually does. The lights are expected to change with the music and be in constant or near constant motion. Intelligent lights are used extensively. Money is seldom a problem. Followspots may or may not be used depending on the style of the band. The audience has come to hear the music, but the show has a very definite visual component, and elaborate lighting effects with smoke or haze and pyrotechnics are common and in some cases expected.

LIGHTING ACCESSORIES— See ACCESSORIES.

LIGHTING AN OBJECT OR AREA—This is a discussion of how many lights-to-an-area are required based on the number of sides the object is viewed from and refers back to the discussion of playing space configurations, as presented in the Preface, being viewed from one, two, three or four sides.

An object lit from only one side only looks acceptable from the side that it is lit from, and it will lack plasticity since there is only one source of light. An object lit from two opposite sides (front and back at 180 degrees of separation) looks acceptable (but not inspired) from

both front and back but looks unlit from the sides. This is not to suggest that there are not times when specials in a thrust theatre will not be used front only or front-and-back. See LIGHTING SPECIAL PROBLEMS for some examples.

An object lit from three points (with 120 degrees of separation) is occasionally suggested for use in thrust and in-the-round situations as an arealighting solution. Used in this way, it looks acceptable (but not inspired) from the three points, most people will find that it looks dark and unlit from the intermediate points. A variant of three point lighting (two frontlights at 90 degrees of separation and a backlight at 135 degrees of separation) is now the most common way to light behind-the-curtain areas in a prosce-

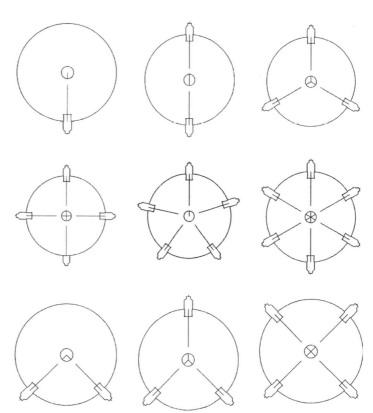

Top row, left to right: One point lighting; two point lighting; three point lighting; *middle row, left to right:* four point lighting; five point lighting; six piont lighting; *bottom row, left to right:* classic Stanley lighting; modified Stanley lighting; four point unaligned lighting.

nium theatre where there is enough distance to hang a backlight (usually everywhere except the upstage row). It is also effective in a corner stage configuration for lighting forestage areas.

An object lit from four points (90 degrees of separation) looks good or at least acceptable to most people from the sides and everywhere else as well. It is the standard for thrust and in-the-round lighting. This is the degree of separation that Stanley McCandless recommended for the proscenium acting areas. Although he only envisioned two instruments coming from the two diagonals, current practice would also include a backlight where the architecture of the theatre permits.

Since proscenium theatres were the standard of the day in 1932, it is unclear what Stanley McCandless would have recommended for thrust and in-the-round configurations. Some have insisted that the light should still come from the diagonals relative to the center audience section (left and right front and left and right back). Others have pointed out that since lighting grids are typically rectangular and aligned to the front of the stage, it makes more sense to have the light come from the front, back and two sides. Clearly in a situation where the audience is equally dispersed around the playing area, half of them see it one way and half see it the other way, and some see it partially in-between these two extremes. The problem comes when more than half see it one way or the other. Lighting students when presented with an example of four-point lighting and asked where they would rather sit have mostly been equally divided on this question. It can still be a hotly contested issue and each lighting designer needs to see and evaluate the situation.

Five-point lighting involves 72 degrees of separation and the fifth point of the star usually comes from the front. It provides nice even lighting, but often raises the question if this is the best use for the fifth instrument.

Six-point lighting involves 60 degrees of separation and provides an even (perhaps too even) lighting. When viewed as three-point lighting with a three-point intermediate fill (i.e. the show has been double-hung but the directions have been offset) it becomes a much more acceptable concept. The fill lights would typically all be the same or very close variants of white light and would be used to partially washout the effect of the other set of three lights that would be more strongly colored.

Is it possible to have too many lights concentrated on a single area? Yes, it is, and when one succeeds in getting light into all the hills and valleys of the actors' faces, all the plasticity that there ever was will have been destroyed. The human eye determines three-dimensional shape by seeing shade and shadow. When all shade and shadow is eliminated, the stage is being lit from too many directions. Stanley McCandless declared 90 degrees of separation to be the ideal compromise. Most professional designers would probably agree. Five and six point lighting is on the borderline of having too many directions. It also raises the question of whether there might be better purposes for those lights somewhere else in the show.

LIGHTING CALCULATIONS— If there were plenty of time between the end of one show and the beginning of another and no budget concerns, the lighting designer could be allowed to hang instruments in one place and then decide after a few rehearsals that they might work better in some other place, and the crew would be called in again to do the actual work of relocating them.

That isn't, however, the way it works. The lighting designer gets one chance, and one chance only, to place the lights in the correct position. Even if the lighting designer were to offer to pay the crew out of his own pocket, there is simply not enough time in the crowded load-in schedule to do the job more than just once.

The reason the lighting designer was hired (at least one of the reasons) is because it is expected that he can predict how lights will behave in different locations. When we talk about how a light will behave we mean *how bright* it will be at its center and *how big* its *beam* will be. There are two ways to do this. The first involves a photographic memory and a lifetime of experiences to draw on. The second method involves figuring it out.

There are really two different kinds of calculations. The *how bright* calculation is discussed as part of the inverse square law. The *how big* part is what is about to be discussed here.

To start, it is essential to know two things: what the *beam angle* of the instrument is, and where the instrument is located as defined by its *horizontal distance* and *vertical elevation*. The beam angle is typically looked-up in the manufacturer's photometric data or in Robert C. Mumm's **Photometrics Handbook.** The horizontal distance can be measured on a plan view (Light Plot) and the vertical elevation is the grid height (or working height of the light pipe) reduced by 5.5' for nose height, reduced by 1' for an underhung instrument and reduced by the platform height (if any).

Let's suppose we intend to place a certain instrument on a 20' grid at 15' in horizontal distance from the aim-point of the area. We've already looked up the instrument and found that it has a beam angle of 30 degrees. So how wide an area of light will that be at nose height?

This is a fair question, and one that any lighting designer needs to be able to figure out. There are three possible methods.

First, one could buy a computer program that would do this, in which case one would enter the three pieces of data mentioned above in a dialog box and hit a "compute" button and the machine would supply more answers than anyone really had questions for. This is a great "at home" method but unless one has a laptop that one plans to take to every production meeting, you will be left speechless when the set designer is asking if you couldn't put this instrument "over there."

Second, one could do a scale drawing, but it's somewhat complicated. Draw a horizontal line 15' long to represent the horizontal

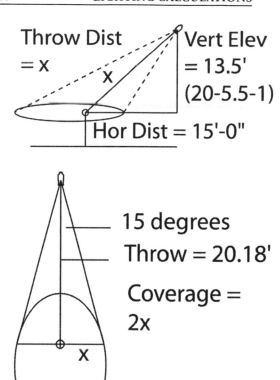

Top: Calculating throw; *bottom:* calculating coverage

distance at the nose height plane. Draw a vertical at one end that is 13.5', which is the vertical elevation (20' grid less 5.5' for nose height, less 1' for underhung = 13.5' of vertical elevation). Measure the hypotenuse to determine the throw distance, which will be 20.18'. Now draw a second triangle with a vertical leg of 20.18 and using a protractor measure the beam angle 15 degrees to each side of the top point. Measure the width of the light "circle" at the base of the triangle to get the diameter of the light, which will turn out to be 10.81'. Again this is mostly an "at home" method as no one really wants to wait while the two drawings are done, even assuming that one had the protractor and so forth with which to do them.

Third, the answer can be calculated on a pocket calculator, which is what will be explained below. The advantages of using the calculator method are that it is lightning fast, one does not need any special equipment other than the calculator itself, and it will make you look like a genius at any production meeting because you will be able to calculate answers while everyone waits and watches in wonder because you will be demonstrating an ability that they won't have. On the minus side, although it is only going to take me a few minutes to write about it, it may take you as long as fifteen minutes to master each of its four steps.

Step One: Getting the Calculator to Work

In order to proceed, you need to have a calculator that has *sin, cos* and *tan* buttons on it, which is commonly called a "scientific calculator." Assuming that you have such a calculator, here's how to use it. Key in a number like "45" and hit the *sin* button. The machine should blink for a moment and give you an answer like "0.7071." Key in "45" again and hit the *cos* button. The sin and cos of 45 degrees are both the same and equal to 0.7071. The tan of 45 degrees is "1." Assuming that you've gotten the machine to produce these answers, you now need to see if you can produce the opposite results. If you know that the sin of an unknown angle is 0.7071, what was the original angle? This is usually phrased as "What's the arc-sine of 0.7071, and the answer is, of course, a 45 degree angle. Most calculators have either an inverse key (*inv*) or a second function key (*2nd*) that provides a second meaning to each designated button. Normally you would key in "0.7071" and hit the *inv* key, followed by *sin*. After a moment of blinking, the calculator should produce the expected "45." The arc cosine of 0.7071 is, of course, 45, and the arc tangent of 1 is 45. If you were asked what the tangent of 20 was, I assume that you could punch the appropriate keys and come up with "0.3640." At this point we're going to say that you understand how to operate the pocket calculator. It does not matter in the least that you know what sin, cos or tan actually mean. As far as you are concerned they are some weird function of a number. It is sufficient that the pocket calculator knows

what these are and can call up the numbers they represent at will.

Step Two: Manipulating Simple Formulas

There are going to be four simple formulas, mostly of the a = b/c variety. If you were told that a = 20 and b = 40, would you be able to figure out that c was equal to 2? Wherever there is a mathematical equation where one side is equal to the other, both sides can be multiplied by (or divided by) a number without changing the equation. Also a number can be added (or subtracted) from each side without changing the equation. In order to actually solve for c, it has to appear alone on one side of the equation. Both sides of the above equation would be multiplied by c (which would yield a*c = b). Then both sides of that equation would be divided by "a" (which would yield c = b/a). Since b = 40 and a = 20, then c =2.

Step Three: What the Greeks Knew about Right Triangles

Triangles have three sides and three angles. In a right triangle one of the angles is 90 degrees by definition. Since there are only 180 degrees in the whole triangle, then the other two angles also have to add up to 90 degrees. The two short sides (on either side of the 90 degree angle) are called the *legs* and the long side (opposite the 90 degree angle) is called the *hypotenuse*. If you know the length of any one side and any other piece of information (either the length of another side or one of the two unknown angles), then everything else can be calculated using one of the formulas below:

1. Pythagorean Theorem, used to solve right triangle problems where the length of any two sides are known: $a^2 + b^2 = c^2$, where a and b are the legs and c is the hypotenuse.
2. Sin   = opposite/hypotenuse, where opposite is the leg opposite the angle   .
3. Cos   = adjacent/hypotenuse, where adjacent is the leg adjacent to the angle   .
4. Tan   = opposite/adjacent.

Step Four: Putting it All Together

Let's return to the original example of a 30 degree instrument at a vertical elevation of 13.5' and a horizontal distance of 15'. The hypotenuse of the right triangle (with legs of 13.5' and 15') will be the throw distance. It can be calculated using formula (1) above. 13.5' squared (which is 182.25) plus 15' squared (which is 225) equals 407.25, and the square root of that is 20.18'.

The second triangle involves a vertical leg of 20.18 and an adjacent angle of 15 degrees (half the beam angle) and we need to solve for the leg opposite the angle. Using formula (3) above: Tan 15 degrees (which is 0.2679)

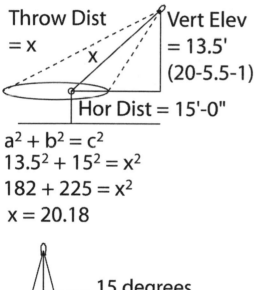

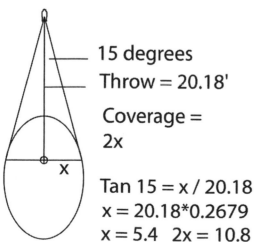

Top: Calculating throw; *bottom:* Calculating coverage.

= opp/20.18. Multiply both sides by 20.18 to yield 0.2679 * 20.18 = opp (which works out to 5.41, which is the radius of the coverage area). Twice that (10.81') is the diameter of the coverage area. A 30 degree instrument (any 30 degree instrument) would have a multiplying factor (MF) of 2 * 0.2679, i.e. 0.5358, which when multiplied by any throw distance would yield the coverage diameter. The multiplying factor is always = 2*tan where is equal to half the beam angle. Most theatres only own one or two sizes of ellipsoidals. Once their MF has been calculated, it can be taped to the side of a pocket calculator or written down somewhere and need not be calculated again.

In a similar way, lighting calculations are often done for lights at perfect 45 degree golden ring positions and at steeper 60 degree positions. An instrument with a throw angle of 45 degrees will be an isosceles triangle and the two legs will be by definition of equal length, so the horizontal distance will always be equal to the vertical elevation and the throw distance (hypotenuse) will be equal to vertical elevation/sin 45 degrees. Sin 45 degrees is of course = 0.7071 and 1/0.7071 (called the *reciprocal* is equal to 1.4142), so the vertical elevation multiplied by 1.4142 will always yield the throw distance. That number can then also be taped to the side of the pocket calculator. For the steeper 60 degree angle, the horizontal distance will always be 0.5774 times the vertical elevation and the throw distance will be 1.1547 times the vertical elevation.

Let's say we have two sizes of instruments that we use on our 20' high grid. One has a field angle of 50 degrees and the other has a field angle of 36 degrees. Their beam angles are, of course, ⅔ of that (cosine distribution) and their multiplying factors are 0.59 and 0.425.

When used in a golden ring position, the 50 degree instruments will have a throw distance of 19.09' (13.5 * 1.4142 = throw distance of 19.09'), which when multiplied by the MF of 0.59 yields a beam diameter of 11.26'. When the 36 degree instrument is used from the same position, it will have the same throw distance, which when multiplied by the MF for that instrument of 0.4251 will yield a coverage diameter of 8.12'.

LIGHTING CONTROL, LOCATION OF— Everyone from Louis Hartmann onward thought the lighting control ought to be out front at the back of the house or balcony where the operator had a clear and unobstructed view of the stage. The problem was it would have been expensive to put it there, so it was tried off right and DC in the orchestra pit and only reluctantly at the back of the house (this only when the cost of putting it there had decreased). It is no longer a hotly contested issue, at least I don't think it is.

The issue that is now contested is whether that is where it should be for the light focusing and for the technical rehearsals. If it is onstage or in the first row of the audience during focusing, one could speak to its operator without yelling, and the operator would be able to do other things like locating and managing the gels and patterns.

If the lightboard is located at a communal tech table in the house with the stage manager and sound operator for the technical rehearsals, then headsets won't be needed and everyone can simply talk in whispers. The lighting designer will not need to ask as many questions because he will be able to see everything that the operator sees.

Opponents of this system say that moving the lightboard involves a lot of work. Most lightboards weigh in at well under 20 lb and their monitors (which are usually separate) are also under 20 lbs. They have a power cord and one or two signal cables (usually 5 wire DMX or something similar). Moving them usually involves throwing the signal cables and a power cable out the booth window and extending them to the tech table where the monitor is re-connected to the board and the board is hooked into power and its signal cables are reattached. Add a worklight and the job is done. That's probably a "lot of work" if none had been envisioned but probably not a lot of work in any absolute sense.

That still leaves open to debate whether the system actually saves any rehearsal time. Those who use the system tend to be the only ones who have tried it both ways and they say it does. I think everyone should try it out for themselves.

LIGHTING CONTROL, OPERATIONS— Over the years there have been three distinct types of dimming control methods: manual dimmers, preset lightboards and computer memory lightboards.

Manual Lightboards

With manual dimmers, there are typically one or more rows of dimmer handles spaced about 6" apart mounted on a vertical surface. Each handle is 10–12" long, has about 90 degrees of travel and typically has a knob at the end that can be twisted to connect or disconnect it from a mechanical mastering device.

If no mastering system exists, then one hand operates one dimmer. Two or three dimmers can be operated together by putting a length of broomstick under the handles or by using knees, elbows or head, but seldom can more than 4–6 be operated at once in this way, as there is often significant friction in the handles themselves. In this situation, it is critically important that the dimmer assignments be made so that dimmers with a similar purpose are grouped together on the board. This is not always possible as some dimmers may be hardwired, which is to say permanently connected to the lights they operate. Footlights and cyc and borderlights were in the past typically hardwired since it was assumed they would be used in every show. Even if each dimmer had a flexible plug on the load side, dimmers were sometimes of different capacities, and this clearly takes precedence for dimmer assignment purposes.

With a mechanical mastering system, an entire row, which could be anywhere between 6 and 20 dimmers, could be operated at once. Assuming that the handles started in the down position, the knobs on the dimmers that would be up in the next cue were set to the locked position (locked onto the master handle). When the cue was called, the master handle brought them all up to the same level, at which point individual dimmers could be unlocked and moved higher or lower as part of several after actions following the main cue. To bring down all the handles, the master handle was first preset in its up position and all the handles that were to be dimmed down were locked on. The handle would then be carefully brought down until the highest reading dimmer clicked on. When the cue was called, the handle would pick up the other dimmers on the way down and would bring them all to zero. On very large lightboards, there might be an elaborate system of row masters, group masters, and finally a grandmaster. The grandmaster could be 3–4' long to provide adequate leverage, and it could require 12 or more hands to bring it down if a lot of dimmers were involved.

An alternate method of mastering was to use a single dimmer of great capacity in series with all the other dimmers. This was not done very often because it effectively doubled the cost of the dimmers, and if it came down to a choice between having 12 dimmers plus a master dimmer or having 24 dimmers, most producers would find the 24 dimmers a better investment. Assuming that the master dimmer handle was down, then the individual dimmers could be preset at their levels for the first cue and then raising the master dimmer handle would dim them up proportionally. Since the master dimmer was a single dimmer, it was no harder to operate than any of the dimmers it controlled. In a similar manner, the entire scene could be brought down smoothly and proportionally by bringing down the master dimmer handle. There would be a switch of some kind so that each individual dimmer could be switched either onto or off of the master, so that the individual dimmer would draw its power either through the master or independently.

A number of different electrical technolo-gies were tried for accomplishing the dimming:

Resistance Dimmers: One of the earliest examples of this was the *salt water dimmer*, which involved a metal weight being lowered into a cylinder of water to which common table salt had been added to provide the resistance. One contact was at the bottom of the container and the other was attached to the weight. The capacity of the dimmer was controlled by the amount of salt present. It was hard to keep the salt in suspension and chlorine gas was released as a by-product. However, the principle was sound. Ward Leonard manufactured a *resistance dimmer* that used high-resistance wire as early as 1897, and by 1910 they were producing a circular 110-step unit that could be positioned on edge in a steel rack. Resistance dimmers place varying resistance in the path of the electricity to reduce the current flow to the load, producing heat as a by-product. They typically are hard to operate smoothly because of the friction as the contact shoe slides over the contact buttons, but they are durable to the point of being indestructible, they work on AC or DC (which was once a more important consideration than it is now) and they usually came with a mechanical mastering system. They were probably the most popular dimmers of all time but certainly the most popular prior to the development of the autotransformer dimmer in the late 1930s, and there are places where they are still in use. They need to be loaded to capacity if one expects them to dim out all the way. This is usually accomplished by adding enough additional instruments to reach the capacity and placing these instruments (commonly called a *ghost load*) in an unused trap room or some other out-of-the-way place where their light won't affect what is happening onstage.

Reactance Dimmers: When an electric current is passed thru a winding, it can induce a current in another winding or core. As early as 1890, it was demonstrated that when an iron core was lowered into a copper winding connected in series with the lights, the lights would dim because a backward EMF would be produced in the core. This was called *reactance dimming* because the induced current "reacted" against the primary coil. It required both AC and DC current, and by 1896, the Earl's Court Exhibition Theatre in London had been equipped with such a system. While nowhere near as popular as resistance dimming, it was a competing system. *Saturable Core Dimmers* were a later variant of this technology that involved a primary, secondary and control coil. Both reactance dimmers and saturable core dimmers needed to be loaded to near capacity and did not respond instantaneously.

Autotransformer Dimmers: These first appeared in the late 1930s but were not in general use until the 1950s. They typically came in multiples of six, created little heat, were relatively light in weight and relatively inexpensive, and typically came with a mechanical mastering system. They were in effect a continuously variable transformer that varied the voltage to the lights and worked more smoothly and produced a more even dimming than resistance dimmers, which they rapidly replaced where AC current was available, and they remained the dimmer of choice up until remote control dimming became possible.

Preset Lightboards

When it became possible to separate the dimmers that did the actual work of dimming the lights (back end) from the controlling mechanism (front end), then it became possible to put the back end in a basement electric room, which saved money on wiring, and to put the control in a place where the operator could see the stage. The lightboard itself consisted of a slider (potentiometer) for every dimmer, which when set would send a low voltage signal to the back end. In the beginning it was necessary for there to be a current carrying conductor for every dimmer, which, if there were 96 dimmers, would be a control cable that that had at least 98 conductors (analog: 96 + common + ground). As time went on, various other data transmission protocols have been developed, the most popular of which is probably DMX 512 that uses five conductors and can control at least 512 dimmers, sometimes twice that many.

Since the potentiometers were relatively inexpensive, it was possible to have two sets of them, one for the present scene and one for the next scene. A master potentiometer could be installed on each preset to proportionally dim it as a whole, and by lowering one at the same time the other one was raised, a smooth crossfade could be produced. To facilitate this, the two master potentiometers were installed side-by-side so that the left hand handle (controlling the upper preset) was installed in the usual way so that its up position meant fully bright and its down position meant off, but the right handle (controlling the lower preset) was installed backwards (so that its up position was off and its down position was fully bright). When pushed up together, they would transition to the upper preset, and when brought down together, they would transition to the lower preset. The handles were typically T-shaped to facilitate their being operated by one hand (called alternately a *split-crossfader* or a *fader pair* or simply the *crossfader*). In theory operating them together like this would result in a smooth (dipless) crossfade. In practice the transition often looked better if the new cue was faded up about halfway before the old lights start fading out. This was called a 50 percent *lead* (pronounced to rhyme with "reed"). If the new lights were faded up all the way before the old lights started to fade out, this was called a 100 percent lead. If the old lights faded out faster than the new lights coming in, this was called a *lag*. A 100 percent lag meant a blackout of the old scene before the new scene lights were brought up. Although two-scene preset boards were the most common because they were the least expensive, there were boards that had anywhere from 5–100 presets and some that had infinite presets in the sense that they used punch cards to define their cues. The crossfader still traveled between an up position and a down position, but there would typically be push buttons to assign each position (up and down) to a numbered preset row.

Clearly while one preset was active onstage, the inactive preset or presets could be *reset*, which meant cleared and then set again from scratch, or *readjusted*, which adjusted only certain dimmers leaving the rest as they were. The fewer dimmers there were, the easier it was to do a reset in the available time between cues. Twenty-four dimmers were usually manageable, but 36 or 48 often involved some very rushed finger-work. To avoid having to do a complete reset, some cues were done manually in the active preset. Often each dimmer had a switch that would keep it on the crossfader or put it on independent. Often there was a master potentiometer to control the independent dimmers, and there would typically be a grandmaster potentiometer that would control the whole board.

Even a simple blackout at the end of one scene followed by some scene change lights before lights-up on the next scene could be tricky. If the old scene was on the upper preset, it would be taken to blackout using the left half of the crossfader (often called the XA). Then the right half of the crossfader (XB) would transition to the scene change lights on the bottom preset. At this point the upper preset would have to be reset for the next scene. The crossfader would then be used to smoothly transition to the new scene or it could be split to provide a blackout of the scene change lights followed by the lights-up on the next scene. If, however, the scene change were very short, it might be necessary to set the next scene up on the lower preset. In this case, after the blackout of the old scene, that same preset would have to be hastily cleared, the scene change lights brought up manually on it and then the transition to the next scene could be done using the crossfader to transition to the lower preset.

Preset boards were the last that would

require a skilled operator, and when they were superseded by the computer memory boards, it effectively brought to an end the age of the designer/operator, which had flourished since the time of Louis Hartmann.

There were a number of dimming technologies that were tried out at this time before they were superseded by the *silicon-controlled rectifier dimmers* that are now the standard (but not the only) current technology:

Reactance-type Dimmers: *Magnetic amplifier dimmers* were another variant of the reactance principle where a small, low voltage device like a potentiometer or autotransformer controls the output of the primary coil. They could be controlled remotely and they could have presets or the presets could be controlled by punch cards. Although they produced little heat, they were cumbersome and expensive. The *thyratron tube dimmer* had a control circuit of gas filled tubes that operated like an electronic switch. It was pioneered by George Izenour from Yale University in the 1940s and is sometimes called the *Izenour dimmer*. This was another heavy and expensive technology that, had it not been for the invention of transistors and subsequently SCR dimmers, might have become more universally popular.

Insulated Gate Bipolar Transistor Dimmers: These are a competing electronic technology, based on the gating principle that do not need a filter choke because they are silent and produce less heat than standard SCRs and do not need to be located in an electrical room but can be hung on the grid wherever needed, which effectively makes them both the dimmer and the distribution system in one package. These are currently being manufactured in America by Entertainment Technology. (*www.etdimming.com*), and they should be better known than they are.

Computer Memory Lightboards

The advantage of the memory board is that it records and remembers the cues and saves them to some kind of storage media (usually tape or a floppy disk). Once the show has been programmed into the machine, the machine will play it back flawlessly, requiring only that a *go* button be pushed to launch each cue.

There will be a computer-type monitor that in its default mode will display the reading of all channels that are active on stage at the moment, usually presented as fractions with channel numbers above level numbers. It also usually displays a simplified cue sheet that includes cue number, time, and a label (cue line), and there are usually status boxes for the primary and secondary fader pair, which among other things display which cue is loaded and what percent complete it is. This is usually called **live mode** or **stage mode**. Typically the monitor can display about 100 channels without having to switch to another page. Since switching pages will almost double the time spent working on each cue, extraordinary efforts will usually be made in the soft patching to see that the dimmers are soft patched so that they share channels and so that less than 100 channels need to be seen. If that is not possible, a second monitor may need to be used. There are a number of other display screens that can be called up, and they are listed more-or-less in the order of their importance:

Blind mode: This looks at a light cue other than the one presently up onstage. Changes can be made and recorded, new cues created or old ones deleted in this view.

Tracksheet mode: This looks at one channel in all the cues of the show presented as a fraction with cue numbers over level numbers. Changes to one or a group of cues can usually be made in this screen. If the desk light always plays at a level of 30 in any cue that it is in, the tracksheet view would be a good way to insure that this was so.

Cue Sheet mode: This looks at the cue sheet and provides an easy and fast way to edit time related settings and to add descriptive labels to each cue. If a *blank disk* was used to clear the machine in preparation for a new show, there will typically be 100 blank cues that will typically all be listed as 5 count

cues. This screen mode is ideal for setting the correct times and correct labels for each of these cues.

Sub Sheet mode: This looks at a list of *submasters* and indicates which if any have been recorded and which if any are set to *inhibitive* rather than *pile-on* mode.

System settings: Usually this is set once and left alone, but it may be that there are a lot of zero count cues in this show, so it makes sense to reset the *default time for new cues* to zero. Perhaps the *level* button is usually set to a level of 50, but for this show it makes more sense for the default to be 75. There can be more than a hundred system settings.

Patch mode: At least once a show, the softpatch has to be done where dimmers are assigned to channels. See SOFT PATCHING for a more detailed discussion.

Disk Reading and Writing: This allows the show to be written to disk or whatever the storage media is or to be read onto the internal memories of the machine from a disk.

Clearing mode: This is used to clear the old show off the internal memories in preparation for entering the new show. There are usually a number of choices. Do you want the patch cleared along with all the cues? What about sub and group assignments, etc?

Park mode: Sometimes called *independent*, it refers to channels that are set at levels undisturbed by other board operations. Where the running lights are controlled on the board, they would typically be parked. Sometimes during a rehearsal situation, the houselights are left on at a glow so that people can see to move around. These levels would typically be parked.

Macro mode: This would be the screen for writing or editing macros or for recording them live.

Help mode: This is a help screen.

Fader mode: This shows the contribution of each fader pair to the overall stage picture and is used for figuring what is contributing what when there is a pile-on situation.

There would be numerous other lesser-used screens that one might never need. Clearly there has to be a screen that includes resetting the clock time. There would be a screen that dealt with the printing of various information, assuming there was a printer, and so forth.

The console itself usually has two split-fader pair in the center flanked on one side by some sliders (submasters) and on the other side by a numeric keypad and some buttons with lighting-specific names. When communicating with the machine, normal English syntax is commonly used, so if for example we'd like see channel 4 at a level of 65, this would be keyed in as "chan 4 at 65," where both *chan* and *at* were the names of buttons. If we wanted to record the stage picture as cue 8, it would be keyed in as "rec 8 enter."

Were you to key in "15" on the keypad, the machine would become confused because it wouldn't know whether you meant *cue* 15, or *dim*mer 15, or *chan*nel 15, or level 15. There are typically numerous number recognition keys: *cue* and *chan* and *time* being the most important, which when pressed before the number is entered, tells the machine what the number means. Others include *sub*master, *dim*mer, *page*, *group*, *type* (of cue), *wait*, *link* and *follow*, which will be discussed later. In the previous two examples, you will note that the machine understands that any number that follows *at* will be a level number. It also understands that whatever number follows *rec* will be a cue number by default unless another number recognition key like *sub* or *group* is used.

A number of the buttons are related to forming a string of numbers. Thus "chan 1 *thru* 30 *and* 42 *and* 43 level" will bring all 32 channels up to whatever the default level is (usually 50). When the number stringing involves *except* and *solo*, it can become quite complex. "Chan 1 thru 20 except 14 and 16 thru 19 solo at 75" means channels 1 through 13 plus 15 and 20 by themselves at a level of 75. Assuming that 1 through 30 had been on at the start, 21–30 would be taken out along with 14 and 16 through 19.

Some of the more important display modes like *blind* and *tracksheet* and *stage* will have dedicated keys. There are often a series of function keys 1 through x that are context sensitive, which is the say their meaning shifts depending on what is being done at the moment. Their current meanings are usually displayed in a toolbar at the bottom of the screen. It is not uncommon for the last one to read "more," which when chosen will act like switching to a new page and will redesignate the meaning of all the other soft keys. There is usually a *macro* key which when followed by a macro number will execute that particular macro as soon as the enter key is pushed. There may be dedicated macro keys for the first 3–5 macros. There may also be dedicated keys for *reading* or *writing* to disk or *printing* or *deleting*. If there aren't they can be created as macros. The five most important keys are *track* and *rec*, which are related to recording, *clear* (as in clear the entry or clear the channel), *release* (as in release the levels as set on the keyboard back to the cue as previously recorded) and *enter* ( ), which is mostly used to confirm an action being taken.

Playback Operations

New operators are traditionally cautioned not to touch any buttons except the go button because that's the only button they'll ever need, which is true up until the time when they hit something else by accident at which point they'll need to know a lot about all the other buttons.

There are typically two fader pair. The primary pair is most often called the AB faders and is located at the bottom center of the board and may have more features than the secondary pair (CD faders), which is traditionally above them. To execute a cue manually, one would put the fader handles in their down position and using the keyboard call forth the cue that was wanted ("cue 47") and then hit the *AB-GO* button to load the cue. At that point, bringing up the fader pair would fade into cue 47.

The uptime has to do with how fast the

new cue will fade up. The downtime refers to how fast the previous cue will fade down, and the reason why there is a split handle rather than one handle is so that the operation of the two controls can be separated and this works the same (or almost the same) as it did on a preset board. Although cues are not commonly run manually during the actual performance of a show, it is used in the cue creation process for things like warming the filaments, which will be explained later.

For performance situations, a fader pair is mostly used in its *timed fade mode*, which is to say the computer controls the timing in a manner previously set. If this is the case, the handles would be left in the up position and hitting the AB-GO button would have the effect of loading & going, i.e. starting the timed fade, which if set to 30 would complete the crossfade in 30 seconds. The second fader pair (CD faders) is a pile-on fader, which is to say that its levels would pile onto the levels set by the AB pair and the highest level would then take precedence. This is abbreviated as *HTP* and is a hugely important concept in board operation and design. It is the opposite of *LTP*, which stands for last action taking precedence, which is the way sequential cues taken on one fader pair work. Theoretically, sunset cues could be performed on the CD faders but this would not allow the new sunset cue to take down any of the existing levels on the AB faders, so as a purely practical matter use of the CD faders is rare and is avoided wherever possible because it complicates the recording process and is prone to error. Many (if not most) shows can be successfully run on the AB faders alone.

Each fader pair, in addition to having a *go* button, will also usually have a *clear, hold* and *back* button.

Clearing a Fader: It would be unusual to need to do this during the performance of a show as it would make the stage go to black (assuming there were no other pile-ons from other faders or submasters), but it is an easy way in a lighting rehearsal to get rid of the current cue and get to a blank screen in-stantly. Simply hit the appropriate clear button.

Holding: This stops the cue is progress. Its most common use is in performance when the stage manager has called the cue in the wrong place or the board operator has hit the go button by accident. Hit the hold button. The cue will stop running wherever it is. Now one can either recall the previous cue and go into it in the time that was originally set for it, or one can simply hold in time and pick up from that stop point in the fade by waiting to *unhold* (usually achieved either by hitting the hold or go button). If it's a rehearsal and they just wanted to go back so they could try it again, hit the *back* button, which will go back to the previous cue in 3 seconds, which is usually good enough for a rehearsal. One can go back several cues by hitting back several times. The default back time can usually be changed to something other than 3. On some machines, back may also understand the "previous" cue to mean the previous one in terms of numerical order; so if one had been in cue 5 and had manually called up cue 15 and had gone into it and then hit the back button, one might well find themselves in cue 14 (assuming there was a cue 14) instead of back in cue 5. If the cues have been linked in a random way so that cue 35 was followed by cue 135 and then by cue 36, and if the back button were hit while in cue 36, the machine might well become confused and might return to the previous number (35) instead of the previous cue. All machines do not work exactly the same way. Read the manual that came with yours to figure out how it does things.

Speeding into Cues: Maybe they want to go back all the way to cue 7. "Cue 7 AB-GO" will load and go on the AB fader, but if cue 7 were a 50 count cue, you'd certainly want to speed into it. The easiest way is usually to take manual control as described previously ("cue 7 AB-GO" and sweep the AB handles down and then back up). An alternate method to fade fast is to go into cue 8 and then back up into cue 7 (in 3 seconds or whatever the default time is). Sometimes one has to start to go into cue 7, start to go into cue 8 and then back into cue 7 again. Sometimes back puts the previous cue on the AB faders, even if it was run on the CD faders originally and it clears whatever is on (or was on) the CD faders. You will need to check how all this works on your machine.

Record Operations

Setting a Channel at Level: The simplest method is chan xx, at 40, at 50, at 55 etc. There is usually a *full* button and a *half* button and a *clear* (kill) button. Instead of the half button, there may be a *level* button, whose default (which can be changed) is set at 50. Holding down the *plus* or *minus* keys after *at* often changes the level a point-at-a-time. There may also be a *wheel* or *touch screen* that can change the level faster. There may also be an individual slider for every channel that can be individually set just like the old preset boards.

At first glance the wheel and touch screen and individual sliders look as if they would be very fast, and they are but it is difficult to set them at a specific level like 45. They are just as likely to pick 43, 44, 46 or 47, which most people don't like because it is hard to get a mental grip on. There is no point in setting anything at full because things never, ever stay at full. If one learns the keyboard entry system described above (at 25, at 30, etc), the other methods can be ignored.

Some designers think on a scale of 10 and then fine tune on a scale of 100. The machine may know that "Chan 4 at 6 " means "chan 4 at 60." Had "06" been meant, then it needs to be entered as "chan 4 at 06." When one types "chan 4 at 6" and pauses, the machine doesn't know for sure if the user is just thinking or if he is done, which is why one has to add either a zero or another number or hit enter when done. If one didn't like the effect and wanted it gone, one could say "at clear." There may be times when an attempt is being made to figure out why a light isn't coming on when it would be preferable to call for the dimmer rather than the channel. This usually works the same way except that the dim button has to be hit first ("dim 98 level").

Once a channel has been set for the first time (14 level) it is usually not necessary to recall the channel number again (at 60, at 55, full, etc). If a keypunch error is made, the entry can simply be rekeyed. It is not necessary to hit chan every time a new channel is selected unless another "number recognition" key like cue or time or group has been hit in the interim. Once all the channels are set to level, the cue setting can be recorded.

There will typically be a color-coding system for the monitor colors. Everything set with the keypad (usually called *captured channels*) will be one color. Channels unchanged from the previous cue may be another color. Channels that either went up or down from the previous cue may be one or two other colors. Channels set by submasters may be a different color from those set on the individual sliders, and the two fader pairs may be colored differently also.

Tracking: Let's suppose that there are five internal cues in this scene. They are essentially the same except that a practical desk light is turned on and then off and this happens twice. If changes are made to the general scene lighting, those changes would need to be echoed to all five cues. Let's say it has been decided that channel 8 looks better at 45 instead of 50. One could call up all five cues (one at a time) and make the change and record it, but there is an easier way called *tracking*. The change is made in the first cue of the series and then the track command (sometimes called *Record-and-Track*) is used to track those changes forward to the other cues. Every time the machine sees channel 8 at 50, it changes it to 8 at 45 until it encounters a cue where 8 is set to a different level (not 50) at which point it quits tracking. Let's say there is a blackout after these 5 cues; the machine will see that channel 8 is not on in the blackout cue and it will stop the track. As should be apparent, tracking is a very powerful tool.

Now let's suppose that it has been decided that channel 10 (which is presently not on) should be at 30 in all these cues. When the change is made in the first cue of the series and tracked forward, wherever the machine sees that channel 10 is not on, it sets it to 30. That's right it tracks right through the blackout and in some cases, if not stopped, it can track all the way to the end of the show. To avoid this, a *no-track blocker* cue is needed. The machine often recognizes 00 as a different level from "clear" (which displays as a blank). There may be an *allfade* cue type, which essentially sets all unused channels at 00. You will want to check that this works with near blackouts, which are really only crossfades (as it is more common to have near blackouts that keep the filaments of the lamps warm), and that it does not also clear the other fader pair, which is usually not what will be wanted. Sometimes levels can be set at 00 or clear only in blind. You need to figure out how your board works.

Record Cue Only: "Rec 2 (or whatever number) ." When the rec button is pushed, the machine usually displays the cue number that it thinks is going to be used. If the machine guessed right, it is not necessary to enter the number again; "Rec " will be fine, but it is probably just as fast and a lot safer to always enter the number and not bother looking. The same system works in blind mode except that one has to hit chan before starting to make level changes (since cue was the last number recognition key hit); it is probably easiest to remember this as part of the going into blind process ("blind 14 chan"). To record blind from a blank screen, "blind 14.5" (there may be a "not recorded" message that will flash), set levels, and then "rec ."

Record-and-Track: "Track 2 " (tracks the change(s) into this and succeeding cues until a new level or 00 is encountered). Sometimes there will be some changes that need to track forward but others that are exclusively for this one cue. It should be apparent that the base cue (the part that tracks forward) has to be done first ("track ") before the modifications for this cue only are set and recorded ("rec "). If all the modifications for this cue are recorded first,

then it will not be possible to track changes forward because those channels will have already been set to their new modified level in this cue, so when the machine encounters their old level in the very next cue it will stop tracking because the level will be different.

Setting Time: This usually has to be done after the cue has been recorded even if it is first recorded in a blank state. The times are usually automatically saved without having to go through the rec 8 process again. The default is usually 5 seconds unless someone has changed it. If this is what is wanted, then no one has to do anything. If this isn't what is wanted, press *time*, enter a number that represents the *uptime*, and press enter. The number can usually be in seconds, in decimal seconds or in minutes and seconds. The machine usually recognizes seconds from 0 to 99; it recognizes decimal seconds from .1 to 59.9 and it recognizes minutes and seconds from 1:00 to 99:59. This is keyed in, in pocket-calculator (or microwave timer) order from right to left; ".1" = 0.1 sec, "1" = 1 sec, "10" = 10 sec, "100" = 1:00, "1000" = 10:00. After one has hit enter, the prompt will ask about *downtime*. If the old cue is to fade out (downtime) at the same speed, hit enter again to cycle by this choice. If the downtime is to be different, type another number and hit enter. The alleged purpose for having separate uptimes and downtimes is to allow the timed fader to do the equivalent of leads and lags. The machine can do leads acceptably well, but doesn't do well with lags. On a preset board doing a 100 percent lag produced a blackout of the old scene. Having the downtime of a timed transition done first will only take out those channels that are going to decrease in the new cue and will leaves up the channels that stay the same between the two cues. As a purely practical matter, if it is unclear how a transition will be timed, it is better to create a blackout cue followed by a lights-up cue. If they are set to follow each other with a follow time of zero, it will be a straight crossfade. If a lag is needed, the downtime wait of the first cue can be set to however many seconds is wanted. A follow time of any positive number and no wait time will create a lead.

There are often three optional keys that could be accessed at this time: *wait, link, and follow*. A wait refers to the time between when the uptime starts fading in the new cue and when the downtime starts taking out the old cue. Normally, they both occur at the same time, so there will be no wait time. One can usually have an uptime wait or a downtime wait, but not both. Usually hitting the wait button once gets the prompt for the upfade time and hitting the wait button twice gets the prompt for downfade wait. Type a number and hit enter. If one needed to link this cue to an out of sequence cue number, one could hit link xx, , where xx was the out of sequence cue number. If one wanted the next cue to automatically follow, one would hit follow, and set a follow time, and hit enter. The follow time is usually calculated from the start time of the first cue, so if one had a 5 ct cue followed by a 7 ct cue and wanted the second cue to start when the first one had finished, the follow time would need to be 5. A follow time of 0 would start both cues at the same time.

Recording Changes During a Rehearsal: Imagine that the current cue is cue 14. Some changes have been made and the modified cue has been re-recorded. The new levels that were set from the keyboard may be in a different color on the screen (and there may be a "captured channels" message). When the channel levels were set from the keyboard, they over-rode the previously recorded levels, and they will now usually stay on when the board goes into cue 15 and cue 16 etc until they have been released. Hitting *rel* once usually uncaptures the last entered channel (its level remains as it was set but its color changes and it won't stay on for the next cue). Hitting rel twice usually uncaptures all the channels and makes the captured channels message disappear. One releases channels after having first recorded, of course. Doing it before recording will return the stage to the last saved version of the cue.

Point Cues: Often a new cue will need to be added between two existing whole numbered cues. Most boards will allow both random linking and point cues. The advantage of the point cues is that they will be in numerical order already and as a result they will be faster because no link information has to be set. Thus 20.1 thru 20.9 can be added between cue 20 and cue 21. If, however, a new cue is needed between 20.1 and 20.2,, then the old 20.2 has to become 20.3 and the old 20.3 has to become 20.4 and so forth until an unused cue number can be located, and this can stop a rehearsal for 15–20 minutes as the board operator re-records cues as new numbers and the stage manager changes all the numbers in the book. As a result it is common practice to use the 5 odd numbers and save the 4 even numbers for future expansion. Before there were point cues, it was common to deliberately skip several whole number cues to achieve the same thing, but that mostly isn't necessary anymore.

Recording the Next Cue Based on This One: If the levels from cue 1 are presently on the screen, and cue 2 is being built from this, then bring up new channels to level, readjust existing levels, and record and release captured channels. Set times, link and follow information (as appropriate). The same procedure is used when a new cue is to be built upon some previous cue. The previous cue is loaded onto the AB fader, the levels are modified and the cue is recorded being sure that it is recorded as the new number.

Deleting a Cue: The machine will do (but generally does not like to do) random linking, so to go from cue 13 to cue 15, it is usually easiest to delete cue 14. If there is a possibility that it might be needed again, it should be re-recorded as cue 714 and then cue 14 can be deleted. Deleting is usually done in blind mode. "Blind 14, del, " (or track) is the usual sequence. There may be an "are you sure?" message which requires that enter be hit again. In stage mode, one would generally want to delete a cue other than the one presently on stage, and sometimes the machine will only delete the current cue. The del key is often not a dedicated button on the lightboard but one of a series of soft keys that mean different things at different times.

Doing Board Notes: The most effective system is blind recording described above because one can clear channels or set them at 00 and see this displayed, and one gets to see the finished state of cues displayed onscreen instantly without having to wait for a timed fade to happen. If, however, the cues have to be seen onstage, one would call the first cue number: "cue 2 AB-GO," and sweep the handles down and up to fade fast. Then one would readjust channels, record and release channels. At this point one could call up the next cue number. If only the time, link, wait, or follow information is being changed for a series of cues, there may be a *cue list display mode* where it would be possible to move around in the fields using the arrow keys and where typing would replace the selection that would be faster.

Loops and Effects

Chase Loops: There are a number of ways to do this. This is best explained as it evolved because the newer methods (*effects, subroutines,* and *macros*) were invented because the old ways were somewhat cumbersome and limited. In the good old days, all that existed were cues. If one wanted to have a loop, cue 1 was linked to 2, and 2 to 3 and then the last cue was linked back to the first one. The assumption was that they would run on the CD faders while other cues continued on the AB faders. Let's suppose there is a fire effect loop (cues 20.1–20.9) that runs from after cue 19 until cue 25 when it stops. There needs to be a "utility" cue (20), which would be taken after cue 19, and it will be a blackout cue (on the CD fader) and the zero step of the loop. Its purpose is to prevent tracking into the loop from previous cues on the AB faders. One would record the steps of the loop (20.1...20.9) as regular cues linked together with or without wait times. 20.9 will be linked back to 20.1. Meanwhile, cue, 21, AB-GO (which will have to be called manu-

ally) will be done as a new cue on the AB faders followed by 22, 23, 24 and 25, at which point (this is where the loop should fade out) the left-hand CD handle can be faded out and the CD masters cleared (one could manually call up another utility cue similar to cue 20 to do this but the manual method is easier). While decimal cues were used in the example; one could call the loop cues 21–29 and renumber the following cues or could call them 621–629 etc, which is often preferable because it makes the back button work better and keeps the loop cues far away from anywhere where tracking will affect them. If the loop is run with the CD handles all the way up in their normal operating position, the loop will run in the times set and at the levels set. If the handles are in some other position one can often adjust the left-hand handle to control the channel levels and the right-hand handle to control the speed. In the good old days, this entire process was further complicated by the fact that the concept of wait times and follow times hadn't really been fully invented yet and a follow cue often had to be a linked cue that had a wait time. There were five major objections to this system. First, it took a lot of cues to make anything happen. If one wanted to flash a light on and off, one needed one cue to turn it on and a second cue to turn it off. The time and links had to be set for every cue. Second, when one needed to edit the loop, it was not possible to see the steps individually one-at-a-time on stage without breaking the links (so one mostly had to do it blind). Third, if one wanted to make changes to the cue on the AB fader while a loop was running on the CD fader, one had to unload the CD fader first because rerecording would record the whole stage picture (including the effects as a pile-on). Fourth, the operation was cumbersome and prone to operator error because one had to manually call up the cue number for the loop (20) and the cue number for the next cue to be played on the AB faders (21). Fifth, there was no way to play a loop twice and then have it stop automatically unless one took a ten step loop and created a 20 step loop (writing a new cue that repeated a previously used one) and then adding a final cue that faded out or stopped the loop.

Subroutines: These work more-or-less like the old system of linked cues with three dramatic improvements. First, in addition to being able to loop the last cue of the sequence back to the first, it can do this for xx number of loops and then it can do something else. It can also *bounce* for xx number of forward, then reverse trips thru the steps, *jump-to-cue*, or *hold-for-go*. Second, the whole subroutine is dealt with as a single cue that has steps. This means that cue 20 (the subroutine that will run the 621–629 loop, hold-for-go, and then run 630 which fades out the CD fader) is linked by default to cue 21, which means that no one has to call up any cues manually either to get into or get out of the loop. Third, additional steps can be added or deleted and the machine will renumber these automatically. Let's say that two new steps are needed, call them 631 and 632, which are out of numerical sequence but no one cares because the machine just asks for a cue number for step 10. It could be any cue from the show. Once the 600 series cues have been created, they can be used in any order. One can create several versions of the loop using the same cues in a different step order. Let's say someone blinks a light (dot, dot, dash) as a signal. In the old days that would have been 6 cues, but in a subroutine one only needs two: on and off. The time information is attached to the step not the 600 series cue.

Any time information attached to the subroutine is typically ignored as the subroutine lasts as long as the sum of its steps, which is important because effects (to be discussed next) don't work this way. Clearly, if one needed to see the steps individually on stage to modify levels, the corresponding 600 series cue could be called up, without breaking or modifying any of the links.

Effects: Most loops are really rather simple problems that involve only a few channels (often only one) where a light has to flicker or pulse on and off or there is to be a flash of lightning or whatever. If one doesn't need to set channel levels at proportional levels, where an on-off (high/low) value will do as well, and there aren't more than 10 channels or groups involved, one may be much better off creating it as an effect. Effects have at least five big advantages. First, the on and off are not two separate steps but one, which means one only has to write half as many cues. Second, one doesn't really write cues, one just tells the machine what channels should be at high setting or low settings, which saves time. Third, the resulting effect can be assigned to a submaster where it can manually be faded in or out. Fourth, if one is doing a chase loop, the machine can automatically set channels to steps and can do positive or negative or alternating chases or reverse chases or bounce chases or build chases. It can also do a random chase that plays back the steps in a random order, which is really good for fire and lightning effects. It can also do a random rate within a range that can be specified.

First, the terminology is slightly different and takes some getting used to. Having gotten used to having uptime/downtime/ (possible wait time)/follow time, one will still have this for the effect as a whole, which is recorded as a numbered cue. However, the steps within have step time/in time/dwell time/out time. This is all about a light coming on, staying on for a while and then going out. In a subroutine or series of linked cues this requires two cues. Taken together they could be graphed as a triangle with its top cut off flat (creating a trapezoid). The left hand slanty side is the uptime; the shorter the uptime, the steeper the angle until at time zero it is vertical. The top represents how long the light stays on and has no name but is created by the follow time of the 1st cue. As the follow time is reduced, the shape tends toward a triangle again, which it does when follow time is equal to uptime. The slanty side on the right is downtime. The bottom is the total elapsed time between the beginning of up and the end of down. Now imagine two of these trapezoids side-by-side with a space between them (steps 1 and 2). The distance between the start of each uptime has no name (it is the sum of the elapsed time of the up, the time it remained on, and the down plus the wait before the start of the second cue), but we are going to call this the *step time*. We're going to call uptime, *in time* and downtime, *out time* and we're going to call the flat top that had no name, *dwell time* (which is really follow time of the first cue less its uptime). When there is a space between trapezoids, step time will be greater than the sum of in time/dwell time/out time. If the trapezoids had their bases touching, step time would be equal to in/dwell/out; and if the trapezoids overlapped each other, the step time would be less than in/dwell/out. If this sounds confusing, it is a reminder that it is essential to visualize the effect before it can be broken into steps. If it flashes on, then uptime will be 0. If it also flashes off, downtime will be 0 and if its duration is just a flash, its dwell time will be something like 0.1. Effects are almost always pile-ons and almost always include only the lights that flash, and almost always have a space between the trapezoids.

Macros: These are for doing repetitive jobs. Each one can typically contain up to about 50 keystrokes, but the whole macro can be linked to another macro or looped back to itself. One can create these blind or live. Blind is usually better when editing an existing macro. Live is often easier for creating the initial macro and sometimes the only method that usually works with soft keys. Often the wheels, touch screens or sliders can't be used for creating macros. A completed macro can be run from a *macro run* button on the board or it can usually be linked to a cue so that it runs at the same time.

A macro can be created for the channel check (described previously). A better macro can be created for the instrument check that will bring up groups of channels (systems) and leave them on for a while before replacing them with other groups. A macro can be

created for *writing* to disk or *reading* from disk or for *printing* or anything that involves switching between fader pairs or any complicated sequence where one would prefer that the machine did it.

Other Features

Clearing the Internal Memory of the Machine: This would be done at the start of a new show to clear away the old show. The easiest way to do this is to have a *blank show disk* that can merely be loaded onto the machine (*read* from disk). Although it may not have subs or groups or patching recorded, it will have system settings and macros (and may actually have one or two cues or patches like houselights or worklights recorded) and usually about 100 blank cues. The advantage of this system is that no one has to worry about what weird thing the last person may have done that no one may have remembered to clear.

There will however be times when someone has created some new macro or something else and as a result it will be necessary to build the new show off the old show disk. First, there are usually some clear functions. Obviously one shouldn't use them unless one is absolutely sure what they do. "Clear show" may sound like a good idea at the time, but it can wipe out houselight and running light and worklight patches, erase all the macros and do a number of other things one would rather it didn't. It is often safer to clear the disk manually using the del button.

The softpatch would need to be cleared, and it can usually be done in one big operation, as in dim 1 thru xx (last lighting dimmer) del   .

Cues can usually be deleted in one big operation from a cue list mode display screen, as in cue 1 thru xx (last cue number) del   .

Sub assignments (if any) can usually be cleared using similar methods from a submaster list display screen.

Groups (which haven't been discussed yet) could be cleared in one big operation.

Macros usually carry through from show-to-show, but unwanted ones could certainly be deleted.

It is always a good idea to save a copy of the old show just in case there was something on it that needed to be saved.

Groups: In much the same way that dimmers were consolidated into channels, channels can be combined into groups. Let's suppose that the entire stage area is used as the playing area even though it is controlled in 8 lighting areas of 4 instruments-per-area, which works out to 32 channels. No one is going to have the time to set 32 channels individually for every scene in the show. The frontlights could be one group, the backlights another and so forth or the scene could be set up once in a very bright configuration (something touches full) and this bright cue could be recorded as a group (and also as a submaster). Then to create a cue the group or sub could be run up to a level where it looked good and could be recorded.

Let's assume that a cue is being built and the submaster controlling the arealights has been run up to a place where it looks good, which puts the frontlights at a level of 53, sidelights at 47 and backlights at 39. These are all illogical readings, so it would not be unusual to at least want one system to have a level that was a multiple of 5 (frontlights at 55, for example). Try as one might to manipulate the submaster slider, it is very hard to make it hit the exact number that is wanted. Had the group been used instead, it could have been set at the specific level because it is called from the keyboard. Let's suppose that a number of specials have now been added and the cue is pronounced perfect and is recorded as a numbered cue and the submaster that created it has been removed because it has served its purpose. Upon second thought, the director decides that the arealighting part of it is too bright. The grandmaster cannot be used because it will dim down both the arealights and the specials. The submaster cannot be used because it would be piling-on to what is already there. In other words the submaster (which works on the highest-takes-precedence prin-

ciple) can make the arealights brighter by piling-on more light but can't make them dimmer. The group control works on the latest-takes-precedence principle, and as a result can either raise or lower the arealight levels without affecting the levels of any of the specials.

Once levels have been brought up on stage and adjusted as appropriate, a group can be recorded in the usual way (rec group xx) where xx is the group number, which will typically be the same as the corresponding submaster number (assuming there is one).

Parking: This puts dimmers or channels at a specific level where it will remain undisturbed by blackouts or other cues. Theoretically a group, cue or submaster can also be parked, but there is seldom a need for that. Parked channels are usually not affected by any board operations (except possible the blackout button, which is primarily for emergency use). They don't get recorded into cues and they often don't display on the screen. There may also be an alternate way to keep channels at a level (independent) that won't be affected by normal board operations, but will allow them to be recorded into cues.

Pile-ons: Pile-ons are typically avoided where possible because they are hard to get out of gracefully, they are prone to operator error, and they are hard to re-record during the rehearsal process (one has to remember to *update* rather than re-record and one has to make sure the correct cue gets updated to). To illustrate, let's say there is a 50-count crossfade (cue 17) in-progress on the AB fader and the desk light needs to be snapped on. One way to do this would be to put the desk light cue (cue 18) on the CD fader. When the long fade is complete on the AB fader, there would then need to be a utility cue (18.5) on the AB fader (basic cue plus desk light) and at that point the CD fader could be cleared. If at any point in the long fade, levels needed to be changed, then changes to the basic cue would have to be updated to cue 17 and any changes to the desk light itself have to be updated to cue 18.

The desk light could also be put on a submaster and brought up by the sub's bump button, but this is still a pile-on situation, and after the long cue is over, there still needs to be a utility cue on the AB fader that will be the basic cue with desk light followed by the submaster being bumped off.

Printing: It is extremely important for the designer to have a printout of what the channels are reading in every cue. If there is an off-line program that works on a home computer, one can simply take the disk home and run the print there. Actually running a print by hooking a printer to the back of the lightboard is often noisy (which is significant when the board is in the house) and slow and uses a lot of paper, as each cue typically prints on a separate page.

Softpatch: This is the process by which dimmers are assigned to lightboard channels. The instruments out on the pipes are plugged into numbered circuits, which in turn are plugged into numbered dimmers. They are often hardwired, in which case the numbers will usually be the same. Let's say that area one has a frontlight (dim 3) and a backlight (dim 87) and two sidelights (dim 42, 51) that work together. Soft patching allows them to be assigned to channel numbers in a way that makes them easy to remember. Frontlights on areas 1–8 can be on channels 11–18. Sidelights can be channels 21–28. Backlights can be 31–38. Not only can an easier-to-remember alias be assigned to the dimmer, but more than one dimmer (the two sidelights) can be combined onto one control channel. It is not unusual for several hundred dimmers to be controlled by a lightboard that has only a hundred channels. Not all channel numbers need to be used, but where there are more channels than can be displayed on one screen (more than about 100) then using numbers in the upper ranges may cause there to be second or third pages of levels, so in the interests of speed and efficiency, efforts are usually made to make sure that the fewest number of pages are used. There may also be a feature that displays only active channels in which case the screen could display the 100 channels that had been used even if their numbers included numbers like 154, and 180–189.

Dimmers that aren't going to be used are typically assigned to channel 0 (unpatch), which turns them off. The dimming curve (called the *profile*) of a dimmer can be changed so that things like fans or mirror ball motors can be operated as if on a switch (*full power at 1 percent*). There is often a level limit capability that can be set so that any particular dimmer will never be higher than 50 percent or whatever, which is a feature that is seldom needed.

Submaster Assignments: Submasters are typically used to run a channel or group of channels manually (as for a flickering light, a lightning flash etc) or to set prototype settings to use as a base to build other cues from. There are usually at least 12 submaster handles but typically 10 or more pages of submasters, which yields more than a hundred actual submaster assignments. These will typically be piled onto whatever cue is on the timed faders. To record onto a submaster, one usually sets up channel levels or brings up a cue onstage and "rec sub 1 rel rel" (or rec, and then hit the bump button under sub 1, rel rel). Submasters can often be loaded with effect sequences (described previously) and the bump button used as a go button. Sometimes the same sliders that are used for the individual channels are also used for the submasters, in which case there will be some kind of *sub mode* button that toggles between *sub mode* and *chan mode*. All the submasters will work in pile-on mode, which is to say anything recorded on them is added-to (piled on to) whatever is already up onstage. In addition usually some of them can be set to *inhibitive mode* in which anything recorded on them will be subtracted from whatever is already set onstage. With normal pile-on submasters, the sliders will be at 0 (down). To bring up a pile-on cue push the slider up manually. There is often a bump button below each submaster. The default for the bump button is usually press-and-hold for on, release for off. It can often also be set to work like a go button with an uptime and a dwell time or it can be disabled altogether so that it doesn't get hit by accident. It may also be possible to set the bump button to *solo*, which would take all other channels to zero.

In a pile-on situation, one needs a way to record some levels to the basic cue on the fader and other levels to the submaster. The channels themselves usually are different colors on the screen, which helps. Often there is a solo and except button for this purpose.

Let's say one wanted the submaster to bump on certain channels to add them to what is already on stage. One could manually bring up the channels to the correct level in the existing cue setting and then do "chan 5 thru 10 solo rec sub 5 ." This would save the trouble of clearing the basic cue off the stage while the pile-on cue (channels 5–10) was recorded separately, and the finished piled-on effect could be seen onstage.

One can do much the same thing to exclude another submaster settings or cue settings from what one wants to record. What is onstage may be a combination of what was set manually and the effect of cue 4 on the AB faders and sub 4. One might want to record everything except what is on sub 4 onto sub 8. So one could do a "rec sub 8 exc sub (or cue or group, to exclude a group or cue) 4 ."

One can often add a *rate* to a submaster to play it back slower or faster than its recorded time; this is mostly useful for effects (described previously). It is often possible to take manual control of rate by hitting the bump button or a function key and moving the rate wheel or touch screen while the cue is in progress.

Miscellaneous: There is often a *flash* button that works like a bump button; press and hold for on, release for off and visa versa if the channel started at a level above 50. There may be an *only* key. "Group 25 and 26 only group 5 at 75 only group 10 at 50" translated means that those channels that are in the group 25–26 subset that are also in group 5 should be at 75 and those also in group 10

should be at 50. There is often a way to do multi-*part cues*, i.e. the cyc is brought up first and then the downstage and then the platform. Usually this feature allows one channel to only appear in one part, which is not usually what is wanted, so a series of follow cues is more flexible. There may be a *quick-step* feature that allows one to step thru the cues without having to wait for fades to happen in the programmed time. *Sneak* is often used during preview performances so that changes can still be made without making it look to the audience as if lights are flashing on and off. Often an alphanumeric computer keyboard can be used to add labels (names) to various things. The most important use for this is to provide cue lines for the on-screen cue list making it easier for the operator to remember what each cue is supposed to do, which in turn makes it less likely that a mistake will be made and either a cue will be missed or the go button will be pushed twice.

LIGHTING DESIGN— The design itself is the way the stage looks on a moment-by-moment basis from the beginning of the performance to the end as a series of static moments. It is documented by three documents and a computer disk. The computer disk shows the level of every channel in every cue in the show and the speed at which the cue was taken. The Light Plot is a plan view of where all the instruments are located, and its companion document the Hook-up Sheet shows how the channel assignments have been made. The fourth document, the Cue Synopsis, indicates where in the script every lighting change is located and describes what in a general way happens visually.

The design is most often communicated by simply being described from the Cue Synopsis but sometimes a lit model is used and sometimes sketches or photographs or a computer rendering are used. Unlike the set and costume designs that are completed usually well before the first rehearsal, the lighting design isn't usually finalized until the lighting designer has seen a runthru, and at that point it is merely a matter of days before the lights will be hung in place for the show. There is not a lot of time for preparing simulations nor a particular need since the actual lights for the show soon will be in position and ready to create the actual cues.

LIGHTING DESIGN, THE PROCESS—

Most lighting jobs begin with the phone ringing. We're going to assume that it has already rung and that both money and the schedule was discussed, and an agreement was reached. Within the next couple of days, the designer would sign a contract, and the theatre would hand him a script. Let's pick up the process at that point. There will be two periods of concentrated activity. Part one will center around the first production meeting. Then there will be weeks where nothing happens except that the lighting designer will go to weekly production meetings. Then just prior to moving into the theatre Part two will start and everything else will happen all at once.

Part One: First Production Meeting

There are five things that will happen here over the course of two or three days, sometimes all within one day:

1. In preparation for the production meeting, the lighting designer will read the script and come up with a list of notes based on the script. See LIGHTING IDEAS for a more complete discussion of this subject.
2. He will go to the first production meeting where he will be given a blank ground plan and inventory of the equipment, a schedule covering the period leading up to opening night, and usually the set and costume designers will explain what the sets and costumes will be like. It would be typical for him to schedule a meeting with the director and to schedule a time to examine the space. See PRODUCTION MEETING, THE FIRST for a more detailed discussion.
3. He will go home and study the set in detail and look over the notes he took at

the production meeting of things related to the costumes and set that might cause lighting problems. This is all in preparation for meeting with the director.
4. He will then spend some time in the space examining the equipment and facilities and verifying the correctness of the information he has been given. See MEASURING THE SPACE for a more detailed discussion.
5. Then he will meet with the director for the first time where he will raise any concerns he may have. See DIRECTOR, FIRST MEETING WITH for a more detailed discussion.

And Nothing Continues to Happen for a Long Time

Many weeks may follow at this point where he will have nothing much of his own to report to the weekly production meetings because he has not done a design yet. It is a time however to make sure that the set and costume designs will not hinder his ability to light the show. It is a time to do *Short Plots*, which are hypothetical exercises in how one would light the space if one had to do it now. This can be considered the lull before the storm.

Part Two: The Set-In

There are six things that need to be done in preparation for the set-in:

1. The final countdown begins with the lighting designer seeing a runthru. See LIGHTING IDEAS for a more detailed discussion.
2. It is followed (sometimes by as little as 15 minutes) by a meeting with the director to discuss what the lighting designer plans doing See DIRECTOR, FINAL MEETING WITH. At this point he would have all the information he is ever going to get that would help in the design process, so there is no reason not to continue onward as soon as he gets home.
3. He will do whatever additional thinking

has to be done and do a handwritten draft version of the plot and hookup.

4. This would be followed by the final version of the Light Plot along with the final Hookup Sheet.
5. This is about the same time that the computer disk would need to be formatted See FORMATTING THE DISK for a more detailed discussion.
6. He would prepare the CUE SYNOPSIS, and give both the director and stage manager a copy at the next production meeting.

There are now four events that take place as part of the lighting set-in that don't involve actors:

1. The lights are hung in place, accessorized and connected to power. See HANGING SESSION for a more detailed discussion.
2. The lights are focused. See FOCUSING SESSION for a more detailed discussion.
3. The levels for each cue are roughed-in. See LEVEL-SETTING SESSION for a more detailed discussion.
4. The roughed-in levels are shown to the director. See DRY TECH for a more detailed discussion.

At this point the lighting can be, and usually is, rehearsed along with the actors. There are four possible kinds of rehearsals:

1. REHEARSALS-WITH-LIGHT integrate the lighting into the show gradually without disrupting the acting part of the rehearsal and usually occur prior to the Dry Tech.
2. TECHNICAL REHEARSALS integrate the lighting into the show using a stop-and-correct method. Usually all other technical elements except the costumes are integrated into the show at the same time.
3. DRESS REHEARSALS are technical rehearsal to which the costumes have been added.
4. PREVIEW PERFORMANCES are considered rehearsals where the theatre reserves the right to stop if necessary, but in most instances they are effectively performances.

On opening night the lighting designer is officially done. Since no changes are usually made after opening night, he is usually done after the note session of the last preview.

LIGHTING DESIGNER— The person responsible for the way the stage looks on a moment-by-moment basis from the beginning of the performance to the end. This person typically specifies where all the lights will be located and decides what color they all will be and how bright in each cue they will be. It is the sum of all these things that determines how the stage will appear to the audience.

LIGHTING DESIGNER, BIRTH OF— Christopher Marlowe didn't have one. Neither did Sheridan or Molière. The question at hand is when did "doing the lighting" get elevated to the level of designer-hood and how did that come about, and why didn't designing the hair or designing the props do the same for those department heads. Or to look at it another way, why didn't the lighting get consolidated and combined with something else like set design?

If you have not yet read the topic called HISTORY OF LIGHTING, you should do that now because the birth of the lighting designer was directly related to various stages in how complex it became to light the stage.

Shakespeare didn't have a lighting designer and by the time gaslight had gotten into the theatre, there still wasn't one. The snuff-boy had been replaced by a *gasman* who was typically a plumber by trade and could pipe the gas where it needed to go. He would also control the flow during the performance to the various areas, which in most cases meant the house as distinct from the stage. The house might easily involve a dozen controls as the orchestra sconces would be controlled separately from the chandeliers and the balconies and boxes controlled by something else. The same would have been true for the stage, as the in-one areas would be controlled separately from the footlights and so forth. When followspots started being used, this added that many more people to the lighting crew. All of them were technicians but none of them designers. While they did whatever setup work needed doing (very little), they were primarily operators.

Electricity, specifically dimmers, required many more pairs of hands to make them work. Louis Hartmann, who was David Belasco's trusted assistant, was probably America's first lighting designer, but the program simply read "Electrical effects by Louis Hartmann" and Louis himself never claimed credit for designing anything he worked on. In his book, he always defers to David Belasco, and says that Mr. Belasco wanted this or that and he (Louis) figured out how to do it.

Stanley McCandless explained how he thought the job ought to be done. If he thought there ought to be a specific designer for the lighting, he did not specifically say so. In fact, he implied that by following his system anyone could achieve the desired results. His system was so simple that it could be learned in an afternoon even by an ordinary person.

While David Belasco had demonstrated in a career's worth of shows that spanned almost three decades how important the lighting could be to the overall show, he had also demonstrated how easy it was to tear a set apart in order to get light into it.

A group of set designers began to think that their designs might fare better if they were the ones who decided how to light them. Robert Edmund Jones and Lee Simonson come to mind in this regard. When they had themselves listed on the program, they gave themselves credit for having designed both the set and the lights, and perhaps without really intending to, they were the ones, more than anyone else, who were actually responsible for elevating the lighting to the level of design. They were not intending, of course, to add a third designer. In fact they were trying to avoid adding anyone new of any kind. They were simply expanding their job title to be more inclusive.

This might have worked quite well except that not all set designers were inclined to accept the lighting as part of their job, and sometimes a really good set designer was not an equally good lighting designer, so the system stumbled. Costumers and directors often thought the combination of set and lighting designer, all rolled-into-one, worried more about how his set looked than he did about how the costumes and actors walking around on it looked. Also the bulk of the lighting work took place just at the time when the set was being installed on the stage, so the combination-designer needed lots of assistants to get everything done. Also, over time the job became increasingly harder. Once the arealighting started being done by fresnels, it had increased the list of what needed to be done but had not really had that much of an impact on the design and planning. Misplaced instruments that caused dark spots could simply be opened wider to overlap more. However, when ellipsoidals started replacing fresnels, it had a huge impact because misplaced instruments were no longer size-adjustable, and so it was possible to place them incorrectly and discover huge gaping unlit places that were almost impossible to eliminate without radically reworking the entire design, and depending upon the enormity of the mistake, there might or might not be time to correct everything that was wrong. If one had to pick a single point at which the job of lighting a show became too complex to learn in an afternoon, the switch to ellipsoidals was that point because the designer now had to accurately predict in advance how these instruments would behave, which meant calculating how big and bright the lights would be.

For a time it became fashionable for the set designer to hire an "assistant" to ghost design the lighting in much the same way as scenic artists did the painting for him. This eventually backfired because the set designer typically had no answers for the directors' questions and the directors quickly realized who had done the actual design and started working directly with those assistants.

In those situations where the set designer either did not want to be bothered with the lighting himself or where he was not asked, the job would of necessity fall to someone else, a third person. Whether he was a real designer or not, could be debated, but the job had been called "lighting design" in the past, so lighting design it had become. A third designer had now officially, and almost entirely by accident, been born.

There was no parade in the streets, and no cigars were passed around to celebrate the event. In fact, all energies seemed to now be concentrated on controlling this new designer to make sure that his "design" or whatever it was he did, did not conflict in any way with the main design idea of the whole show, i.e. the set and costume designs.

It was about at this point that the idea of having production meetings came into being. Previously the stage manager had delivered messages back and forth between the director and the various concerned parties, which included the two principle designers but also included front-of-house staff or administration staff or anyone else like the prop master or the lighting person or the sound person, etc. That was fine for the director but it left no mechanism for the two principle designers to address the sub-designers and other technical workers. The general idea of the production meeting was that the principle designers along with the director would explain to department heads and sub-designers what the plan for the whole show was. Then the sub-designers like the lighting designer would submit their proposed designs for discussion to make sure nothing that they were planning would interfere with the main design.

In theory there was nothing wrong with this, but it failed to take into account that the lighting designer did not do his design at the same early date as the set and costume designers and as a result would not have anything to submit until after the meetings were long over. As it worked out, it became a forum for the lighting designer to make sure that the set would not be in the light path or in other ways interfere with the lighting

without submitting the lighting design as a whole to any kind of critical scrutiny.

It was never really clear what a presentation by the lighting designer would have consisted of anyway. The Light Plot is completely unreadable even to other lighting designers without hours of deciphering. Mostly the lighting designer describes what the scene will look like. The descriptions are usually so vague, like a "bright moonlit night" that they have to be seen to be fully appreciated. Directors mostly accept the vague descriptions knowing that they will have a dry tech session where every cue will be seen and approved.

LIGHTING DESIGNER, GETTING A FIRST JOB— The most common way to get a job is to get recommended for it. In other words, a teacher or mentor or someone who knows the people who actually hire lighting designers suggests that this person ought to be given a chance. If the new lighting designer doesn't do well, there may not, of course, be other chances unless they are a relative or have a personal relationship with someone of importance at that particular theatre, in which case it won't matter at all whether they can do the job or not because it will be theirs for life.

Why would anyone else hire someone who was totally inexperienced? The answer is they wouldn't. You won't read this everywhere but almost everyone who has been a lighting designer has had to invent a resume before he actually had one. Lest there be any confusion, this means that the would-be lighting designer pretends he worked at places where he didn't or more commonly that he was the lighting designer at places where he worked as some kind of technician.

LIGHTING DESIGNER, GETTING HIRED BACK— It is a sad truth that the people responsible for hiring the lighting designers often cannot tell the difference between a good lighting design and a bad one. They very often haven't even seen the shows or if they have, they can't remember what the lighting looked like. So what then do they base their hiring on? A lot of it is based on demeanor.

It should be obvious that the lighting designer should not fight or argue with anyone else on the production design team or do anything else that will create an adverse memory. This is not to say that he can't have differences, but they have to be resolved in a way that no one recalls that there was any conflict. Second, the lighting designer needs to figure out who has the most voice in the hiring process, and he needs to try to make a friend, or failing that, make sure he doesn't create an enemy. This person is typically NOT the show's director, who often has very little say in who gets hired. Third, the lighting designer should take advantage of anything that will impress the cousins from the country, which includes using a CAD program and doing math calculations on a pocket calculator. The designer's paperwork should be immaculate, and he should be good at communicating with people both on a one-to-one basis and at a group meeting. DIPLOMACY covers much of this is more detail.

Many lighting designers feel that hand-drawn light plots and hand-written paperwork are just as good as CAD drawings and typed (printed) paperwork. They are for every purpose except that of getting another job. For the purposes of getting the next job, the lighting designer may have to do some things that don't seem to directly relate to the job. Of these things demeanor is of first importance. Perfectly awful lighting designs go undetected because the lighting designer pretended he liked everything he saw and was always friendly and happy. While it is normal for a lighting designer to have doubts about what he's done, he needs to keep these thoughts to himself and present a confident public image.

When David Belasco found a lighting designer that he liked, he had him light every show that was done at his theatre for 28 years. This kind of loyalty has since gone out of fashion, and the job would now more likely be shared between several different designers. In that way, they are all kept humble and if one were to leave or get a better job somewhere else, then the loss would be less significant.

LIGHTING DESIGNER, QUALIFICATIONS— These are not the qualifications for getting the job or getting hired back, which have both been discussed above, but these are the qualifications that one actually needs to do the job in a way that people one respects will think the job was well done. There are five general areas of concern: Having ideas, technical know-how, working within the time constraints, working with others, and communicating the vision.

One has to have ideas, lighting ideas. Although this is dealt with in considerable detail in LIGHTING IDEAS, unhappily no one can explain where they come from exactly or how to reliably get them, but it is impossible to produce inspired lighting without them.

Once one has the idea or image of how the scene should look, then one needs the technical know-how to understand how to make it happen. The good news is that once an effect can be imagined, one can usually learn how to produce it.

None of the other designers work with similar time constraints. It is as if the lighting designer is in a race, but everyone else has had a big head start. As a result the lighting designer has to do everything right the first time, make no mistakes along the way and somehow overtake the field. In practice, most lighting designers are calm under pressure and capable of instant decisions, and they tend to be excessive planners, planning for many contingencies. Most good designers make the whole process seem effortless, but even so, as simple a mistake as using the wrong color in a color wash has to be recognized as a mistake and dealt with. If allowed to continue into a second rehearsal, it will severely limit the time left to try other solutions.

Lighting designers need to be diplomats. If they are to see their vision produced onstage, they need to get agreement from a number of other people, and they need to do this in a way that hopefully does not anger or alienate their co-designers or the director.

In dealing with the director, the lighting designer has to have the storyteller's gift to help the director see the same image of the scene or, failing that, to help the director believe that the lighting designer at least knows what it should look like. In a similar vein, during the first 10–12 weeks of rehearsal the lighting designer does little else but attend meetings without producing the slightest shred of evidence that he or she is competent to do the job. This requires projecting self-confidence, and this may be particularly hard in a situation where the lighting designer is having trouble getting ideas and is suffering from self-doubts.

LIGHTING FOR THE STAGE— The question at hand is how is lighting for the stage is different from the way a sunny day is lit or the way a skating rink or factory is lit. There are at least four factors involved.

First, the sunny day, the skating rink and the factory are all lit from directly above because it is horizontal surfaces that need to be lit. In the theatre, the primary concern is vertical surfaces, and light from directly above does not work well for this.

Second, the day, the rink and the factory all rely on the light from above then bouncing around and being reflected by everything that it comes in contact with so that all the actual shadows are softened. In the theatre, an attempt is made to eliminate all bounce light because it cannot be controlled and bounces out into the house or onto things that no one wants seen. To make the scene seem real, it is then necessary to simulate the effect of bounce light by direct lighting in a shadow color. This can only be partially effective as the angle will be wrong. The shadow color will have to come from the place where the instruments are (above) whereas in real life the reflected light comes mostly from below. This is further complicated by the fact that if there is a sunny side

and a shady side to something, everyone in the theatre wants to feel they are on the sunny side. As a result, the shadow colors have to be more muted than they would be in real life or in a painting that is always viewed from the front.

Third, because of the Bounce Light Problem and because of a potential Glare Problem (both explained in more detail elsewhere) an attempt is going to be made to keep the light levels low. Both Stanley Mc-Candless and Louis Hartmann warn that in their modern age of electricity (1920s), it had suddenly become possible to flood the stage with light but that in most cases this was a bad idea as many things were more interesting when only partially seen. A sunny day in real life is about 5000 fc bright. In the theatre, it will typically only be 50–100 fc bright. At the same time, a night scene in real life would only be a fraction of a candlepower bright, but in the theatre it may have to be 4–5 times brighter, which is part of the Audience's Right To See, which is explained in more detail elsewhere. See LIGHT, QUANTITY OF for a more detailed discussion of light levels in the theatre.

Fourth, the light used in the theatre will have more color than either natural or most artificial light because it is trying to differentiate between source light and reflected light (through the use of color).

LIGHTING IDEAS— The question is where do a lighting designer's ideas or inspiration come from, and how is it possible to encourage this process. Ideally, the lighting designer will eventually see the whole show played out like a moving picture in his head, and he will merely reproduce these images onstage with light.

First, it is essential to distinguish between the ideas or images and the technique that it takes to render them onstage. If for example one were given a postcard from an art museum by any of the many painters who use light so well and were told that this is both a picture of the set and a static moment for which it will be necessary to reproduce the lighting, one could or should be able to do this because it is purely a matter of discerning the direction and color of the light and copying it. If one can't do this now, one could certainly be taught to do it because it is purely a matter of technique, and technique can be learned.

The image or idea came from the original artist's imagination, no one can be taught how to get this kind of idea, but in the theatre they can be stimulated and encouraged by three sources: the *script*, the *set* and the *runthru*.

The Script

Chronologically, it will be the script that will become available to the lighting designer first. He will have only one chance to approach it from the point-of-view of a first time audience. Inasmuch as one is trying to conjure forth elusive ideas, most designers will clear away all distractions, choose a time when the phone and the door can be allowed to go unanswered, and accord the event the proper respect and as a result will read the entire play at one sitting, without the benefit of radio, TV, or snacks.

There is an ideal time to do this, and it is not the day the script arrives in the mail. It is the night before (or morning of) the first production meeting because then all the characters, situations and anything else will be clearest in the designer's mind. If the designer is new to this particular theatre, he will be expected to prove in some small way that he has indeed read the script. If he doesn't volunteer something at the first production meeting, someone is likely to ask him a skill-testing question that he could not begin to answer unless he had actually read the script like, "Do you think Mary's hat will be a problem?" If he's not read the script, he won't know who Mary is or what kind of a hat she will wear or why it is required that she wear one at all. More to the point, if he read the script a month ago, he could easily have forgotten the characters' names or the intricacies of the plot by this point, and so even though he actually did read the script,

he will leave the impression that either he didn't or didn't read it very carefully. Neither impression will be the way he wants to start off in a new job.

There is a considerable difference of opinion as to how many times the script should be read. Some believe that the designer will be left with the sharpest visual images if he reads the script just once and never touches it again except to look up references or cue lines. Others suggest that he should read the script weekly or daily or as often as possible. The actual truth is that scripts as a whole provides a wealth of information for the actors and director, considerably less for the costume and set designers and next to nothing for either the lighting or sound designers. What little is left for the lighting designer is usually conveniently left in the stage directions preceding each numbered scene where the information can be effortlessly extracted.

All would probably agree that the script should be read as many times as necessary until all its ideas have been extracted. All would probably agree that when the designer was done, he should be able to pass a test on what he has read, because, as mentioned above, there often is a thinly veiled test of sorts. He should know how many different scenes there are and which ones probably repeat the lighting of an earlier one. He should know how many different locations there are going to be in this play and how many different ways he will be expected to light each one (i.e. if its time of day, season of the year, or some other factor is different). While a play might have 20 *scenes*, it might only have 11 *locales* and these could require 16 different states of lighting, which are commonly called *looks* and which we take to mean the significant or major cue settings upon which other derivative cues (sub-looks) may be based. There is no correlation between the number of looks in a show and the number of cues it may have: it all depends on how many times each look is repeated and how many cues are simply slight or insignificant variants of the original look. Plays essentially consist of a series of static cue settings, which flow from one to another in a rhythmic and dynamic way. Yes, sometimes the sequence of cues may follow each other in such rapid succession that it creates the impression of fluidly moving lights, but the cues themselves are static and this is the way the lightboard records them and the way they are commonly discussed.

Most designers highlight (or otherwise mark) in the script all references to lighting, time of day, season of the year, location, looking out windows or anything else related to lighting, even if they don't intend to do it that way. There are really three kinds of clues embedded in the script, some more important than others: Of the highest order are those things that are embedded in the text of what one character says to another, as for example, "All this rain depresses me." There can be no question that these come from the playwright, and the designer must either do these the way the playwright envisioned or he must convince the director to change the playwright's lines. These are commonly called the *obligatory cues.* The stage directions are quite a different story, and for the most part can be treated as suggestions from a previous production. Few of these come from the playwright; most were written by an editor or the stage manager prior to the publication of the script to try to make it easier for the reader to visualize the finished product, so they fall into two categories based on whether one intends to do what they say or not. The director and all the actors have also read these same stage directions, and they tend to assume they've been written in stone, so if the lighting designer plans to deviate from anything written there, he needs to explain this to the director.

It is not unusual for the lighting designer to make a running list of possible specials while he reads, which will read something like "possible window special," "possible isolation special on so-and-so scene 11." These are things he thinks he might want to do. Most designers will organize this by scenes and will indicate the time, place and any situational information explicit in the script (often in the stage directions at the beginning of each scene). This constitutes the lighting designer's script analysis, which can be called a *script list,* although there isn't a universally agreed upon name for it. These are the designer's personal notes and can be organized any way that makes sense to him.

Any play written before 1960 is unlikely to have many stage directions that involve lighting at all, but the lighting designer and the director are going to have to imagine what the playwright would have wanted done had he written his play now. In essence the play is going to be adapted to a current-day production, at least in terms of its lighting.

You will notice that the script analysis did not include a "spine" or meaning of the play or a graph of the tensions of the characters in the various scenes of the play. Most plays being done these days are one of the sub-genres of realism where the lighting is expected to be motivated and to simulate real sources. Most directors do not expect or want the lighting to try to express the theme or meaning of the play, and there is considerable question as to whether this is even possible, and if it were, what it would entail. See LIGHTING, ART OF for a more detailed discussion.

The Set

Once the lighting designer understands what the set is going to be like, he is in a position to start thinking about how he might go about lighting the show, at least in terms of arealights and sometimes also in terms of color washes.

He will be using the LIGHT-THE-SET METHOD (described separately) because it is the only method available at this early date. He could theoretically deliver a completed lighting design on the day after having seen the set design because the system is based on the principle that if one has lit every place on the set that an actor might chance to be, then by coincidence (or design) the entire show has been lit (or any other performance that could be done on that set), and the system does not require that the designer either read the script or see a runthru.

Not reading the script and not going to see any rehearsals would not, of course, make the lighting designer popular with the director, and it would generate no show-specific specials because he would be totally ignorant of what the play was about, so this is not being suggested as a final method but as a way to stimulate thought about what might or could be done. There have been designers who have read the script diligently and gone to numerous runthrus who could not equal the results produced by someone else using this method alone, so it has a definite place in the planning process.

If the theatre does not own its own lighting equipment, then a shop order has to be prepared at an early date to rent what will be needed. This is the method that will have to be used to prepare the estimate.

In the schedule, there is usually a long time between when the set design is unveiled and when the lighting designer sees a runthru. It is important that the lighting designer continues to think about the show during this time on at least a weekly basis. The ultimate purpose is to conjure up ideas and alternate ways to do the same thing. He is thinking about how he would light this play if he had to light it tomorrow without having had the benefit of having seen a runthru. If there is going to be a problem lighting the high platform because actors' shadows will be cast back onto the drop or there will be spill light out in the house, now is the time to bring up these issues while there is still time for changes to be made to the set. Maybe it never occurred to anyone that moving the high platform downstage a foot might help out the lighting enormously.

The plot will, of course, be incomplete because (until the lighting designer sees a runthru) he has no idea where most of the specials will need to be. What is remarkable, however, is the vast number of instruments that he will be able to place because they are going to be the arealights or washes (i.e. light the actors wherever they may be on the set),

which makes them set-dependent rather than production-dependent.

The Short Plot does not require mapping the location of the instruments but assumes that there will be a hanging position at the ideal location. It is typically done on the back of an old envelope or on a piece of scratch paper. Available equipment is listed by type across the top and proposed uses down the side and the quantity used constitutes the body of the table. How many instruments will it take to frontlight this set, light it from the right, from the left, from the back? What are the known or suspected specials? By totaling the columns one can tell how many instruments have been used and how many are left over to be used for something else.

Short Plots are typically done after every production meeting from memory without consulting any of the previous versions. In this way a collection of slightly different variants can be compiled. It is not uncommon to assign tentative gel colors to the various systems, and it is not uncommon to figure out what channels will eventually control these things. In this way, not only are the available instruments accounted for but also the available channels and sometimes the number of barndoors and other accessories.

When the time comes to actually do the draft Light Plot, the collection of Short Plots is used as the basis for this, and the process of having done them is supposed to reduce the fear and stress of having to draw the light plot in an afternoon or a day or whatever the schedule calls for.

In rare situations where time between the runthru and the time the lights need to be hung is very short, the Short Plot may be expanded into an actual light plot (preliminary plot) with instrument numbers, circuit numbers and all other numbers. The idea is that after the designer has seen the runthru, any changes will then be pen-and-inked onto the plot along with the location of the specials. Doing it this way does not always result in the best circuiting choices and is not as easy for the crew to read, but sometimes there is simply not enough time to do it any other way.

The Runthru

Assuming that the designer has been doing Short Plots on a regular basis, the tentative design will have gotten better over time and presumably will get a whole-lot better after the runthru has been seen. What has already been done for practice is about 80 percent of what the finished product will be.

Is it known where the cues will go in the show? Well no, not all of them. It is however known that the houselights will go to half at the start of the show, that they will go out, that there will be lights-up on Scene 1. When actors hit light switches, lights will appear to go on or off, and these all constitute light cues. One also knows there will be curtain calls at the end of the show, followed by the house lights coming up and a postshow cue being put onstage.

This is called a *draft Cue Synopsis*, and depending on how much time there is before and after the final meeting with the director, it may or may not make sense to do this initial draft version. If a draft is done ahead of time, it can be used as a reference document while watching the runthru and it can become the discussion document at the light meeting, after which it would have to be corrected (all the cues renumbered, etc) before it was passed out in its final form.

If the script is to be used as the discussion document at the light meeting, then it will have to have the cues written in (usually an extra step). There are differing schools of thought about whether the Cue Synopsis should be done before or after the lighting meeting. It is not even universally agreed that there even needs to be a Cue Synopsis (as a written document) at all, except in the sense of the lighting designer delivering it orally. See CUE SYNOPSIS for a more detailed discussion.

The first runthru involves the lighting designer with a legal pad and an open mind, sitting in to watch it. This is the one and only time that the production can be seen as the audience will see it as if for the first time. Most designers understand the importance of these first time impressions and accord the occasion the respect it deserves.

Regardless of how many times one has chosen to read the script, re-reading it on the eve of seeing the runthru is a hideously bad idea as it potentially will contaminate what is being done in this production with what they did in some previous production. Most designers try to forget the script as much as possible at this point. They do however need to refresh themselves on what the set will look like and what all the tape marks on the floor mean, and they do need to remind themselves of what the actors' names are because in a rehearsal situation they are often referred to by their real names.

If the show is particularly complicated like a musical where cues are likely to come on a certain part of the music or a certain bit of choreography, making a tape (either audio or video but preferably the latter) will greatly enhance the chances that the cues are placed in the correct place. Seeing the runthru is not supposed to be a memory test for the lighting designer, who is often writing on his pad at the critical moment when something else is supposed to happen. Theoretically the lighting designer could come back to see another rehearsal, but they may not be doing runthrus and even if they were, they could not predict when they would get to the part that he needed to see again. If he has the runthru on tape, he can fast forward to the part he is interested in.

When the playwright writes the script, he divides it into acts and scenes that make sense to him at the time, but this is not always the way the production may appear to the audience. The audience does not have the benefit of having read any of the stage directions and perceives acts and scenes mostly based on what the lighting does. When one watches a runthru, one usually wants to completely forget about the acts and scenes and watch for *perceptual units*, which are units of action that will be perceived by the audience as being part of the same scene (whether written that way or not). Sometimes there may be a sequence of three written scenes that flow as if they were one. Sometimes there may be one written scene that has three separate parts that will be separated by three different lighting cues and will appear as if they were separate scenes. This has to do with the way the play has been staged, whether there are prop or costume changes and many other factors. In other words, a lot of other people may have done things that will affect how the audience will perceive what they see.

The first runthru as the name implies is usually the first time the scenes have been done in their playing order sequence without there being a stop after each one. The actors are usually nervous enough about this, so the addition of "visitors," even if they are only the show's designers (often only the lighting and costume designers), may seem a lot like having an audience. The addition of a video camera, unless the actors are used to this, may cause an unpleasant scene, which the actors almost always will win. It also may be against a strict interpretation of the rules (either the actors' union rules or the theatre's internal rules). In any event, the actors will typically behave differently if they think they are being taped, which is reason enough for it to be handled discreetly. As a purely practical matter, the camera can often be put in the control booth or in the balcony or somewhere else where it can be turned on at the start of an act and otherwise left unattended.

Regardless of whether the rehearsal is being taped or not, the lighting designer typically makes copious notes and draws little sketches of where everyone is as he watches the run. Every time he thinks the lights should change, he'll write down the cue line with a description of what he thinks should be different. Sometimes he won't know specifically what he wants to be different. He will just know that something has to change because there is a passage of time or because the actors are supposedly traveling from one place to another or for some other reason. He may see opportunities where it would be helpful to have a special. He may have an image of color and direction for a particular special. By lining up the aimpoint of a special with some other object or person either in front or behind, it is often possible to light two things with one instrument simply by picking the appropriate angle.

If the show is fluid and stream-of-consciousness style, then the designer has to try to identify the perceptual units without reference to the Cue Synopsis. If the show is more conventional and the scenes as written are the scenes as perceived, then he may simply correct a draft Cue Synopsis as he watches, changing as necessary the timing, cue line or description.

The whole question of how frequently the lighting designer should attend rehearsals is a hotly debated issue although everyone would probably agree that it is up to the individual lighting designer to decide how often he needs to do this. In order to estimate timings, the scenes have to be run in order more-or-less the way they will be in performance (in other words to be entirely useful, it has to be a runthru rather than an ordinary rehearsal situation). What about changes that are made to the production after the lighting designer has seen the run? This is exactly the reason why in most schedules the designers' run is scheduled a couple of days before the Light Plot is due and when the instruments are on the verge of being hung. The production usually will change all the way up to opening night, but once the lights have been hung and focused, the ability to respond to those changes is greatly reduced because the time available is ever diminishing, and in the real world, it may simply not be possible to incorporate every last minute change or new idea.

If the lighting designer is meeting with the director after the run, then he will usually revise his act one notes during the intermission break and revise or review his act two notes while the director is giving actor notes after the run.

When one has experienced the three sources of inspiration and discussed the show with the director, then one has gotten as much input as one is ever going to get, and it would now be time to do the Light Plot and otherwise finalize the plan for the lights.

LIGHTING INSTRUMENTS— See IN-STRUMENTS.

LIGHTING MAGAZINES— See MAGA-ZINES.

LIGHTING PLOT (BRITISH: *lighting lay-out* or *lighting plan*)— See LIGHT PLOT.

LIGHTING POSITIONS— See HANGING POSITIONS, IDEAL.

LIGHTING REHEARSALS— In its most generic meaning, it refers to any rehearsal that includes the stage lighting whether actors are present or not. Rehearsals that don't include the actors are more commonly called *dry techs* and rehearsals that do include them are more commonly called *technical rehearsals* (*techs* for short) and typically also include all other technical elements except the costumes. Technical rehearsals that include the costumes are mostly referred to as *dress rehearsals*. Anything called a lighting rehearsal suggests a remedial session designed to work out specific lighting problems.

LIGHTING SEATS— The lighting designer is supposed to light the stage so that it can be seen from every seat in the house, and as a consequence is expected to sit in many different places, but there are often only two or three rehearsals in which to do this. The lightboard operation has to have reached a point where it is going well enough that the designer feels free to abandon his position behind the lightboard monitor for positions out in the house. Once preview performances start, movement is limited to moving between acts, so that leaves just a very few rehearsals in which to try out perhaps 500 seats.

It isn't, of course, necessary to sit in every one of them. It is only necessary to sit in some typical seats, and it is not necessary to sit in each one for very long.

Typical seats would include front row at the two ends and center, the center back of the house and the front and back of the balcony. If the balcony curves around the stage, it would then be necessary to include the first row end seats in the balcony also. The lighting from the balcony usually looks terrific because the stage is being lit from the same direction as it is being viewed from (above). The balcony is mostly checked to see that the extreme seats cannot see backstage or over the set.

The front row of the orchestra is quite a different story as the audience is mostly looking up at the action, which is lit from above, and it is the first row that is going to be most aware of the facial shadows and also a location that sees too far into the wings or up in the flies.

One would want to sit in all of these seats, at least for 15 or 20 minutes each. If the side-lights appear too dim in scene one, they will probably be too dim in many other scenes built off of this cue. After all these initial changes have been incorporated, then it makes more sense to spend a whole act in one of the problem locations.

LIGHTING SPECIAL PROBLEMS— There are a number of common theatrical situations that cannot successfully be lit in the conventional way but require special techniques. A problem common to many of them will be where the shadows fall. The rule of thumb is that actors need to stay 8 feet away from vertical surfaces if shadows are to be kept off the surface. This is based on lighting from the golden ring positions (45 degrees above), where the shadow will extend as far back as the actor is tall (usually assumed to be 6 feet) and then 2 extra feet are added because the lit area is seldom cut off at head height but extends upward so that the actor can raise his arms or stand on a chair. As the actor moves closer than 8 feet to a vertical surface, his shadow will begin climbing up the surface until the point where the actor is less than a foot away at which point the shadow will be full-sized. Often lighting positions steeper than 45 degrees are used to reduce the length of the shadows, but this creates more pronounced facial shadows and decreases visibility.

Aisles and Runways

When the aisles are used as playing areas, it is important to distinguish between audience aisles (part of the audience egress plan, where doors or other scenery are not permitted) and aisles or vomitoria that are actor-only entryways that are often terminated by a piece of scenery like a door or window. In proscenium configurations, entrances for performers from the house are rare. In theatre-in-the-round, they are the only entryways there are. In thrust configurations there are often as many as three downstage entryways, which may or may not also be shared by the audience.

The problem here involves the seated audience on either side that needs to be kept in relative darkness. The only way to do this is to use two-point lighting to light the aisles along their line-of-travel. The light from onstage tends to come from the lighting grid and the light from the offstage tends to come from a FOH eyelevel position on a wall or underside of the balcony, but there may not always be house positions that could light the aisles from the house side. Sidelights would spill into the audience and so can't be used unless the aisles or vomitoria have high sidewalls. Because the front and backlights produce cones of light, they are usually cut to the armrests of the audience seating on both sides of the aisle. At the nose height of a standing actor, this translates into a lit path only about 16–20" wide, so although the aisle might be considerably wider, the actors will only be lit if they stay very close to the centerline of the aisle.

A runway that runs directly out into the audience can be lit from the front but not backlit unless there is 8 feet or so of light moat between the DS edge of the runway and the first row of audience, which there usually isn't.

A similar if not identical problem can be encountered onstage where a central US/DS

corridor needs to be lit without spilling either into a SL or SR area. Again it needs to be lit along its line-of-travel, but as it is onstage there are usually hanging positions that will be in the right place.

Two-point lighting is not particularly good lighting, but sometimes it is the best available when there are other requirements that need to be met first.

Alcoves

These are places that recess backwards or off into the wings and have ceilings or headers that prevent light from traveling into them well. If the header is lower than the ceiling it may be possible to conceal sources right behind it. Small floodlights are often used for this purpose but they will all have Distance Problems because of their closeness. Where this is not possible, the alcove or recess badly needs a ceiling mounted practical light to assist in casting light into its depths.

Backings & Glows

Door Backings: The traditional method involves a cliplight or flood of some kind mounted high above the door on its offstage side. When the actor approaches the door from the offstage side, he becomes increasingly brighter as he gets closer to the door, and then there is a dead spot just before he gets to the door where he cannot be hit either by the flood above the door or by instruments from the onstage side coming through the door. This is clearly a less than ideal situation.

The lighting in these areas can be greatly improved by indirectly lighting them. The area above the door on the off-stage side needs to be painted white. An instrument needs to shoot above the heads of the actors to hit this area above the door (and the false ceiling) and bounce this light back onto the entering actor. The instrument needs to be high enough so that it is out of audience sight lines. This is not always possible. Sometimes one might have to mount an instrument on the upstage backing wall that directs its light at the back (upstage side) of the downstage masking wall. The light has to be contained so that it only gets out of the light box through the door opening and any direct light has to be above the heads of the actors so that no unwanted shadows are created.

Glow Through a Glass Block Wall: This is a situation in which the glass block or pebbly Plexiglas is so obscure that it may be possible to bounce light directly off the back of a light box without actually being able to see the back of the box. A white flat or surface is placed at least 3–4 feet back from the glass block, the further back the better. It is lit by PAR's, floods or plain light bulbs mounted to the sides of the area of glass block. Sheets, muslin, or other flats are used to enclose the sides so that the light does not spill out of the box.

Glows Under Platforms: A glow by definition is indirect illumination. The problem with putting lights under platforms is usually one of space. The lights need to be placed where they cannot be seen by the audience, and they have to be aimed at a surface that can't be seen either. Everything that can't be seen has to be painted white or silver so that it will encourage light to bounce. The best solution is usually instruments on the deck (masked if necessary) pointing at the underside of the platforming. The alternative is to mount the lights on the underside of the platforming aimed at the floor, but this doesn't usually work as well because the actors moving around on the platforms cause the attached lights to move also.

Window Backings: The problem is even easier here because actors usually aren't seen here. It is only the backing flat that needs to have light on it. It can often be directly lit by a flood mounted above the window on the offstage side (traditional method). If the space is too cramped for this, it may be possible to place floods on the backing flat lower and higher than sightlines that bounce light off the backstage side of the window wall, which usually creates a much more even lighting.

Cycs and Drops

Let's say there is a sky cloth against the upstage wall of the stage. At the very least, the actors have to be kept 8' downstage of it to prevent their shadows from the arealighting projecting onto it. Lest there be any confusion, that's 8' of stage depth where no acting can take place.

How will actors get from one side of the stage to the other? If they need to pass behind the sky cloth, this will add at least another 2 or 3', and if the sky cloth is in fact a cloth rather than a hard (plywood-like) unit, then the actors will have to be very careful when they cross behind that they do not cause the fabric to ripple in the air currents they will create. If the cloth needs to be backlit as well as front lit, then one has to allow at least another 3–8'. As a general rule direct backlighting does not work as well as indirect backlight. Both are discussed below.

So far as much as 18' of depth has been used up (8' for acting area shadows, 2' for passage behind, plus 8' for backlight and the sky still shows no signs of being a "distant" sky. When one or more gauzes (scrims) are hung in front, it softens the view and makes the drop seem to be more distant. If there is to be a gauze, then it needs to be at least 3–8' downstage of the sky cloth because the lights need this much room to light it, and now the actors need to be kept 8 feet downstage of the gauze, which puts the unusable stage depth, for those of us still counting, at 26', which is often the entire depth of the stage. Harold Ridge in his book, **Stage Lighting Principles and Practice**, published in London in 1935, estimated this distance at closer to 30' and indicated that although stages on the continent typically took this into consideration, the English stages of the time did not. For the most part, American stages don't allow for this kind of depth either. As a small historical footnote, this has not always been the case. In Italy in the 1600s it was common for the stages to have a width-to-depth ration of 2:3, which for a 30' proscenium opening would have meant 45' of depth.

First, there needs to be a frank discussion with the director and ultimately the set designer about how much unusable stage depth is going to be expended on creating the effect.

Second, once that has been decided there still has to be a discussion about how best to utilize this space. Even when backlighting and a passage behind are eliminated, this still leaves about 16 feet of unusable space.

The traditional way to light a drop or sky cloth dates back to the days when there was a row of candles at the top and another in a sunken trough below. This is called the *skim-the-surface-method* for obvious reasons and involves light sources both top and bottom. It can be done in as little as 3 feet of space but clearly will look better if more space can be spared. Striplights are traditionally used for this purpose and the bottom row traditionally lights the bottom half of the drop and the top set lights the upper half, which may not be the best way to do this. Most first year lighting students would understand that this is a variation of the near, middle, and far tormentor lighting problem discussed later, where lighting the near area is always less successful than lighting the far area because of the Distance Problem. So cross-lighting, although not the traditional way to light the cyc, will usually produce the best results, i.e. the lights at the bottom illuminate the top half and visa versa.

Louis Hartmann complained at length about four-circuit striplights being inferior to three-circuit striplights because the light sources were so widely separated that the colors did not have a chance to blend before they were seen in the context of their adjacent color. We commonly refer to this as the *Veeing Problem* in striplights, and it means that we see the individual cones of light from each color circuit as a "vee" against the background. This is particularly noticeable on the floor units because there often is no trough to hide them in and the groundrow that masks them is usually only high enough to hide the units themselves. Putting the same color in all circuits would go a long way to

eliminating this problem as would replacing the groundrow with a high fence.

Even when cross-lighting techniques are employed as described above, the fact that the lighting is skimming across the surface will result in the imperfections (wrinkles) in the surface being more visible. This is a significant concern where a cloth is involved.

The second method is called the *over-the-head method* and it needs at least 12–15 feet of throw distance. Stanley McCandless said it was the best way he knew of to light a cyc, and it is certainly the way paintings are most commonly lit in an art museum. The instruments (Stanley McCandless suggested floods but today we would be more likely to use wide-angle ellipsoidals) are placed as far downstage as possible so that the light trav-

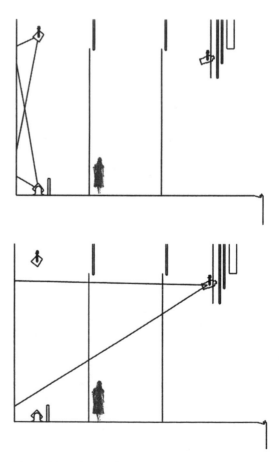

Top: **Skim-the-surface cyc lighting;** *bottom:* **Over-the-head cyc lighting.**

els above the heads of the actors and hits the drop as close to perpendicular as possible. This is not always possible for every show or every venue, but where it is, it provides excellent drop lighting.

Cycs or Drop Backlighting

This is another problem made worse by too little space. The lights have to be out of sight around the perimeter. There are two methods of doing this. The first and usually brightest, but least even, method involves putting the instruments top and bottom at the extreme upstage of the space and direct lighting the back of the cyc. The second method involves making the back wall reflective and putting the instruments at the extreme downstage of the space and directly lighting the reflective back wall. The light has to be contained, especially on the sides. Even given all of these things, it is still extremely

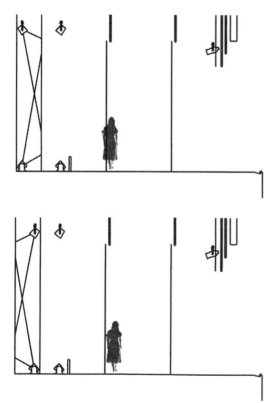

Top: Directing backlighting a drop; *bottom:* indirect backlighting a drop.

hard to get light onto the center of the cyc or drop. Having said that, cross-lighting (for either method) usually produces better results, i.e. lights at the bottom are used to light the top and visa-versa.

High Platforms

High platforms (7'0" +) are almost always placed as far upstage as possible because they would otherwise block sightlines. There is almost always a perimeter safety rail at about +2'6" (otherwise the audience tends to worry about the actors' safety). They pose three problems. First, the heads of the actors are typically within 3–4 feet of the lights that will light them, which runs afoul of the Distance Problem and limits coverage. There is really no solution to this except to use instruments that have wide beam angles (fresnels or floods) and to accept the fact that at throw distances of 4 feet a fresnel even with a field angle of 65 degrees would have a beam coverage of only about 3 feet, which means there would need to be a lot of instruments. Second, the shadows of the actors will be projected onto the scenery piece that is immediately behind the high platform, which is often a sky cloth of some kind. Third, the safety rail on the front allows only a view of the actors from about the waist up even when they are at the extreme downstage edge of the platform, and this gets worse as the actors move upstage on the platform, so really the only good acting location is on the downstage edge of the platform. While this is primarily a problem for the director, it also affects the lighting designer. If the director will agree to use only the downstage edge of the platform, then it simplifies both the coverage problems and the shadow problems.

If, for example, the platform is 8' deep but the director has agreed to confine movement to the first 2', then the shadows will be mostly on the platform floor and will certainly climb no higher than 2' up the back wall, in which case the platform can be primarily lit from standard golden ring positions. This will not look as good as normal lighting on the stage floor because the audience is looking upward at something that is lit from above, and as a result, they will be more aware of raccoon eyes and harsh facial shadows. There badly needs to be some kind of low angle fill. Sometimes eyelevel sidelight (eyelevel at the height of the high platform) can be used. Assuming the high platform has side walls no higher than waist height, the shadows would then be projected into the wings left and right where, if the levels were low enough, they might be undetected on the black velour masking (assuming there was black velour or other light absorbing material there).

If the platform must be lit all the way to the back, then shadows will fall on the back wall of the platform or if there is only a waist high wall back there, they will continue backwards and will usually hit the sky cloth (again assuming that this is what the backing is). A valid question at this point is, "Does it matter if the shadows fall on the backing below the level of the high platform?" If the entire front of the high platform is masked with a solid masking and this masking is carried all the way across the stage, then this would block the audience's view of shadows that fell below the level of the platform, and it would not matter that shadows fell on the sky cloth or the actual floor of the stage as long as it was upstage of the masking.

Successfully lighting a high platform requires a great deal of skill. It requires an early discussion with the director and ultimately the set designer so that the platform depth, the height of its backing wall and sidewalls can be decided upon. Its distance from the cyc or other scenery backing piece has to be decided upon and masking options have to be discussed, all before the carpenters begin building it and before the set design is finalized.

Scrims and Gauzes

When lit from the front they appear to be an opaque drop, but when lit from the rear, they become transparent and can be seen through. At least that is the theory. In prac-

tice, they have to be lit from the front from a very steep skim-the-surface angle or the light will go through the holes and light the scene behind before it is time. Often they have to be backed by a black curtain to prevent anyone seeing through them. There needs to be 6–8 feet of unused depth immediately behind the scrim to allow the instruments that light the scene behind the scrim to spread out. There is seldom anywhere near that much depth, so the scene behind gets lit from the two sides and the top. As a result, there will typically be a light cue that reduces frontlight on the scrim so that the black masking curtain can be flown out. Then there will be the cue that bleeds through the scrim. Then because the lighting behind the scrim is so inadequate, the scrim will be flown out and a third light cue will add frontlight to the scene.

Staircases

Staircases are almost always as far upstage as they can be so that they do not block sightlines. They tend to run either left/right or directly upstage. They never (almost never) begin upstage and get higher as they come downstage (again for sightline reasons). There are really two difficulties here.

First, if the staircase runs left/right (or right/left) then there is usually an upstage backing wall that the shadows of the actors will fall on. Second, inasmuch as staircases move upward in elevation, they inherit at their upper levels the same problems as a high platform, as was just discussed.

For reasons that escape me (and will escape you too), they are often lit along their line-of-travel as if they were an audience aisle or a runway. A light is mounted at the top of stairway aimed at the actor's head at the bottom of the stairway along the line-of-travel so that the actor is always in this light as he ascends. At first this may seem to be a very sensible idea, but it runs afoul of the Distance Problem because when the instrument is dimmed up to the level needed to illuminate the actor at the foot of the staircase, it will be way too bright by the time the actor is at the top of the stairs and usually only about 4 feet away from the instrument (assuming it is a high staircase). There is usually no way to run a light from below upward along the line-of-travel of the staircase because there is no position to put such a light in, but even if there were a place to put it, it would have the same problem, which is that the actor would be bright on the near side and dim on the far side.

On the whole, most staircases can be lit by two instruments-per-area from front-left and front-right positions, which is the standard of Stanley McCandless' method. There will be shadow problems on any backing wall. In the case of a stairway that goes up as it goes upstage, it is possible to light this from golden ring front and 90 degree side positions, but there will be spill light off the sides onto the floor below regardless of whether they are lit by two instruments or three.

Tormentors

The tormentors are the first vertical masking units behind the front curtain. It was traditional, and in some venues still is, to locate booms or towers here for sidelighting. The same thing is often done out on the apron in front of the curtain and on the box booms and sometimes in slots in the sidewalls of the house. These all involve lighting an entire zone (near, medium and far locations from a single pole), and for the purposes of this discussion are all cases of *tormentor lighting*.

Stated simply the problem is that each instrument will have a different throw distance but the size and brightness of each component area is hoped will be the same. Unhappily, each instrument will also have a different throw angle because the pole is usually too short. Booms are seldom taller than 21', which is the standard length of the pipe. While it is possible for the near area (and sometimes the next one) to have a throw of 45 degrees, the rest, even if clustered at the top of the pole, will have throw angles of less than 45 degrees.

The first question that has to be dealt with is where on the pole should the instruments be placed. The method just suggested will usually work acceptably if there is only this one system of lights that needs to be located on the boom. Sometimes there will be two or three colors, and if that were the case, it would be more usual to cluster the three near colors at the 45 degree position, cluster the far colors at the top and put the mid-stage clusters equally-spaced in-between. A third alternative would be to have all throw angles match the throw angle of the far area (usually 35 degrees or thereabouts). The gentler angle casts longer shadows and makes the distance problem more pronounced on the near instrument, but the left-right coverage is better, and if it is a choice between covering the zone in three areas rather than four, it is sometimes worth doing as the visual differences between these methods are often too small to be noticeable from the audience.

The second question is what kind of instruments should be used. Ellipsoidals are preferred so that the light can be cut off the far-side masking. The usual advice is to use a wide angle (50 degrees) for the near, a narrow angle (30 degrees) for the far and medium angles (40 degrees) for the intermediate area or areas, but this does not always work out as expected, especially in the near area.

Let's take a typical case where the stage is 30' wide, the boom is 2' offstage and 20' high. Assuming that there would have to be four areas across, this would make each one 7.5' in diameter. This puts the center of the near area at 5.75' (3.75 half diameter + 2' offstage) from the boom and if the instrument is to be at a 45 degree angle and yoked forward from the boom, it would have to hang at 10.25' (5.5 nose height + 4.75 horizontal distance reduced by 1 because instrument is yoked forward). This puts the throw distance at 6.7' and will produce a beam diameter of less than 4' and a brightness of well over 500 fc, which is way too small a coverage area and way too bright even taking into account that it will be controlled on its own dimmer.

Sometimes a fresnel will be used for the

near area, but fresnel lamps typically burn cooler (at a lower Kelvin temperature). As a result it would be hard to get the colors to match and the instruments to look right together. Sometimes fresnels are used for all the tormentor instruments. One would certainly need to check that this would be bright enough in the far area without having to double-up on instruments there. Barndoors would have to be used, but their ability to cut light off the masking is nowhere near as good as the shutters of ellipsoidals. If there were zoom ellipsoidals in the inventory, they might be used to advantage here even though they are typically less bright than their fixed lens counterparts.

Even with the near instrument being a fresnel, the performers are usually going to step out of its light before disappearing into the wings. To solve this a small (100–300 watt) flood may be mounted on the boom at eyelevel and dimmed up just enough to cover the gap between when the performer steps out of the near instrument and vanishes out of sight behind the masking.

Tormentor lighting requires a lot of careful planning. The choice of instruments is critical, but the use of different brightnesses of lamps and the possibility of doubling instruments needs to also be considered. Even when all the instruments have been balanced on the lightboard, there is no way to correct the brightness variance within each area itself. It will always be brighter on the near side and dimmer on the far side. The next overlapping area will always be brightest at the point of overlap, which means a ridge of brightness at every overlap point.

Better sidelighting can almost always be obtained from a pipe running across the areas from above, but the assumption is that such a pipe is not available or is already loaded to capacity, and it is a choice between using the tormentor positions or not having a position to use.

Tormentor lighting should not be confused with *wing entry* lighting, which will be discussed next.

Wing Entries

This is provided to make sure that the performers are lit on exits up until the point they vanish from view behind a wing piece and on entrances to make it appear that they came from a lit place. A SR wing entrance would be lit from the onstage side from the top of a boom SL, and it would be lit from the offstage side from an eyelevel flood on a boom SR and just out of sight of the audience. This is exactly what was just discussed relative to tormentor lighting except with wing entry lighting no attempt is being made to light mid-stage or near areas from the near side. The wing entries are being highlighted to compensate for the arealighting dropping as it approaches and is being cut off of the wing pieces.

Wing Washes

The purpose of a wing wash is to light the painted scenic piece. As a result it lights from the opposite side of stage only (as for a wing entry light but without the near side light) and lights all the way up to the point where the leg vanishes behind a horizontal border-masking unit. It will also light an actor who stands in front of the wing, but it may also cast his shadow back onto the wing piece.

LIGHTING SYMBOLS— See SYMBOLS (lighting).

LIGHTING TABLE— See TABLE.

LIGHTING TOOLS— See TOOLS.

LIGHTING UNITS— See UNITS (lighting).

LIGHTING WRENCHES— See WRENCHES.

LIGHT-LEAK—Any light produced by a stage instrument that goes where it is not wanted. While it can be used to refer to light that is leaking through joints in the scenery, it is most commonly used to refer to light that leaks out of the instruments themselves through vent holes and other openings. Black foil and gaffer's tape is usually used to combat these.

LIGHTNING EFFECT—See EFFECTS, KINDS OF.

LIGHT-THE-SET METHOD (of Lighting Design)— This is said to be the method that set designers used that caused them to lose the right to supervise and hire the lighting person. See LIGHTING DESIGNER, BIRTH OF for a more detailed discussion of this. To say that someone used this method usually is intended as a slur on the light design. It suggests that there were not enough specials specific to this particular play because the designer didn't bother to see a runthru or read the script but instead simply provided light on all parts of the set so that the actors wherever they might choose to go would always be lit. The lighting would work equally as well for this particular play as for any other that could be done on this set. When theatres are rented out to other groups, it is not unusual to provide this exact kind of non-show-specific lighting, which is then called either *basic lighting* or a *rep plot*. It is also the method used in the preparation of Short Plots. Stanley McCandless' method was intended to be a basic lighting plan that could work with minor modifications for every play. See LIGHTING IDEAS/Set and INTUITIVE METHOD for a more detailed discussion.

LIGHTS-UP–LIGHT-DOWN SHOW— A show with no internal light cues. Older plays were written at a time when the candles were lit before the audience came in and snuffed-out after they had left, so no requirements were made of the lighting. Plays written after about 1950 begin to reflect an increased reliance on the lighting.

LIMELIGHT— A vintage followspot method that involved a piece of limestone heated to incandescence by a combination of bottled hydrogen and oxygen with a lens and housing attached. It was in common use for a longer period of time in Great Britain than here in America. It was superseded by carbon arc lights, which were less expensive to operate.

LINE—(1) An electrical cable. (2) A row or zone of lighting areas running from left to right or a column running upstage and downstage. (3) A spotline meaning a rigging line or rope. (4) The opposite of *load*, i.e. the side that the electrical current is coming from.

LINE-OF-THROW— A straight line between the actor's nose and the source of light (instrument) whose length is called the throw distance, and the angle between this line and the nose plane is the throw angle.

LINE-OF-TRAVEL— This is used to describe narrow walkways (like audience aisles or staircases) where movement is only anticipated in two opposite directions. The lighting then is either oriented at both ends of the line-of-travel or from the side perpendicular to the line-of-travel.

LINK— This is a computer lightboard term that refers to linking cues together. This is usually only necessary if the cues are out of number sequence or if there are intervening cues that need to be skipped. The linking is sometimes not recognized by the *back* command, which may revert to the next lower number in sequence instead of back to the previously launched cue. See LIGHTING CONTROL, Computer Memory Lightboards for a more detailed discussion.

LINNEBACH PROJECTOR— A vintage shadow projector. See PROJECTORS, KINDS OF.

LIVE— Connected to electrical power. It is used synonymously for *hot*. However, apparatus with exposed electrical parts are always called *live front* (opposite of *dead front*) and never hot front or cold front.

LIVE FOCUS— See FOCUS, KINDS OF.

LIVE MODE— Also called *stage mode*. This is a computer lightboard term that refers to the display screen being set to view the cue currently up onstage.

LOAD—(1) Any electrical device using power is called a load or electrical load (2) Opposite of *line* side. The load side always has male connectors and the line side has female connectors.

LOAD-IN and SET-IN (BRITISH: *get-in and fit-up*)— The period of time between when the theatre space becomes available for this particular show and opening night. The set has to be installed onstage, costumes arranged in dressing rooms, props tables set up and the lighting equipment has to be brought into the space (often off-loaded from trucks), hung, focused and integrated into the show.

Technically, when the trucks are unloaded, the load-in part is over and the set-in starts. In actual conversational usage, the terms *load-in*, *set-in* and *changeover* are used to convey subtle differences of meaning. If the crew call is referred to as a *load-in*, this already encompasses the idea of the set-in and further suggests a touring show or rental house situation where there are large trucks involved. If it is called a *set-in*, it suggests that there are no trucks, that it is in in-house operation and that the stage is bare at the start. A *changeover* describes a crew call where the strike of the old show is combined with the set-in of the new show, and this is almost always an in-house operation. For the purposes of this discussion we're going to ignore these subtleties in the terms and discuss how the process itself may be different.

While there is a current show running, the theatre space may only be in use for the few hours of the performances. However, once the show is over and the theatre is dark, not only are there no revenues coming in but the labor expenses are skyrocketing because of the extra personnel, so there is tremendous pressure to get the technical elements in place as fast as possible so that technical rehearsals can begin with the actors.

As many activities as possible are allowed to go on concurrently. As a result, the load-in period is typically characterized by too many people, all trying to do way too much, in too little time, and this can extend around-the-clock as crews rotate their rest periods.

There are four models here. I think it makes most sense to discuss them in the order of their relative efficiency:

Touring Show: A touring show that arrives at the loading dock at 10 A.M. expecting to do a show that evening will have an experienced core crew who will supervise the local crew who are providing the bulk of the actual labor.

From a lighting standpoint, the first thing that will happen is the lighting equipment will be off-loaded from the trucks and placed in temporary storage in and around the stage area (usually leaving the actual stage space clear). While this is going on, the head lighting person of the core crew will be checking out the facility with the house electrician and preparing a list of things that need to be done.

The lights will typically already be mounted on pipes or trusses that are in sections that can be easily connected together, tested, and flown out.

Part two of the set-in will involve the hanging of the lights. It can be done concurrently with the scenery being installed, as both activities require the worklights being on. If the show has its own lightboard, this will have to be hooked-up too. The pre-wired trusses will then have to be cabled to the location of the dimmers.

Part three of the lighting set-in will involve the focusing of the lights. This will typically be done with the trusses at chest height by aiming them at a specially marked focusing cloth.

Part four will involves a cue-to-cue rehearsal (with or without the actors) where the already programmed show is played back cue-by-cue and adjusted as necessary. Even if there is no computer lightboard, the cues will have been documented in such a way that they can simply be run one-after-another.

At this point everyone will take a dinner break and come back to run the evening show. The touring show has special equipment and methods designed to deal specifically with their situation. They also have done it all before. A show being put together for the first time cannot hope to match this kind of speed and efficiency.

Rental Theatre: The New York model involves a theatre (almost always proscenium) that is rented "with bare walls" and until relatively recently with DC current only and with few, if any, hardwired locations to plug lights into.

The load-in would be from a truck coming from the lighting equipment rental house and would include dimmers and a mountain of cable. There might be boxes or racks of instruments but they wouldn't be pre-mounted or pre-wired. They would be off-loaded and given a temporary storage place.

In part two (the hang), they would be placed on the chest high pipes. They would be gelled, a pattern (if any) inserted, an accessory (iris, barndoor or tophat being the most common) added, and the cabling carried at least to the end of the pipe and somewhat beyond. Even when this is carefully planned out and even when cables are bundled together in advance and gels are filed in the order in which they will be needed and so forth, this is clearly a time-consuming process as the pieces are assembled for the first time.

When it comes to the focus (part three), there will be no specially marked ground cloth. The lights will have to be focused at their trim height, which usually means accessing them by some kind of ladder or lift.

Part four (integrating the lights into the show) will also be more complicated because there will not be a show already on disk. Each cue will have to be built one-channel-at-a-time and recorded.

Regional Theatre: regional theatres, which include any theatre that does a season of shows, will often combine the load-out of the old show with the load-in of the new show. See CHANGEOVER PERIOD for a more detailed discussion of how this might work.

While there may be a load-in of the set as it is trucked in from the scene shop on the other side of town, there will typically be no load-in of the lights as they will either be in a storage room or in the place where they were used for the previous show. The dimmers and lightboard and an extensive distribution system of plug-in points will typically be owned by the theatre.

Hanging the lights will proceed more-or-less as described above except there likely will be receptacles to plug into, which will greatly reduce the cabling. In houses that do not have flying capabilities, the lights are hung on a stationary grid from ladders or lifts and this will increase the time required to hang them.

The focusing will proceed as described above for the rental house as will the integration of the lights into the show.

Educational Theatre: Educational theatres, which includes any theatre that does complicated theatrical shows occasionally but smaller events from time-to-time in-between shows will often have a basic light plot that will typically be in place at the starting point of the load-in and that will have to be restored at the end of the load-out. In fact, the show specific lighting may merely have augmented what was already there.

Inasmuch as the set may be built and assembled on the stage itself, there may not be any actual trucks to load or unload.

In all other ways, the lights are hung, focused and integrated into the show as described above.

LOAD-OUT (BRITISH: *get-out* or *derig*)— The period of time between the end of the last performance and the time when the space is returned to its condition prior to the load-in.

Load-outs are relatively fast. When this occurs after the last performance as it often does, it is commonly called *strike night*. While set, costumes, props and anything else related to the show may be struck on strike night, the strike of the lighting equipment may be delayed until later.

The lights may for example be left in place to cover intervening events until it is time to set in the next show. As a purely practical matter, the theatre usually has no space to store all their lights except in-the-air, so taking them down doesn't make much sense unless they are to go right back up, and if that is the case, one of the strategies discussed in STRIKES, KINDS OF will be both faster and more efficient.

Even when the next show is ready to go in at once, it often makes more sense to delay the strike of the lights until at least everyone else is done striking, which often means a delay until early the next morning. There are several good reasons for this, which are discussed in STRIKE THE LIGHTS, WHEN TO.

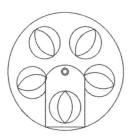

LOBSTERSCOPE— This is a vintage effects machine that can easily become confused with a *sciopticon* or a *stereopticon*. The lobsterscope has no lenses but is a colorwheel with eye-shaped openings where the gels would have been that is rotated rapidly either by hand or by motor or by clockwork to produce a flickering effect.

Lobsterscope

LOCALES— This refers to how many places in which the play takes place. It is not in the least unusual for a drama to occur in the same place throughout, only at different times. If there are three times of day when a scene takes place, then there will be at least three different lighting looks. See LIGHT-ING IDEAS/Script for a more detailed discussion.

LONG FOCUS or THROW— This refers to instruments that have narrow beam angles and are designed to be used at long throw distances. It is however a confusing term and hard to correlate with either a lens focal length or a beam angle. Describing lights by their beam angle or field angle, which is the current practice, seems to be far less confusing and considerably more specific.

LOOKS— A distinctively unique state of lighting that may have many variants. Typically the morning library scene would be considered a different look from the afternoon library scene, but if all that happened in the afternoon scene was that a window drape was opened or a practical light was turned on, then this would be considered

simply a variant of the basic cue. In the same way that an actor may count his lines to determine how big a part he has, a lighting designer may think of his show in terms of how many different looks it contains. See LIGHTING IDEAS/Script for a more detailed discussion.

LOUVERS— An add-on lighting accessory that looks and works like Venetian blinds. See ACCESSORIES for a more detailed discussion.

LOW ANGLE FILL— This is the generic term for any lighting that tries to get light in under hat brims. Traditionally, the balcony rail was the favored position for this, but in houses without balconies, it can be over-the-head of the last row of audience, which is to say on the back wall of the house or from a booth at the back. If run up too high, it will cause a shadow of the actors on the back wall of the set, but if carefully controlled, it can do much to reduce the occurrence of raccoon eyes and to get light in under hats.

LOW VOLTAGE— In theatrical usage, anything that does not produce an electrical shock that can be felt (30 volts and below) is considered to be low voltage. This includes most speaker and mic and intercom lines and phones and practical doorbells and cuelights and other kinds of signal lights.

LOW VOLTAGE WIRING METHODS— Low voltage wires (other than sound/audio) can use zip cord or bell wire and can be connected together with wirenuts outside of electrical boxes. Sound wires have their own sets of connectors for various purposes and are often run in conduit to isolate them from AC hum caused by running them parallel to the high voltage lighting lines and often the wires themselves are shielded.

LTP— Abbreviation for LAST-TAKES-PRECEDENCE.

LUG— A terminal for a large wire usually allowing it to be attached to a bus bar.

LUMEN— This is a unit of *luminous flux*, which measures the amount of light produced by a source in all directions. A lumen of light evenly distributed over a square foot of area produces a footcandle of *illumination*.

LUMINANCE— When light hits an object, some of it is reflected. Various object surfaces have coefficients of reflection to describe how reflective they are. Luminance measures the quantity of light being reflected and in terms of calculations simply involves the footcandles of light hitting the surface being multiplied by the reflectance coefficient, which then yields the luminance measured in footlamberts. For the most part, lighting designers are not concerned with measuring luminance with any device other than their eyes.

LUMINAIRE— This is an international word for a lighting instrument and has yet to catch on here in America with the technicians who hang and focus them. The term can be encountered in scholarly monographs, but it isn't something likely to be heard over the sales counter at the local theatrical supply house, at least not yet.

LUMINESCENT— Anything that gives off visible light when stimulated with ultraviolet or some other non-visible form of electromagnetic energy.

LUMINOUS FLUX— This is a scientific word to describe the amount of light emitted by a source (lamp) in all directions as measured in lumens. It is often found in theatre supply catalogs as part of various lamp descriptions, and as such provides an approximate way to determine how any given instrument might perform with a different type of lamp. Usually, the manufacturers will provide much more accurate lamp coefficients as part of their published photometric data so that this kind of approximating isn't necessary.

In a theatrical situation, by the time one has put a light source inside an instrument and bounced its light off a reflector and passed it through a lens system, its luminous output is a meaningless number because all

that matters is how much of that original light is now coming out the front of this instrument. This has to be measured in a laboratory situation and will be measured as an *intensity* of this source in candelas.

LUX— This is the metric equivalent for footcandle, but rather than being a lumen per square foot, it is a lumen per square meter. Multiply lux by 0.0929 to get footcandles or multiply footcandles by 10.7643 to get lux.

MACRO— This is a computer lightboard term that refers to a series of keystrokes that are recorded into a playback unit that can be recalled at the stroke of a single key or stroke of just a few keys. Routine procedures like reading from disk, writing to disk, printing or doing an instrument check are all common justifications for creating a macro. A macro can, also, usually be linked to a cue and can perform a complicated series of cues.

MAGAZINES (Lighting)— We're talking about periodicals relating to stage lighting. *Theatre Crafts* was enormously popular in 1970s and '80s and dealt with all things technical. In additions to its articles, its advertisements were a whose-who of North American manufacturing. After its demise, *Lighting Dimensions* (which had been architecturally oriented) became the lone survivor and has since increased their performing arts content. They list advertisers and provide contact information. (*www.etecnyc.net*). *Theatre Design and Technology* is the journal of the USITT and is published quarterly.

MAGIC LANTERN— A vintage name for a slide projector. Where this term is used, it refers to the kind of slide projector that had a manual slide holder that slid back and forth.

MAGIC SHEET— See KEY SHEET.

MAGNETIC AMPLIFIER DIMMERS— A vintage dimming technology based on the reactance principle. See LIGHTING CONTROL for a more detailed discussion.

MAIN or MAIN DISCONNECT— The switch that turns off the power to the dimmer boards. In the days of manual boards, this would have typically been located wherever the dimmers were operated from and would probably have been turned off at the end of each day. Now it is more likely to be in a basement electrical room, where it would be customarily left on.

MALE CONNECTOR or PLUG— These are the ones with prongs as opposed to holes. They are also on the *load* side as opposed to *line* side of the electrical current. A male connector (on an instrument) plugs into the dimmer or source of power. A female connector (on the plugging channel) is what the instrument gets plugged into. Female connectors are almost always electrically hot. Males aren't.

MANUAL BOARD— Any lightboard where the dimmers that do the work are directly manipulated. This is the opposite of a *remote-control* lightboard. The two most popular manual dimming methods were the resistance dimmers up until the 1950s when the autotransformer dimmers became popular.

MARK IT— A vintage term dating back to the days when dimmers did not have calibration markings, meaning do whatever has to be done so that the cue can be repeated again later (making colored marks to line up with the dimmer handle). Used synonymously with *write it*, which is another vintage term dating back to the days when each cue had to be written after it had been approved. *Record it* is current usage and reflects the fact that the machine keeps track of cues and repeats them on demand.

MASKING CONVENTION— This is a theatrical convention that applies only to proscenium theatres, where it is customary to mask or conceal all lighting instruments from view by the audience. Often extraordinary efforts have to be made in order to achieve this. Often perfectly good instrument locations have to be abandoned be-

cause they cannot be entirely concealed from view. In thrust and other forms of open staging, no such expectation exists and instruments can be placed wherever needed, which is a huge advantage.

MASKING TAPE— See TAPES, KINDS OF.

MASKS or MATS— In modern usage, it would refer to any opaque material placed at the front of the instrument to alter the beam path of the light. This could be a crude barndoor made out of black foil or it could refer to some kind of pattern (i.e. a homemade donut of some kind). Originally it also referred to mats placed inside the lights but they are now referred to as *gobo patterns*, whether homemade or not. Neither word is used much anymore as commercial add-on accessories with other specific names are more commonly used.

MASTER DIMMER— This refers to a dimmer that electrically controls a group of other dimmers. The other dimmers can be set at their playing levels and then all can be dimmed up at once by using the master dimmer. On remote control lightboards, various potentiometers are used to simulate this effect. See LIGHTING CONTROL for a more detailed discussion.

MASTER ELECTRICIAN (Abbr. M.E.)— This is the answer to the question, "Who's in charge around here?" The title will vary from venue to venue and he or she may be called the *head* or *chief* or *production* electrician. In the case of touring shows this usually refers to the headman for this production as opposed to the house electrician who is hired by the facility and is the facility's headman.

MASTER ELECTRICIAN, MEETING WITH— Around the time that the lighting designer is seeing the runthru and talking to the director, he needs to meet with the master electrician. The alleged purpose of the meeting is to discuss how the master electrician would like to have the Light Plot done. What scale does he want? Is blue line okay? Are tiled pages okay? How much informational detail does he want? How many copies does he need?

Of all the people who work at this theatre, this is the person who knows the most about how the lights work in this space. If the lighting designer can get a conversation going, he may be able to learn why the last designer wasn't hired back or what some of the common mistakes are in addition to a whole lot of other useful things.

This person may also be a lighting designer in his own right. He may even think he ought to be doing this particular show. One may not be able to make a friend here, but one should try very hard not to make an enemy.

Most designers will describe how they "usually" do the Light Plot and inquire if this is okay. This limits the differences to the things that really matter at the same time that it demonstrates that the designer understands what is traditionally required. Since the master electrician is in charge of the crew, it goes without saying that the designer is well advised to give him the paperwork at whatever scale or format he says he wants. It was for a time fashionable to give the master electrician a simplified light plot (electrician's plot) that only contained the information that he needed to know, thus saving the everything-plot for the lighting designer. The assumption was that his tiny mind might become confused by the complexity of the full light plot. If the master electrician specifically asks for a simplified plot, he should be given one. Otherwise it is probably fair to assume that his mind is no tinier than anyone else's and he can probably deal with the power of the full plot. He may however ask for an increased scale, as plots that contain all the information can be hard to read at smaller scales.

In a similar vein, the directions in which instruments on the plot point are sometimes simplified to include only the four cardinal points and the instruments are spaced equidistantly along their support pipes (usually 18" apart) thus 28 instruments always fit on a 42' pipe (pretty much regardless of which way they will point) and the final product looks incredibly neat and tidy. Again the underlying assumption is that the tiny minds of the stagehands would be compromised if they had to deal with the added complexity of a fully loaded pipe where instruments were placed where they needed to be and where there were perhaps gaps between clusters of instruments.

Most CAD programs by default would point the instruments toward their aimpoints at whatever weird angle that turned out to be, but this can, of course, be overridden. Hanging the instruments only at the cardinal points almost guarantees that each and every one of them will have to be re-aimed during the focus, which creates more work for the crew (which depending on one's point-of-view is either a good thing or a bad thing). The even spacing of the instruments however has more of an impact on the design because instruments are being deliberately moved from their ideal positions (not because they won't fit but) because they don't look neat and tidy. Where a 42' pipe is broken into ten 4' bays, then anywhere between 2 and 4 instruments can usually be placed in each bay depending on the size of the instruments used and which way they all face (which is, after all, the point of doing the drawing in scale), and in this way about 40 instruments can often be put on the same pipe without them interfering with each other

The designer will also want to discuss what the master electrician expects him to do during the hanging session and during the focusing session. It is not uncommon for the master electrician to want to conduct the hanging session in private on the assumption that if the designer is present, he will make changes. And that is exactly the reason why the designer does want to be there. Lighting designers are not perfect. They sometimes make mistakes. The sooner they recognize that these are mistakes, the sooner they can be corrected. Rather than come in the next day to discover that a whole hanging position is behind a ventilating duct, the designer thinks it would be better to at least be present to answer questions during the hang. The designer also needs to get a feel for how good the crew is, which will affect the focusing session. Union rules often prohibit the lighting designer from touching the instruments, but there are often other things of a generally useful nature that he can do while there.

The lighting designer is usually nominally in charge of the focus session and is typically expected to stand in the aimpoint of the lights. It is often easier to see the lights from some other position out in the house, so the designer may want someone else to stand in the lights. If the master electrician doesn't want to provide anyone from his crew, it may be up to the lighting designer to bring an assistant.

Whatever the situation will be, it is important that it be understood by all parties. Who will format the disk? Sometimes the designer will be allowed to do this and sometimes the master electrician or one of his crew will do this. It is important to know at this point who this will be.

If the designer plans to create focusing cues, both the number of ladder crews there will be for the focusing session and the ladder travel path may have to be discussed.

MASTERING— This refers to controlling individual dimmers as a group and there are two kinds: *mechanical mastering* (sometimes called *interlocking*) and *proportional mastering* by means of a master dimmer or master potentiometer. In the days when manual dimmers were used, the mastering was mostly mechanical and was crucial to the execution of each cue. Now it is mostly electronic (and proportional) and while still crucial, it is completely taken for granted.

MAT— This is a vintage and generic word to describe any attempt to shape the beam of light, and it is not used much anymore because there are now much more specific terms like barndoor and tophat and spill rings and black wrap that describe better the actual method being used. Also sometimes called a *mask*.

MATRIX PATCHING— A kind of hard patch panel that allowed any number of circuits to be patched to any dimmer. At the time, it was typical to provide each dimmer with 2–4 plug-in points. Many dimmers had only one thing plugged into them, so the other three plug-in points were wasted. On special dimmers, it might be necessary to have as many as six or eight things plugged in, not at once, but they would all be plugged in at the beginning of the show and individual circuit breakers would be turned on and off to control what lights were then active. To plug more than four in at once, there had to be some kind of two-ferring device. Matrix patching eliminated all this as it made it possible to connect as many or as few circuits as were needed onto any one dimmer by means of contact shoes from the circuits being affixed to one of many bus bars that represented the dimmers. While matrix patching was a big deal at the time (1960s and 1970s), it is now obsolete because patching now involves hiring an extra technician, and as a result it is mostly not considered worth doing anymore.

MATRIX SYSTEM— This is a modern computer lightboard method that allows the operator (for cue-setting purposes) to have both color control and area control. Let's assume there are six areas and four systems. The areas are put on subs 1–6. The systems on 31–34 set to inhibitive mode. To set areas, raise the area subs to a balanced level. Area 3 (sub 3) or any other area could be allowed to be brighter or dimmer than the other areas. Now the color systems can be balanced until the stage looks right. While the four system subs typically remain unchanged throughout the show, they don't have to, but could be changed to create different looks. Once a system balance has been achieved, the areas can be proportionately set to this balance and brought up, which will serve as the basis of individual cues. Once all the cues are set, the subs used for building them have served their purpose and can be erased.

MAXIMUM OVERALL LENGTH— This is a lamp measurement from a point on the base to the extreme far end of the lamp. See also LENGTH TO CENTER OF LIGHT. Both are important measurements when trying to determine if a particular lamp will fit and work but both are included in the three-letter lamp code.

McCANDLESS, STANLEY — Probably the most famous name in American stage lighting. He began as an instructor of lighting at the Yale school of drama. In 1926, when they built their new state-of-the-art theatre complex, he helped design the switchboard and other lighting related systems. He is best known for his slender volume entitled **A Method of Lighting the Stage**, first published in 1932. It went through at least four editions and numerous printings and is probably the most widely read and still one of the most sought-after and authoritative books on the subject in the USA today despite the fact that huge portions of it that dealt with the equipment of his day are now obsolete. His ideas were better than his ability to write about them, however. As a result, he understated some of his most important observations (such as the over-the-head method of cyc lighting and the evil effects that resulted from having too much light), and some of the terms he used were subsequently misunderstood and misinterpreted (*naturalism* and *composition* and *motivated* or *motivating* lights are good examples of this), and he was simply mistaken and wrong about other things (like the use of complementary colors in arealights) — all of which will be discussed in the next topic, which deals specifically with his method. He also wrote **Syllabus of Stage Lighting** in 1953, which was essentially an outline of what he taught in his classes. Again, much of it dealt with the equipment of his time and is only of historical interest now.

McCANDLESS METHOD — In 1932 Stanley McCandless of Yale wrote a slender volume called **A Method of Lighting the Stage** in which he presented a cookbook-style recipe for stage lighting in general, and arealighting in particular. This was the first time that anyone had ever suggested that there might be a single, learnable, right way to do the stage lighting, not the only way but simply one right way in a sea of wrong ways.

Current practice had been to pour light onto the stage from every available opening: doors, windows, from the area just behind the proscenium arch and from the balcony rail in the house (if there was one) and from vertical pipes along the side walls of the house more-or-less where the boxes were (box booms). The problem was mostly that the set designers had not learned yet to leave slots in the walls and ceilings sufficient to get light onto the set. The sets were painted canvas, and looked best when lighted from the front.

Thanks to the ideas, visions, and theories of Adolphe Appia, a Swiss designer and Gordan Craig, an English designer, something called the *new stagecraft* was coming to America and would be embraced by a number of American designers such as Robert Edmund Jones and Lee Simonson in which painted scenery would be replaced by three dimensional units (platforms, steps, ramps, draperies) so that the shadows would no longer be painted on but would be created by light hitting the objects and the settings would look different when lit differently. Where this kind of scenery was to be used, there were several different schools of thought as to how best to light it:

- **Front Lighters** thought it was a question of which direction the sun (or artificial light source) was to come from, and the answer was that it should always come from the side on which the audience sat (front). A few sidelights from the wings would take care of revealing the three dimensional shape of the objects, but essentially they would look three-dimensional because they WERE three-dimensional.

- **Cross-Lighters** believed that the light source should come from over the audience's left (or right) shoulder so that the directional quality of the light was more obvious. It was pointed out that this was the system most commonly used by the great classical painters. This required not one wash but two, colored slightly differently and controlled separately and required twice as many instruments. In practice the left side of the light pipe was often used for the wash from the left and the right side, for the wash from the right.

- **Side-Lighters** believed that it was possible to get the best definition of three-dimensional shapes by lighting from the two sides in different colors. This produced a pied effect where one side of the face (or object) would be one color and the other side a different color. This would then be washed out by the use of a neutral front wash. This involved three color washes that all had to be controlled separately (or the front at least had to be controlled separately from the sides) and that required three times as many instruments.

None of these systems involved the use of individual lighting areas. This is because the entire stage was used for every scene in the plays of the time, and so the whole stage was in effect a single area. It could not be lit by only one instrument because the instruments did not open up that wide, but since fresnels were being used, their size was adjustable, and it was decided on a case-by-case basis how many instruments could be spared for each directional wash. No mention was made of ideal angles or ideal colors. Control was to be done by color wash, where the fewer dimmers used, the fewer hands it would require to run the show.

Stanley McCandless thought frontlighting alone was too skimpy. He thought that two sidelights and a frontlight, with 45 degrees of separation instead of 90 degrees, washed out too many beneficial shadows. He liked cross-lighting the best. He was careful not to say that this was the only way to light the stage. He merely said that it was economical on equipment required, and it had been tested on numerous productions and it worked every time. He said students just starting out needed a system they could start with and have confidence in. The highlights of his method are these:

- Each instrument, when aimed at the stage, will produce an oval of light on the floor, which is usually adjusted to be 8–12 feet in diameter, and this constitutes a lighting area. He was, of course, thinking of fresnels (since ellipsoidals had not been invented yet) whose beam size is adjustable. It was however important that the area size, once decided upon, be uniform from area-to-area as big areas were going to be dimmer than small ones, and making them all the same size eliminated many of the problems of making them appear equally bright.
- The stage is lit based on how many lighting areas it would take to light it. He believed this usually worked out to either 2 rows of 3 (6 areas) or 3 rows of 3 areas (9 areas) although this was set-dependent, as one was likely to need additional special areas in hallways, alcoves etc. He discussed this at some length and worked through several examples to show how it would work.
- Each area could be best lit by two instruments. Both would come from an elevation (tilt) of 45 degrees above. One of them would come from an azimuth (pan) of 45 degrees to the left and the other from a pan of 45 degrees right. This would make their angle of separation 90 degrees in plan view.
- One should be an appropriate warm-colored light, the other its complementary cool (shadow) color because when mixed together they would theoretically produce white light. He presented Red, Blue, and Green as the primary colors of light from which all other tints and shades could be made, and this is where the idea that complementary colors produced white light came from (which as is discussed in COLOR, is not exactly how it works out in practice).

The most remarkable part of his system was the concept of there being lighting areas and that all lights aimed at that area would converge at its center and that these areas would all be controlled separately on the lightboard. Since the plays of the time all used the stage as one big area, it is hard to see what he had in mind exactly. There is no doubt that he was predicting a future use, which has since proved true as playwrights and directors now routinely use portions of the stage for scenes instead of using the whole stage for every scene.

More than this though, he was trying to provide a way, even when the stage was used as one big area, for there to be lighting emphasis on one or more specific areas. Previously this had been done by followspots, but he hoped to provide an alternate and more subtle way to achieve the same objective. Today we would call this "reducing the light in areas that aren't being presently used" as a way of changing the stage picture. Adolphe Appia had envisioned the lighting (of a Wagner opera) being similar to a musical score that continually shifted during the performance. Stanley McCandless quite clearly said this was not possible with the technology of his time but did not rule out the possibility that this might occur in the future. He also predicted a time would come when it would be possible for each instrument to have its own dimmer. Both are now possible.

He defined the purpose of lighting and said it had four functions: visibility, naturalism, composition, and mood.

It was a system designed for use in a proscenium theatre, which was what the theatres were at the time. He did not deal with other theatre configurations because they simply did not yet exist.

There were however some problems with his system that surfaced almost immediately, some of which he was already aware of and some not. The following list touches on most of the major areas of contention:

First, he had become interested in what we would now call the "psychology of color," which is to say, "Red means war, green means jealousy, yellow means cowardice, etc." He postulated that stage lighting could create a "mood," which he defined as an emotional response from the audience. He did not present any rules for how to achieve this. In fact, he admitted he didn't know how to achieve it, but he suspected the primary tool was going to prove to be color. It is now many decades later, and we are still no closer to having any reliable science on this subject. The essential problem is that "green" reminds some people of the tranquility of green grass while at the same time it reminds others of green aliens either those from outer space or those that use the cards of the same color and come from places like Mexico. This is not to say that color cannot be used symbolically in the context of a play, but if that is what is being attempted, then it is essential to establish early on that the colors are coded and to demonstrate for the audience what that code is.

Second, there were a whole series of color related problems. Stanley had embraced the Red, Blue, Green (trichromatic) system of color, but it was not by any means the only color theory (either then or now). It was also only a theory in Stanley's day, and it is only a theory now. The Munsell system uses a five primary system to describe and catalog color. The TV and computer screens of today use a system based on Cyan, Yellow and Magenta pixels. The continental Europeans at the time were mostly using a red, green, white system or a red, green, white and yellow system. Secondary colors are not supposed to be able to produce primaries. That's why they are called *primaries* in the first place, so how could cyan, yellow and magenta ever possibly create a working system?

From a practical point of view, red, blue and green striplights were never able to produce much other than the individual colors themselves, certainly not all the colors of the spectrum. If one wanted a purple sky, one needed purple gel. Nothing looked good in green light. The green rondels or gels were promptly replaced by amber or white (nocolor) because they were more useful. Red, blue and green combined did not really produce a white light, but rather a whitish light that was dim and did not look quite right. Areas were supposed to be lit with complementary tints, but the contrast was often (if not always) way too severe, and it just did not look natural or pleasing. They did not in fact produce white light as they were supposed to but retained the color overtones of the original parent colors. This resulted in the practice of using different colors from each side even if they weren't really the complementary colors. The whole concept of warm and cool colors was also vague and hard to understand. Was Surprise Pink a warm or cool color? At what point did violet get enough red in it to be considered a warm color (magenta)? At what point did yellow get enough green in it to become a cool color?

Third, it was never possible to achieve the ideal 45 degree angles left and right at the extreme edges of the stage because (a) there were no pipes that extended far enough to the sides and (b) even if there had been, the light would have been cut off by the proscenium arch or would have been behind a black masking curtain onstage. So the areas on the sides of the stage were lit from the front (often the 2nd or 3rd instrument in from the end) and from 45 degrees from the inside (left or right as the case might be). Stanley knew this and mentioned it (even drew a picture of it in his book), but he did not explain what this would mean when these lights were paired on the same dimmer. The light that came directly from the front had a shorter throw distance, which meant it was also going to be brighter (inverse square law). In order to balance the lights, the one from the front was going to have to be gelled down so that it would match the brightness of the other light that traveled the longer distance.

Proscenium theatres did not have lighting grids. They had lighting pipes and these ran left and right. There might be a ceiling cove out in the house (which did not raise or lower) and then usually 1 or 2, possibly 3, lighting pipes on stage. Raising or lowering them changed the throw angle but often their height was determined, not by the ideal lighting angle, but by the height of scenery and the ability of borders to mask them. Even had it been possible to set their height based on an ideal angle, the ideal height for lighting something from the front (from 45 degrees above) is different from the ideal height for lighting it from 45 degrees from above and 45 degrees off to the side. The pipes were hung like trapezes and there was no way to yoke instruments forward or back as this would simply have changed the center of gravity and rotated the whole pipe. So while Stanley knew what the ideal angle was, the architecture of the theatres had not caught up with his thinking, and there was no practical way in the real world to achieve what he envisioned.

Fourth, dimmers were expensive and are-alights were always ganged together so that as many as possible could share the same dimmer. If the whole stage was always used as one playing area, one could gang together all the lights from left on one set of dimmers and all the lights from the right on another set of dimmers. One set could use warm colors and the other set could use a cooler color and the balance would be achieved with the dimmers. If the play required area control, then one usually ganged the warm and cool of each area together on the same dimmer as Stanley had suggested. Warm colored gels typically transmit more light than cool colors so unless one were to double gel on the warm side, the result would look unbalanced. As mentioned before, one had to double gel the light that came from the front on both end areas to lessen its brightness. Double gelling also darkened the color produced. Modern practice would be to use gray gel, which didn't exist then, assuming we had a similar shortage of dimmers (which for the most part we don't).

Fifth, Stanley knew that one had to overlap areas to get good coverage. If he knew by how much, he did not say. If he knew the difference between a field angle and beam angle, he did not say. Essentially he encouraged one to overlap instruments by an amount that looked good. Mostly he assumed that fresnels would be used, which are zoom-type instruments with very even drop-off to the side; so one could pretty much set the area width at whatever was wanted. Today we mostly use ellipsoidals, and they have a steep drop off at the edge, and we cannot be quite so cavalier about how they get overlapped.

Sixth, when Stanley's method was applied to thrust theatres, it was not immediately apparent that it needed to be rotated so that the light came from the front and two sides and (when appropriate) from the back. Instead, it was often assumed that it should come from the diagonals of the stage (as had been suggested for a proscenium situation), which is in most cases a hideously bad idea. This is called *defying the grid* and is discussed separately.

Since Stanley's method did not entirely work as it came out of the book, it got modified in real world usage. It was still a cook-book-style recipe for arealighting the stage, and Stanley still got all the credit for the ideas even though some of them had been somewhat modified. Here are the four highpoints:

1. The idea that the areas had to be 8–12 feet in diameter was replaced by the idea that the beam diameter of one of the arealighting instruments (ellipsoidals) determined the size that the lighting areas would be. The beam diameter, of course, varied with the throw distance. The manufacturer provided the information on this, and it is also available in book form, and it can be calculated. In any event, if one knows what kind of instruments they have, they will come to know (if they don't already know) how big the pool of light will be on the stage at the nose plane.

2. The whole idea that the entire stage was divided into lighting areas based solely on how many beam diameters it would take to cover it was modified to take into account how the set was most likely to be used, so that the division into areas had

to make sense within the context of the play. In other words while it might be more efficient to light each zones with 4 areas, this might not make sense if the play had a lot of scenes that took place center because the center areas would be split across the centerline.

3. Areas upstage of the proscenium still needed to be lit by at least 2 instruments-per-area, but this was expanded to include an optional backlight. Backlighting did not really become popular until the movies and TV started using it to help separate the actors from their background. Areas downstage of the proscenium (thrust and arena theatres) needed to be lit by 4 (on rare occasions 3) instruments-per-area and these worked better when aligned with the grid.

4. The idea that left and right lighting systems needed to be complementary colors was modified so that when there were more than just two systems that surrounded the acting area, adjacent systems would be different (although not necessarily complementary colors). In a four-instrument situation, this meant that front and back could be the same color and sidelights left and right could be the same color or all four could all be different colors.

M.E.— Abbreviation for MASTER ELECTRICIAN, the electrician in-charge. It is slang and used mostly by crewmembers among themselves. It tends to remind everyone else of a medical examiner.

MEASURING THE SPACE— This is always called something else like a *familiarization session* so that it doesn't sound as if the new lighting designer doesn't trust the accuracy of the materials he has just been given (usually at the first production meeting), but that is precisely the reason and the only reason why the new designer wants to personally measure and count anything.

Lighting designers who have been in the business for a while will have countless stories about the time they didn't bother to do this and discovered this huge mechanical vent blocking an entire hanging position or the time when the theatre listed a whole set of instruments that had subsequently been given to the touring show and so were no longer available. All this makes for a funny story if discovered in time. On hang night, the unexpected loss of 12 instruments won't be a laughing matter, and the plot will have to be reworked in the matter of a few minutes, and it will probably put the lighting designer in a bad mood for the rest of the session.

Start by taking the set designer's ground plan and the blank light plot of the theatre (assuming they are two separate drawings) and hold them up to the light (or put them on a light table) to see that the theatre outlines match. You'd be amazed at how often they don't. Even if they do match, you'd be amazed at how often they are inaccurate, incomplete or just plain wrong.

To measure the space without assistance, one needs a hammer and some small nails and a 50–100' tape measure with a ring on the end (that can be hooked over a nail), some string and a plomb bob.

When all the lights have been hung and focused and turned on for the first time and nothing looks right, this is not the time one wants to discover that the catwalks are really 2 feet lower than where they were drawn. "You know someone ought to change that on the Tech Specs."

"I thought we'd already changed it, but you must have gotten one of the old versions. Sorry."

Everyone will be sorry that the incorrect information was given out, but it will be the lighting designer who has just spent eight hours hanging the instruments in the wrong place and now there won't be the time or the manpower to change any of it. The staff who send out information packets are not expected to be technically knowledgeable and often don't realize they are sending out old drawings that date back before the last major remodel. They won't lose their jobs because they grabbed the wrong drawing by accident, but the lighting designer won't be invited back to do another show unless the lights look good, and no one will be interested in hearing excuses. In the end they will say that the lighting designer should have checked. He should have, and here's a list of things he should check:

1. Height, width and depth of the stage in enough detail that one could draw it including the location of the proscenium arch (if any) and the position of the first row of seats outward from the stage.
2. Height, length and location of light hanging pipes. There is usually one on the centerline. Drop a plumb bob down to the stage to see that it actually falls on the centerline of the stage (you'd be surprised how often it doesn't), determine where in an upstage-downstage location it is and what its height is. Based on this, one can do the rest of the measurements up in the grid or at the counterweight rail. For locations like house coves, put an angle measure (angular bubble level) on a music stand at nose-height and sight along it to the cove position to get the throw angle and then measure the throw distance with a piece of string hooked around the pipe up there with both ends coming down to your nose. The advantage of this system is that you don't have to go back up to the cove to unhook the string as pulling one end will release it. One can then make a scale drawing (or calculate) to arrive at vertical elevation and horizontal distance.
3. No-hang zones. Sometimes the lighting pipes will be where they are supposed to be, but some sprinkler pipes or something else will be in the way, and it will not really be a hanging position at all. This is especially true if one intends to overhang any instruments. Always be sure there is adequate space, and that there aren't any obstructions.
4. Are the circuits, where they are supposed to be? Are any of them blocked by ducting? Do they all appear to be working (not taped over with a "Do Not Use" tag)?

5. How are the electricians going to know where on the pipe to hang the instruments? They will, of course, be looking at the Light Plot, which is drawn to scale, but one doesn't really want them to have to scale the plot and then transfer those distances to the pipe. They should be able to see and judge positions by eye. Usually this is done on long pipes by putting colored tape every 4' along the pipe starting at centerline. If there is a plugging channel with numbered circuits hung above the pipe, it may be possible to judge positions off of that, assuming they have been correctly drawn on the plan.

6. Count the instruments. Usually they are in position for the show that is currently in performance. Count the instruments that are in-the-air and then count the ones in storage and ask about where the others (if any) are. If they are missing or broken, one would want to know now while there is still time to get them found or fixed.

7. Look at the storage room. Do the instruments appear to be in good repair? Are the gels neatly put away and labeled? What can be seen here is a good indicator of what one can expect to find in-the-air. Do there appear to be extra cables and two-fers and sidearms and barndoors or anything else that might be needed later?

8. Measure the sightline height of the first and last rows relative to the stage floor. Do this for the balcony too if there is a balcony. This may have to be done by sighting along a level table-top toward an 8' 1 · 2 with one foot markings placed vertically in the seats

9. Turn on all the exit signs, aisle lights, orchestra lights or anything else that normally stays on throughout the performance and look at a blackout onstage to see how black it really gets.

10. This whole process should take an hour, two at most. Regardless of how long it takes, the time spent looking, examining and measuring is never wasted. When one does this personally or is present while it is being done, then there won't be as many things to be surprised by later.

MECHANICAL INTERLOCK— See MASTERING.

MEDIA, COLOR— See COLOR FILTERS or MEDIA,

MEDIA, STORAGE— See STORAGE MEDIA and DISKS.

MEDIUM (BI-POST, PREFOCUS, SCREW or CANDELABRA)— Lamp bases of various kinds. See LAMPS.

MEMORY HEAD— Another name for the front end of the memory lightboard. See LIGHTING CONTROL.

MERCURY SWITCH— One of the first silent switches, it poured a vial of mercury onto the two contacts to complete the electrical circuit and poured it off the contacts when the switch was reversed. When used in its generic sense it refers to any silent switch. It is important that the prop switches provided on the set for the actors to use be silent so that the sound of a click cannot be associated with when the lights controlled by the lightboard change. See PRACTICALS for a more detailed discussion of the circumstances in which actors might actually activate switches.

MERCURY VAPOR LAMP— A special lamp used to produce ultraviolet light. It requires both a warm-up period and a cool-down period after use before it can be started again.

MF— Abbreviation for MULTIPLYING FACTOR, which usually refers to a number which when multiplied by the throw distance, will yield the diameter of the lit area.

MICA— Also called *isinglass*. Up until the mid–20th century, this was one of the few heat resistant material that was also transparent. It is a silicate mineral that is layered.

It was used to create color media for anything that had a live flame. Louis Hartmann talks about using several layers of it to adjust the brightness of the arc lights.

MILITARY BRIEFING MODEL— Production meetings are typically based on one of two models, either the *military briefing model* or the *knights of the roundtable model*. See PRODUCTION MEETING for a more detailed discussion.

MIMIC LIGHTS— See PANEL LIGHTS.

MINIATURE CANDELABRA— Often called *mini can* for short. This is a kind of lamp bases. See LAMPS.

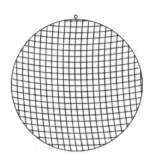

MIRROR BALL— A sphere usually 12–24" in diameter covered with mirror facets. When attached at the top to a mirror ball motor, it will turn slowly and any light aimed at it will be reflected 360 degrees around the room. It is strongly associated with ballrooms and dancing but is used as a special effect in the theatre.

Mirror ball

MISSING INSTRUMENT REHANG— One of four methods of changing the lights from one show to the next. See STRIKES, KINDS OF for a more detailed discussion.

MODE— This refers to what the monitor screen displays on a computer lightboard. See LIGHTING CONTROL/Computer Memory Lightboard.

MODELLING— Another (perhaps less descriptive) word for *plasticity*, which is to say making three dimensional objects appear three dimensional from a distance by the use of different colors from different directions. See VISIBILITY for a more detailed explanation.

MODESTY WALL— This is an 18–24" wall that separates the first row of audience from the stage area. It prevents small props or liquids from getting spilled into the audience and effectively prevents the audience from stretching their legs into the stage area. Lighting units or sound mics are sometimes mounted to it or concealed inside it. Its primary function as the name suggests is to prevent seated audience on the opposite side becoming visually distracted by the opposite-side audience.

MODIFIED PROSCENIUM LIGHTING— See LIGHTING, KINDS OF.

MOGUL— A large size of lamp base. There is a mogul screw base and a mogul bi-post base, neither of which are seen much anymore as the emphasis has been on creating smaller more compact lamps.

MOL— Abbreviation for MAXIMUM OVERALL LENGTH, which is a lamp measurement from a point on the base to the extreme end of the lamp.

MONITOR— The TV-type screen that displays the visual component (visual interface). of a computer lightboard or any other kind of computer for that matter.

MONOCHROMATIC— Using one color, especially in regard to monitor screens which (when they are monochromatic) typically have green or yellow lettering against a black background.

MOOD— Also called atmosphere, it is based on the ideas of Adolphe Appia who postulated that the lighting could or might have an emotional effect on the audience. Few would deny that plays that end sadly can leave their audience in tears in a reasonably regular and predictable way. Books, movies and TV can do the same thing, but this is mostly because the audience identifies with the principle character or characters and imagines how it would feel to be in that person's sad predicament. What part the lighting might play in this (if it plays any part at all) is unclear. There is certainly no lighting cue that can be put on the stage that will bring an audience to tears in and of itself.

If the lights are noticeably inappropriate to the scene, they could call attention to themselves to such an extent that it might ruin the mood being created by the actors. There is a huge difference between not ruining an effect being created by someone else and actually being able to create a discrete mood with the lighting alone. First, how would it be done, and specifically which of the variable properties of light would be used? Stanley McCandless thought it should be a function of stage lighting and thought it might have something to do with color. "I'm feeling blue," is an idiom in the language, but when people see the color blue on objects, they do not automatically associate it with sadness. Who would want to own a car or wear blue clothes if it were a sad and depressing color, so science has as yet failed to discover any universal subconscious emotional responses to colors.

Almost every stage lighting book since Stanley McCandless has reiterated that the lighting should create a mood but no one has as yet offered a method for achieving that, and in many cases they have not even bothered to define what they think a mood might be. Some people think that morning and afternoon constitute moods. Most people, when asked to name five moods (emotional responses they expect the audience to have), become stumped after "happy" and "sad." Richard Pillbrow (See bibliography) said in essence that when you'd gotten the time, place, situation and everything else right, then the mood would take care of itself. New designers need to ponder this question and decide for themselves what they think. See LIGHTING, FUNCTIONS OF for a more detailed discussion.

MOON EFFECT— See EFFECTS, KINDS OF.

MOSAIC FUSION— This describes tiny dots of different colors that are placed so closely together that they cannot be separately focused by the eye and as a result are interpreted by the eye as being a single intermediate color. Newspaper photographs are created this way, as is everything printed on an inkjet printer, and many other things as well. See COLOR MIXING for a more detailed discussion.

MOTIVATED LIGHT— A vintage textbook term, always confused with motivating light, which means a reinforcing light. See REINFORCING LIGHT for more detail.

MOTIVATING LIGHT— A vintage textbook term, always confused with motivated light, which means a practical light, where the source of the light can be seen. See PRACTICALS for a more detailed discussion.

MOTOR-DRIVEN DIMMERS— A vintage system of remotely controlling dimmer operation used mostly on things like houselights that moved at one speed.

MOTORIZED LIGHTS— These were the forerunners of the present *intelligent lights.* They were mostly used in TV studios or repertory situations where time to change the lights was severely limited. The lights could be raised and lowered, tilted and panned from a remote location. They were also used in hard to get to locations where their high initial cost was balanced against the continued high labor costs of getting to the location.

MOVEMENT (as a controllable property of light)— Although it is not one of the eight variables of a static lighting moment, it is a controllable property by means of light cues. In fact, movement or change is what defines a light cue. Whenever a light cue is taken, then one or more lights have had one or more of their eight variables changed. What lightboards mostly do is change intensity, but the effect onstage is not necessarily one of it being either brighter or dimmer. If, for example, a blue wash is brought down and a red wash is brought up, the effect will be that of a color change even though the mechanism was a change of intensity. When an operator is involved, as with a followspot, then the range of what can be changed increases, but it will still be one or more of the eight variables of light. See VARIABLES OF LIGHT.

MOVING LIGHT— In its most generic meaning, any light that has an operator can become a followspot and thus a moving light. The term is usually reserved to mean some kind of motor driven remotely controlled system like the early forerunners of intelligent lights. See INTELLIGENT LIGHTS for a more detailed discussion.

MULTIMETER— See ELECTRICAL TESTERS.

MULTIPLE (stagepin receptacle)— Also called a *three-way tap*, it is a female connector that has receptacles on the three sides that don't have the cable coming into it. It has fallen out of common usage because a three-fer can be made up from three female connectors and Teflon wires in a flexible sleeve. Not only is the made-up three-fer vastly cheaper, it is also much more versatile because it can reach instruments that are further apart without using extra jumper cables. This is especially true if the three-fer is made up "daisy-chain style" rather than "spoke-style." See TWO-FERS for a more detailed discussion.

MULTIPLE-CONDUCTOR CABLE— Sometimes called *borderlight cable* because that is where it is most commonly used, but it is also used to supply power to plugging channels that are attached to electric pipes. Any cable that has more than two current carrying conductors (plus a ground wire) is considered a multiple-conductor.

MULTIPLEXING— Sending several discrete signals over a single pair (or limited number) of wires, especially in regard to dimmer control. DMX 512 is probably the most common protocol for this.

MULTIPLYING FACTOR (Abbr. MF)— A number which when multiplied by the throw distance will calculate the diameter of the pool of light. It is often found in photometric data and manufacturers' cut sheets. It is always 2 * Tan   where   is equal to half the beam (or field) angle. Where beam or field is not specified, it can be assumed to be for the field angle. Multiply the MF for the field angle by 0.66 to get the MF for the beam angle for ellipsoidals adjusted for flat field, which is mostly all of them.

MUSICAL, LIGHTING OF— See LIGHTING, KINDS OF.

NANOMETERS— These used to be called milli-microns, which seemed to better suggest their extreme smallness, but the name was changed so that it would end in "meters." Nano comes from the Greek and means dwarf. Nanometers are used to measure the length of lightwaves, which vary between about 380–780 nm.

A nanometer is a billionth of a meter. Imagine the thickness of a piece of paper divided into 75,000 parts. Each part would be a nanometer. Another way to visualize this is to hold your thumb at the 7.5" (187.5 mm) mark of a ruler and imagine that the distance represents the thickness of a piece of paper. If that were so, then the entire visual range (all 400 nm of it) would fit between any two millimeter marks.

NATIONAL ELECTRIC CODE (Abbr. NEC)— A code governing electrical wiring and devices and installations of all kinds. It is produced by the National Fire Protection Association and revised every few years. States and building code districts then adopt it into law, occasionally adding or subtracting material of their own.

NATIONAL ELECTRICAL MANUFACTURERS ASSOCIATION (Abbr. NEMA)— This is the organization that sets the standards for electrical connector configurations.

NATURAL SOURCES— See SOURCES.

NC— Abbreviation for NO COLOR and usually not capitalized (nc).

NEGATIVE— Used in reference to DC current, it is the side from which the electrons flow. It is typically color coded black and is also called the *common* terminal.

NEGATIVE MIXING— This is a color cataloguing technique to match a test color to a three-color primary system. Suppose that a brilliant yellow color on one screen is to be color matched to a combination of red and green on the other screen. There is no way that the red and green alone can effect such a match. However, if blue is added to the yellow side of the screen, its color can be so desaturated that a match can be made and the color catalogued as a mix of red, green and negative blue.

NEMA—Abbreviation for NATIONAL ELECTRICAL MANUFACTURERS ASSOCIATION, which is the organization that sets the standards for electrical connector configurations.

NEON— A gaseous discharge system that involves a high voltage and which can't be dimmed. It is used on stage (as everywhere else) for neon signs. While the red-orange color is the most common, there are other possible colors.

NEON ELECTRICAL TESTER— See ELECTRICAL TESTERS.

NEUTRAL— By law, all neutral connections are color-coded white. The white wire of the instrument cord is connected to the white (silver colored) screw on the connector, which in turn is connected to a neutral bus bar in a disconnect box, which in turn is connected to a metal rod or pipe sunk in the ground.

NEW STAGECRAFT—This was the name given to the ideas of the French theatrical impressionists after those ideas had been reworked by Adolphe Appia and Gordan Craig and brought to America. If this sounds somewhat roundabout, then it partially explains why the ideas sometimes appear to be confusing, illogical and contradictory. It will probably be best to start with the impressionists in Paris in the 1880s and '90s.

A group of French artists and intellectuals wanted to free the performing arts from the bonds of realism, much as the painters had freed painting from its ties to a representation of realism. Theatrical realism had in their opinion run its course and was now depicting trivial domestic events (instead of epic myths and legends) in a chronological and totally predictable way (the well made three-act play). It was attempting to affect the emotions of the audience by creating an illusion of realism that left nothing to the imagination and that relied on highly emotional acting.

The impressionists, on the other hand, wanted to affect the emotions directly through a combination of music, poetry and light. Music and poetry had for a long time been credited with creating feelings in its listeners. Aristotle had postulated a connection between colors (light) and music, and there was a popular feeling that science was on the verge of demonstrating what that exact correlation was. A popular entertainment of the time was called "color music" where music was visually accompanied by a light show where colored lights were played upon a sculpture of some kind. The impressionists gravitated toward dream plays that moved in stream-of-consciousness style like Strindberg's *Dream Play* or Ibsen's *Peer Gynt.* They disliked painted scenery because it was representational, preferring instead more abstract platforming with steps and shapes and draperies that were vague in their location and left more to the imagination. In terms of lighting, they were fascinated by the dreamlike quality provided by scenes set behind scrims, by images created by lantern slides and by scenes plucked out of darkness. While they combined the spoken word with movement, the words were often provided by a narrator and the movement by dancers. They did not want to use the realistic acting techniques of the past, and so the actors were in a sense choreographed puppets, which is presumably the origin of Gordan Craig's idea that Übermarionettes should replace live actors on the stage.

The Impressionists (sometimes called Symbolists) eventually gave up their theatrical experimentations and moved on to other things leaving behind little except some newspaper clippings that chronicled their efforts. Were they simply faddists, as David Belasco suggested, whose fad had simply come to an end and whose audience was now ready to move onto the next new fashionable thing, or had they discovered some viable alternative to realism but had simply not gotten around to writing about it? In any event, their ideas had caught the fancy of Gordan Craig and Adolphe Appia, who made these ideas their own. While they wrote about them independently, the similarities between their ideas was the result of their having gotten their inspiration from the same source.

While one could not ask for two more devout believers in the cause, they were both set designers, which may have affected their emphasis. They didn't explain the underlying ideas very well. Why, for example, was it perfectly okay to act in front of a two-dimensional lantern slide image but totally unacceptable to act in front of a two-dimensional painted drop?

In any event, it was in this way that the ideas (which had now become theirs) arrived in America where they were accorded a mixed reception. Appia's book (**Musik und die Inscenierung**) was available only in what was said to have been a bad translation and Craig's book (**Art of the Theatre**) while fervent, was also bombastic and not particularly easy to read. David Belasco called it "inexplicable," by which he meant incomprehensible, and he devoted an entire chapter (*Holding the Mirror Up to Nature)* to this subject in his own 1919 book (**Theatre Through Its Stage Door**). There was no question here in America of replacing realism or revolutionizing the performing arts in general. There was no outcry against trivial plots, or well-made plays or emotional acting. There was no danger of actors being replaced by super-marionettes, and there wasn't room in the theatrical command structure for a set designer who thought himself a puppet master as the job had already been filled by the play's director.

Only the ideas that related to scenery and lighting were considered at all, and the message of the *new stagecraft* seemed to involve doing three things: (1) firing the scene painters (2) getting rid of the footlights, which Appia had declared a "monstrosity" and (3) providing an expanded (but not a clearly defined) new role for the lighting.

Firing the scene painters and replacing the painted backgrounds with three-dimensional scenery pieces had the initial effect of making the existing realism more like real life, which was the opposite of what the impressionists had wanted to happen. The box sets of the time now incorporated platforming and steps, the walls did not undulate in the ambient wind currents backstage, and the molding and trim were now real, and although shadow lines still had to be painted on to make them read as three-dimensional to the back of the house, they were actually made of real wood. Making the sets more solid also made them more cumbersome and harder to move and change.

Doing an outdoor scene, which in the past had simply involved a painted drop made to look like an outdoor scene instead of an indoor scene, now involved building rocks and trees. This put tremendous pressure upon the playwrights to locate their plays in one indoor location and to leave it there for the duration of the play and not to have any outdoor scenes at all since they were so much harder to do. This resulted in fewer locales and less scenery, and without painting techniques being used, it made it particularly hard to create a credible looking sky in the background. There had really been nothing inherently wrong with acting in front of a painting. It was not intended to be realistic, which should have appealed to the impressionists. It was, however, accepted as a theatrical convention by its audience and it allowed very fast scene changes from one locale to another and firmly established the time, place and situation of each scene. The goal of leaving more to the imagination of the audience was not even partially realized until the architecture of the theatres changed in the 1960s, and then there literally was no longer a place to put the scenery.

Both Louis Hartmann and Stanley Mc-Candless argued eloquently against getting rid of the footlights, but no one at the time was in the mood to listen. Their subsequent elimination has proved to be a huge inconvenience (some would say mistake) as there is now no mechanism to soften harsh facial shadows, which have been made worse by the increased use of ellipsoidals.

The expanded role for the lighting designer included (1) creating the mood unassisted by either music or poetry, which had been part of the original impressionist package but was not part of realism or realistic plays (2) establishing "unity" but again the unity was supposed to be with the music and poetry, which were both now missing from the package. Regardless of whether one believes that mood and unity ought to be part of the lighting designer's job, the suggestion that the lighting should do more than just provide the base illumination and the subsequent search for what that expanded role might entail has undoubtedly had the effect of improving the overall quality of stage lighting because the lighting person's elevation to designer status has brought with it the challenge to prove that the promotion has been justified.

NEW THEATRE LIGHTING— This is a vast subject where each choice made along the way limits all the subsequent choices until in the end one runs out of choices altogether and is stuck with whatever has somewhat inadvertently been created.

For the most part the lightboard is being put in a large control booth with an excellent view of the stage. Hanging positions are being provided in the necessary places for instruments. Each circuit is being given its own dimmer. These were some of the complaints of Louis Hartmann and Stanley Mc-Candless that no longer apply.

The following comments represent areas where the present-day ideals are not being met as well as they might be. It deliberately skips *under-equipping* on the grounds that everyone knows this one but has accepted the idea that these things will be added later, except for the most part they never are.

1. **Inappropriate Equipment:** This comes about as a result of a popular misconception that since no one knows what each show will be like, no one could possibly predict in any exact way what lighting instruments might be required to light it. As a result, a big collection of this-and-that is put together that includes such old favorites as striplights, scoops, cyc lights, some fresnels, and a nice collection of mismatched ellipsoidal in various sizes. If the money wasted on useless equipment were channeled into badly needed equipment, better results would be obtained. The idea that no one can predict how to light the space is absurd. Theatres typically provide what is called a basic light plot for their off-season rental customers. Any first year lighting student should be able to take a blank light plot for an unknown theatre and figure out how many areas it would take to light the flat floor and what equipment would be needed. He should then be able to estimate washes and specials and come up with an overall equipment recommendation. Unless the hanging positions are at radically different heights, the ellipsoidals should be the correct size rather than varying sizes.

2. **Hard-to-Get-to Hanging Positions:** In most hanging and focusing sessions, more than half the time spent is expended getting a ladder, lift or other device in a position to get to the hanging location. This means high labor costs for the life of the building, and in practical terms these positions are used only as a last resort because they require too much time at a time when it is severely limited. The technician should be able to walk to every hanging position. This means catwalks, and they should be in more common use than they are.

3. **Pipe Grid Spacing & Height:** Pipe grids

are usually set up on 48" centers or something that appeals to the architect when in fact they should be spaced so that they are on the centerlines of the lighting areas in both directions. Grid heights less than 20' begin to run afoul of the Distance Problem (unfixable), and require more instruments to cover the area because of reduced coverage, and they will have blending problems that all the frost gel in the known world won't be able to fix. Keeping the grid high enough has to be solved at the architect-planning stage.

4. **Reach Up and Plug It In:** Once an instrument is hung, one should be able to reach up and plug it into a waiting receptacle. Often there is a receptacle within reach but it is a second drop point for a circuit that has already been used elsewhere. Due to the popular misconception that no one could predict what circuiting would really be needed, a random system where each circuit repeats every x number of feet is often adopted, but as pointed out earlier, first year lighting students should be able to figure this out. Each arealight is going to have its own circuit, so there is absolutely no reason for those circuits to repeat at all. We're talking about the design of the plugging channels, and for the same money a more useful configuration could often have been designed.

5. **Each Dimmer Should Be Used for Each Show:** Circuits that show up in weird places like the light booth, the trap room, a floor pocket or the back of the house may get used once every five years, so they need alternate drop points so that their dimmer will get used on a more regular basis. Otherwise an expensive dimmer will remain idle.

6. **Light Moat:** Provision should be made so that the stage can be lit from the inside toward the perimeter without light spilling into the house. This means a wide walkway between stage and audience or raising up the first row of seats or a combination of these.

7. **Floor Pockets:** These are expensive units,

they typically get buried under platforming, and usually it is some household lamp or appliance that needs to get plugged in (PBG connector). As a result an extension cord is run under the platforming and brought up through a drilled hole somewhere. For the money spent, an impressive array of PBG circuits can be made available in a recessed cavity in the wing walls or somewhere else backstage where they won't get blocked.

8. **Footlights:** They are out of fashion now and have been for some time, but we have continuing problems getting light into eye sockets and under hat brims, and these problems would all go away if we had some means to bring in light from below (from the footlight position). It is hard to believe that no one has figured out how to solve this problem yet.

NICHROME WIRE — A high resistance wire used in resistance dimmer boards and household hotplates and toasters.

NICOPRESS SLEEVES AND TOOLS — A tradename for an aircraft cable crimped fastener system that locks the cable back onto itself to form a loop, as for instrument safety cables. The sleeves are typically made of brass in $\frac{1}{16}$, $\frac{1}{8}$ and $\frac{3}{16}$ sizes (many other sizes too but these are the ones most commonly used in the theatre). The crimping tool has no name other than a *nicopress tool*, and it is about the size of a bolt cutter for the sizes of sleeves mentioned. Properly crimped sleeves are very secure and cannot be removed except by cutting the aircraft cable.

NIGHT LIGHT — This usually refers to a light left on at night to allow people to walk through the darkened theatre or other workspaces. The traditional method involves a stand with a bare light bulb enclosed in a wire cage, and this is traditionally carried out on stage with a trailing cord and set somewhere close to center stage. This is not however the only way to solve this problem. Sometimes a garage-type shaded light is lowered in from above. Sometimes there may be a fluorescent fixture above the grid that is left on.

NIGHT VISION BLUE CONVENTION—

Refers to the symbolic use of blue colored light to represent both nighttime scenes and other scenes where an "invisible" form of light is needed.

In real life, there is no natural source of blue light anywhere outdoors at night. In the absence of artificial sources, there is either moonlight or no moonlight. Moonlight is a reflection of sunlight and it appears to be a colorless white light, but there isn't much of it (0.02 fc or thereabouts). In other words no one could read in such light, but one could probably make it across the back yard without walking into a tree or piece of lawn furniture. A non-moonlit night is lit only by starlight, and it was on just such a night that George Washington moved an entire army across the Delaware River undetected by the British sentries on the other side.

For theatrical purposes, the audience loses color perception at about 1 fc and would consider anything less than this unacceptably dim. By using light that is blue in color, the audience has come to understand that this is light being provided for them to see and that the actors are going to pretend that they don't see. As a result, there may be a night scene in which the actors are feeling their way along the walls, although the audience can see them well enough in the blue light. The actors are only acting because they can see as well in blue light as anyone else. Blue light is typically used as scene change light, and in that case, it is being provided for the crew to see marks on the floor and horizontal surfaces while the audience is supposed to pretend that they can't see what the crew is doing.

There is some scientific justification for this in the sense that blue is right on the edge of visual perception and the human eye does not see it as well as it does other colors of light. It should come as no surprise that the colors the human eye sees the best are the three colors used in a traffic light. Blue when faded down to low levels can appear grayish in a way that most nearly approximates the monochromatic grays that objects take on when color perception is lost. Whoever first started doing this, predates Louis Hartmann who talks about it as a firmly established practice in his day.

NO COLOR (BRITISH: *open white*)— No color media is being used, which is abbreviated on plots and paperwork as *nc*.

NON-CONDUCTOR— More commonly called an insulator, it is any material that resists the conduction of electricity like plastic, rubber, ceramic and glass.

NON-DIM or NON-DIM CIRCUIT— A circuit controlled by an on/off switch. On modern lightboards it is commonly a dimmer whose dimming curve has been defined so that it works like a switched circuit (full at 1 percent). Non-dims are typically used for motors, fans, florescent lights or anything else that may be damaged by being dimmed. It can also be used for worklights or running lights that could be dimmed but generally don't need to be.

NORMAL— In its specific scientific meaning, it means that a line is perpendicular to a plane in all directions. Trapezoiding is caused by the projection screen not being normal to the centerline of the projector. Illumination levels found using $I = E/d^2$ are only accurate if the lit surface is normal to the *centerbeam* of the light (at that point).

NOSE HEIGHT or PLANE— The horizontal plane at the height of the actor's nose, which is taken to be 5'6" for adults and is the normal aimpoint for the lights.

NO-TRACK BLOCKER (or blocking) CUE— A computer lightboard term referring to a cue whose unused channels have been set positively to off (often displays as 00) rather than clear (which often displays blank). The point is to introduce a barrier that will stop levels tracking forward from previous cues. All blackout or near blackout cues are usually set this way. See LIGHTING

CONTROL, Computer Memory Lightboards for a more detailed discussion.

NUMBER SHEET— A designer's worksheet that has numbers from 1 to 100 (or whatever fits on a page) with a space to write something after the number. These are used to keep track of the number of instruments used, number of circuits used, number of gels used or anything else that needs keeping track of, and it would look something like this:

Number sheet

This is a worksheet for the lighting designer's personal use. He could use a piece of scratch paper and write down the numbers each time but having a form is easier. It is merely an aid for him to see how all his available instruments or channels or anything else he needs to count are going to get used up. It is easy to erase and correct and keep current.

NUMBERING & LABELING— The tradition on a proscenium stage is to number from SL to SR and from the proscenium outward and in the case of booms, from the top down. Labeling in the context of portable equipment is done primarily to give it an id number so that if one of the fresnels has a cracked lens a note can be made that instrument #84 or #F20 (or whatever the numbering system) has a problem. In addition, if some of the ellipsoidals don't have gobo slots or don't have wide gobo slots, then these instruments are prominently marked so that they will not be hung in a place where a gobo is needed. This kind of labeling is usually

done with colored tape around the yokes of the instruments, and it is usually prominent enough to be seen both by the ladder electrician and from the deck. See also AREAS, NUMBERING OF.

OBJECTIVE LENS— An image-forming lens used in projectors to focus a slide.

OBLIGATORY CUES— Those cues without which one cannot do the play as written. These include lights down at the beginning to allow actors to get into place, it allows for lights being turned on or off as part of the business of the play and it provides for scene changes and a restoration of light. It also includes the cues that are referred to in the text of what the actors say to each other. See LIGHTING IDEAS for a complete discussion of this subject.

OCCUPATIONAL SAFETY AND HEALTH ACT OF 1970 (Abbr. OSHA)— The act of Congress establishing safety rules for all businesses and industries in America.

OCTAGONAL BOX— An eight-sided electrical box used most often for the facility's lighting fixtures (like makeup mirror lights) as opposed to the facility's switches and outlets, which are more commonly put into foursquare boxes.

OD— Abbreviation for the OUTSIDE DIAMETER of a pipe. Pipes however are most commonly referred to by their INSIDE DIAMETER (ID).

OHM— A unit of resistance to the flow of electricity, named after Georg Simon Ohm (1787–1854).

OHM'S LAW— E = IR. See ELECTRICITY.

OLD WIVES TALES— In order for something to achieve the status of an old wives tale, it has to be a fact-like phrase that sounds reasonable, it has to be oft repeated and it has to be of questionable merit. These are the kinds of things that directors, who don't know any better, might say to fill a silence.

1. Comedy needs to be bright and tragedy should be dim or at least dimmer. Let's

say we ran the grandmaster down to half for a tragedy. How would that be? It would be fine except that no one would notice the difference. All theatre lighting relies on relative levels. It is not possible to create the real daytime levels of 3000–5000 fc, but this does not seem to matter because an average audience accepts something as low as 70 fc as being a daytime reading. The human eye is not a good measuring device for quantitative levels, so running the grandmaster at half would make daytime scenes 35 fc and night scenes 5 fc. It might look as if the theatre didn't have quite enough equipment, but otherwise it simply wouldn't be noticed.

Act I, Sc vi of **Macbeth** begins with the line, "This castle hath a pleasant seat." Does this sound like it ought to be a dark or gloomy scene? Should it be deliberately made so because this is supposed to be a tragedy? No one would want every scene in a show to have the same underlit (or any other) quality. It is the differences and contrasts that produce dramatic interest. The original idea dates back to something said by Leone di Somi in the 1500s, which was contained in his description of a show that he had done where he had begun with the stage brightly illuminated but at the first unhappy event, he had dimmed down the lights all at once, which had produced the effect of horror in the spectators and had been widely praised. As a purely practical matter, if the audience can't tell whether the scene is happy or sad unless the lighting helps out, then the show has more problems than the lighting will ever be able to fix, and sometimes it will be far more interesting for the lighting to not mimic the happiness or sadness of the scene at all.

2. In order to see better, put more light on the stage. Often what is needed is less light in order to see better. See VISIBILITY for a more detailed discussion.

3. The lighting needs to wash out the shadows. Inasmuch as the shade and shadow reveal the shape of the objects, when all the shaded areas are washed out, a sphere will look like a circle. Occasionally shadows on the background scenery may have to be washed out, but even then care has to be taken in this process that the background does not become brighter than the actors. See VISIBILITY for a more detailed discussion.

4. One of the functions of stage lighting is to direct where the audience will look by making whatever they should be looking at brighter. This has its origins in the role of "light" in paintings. Paintings don't move and paintings don't speak. The rules are different in a theatrical presentation, and what is brightest is way down on the list of things that will attract an audience's attention. See LIGHTING, FUNCTION OF for a more detailed discussion.

5. One of the functions of stage lighting is to create a mood for the scene. Few would question that scenes may have moods, but they are created by the actors guided by the director and using the words of the playwright. Where is the role of stage lighting in all this? Must the lighting reinforce something that has been made obvious by someone else? Or might it be more interesting for the lighting to do something else? Which variables of light control the mood? Is it possible to make the ending of Hamlet seem joyful by using the lighting when at the same time the corpses are being stacked up like cordwood? See LIGHTING, FUNCTION OF for a more detailed discussion.

6. The idea that the additive mixture of red and green light produces yellow light and the overlapping three-circle diagram that is almost always provided to illustrate this process. Does no one check this stuff out anymore before they include it in their book? Just because Munroe R. Pevear and Stanley McCandless believed that this was so, does that make it so? Have you personally tried it out? Because if you had, you might have reached the same conclusion that Sir Isaac Newton reached in 1666

when he said that mixing green and scarlet did not produce the intermediate color of yellow. They can't both be right. This is a question of fact that can be easily tested in the context of stage instruments and stage colors. See COLOR MIXING for a more detailed discussion.

7. Green light on a red object will turn it black. Does no one check this stuff out anymore before they include it in their book? According to the theory of selective absorption, this is what is supposed to happen, quite true. Unfortunately this is not what actually happens. Thanks to color constancy, the eye sees the red object as a red object, even when the theory of selective absorption says that objects don't have any color at all. See COLOR ANOMALIES/Color Constancy for a more detailed discussion.

8. Unity. Who could possibly be against unity? Shouldn't there be unity between all the production disciplines? It certainly seems as if there should. This is an idea that dates back to Adolphe Appia relative to the operas of Richard Wagner, but it has never been explained very well, and it is unclear by what means it would be effected. How can the lighting achieve unity with the costume design? Or with the set design or with the show as a whole as presented by the director based on a play by the playwright. If this concept has any relevance to the lighting, then it needs to be explained better.

9. The evenness of light. This used to be a litmus test for the lighting designer whereby he proved that he was a master of his craft. When borderlights provided the majority of the light, it was very evenly dispersed, but no one thought that looked particularly interesting. Sir Henry Irving went to great lengths to make sure that his lighting had pockets of brightness and darkness, and it was something he was famous for and theatre practitioners came from far and wide to study his methods. When fresnels started being used to provide the arealights, it suddenly became very hard to achieve the evenness of the old borderlights, so to say that someone's lighting was very even was a compliment because it showed that the designer had tamed the fresnels with their hot centers and positioned them in a way that looked more-or-less even. Now that we are using more ellipsoidals that have much more even fields than ever before, it is no longer difficult to achieve evenness, but evenness is seldom interesting, so saying that someone's lighting is even is now the equivalent of saying that it is "boring." There are times when the lighting should be even and boring and other times when it should be textured in a controlled way.

10. Painting with light. This is something that David Belasco said in the introduction to Louis Hartmann's book, and it was intended as a flattering bit of hyperbole, which it is, but he may not have originated the phrase. It has not, however, been possible to actually do anything with stage lights that in the least resembles the subtlety with which paint can be applied to canvas. In fact, it has been this false belief that has resulted in exaggerated expectations of what the lights should be able to do but aren't able to do. (White sky-cloths are a good example of this, where it has been left to the lighting designer to make them look like the sky.)

11. A lawyer friend of mine who is as shocked as I am that catwalks are not the standard method of getting to the instruments thinks that this subject should be explained in terms of billable hours. His complaint is that all methods of access to the lighting instruments are usually discussed as if they were equally good (i.e. safe) or as if safety were not or shouldn't be a concern. There are three points to be made here. First, while we all know several different ways for a ladder accident to occur, we may even have witnessed one or been in the building when one happened, none of us have

ever heard of a catwalk accident nor could we imagine what it would entail. In other words catwalks are as safe as the balcony outside your bedroom window, but ladders are not. Second, no one wants to think that someone who worked for their theatre would later bring a lawsuit, but if that person could no longer work anymore, they might feel they had no other choice. If it were you who couldn't work and had ever mounting bills, you might not feel that you had any choice either. Third, defending against a lawsuit (especially one involving safety and an injured party) ends in only one of two ways, neither one of which turns out well for you, the client. Either you will celebrate the win by giving your lawyer vast sums of money or you will lose and in addition to having to pay your lawyer, you will have to also give vast sums to the person who sued you. In terms of a small non-profit theatre, this can break the bank and end the dream. The good news is that it is avoidable at a fraction of the price, and as a by-product, the use of catwalks will also lead to better lighting.

OLIVETTES— Said by Theodore Fuchs to have been named after the production in which they were first used, which would have been the Bijou theatre's production of Edmund Audran's musical **Olivette** in 1881. They began as a trapezoidal shape of open box arc light, painted white inside but having no actual reflector. Louis Hartmann used four of them in the 1906 production of the *Rose of the Rancho*, and their position on the ground plan behind a high garden wall suggests that they were the arc-type and had operators. When the new 1000-watt lamp was invented in 1913, Louis Hartmann talks about replacing the arc units in the olivettes with the new lamp. This is the same lamp that was supposedly made at the special request of David Belasco and that David Belasco had exclusive use of for two years (which would have been 1914–15, which would cor-

roborate its first commercial use in 1916 in a Caliban floodlight). The olivettes were a grandparent of the scoop, and a huge step forward from bunchlights. It is also possible that there were gas versions of the olivette that were perhaps called something else.

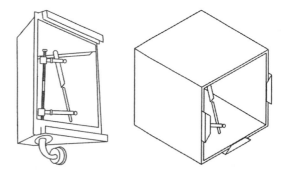

Left: Olivette arc-type; *right:* Open box arc

OPEN BOX ARCS— As the name suggests, these were large open boxes painted white inside (no other reflector) powered by an arc light and used for floodlighting pre 1905, when the gallery reflectors were invented, which were said to have been an improvement. They were typically mounted on short stands, and they required an operator.

OPENING or OPENING NIGHT— The night that the production is officially open to the paying public and the night on which the reviewers are expected to come. While audiences that come to preview performances pay, they pay less and the understanding is that the play is not quite finished yet. It is considered extremely bad form for a reviewer to come prior to the official opening. An opening night audience often consists of board members and other highly placed friends of the theatre, and it is not unusual for there to be a party in the lobby or onstage either before or after the performance, or both. The lighting designer's job is usually over as of opening night and in some venues the designers' paychecks are distributed after the performance. By tradition no changes are made after opening night. While the director can pretty much do as he pleases in this regard, it would not be thought proper for a lighting designer to appear in the booth after opening night with a list of notes, so the lighting designer is effectively done with the show at the end of the note session of the last preview.

OPERA, LIGHTING OF— See LIGHTING, KINDS OF.

OPERA GLASSES— Vision-enhancement devices (binoculars) designed to assist sight when either the distance is too great or the viewer's personal eyesight is not good enough.

OPERA GLASSES TEST— Is it you or are you just too far removed from the action onstage to see it properly? Take the test and find out. Have someone hold up a card with one-inch print on it. A normally sighted person will be able to read this at a distance of about 50'. If this does not include you, then you may need to compensate and sit closer. Since operas are typically performed in facilities that place audience members at distances in excess of 50 feet, you are well advised to bring your opera glasses if you hope to see properly. If "one-inch print" seems like an arbitrary standard, then look at two people talking to see if you don't agree that 50' is the extreme limit at which you are still able to make out faces well enough. All potential lighting designers need to know if they are normally sighted or not, and they need to know where the limits of acceptable visual acuity are.

OPERATOR— Anyone who operates theatrical equipment during a performance is considered an operator. In terms of the lighting, this means a board operator. Where followspots are used, it means one or more followspot operators. Where floor instruments are moved or changed, it will involve floor electricians.

OPTICAL AXIS— The centerline through the lens system, lamp and reflector which all are supposed to line up.

OPTICAL SYSTEM—(1) The entire lens, lamp, reflector package in an instrument, which includes everything except the housing, the socket and the connector. (2) The lenses and whatever holds them in place.

ORCHESTRA LIGHTS— There are really three distinct types of lights that could be called orchestra lights. The first is the light or lights on the conductor. At the very least, he needs to be given an isolation spot from the front as a light for the curtain call. This is often enough for the actors and musicians to see him by during the performance, also. If it lights him rather too well from the front, it may be possible to light him from upstage or from the sides during the actual performance.

The second type of orchestra light is the light that illuminates the orchestra when they stand up for their curtain call. Often the followspots are called upon to do this, as it may seem hardly worthwhile to dedicate house instruments for this tiny moment, unless there is no other choice.

The third type of orchestra lights refers to what the musicians use to read their music by and this is a more complex issue. While many other systems have been experimented with, music-stand-lights appear to be the system that reduces the total amount of light the best and puts it directly on the music that needs to be seen. It's also the method musicians appear most comfortable with and like the best.

ORCHESTRA LIGHT PROBLEM— The light from the orchestra pit can have a catastrophic effect on blackouts and dark scenes. There are really only three solutions to too much light coming from the pit:

Change the Color of the Light

If the light coming out of the pit were blue, there could be a whole lot more of it before it began to be objectionable. Blue is right on the edge of the visible spectrum, and the eye does not perceive it as a light color in the same way that it sees white or other colors of light. It would not need to be very blue for it to begin to have a positive effect. Something as pale as ¼ CTB (G885 with a transmission of 60 percent) can work wonders. Even ⅙ or ⅛ CTB would be better than nothing.

Make the Light Dimmer

This can be done by changing the lamps, employing gels or by installing a dimmer somewhere.

Changing the Lamps: This can usually be ruled out on the basis of cost alone. The tube lights that typically go into orchestra lights come in 25 and 40 watt sizes and cost about as much as a household dimmer that could control the entire pit. Musicians can read wattage numbers on light bulbs as well as anyone else, and are going to be very aware if a deviant lamp is installed. As a purely practical matter, they usually carry a spare in the size they are accustomed to having in case they have a mid-show burn-out.

Employing Gel: Putting a neutral gray gel (which dims the light without changing its color) over the opening on the music stand lights has the advantage that parts of the gel can be further cut away to allow even more white light to come through, which allows different musicians to have different levels of light depending on their individual needs.

Installing a Dimmer: Simply putting the music stand lights on a dimmer is usually the simplest and least expensive method. It is also the least obtrusive way to handle the problem, as no one can tell, just by looking, that a 40-watt light bulb has been dimmed down to 80 percent. It does not however provide a way for some musicians to have more light than others. Neither does the commonly existing system of giving everyone a 40-watt light, but it would be an improved system if it did.

Prevent the Light from Leaving the Pit

There are really four things to consider in this regard: the architecture of the pit, its covering material (if any), reflection within the pit and shielding on the music stand lights.

Pit Architecture: It is essential to actually inspect the pit area. Sometimes the pit can be made to sink lower. Sometimes the pit contains platforms that could be removed or lowered. Sometimes the pit wall that separates the pit from the house could be made higher. The pit's floor level (when it is adjustable at all) is usually set, based on two things: first, the conductor's head has to be above the height of the stage floor so that the actors can see him. Second, the heads of the standing orchestra need to be seen above their masking wall for the curtain call. Also, inasmuch as some of the musicians have to stand to play their instruments, their heads need to be below the height of the stage floor during the performance.

Pit Coverings: Pits are usually open on their top, which is usually the way the musicians like them to remain, but this is how the objectionable spill light is getting onto the stage. No one is suggesting that the cover needs to be plywood, although this would effectively stop the light leak problem. Some kind of black scrim-like material is usually the covering most often mentioned. From a lighting point-of-view it can be demonstrated that it would be quite effect at containing the light and reducing the spill, but it will likely be hugely unpopular with the musicians because they will have to look at the conductor through it as he stands like a tank commander half-in and half-out of the tent. There are several weights of netting, but this is a method of last resort. Often the mere discussion of netting of any weight makes the idea of dimming the lights in some way seem more possible to the musical director.

Reflections: Light reflects best from light colored surfaces. The walls and floor and platforming in the pit should be a dark, nonreflective color that approaches black (*theatre brown*). The main sources of reflectance are usually the white sheet music, white shirts or blouses and shiny musical instruments. Although one is unlikely to make much headway at changing any of those, it won't do any harm to talk about them.

Shielding: Not all commercially made music stand lights are of equal quality. Some can be rotated and adjusted better than others. The light needs to be directed at the sheet music, and it should not spill on anything else. One needs to determine if some judicious use of black wrap and gaffer's tape would improve the situation significantly.

If this were purely a lighting problem, it could be solved in an afternoon using any one of the several methods suggested above. However, the musical director is the person responsible for how the sheet music will get lit, and the lighting designer in on the verge of asking that this be done differently than it has been in the past.

This is a perfect example of a situation where diplomacy may make the difference between success and failure. The musical director will need to be consulted and will need to approve of any plan that involves dimming the music-stand-lights or modifying the pit in any way. If this is approached in the wrong way, the musical director may simply refuse to help and will simply say that the musicians need to be able to read their music and that will be an end to it because the only other alternative would then be to find another musical director.

The actual stage lights for the show have not been hung yet, and no one really knows for sure that the orchestra lights will adversely affect the blackouts. If, however, there is any possibility that they may cause a problem, then a contingency plan should be discussed now before time and tempers get short. Better to install a dimmer now and later discovered it does not need to be used than to try to deal with the problem for the first time at the first technical rehearsal when there will be so many other things that will need to be dealt with.

At some suitably early date, as part of the measuring-of-the-stage session, the lighting designer will have turned on the musicians' lights as well as the exit signs, aisle lights and any other emergency lights that might remain on during a performance to see if (or how badly) they might affect a blackout.

If, and only if, there is a potential problem, the first step would be to examine the music stand lights to see what kind of lamp they use, to see how they are shielded, to see whether they are on a dimmer already or could easily be put on one and to generally snoop around the pit.

At this point one could approach both the master electrician and the stage manager separately in a casual setting and ask what kind of orchestra lights are typically provided and whether that was ever a problem? Did they ever find that too much light came out of the pit and what if anything did they ever do about it? If there are stories there, this should elicit them.

Also, as part of the research, one would want to engage the musical director in a casual discussion about anything except orchestra lights, just to get a feel for how flexible he might be. One could, for example, ask what is usually provided for the conductor during the performance and curtain call. The musical director will describe what he would like to have rather than what he usually gets. Having asked his opinion, it would be polite to agree to light the conductor and his orchestra at the curtain call any way he sees fit. If he is going to be asked for a favor later (as is likely), it would be an advantage to have done something nice for him first.

Step two would be to ponder the problem and come up with a number of solutions in one-two-three order. Only the lighting designer has any sense of how significant the problem might be and therefore how drastic the corrective action might need to be. Often shielding alone is enough, possibly shielding plus a gel or shielding plus a gel plus a dimmer. The musical director will usually be understandably nervous about having any power circuits from the pit connected to the lightboard. In his place, you would be nervous too. If he agrees to a dimmer, it should be a household dimmer or some other portable unit placed wherever he says he wants it so that either he, or a trusted assistant, can manipulate it.

The platforms that one finds in pits are usually placed there for good reasons, usually to allow musicians to see the conductor, and the conductor usually stands on a raised platform to see the stage. Raising the pit wall might decrease spill into the house but is unlikely to have much effect on spill onto the stage. As a general rule, the orchestra pit will be 1–3' lower than the first row of audience. Neither the stage nor the pit wall can be higher than the eyelevel of the first row (48") or it will block their view of the actors. Before one wastes any time trying to redesign the orchestra pit, make sure that sinking in further downward x number of inches will actually improve the lighting problem. Often it won't and so the whole question of pit height and its internal platforming becomes irrelevant.

Step three is going to be to involve the director. Within days of the first production meeting, the lighting designer typically meets with the director for the first time. This is discussed in detail in the topic DIRECTOR, FIRST MEETING WITH. If there is going to be a potential problem with the light in the pit, then the director should be made to look at the effect of the orchestra lights to make sure that he agrees that this may be a potential problem. This should precipitate a discussion of possible solutions. The director needs to be fully briefed on the possible solutions because he is the one who is going to have to sell the idea to the musical director.

If the director agrees that there may be a problem, then step four would be to schedule another demo with the musical director to again look at this and to discuss how best the problem might be solved, if in fact, it proves to be a problem (no one knows how bright the show itself will be or how dark the dark scenes will be yet, so at this point it is still only a contingency plan). What does the musical director think about blue gels in the ⅛–½ CTB range? What does he think about something darker like x364 but with 5 or 6 paper punch holes in it? The musical director should be allowed to pick among the possible solutions any way he'd like. He may already have encountered this problem before and have a way that has proved to work in the past.

The idea is to win over the musical director, so that he is looking out for the interests of the show at the same time as he is protecting the interests of his musicians. By giving him total control over any dimming device, one can then expect him to deflect or handle any future complaints from individual musicians and allow them to cut away more of their gel (or whatever the system turns out to be). Once the director and musical director have gotten together to discuss this, the lighting designer can fade into the background.

Often a final decision will be deferred until the actual light cues are integrated into the show so that everyone can see how much of a problem it will be. It may be only one or two scenes that will eventually be affected, and as such it might not be a big deal at all.

Clearly whoever runs the wires in the pit would need to aggressively tape the music stand lights into their dimmed power strips and would need to tape over unused outlets to discourage anyone else from plugging musical equipment into these outlets. The musical director would need to explain to his musicians what was going on.

If the director can't be made interested in this subject, it is either because he doesn't see it as a potential problem or because he has plenty of other things to argue about with the musical director that are more important than this or he thinks he'll lose. He may be right about one or all of those things.

If the lighting designer wanted to pursue this on his own, he could have a very casual conversation with the musical director where he asked if the musical director had ever considered putting the pit on a dimmer or using gels. If this is a hot-button issue, he could then gracefully disengage without ever getting to the point of asking for anything. The musical director may in fact know a lot about orchestra lighting in general, and the lighting designer may learn some things he didn't already know that will help him, not only now, but in dealing with other musical directors.

OSHA— Abbreviation for the OCCUPA-TION HEALTH AND SAFETY ACT of 1970, which is an act of congress establishing safety rules for all businesses and industries in America.

OUT—(1) When used as an adverb as in "Instrument Nr A-18 is out," it means unlit. (2) When used as a noun, it is either short for to the *load-out* or (3) short for *fade-out*.

OUT TIME— This is a computer lightboard term that refers to how long it takes a step to dim out all the way as part of the in time/ dwell time/out time/ step time process.

OUTLET— This is a generic term referring to the female receptacle of a permanent (and usually flush-mounted on the wall) electrical circuit. While it could be used to describe a 240-volt outlet for the stove in the green-room or a 30-volt intercom outlet, it usually is used to refer to convenience outlets, which are spaced every 10–12 feet around the perimeter of offices and workrooms and are connected to non-dimmed 120-volt power.

OUTSIDE DIAMETER (Abbr. OD)— In the context of pipes, it refers to the distance between outside walls. When "1.5 inch pipe" is talked about without any other qualifier, it most commonly refers to the INSIDE DIAMETER of the pipe. Schedule 40 black pipe is most commonly used and the OD of 1.5" pipe is about 2", and it is this 2" OD distance that the c-clamps must fit around.

OVERCURRENT DEVICE— A fuse or circuit breaker that will protect the dimmer and the rest of the electrical circuit from an overload. When the circuit is loaded beyond the capacity of the overcurrent device, then either the fuse blows or the circuit breaker trips.

OVERHUNG— This refers to hanging an instrument above a support pipe (yoke forks point upward) as opposed to the more common underhung position, which is the system favored by gravity. See YOKING for a more detailed discussion.

OVERLOAD— An electrical load in excess of the capacity of the wire or dimmer or connectors. Since all such electrical circuits are also supposed to either have a fuse or circuit breaker (overcurrent device) that is the weakest link, the fuse or circuit breaker is the part that is expected to fail.

OVERRIDE (manual)— To take manual control of a light cue or lightboard function that otherwise would run in a preset, timed way. In a rehearsal situation, it would not be unusual to speed-up a two-minute cue by taking manual control so that the rehearsal can start. In a live performance, the occurrence of something unexpected often requires taking manual control. When the stage manager calls for an extra curtain call, this will typically be run manually as there are usually no pre-programmed cues for this.

OVERRIDE SWITCHES— Both the night light and the stage worklights need to be controlled from backstage. To prevent them being turned on during a performance, the switches are sometimes recessed in the wall, or sometimes put inside a glass case, or they could have an override switch (usually in the booth) that would have to be turned on first. The override switches would be hooked in series with the backstage switches. Override switches typically have mimic lights to indicate that they were engaged.

OVER-THE-HEAD METHOD OF CYC LIGHTING— Described as early as 1932 by Stanley McCandless, it involved lighting the cyc above the heads of the actors from a downstage position where the lights were almost normal to the cyc or sky cloth. See LIGHTING SPECIAL PROBLEMS/Cycs and Drops for a more detailed discussion.

PAGE— This is a computer lightboard term that refers to any listing that will not fit on one screen. The screen can usually display about a 100 channels and their settings. Where there are more channels than that, they will be on a second page. There are often only about a dozen submasters but many pages of assignments. There are often buttons for *next* and *previous* pages.

PAIRING— See GANGING.

PAN— To move left or right. Used to describe the movement of intelligent lights or to describe the ability of a stage instrument to pivot left and right on the large yoke attaching bolt.

PANEL LIGHTS— This is a generic term that refers to any of a number of usually low voltage lamps or LED's, whose purpose is usually to give the user/operator of a piece of equipment information. These are also called *indicator lights* or *status lights* or *mimic lights* if the on-off state of the light mimics the on-off state of some other device. The most common mimic light is a power-on light that indicates when an apparatus (be it a coffee pot or a computer or a feature on a lightboard) is turned on. Panel lights also by extension refer to the lights that illuminate meters or other graphic displays like the VU meters on a sound mixer.

PANIC ATTACK— A mental state usually caused by stress and lack of sleep wherein the designer has a complete loss of faith in the whole design and every cue looks worse than the one before, and no corrective action seems to suggest itself, and the designer becomes lost in a sea of indecision. It is most likely to occur during a rehearsal-with-light or the dry tech, especially when it comes at the end of a long day.

Of all designers, the lighting designers have the least time in which to do their job and are often under tremendous pressure to get everything right the first time. Sometimes they stay up all night because it seems to be the only way that the job will get done. Most people can still function adequately after 24 hours without sleep, but everyone has a breaking point; it is just a question of where it is. When the body reaches a point where it can go no further, the brain simply shuts down and refuses to function, leaving one in the state described above. Although this is an extremely common problem, it is not discussed much because no one would want to hire a lighting designer who had some kind

of "mental problem" that incapacitated him during tech week. It is for the most part preventable, but that is not much of a consolation when one is already in its grasp.

In most cases, the lighting is not as bad as it may appear to be and can be successfully dealt with later (any time but now). Attempting to continue to work in this state simply compounds the errors that will be made, which will have the effect of reinforcing the idea that everything that was touched became worse.

The designer needs to go home and get some sleep, but this often seems impossible in the middle of a rehearsal. It's not. All the designer has to do is jump up from the tech table and run for the rest rooms, saying something like, "...going to be sick." He can return several minutes later wiping his mouth with a piece of toilet paper. He can then apologize, and say he thinks it might have been the clams he had for dinner. He can then collect a copy of the disks, make arrangements for tomorrow and go home. Everyone will understand because migraine headaches and stomach attacks are generally understood as things that could happen to anyone.

Things will usually be better by the morning. The lighting designer is a trained professional. Even on days when the lighting may not be inspired, it will at least be competent in the sense that the actors will be lit so that they can be seen from anywhere in the house and the cues will appear to be consistent with the time, place and situation of the play.

PANIC SWITCH— This usually refers to a front-of-house switch that would allow the house manager to override the houselight dimmers and turn on the houselights in the event of an emergency. There are, of course, times when the performance needs to be interrupted and the houselights turned on for a medical emergency or something similar, but this is usually coordinated by headset with the stage manager so that as the house manager walks out onto the stage to explain to the audience what is happening, the lightboard operator is bringing up the houselights, so although the panic switch exists, it is rarely if ever actually used for its intended purpose. Having a houselight switch in the front-of-house is however handy when the lightboard operator has left the building before the last of the patrons, and it falls to the house manager to lock up for the night. It is handy for the carpentry crew working alone during a load-in and not having access to the booth. The switch itself is often recessed in the wall or protected by a plastic box so that it is more difficult to activate it by accident.

PAPER SIZES— There are four standard paper sizes as they relate to lighting or really any theatrical drawings: A-sized paper is 8.5 · 11, B-sized paper is 11 · 17, C-sized paper is 17 · 22 and D-sized paper is 22 · 34. Of these, B-sized sheets are usually the biggest size that anyone can deal with without having to fold them. We're talking about ladder crews where there is no convenient drafting board on which to place the drawings. B-sized sheets are also the largest size that can usually be photocopied on a standard copy machine, which explains in large part why this is such a popular size.

PAPER TECH— Where this exists, it is a meeting held sometime between the lighting designer's final meeting with the director and the dry tech at which the stage manager writes the technical cues into the book. Typically the director, stage manager, sound and light designers are present along with possibly the operators, possibly the technical director, and possibly others. Even if the lighting designer has prepared a written Cue Synopsis, he will be expected to be there to discuss whether the light cues should come with or be followed by sound cues, etc.

If the paper tech precedes the level-setting session, then the light cues will be exactly as written on the Cue Synopsis. If it occurs after the level-setting session or after rehearsals-with-light, then there may have been numerous changes and the lighting designer may

reissue a corrected Cue Synopsis. The changes are usually pen-and-ink changes or otherwise clearly indicated, so that the director and stage manager don't have to cross-compare with their earlier version to determine what is different. In fact there is really no reason for the stage manager to have the earlier version if he or she plans to wait until this session to put cues in the book.

Sometimes the suggestion will be made that this should or could also incorporate the otherwise private lighting meeting with the director, but most designers will want to have that be a separate meeting.

PAPERWORK— The documents that define or explain the lighting design. Lighting design used to involve no paperwork at all (except for a few handwritten notes about how to run the lightboard, which is to say a handwritten Cue Sheet). Lighting designers are now somewhat notorious for producing way too much paperwork, as can be seen from the list below.

The four most essential documents are probably the Light Plot, the Hookup Sheet, the Cue Synopsis and the Channel Reading By Cue Sheet. Taken together, these four items define the entire show in a way that makes it possible to recreate and remount the design at some future time.

As long as there was just one lighting technician who did all the work by himself, there was no real need for paperwork. While he might have had lists and sketches and notes for his own use, he didn't have anything he intended to share with anyone else. As he acquired a crew, he needed documents that would tell them what he wanted them to do. There were documents that then related to the crew that would hang and focus the lights, and there were documents that related to the crew that would run the lightboard and followspots and floor instruments. As time went on, there were documents that were meant for the director (and/or stage manager and fellow designers), and there were his own notes and lists that helped in the design process.

This was further complicated by the fact that everyone invented their own system of documentation and then felt free to copy and modify everyone else's system as they encountered it, and many of these systems overlapped. The technology also changed, so the Cue Sheet paperwork for example was forced to change when manual boards were replaced by preset boards.

Hang and Focus Group

Circuit Schedule: This is a re-sort of the instrument data (contained in the Hookup document) in circuit number order. It is used to hard patch circuits to dimmers where the incoming circuits are a bundle of loose cables and where the intention is to grab the first one and plug it into its appropriate dimmer. It is also useful for making sure that no circuit has been used in more than one dimmer and for identifying unused circuits.

Dimmer Schedule: This is a re-sort of the instrument data in dimmer order. It is used as an aid in hard patching circuits to dimmers where these are not the same. It is not necessary where circuits are hardwired to their dimmers and both share the same number.

Focus Charts: These are usually pictographs of how each instrument is focused to include sharpness, aim-point and shutter cuts as seen from the back of the instrument. They are usually not necessary unless the show is to be recreated at some future date or is to have a long run, in which case it often takes the form of pen-and-ink additions to an enlarged Light Plot. Where they are created, they document what has already been done and are often part of what the assistant is expected to do.

Hookup Sheet: Also called the *Plugging and Softpatch Sheet* or the *Channel Schedule,* this is a spreadsheet of all the data about the instruments in dimmer order for manual boards and in channel order for computer boards. It is used by the electrician to hard patch or soft patch the show. It is used by the board operator as a Pre-Show Instrument Checklist, and it is used by the designer as a

list of what all the channels control (Cheat Sheet). See HOOKUP SHEET for a more detailed discussion.

Lighting Sectional: This is a sectional drawing of the theatre usually at the centerline showing the location of typical instruments and often showing beam coverage upstage and downstage. It is used by the designer as a tool for locating the hanging positions. It is usually not necessary for the crew hanging the show and usually is not provided to the master electrician unless specifically asked for, but it is often created by the designer as a worksheet.

Running Group

Cue Sheet: This is a step-by-step description of how two hands (or however many hands) are to execute each cue in the show. When manual boards were replaced by preset boards, the format changed and a *Reset Sheet* was added. When computer boards replaced preset boards, the cue sheet was created onscreen by the machine and ceased to become a document that was provided in hardcopy form. See CUE SHEET for a more detailed discussion

Floor Cards: A step-by-step list of color or focus changes for floor instruments (usually on rolling stands) during the show. This is not necessary if there aren't any floor instruments that are changed during the show.

Followspot Cue Sheets: A step-by-step description of what one or more followspots do during the course of the show, which would include pick-up points, size, color and anything else necessary.

Pre-Show Check List: Also called an *Instrument Check List,* this is a step-by-step list to check to see that all lights are working prior to each show. Often this consists of a set of pre-show check cues on the computer that run in some kind of sequential order, while the electrician on the floor uses the Instrument Check List to check that everything is working. Sometimes an assistant brings up channels or dimmers one-at-a-time as the electrician on the floor calls for them. If the check is done in channel order, then the Hookup Sheet can be used as the check sheet. See HOOKUP SHEET for a more detailed discussion.

Replug Tracksheet: A table showing the dimmers that get replugged across the top and the cues at which that happens down the side. Used by the board operator to determine the state of the replugs at any given point in the show. This was mostly for use at rehearsals where a scene might be rehearsed out of sequence. It is now obsolete unless there are replugs.

Reset Sheet: This is a chart showing every dimmer with a space below where the level gets penciled in. It was used by the board operator to reset the presets. It got erased and corrected many times prior to opening. Now it is obsolete unless one is working with a preset board.

Director's Group

Cue Synopsis: Considered by many to be an optional document, it describes the effect of each cue in the show and includes script page, type and speed of the cue. It is used as a confirmation document for the director that puts in writing what the lighting designer has told him orally. It is used by the stage manager to put cues in the book. It is used by the lighting designer in the cue-setting session as a reminder of what areas to light and what the time, place and situation is, and it is used by whoever formats the disk to create blank cues for the show. It includes all information contained in the onscreen cue sheet and can be used as a cue sheet where the onscreen one is not sufficient. See CUE SYNOPSIS for a more detailed discussion.

Design Concept Statement: Optional unless the show is going to be recreated at some future time, it is a short essay that describes the number of areas and the lighting systems that will light them in plain English with descriptive color names instead of color numbers. It will also describe the specials, and what they are supposed to do in which scenes and anything else that relates to the logic of the design.

Director's Keysheet: Also called a *Director's Magic Sheet*, it is an optional letter-sized plan view of the stage showing the position of the areas and/or specials with descriptive color names, tailored for the director's use in staging the show so that the actors are placed where the lights will be. See KEY SHEET for a more detailed discussion.

Designer Worksheet Group

Channel Reading by Cue: A spreadsheet with channels across the top and cues down the side, showing the level of every channel in all cues in the show. This used to be handwritten and much corrected. Now it is usually a manipulated computer printout from the lightboard. It is used by the designer to examine and compare cues and to restore lost cues. See CHANNEL READING BY CUE for a more detailed discussion.

Cheat Sheet: A list of the channels in numerical order (often made to look like the monitor screen) with notes as to what each channel controls. This is very similar to the Hookup Sheet, which does the same job although it doesn't look like the monitor.

Cut List: A list of gel cuts necessary, sorted by size and color number. It is typically handwritten and handed to whoever is going to cut the gel. Often a re-sort of all the instrument data in color order is viewed onscreen and counted in order to make this list. The gobo patterns to be used are also usually noted, as they will be pulled from stock or purchased along with the color. See CUT LIST for a more detailed discussion.

Key Sheet: Also called the *Magic Sheet*, it is a small plan view of the stage indicating the aimpoint of the areas and all the specials with gel colors, channel numbers and often group or sub numbers. It is used as a memory aid by designers who haven't memorized what their channels do.

Number Sheets: A blank form that numbers things from 1 to 100. They are used to count anything that needs to be counted and kept track of to insure that too many aren't used like channels, circuits, barndoors, patterns etc. See NUMBER SHEET for a more detailed discussion.

Script List: Designer's notes based on a first reading of the script. Used as an aid in designing the show. See LIGHTING IDEAS for a more detailed discussion.

Short Plots: A table that lists available equipment across the top and proposed uses down the sides. It is used as an aid in determining how best to apportion the available equipment. Different versions are created weekly and eventually used for reference when creating the plot, and they are all discarded when the final plot is complete. See SHORT PLOTS for a more detailed discussion.

PAPERWORK REDUCTION— While this may be a huge ironic joke at the Internal Revenue service, where the phrase may have originated, it is a vitally important issue to the lighting designer. A huge amount of precious time can be taken up creating paperwork that no one will ever read. A lot of designers believe that producing lots of paperwork helps them appear competent and helps them to get jobs. For this to work, the people that hire the lighting designers would need to be aware of this plethora of paperwork, which is not typically what happens, as most of it is given directly to the master electrician and is often seen by no one else.

In any event while paperwork requires a disproportionate amount of time to create, distribute and revise, it contributes very little to the way the show will eventually look. The fewer documents produced, the fewer people these are distributed to, then the more time there will be that can be devoted to the design itself.

Some designers believe that the Plot and the Hookup Sheet are all that are needed. Others might add the Cue Synopsis and the show disk to this list. Certainly in terms of recreating a show that was previously done, more than this would seldom be needed.

PARABOLIC ALUMINIZED REFLECTOR LAMPS (Abbr. PAR)— A whole class of sealed beam lamps characterized by their rugged construction. Many different wattages, lamp bases and beam angles are available. They are used extensively in parcan units and in striplights.

PARABOLIC REFLECTOR— One of three common reflector shapes. See REFLECTION, LAWS OF.

PARALLEL CIRCUITS— When two or more lights are hooked up independently to the same source of power, they are said to be hooked in parallel. They burn at full brightness and if one burns out, the others still continue to stay lit. This is the system used on C7 and C9 Christmas tree lights. In a parallel circuit $1/R_T = 1/R_1 + 1/R_2..., I_T = I_1 + I_2...,$ and $E_T = E_1 = E_2....$

The opposite of this is *series circuits* in which two or more lights are daisy-chained together with only one path to the power. Miniature Christmas tree lights are made this way. When one burns out, the rest go out as well, as their path to the power has been broken. Also each additional light added makes the rest dimmer.

The schematic below represents a cuelight system that allows the stage manager to signal either to stage left or stage right. The stage left (and stage right) circuits are each hooked in parallel to each other but the two lamps and switch of each circuit are wired in series.

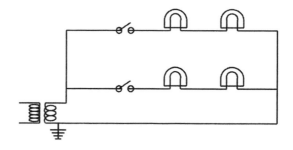

Cuelight system

PARALLEL-BLADE CONNECTOR (Abbr. PB or PBG)— The common household connector that features two flat blades (also called an *Edison connector*). When it includes a third grounding prong, it is becomes par-allel-blade grounded. See CONNECTORS, KINDS OF for a more detailed discussion.

PARCAN— A stage instrument that uses a sealed beam lamp that often looks like an automobile headlight. These typically are pointed in the correct direction and no other focusing or control is possible except that the entire lamp can be rotated, and the facets that make up the lens system (commonly called *bottles*) then can be oriented either horizontally or vertically or anywhere in-between. Parcans typically accept a gel or a barndoor or tophat.

There are several sizes of parcan instru-ments based on the kinds of sealed beam lamps they accept, and wattages typi-cally range between 50 and 1000. Addi-tionally, the lamps can be had in one of five oval beam spreads from wide flood to very narrow spot. Inasmuch as the instruments consist of little more than a socket and housing for the lamp (which is the reflector, lens and light source combined in one), they are the least expensive of the stage spotlights. The lamps are long-lived, but about 50 percent more expensive than their fresnel counterparts, and the light qual-ity is generally not as smooth as that pro-duced by a fresnel or an ellipsoidal, and unlike the fresnel, the beam size is not adjustable. See INSTRUMENTS for a more detailed discussion.

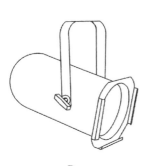

Parcan

PARK— This is a computer lightboard term that refers to setting a dimmer or channel or a group of them at some specific level where they will remain undisturbed by most board operations. If there are music stand lights, they would commonly be parked to insure that they remained on all the time at what-ever their level was supposed to be.

PART CUES— This is a computer lightboard term that refers to doing a single cue in such a way that certain channels come up first, followed by a selected list of others and so forth. Usually, it is not possible for a chan-nel to appear in more than just one part. As a result, a series of follow cues usually achieves the same end but is more flexible and capable of being changed more easily if it doesn't work out.

PATCH BAY— This term refers to sound patching systems permanently installed in sound racks where typically the inputs and outputs from the backs of various equipment are extended to one or more patch bay on the front of the rack for convenience in inter-connecting the equipment. Lighting patch bays are typically called *patch panels*.

PATCH CORD— A jumper cord often con-sisting of only one current carrying conduc-tor used to patch a load into a dimmer in what is commonly called a *hard patch* sys-tem. The patch cord is sometimes hardwired into either the dimmer or more commonly the load and these cords sometimes self-retract into the patch panel box.

PATCH MODE— This is a computer light-board term that refers to a display screen where the softpatch can be set.

PATCH PANEL— This is an electrical device that allows all the circuits to be connected to any of the dimmers. It is often set up like a telephone switchboard with patch cords that interconnect two other connectors. It could also be a series of sliders that connect to one of a number of bus bars that each represents a dimmer. Many loads can be connected to one dimmer, but any given load can only be placed on one dimmer.

PATCHING— Where the word is used alone, it generally refers to hard patching. See HARD PATCH or SOFT PATCHING.

PATTERN— Short for GOBO PATTERN.

PBG— Abbreviation for PARALLEL BLADE GROUNDED.

PC— Abbreviation for PLANO-CONVEX.

PCP— Abbreviation for PEAK CANDLE-POWER.

PEAK CANDLEPOWER— Also called *beam candlepower*, it is the commonly understood word for what the scientists call *intensity*, and it is measured in candlepowers, which are now called candelas in scientific circles.

PERCEPTUAL UNITS— This refers to the way the audience will perceive a given sequence in the action of the play. The audience does not have the benefit of seeing where the playwright chose to declare a scene or an act, so they sense these all as *perceptual units*, and lighting designers usually make sure that there is a light change at these points.

PERIMETER LIGHTING— In the context of thrust or arena configurations, there will be two kinds of perimeter lighting. The most common is light from the outside (audience side) aimed in at the stage, and where "perimeter washes" are referred to, this is usually what is meant. The second kind involves lights from the center of the stage (from the inside) radiating outward toward the audience, and this kind needs to be carefully focused to prevent unwanted spill falling into the house. In a thrust situation a perimeter wash typically comes from three directions and in an arena situation it would typically come from all four directions.

PERSONALITY FILES— Different brands of intelligent lights use different numbers of control channels to control the various attributes of the lights. Personality files come either from the instrument manufacturer or from the manufacturer of the lightboard (or other controller) and are in effect an initiation file for the controller that tells it how to manipulate the light. Using a personality editing feature, custom personalities can be created.

PEVEAR, MUNROE R.— A Boston architect who in the 1910s is credited with having invented the idea of having borderlights wired in three circuits so that red, green, blue color mixing could be done. He owned the Pevear Color Specialty Company, which among other things manufactured a line of gelatine colors, which were said to be of exceptional purity. He also developed a soft edged spotlight by grinding down the edges of the lens, a special tormentor spotlight, a teaser spotlight, a footlight unit that could light either directly or indirectly, and color mixing cyc lights.

PHANTOM CHANNEL— Any channel that is not connected to a load but is set at various numerical levels as a date or show code. See CODES, DATE or SHOW for a more detailed discussion.

PHANTOM LOAD— Another name for a *ghost load*. Some older and now obsolete dimmer systems (most notably resistance dimmers and to some extent autotransformer dimmers) would not dim out all the way unless they were loaded either to capacity or in the case of the autotransformers to a point where the dimmer recognized that there was a load. The most common solution was to add a phantom load, which was one or more floodlights in a hallway, workroom or other location where they would not be seen onstage.

PHASE (electrical)— Refers to a unit of time relative to the rotation of an AC generator. In a three-phase situation, the peak points of the cycles are at 120 degrees of separation, thus occurring at slightly different times for each of the three hot legs.

PHOSPHORESCENT— Any substance that absorbs light and then re-radiates it after the source has been withdrawn. This typically refers to glow tapes and paints that glow in the dark and are used to spike the location of scenery and props.

PHOTO CALLS— A time when photographs of the performers are taken. Often these are taken early in the rehearsal process and are used for publicity purposes. Where this occurs onstage, some kind of scenic backing has to be found, costumes (even if they aren't the actual costumes) are used, and some stage light is turned on.

Production photos (designed to be given to the reviewers for inclusion in their reviews) are customarily taken at a dress rehearsal as the show is running, but there may also be a photo call after this rehearsal to take shots that might have been missed. Most film, even a very fast film like ASA 400, may fail to get a good picture in low light conditions, like those often encountered in the theatre. These shots would be part of the photo call and more light would be added.

PHOTO FLOODS— These are floodlights designed to be used photographically, and the term refers to both the lamp and the fixture. The lamp is usually an R-type sealed beam lamp with a thin filament, which will make it very bright but very short-lived. The fixtures usually have built in barndoors and the housing makes no attempt to prevent any spill light, as spill light is not a problem when photographs are taken.

PHOTOMETER— See LIGHT METER.

PHOTOMETRIC DATA— This refers to the information manufacturers provide to potential customers regarding how big an area will be covered at varying throw distances and how bright it will be in the center of the area. They all more-or-less look something like this:

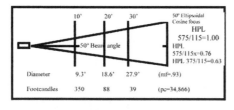

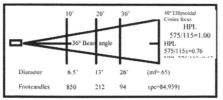

Photometric data

In the old days, each manufacturer did their own testing and published their own findings. Now they mostly send their instruments to an independent lab for testing, but the way they report the results is still up to them. Data sheets are primarily sales tools, whose purpose is to convince the potential buyer that this company's instruments are better than those of their competitors.

In photometry, *beam* has a specific scientific meaning, which is the central part of the cone of light up until the brightness has decreased to half of what it was at center. The outer part that encompasses brightnesses ranging from 100 percent to 10 percent is called the *field*. When the instrument is adjusted for a *flat-field* (sometimes called *cosine*) distribution, its beam will be ⅔ the size of its field. Sometimes this is explained in fine print or as a footnote somewhere. Sometimes it is assumed the buyer already knows it.

The manufacturer typically uses the brightest lamp available and provides correction factors for other possible lamps. A multiplying factor (MF) is often provided, which when multiplied by the throw distance will yield the field (or beam) diameter at that distance. The MF is always equal to 2 * Tan , where is equal to half the field (or beam) angle, which is explained in more detail in LIGHTING CALCULATIONS. The *intensity* of the instrument is always noted. Sometimes this is called *peak candlepower* or *beam candlepower*. The illumination levels given at 5, 10, 15 feet and so forth are simply the result of applying the inverse square law and are accurate in the sense that they fairly represent the amount of light that an actor would get from an eyelevel light (where the actor's face was normal to the centerbeam of the light). The buyer must beware when reading all this data, however, because some of it can be misleading. In the drawings above, there are at least three things that are not presented as clearly as they might be.

First, the cones of light are not to scale so the one in the upper drawing, that is supposed to represent a 50 degree instrument, looks the same as the one on the bottom, which is supposed to represent a 40 degree instrument. While this is a common practice, it is clearly misleading.

Second, the so-called 40 degree instrument is really a 36 degree instrument. There are many so called "40 degree" instruments whose actual field angles hover between 36 and 40 degrees. Just because the instrument itself has a big white "40" painted on its side doesn't mean this is what it actually is.

Third, what is called the beam is really the field even though they either don't say so or call it by the wrong name (as was done here). The multiplying factor is thus the multiplying factor for the field diameter.

Many professionals who should have known better have looked at a manufacturer's data sheet and concluded that a 50 degree instrument at 13.5 feet would cover about a 12.6' area, only to discover much later that it would only cover ⅔ of that (8.4'). As a purely practical matter, lighting designers seldom care where the fields will be because they will mostly fall victim to shutter cuts.

Robert C. Mumm has written a book called **Photometrics Handbook** in which he has compiled photometric data from instruments past and present and has presented it in a concise and uniform format. It is the first place that many designers turn when confronted by an instrument that is unfamiliar to them.

PIANO BOARD— This is a road box with 12–14 resistance dimmers with switches and master handles that is about the size and shape of an upright piano. It represents about all the dimmers that one operator can be expected to operate. Until relatively recently, the major New York City theatres provided DC current only, which insured the survival of the piano boards (which work on either AC or DC) long after they should have vanished from the theatrical scene. See LIGHTING CONTROL/Manual for a more detailed discussion.

PICK UP and PICK UP POINT— This refers to followspot operation where the light is put on a performer or object for the first time. The place on stage where that occurs (usually at one of the side wings on a proscenium stage) is called the pick up point.

PIE FORMULA— $P = IE$ where $P = $ power in watts, $I = $ current flow in amps and $E = $ electromotive force in volts. See ELECTRICITY for a more detailed discussion.

PIGTAIL— A short piece of cable as from a plugging channel or a drop box usually with a female connector on the end.

PIGTAIL TESTER— See ELECTRICAL TESTERS.

PILE-ON— This is a computer lightboard term that refers to the stage picture being the result of several input sources, such as submasters, fader pair and direct keyboard entry. The sources are usually color-coded on the display screen. Where the same channel is controlled by two input sources, then the highest reading takes precedence (*HTP*).

PILOT LIGHT— This refers almost exclusively to the tiny gas jet on gas appliances that always remains lit. When used in an electrical context, it would refer to a panel light of some kind. The electrical kind are more commonly referred to as *panel*, *status* or *indicator* lights.

PIN CONNECTORS— Short for *stagepin* connectors, they are special electrical connectors made for stage-use that are both inexpensive and durable. See CONNECTORS, KINDS OF for a more detailed discussion.

PIN SPLITTER— A special tool designed to separate the pins on a stagepin male connector. A pocketknife or matt knife can also be used for this purpose.

PIN WIRE— This is a moderately flexible wire about the thickness of a wire coat hangar and usually pre-cut into 6" lengths and used in the loose pin hinges that typically attach a rolling ladder to its platform. Where sidearms are made up on site, pin wire is sometimes used in place of a cotter pin or rivet or bolt and is put through drilled holes at either end of the ½" pipe to provide end-stops so that neither the c-clamp nor the sliding tee can slip off the pipe by accident.

PINSPOTS—(1) In the context of a follow-spot, any spot smaller than a headspot. This is typically achieved by means of the iris, and it usually means "as small as you can make it." (2) Another name for *rain lights*, which are sealed beams with narrow beam angles.

PIPE CLAMP—This is a generic and some-what vague term that most commonly would refer to a c-clamp, but it could also refer to a *crosspipe connector* or a *pipe hanger* or a two-piece *yoke clamp*.

PIPE CLAMPING or ATTACHING BOLT—This is the ½–13 square-headed bolt (usually about 3" long) that attaches the c-clamp to its support pipe.

PIPE ENDS—This refers to a hanging position on the extreme ends (left and right) of pipes in a proscenium house, usually higher than the booms that may be at that same approximate location.

PIPE FITTINGS—The pipes that are used to create hanging positions for lighting instruments are in reality plumbing or natural gas pipes that have been adapted to this use. Many pipes are used without fittings of any kind, but when the pipes need to be connected together, then using the pre-made fittings is usually the easiest method. It is a modular system with special terms of its own.

    Couplings: Interconnects two straight pipes to each other to make a longer pipe.

    Crosses: Interconnects four pipes at 90 degrees to each other.

    Elbows: Interconnects two pipes at 90 degrees to each other (sometimes 45 degrees).

    Flanges: Connects a pipe to a flat metal plate that can be bolted to a floor or wall.

    Nipples: Short pieces of pipe, threaded at both ends.

    Tees: Interconnects three pipes at 90 degrees to each other.

    Unions: This is a three-piece unit for connecting two straight pipes together. One piece is attached to each of the pipe ends to be attached together, and the third piece locks them together without rotating either of the two original pipes.

PIPE HANGER—It typically has two halves, which bolt together around a pipe and is then attached to the aircraft cable used to suspend the pipe or trapeze.

PIPE STAND—A less commonly used name for a *light stand*, which is a short boom (vertical pipe), usually with at least one cross-piece across the top, usually 10 feet or less with a heavy iron base, which is intended to be screwed to the floor. Occasionally the stand telescopes. Occasionally it has casters, in which case it would more commonly be called a *rover* or a *rolling light stand* (or *rolling pipe stand*). It is rarely high enough to require securing at the top.

PIPE WRENCH—This is an adjustable wrench with serrated jaws for use on pipes. It is shaped like the letter "F" where the short bar raises and lowers relative to the top, which remains stationary. It may also be called a Stilson wrench, which is a trade-name.

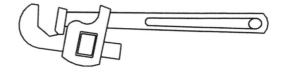

Pipe wrench

PIPES (BRITISH: *barrels, bars* or *battens*)—This refers to pipe battens in a fly house. Most commonly they are schedule 40 black pipe that have a 1.5" inside dimension and a 2" outside dimension and come in 21' lengths, which makes 42' a very common pipe length in a proscenium house.

PIT WALL—The modesty wall that separates the orchestra pit from the first row of audience, usually about 3' high, but this will vary depending on how sunken the main floor of the pit is and how high the stage is (relative to the first row of audience).

PLAN or PLAN VIEW— A generic term referring to any drawing that shows a horizontal slice of the stage or part of the stage as seen from above looking down as if through a glass ceiling at the height of the slice. In terms of stage lighting, the plan view is called the Light Plot, and it is a slice taken above the highest instrument location so that it shows both the instruments and their hanging positions and the outline of the stage below. The plan view drawing provided by the set designer, which is typically a slice taken above the highest piece of scenery is called a Ground Plan.

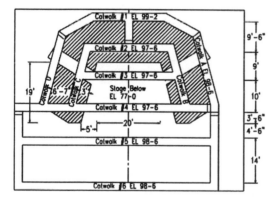

Plan View of a thrust theatre with catwalks and two entries from the house.

PLANO-CONVEX INSTRUMENTS (Abbr. PC)— A vintage instrument that used a plano-convex lens and a spherical reflector and usually a screw-base type lamp. These are now obsolete, having been replaced by fresnels. See INSTRUMENTS/Lensed Instruments for a more detailed discussion.

PLANO-CONVEX LENSES— An image-forming lens that is flat (plano) on one side and humped out (convex) on the other. They are sometimes installed in pairs with convex surfaces almost touching to reduce the overall focal length of the system. See LENSES, KINDS OF for a more detailed discussion.

Left: Plano-convex instrument; *above:* Plano-convex lens

PLASTICITY— This refers to light that reveals the three-dimensional shape of objects, which depends on having proper angles of separation between instruments and using different colors to ensure that the hills and valleys of the object (usually a face) look different. It was originally based on Adolphe Appia's concept that there were two kinds of light. There was a diffuse, shadowless light that was everywhere, and then there was a form-revealing light that created shade and shadow and thus revealed the shape or form of the objects. Both Stanley McCandless (1932) and Theodore Fuchs (1929) use the word in their respective books.

PLATFORM LADDER— See LADDER, PLATFORM.

PLOT— Short for LIGHT PLOT, meaning the drawing by that name, but the plot also refers to the state of the equipment in-the-air and as such is the equivalent of what in British practice might be called the *lighting rig*, so one might say that the plot was not setup to accommodate a second color wash.

PLOTTER— A computer printer that uses special felt-tip pens of various weights and colors and produces drawings rather than documents. Plotters typically are used for paper sizes larger than B-sized (11 · 17).

PLUCKING SCENES OUT OF DARK-NESS— A theatrical lighting technique (*clair obscure*), perfected by Henry Irving using gaslight, it became one of the signature marks of the *new stagecraft* as it related to the use of lighting. Only an isolated part of the scene is lit, and the background is obscured in darkness. It is still a tremendously valuable tool, but it only works where the light levels can be kept relatively low.

PLUG FUSE— Another name for a screw-in type fuse. They are no longer allowed in new construction, but some are still in use in older facilities.

Plug fuse

PLUGGING BOX— Another name for a DROP BOX.

PLUGGING CHANNEL (Abbr. PLUG-CHAN)— An industrially made electrical gutter with a 4x6 or thereabouts cross-section that has plug-in points every foot or so, either pigtails or flush-mount receptacles. These are typically located above the light-

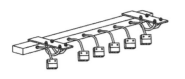

Plugging channel

ing pipes or grid so that one can reach up and plug in an instrument. Short sections (8–16") are usually considered drop boxes. In some cases, they may replace the light pipes entirely in the sense that the instruments are suspended directly from special hangers attached to the channel itself. Ariel Davis was one of the first manufacturers to do this, and they called their product Channel Mount.

PLUGGING PANEL— Another, although less common, name for a PATCH PANEL.

PLUGGING STRIP— You probably have one on your computer. It is a household hardware item that has about five PBG female receptacles mounted on a plastic bar about a foot in length along with a 15-amp circuit breaker/switch and a short cord with a male connector. They are used backstage to provide extra outlets or as a means of turning off a set of running lights or as a means of running power to onstage practical lights of one kind or another.

PLUGS— A very generic term for male electrical connectors of all kinds. See CONNECTORS, KINDS OF for a more detailed discussion.

POCKET (BRITISH: *dip*)— A recess in the wall or floor containing electrical receptacles or sound connectors. The electrical receptacles are most commonly stagepin receptacles but could be PBG or TLG. The recess typically has a hinged metal cover that allows cords to come through slots.

POINT BLANK— An artillery term meaning at zero elevation. Hence an instrument that is point blank or at point blank range is extremely close.

POINT CUES— This is a computer lightboard term that refers to cues that are added between existing whole-number cues. If added cues were needed between cue 30 and 31, they would be cues 30.1–30.9, hence the name.

POINT LIGHTING— As in one-point, two-point and so forth meaning lit from one point or from two points, etc. See INSTRUMENTS-PER-AREA and LIGHTING AN OBJECT OR AREA.

POINTS OF THE COMPASS— Maps are viewed with North at the top. In a similar way, plan views of the stage are typically viewed with upstage at the top of the drawing. In arena situations, the director picks a place to sit and the near area becomes downstage and the further area becomes upstage (sometimes called 12 o'clock or North). When the lighting is said to be aligned to the points of the compass, it comes from the front, back and two sides. When it is not aligned, then it comes from the four 45 degree diagonals, i.e. NW, NE, SE and SW.

POLARIZED—(1) For many years, AC connectors had only two blades or pins and could be connected in one of two ways. When grounding prongs were introduced, it became possible to connect them only one way. Certain classes of appliances were still allowed to use a two-contact parallel-blade plug because they had no metallic housing to ground anything to, but they were from about 1964 onward required to use a plug that had one blade wider than the other so it would only go in one way to insure that the unswitched white wire got connected to the unfused neutral.

POLE—(1) A vertical lighting pipe, more commonly called a *boom* if tall or a *light stand* if short. (2) The positive or negative electrode on a battery. (3) On a switch or relay, pole refers to the number of circuits that will be switched at once.

POOL OF LIGHT—A generic term that refers to whatever shape the light may be as it hits the stage. In the case of downlights, it will usually be circular. In the case of instruments located on the golden ring, it will be egg-shaped. Also called a circle of light even when it is not actually circular.

PORT—A recess for lighting in the sidewalls or ceiling of a proscenium house, more commonly called *coves*.

PORTABLE LIGHTBOARDS—This used to be a very important lightboard feature, but most control heads are now portable and can be carried by one person with ease. Contrast this to "portable" piano boards that require four people and wheels to move.

PORTALS—(1) A complete portal or show portal is in fact a second proscenium arch somewhat behind the permanent one. It consists of two leg pieces and a top header. (2) More commonly called *slots* or *coves*, they are openings in the sidewalls of a proscenium theatre that provide a concealed boom hanging position usually accessible from the back for focusing and maintenance.

POSITIVE—Used in reference to DC current, the positive is the side to which the electrons flow and is typically color-coded red.

POST-MORTEM—Where it exists, it is a final production meeting after the run of the play is over to discuss what went wrong and how to avoid making the same mistakes next time, which, on the face of it, sounds like a worthy idea.

In actual practice, the event is usually somewhat more sinister. If all had gone well with the production, everyone would have gone out for a drink to celebrate instead of gathering for a post-mortem.

The answer to, "What went wrong?" is almost always that so-and-so is completely incompetent and did not do his job or did not do it very well, and everyone at the meeting, by this late date, will already know this. If the meeting had actually been intended to uncover facts for a bewildered management, the designers would have been interviewed separately and confidentially, but that hasn't been done.

The person responsible for the mistakes is usually upper management, the director or someone being protected by the director or in educational situations, someone with tenure, so the purpose of the meeting is most often to white wash and rewrite the events of the past.

Had it been a low level flunky, like the lighting designer or sound designer, who had made the mistakes, they would either have been summarily let go or simply never invited back.

The post-mortem is aptly named, as a funereal gloom usually pervades the event. Otherwise talkative members of the production design team will have nothing to say. The answer to, "What went wrong?" will be a heavy silence because the real question is, "Who dares accuse us?" and everyone knows it. The designers at the low end of the pecking order fear for their jobs, stare at their shoes, count the minutes until the end of the meeting and wisely try to say nothing that will get them in trouble.

POTENTIOMETER—Sometimes called a *pot* for short, this is a variable resistor (almost always low voltage) that finds its way onto lightboards as a slider to control brightness. It works on exactly the same principle as a *rheostat* or a *resistance dimmer*.

POUNCE WHEEL—See TRACING WHEEL.

POWER—A scientific word referring to the ability to do work as measured in horsepower, where 1 hp = 745.7 watts.

POWER FORMULA—Also called the PIE formula and the West Virginia formula. See ELECTRICITY.

PRACTICALS— Any light source that is visible onstage. This usually means chandeliers, wall sconces, desk lights and so forth, but it would include the light inside a radio or refrigerator or a lighted Christmas tree. Practical is extended to mean any electrical device controlled by the lightboard, which would additionally include ceiling fans and hot electrical outlets into which are plugged various appliances. These are frequently (but not necessarily) things handled by or controlled by the actors.

There is a very hazy dividing line between these items and "lighted props or lighted costumes," which is usually based on whether the device plugs in or is battery powered. Flashlights would be the most common example of these, and they would typically be considered to be a battery-powered prop, as would a hand-held battery-powered candle, even though it might have been wired-up and be recharged on a regular basis by the electrics crew and might be the only light on, onstage. The same would be true of a costume that had a lighted headpiece. While the electrics crew might have done the electrical work and might be the one maintaining the charge of the batteries, the item itself would be considered in most instances to be a costume rather than a practical light.

Practical lights are often reinforced. See REINFORCING LIGHT for more detail.

It is traditional for the actors to not actually manipulate the on/off switches on practical lights, but this is a question that is open for debate. While it is best that they not turn on or off practical lights that are reinforced by the lightboard because it will be impossible to synchronize the two actions, there is no valid reason why they shouldn't turn on or off unreinforced lights. It is often argued that they might forget, but if they are trustworthy enough to remember their lines, and their blocking, it seems inconsistent to suggest that they can't be trusted to make a light switch work. When actors turn on and off their own lights, it always looks perfectly synchronized because it is, and they (the actors) usually feel more confident about the process. The same cannot be said of the stage manager and the lightboard operator, who may try very hard but do not always succeed. The standard method of working a light switch involves the actor holding his hand over the switch until he sees the lights go on (or off) unless it doesn't happen, in which case he has to improvise.

PREFOCUS BASE— A lamp base invented in the early 1930s, which allowed the new bi-plane lamps to be exactly aligned with their reflectors.

PRE-FOCUSING THE INSTRUMENTS— This refers to pointing the instruments in the correct general direction at the time they are hung. This insures, or goes a long way toward insuring, that the instrument will not hit another instrument, and it makes it easier to recognize which instrument is which during a troubleshooting session. It also helps establish the correct center of gravity on a suspended pipe. This should not be confused with *dead focusing* that actually does a final focus by aiming the instruments at the floor.

PREHEAT— This refers to warming the filaments of the lamps to improve response time.

PRELIMINARY PLOT— See LIGHT PLOT, PRELIMINARY.

PRESENTING THE DESIGN— The assumption is that the lighting designer sees each cue as a snapshot in his head. The question is how to make this clear to someone else, like the director. It has been suggested that the lighting designer might draw sketches or storyboards. Where this has been done, it has usually been done by a set designer who was also rendering his set, but if the lighting designer happened to be a gifted graphic artist, he might indeed do this. He might do a computer simulation. The most common method, however, is for the lighting designer to describe the cues to the director in broad terms explaining how this cue is different from the last one.

In the context of a lighting class where everyone present is knowledgeable, it would be more common to use a shorthand code to describe the system of arealighting used and to locate the positions of the various specials. "Modified Stanley aligned to the stage with three rows of four areas. The two rows DS of the proscenium using positions 1, 3, 5 and 7 and the one row upstage using positions 2 and 8. The UC special is an out-of-focus foliage gobo from position 5." Modified Stanley refers to three instruments-per-area US of the proscenium (where possible) and four instruments-per-area DS of the proscenium. In this case, a backlight US of the proscenium is not possible so those four areas are lit by the front-left and front-right positions on the golden ring (positions 2 and 8, starting at the front with nr 1 and going clockwise to end at nr 8, front-left). The two rows of arealights on the thrust are lit from front and back and left and right rather than front-left, front-right and back-left, back-right. This is what *aligned* with the stage refers to. The foliage gobo is a backlight coming from center back on the golden ring. In a classroom situation (as well as in life) it is essential that lighting designers see and recognize the system being used and be able to explain it quickly.

PRESET— This is a remote control lightboard term that refers to a complete set of sliders that represent every dimmer. Most remote control lightboards have at least two sets of these presets so that the one that is not active can be reset. Some preset boards have a vertical wall full of presets. Presets don't exist on a computer memory lightboard.

PRESET BOARD— A remote control lightboard that has presets and is not a computer memory lightboard. See LIGHTING CONTROL, Preset Lightboards for a more detailed discussion.

PRESET SHEET— Another name for a RESET SHEET.

PRE-SHOW CHECK— At about an hour prior to curtain time, the board operator is expected to check all the channels to make sure that they are all working and to change any gels or lamps that may have burned out before the house is opened at half hour. With a manual lightboard, this required an assistant to raise the dimmers one at a time while the electrician stood on stage and looked up. On a computer memory lightboard this is typically done as a series of cues that run in sequence with wait times between each one. While it might be each channel that is brought up individually, it is much more likely to be a group of related channels or a whole position that is brought up at once, as this is faster. The board operator consults his Pre-Show Checklist (usually the Hookup Sheet) as each cue is turned on.

PRESSURE CONNECTION— Before there were strain reliefs, there was a method (that has now fallen into disuse) that connected the wires to the screws inside a connector in such a way that they would not pull loose. See CONNECTION, MAKING ONE.

PREVIEW PERFORMANCES— For a reduced ticket price, audiences are allowed to see the final dress rehearsals of a play. While the theatre reserves the right to stop and correct anything that goes wrong, this seldom happens, and previews become simply the first performances where the actors adjust to the responses they are going to get.

PREVIEWING LIGHT CUES— Another name for viewing cues in *blind mode*. See LIGHTING CONTROL, Computer Memory Lightboards.

PRIMARY COLORS— See COLORS, PRIMARY.

PRIMARY CURRENT or WINDING— This is a winding or coil that is typically hooked in series with the load on a transformer or reactance dimmer.

PRINT or PRINTOUT— This is a computer lightboard term that refers to a hardcopy that has been printed on a computer printer from the data either on the internal memories of the machine or on the storage media. Current practice tends toward producing a floppy disk that can be printed from a home computer, which replaces the older practice of hooking up a printer to the lightboard. Although a variety of data can be printed, the channel readings in every cue are the most crucial thing that needs printing because two cues cannot be successfully compared onscreen without it.

PROBLEMS (lighting)—These are all discussed in detail as separate topics in this book but they are collected here as a convenience in finding them all:

Bounce Light Problem: Where light is permitted to bounce, it cannot successfully be controlled and bounces out into the house or onto other things that should remain in darkness.

Distance Problem: At throw distances of 20' and below, the movement of the actors to and fro in the light makes them appear brighter or dimmer as their distance to and from the light varies. This is most noticeable in sources like the footlights and can be calculated using the *inverse square law*.

Glare Problem: When the contrasts exceed a 20:1 ratio, the pupil in the eye has to readjust, and the darker areas become black holes.

Raccoon Eye Problem: Where the lighting comes from too steep an angle from above, the actors' eyes can look like black holes. This can only be alleviated by footlights or something just like them.

Veeing Problem: When striplights are placed too close to the surface they are meant to light, the colors do not have a chance to blend and the cones of light can be seen as visible "vees" on the surface.

White Color Problem: Where the actors' faces are seen against a lighter background (either a white shirt, or a white wall or a white floor) the face appears dim in contrast, but all attempts to increase the level of light simply continue to create the problem at a brighter scene level.

PRODUCTION CONCEPT—See CONCEPT, PRODUCTION.

PRODUCTION DESIGN TEAM—This consists of the director, the stage manager and his designers and various invited others (often the department heads and numerous assistants). Sometimes the business manager or whoever controls the budgets wants to be there. It can often be quite a large group. They typically meet regularly to share production ideas and discuss areas of mutual concern.

Historically, there were only two designers, sets and costumes, up until somewhere between 1930 and 1960. When it became apparent that lighting was something that needed to be planned and considered ahead of time. There was initial disagreement about who would control the lighting, but amongst the contenders (set and costume designers and director) the set designer prevailed for a while until it became apparent that the set designer mostly lit his own set and did not pay attention to the costumes or the actors' faces as much as he should have. The director and theatre managements eventually exercised their prerogatives and made the lighting a technical position that was responsible to the director alone. This was extremely fortunate because to this day the props master is also responsible to the set designer and the costume designer. Every found prop has to be further approved by the director and often by the individual actors. More than half of a prop person's time is typically taken up returning props that have been rejected by one or more of his masters before ever appearing onstage.

The lighting designer avoided this fate and got promoted to the status of a "co" and almost-equal designer. The other contributing factor was that the technical knowledge required (especially relative to how the lightboards worked) skyrocketed leaving many would-be lighting designers confused and unequipped to deal with the problems. It used to be said that stage lighting was so easy to do that anyone could learn how to do it in an afternoon. When that ceased to be true, the lighting technician became the lighting designer. See LIGHTING DESIGNER, BIRTH OF for a more detailed discussion.

PRODUCTION MEETING— A meeting of the production design team, usually at a specific time each week, beginning a week or two before the first rehearsal and usually ending once the show has moved onstage. The frequency of the meetings and the participants will vary from theatre to theatre, as will the actual length of the meetings and the subjects they discuss, although they are supposed to concentrate on areas of mutual inter-departmental concern.

They are usually based on one of two models (or some variant of these two): the *knights of the roundtable* model or a *military briefing* model.

The knights-of-the-roundtable model is the one most often described in books and the one least often seen in real life. The team would theoretically discuss all aspects of the production together. The director would present his concept of what the play was about. Everyone would have an opportunity to comment and discuss. In fact they would be encouraged to do so on the assumption that the pooled knowledge of the team would be greater than any one person's individual knowledge. Designers would present for discussion each aspect of their design, and everyone would comment and discuss. At one point there might be a discussion of whether the stage floor should be particleboard or oriented strand board. At another point they might discuss whether a particular costume should have hooks or snaps. Eventually it would turn to a discussion of whether Roscolux 60 (no color blue) was the right arealight color.

This kind of meeting requires an exorbitant amount of time as each person who wants to express their opinion gets their chance to do so, usually with very little control placed upon how long anyone can talk. Although each designer could theoretically make the final decision on an issue in his or her area of concern, as a purely practical matter there will be tremendous social pressure to follow the will of the majority, and so the decisions become things that are voted on.

It should be remembered that everyone present has been hired to do one small part of the project, presumably because of their unique abilities. Most designers derive satisfaction from seeing their individual ideas presented onstage, and few want to simply execute someone else's ideas. While it can be taken as a given that if provided the opportunity, any two people could offer two different opinions about how something ought to be done, but there is no reason to believe that these opinions might be better than the expert opinion of the designer concerned. The reason this kind of meeting is not more common is because the director is usually not interested in how someone else (perhaps you) would direct his play if given the chance. The set designer is not interested in how someone else would have designed the set better. Most lighting designers are not all that interested in how someone else would have done the lighting job either. While many designers have an open-door policy in regard to listening to differing opinions about how the job ought to be done, they usually like to hear these ideas or suggestions in private where there is no social pressure to accept them, and this also saves considerable time as it reduces the list of what needs to be discussed in the production meetings themselves.

In the military briefing model, the sharing of production ideas is done from the top down with the lower ranks asking clarifying questions and giving status reports. The show's director may be thought of as the colonel. He in turn answers to other brass hats like the artistic director of the theatre and the board of directors, but in terms of this one particular show, he is the highest ranking person that any of the designers will ever get to see on a working basis. He is certainly the lighting designer's immediate boss.

The four designers are all lieutenants of sorts, but the lighting designer and sound designer are often sub-lieutenants or lieutenants, jg, which is to say that while all designers may be equal, some are not quite as equal as others.

Every department has a sergeant who is in charge of that particular department. In the case of the lighting, this person is most typically called the *master electrician*, and he or she is responsible for the various members of electrics crews who are the enlisted personnel.

The technical director would be the equivalent of a sergeant major and is responsible for all things technical and specifically for supervising the costume shop manager and the master electrician and other department heads.

In this kind of a production meeting, the director explains what he thinks the play is about, and everyone for the most part says, "Yes, sir. How may I be of assistance, sir?" The set designer briefs everyone on what the set will be like. The actual set itself was worked out in private with the director at a meeting that no one else was invited to attend. This is not to suggest that it was in any way a secret meeting. It was simply a meeting that was so specifically related to the set that it was thought that no one else would be interested in attending. This is usually correct. If the costume designer thinks that a particleboard floor will be too slippery, he has in no way lost his opportunity to inquire about the floor and effect a change.

While the costume designer briefs everyone on the costume design and usually passes around sketches, the sound and lighting designers usually escape ever having to present their plans to the rest of the team but for slightly differing reasons.

The sound designer typically has nothing in common with his fellow designers except the schedule as it relates to when he will have a quiet stage and house in which to playback sound levels. While he could present his ideas and play a CD's worth of music and effects, no one except the director is really affected by the sound, and the rest of the designers are usually happy to let it be a technical rehearsal surprise.

Whatever the lighting designer does affects how the costumes, sets and actors will look and there is intense early interest in this. The lighting designer, however, usually knows very little about the final lighting design until he has seen a runthru. While he may have a preliminary arealighting plan, he is unlikely to have specials or colors or even be very sure that the original plan will survive the runthru. As a result, the lighting plan is typically finalized right around the time when the load-in starts, production meetings end, and everyone becomes furiously busy. While theoretically a special meeting could be called to let the lighting designer brief everyone on the lighting plan as decided upon by the director and lighting designer, they are within hours of seeing the plan executed onstage, so it usually makes more sense to wait.

Most production meetings are based on the military briefing model although this may not be explicitly stated and although the pecking order according to rank may not be immediately obvious. Assistants of all kinds, who are privileged to be allowed to listen in, are often told in private to keep their opinions and comments to themselves and to save them for later. The set designer who tells the group that the floor material is still under consideration does not want to hear his assistant remind him that the shop order was placed yesterday, and so it is not really under consideration at all anymore.

There is an unwritten and, for the most part unspoken, pact or agreement between designers that they will respect each other and allow their fellow designers to do their part of the project unhindered and that this is the way they in turn wish to be treated. As a result, most designers do not comment about things outside their areas of concern unless it directly affects them.

Some set designers can remember back to the days when the lighting was considered part of the set design. Even if they can't actually remember those days, they sometimes think they should have some special oversight of the lighting. This is in clear violation of the unspoken designer's pact discussed above, and most lighting designers will not willingly submit to this anymore.

PRODUCTION MEETING AGENDAS—
The alleged purpose of production meetings is to discuss items of mutual concern to all departments or at least two or more departments. While there is a lot of talk about coordinating all design elements together, these areas of mutual concern are rarely enumerated and perhaps that is because there are really so few of them.

Clearly the schedule, especially as it relates to time in the theatre space itself, is the most impressive subject for discussion (although it rarely affects the costume designer).

As to issues one might have in common with the costume designer, three come to mind: big hats or hair styles that will shade the faces, costume colors around the face that are lighter than the actor's face that will make the face look dim, and an assurance that the lighting colors won't distort the costume colors. Sometimes there will be a discussion of the lighting colors helping to bring out the colors in the costumes, and while this sounds good at a meeting or in a book, in practice it is not possible to light the costumes one way and the actors trapped inside them a different way. Lighting colors are chosen primarily for their effect on the actors' faces. Any other color used would usually need to be consistent with the time, place and situation of the scene, which leaves very little leeway for some other set of colors.

In regard to the set designer, the list includes light colored backgrounds that will either appear to be the same color as a face (and thereby make the face disappear) or colors that are lighter than a face that will make the face appear dim. Regardless of whether a face can be seen against the background of the floor (as from the balcony), light colored floors are also going to bounce light, which is usually a bad thing as it tends to bounce into the house, but the lighting designer will always have a preference about floor color as it relates to bounce light. The lighting designer is also concerned with anything that hangs in the light paths and is going to cause shadows. This includes things like false beams and chandeliers and suggestions of rooflines and anything else of that kind.

While all of these are valid areas of concern, most lighting designers will consider it more prudent to broach them in a private meeting with the director first. This is all part of something called diplomacy, which is discussed separately. Children who want permission to go to some event that is past their normal curfew time know which parent to plead their case to first. In the structure of the design team, most lighting designers know how to do this too, and they will typically not discuss anything controversial or anything that they really care about in an open and uncontrolled meeting unless they have had a chance to discuss it with the director first.

PRODUCTION MEETING, THE FIRST—
The first production meeting is usually the time the lighting designer gets to see the ground plan or model for the first time along with the sketches of the costumes and gets a copy of the schedule. If this is his first time in this theatre, it may also be the first time he has seen the playing space, and it is usually the time when he gets an inventory of the available equipment.

The way a production meeting usually works is that they go around the room (in pecking order) and everyone gets to say something. It starts with the director who either explains why he picked this play or presents some general vision for the play or tells everyone how it is going to be different from what they may have read in the script (set in the '40s, set in a bingo parlor, set in North Africa, whatever).

The stage manager may be next, and one can tell a lot about the stage manager (and by inference, the theatre) by how the stage manager distributes information. The lighting designer should receive a packet or folder of information. He probably cares most about the schedule and a blank Light Plot and the Inventory of the equipment, or if the theatre does not own its own equipment, the budget figure for rental equipment. However, there may also be a copy of the contract, the comp policy, a draft bio for the program (or request to provide one), possibly their policy about alcohol/tobacco/rudeness to one's co-workers, contact sheet, cast list and other similar documents.

The set designer will then usually explain what the set will look like. The lighting designer is free to ask whatever questions might be necessary to make sure he understands what and where the platform levels are, where any practical lights may be or anything else that is going to affect the lighting like hanging scenery that might get in the light path. He will make sure he knows in a general way what color the set and floor is going to be.

The costume designer usually gets to go next and will explain what the costumes will be like.

It will probably be the lighting designer's turn at this point. He usually does not need to explain to everyone why there is no lighting design yet. Since he has just received a copy of the ground plan of the set, no one expects him to talk about his design ideas because everyone knows he couldn't possibly have any yet. While the lighting designer theoretically could remain silent, he'll usually want to say something that will indicate that (1) he's read the script and (2) that suggests that he will be a team player. Most lighting designers concentrate on the schedule and ask when this or that activity (something that has not been listed like the hang or focus times or the first runthru) will take place. If there is reason to believe that the ground plan of the set might be available on disk, the lighting designer might inquire about this, as it would save him hours of recopying work. Most CAD programs can save drawings in DXF (drawing exchange format) as well as their own native format, which as the name suggests allows them to be shared by other CAD programs. If it's the kind of show that does not have scenes but flows in stream-of-consciousness style, the lighting designer may ask for a *scene breakdown* that shows the French-scenes and

numbers them for convenience and indicates who is involved in each one. It is also typical for the lighting designer to ask for a lighting meeting with the director within the next day or so, and if he is new to this theatre, he will want some time alone to examine the space. Asking for the meeting with the director serves two purposes. First, by requesting a meeting real soon, it deflects whatever is on the director's mind or anyone else's for that matter vis-à-vis what the lighting designer hasn't said about his lighting design for this show, and second it establishes the precedent that the lighting designer intends to deal exclusively with the director in all design matters and not here in an open meeting. See DIRECTOR, FIRST MEETING and MEASURING THE SPACE for a more detailed discussion.

There are a lot of issues that could be raised at this first meeting, but there is usually a lot the lighting designer doesn't know yet. To raise these issues in a public forum like this is to risk having them not go the way the lighting designer would like them to go, so these issues will typically be saved for the meeting with the director.

PRODUCTION TABLE— See TABLE.

PROFESSIONAL THEATRE— Theoretically, the professional theatre pays its workers and the amateur or non-professional theatre does not, but the demarcation line is somewhat blurred. Everyone would probably agree that a company that hires Equity actors and employs IATSE stagehands is a professional theatre. But what about a summer stock company that hires Equity actors but uses non-union technicians? As a purely practical matter, it is very hard to find someone who will work for nothing at all because at the very least they will have transportation/parking expenses and possibly babysitter expenses and so forth, so it is more typical for everyone to sign a contract and for there to be stipends in the under $100 category to cover expenses. As a purely legal matter, unless money has changed hands it is very hard to argue that a legally binding contract exists, which means that the free labor may at any time simply feel free to not show up anymore.

PROFILE—(1) This refers to a dimmer profile. See DIMMER CURVE. (2) In the context of a lighting instrument, it would refer to a profile spot, which would be a foreign-made ellipsoidal.

PROGRAMMING— In the context of a computer lightboard, the process of entering the show specific information onto the internal memories of the machine is often referred to as programming the machine, but has nothing to do with computer programming in its more general sense, which involves writing computer code.

PROJECTION BOOTH— See BOOTH.

PROJECTIONS— While this was once thought to be something that a novice could learn to do in an afternoon, it is now a very complex process involving expensive equipment and requiring specialized knowledge.

The actors have to be kept away from the projection surface so that the light that lights them does not also light the screen or create shadows on it. The projectors even the really expensive ones can't compete with full stage lighting, so the scene level has to be brought way down to make the projections effective.

The projectors need to be located normal to the surface of the screen and the audience viewing the image also needs to be normal to the screen as well. Projections from the rear will appear dimmer and will need to insure in some way that the audience cannot see the light source through the screen.

Often touted as an inexpensive way to produce scenery, in most cases, their use turns out to be an extremely expensive way to produce scenery. See FORMULAS for the three formulas related to projections.

PROJECTORS, KINDS OF— There are three general kinds of projectors that have at one time or another been used:

Linnebach Projectors: These are lensless, direct lighting shadow boxes. They are

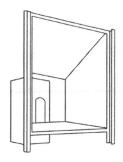

Linnebach projector

named after their inventor Adolphe Linnebach, who was the technical director at the Munich Opera in the early 1900s. The first commercially manufactured model was introduced in this country by Kliegl Bros. in 1922. They typically have a black metal housing with a lamp at the extreme back and an 18 · 20" or thereabouts painted glass slide mounted about 16" in front of the lamp. They are painted black inside and the effect produced is soft-edged and vague. They can easily be homemade and the slide can be any size. The bigger the slide, the larger the coverage area. Also the closer the lamp to the slide, the larger the coverage area, but also the less distinct the slide image will be. Homemade models can be tailored exactly to the needs of the theatre in regard to where the projector has to be placed and how big its image needs to be. As with all projections, in order to minimize the image distortions and brightness differences, the projector needs to be as nearly normal to its projection surface as possible. The slides are traditionally painted rather than being photographic.

Carousel Projector™: This is a trademark for a Kodak slide projector with a circular slide tray, but this discussion is meant include other brands and other styles of slide trays as well. These are made for presentation purposes in a boardroom situation and have found their way into theatre use because they were readily available and not prohibitively expensive. For stage use, the fan is usually separated from the light so that the light can be dimmed on a dimmer, while the slide changing mechanism and the fan are provided with full power. It is customary to also add a relay that cuts off power to the lamp when the fan is not running. This is to try to make it harder for someone to operate the light without the fan and thus burn up a projector costing several hundreds of dollars. Often by installing a better fan, a brighter light can be used. The 4–6" focal length zoom lens that usually comes with the projector is usually not wide angle enough for stage use, so some kind of f-1 lens needs to be used, and these can often cost as much as the rest of the projector. Even after doing all these things, the fan and slide change noise will usually be objectionable so the projector will be encased in a sound deadening box that will usually reduce but not eliminate the sound. The image even with a significantly brighter lamp will probably still not seem bright enough, and, of course, the projector needs to be placed normal to its projection surface, which is almost never possible. The edges of the image will always be dimmer and out of focus because their throw distance is longer.

A standard ellipsoidal becomes in effect a slide projector when a gobo pattern is inserted, even if its slide is mostly monochromatic. Standard overhead projectors that one finds in the classroom including the kind that projects the contents of a computer screen have been experimented with and work up to a point, but they all need operators to change the slides, which may not be all that much of a problem as it is the way most dedicated scenic projectors work as will be discussed next.

Scenic Projectors: Dedicated scenic projectors have been made since the early 1900s when the first stereopticons and sciopticons were introduced. The Great American Market here in America and Pani of Austria both make several halogen models and several HMI models. The slides can be photographic and they are typically hand inserted in a carrier that slides back-and-forth in the tradition of lantern slides. Prices of a basic halogen unit (without lamp) start in the

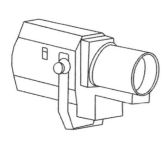

Scenic projector

$4000 range, and a nicely equipped pair would cost somewhere in the $12–20,000 range. An HMI 575 watt unit will start at about $8000 and a brighter 2.5 kw HMI unit will start at about $24,000. While this is expensive compared to other lighting instruments, it could easily pay for itself within a year or so if it were to replace other scenery for many shows in a large venue like an opera house where it takes a lot of scenery to cover a big stage and a lot of stagehand hours to put it there. Usually the more difficult problem is finding a suitable projection location for the two projectors and the operator, a booth built into the balcony rail position is ideal but it usually has to be planned for in the original design of the building.

PROMPT BOOK—The stage manager's copy of the script. See BOOK.

PROPERTIES OF LIGHT—See VARIABLES OF LIGHT.

PROPORTIONAL DIMMING or MASTERING—This used to be an important feature of early dimmer boards. Mechanical mastering brought all dimmers up or down to the level of the master handle whereas proportional mastering could maintain the percentage of difference between individual dimmers. Now modern lightboards always dim proportionally by default.

PROSCENIUM LIGHTING—See LIGHTING, KINDS OF.

PROSCENIUM STRIPS—This refers to the vintage practice of mounting striplights vertically just behind the proscenium in essentially the tormentor position.

PUNCH—This refers to the relative brightness of a light or group of lights and is a combination of wattage, color and contrast with the existing lights.

PURITY—One of the three perceivable properties of color. It refers to the amount of pure color in the mix. It is sometimes referred to as *saturation* or *chroma*. See COLOR for a more detailed discussion.

PURPOSE— See LIGHTING, FUNCTION OF.

PYROTECHNICS— Anything that involves direct combustion to produce a light or sound. Mostly a metal box of some kind is used to contain the explosion and it is typically set off by an electric spark. To do this legally, permission usually has to be obtained from the local fire department and sometimes a special license is required. This used to be something that was simple and uncomplicated to do. Now there is a good deal more to it. How much smoke is wanted? What color should the smoke be? How big should the bang be? Effects now have names like *gerbs* and *marroons*. There are several kinds of flash pots or explosion chambers to choose from. Customers can now buy pre-packaged explosive blends that only need to be detonated following the included instructions. When it is remembered that pyrotechnics is a form of bomb making, the wisdom of using a pre-packaged blend becomes more obvious.

QUADRUPLEX— A receptacle with four outlets, usually PBG or TLG.

QUALITIES OF LIGHT— See VARIABLES OF LIGHT.

QUARTZ-HALOGEN or QUARTZ-IODINE (1959)— Now called *tungsten-halogen (TH)*, they are lamps that have tungsten filaments and the glass envelope is filled with a halogen-type gas to prevent the blackening of the lamp. They are now considered the standard of the industry.

QUICKSTEP— This is a computer lightboard term that refers to being able to step through all the cues in the show at a zero count, thus ignoring all the recorded time information. This is typically used to determine what has changed between two sequential cues.

RACCOON EYE PROBLEM— A condition where the actor appears to have black, unlit holes where his eyes should be. It is caused by the light coming from above (golden ring positions) and being unable to reach into the eye-sockets. Inasmuch as there is often no other place to put the lighting instruments, it is for the most part unavoidable. Its effect can be somewhat diminished by gentler angles and by adding light from eyelevel or below, but many (if not most) theatres have neither hanging positions for this (i.e. balcony rail) nor footlights, anymore.

In life, the eye-sockets are lit, even in bright overhead sunlight, by the ever-present bounce light. In the theatre, bounce light is, where possible, eliminated because of its proclivity to bounce out into the house or onto things that should remain in darkness, and its effect is simulated by direct light from other golden ring positions. See BOUNCE LIGHT for a more detailed discussion.

RACEWAY— Another name for a WIREWAY.

RACK (dimmer)— A metal cabinet that encloses the dimmers and their circuit breakers. It typically contains some multiple of 12 dimmers (96 is usually a full rack) and has a door that can be shut and often locked. It is typically put in a basement electric room or wherever power from the street enters the building.

RAIL— See BALCONY RAIL.

RAIN LIGHT— A narrow beam, sealed beam unit often working on 6 volts used primarily for throwing light onto a mirror ball.

RAINBOW COLORS— These are the colors that can be seen when the sun's rays pass through drops of water. Sir Isaac Newton, who is credited as the first person to separate white light into its component colors, said there were seven colors: red, orange, yellow, green, blue, indigo and violet. Indigo is usually dropped from the list these days, making six.

RAT HOLE— A colloquial name for a drilled hole in the scenery or floor through which electric cords (and sometimes their connectors) are passed.

REACTANCE DIMMERS— A vintage dimming technology dating back to 1890 when it was first demonstrated. It required both AC and DC current. See LIGHTING CONTROL, Manual Lightboards for a more detailed discussion.

READ—(1) Also sometimes called *load*, this is a computer lightboard term referring to the process of reading a show from the storage media onto the internal memories of the machine. This is usually not necessary unless a show disk has been modified off-line on a home computer or if the theatre is doing several shows in repertory. (2) Colloquial for "be visible." Often fine detail like molding on the walls does not appear three-dimensional from the back of the house. In this sense it is said to "not read" from the back of the house.

READINGS— This refers to the dimmer calibration levels from 0 to 100, which are supposed to approximate percentages of brightness.

READJUST— This is a command that dates back to preset lightboards and refers to leaving a preset intact except for specific changes that have been noted. It is the opposite of a *reset* that refers to clearing a preset and resetting all sliders from scratch. Resets are usually gathered together on a reset sheet. Readjustments are typically noted on the Cue Sheet itself under a heading of things to do to prepare for the next cue (advance).

READY— Also called a *stand-by*, this is the second announcement of an upcoming cue. It follows the *warning* and precedes the *go*. See CUES, CALLING OF for a more detailed discussion.

RECEPTACLE— This is the female outlet of an electrical circuit. When this term is used, it suggests that the receptacle is recessed in the wall or floor or flush mounted on a plugging channel as it would be more common to call a female connector on a short piece of cable a *pigtail*.

RECORD— In the context of a computer lightboard it refers to putting the cue into the internal memories of the machine. At the end of a day's rehearsal the whole show will usually be *written* to disk as a backup.

RECTIFIER— An electrical device that changes AC current to DC current.

REFLECTANCE— The ability of a surface to reflect light. It is usually measured as a percent or decimal coefficient, which when multiplied by footcandles of light hitting the surface will give footlamberts of reflected light leaving the surface. A pure white surface can reflect 70–90 percent of the light hitting it while a black velour might reflect only 1–5 percent. Surface texture is the other factor. Smooth shiny surfaces reflect more than rough, uneven ones.

REFLECTION, LAWS OF— There are several. The most famous of these deals with flat reflectors and says that the angle of incidence will be equal to the angle of reflection. Reflectors inside instruments are not, however, flat. They are typically spherical, ellipsoidal or parabolic. Here are the explanations of how they all work:

Ellipsoidal: When the lamp is placed at one focus, all the light that hits the reflector will be reflected to the other focus (the gate of the instrument).

Parabolic: When the lamp is placed at the focal point, all rays of light are projected outward in parallel lines. Beam projectors and some floodlights have this kind of reflector.

Spherical: When the lamp is placed at the focal point (center of the sphere) all rays of light will be reflected directly back through the lamp at the same angle. Fresnels and PC's have this kind of reflector.

REFLECTION and ABSORPTION— When light hits an object, some of the light will be absorbed by the object and turned into heat, some will be reflected and some may be transmitted through the object. Opaque objects do not transmit light but glass, water, thin paper, fabrics and many plastics do. Shiny objects (like a watch face) reflect light in a mirror-like way. This is called *specular* reflection, and the angle at which the light

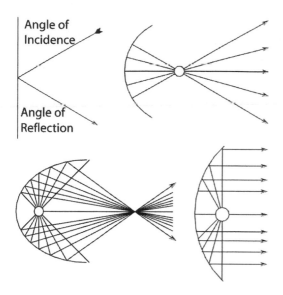

Top, left: Flat reflector; *top, right:* Spherical reflector; *bottom, left:* Ellipsoidal reflector; *bottom, right:* Parabolic reflector.

hits a flat surface will be the same as the angle of the reflected light leaving the surface. This is usually phrased as *the angle reflection is equal to the angle of incidence,* and it is a law of physics. Specular reflection in the theatre is usually caused by shiny serving trays or some other shiny prop and is particularly annoying because it flashes light from the stage instruments in a distracting way. Specular reflection can be eliminated by dulling down the surface with a soap solution or a commercially made dulling spray. When light hits a non-shiny surface, the light is reflected in all directions and this is called *diffuse reflection.* In real life, this reflected light allows us to see objects that are not in direct sunlight and allows us to see on overcast days. In the theatre, diffuse reflection is responsible for bounce light, which tends to light the audience and parts of the playing area that would be better left in darkness. Although it cannot be completely controlled, its effects can be lessened by reducing the overall brightness of the scene and by using dark colors that reflect less light, which is why most theatre draperies are dark colored velour. The amount of light reflected is always less than the amount that originally

hit the object. This is called the *coefficient of reflection.* The moon for example is a very poor reflector, reflecting only about 7 percent of the light hitting it.

REFLECTOR DROPS— Usually a white cloth drop that hangs upstage of a set of lights that light it directly, thus indirectly backlighting the drop or cyc downstage of the lights. Sometimes the back wall of the theatre is painted white and used in place of a reflector drop. Sometimes the back of an unused drop is used. See LIGHTING SPECIAL PROBLEMS, Cycs or Drop Backlighting for a more detailed discussion.

REFLECTOR LAMPS (PAR and R-TYPE LAMPS)— Lamps that have a built-in reflector (usually parabolic) and a built-in lens. See INSTRUMENTS for a more detailed discussion.

REFRACTION— A scientific word that refers to the bending of light rays as they pass from one medium into another, as from air into glass in a lens.

REHEARSALS-WITH-LIGHT— These are typically the first rehearsals on the stage with the set and props. There will also be stage light (rather than worklight) provided, and the lighting designer will typically set levels on the fly, but this is usually based on something already created at a level-setting session that is now being tried out and adjusted. Unless the lights go out, no one ever stops for lights or pays all that much attention to them at all. The stage manager could theoretically call the cues but usually has other more pressing things to do, so it is the lighting designer who decides when to take cues. For beginnings and ends of acts, the stage manager usually continues to say something like, "The houselights are going out and the stage lights are coming up; actors go." While the lights could mimic this, they are usually already set to the first cue of the act and the house is generally already out. If the objective is to have everyone ignore the lights, then it should not begin like a technical rehearsal with cues but should just start in its first cue, at least that is the theory. If at the end of the rehearsal the actors can be given their notes in the lobby or the greenroom, then some of the numerous board notes can then be worked out on a darkened stage.

In his book, Louis Hartmann describes how he and David Belasco would painstakingly set each cue in the absence of the actors until everything looked just right, and then the actors would be brought on. In the early years (circa 1910), they would have to add footlights and borders to provide just enough light to see the actors by, but in later years they began using arc lights (followspots) on the actors along with an elaborate system of mica slides that dimmed the arc light in gradations (like gray gel) to make it more subtle. In any event, what has not changed over the years is that when the roughed-in cues are seen for the first time on the actors, they usually have to be adjusted so that the actors can be more clearly seen. While it is possible to create spectacular cues for use during an intermission when no one is acting on the set, it is considerably harder to equal these cues when the actors are present.

REINFORCING LIGHT— This refers to the stage lighting that reinforces the effect of a practical light. The actual chandelier needs to appear to be lit, but the actual light hitting the stage comes from stage instruments whose job it is to simulate (reinforce) the effect of the practical light. In many cases the reinforcing lights are used alone, and the actual source is imagined rather than seen. This is particularly true in thrust and in-the-round situations where chandeliers cause glare problems and get in the light paths of the stage instruments.

RELAY— This is an electrically activated switch (sometimes called a *contactor*). There is an electrical coil, which when energized results in an electromagnet closing two normally-open (or normally connected to something else) contacts, which then closes the switch to whatever device the relay is intended to run. In the past, the houselights were typically on a relay because they drew so much current that the switch or switches that would operate them would have to have been huge. By using a relay, low voltage wire and switches could then be run to all the auxiliary switch locations, thus saving on wiring costs. This is still done is some places.

RELEASE— This is a computer lightboard term and frequently a button name that refers to releasing channels that were manually set on the keyboard (*captured*) and returning to the most recently recorded version of the cue.

REMOTE CONTROL— Any device that can be operated from a far away location, such as fog machines, mirror balls etc. It is most commonly used in the context of lightboards and refers to preset lightboards and computer memory lightboards where the control portion (*front end*) is remote from the dimmers themselves.

REP PLOT— As the name suggests, it is a light plot made to serve several shows (as in a repertory situation), where there is simply not the time to completely change all the lights. This usually means that the arealights are the same for all shows. In this respect, it is identical to a *basic lighting plot* that the theatre would provide for outside groups who were renting the space. Typically there would be specials used exclusively for each of the shows and there would be specials that would be shared and could easily be regelled and/or re-aimed for each show. It is time, or the lack of same, which effectively limits how much lighting work can be done between shows.

REPATCHING— Pulling out one plug and replacing it with one or more other plugs. Sometimes it works just that way or it can involve turning off a number of circuit breakers and turning on another set. It can also involve a switchbox arrangement where an A, B, C, and D setting can be switched on in any combination.

REPLUG TRACKSHEET— This is a record of the state of the replugging at any moment

Replug Tracksheet	ALCHEMIST		
CUES	B	5	16	24
9a—Desk Lt	a	b		
9b—CC spec				
15a—Street Lt	a		b	c
15b—Balc				
15c--Toplight				

Replug tracksheet

Reset sheet

in the performance, showing replug dimmers across the top and what is plugged in down the side based on what cue it happens after in the body of the table. When the rehearsal starts in the middle of an act, the replugs can then be reset to that point.

REPLUGGING— See REPATCHING above.

RESET— This is a command that dates back to preset lightboards and refers to clearing a preset and resetting all sliders from scratch. It is the opposite of *readjusting* that refers to leaving a preset intact except for the noted changes. Resets are usually gathered together on a Reset Sheet. Readjustments are typically noted on the Cue Sheet under a heading of things to do to prepare for the next cue (advance).

RESET SHEET— This is a document (usually a table with two rows) that shows the channel numbers and has a blank space for what their levels are set to in this cue. There will typically be 4 or 5 resets to a landscape-oriented page and each reset will be given an identifying number that relates to the cue number in which it is first used onstage.

RESISTANCE— This refers to resistance of a conductor to the flow of electrical current as measured in Ohms.

RESISTANCE DIMMER— A vintage dimming technology that transformed electricity into heat by putting resistance in the current path. See LIGHTING CONTROL/ Manual for a more detailed discussion.

RESPONSE TIME— The time it takes between doing something and seeing something happen. While this could refer to the time between when the stage manager calls a cue and when something can be seen to change onstage, it more commonly refers to the time between a button push and seeing something change onstage, which is caused mostly by the lamp filaments warming up.

RESTORE— See FADES, KINDS OF.

RETRIEVING LOST CUES— Let's say that it's the middle of a rehearsal of act one, numerous changes have already been made, and a cue gets erased or recorded over by accident. When this occurs, the safest and least time-consuming method would be for the lighting designer to read back the channel levels to the board operator. Here's where having the hardcopy printout pays off.

Where there is no hardcopy printout, the cue can theoretically be retrieved from a previous disk, but this has to be done ever so carefully or all changes made so far today could also be lost. One has to be especially concerned because a board operator, who has already made one rehearsal-stopping error, is now about to embark on an even more difficult and complicated procedure.

First, two copies of the show as it now exists (partially improved over yesterday but with a missing cue) needs to be recorded to disk and clearly labeled.

Second, whatever disk was used to load the show at the top of rehearsal today needs to be reloaded on the internal memories of the machine, and the missing cue needs to be made current onstage.

Third, the partially improved show now needs to be re-loaded onto the machine and the cue currently onstage (the lost cue) can now be recorded.

This only works for one lost cue at a time. If several cues have been lost, then the disk used at the top of today's rehearsal would be loaded onto the machine and the rehearsal would continue. This would leave a complicated mess of having half the show on one disk and the remainder on another that would have to be resolved outside of rehearsal usually by re-entering manually all the cues from one disk (the shortest) onto the other disk by having them read back from a hardcopy printout.

RETROFIT LAMPS— Any lamp that replaces an older style lamp that is no longer made. There are retrofit lamps for chimney top ellipsoidals and for GLC lamps so that they will fit into HPL sockets.

REVERSE or REVERSING— When used in a computer lightboard context, it refers to a chase sequence that has gone in 1, 2, 3 order that is now reversing and going in 3, 2, 1 order.

REVERSE VIDEO— A vintage technique used on monochrome monitors that put black letters against a yellow or green rectangle for emphasis, assuming the normal display was light colored letters against a black background as it often was. The use of different colors on a color monitor has made this practice obsolete.

RHEOSTAT— Another name for a RESISTANCE DIMMER that puts a continuously variable resistance in the current path.

RIDE THE LEVELS— This refers to the practice of dimming sources when the actor moves toward them and raising the levels as he walks away in order to make the perceived brightness appear to be the same. This is only necessary where the sources are placed very close to what they are lighting (as from the footlights or tormentor positions).

Sound operators, who are controlling live mics, do this all the time to make the perceived volume appear the same, and it is a significant part of their job.

Louis Hartmann talks about having his operators do this as a way of solving the Distance Problem. It has fallen into disuse in the current age of computer lightboards, where the attitude often is to let the machine do it in the default manner instead of finding a way to make the machine do what needs to be done. Riding the levels still works, and in some ways it works better now because the board operator usually has less to do and has a better view of what he's doing.

RIGID CONDUIT— A heavy-duty conduit that is threaded like water pipe and is sometimes hard to tell apart from water pipe.

RIM LIGHT— See BACKLIGHT.

RISERS— On a fresnel or step lens, the vertical part of the rings are called risers and are often painted black so they can act like spill rings.

ROCK CONCERT LIGHTING— See LIGHTING, KINDS OF/Performances with Live Musicians.

ROLLING LADDER— See HANGING POSITIONS, GETTING TO.

ROLLING LIGHT STAND (or less commonly a ROLLING PIPE STAND)— A short boom (vertical pipe) on wheels, usually with at least one crosspiece across the top, usually

Rolling light stand

10 feet or less in height. Occasionally the stand telescopes. Also called a *rover*.

RONDELS (sometimes ROUNDELS) — Glass color media, usually for striplights. They typically come in limited colors, i.e. red, amber, green and blue. They are a vintage product but they don't fade or melt and they last until they are dropped and broken, which requires a determined effort because they are a heavy ashtray-weight of glass and they do not break easily.

ROPE LIGHTS — Another name for tube lights. See TUBE LIGHTS for a more detailed discussion.

ROSCO LABORATORIES — American manufacturer of color media since 1910 and now a maker of special effects and dimming equipment.

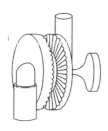

Rosette

ROSETTE — A serrated wheel that was bolted to another serrated wheel as part of a vintage system (swing joint) of locking an instrument in place in two directions, as to a stand or sidearm. These were often found on olivettes and old time striplights but are now obsolete.

ROTA-LOCKS™ — A brand name for a device that will lock two pipes together at a 90 degree angle as on a grid or as a crossarm on a boom. Not to be confused with Roto-lock™, which is a brand name for a coffin-lock device used to connect two theatrical platforms together.

ROUGH FOCUS — Often the actual scenery isn't available at the focusing session or the exact positions where the actors will stand are not yet known, so the instruments are said to be rough focused because they are

focused based on a guess, and it is generally understood that they may have to be refocused later.

ROVER — A rolling light stand, commonly used in the wings of a proscenium theatre and frequently moved around and regelled during the course of the performance, thus doing a job that it would otherwise have required several stationary stands. Fewer stands in the wings mean fewer that the performers could run into.

ROWS (of areas) — This refers to rows of lighting areas. Each row runs across the stage left and right, and the rows themselves run from downstage to upstage. Usually they are arealights but occasionally washes. They are also called *zones*.

RUN — As a verb, cues are run, cables are run, shutters are allowed to run. As a noun it refers to the run of the show in weeks or the running time of a runthru or performance

RUNNING A CABLE — Unless there is a compelling reason to do something different, cables are always started at the plug-in point and run toward the instrument location where the slack (if any) can be used to reposition the instrument if that were to become necessary. Also it is the female end of the cable that will have tie line attached to facilitate tying up the extra slack. Cables are typically made up into lengths that are increments of 5' and most experienced electricians can tell at a glance if they need a 10 footer or a 15 footer. At some point (either now or later) the cable has to be tied to the pipe, and this can become a tedious process. If there are to be lots of cables, it probably makes most sense to do it after all the instruments have been hung and tested. If there will be just a few, then they can often be wound spirally around the lighting pipe (about one spiral per 3-4' of length). This requires no tie line and is very fast and also very neat, often more tidy than a cable bundle tied up every foot. By varying the frequency of the spirals the excess cable can effectively be used up so that nothing at all will need to be tied up.

RUNNING CREW— Anyone who works during the performance of the show. In the context of the lighting, this would include the board operator and followspot operators (if any) and floor electricians (if any).

RUNNING LIGHTS— Small, well shielded backstage worklights, often dim and often blue, placed close to the surfaces they are supposed to light (usually table tops and a path along the floor). They can be C9 Christmas lights or 7.5-watt night lights or 11-watt sign lights or something that has been heavily gelled down. They are often put in a bedroom pinup light fixture that has a can on a yoke, mounted to a tiny round base that can be screwed to the wall or a horizontal surface. They are also called Equity lights because they were required by the actors/stage manager's union for backstage safety.

RUNNING TIME— The amount of time from curtain up to curtain down on each act as recorded by the stage manager each night.

RUNTHRU— This refers to a rehearsal where all the scenes are performed in sequence, and it is usually the intention to not stop unless things become hopelessly confused and there is no other choice. The lighting designer and often the other designers (costumes especially) may want to attend the first runthru, and it is not uncommon to plan such an event just for them, in which case it is commonly called the *designer's run* whether it is the first or not. See LIGHTING IDEAS for a more complete discussion of what the lighting designer does during such an event.

RUNWAY LIGHTING— See LIGHTING SPECIAL PROBLEMS/Aisles and Runways.

SAFETY CABLES— The purpose of a safety cable is to provide an alternate way to support a 20 lb instrument in case its 600 lb-test c-clamp were to fail in an earthquake, in which case the instrument could theoretically fall to the ground. This makes about as much sense as chaining your car to a tele-

phone pole in case its brakes should fail while you are at the grocery store, but we're going to ignore that. Politicians tend to vote for anything that has "safety" in its name, and rightly or wrongly safety cables are now the law of the land in most parts of this country. The labor unions tend to like them because they add several extra hours to either the hanging process or the striking process, thus providing more work for the members. The manufacturers like them because they provide yet another add-on sale.

They are typically added last and removed first, and while this does not violate any laws and is not a criminal offence, it should be obvious that the time when an instrument is most likely to fall (and hurt someone) is when it is either being installed onto, or being removed from, a light pipe, and there is actually a way to use them that makes this process safer. See HANGING AN INSTRUMENT for a more detailed discussion of this subject.

SAFETY CORDS— These tie tools to the body of the electrician who is going aloft to make it harder to drop them from above.

There are really three styles of these: key chain style, bracelet style and necklace style.

The **bracelet style** involves a wrist loop at the end of the wrench or tool, so that the tool hangs from the wrist when not in use. This is particularly handy when working on a catwalk or somewhere where it is not necessary to climb, as climbing simply bangs the tool against the ladder at every step. There are commercially made spiral coiled plastic wrist straps made for keys, but they usually have plastic dog clips and are not sturdy enough for lighting tools.

The **key chain style** is probably the most common. The end of the crescent wrench is tied to the belt line with a 36" piece of tie line or something similar, which allows the wrench to be used over the head or put in a back or side pocket. This leaves a longish loop that can snag on instruments or parts of the ladder. Another variant uses coiled telephone cord to which dog clips have been attached at each end, and this considerably reduces the snagging problem.

The **necklace style** goes around the neck. This may work best for a small pocketknife tucked under at least one layer of clothing. If whatever is worn around the neck is outside the clothing, it will snag from time-to-time. While it is one thing to be brought up short by the wrist or belt loop, it is quite another to be snagged by the neck by a garrotte-like cord.

SALTWATER DIMMERS— A vintage dimming technique where the amount of salt in the water controlled how well the solution would carry current. It was a variant of resistance dimming that is often mentioned in books but had a remarkably short life in the theatre as it released chlorine gas as a by-product. See LIGHTING CONTROL/Manual for a more detailed discussion.

SATURATION— One of the three perceivable properties of color. It refers to the amount of pure color in the mix. It is sometimes referred to as *purity* or *chroma*. See COLOR for a more detailed discussion.

SAVE—(1) In the context of a computer memory lightboard, saving refers to writing the contents of the internal memories of the machine to the disk or other storage media. (2) In colloquial usage, it means "to turn off" an un-needed instrument or channel, presumably to save the gel or to save the lamp from burning out.

SCAFFOLDING— A commercially made climbable structure that almost always rolls. See HANGING POSITIONS, GETTING TO for a more complete discussion of this subject.

SCALE DRAWINGS— Technically, any drawing that is drawn to scale. The Light Plot and Sectional, which are to scale, would more commonly be identified by name. So where this term is used, it usually refers to letter-sized sketches made for the designer's personal use. Often doing a small scale drawing and measuring with a scale ruler pro-

vides an answer to beam coverage or throw distance faster than figuring it out mathematically.

SCALE RULER— These are typically triangular and have six edges, one of which is devoted to full-scale inches. There are five edges for scales, and it is common to have one size start on the left and a size twice as large start at the right side. Thus ⅛ scale might start at the left and ¼ scale at the right (or visa versa). There are two kinds of scale rulers that look amazingly similar, but aren't. The Engineer's scale divides inches into tenths and hundredths of an inch and has scales like 10, 20, 30, and 40. The Architect's scale divides inches into sixteenths and thirty-seconds and is the scale universally used in the theatre.

CAD drawings can be drawn to any scale, but it is important to remember that the electricians who use the drawing can only decode the distances if they have that particular scale on their ruler. For manual drafting, lighting templates typically can only be found in ½" and ¼" sizes.

SCALLOPING— See VEEING PROBLEM.

SCENE BREAKDOWN— This is a document usually prepared by the stage manager, which breaks the play down into French scenes (scenes triggered by the entrance or exit of a character). Each French scene is then numbered for easy reference. The director and stage manager use it to plan rehearsals. The costumer uses it to calculate when someone could make a costume change or come for a fitting. The lighting designer uses it to determine where to place cues, as they are most likely to occur at the beginning or ends of French scenes rather than in the middle of them.

SCENE CHANGE LIGHTS— The lights provided for stagehands to change the set and re-position the props and for the actors to get into their places in preparation for the new scene. Where any lights at all are provided, they usually come from directly above and are typically blue in color. Coming from above allows the stagehands to see horizontal surfaces and spike marks on the floor but denies the audience a view of faces. Lights that are blue are harder for the eye to perceive as being light and have been established over time as being the color of scene changes. This is for *à vista* scene changes, as scene changes that take place behind a curtain would be lit by behind-the-curtain worklights.

SCENE LEVEL— This describes the general relative brightness of the scene. Once this has been established, the component areas can be raised or lowered to fine tune the overall stage picture.

SCENERY BUMPERS— Three to five metal hoops attached to light pipes to deflect flown scenery and prevent it from knocking the lights out of focus.

SCENES—(1) One scene is differentiated from the next by either a change of time or a change of place or both. Often set pieces and props have to be moved around or the actors need to change places in preparation for the next scene. If that is the case, the lights typically fade out or down to either scene change lights or a blackout and then are brought back up for the new scene. Even if no props or actors move, the lights still need to change in some way to indicate to the audience that it is a new scene. The most common method would be to dim out the lights and then bring them right back up. (2) In the context of a preset lightboard, this refers to the number of sets of presets there are, thus a two-scene preset has two sets of presets, and a five-scene preset has five and so forth.

SCHEDULE— This usually looks like a calendar that has cryptic notes written in below certain days. It is usually prepared by the stage manager and is simply given to the designers (and everyone else working on the project), but it includes rehearsal times and places, when the various designs are due, when the photo calls are, who has the stage when on what days and for what purpose. In the context of the lighting, it should include all production meetings, the hanging session, the focus session, the designer's runthru, the level-setting session, the rehearsals-with-light, the dry tech and all succeeding technical and dress rehearsals and potential additional crew calls. The lighting designer needs to study it carefully and ask any questions or present any concerns early in the rehearsal process. Once everyone has initially acquiesced to it (or failed to complain about it), it is very hard to then get it changed later.

SCHEMATIC DRAWING— One of two methods of drawing an electrical wiring diagram, the schematic drawing uses symbols to represent electrical devices and presents the wiring as rectangular circuit loops. The intent is to allow the reader to follow the path of the current to understand how the circuit works. See WIRING DIAGRAM for a more detailed discussion.

SCIOPTICON— This is a vintage effects machine that can easily become confused with a *lobster-scope* or a *stereopticon*. The sciopticon is attached to a spotlight and has a circular effects wheel that is rotated in front of the lens, and there is an additional set of condenser lenses on the effect head.

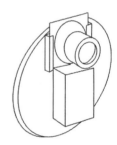

Sciopticon

SCOOP— A large floodlight, typically in the shape of a half sphere (or end of an ellipse). The inside is typically painted white (but could have an ellipsoidal or parabolic reflector). 250–1000 watt lamps are used and the scoop usually has a slot for a gel frame. This is a vintage instrument that is still in use, mostly for drop lighting. Sometimes the lamp can be pulled back inside an

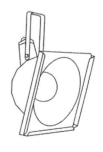

Scoop

attached can to lessen the beam spread. Otherwise, they are pointed in the correct general direction and the job is done. The gel frames are large, and it is usually only possible to get one *cut* out of a sheet of gel making them expensive to color or re-color. There are other more compact cyc lights that spread light as well, if not better, but require less gel. While the expense of large cuts of gel is a consideration, it is the availability that is more serious because re-coloring 50 scoops will involve 50 sheets of gel, and the local distributor may not stock gels in that kind of quantity. Like other floodlights, the considerable light they produce cannot be controlled very well.

SCOTCH TAPE— See TAPES, KINDS OF.

SCR— Abbreviation for SILICONE CONTROLLED RECTIFIER DIMMERS.

SCREW BASE— The normal base for household light bulbs (medium screw), although there are three other sizes, one of which is larger (mogul screw) and the other two are smaller (intermediate candelabra and miniature candelabra). See LAMPS for a more detailed discussion.

SCRIM LIGHTING— See LIGHTING SPECIAL PROBLEMS/Scrims and Gauzes.

SCRIPT— The text of what the characters say to each other along with explanatory notes, called *stage directions*, written by the playwright, the stage manager or the publisher to make the play more understandable for a first-time reader.

SCRIPT LIST or NOTES or ANALYSIS— These are the lighting designer's notes based on the first reading of the script as they relate

Script List	MOOSEHEAD
Sc 11 INT GRAND HOTEL LOBBY, night (1975)	
Practical desk light (stg dir p 4)	
2 chandeliers (stg dir p 4)	
Dark outside front door (text p 7)	
Sense of fading decadence	
Raining outside (text p 9)	
Possible internal cue to iso when Lorie ENR p 12	

Script list

to the stage lighting. While there is no set format for these, they typically are organized in chronological order by scene. See LIGHTING IDEAS for a more detailed discussion.

SCROLLER (color)— An accessory that attaches to the front of an instrument and changes the color of the light by means of a roll of colored plastic of varying colors taped or glued together like frames of photographic film that rolls from one cylinder to another like a scroll. Scrollers are motor driven and typically run off a DMX signal and can randomly access any frame on the roll. It is used in places where it is not possible to have a technician simply change the gel frame. The idea for this dates back to 1900 when Louis Hartmann used a manual scroller of sewn together silk in front of an open box arc to create the slightly under three minute transition to dawn cue in David Belasco's production of *Madame Butterfly*. See COLOR CHANGING for a more complete discussion of this subject.

SEALED BEAM LAMP— Any of a number of lamps where the reflector (usually parabolic), the lens system and the light source are combined into the lamp. They are typically used in striplights, parcans and certain floodlight type lights. R40 type lamps are typically the ones used in striplights and they are relatively delicate in terms of impact damage. PAR type lamps are made to be used outdoors and are extremely rugged and impact resistant.

SECONDARY COIL or WINDING— On a transformer there are two coils of wire. The primary is the input coil and the secondary is the output coil.

SECONDARY COLOR— The intermediate colors created by mixing two primary colors. Colors made by mixing three primaries are called *tertiary colors*.

SECTIONAL DRAWING— Short for CROSS-SECTIONAL.

SEGUÉ— A musical term, which when applied to a light cue, means an "immediate follow." It is more likely to be encountered in a performance situation that has live musicians like opera or ballet than in a dramatic production.

SEINING LINE— A marine product intended for use making and repairing seine nets. It is three-strand polypropylene and comes in a dizzying array of sizes from almost invisible trick line up to something about ¼" thick, and it is amazingly strong. It is either black (tarred) or dark green and is sold by the pound, so $3 can buy several miles of it. It makes excellent tie line or packaging cord. It does, however, need a stopper knot or whipping tape to prevent unraveling.

SELECTIVE ABSORPTION, THEORY OF— This dates back before the days of Sir Isaac Newton to the 1630s and the work of René Descartes, who believed that objects were colorless and their color was the result of an interaction with the light hitting them. Prior to this, the common belief had been that light was colorless and merely illuminated the objects and that color was a property of the object itself. According to the theory of Selective Absorption when a white object is lit by white light, it reflects most of the light hitting it, and as a result appears to be white. Were the same object to be painted blue, it would absorb all wavelengths of light except blue ones, and so the object would appear to be blue. Selective absorption is the underlying principle behind the scientific explanation of color perception.

This theory appears to be entirely correct when it comes to explaining how light passes through gels because a saturated dark blue gel usually has a transmission rate of only 1–4 percent. It is easy to see that the ungelled light was extremely bright, but as soon as the gel was put in place, it became very dim. It is also clear that the gel is absorbing the light energy and turning it into heat because the gel is often heating to its melting point.

When the theory is applied to surface colors, however, it does not seem to explain what the eye perceives. First, the eye perceives surface colors as distinct from light colors. According to the theory of selective absorption, a red car and a white car both lit with red light should appear amazingly similar because they are both reflecting almost all of the red light hitting them, and as a result should both look red. Instead the red car looks red and the white car looks like a white car lit with red light. Second, a dark blue object that is absorbing 90 percent of the light hitting it should appear very dim next to a white object that is absorbing only 10 percent of the light and reflecting the rest. While it is true that light colored objects reflect more light than dark colored objects, the difference is relatively slight compared to the percentage of light that is theoretically being absorbed. Take the case of yellow light. It has an extremely narrow wavelength band so there is very little of it in white light. If all wavelengths were absorbed except this narrow yellow band (and other colors that could combine to produce this color), then yellow should appear very dim, whereas quite to the contrary it usually appears quite bright.

SELECTIVE VISIBILITY— See VISIBILITY, SELECTIVE.

SELECTOR SWITCHES— A generic name that includes both rotary switches and the multi-position linear switches like a double-throw switch with a center-off position. See SWITCHES, KINDS OF for a more detailed discussion.

SELLMAN, HUNTON D.— Technical Director at the University of Iowa, who wrote the second American textbook on stage lighting in 1930. Actually two books were contained in one volume, which was called collectively **Stage Scenery and Lighting**. Part I was called **Stage Scenery** and was written by Samuel Selden. Part II was called **Stage Lighting** and was written by Hunton D. Sellman. Part II ran to 175 pages and covered electricity, optics, reflection and instruments and dimmers. The copyright was renewed in 1958 and 1964, and in 1972 the book was completely revised and reissued as a separate

volume called **Essentials of Stage Lighting.**
It is, of course, the earlier volume that is
most interesting from a historical viewpoint.
Although he mentions the books of both
Theodore Fuch and Louis Hartmann in his
bibliography, he most clearly presents the
lighting techniques of his time (prior to the
Stanley McCandless method) in a very clear
and straightforward manner. An example of
how to light an interior set is given in which
six spotlights are used on four areas that we
would call *accent* areas today. The rest of the
light was to come from borderlights with the
tiniest touch of footlights (but only if necessary to soften facial shadows).

SERIES CIRCUITS— When two or more
lights are daisy-chained together with only
one path to the power, this is said to be a
series circuit. Miniature Christmas tree
lights are made this way. When one burns
out, the rest go out too, as their path to the
power has been broken. Also each additional
light added makes the rest dimmer. In a
series circuit, $R_T = R_1 + R_2...$, $I_T = I_1 = I_2...$,
and $E_T = E_1 + E_2....$

The opposite of this is *parallel circuits* in
which two or more lights are hooked up independently to the source of power. They burn
at full brightness and if one burns out, the
others still continue to stay lit. This is the system used on C7 and C9 Christmas tree lights.

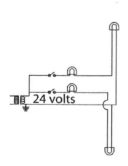

The component dia-
gram at left represents
a cuelight system that
allows the stage man-
ager to signal either to
stage left or stage right.
The stage left (and stage
right) circuits are each
hooked in parallel to
each other but the two
lamps and switch of
each circuit are wired
in series.

Cuelight system

SET LIGHTS or SPECIALS— See SPE-
CIALS, KINDS OF.

SET-IN— This is a load-in where it is an in-
house operation and trucks from faraway

places are not involved. Often the scene
building, costume building and prop building shops are in other parts of the same
building and are simply rolled down the halls
and put on an elevator. Even if they aren't,
and even if actual trucks are involved in
transporting the components, if it is an in-
house operation, it would be more common
to call it a set-in rather than a load-in. See
LOAD-IN AND SET-IN for a more detailed
discussion.

SETTING LEVELS WITH MATH— This
refers to setting cues blind. It is either used
when it is not possible to have a level-setting
session, or it is used as the starting point to
save time at the level-setting session. The levels of the various systems (frontlights, sidelights, backlights, etc) are set equally bright
after having taken into account the effect of
the various throw distances and gels. This is
used as a starting point.

If the frontlights, sidelights and backlights
all used the same kind of instrument and
these were hung at the same perfect golden
ring positions and had gels of equal transmission, then balancing the frontlight setting to the sidelight or backlight setting
would simply be a matter of setting the
channels at the same brightness level. In real
life, that rarely happens.

Let's suppose that the same 32,000 candela
instrument is used throughout and that the
vertical elevation is 11.3'. By looking at the
instrument locations on the Light Plot, the
frontlights appear to have a horizontal distance of 12' but backlights only have 7' and
sidelights have 10'. Since the horizontal distances are different, the throw distances will
also be different and as a consequence the
brightnesses will be different. The frontlights
will deliver 118 footcandles (fc) of light but
since the gel only has a 67 percent transmission rate, the brightness after gel will be 79
fc. Sidelights with 61 percent transmission
gel will produce 86 fc and backlights with 65
percent transmission will produce 118 fc.

We would be most interested in the frontlights because they are the dimmest of the

three systems. We'll assume that they will run at full and produce 79 fc. The question is at what dimmer levels would sidelights and backlights have to be set to produce 79 fc of light, since at full they produce 86 and 118 respectively. This is a ratio problem similar to, "If a 2 lb box of cereal costs $3, what would a 1 lb box cost?" and would be phrased this way, "86 fc is to 100 percent as 79 fc would be to x," where x would be the reduced dimmer reading. When the equation is solved for x, then $x = 79 * 100/86$ or 92 percent. By a similar process, the backlights would need to run at 67 percent. This creates the brightest possible version of this cue, which could then be assigned to a *sub* or *group* or both and run (proportionally) to any lower level that was wanted. Building blocks, that have been set blind, always have to be checked out visually before they are depended on. See FORMATTING THE DISK for a more detailed discussion.

SET-UP— More commonly called the *advance*, it was whatever the board operator had to do in order to set up for the next cue. This included replugs, resetting presets or whatever else might have been required. With computer lightboards, there typically is no set-up or advance.

SHADE AND SHADOW— This is how we perceive three-dimensional shapes. This is more commonly referred to as *plasticity*. See VISIBILITY and PLASTICITY for a more detailed discussion.

SHADES— See TINTS, TONES or SHADES.

SHADOWLESS LIGHT— This dates back to an Adolphe Appia idea that there were two different kinds of light: one was form revealing and shadow making (*gestaltendes Licht*), and the other was diffuse and shadowless as produced by footlights or striplights (*verteiltes Licht*). This was only true of the old time border and footlights that were painted white inside. Once specular reflectors and sealed beam lights became part of the package, the light produced ceased to be shadowless anymore.

SHADOWS— This typically refers to the actors and scenery pieces, that are being lit by a source of light, thereby blocking the light from hitting whatever is behind them. This creates an unlit area in their approximate size and shape on the backing, which is called either the *shadow* or *cast shadow*. Part of the purpose of using the golden ring positions is to insure that these shadows fall on the floor where it is harder for them to become distracting.

SHAFT SET SCREWS— These are the 5/16–18 square headed bolts (usually ½" long) that are used on both sliding tees and c-clamps to lock the position of the pipe or shaft.

SHAPE— One of the eight variables of light. It refers to the ability to shape the pool of light produced by the instrument. A barndoor can be added as an accessory to a fresnel or parcan and can shape the light in a more-or-less rectangular way. Since the edge-quality is soft on these instruments, it reduces light in one or more directions but does not cut it off entirely. The framing shutters on an ellipsoidal do this job not only in a rectangular way but in a trapezoidal way that is much more flexible. Gobo patterns also can be used to alter the shape of the light. See VARIABLES OF LIGHT for a more complete discussion of this subject.

SHARP FOCUS— This is another name for *hard focus*. The opposite of hard focus is soft focus. The opposite of sharp focus is also soft-focus as there is no similar term like "dull focus."

SHIELD (light)—(1) Anything that is used to control spill light. The most commonly used material is blackened aluminum foil or any dark-colored, non-flammable material of any kind. (2) If the shield refers to a HEAT SHIELD, then the intent is to filter out infrared radiation usually in order to lengthen the life of the color media.

SHINBUSTERS— Also sometimes called *kickers*. These are low hung sidelights from the sides or diagonal sides, most commonly used in dance performances. The name says it all. The performer exits to the wings temporarily blinded by the battery of sidelights located there but is spared serious injury because the sidelights are mostly above head height and have been suspended from above on lighting ladders rather than being supported on booms attached to the floor, so there is no vertical pole to unsuspectingly run into. This is where the shinbusters quietly lie in wait on the floor because they have no other place to be, and they are especially dangerous if they don't happen to be in use at the time. They are typically decorated with fluorescent glow-tape or small running lights to warn of their dangers during blackouts, but they rack up a high score of injured dancers just the same.

SHOCK— In reference to electricity, this is a situation, where a person instead of a wire becomes the conductor of electrical energy. The whole elaborate safety procedure of providing green wires to everything that has resulted in three-pronged connectors on everything was done to provide an alternate route for the current. The most common cause of electrical shock is touching wires that are supposed to be disconnected from power but aren't. If one treats every wire as if it were hot, unless it has been tested, then there will be little problem with shocks. This is after all what the electrical testers were designed to do.

SHOE— Also called a *brush*, this is the sliding contact on a resistance dimmer board, usually made of brass.

SHOP ORDER— This refers to the rental contract for the equipment needed and includes cables, gel frames, c-clamps, two-fers and everything else that might be needed. Because it has to be prepared ahead of time, it has to take into account contingencies since the show won't have been designed yet. Once the run of the show has officially started, any extra equipment is typically returned to avoid continued rental charges.

SHORT CIRCUIT— The current runs virtually unimpeded from hot wire to neutral and so much current flows in this resistance-free environment that the capacity of the wire is exceeded and a circuit breaker trips.

SHORT FOCUS or THROW— This refers to instruments that have wide beam angles that are designed to be used at short throw distances. It is however a confusing term and hard to correlate with either a lens focal length or a beam angle. Describing lights by their beam angle or field angle, which is the more common current practice, seems to be far less confusing and considerably more specific.

SHORT PLOTS— A system of lighting the stage without reference to the actual location of the instruments but otherwise accurate as to numbers and kinds of instruments used to do what specific jobs. The *light-the-set method* is commonly the basis for this. This is a working document seen by no one except the lighting designer and perhaps his assistant. It is often done on a piece of scratch paper, and would typically look something like this, where instruments are listed across the top and potential uses down the side:

SHORT PLOT	50° (16)	36° (6)	6x9 (24)	6 Fr (22)
Front (x60)	6			
Rt & Lt High Sides (x53)	6			
Back (x51)	4			
Rt & Lt Low Sides (x64)				12
Night Wash			8	
Day Wash			8	
Sconce Reinf (x09)				2
Fire Reinf (x321)				2
Iso spec Lorrie			1	
(number unaccounted for)	0	6	15	8

Short plot

The first time the designer does one of these, he may ignore the actual quantities of each kind of instrument that actually exist in the inventory and pretend that he has unlimited quantities. This usually results in using more instruments than actually exist. By cutting this down until it more-or-less matches what will eventually be available, it provides a handy list of additional specials that might be useful in case some of the specials that have been planned for turn out not to be needed.

SHUTTERS, FRAMING— See FRAMING SHUTTERS.

SIDEARM (BRITISH: *trunnion arms*)— This is a short piece of ½" pipe with a C-clamp at one end and a sliding tee along its length. When an instrument yoke is attached to the sliding tee, then it becomes a means to hang lights sideways from a pipe. Where booms are involved, the use of sidearms replaces crossarms. Where these are used on a grid, they provide in-between hanging places. On catwalks they provide an outboard instrument location for sidelights where their light will not hit the catwalk structure. When these are made up in the field, there needs to be some kind of rivet or cotter pin or bolt or pin wire inserted into each end of the ½" pipe to provide an end-stop for both the c-clamp and the sliding tee so that they cannot slide off the pipe when their set screws are loose. Although they can be as long as 48 or 72", they are more commonly closer to 18" as the longer lengths apply a lot of torque on the lighting pipe and are harder to keep locked in place.

Sidearm

SIDELIGHT— Any light coming from the side. On a proscenium stage, this means from booms or boom-like structures in the wings.

SIGNAL LIGHTS— More commonly called *cuelights*, these date back before the existence of headsets and were used to signal remote locations when to take cues. The cuelight going on was typically the signal to stand by and the light going off was the signal to take the cue (go). While not used as much as they once were, they are still in use, especially for cueing actors' entrances in situations where they can't see the stage.

SILENT SWITCH— Any switch that does not make a noise when activated. At one time these used to be exclusively mercury switches. Any practical switch located on the set ordinarily needs to be of the silent type because it shouldn't make a noise when activated by the actors, assuming that they activate it, as the click will be heard by some of the audience and usually won't be synchronized to the light cues. See PRACTICALS for a more detailed discussion of the circumstances in which actors might actually activate switches.

SILHOUETTE— This is created by having an unlit person or object stand in front of a lit background. This should not be confused with backlighting where the person or object is actually lit from the rear and the background is unlit.

SILICON CONTROLLED RECTIFIER DIMMERS (Abbr. SCR)— This is the most popular dimming technology in use today, as it is relatively inexpensive and relatively easy to maintain. It relies on semi-conductors limiting the passage of current in a continuously variable way by turning the current on and off many times a second. See LIGHTING CONTROL, Computer Memory Lightboards for a more detailed discussion.

SIMULTANEOUS CONTRAST— A complicated color anomaly whereby colors seem to become more separated from each other in hue and whereby the cast shadow is outlined in the complementary color. This is discussed in more detail as one of several COLOR ANOMALIES.

SINGLE PHASE— This is electricity supplied as to residences in which the peak of the 60 MHZ cycle occurs at the same time for both hot legs. Most theatres will be supplied by three-phase current where the peaks of the cycles are offset by 120 degrees between the three hot legs. See ELECTRICAL SERVICES for a more detailed discussion.

SINGLE POLE or SINGLE THROW SWITCHES— See SWITCHES, KINDS OF.

SIXTY CYCLE CURRENT— Normal AC current that reverses direction 120 times per second, which equates to 60 complete cycles per second.

SIZE— One of the eight variables of light. It refers to the size of the light pool, which is adjustable on a fresnel or zoom ellipsoidal but can only be changed on a standard ellipsoidal by replacing the lens tube assembly or by using a gate reducing gobo pattern or by using the shutters in a trapezoidal way. See VARIABLES OF LIGHT for a more complete discussion of this subject.

SKETCHES— It is suggested from time-to-time that the lighting designer might provide sketches for each scene or look, but there is considerable doubt that this is possible. Historically, efforts made to indicate lighting in sketches by designers, such as Adolphe Appia, Gordan Craig, and Robert Edmund Jones, have not been entirely successful. Their sketches for the most part have been vague and obscure, highlighting only a very few lit spots in a sea of darkness, putting light only where it was wanted and deleting inconvenient shadows, while at the same time showing shadows falling where it would be impossible to have any. While these drawings are evocative and interesting to look at in the context of graphic art, they are certainly not realistic representations of how the scenery would (or did) look under light. They are also, almost without exception, in black-and-white.

SKIM-THE-SURFACE METHOD— The traditional method of lighting a cyc or drop that involves having lights top and bottom (often striplights) skimming the surface. See LIGHTING SPECIAL PROBLEMS/Cycs and Drops for a more detailed discussion.

SKIN TONES, LIGHTING OF— Almost everyone agrees that in a dramatic presentation, it is the faces of the actors that need to be lit. In order for this to occur, they must first be seen against a contrasting background that makes them stand out and second, where possible against a background that is darker than the face because this will make the face appear to be brighter even though both face and background are lit the same. Faces usually are closer to the light sources than the background and as a result, receive more illumination. The problem, when there is a problem, results from the faces not being as reflective as the background.

Black faces are the hardest to light because they absorb more of the light that hits them and reflect less. Attempting to provide an even darker background for them to be seen against usually results in the phenomenon of the scenery appearing to talk, as the faces become incorporated into it, as described for white faces in the *White Color Problem*. In this situation making the face stand out from (be a contrasting color to) the scenery is way more important than whether the background color is darker or lighter.

Even in a production with an entirely black cast, some faces will be lighter and easier to see than others. There is also no such thing as a purely white face either, unless one means perhaps an albino face. Caucasian faces tend to be varying shades of pink, yellow and tan. They absorb and reflect light differently and some will always appear brighter in any scene than others. Pink faces and pink bald heads are particularly troublesome because there is usually pink, amber, or lavender in the lights, and these surfaces will pick up the pink or reddish color and accentuate it to the point where it may be necessary to change gel colors.

The reflectance of surface colors is determined entirely by the color and roughness of the surface. While set and costume colors can be altered to help make the actors' faces stand out, the faces themselves will always be the color that they are, and the lighting designer has very few tools with which to try to alter this.

Having said all that, the human eye can be made to focus on things that are hard to see even if that is not particularly easy. Anyone who has ever driven a car West just before sunset will instantly recognize how it was possible to focus one's attention on the road at a time when the sun was coming from an eyelevel front position. In a similar vein, while it may be harder and more fatiguing to concentrate one's attention on a face that is not as reflective as its background, it is still possible to do so, and in terms of audience focus, they will in most cases watch the speaking actor regardless of whether he is easy to see or not.

SKY, THE LIGHTING OF— See LIGHTING SPECIAL PROBLEMS/Cycs and Drops.

SLIDE PROJECTORS or PROJECTIONS— See PROJECTIONS.

SLIDE TAPE— See TAPES, KINDS OF.

SLIDING TEE— A hardware item for making a sidearm out of a c-clamp and a piece of ½" pipe. It is a metal cylinder tapped for a ½" bolt (yoke attaching bolt) that can slide along a ½" pipe and can be locked in place by two square headed setscrews.

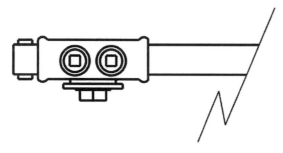

Sliding tee

SLOTS—(1) These are recesses in the walls or ceiling of a proscenium theatre for mounting lighting instruments, more commonly called *coves*. (2) The grooves at the front of a lighting instrument that hold the color frames in place (color slots or gel slots).

SLOW MOTION EFFECTS— See EFFECTS, KINDS OF.

SLOW MOTION WHEEL— A vintage grand mastering system that involved a gear dri-

ven wheel about the size of car steering wheel that would be turned instead of a huge baseball bat-sized handle that was pulled down. The fact that the wheel was geared allowed it to turn easier but required faster movement because it had to be turned many times.

SNAKE—(1) A bundle of sound cables is commonly called a sound snake. Theoretically it could be applied to a bundle of lighting cables but this is rarely heard. (2) A flexible wire coil used to clear blocked drains is commonly called a plumbing snake. (3) Theoretically the flexible metal wire used to pull conduit wire through conduit (*fish tape*) could be called an electrical snake and everyone would understand what was meant, but this is not a common usage.

SNAP CUE— Any zero count cue taken as if switched on.

SNAP HOOKS— A fastening device with a spring activated tongue. See DOG CLIPS.

SNEAK— To slowly bring up a channel or entire cue. This is frequently also the name of a computer lightboard board button that will do this. Often the default sneak time can be set.

SNOOT— Another name for a tophat, one of several lighting add-on accessories. See ACCESSORIES for a more detailed discussion.

SNUFF-BOY— Earliest known lighting job in the theatre. The snuff-boy, equipped with several lengths of snuffers, was responsible for extinguishing candles that had begun to smoke or otherwise misbehave. Theoretically, it did not matter whose scene he needed to interrupt. He was authorized to go out onstage whenever there was a problem and do his job. He, also, usually was the person who lit the candles at the top of the show, snuffed them out at the end, recycled the stubbies and put new candles in everywhere in preparation for the next performance. His job was eventually replaced by a gasman, who was usually a plumber by trade or who had plumbing experience. The gasman ran the rubber gas lines to the various gas jet fixtures and operated the gas table, which controlled where the gas went and, as such, was the equivalent of a dimmer board for gas.

SOCK — A padded bag, sometimes an actual sock, that is put over the delicate ends of connectors to protect them from snagging or mechanical damage. When the lightboard control cables are lowered out the booth window to the tech table below, someone will usually have put a sock on the cable ends. Socks are occasionally put on ladder feet to protect the floor surface, but this has to be done ever so carefully to insure that it does not compromise traction and make the ladder more dangerous.

SOCKET — Any device that holds a lamp in place and connects it to power.

SOCKET ADAPTOR — This mostly refers to the four sizes of screw-in sockets that can be adapted downward and less commonly upward, but it would apply to any adaptation from one socket style to another.

SOFT EDGED or FOCUSED — The edge of the light appears to fade gradually into the background in a way that makes it difficult to determine where the lit area is and where it has disappeared. Fresnels are soft-edged. Ellipsoidals are usually considered hard-edged although they can actually be either.

SOFT LIGHT — (1) Soft edged light as described above. (2) Light that has a very even field, which is true of all light that comes from a long distance. (3) The equivalent of Adolphe Appia's *verteiltes Licht*, which would be a shadowless light similar to what comes out of borderlights and footlights that have no reflectors.

SOFT PATCHING — Soft patching only exists on a computer lightboard where it is channels (not dimmers) that are controlled, and it is the process by which the available dimmers are assigned to channels. This could be done on a one-to-one basis with dimmer 1 being assigned to channel 1 and so forth, and this is often the default setting. However, soft patching provides a unique opportunity to assign channels in a way that will make them easy to remember. Channels 1-10 could be for specials. Channels 11-20 could be frontlights. Channels 21-30 could be sidelights. It makes no difference what the system is as long as it makes sense to the designer. It could vary by show or could remain essentially the same for all shows. Since more than one dimmer can be assigned to one channel, it allows the channels to act as control areas so that instead of having to set 100 dimmers for every cue, one only has to set 20 channels. Soft patching is a tremendously valuable tool.

SOLDERLESS CONNECTORS — See WIRENUTS.

SOLID STATE — In the context of dimmer boards, this refers to dimming systems that use the gating principle to rapidly turn on and off the current as occurs with the SCR or Triac or IGBT dimmers.

SOLO — This is a computer lightboard term that refers to the remainder of the stage being dimmed out while the designated channel or cue plays alone (solo).

SOURCE LIGHT — Another name for a PRACTICAL light.

SOURCES (natural) — It often seems there is only one, the sun, because it is the only natural source that is non-flickering, colorless (nearly colorless) and bright enough to read by. A sunny day is usually about 5000 footcandles (fc) bright. At noon on the equator, it can approach 10,000 fc, and even an overcast day is about 3000 fc bright. The moon is not a source at all but merely a reflector of sunlight. While its light is colorless and steady, it is only a few hundredth of a footcandle bright, just barely enough to allow one to see large objects like trees, bushes or yard furniture. Other natural sources include: lightning, which is bright but not sustained; the northern or southern lights, which are pale colored, flickering and dim;

starlight, which is exceptionally dim; and firelight, which is yellowish and flickers. Most of these sources at one time or another have to be depicted onstage.

SOURCES OF INSPIRATION— These include the script, the set and the runthru. See LIGHTING IDEAS.

SOURCES OF LIGHT— A lamp (or to be more specific, its filament) is the source of all tungsten-halogen theatrical light. However, when the lamp is inside the instrument and a lens is involved, the source of light is taken to be the front of the lens for fresnels and the gate for ellipsoidals

SPECIAL AREALIGHTS— See AREAS, SPECIAL.

SPECIAL EFFECTS— See EFFECTS, KINDS OF.

SPECIAL PROBLEMS, LIGHTING OF— See LIGHTING SPECIAL PROBLEMS.

SPECIALS, KINDS OF— All instruments that aren't arealights (either regular are-alights or special arealights) are considered specials. These divide into two general groups: washes and all other specials. Other specials include accent specials, isolation specials, set specials, practicals, reinforcing lights, backing lights, cyc or drop lights, wing lighting and anything else that falls into no other specific category.

Accent Specials (sometimes called Emphasis Specials): One or more lights used to provide more light at a particular place, usually related to doors, windows or furniture pieces or on less representational sets to sitting or leaning places, often in a color slightly different from the surrounding arealights.

Practicals: Usually these are chandeliers, wall sconces and floor or desk lamps but can be any source seen by the audience. See PRACTICALS for a more detailed discussion.

Reinforcing Specials: One or more instruments whose light appears to be coming from a practical light source. Also an instrument whose light appears to be coming from an invisible practical source, as is the case in thrust theatres, where the invisible sidewalls are often assumed to have windows or lighting fixtures on them. The reinforcing lights, used alone, are supposed to suggest the presence of these sources.

Set Specials: One or more instruments used to light parts of the set. Many times the spill from the arealights is sufficient. In those cases where it is not, other instruments are used for specifically that purpose. The lighting of wing pieces, backings and drops (although they would fall into this category) are discussed separately. See LIGHTING, SPECIAL PROBLEMS for a more detailed discussion.

Specials, Isolation: One or more lights used to isolate an actor (or object), usually tightly focused and a slightly different color from the arealights which are often on at the same time but at a lower level. At the appropriate moment, everything else may fade away to reveal the special alone isolating the actor.

SPECTROPHOTOMETER— A spectrometer, for short. This is a scientific device that breaks light into wavelengths and records the results on a spectrogram. Louis Hartmann talked about this and had obviously been allowed to see one, but theatre lighting technicians don't have access, nor a need to have access, to this kind of equipment.

SPECTRUM or SPECTRAL COLORS— The component colors of white light. See COLOR SPECTRUM for a more detailed discussion.

SPECULAR or NON-SPECULAR REFLECTION— Mirror-like or non-mirror like reflection. See REFLECTION AND ABSORPTION for a more detailed discussion.

SPEEDTHRU— Also called an *à italien* rehearsal. This is a rehearsal where the actors typically say their lines as fast as possible. Where this occurs onstage with movement, it is pointless to have it also be a lighting rehearsal because the timings will all be off.

SPHERICAL REFLECTOR— One of three common reflector shapes. See REFLECTION, LAWS OF.

SPIDER— This is a vintage colloquialism that refers to a multiple female connector of some type, usually a pin-connector, as the PBG kind is more commonly called a *three-way tap*.

SPIKING THE STAGE— This refers to putting marks on the stage for focusing purposes. At the very least the center of all areas and specials have to be established. This is often considered part of the focusing session, so while the full crew is standing around drinking coffee, the lighting designer and an assistant are crawling around on their hands and knees moving tape measures around with sweat pouring down their faces.

Often by demanding that the stage manager provide marks for the furniture and isolation specials another time can be found in which this can be done. If that is the case, then the lighting designer can be making area marks while the stage manager is locating furniture positions. The marks do not have to be on the stage surface itself. They can often be made on the front edge of the stage (or front seats in the house) and in the wings at the locking rail. The lighting designer can then sight off these marks and drop a numbered card at that position onstage (as part of the focusing session).

Regardless of who places the marks, there is no guarantee that these won't change in the course of rehearsals and everyone usually accepts these as only the starting points. When tempers run hot, lighting designers can sometimes be heard to say that the light is right on the mark given them by the stage manager although it is unclear what lasting good is achieved by this as the light (if it is in the wrong place) will surely have to be moved regardless of who located its position.

SPILL or SPILL LIGHT— Any light that goes where is it is not wanted is considered spill light, but this most commonly is applied only to direct light that has not been adequately controlled rather than bounce light, which bounces in all directions and also spills where it is not wanted.

SPILL LIGHT PREVENTION— See ACCESSORIES.

SPILL RINGS— One of several lighting add-on accessories. See ACCESSORIES for a more detailed discussion.

SPLICES— Once common in both ropes and wires, they have now all but disappeared. Ropes are now continuous, and electrical wires are now supposed to be wirenuted together inside an electrical box (by code), although low voltage wires (signal and sound wires) may still be tied together and wire-nutted outside of electrical boxes.

SPLIT-FADER or SPLIT-CROSSFADER— See CROSSFADER.

SPOKE-STYLE— This mostly relates to how two-fers and three-fers are made, but it could also refer to the way the wiring inside a light box is done. When electrical devices are hooked together in a spoke style, the power for the second and subsequent devices is drawn from the original point. The opposite of this is *daisy-chain style* (often seen in C7 and C9 Christmas tree lights) where each female socket draws its power from the previous one. This has nothing to do with series or parallel circuits as all connections are in parallel. See TWO-FERS for a more detailed discussion.

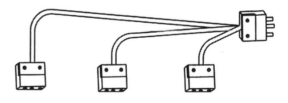

Spoke-syle three-fer

SPOT LINE— A single rope line (rather that a line-set) that is intended to lift only a single item like a cable cradle.

SPOT MARKS— Marks placed on the walls of the booth (or followspot location) to help with difficult spot pick ups, usually pick-ups made in the dark. To make it work there has to be a stray shaft of light coming from the spot that will hit the walls of the booth, which usually means someone drilled a hole in the instrument housing.

SPOTLIGHT— An entire class of lensed instruments. See INSTRUMENTS for a more detailed discussion.

SPOTTING LIGHT— A dim light in a recognizable color, usually coming from the balcony rail or back of the house, that serves as a beacon for dancers to help them find front.

SQUARE LAW— Not to be confused with the inverse square law, this relates to a dimmer curve and correlates human perception to the calibrations on the curve so that at quarter bright, the light appears to be 25 percent bright and so forth.

SQUID— Named for their shape (a small ball with two thin leads), they are electrically operated igniters (electric matches) used to detonate pyrotechnic devices. Squib™ is a tradename for one brand of these.

SRO— Abbreviation for *standing room only*, and as such this is synonymous with being sold out. In response to a question about how the house was last night, "We were SRO," would indicate it was full.

STAGE CREW— Depending on its usage, it may describe everyone involved in either the building part or the running part of the show, or it may be used to mean just the running crew or just the scenery running crew. It would not include designers. It might or might not include dressers, followspot operators and production assistant who are all part of the running crew. This is a vague and imprecise term that one is most likely to encounter in non-professional situations, as professional theatres involve clearly defined departments and titles.

STAGE DIRECTIONS—Anything in the script that isn't the text of what the characters say to each other is considered to be a stage direction. Some of these were written by the playwright to clarify to whom char-

acters are speaking and what their emotions might be at the time. Other stage directions are typically added before the script is published to make the reading of it more visual for the reader. The stage manager is often asked to help in this regard. When there is a sketch of the set and stage directions that relate to it, this was usually provided by the stage manager and is based upon what was done in the first production.

STAGE MODE— Also called *live mode*, this is a computer lightboard term that refers to the display screen being set to view the cue currently up onstage.

STAGE PLUG— In the old days this referred exclusively to floor plugs (now obsolete and illegal), but now it would be taken to mean a male stagepin connector.

STAGE TIME— The period between load-in and opening is considered stage time as it relates to what crew or crews are working on the stage. Since stage time is precious, many things are done ahead of time so that less of it is used up.

STAGEPIN CONNECTORS (Abbr. 2P&G)— Special electrical connectors made for stage-use that are both inexpensive and durable. See CONNECTORS, KINDS OF for a more detailed discussion.

STAGGER-THRU— A runthru that is not expected to run smoothly without having to stop.

STAIRCASE, LIGHTING OF— See LIGHTING SPECIAL PROBLEMS/Staircases.

STAND or STANDARD— More commonly called a *light stand*, this is a vertical pipe mounted on a heavy iron base to support one or more lighting instruments. It is usually less than 10' tall, and it may telescope, but if it were on wheels, it would be more common to call it a *rolling light stand* or *rover*.

STAND-BY— Also called a *ready*, this is the second announcement of an upcoming cue. It follows the *warning* and precedes the *go*. See CUES, CALLING OF for a more detailed discussion.

STANDING ROOM— In a situation where the theatre is sold out of tickets, it is sometimes possible to allow audience to stand at the back of the theatre or back of one of the balconies and watch the show from there, usually at a reduced price. The local government (city) that issues the building occupancy permit decides whether this will be permitted or not, and if so, how many people will be allowed to stand. Selling standing room is usually only permitted when all the other tickets (to the assigned seats) are gone.

STAND-INS— See WALKERS.

STANDOff (color)— A motion picture industry name for a *color extender*. See ACCESSORIES.

STANLEY— Short for Stanley McCandless whose method almost everyone involved in stage lighting has heard of and is familiar with. Standard Stanley (Classic Stanley) involves there being two instruments-per-area upstage of the proscenium from front-left and front-right on the golden ring. Modified Stanley involves there being three instruments-per-area upstage of the proscenium (backlight where possible) and four instruments-per-area downstage of the proscenium (as for thrust or arena lighting).

STARS— See EFFECTS, KINDS OF.

STATES OF LIGHTING— Although highly descriptive, this is mostly heard only in British practice and is commonly called *cues* or *completed cues* or *static moments* in the USA. It refers to the way the stage looks when the cue is complete. None of the American words convey the idea that the state of the lighting can be a moving or changing state as long as this is done in a predictable and regular way.

STATIC MOMENTS— The action on stage is not static. The lighting is (usually is but not always as will be explained below). A static lighting moment may last for a fraction of a second or for an entire act. The lighting of an entire show is typically described as a series of static moments where the lights look one way until something happens, at which point they change and look some other way. This in fact is the way the computer lightboard records them and the way lighting designers describe them to the director.

If it is a 5-count cue, then there is technically a 5-second transition period when the audience is between cues. This is usually ignored as it is typically short and covered by actor movement and considered a necessary prelude before the cue actually becomes static.

There are times however when the count is longer and where the transition is the cue itself. This is especially true for followspots. They pick someone up and follow them until they are told not to. Following one character is one cue. Even though it is not static, it is a static moment in the sense that the lights are doing one thing only. In the same way a scene that takes place in the flames of a fire or as the lights are fading out on a 50 count, are static moments in the sense that the lights are doing only one thing even though the lights themselves are changing. .

STATUS LIGHTS— See PANEL LIGHTS.

STENCILS (lighting)— See TEMPLATES.

STEP LENS— A variant of the fresnel lens, not used much anymore. See LENSES, KINDS OF.

STEP TIME— This is a computer lightboard term that refers to the amount of time between steps in an effect or subroutine. It is the sum of the in time/dwell time/out time plus the amount of time before the next in time. If steps overlap, the step time will be less than the sum of the in time/dwell time/out time of the step in question. See LIGHTING CONTROL/Computer Memory Lightboards/Effects for a more detailed discussion.

STEPLADDER— A ladder that folds flat for storage and opens up forming a letter "A" when in use, typically in sizes from 2–20 feet. See HANGING POSITIONS, GETTING TO for a more detailed discussion.

STEREOPTICON— This is a vintage effects machine that can easily become confused

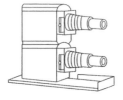

Stereopticon

with a *sciopticon* or a *lobsterscope*. The stereopticon involves two slide projectors, which either creates an image with 3D overtones or allows one static slide image to dissolve into another.

STICK— The raiseable vertical center portion of an A-ladder, sometimes called the *fly section*.

STILSON WRENCH— A tradename for a pipe wrench.

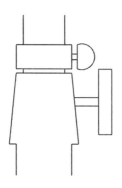

Stop collar

STOP COLLAR— A metal cylinder with a hand operated setscrew, used on telescoping light stands to lock the position of the telescoping upper portion while still allowing the upper pipe to swivel left-and-right.

STOP-AND-GO REHEARSAL— This is a technical rehearsal (often the first one) where the understanding is that the show will run without stopping unless the actors need to stop or the director, stage manager or a designer asks to stop. If sound and light cues have already been integrated into the show during rehearsals-with-light, these rehearsals often run with surprisingly few stops. The guiding principle at work here is that rehearsal time where the cast works together is precious and the cast should not be made to stand around and wait while the lighting designer refines a cue.

In this kind of a situation, while the lighting designer will exercise restraint and take notes wherever possible, there will be times when the run needs to be stopped. If actors are not standing where the lights are, either the lights need to be reworked or the director needs to tell the actor to find his light. Often there may be a very fast sequence of

cues that has to be stepped through with the actors in slow motion. Often transitions are of a fixed length of time, and if the lights for the new scene are coming up before the actors are fully in place, either the time needs to be lengthened or the actors need to move faster.

STOPPING DOWN— This refers to reducing the aperture size of a lens. On an ellipsoidal it can be done in a hard-edged way either with the framing shutters or a gate reducer or an iris or in a soft-edged way by using a donut in the gel frame.

STORAGE MEDIA— This is an academic word that refers to the tapes or disks used in computer lightboards to store the show information. These are usually removable, but in the early years this was not always the case. They would always be called either the *tape* or the *disk* by the people handling them.

STRAIN RELIEF— A device that attaches an electrical cord or cable to a lighting instrument or appliance. As the name suggests, the purpose is to prevent there being any strain placed on the actual electrical connection inside. In the old days, it was common practice to simply tie a knot inside the appliance with the electric cord and the underwriters knot was devised for just this purpose, but this is no longer permitted by the electrical code.

STRAINER— A metal plate with holes in it (inserted in the gel frame) to limit the quantity of light. This is a countermeasure to incandescent color change that dims the light without losing the purity of the color. Gray gel is sometimes used to achieve the same thing, but the gray gel method appears to also desaturate the color whereas the strainer doesn't.

STRAND LIGHTING— The first British manufacturer of electric stage lighting supplies, established it 1914 as Strand Electric and Engineering Company Ltd. Strand, eventually, bought out Century Lighting Company in New York, which for a time became Century Strand, and is now just Strand Lighting again.

STRANDED WIRE— Any wire that is made up of many small strands, thus making the wire flexible. Stranded wire is used almost exclusively in the theatre in all type S cable.

STRIKE— To remove something from the stage. Its opposite is *set*, as in, "Could someone set the furniture for this scene." As it relates to lighting, strike refers to removing some or all of the lighting equipment. If a light did not perform as hoped, it might have its gel struck or its barndoor struck or the whole instrument and all its accessories could be struck. This would only be done if the instrument were to be rehung in a different location. Otherwise, instruments that don't prove useful are usually simply abandoned in place until the show is over and everything is either struck in one operation or repositioned, unless they are rented, in which case they would be struck and returned shortly after opening night.

STRIKE, LIMITED— One of four methods of changing the lights from one show to the next. See STRIKES, KINDS OF for a more detailed discussion.

STRIKE AND REHANG— One of four methods of changing the lights from one show to the next. See STRIKES, KINDS OF for a more detailed discussion.

STRIKE NIGHT— The night when the set and everything else connected to this show is by tradition struck and either put back in storage or put in a pile to be disposed of or recycled. This is typically the last night of the run and takes place after the final performance and often runs to midnight and beyond, into the early hours of the next morning. The strike of the lights may or may not occur on strike night. There are compelling reasons why it should not, as described next.

STRIKE THE LIGHTS, WHEN TO— By tradition the lights are struck following the last performance as is the set and everything else related to the production. There are however compelling reasons why the lighting strike should be delayed (at least until the next morning).

First, the filaments of the very expensive lamps are most vulnerable to damage if they encounter impact while they are hot, as they would be after a performance. If even one lamp were saved, it would probably be worth it to have had a delay.

Second, strike night is often characterized by too many people all trying to find something useful to do. In terms of lighting, usually a clear floor is needed and all the available ladders are needed. On strike night, most of the ladders will already be in use and the stage floor will typically be awash in extra help.

Third, the majority of the lighting crew will probably be tired and at the end of their working day, which translates into thinking and working slower.

Fourth, there will be a lot of noise and it will be hard to communicate. This is probably less of a concern because it is really only the ladder assistants that need to communicate with the ladder electricians, but there will certainly be less stress by the next morning.

STRIKES, KINDS OF— In its most specific meaning, striking the lights refers to taking them down, and in this context there are no differing kinds of strikes as the existing instruments are simply removed from their diverse locations.

When the strike is immediately followed by a rehang, then there are four distinct or relatively distinct ways to do this.

Strike and Rehang: As the name suggests, all the instruments are struck and when the grid or pipes are bare, they are put back up again, often in the same positions or approximately the same positions. This is sometimes said to be the least confusing method to get the job done. This is also usually said by the same people who benefit most from it taking the longest. This system involves two ladder trips for every light in the show.

Limited Strike: In this system, there is a strike of the old show but lights that are in approximately the right place are left up, but stripped of their color, accessories and cable.

Missing Instrument Rehang: In this system, one goes across the hanging positions striking anything that shouldn't be there and hanging anything that should. In the event that the instrument that should go there has not been struck from the old show yet, a ribbon or tie is left to mark the place. This involves only one ladder trip for most instruments.

Full Rehang: By cleverly controlling the path of the ladders, it is often possible to assure that a missing instrument rehang will have few if any missing instruments. In this sense it becomes a full rehang and involves only one ladder move per instruments with many of the instruments already being in place.

STRIKING AN INSTRUMENT— First, the c-clamp can be loosened and unhooked and the hauling rope can be attached leaving the instrument hanging by its safety cable. The safety cable could now be released and the jumper cable and any accessories likely to fall off during the lowering process could be threaded on and the safety cable could then be reattached to itself around the yoke of the instrument (but not around the support pipe anymore). At this point the instrument is ready to be lowered down. The above procedure is a safety strategy for instruments that are in-the-air when the electrician may not have two hands free. When working on catwalks or on the stage floor with an electrics pipe at chest height, the safety cable is unclipped first and the jumper cable and accessories are removed and put in a box on the floor, at which point the instrument can be detached from the pipe and put on the floor also or carried away.

STRIPLIGHT— Any borderlight or footlight made up of modular units 6–8 feet in length. They are commonly calls *strips* and are now used for footlights, borderlights and cyc lights or cyc foots. The striplights typically

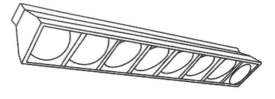

Striplight

have c-clamp sidearms at each end to attach to support pipes and have some provision so that they can be connected end-to-end to create longer lengths.

STRIPPING OUT ACROSS THE STAGE— In the context of a followspot, this would typically involve widening the focus with the trombone handles and narrowing the height with the douser to cover a narrow band from left to right across the stage.

STROBE— An effect that flashes bright light, using xenon, on and off many times per second. It is used to create slow motion effects or lightning flashes. Audiences find it particularly annoying, and where it is used, there is usually a warning sign in the lobby, as it is said that it can cause epileptics to have a seizure.

STUD—(1) A bolt whose head has been replaced by screw threads so that it can be screwed into a wood member by grasping the center with a vice-grip and turning. Toilets are commonly secured to the floor using studs. When these are inserted into the wall backstage or underside of the balcony, they provide hanging positions for instruments by sliding the yoke onto the exposed threaded bolt-part and adding a washer and wing nut. (2) Some striplights already have studs coming out their sides (often attached to rosettes).

STYLE— In its most generic sense, it refers to the unique manner in which something is done. Individual directors have a distinctive style. So do designers and actors and everyone else. Playwrights have a style and so do plays. In the context of stage lighting, styles of plays fall generally into one of two categories: realistic plays and everything else, which is to say non-realistic plays.

In realistic plays, the lighting is supposed to look as if it came from logical sources (sun or artificial sources) and the cues theoretically need to be motivated by the sun passing behind a cloud or someone hitting a light switch or something similar. In practice, the audience understands that it is only a play. They know it is not really as bright as a sunlit day. They know it will never be as dark as an actual nighttime scene. They know the colors in the lights are exaggerated from what they would be in real life. They understand that, sometimes, light cues are taken for theatrical reasons that don't correspond to the supposed realism.

In non-realistic plays or presentations, the time, place and situation is often either vague or unimportant. Light cues can be motivated by the music if there is music or by a change in the imagined emotional state of the main character. Dance performances, opera and children's theatre often operate this way. While historic categories of play or performance styles can be considered as an indicator, it is the style of the particular production that really matters. Just because it is an opera does not mean that it will be done in the traditional way. See LIGHTING, KINDS OF for a more detailed discussion.

SUB— Short for SUBMASTER.

SUB SHEET MODE— This is a computer lightboard display that allows the operator to view and alter submaster assignments.

SUBMASTER— Commonly called *subs* for short. (1) On a manual lightboard that had mechanical mastering, it was common to call all master handles that weren't the grandmaster a submaster. Where there were three levels of mastering, submaster typically referred to the middle level that controlled a group of row masters and was in turn controlled by the grand master. (2) On remote control lightboards, submasters are sliders that can be loaded with groups or channels at varying levels (cues) or effects. See

LIGHTING CONTROL for a more detailed discussion.

SUBROUTINE— This is a computer lightboard term that refers to a group of cues (called *steps*) that are automatically run as part of one operation. See LIGHTING CONTROL, Computer Memory Lightboards for a more detailed discussion.

SUBTRACTIVE MIXING— Both the mixing of paint colors and the placing of two colors of gel in a single frame are considered to be forms of subtractive mixing because each component subtracts or filters out a subset of colors. See COLOR MIXING for a more detailed discussion.

SUNDAY— A small loop of rope or cordage tied back to itself in a way that creates a loop about 10–14 inches in diameter. They are most commonly used to hang a pulley (like for the light hauling rope) aloft. The Sunday loop is ring hitched to the pulley and then ring hitched again to the grid or ladder rung. Sundays are also used to temporarily attach dog-clips to accessories of various kinds (like a barndoor or a bucket of tools).

SUNLIGHT EFFECT— See EFFECTS, KINDS OF.

SUNNYSIDE CONVENTION— This is a theatrical convention designed to make each audience member think that they have one of the best seats in the house. It is a standing joke that while no one wants to pay enough to have good seats, at the same time no one is prepared to accept that the seats they have already bought will be bad. Directors have to make sure the cheap seats always get to see a few faces instead of a lot of backs. Lighting designers have to make sure that the scene looks lit from all directions. Where there is a sunny side and a shady side to the action, the audience if given the choice (as in a festival seating situation) would surge toward the side from which the scene looked sunny. In a proscenium configuration, this is no problem as everyone can be on the sunny side of the action. In the other configurations, the brightness differences are commonly evened out to reduce the contrast and obscure which side is the source side of the light, letting the differences in the colors of the light from the different directions reveal the shape of the objects and represent in a vague way the shadier side. Ideally everyone in the audience will feel they were on a sunny enough side so that they will not even be tempted to think about it at all.

In circumstances where an actor is lit by a single spotlight, it will be very clear where the sunny side is as there will be no light whatsoever on the other three sides. An audience on the sides will usually tolerate this if it is of short duration, but they will not want to see a whole scene done this way. They are also more likely to tolerate it if the actor remains with his face toward the light rather than having him turn and look at the side sections, thus drawing attention to the fact that he is not lit from that direction at all.

SURGE and SURGE PROTECTOR— An unexpected voltage spike. This is not usually a problem for lighting equipment but is a serious problem for computers and other electronic equipment. Most computers use special plugging strips that incorporate some kind of surge protection. Lighting computers are no exception.

SWATCH BOOK— More commonly called *gel books*, they are free samples about 1 · 4" in size of all the colors in a manufacturer's line of color filters, which will typically be about 100 colors. They are used by designers to compare and pick the colors for the show, and they usually specify a transmission percentage and a graph showing what wavelengths of light are passed in what approximate quantities.

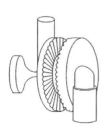

Swing joint

SWING JOINT— This is the vintage system of two rosettes tightened against each other to limit movement in two directions. This has

been replaced by disc locks on instrument yokes.

SWITCH OUT— This is a vintage term that refers to pulling the switch on a dimmer, or bank or main rather than pulling down the dimmers. It would now typically be referred to as a zero count fade out.

SWITCHBOARD— A vintage name for a *dimmer board* dating back to the days when there were more switches than dimmers.

SWITCHES, KINDS OF— There are two concepts here. The first deals with how many things can get connected or disconnected with one throw of the switch handle. That's called *poles*, and theoretically each one could be connected to a different voltage or electrical phase (as long as it is within the amp carrying capacity of the switch contacts) because there is no cross-connection between poles. The second concept involves how many things one pole can be connected to. In the case of a rotary switch, one pole can be connected to as many things as there are contacts (i.e. positions on the switch). In the more common switch that has a handle that is either up or down, then the maximum number of positions (*throws*) is two with the possibility that there could be a center off position, which is usually not counted. Thus typical descriptions of switches are: single-pole double throw switch (SPDT), four-pole single throw (4PST) and so forth.

SYMBOLS (electrical)— These are used in schematic drawings, which are simplified drawings designed to allow the viewer to follow the current path. Typical symbols are shown below and include battery, switch, fuse, relay, diode, variable resistor, resistor, light and so forth.

SYMBOLS (lighting)— These are the representations of lighting instrument that appear on the Light Plot (or Sectional drawing, if any). If the drawing is manually drafted, a commercially made plastic template is typically used. The USITT publishes a list of what it considers the standard symbols to be,

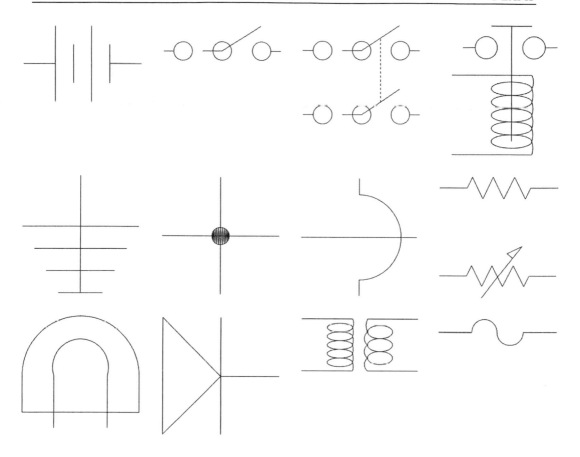

Top, left–right: Battery; SPDT switch; DPDT switch; SPST relay; ***middle, left–right:*** Grounding; Wire junction; No wire junction; resistor (top) and dimmer (bottom); ***bottom, left–right:*** Light or load; Diode; Transformer; Fuse or CB

and these are what are most likely to be found on the commercially made templates. These are published in the back of many lighting books (such as Robert C Mumm's **Photometrics Handbook**) and they can be downloaded from Altman Stage Lighting along with the symbols drawn by Altman for their own equipment (www.altltg.com). If the drawing is done on a CAD program, the lighting designer can either draw his own symbols or use a symbol downloaded from a manufacturer. The advantage of custom drawn symbols is that they can often be made to look more like the silhouette of the lighting instrument, which is more likely to result in fewer errors and faster instrument placement at the hanging session. See TEMPLATES for samples.

SYSTEM—A group of instruments with a common purpose and usually a common color doing the job that one instrument (if big enough, but none are) could theoretically do. They are mostly directed at the whole stage from a specific direction, but they can cover a part of the stage as well.

SYSTEM SETTINGS—This is a computer lightboard term that refers to user preferences and default settings like default cue time. There is usually a display screen where these can be viewed and modified.

T LAMP—One of a number of lamp bulb shapes but historically important because the tubular lamps were the ones first used in ellipsoidals. Compact ellipsoidals could not have been developed if this kind of lamp had

TABLE 306

not been invented. The lamps were slimmer in profile and could be burned base up. See LAMPS for a more detailed discussion.

TABLE (Lighting or Production or Technical)— This is the table out in the house used by the director, stage manager, lighting designer, and sound designer or some combination thereof. It is used during technical rehearsals and removed before the first preview.

In the good old days, the lighting operator and sound operator were confined in a booth at the back or to the side of the house.

During the period when the sound and light cues were being integrated into the show, the director and stage manager would have a table set up in the house that more-or-less duplicated what they had had in the rehearsal room, where they could talk in whispers to each other and where the stage manager could talk by headset to the booth crew, the backstage spaces and the actors onstage via the house speakers. Call this phase one, and the table was most commonly called the *production table*.

When lighting equipment reached the point of having monitors, one was usually provided for the lighting designer in some remote corner of the house along with a desk to put it on (*lighting table*) where he could jabber away to the lightboard operator and not interrupt the rehearsal. Similarly, the sound designer was often given a headset (but no desk) in some other remote corner of the house so that he also could jabber away to the sound operator. Call this phase two.

At some point, it became possible to have the actual lighting control part of the lightboard located down in the house. This was a huge improvement for the lighting designer because then he could sit behind the board operator and whisper what he wanted done instead of having to wear a headset. The stage manager could sit next to the board operator and give light cues by hand signals or in whispers. By the time the sound designer had figured out how to get his operator down there also, the table was being

described as a *tech table* where the stage manager sat in the middle and gave cues to the sound operator on the one side and the lighting operator on the other side, and this usually replicated the situation in the booth. While the sound and lighting designers mostly sat behind their operators, the director was often driven off and found himself alone with a notepad, a flashlight and a headset (that he would never use unless he wanted to stop the whole rehearsal) in some remote corner of the house where at least it was quiet.

Every theatre gets to decide how many tables they intend to set up in the house and who will be given headsets and lights. The set designer and costume designer by tradition have no one they need to talk to, so they are abandoned in the house to take notes as best they can, providing their own flashlights. The sound and lighting designers typically have a cue-per-page or cue-per-minute and need to talk to their operators almost constantly.

As a purely practical matter, the tables are there to support equipment. If the designers (light and sound) can see the actual, real equipment then they don't need to have any monitors or other simulations and can merely sit behind the operators and take notes or whisper to them without any need for headsets.

TAILING DOWN—This is a seldom-used term that refers to suspending something (a pipe, ladder, trapeze) down from some other hanging position.

TAKING A LEAD—Think of a baseball player part way to the next base as the pitch is delivered. It is said that he "took a lead." In the days of manual and preset boards, it was common practice to slowly sneak partway into the next cue on the standby so that when the go was given, the lights onstage would visually begin to change almost instantly. This only worked if the next cue was a crossfade. It had the effect of warming the filaments of the lamps for the new scene. When it was artfully done, no one was aware of the technique. This is sometimes referred to as *anticipating* the cue, but anticipating the cue suggests that it is taken slightly early while *taking a lead* involves advancing just a tiny bit into the next cue and waiting.

TAKING NOTES— This is in the context of a darkened theatre and is not as easy to do as it sometimes appears it ought to be. If it is a technical rehearsal of some kind, a flashlight or lighted pen is what is needed (the flashlight system requires one hand on the flashlight, one hand on the pen and one hand to hold the notepad whereas the lighted pen combines the light and pen in one hand and is more suited for two-handed people). If it is a preview rehearsal, it will have to be done in the dark. One system involves a small pad with one note being written per page. Another system involves writing a note in each of the 4 margin areas of the program, thus getting four notes to a page. Another method involves keeping one's left thumb at the start location of the next note, but still this limits the number of notes per page to about six.

Notes written in this way, even if they are legible, are not yet entirely readable. While the lighting designer may have written down "library scene needs to be brighter," he needs to translate that at intermission into a form that will make sense to a computer like "Group 4 at 65 in cue 14."

TAP AND DIE SET— This is a very useful electrician's tool for creating a hole in a piece of metal that a bolt can be tightened into (tap) or repairing a bolt that has been cross-threaded and now is reluctant to go into its tapped hole (die). Instrument bolts (or hand wheels with threaded studs) are typically hard to find or expensive or both. A tap and die set allows them to be repaired in a mat-

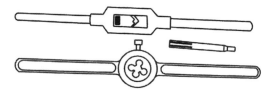

Tap and die set

ter of minutes. When a threaded opening has been damaged beyond repair, it can often be re-tapped for the next larger standard-sized bolt, thus putting the instrument back in service (even if with a deviant bolt).

TAPES, KINDS OF— With the possible exception of photographic slide tape, none of these tapes are exclusively used for lighting purposes but have more general uses. Most of them will need little introduction as they are commonly used in the theatre in the same way they are used in the home or office:

Cellophane (Scotch™) Tape: Used as an expedient to tape gels together and to provide a more durable seal over Avery labels used to mark instrument yokes.

Duct Tape: True duct tape is silver colored and is used commercially on heating ducts. It is mostly used as a cheaper substitute for gaffer's tape (described below), but it is harder to tear off pieces by hand and harder to pick off later.

Electrical Tape: A plastic tape that does not conduct electricity, used to secure wirenuts and cover over any exposed wires and sometimes used to repair wire insulation accidentally cut. In colors other than black, it is used as a marking and color-coding tape to color code wires, cables or instrument yokes.

Friction Tape: A sticky cloth tape once popular for covering splices in electrical wires and providing bulk to the splice. Splices for the most part are only allowed inside electrical boxes and wirenuts have for the most part replaced friction tape.

Gaffer's Tape: A general-purpose cloth tape in black or a dizzying array of colors. It is used to tape down cables or pieces of carpet that cover wires. It is used to attach black foil to lighting instruments. It can also be used to mark instrument yokes or cables.

Masking Tape: Used mostly to label things or to tape over switches or outlets as a reminder that they aren't to be used. There is also a photographic version that comes in a black color and is useful for bundling together in-view cords in a way that they can be separated easily later.

Slide Tape: A silver tape capable of intense heat. It is used to mask areas on a photographic slide or a gobo pattern.

TECHNICAL REHEARSALS— This refers to rehearsals onstage using set, props, lights and sound (but typically not costumes or make-up). These typically run for a whole act without stopping, although the director may stop or not, as he chooses. The rehearsal will also stop if the light or soundboard crashes or malfunctions or if an actor gets hurt, but for the most part all concerned parties write notes. Even when the lightboard is out in the house and the designer is sitting a row back behind it, he will typically take notes rather than interfere with the stage manager's calling of the show unless he actually needs to see a change, in which case he will pick a non-busy time to whisper to the lightboard operator.

TECHNICAL TABLE— See TABLE.

TECHNICIAN— Anyone involved with wiring, electricity or computers. It could either be part of the set-in crew or part of the running crew, usually involving electrics, sound or headsets and communications. Crewmembers involved with props, costumes or the set would not typically be called technicians. Sound and lightboard operators are technicians, as are followspot operators but they would all be more commonly referred to by their job titles, whereas a technician suggests an unknown assistant to somebody.

TEE— See PIPE FITTINGS or SLIDING TEE.

TELESCOPTER— Another name, possibly a tradename, for a manual lift. See HANGING POSITIONS, GETTING TO/CHERRY PICKER.

TEMPLATES (lighting)— (1) These are stencils of lighting instrument symbols in either plan view or side view. They are typically made out of plastic (sometimes cardboard) and are commonly available in ¼ and ½ inch sizes. They are used in manual drafting to place instrument symbols on drawings.

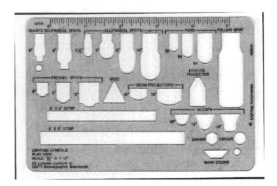

Lighting template

While the symbols attempt to suggest the shape of the instruments, the primary concern is that a drawing pencil be able to follow the pattern in an unbroken path. (2) Gobo patterns are sometimes referred to as templates.

TEMPORARY WIRING— At one time, all wiring to the stage lighting instruments was considered temporary wiring that was run with bundled extension cables. This is still the case in some rental houses. In most modern theatres, there is a distribution system whose attempt is to put circuits where they are needed so that very little temporary wiring is necessary. Temporary wiring now is mostly only needed for lights placed out of range of the common grid locations and practicals on the set that are typically wired from floor or wall pockets. Let's take the case of a practical desk light. When it was found at the second-hand store it had five feet of lamp cord attached with a PB connector. It is often left in this state and its cord is permitted to vanish behind a furniture piece where it goes thru a *rat hole* in the wall or floor and connects to a 16 gauge extension cord that travels under the platforming or behind the set to a wall pocket where it plugs into a fused plugging strip that is connected to a stage circuit (which may require an adapter). Is this safe? Is this legal?

Let's digress to talk about how electricity is used at home. There are convenience outlets everywhere. It is common for the entire upstairs set to be on one 20-amp circuit, where only the circuit breaker and the conduit wire is rated at 20 amps. When a bedside lamp is plugged into an ordinary lamp cord extension cord, what is the weakest link in the system? It, of course, is the 18-gauge lamp cord that is supposedly rated at only 300 watts. Someone who didn't know any better could theoretically plug a 1500-watt steam iron into the same extension cord and while the circuit breaker wouldn't trip, the lamp cord would overheat and could theoretically start a fire. The reason there aren't more house fires caused by this is (1) people do know better and (2) all electrical wiring (but especially lamp cord) is massively underrated in terms of its ampacity since in most circumstances it can carry 1000 watts without even getting warm. If anyone thought this was a problem, they could ban lamp cord (as it has been banned in the theatre) and require that all household extension cords be rated for 20 amps, but none of this is considered that much of a problem in the home.

If this is permitted in the home, why isn't it permitted in the theatre? The NEC has never come up with a set of rules for truly temporary wiring like in the theatre. As a result theatres are theoretically expected to wire things by permanent wiring rules, which means every splice would be in an electrical box and the size of all cords used would be governed by the circuit breaker size on the circuit, i.e. 20 amps.

In answer to the original question, the desk light wiring is safe and it is legal in most places by home rules but not legal by theatre rules. Local fire departments are charged with enforcing building code rules. For the most part, they only write up violations that are in plain sight and clearly dangerous and turn a blind eye to the rest.

TERMINALS (CRIMP-ON) — These are commercially made wire ends, which are made in rings and spades and other shapes that can connect to each other and can be used as low voltage connectors. They are attached by means of a crimping tool, which relies on friction to stay attached.

TERTIARY COLOR — A color derived from mixing three primary colors. In the tri-color system orange and yellow-green would both be considered tertiary colors as yellow is the secondary color that they lie on either side of, and they are a mixture of the secondary and a primary (i.e. three primaries).

TEST-AS-YOU-GO — This is a method typically used at the hanging session in a proscenium house where each pipe is tested to see that each instrument works before it is flown out. In other circumstances, especially in reference to positions that are hard to get to, all the instruments at that position might be tested before the ladder (or other access) was removed. Where there are objections to test-as-you-go, these are usually based on wanting a cold grid for safety. As a purely practical matter, there are so few locations that need to be tested that it is easy enough to bring everyone down off of the ladders while they are being tested, and it will still save time.

TESTERS   See ELECTRICAL TESTERS.

TEXTURE — This is one of the eight variables of light and refers to a light/dark texture as created by a gobo pattern. Unless the image of the lamp filament is a factor, texture always refers to either imperfections in the lens or a gobo pattern.

TH — Abbreviation of TUNGSTEN-HALOGEN LAMPS.

THEATRE BROWN — Everyone always talks about painting everything that shouldn't be seen black, but black is not a particularly visually pleasing color. A very dark brown often produces warmer, more pleasing results.

THEATRICAL CONVENTIONS — Or at least the ones that have some effect on the lighting. There are at least five:

1. **Audience Separation:** It has been traditional for the stage to be lit and the audience to be left in darkness. This has not always been entirely possible throughout history but once it became possible (from

about 1850 onward), it has been done ever since.

2. **End of Scene Convention:** Where a front curtain is present, it is closed to indicate the end of a scene. The lighting often mimics what the curtain does, or in the case of a fast curtain, the lights sometimes blackout as the curtain starts to close. In the absence of a curtain, the lighting is supposed to go to black or to a very low reading to indicate the ends of scenes. Even in theatres that still have curtains, they are not always used for this purpose.

3. **Masking Convention:** This applies only to proscenium theatres, and it requires that stage lighting instruments be concealed from the audience's view. In recent years, this has been relaxed as regards to some front-of-house instruments.

4. **Night Vision Blue Convention:** The use of blue as a color of light to symbolize either a night scene or any other scene where the actors are assumed to have next to no light but the audience is provided with light so that they can see the action. Blue light is also used for scene changes.

5. **Sunnyside Convention:** In theatres where the audience views the action from more than just one side, the directional nature of the lighting is made less pronounced so that no one has the impression that their seats were on a shady (unlit or underlit) side.

THIN WALL CONDUIT— See ELECTRICAL METALLIC TUBING.

THREE-CIRCUIT STRIPLIGHTS— See BORDERLIGHTS, THREE-CIRCUIT. While *striplights* refers to the fact that the units are modular and *borderlights* refer to the overhead position without reference to whether the units are modular or not, the circuiting method is the same.

THREE-WAY TAP— This is the generic term that could apply to all connector types (although it most commonly would refer to a PBG device) to describe a connector with three females outlets, thus allowing three things to be plugged into the same outlet.

THRESHOLD OF BOUNCE— The brightness level at which the light hitting an object will be reflected away with enough strength to throw light on some other object (usually a first row audience member). See BOUNCE LIGHT PROBLEM for a more detailed discussion.

THRESHOLD OF VISIBILITY— The brightness level at which the light hitting an object will allow the audience to see the object adequately. Scientists tend to be interested in the point where one can make out the shape of an object. In the theatre (and at the optometrist), the standard is much higher and it is not uncommon to expect to be able to read print of an appropriate size unless there is a compelling reason why this standard of visibility should be set lower.

THROW—(1) Short for throw distance. (2) In the context of a switch or relay, it refers to how many things each pole can be connected to. Many, if not most, switches have two positions or throws. These usually correspond to on and off, but this is not always the case. An emergency light switch, for example, would merely transfer the load between standard current and battery power.

THROW ANGLE— The angle between the line-of-throw and the nose height plane. The actor's nose is a point in space on a horizontal plane called *nose height* which hovers 5.5' above the floor. The source of light (instrument) is on a horizontal plane usually taken to be a foot above or below the supporting pipe height depending on whether the instrument is overhung or underhung. Light travels in straight lines, so if one were to connect the actor's nose to the source of light, one would have the line-of-throw, and the angle between this line and the nose height plane would be the throw angle.

THROW DISTANCE— The distance between the actor's nose and the source of light.

THRUST LIGHTING— See LIGHTING, KINDS OF.

THUMBSCREW— A bolt with a head that sticks up like a Mohawk haircut to provide a flat surface to grasp so that it can be hand tightened.

THYRATRON TUBE DIMMERS— Also called *Izenour dimmers* after the man who researched their development in the 1940s. They were an electronic variation on the reactance principle of dimming, and they were eventually replaced by SCR dimmers, which were less expensive to purchase and maintain.

TIE LINE— Often this is black Venetian blind cord or black polypropylene seining line, but it can be any cordage that is used to tie up cables to pipes.

TILING— A process of assembling the original of a drawing by taping together smaller pieces. Most commonly this is two letter-sized pages being taped together to create a B-sized drawing, but C or D sized drawings can be tiled together in a like manner. Although copy machines mostly accept B-sized originals with no problem, most computer printers can only print letter or legal size, and wide format printers or dedicated plotters are five to ten times more expensive. When this ceases to be true, tiling, which no one particularly enjoys doing, will go out of fashion overnight. However, when it is artfully done and the result is photocopied, it is almost impossible to tell that the original was taped together.

TILT— This refers to the up/down movement of an instrument, which usually means the body of the instrument is pivoting up and down within the confines of the stationary yoke.

TIME— In the context of computer lightboards, it refers to setting uptime and downtime for each cue (often the same). In the days of preset lightboards and earlier, this was more commonly referred to as the *count*. Now either count or time can be used interchangeably, as in, "What was the count (or time) on cue 14?" Setting the time is also

commonly understood to include follow and wait information as they are related to time.

TIMED FADER— When preset boards were first invented, their crossfaders could only be used manually. As time went on, it became possible to set a time (usually on a rotary switch) and then hit a button so that the machine would take the cue in the set time. This was particularly useful for long fades. In modern usage, the term has lost most of its meaning as all crossfaders now can operate either manually or as a timed fader. It would be more common now to refer to *crossfaders*, *faders* or *fader pairs*.

TINTS, TONES or SHADES— In the context of color mixing, lighter values of a hue are called *tints*, darker values are called *shades* and grayed down colors are called *tones*. In practice, the addition of white or black not only lightens or darkens the color but also makes it less pure at the same time. This is why the color solid tapers to a point as it approaches either the white or black endpoints.

TLG— Abbreviation for *twist lock ground*, one of three kinds of connectors commonly used it the theatre. See CONNECTORS, KINDS OF for a more detailed discussion.

TOGGLE SWITCH— A switch with a handle (the toggle) that has two positions (usually, but not always, on and off). See SWITCHES, KINDS OF for a more detailed discussion.

TONES— See TINTS, TONES or SHADES.

TONING LIGHTS— Groups of colored lights intended to make the entire stage (or part of the stage) appear to be colored or tinged in that color. Toning lights typically come from either directly above or from a steep angle to avoid making the faces a weird color. Although any instrument could be used for this purpose, it was common practice to use the borderlights for this. There was a long period of time, after the use of spotlights as are-alights had become common practice, when no one knew what exactly to do with the rows of borderlights that usually still existed.

They were often used as worklights. If they were still divided into circuits by color, then their blue circuit was used to suggest night scenes and their red or amber circuit was used to augment or tone daytime scenes. In the absence of borderlights, any toning that needs to be done is typically handled by color washes.

TOOLS— When people think about climbing ladders or going aloft in any other way, they usually empty their pockets of everything that would add weight to the climb or that might fall and hit someone else. In addition to a lighting wrench (discussed separately below), a pocketknife is often taken to cut tie line or spread pins on a pin connector, a handkerchief to handle hot things and staunch the blood, some extra tie line in the belt loops and possibly gloves. The tools need to have some kind of safety cords to prevent them slipping thru sweaty fingers. See SAFETY CORDS for a more detailed discussion.

In the context of what to have sent up to repair an instrument that isn't working, this would include (in addition to a spare lamp) a 4-way screwdriver to take apart the connector, a multimeter, a wire-stripper/crimper and a pair of lineman's pliers, which are amazingly good for removing a medium prefocus base from its socket after its bulb portion has been broken or twisted off. If the problem is found to be in the socket, then either the whole instrument or the lamp cap assembly will typically be sent down to the deck for disassembly as sockets are notorious for being made up of tiny component pieces that can fly in all directions. See TROUBLESHOOTING for a more detailed discussion.

TOP-DEAD-CENTER— One of the 26 possible hanging positions on a hypothetical glass sphere (position 25, a downlight). See HANGING POSITIONS, IDEAL for a more detailed discussion.

TOPHAT— One of several lighting add-on accessories. See ACCESSORIES for a more detailed discussion.

TOPLIGHT— A light from position 25, top-dead-center. See HANGING POSITIONS, IDEAL for a more detailed discussion.

TORCH EFFECT— See EFFECTS, KINDS OF.

TORMENTOR INSTRUMENTS— Any instrument that is used at the tormentor position. In the early 1900s when electricity was just finding its way into theatres, the light bridge position just behind the proscenium and the tormentor positions to the two sides were the only openings to get light into a box set that had a ceiling, and so while it was not a very good position, it was one of the best available.

TORMENTOR LIGHTING— See LIGHTING SPECIAL PROBLEMS/Tormentor Lighting.

TOUCH SCREEN— In the context of a computer lightboard, it refers to a location on the lighting console where finger movement on a screen up and down triggers channel levels to move up and down. It often has a coarse/fine setting and is essentially a more refined version of the wheel, which it usually replaces. It may also be sensitive to left-right movement and can control more than just channel levels, especially in the context of intelligent lights.

TOWER— This, of course, is one or more booms or poles linked together in a tower-like structure. Where this has been done, then its purpose is usually to provide a wider more stable footprint with more hanging locations, that does not need to be supported from above. Towers may or may not permit one to climb them directly without using a ladder. They are most commonly used for outdoor events.

Lighting tower

TRACING PAPER— Any drafting paper that is thin enough to see through to the drawing layer below.

TRACING WHEEL—Sometimes called a *pouce* wheel, it is a small tool where a wheel with needle-sharp points rolls over something to mark it with a series of tiny holes. This is used on deep colored gels to provide ventilation. See COLOR MODIFICATIONS for a more detailed discussion.

Tracing wheel

TRACKING—This is a computer lightboard term that refers to a recording process where changes made in the present cue are recorded, and the machine remembers both the original and modified levels of all channels changed. It then makes these same changes in all successive cues where the original channel levels are the same until it encounters a different starting level for any channel, at which point it stops tracking that channel but continues to track the other channels until different levels are encountered for all. See LIGHTING CONTROL, Computer Memory Lightboard for a more detailed discussion.

TRACKSHEET—(1) In hardcopy form, this at one time meant a spreadsheet where columns represent channels and rows represent cues and the data showed the levels of all the channels in any particular cue, but that is now called a *Channel Reading By Cue Sheet* to distinguish it from this next item. (2) In the context of a computer lightboard it now refers to a display mode where the levels of a single channel can be viewed in every cue in the show and edited.

TRANSFORMER—A device that changes the voltage of AC current either up or down. In the theatre 120-volt current is transformed downward to run doorbells, buzzers, telephone ringers, cuelights and certain kinds of sealed beam lamps. It is transformed upward to operate special effects like neon tubes.

TRANSITIONS—See FADES, KINDS OF.

TRANSMISSION PERCENTAGE—This refers to the ability of color filters to transmit light as expressed as a percentage.

TRAPEZE—This is usually a short (2–4 foot) piece of pipe that has been temporarily suspended to serve as a lighting position. In a proscenium situation, they are often hung perpendicular (in plan view) to the other light pipes in the wing areas, and sometimes they are suspended parallel and beneath another light pipe to provide a second, lower hanging position.

TRAPEZOIDING—Sometimes called *keystoning*. When a projector of any kind (ellipsoidal with a gobo pattern or dedicated slide projector) is not perpendicular in all directions (normal) to its projection screen, the image will be distorted. If the gobo pattern is foliage or anything that is intended to be taken out of focus, this may not matter. If it is a French window pattern and is projected on the floor from a golden ring position, then the top of the window will be wide and the bottom narrow (like a keystone) and the sides will slant outward from the bottom up. This is caused by the fact that the top of the image travels further and spreads out more.

Were trapezoiding the only problem, it could be corrected by a custom made pattern that was photographed at the reverse

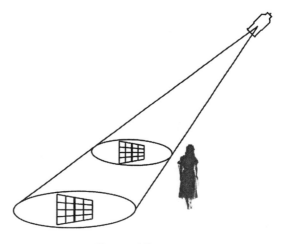

Trapezoiding

angle. Ignore for the moment how expensive this would be and how carefully it would have to be planned and coordinated weeks ahead of time. Even so, it might be worth doing except that there are two other problems. The bottom of the image will be brighter because the light did not have to travel as far (inverse square law), and it will not be possible to get both the top and bottom in focus at the same time, again because the distances are different.

As a purely practical matter, it usually makes most sense to put the middle or top in hard focus because the bottom is going to be brightest and the hardest to blend with the other lights. By putting it out of focus, its hard lines are softened somewhat, which makes the blending easier.

If horizontal lines in the pattern do not appear to be parallel but appear to curve, this is not a result of trapezoiding but is usually caused by the curvature of the lens and is not correctable without a more sophisticated lens train. It can be somewhat lessened by doing what the photographers call *stopping down*, which involves either a gate reducer in the gobo slot or a donut in a gel slot.

TREE— A lighting tree involves a vertical pole with one or more horizontal "branches" (*crossarms*). It most often sits on the floor, but it can be suspended (upside down) from above, in which case it would be more common to call it an *inverted tree*.

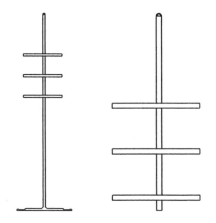

Left: Lighting tree; *right:* Inverted tree

TRESTLE LADDER— The ladder manufacturer's name for an A-ladder. Although there are a lot of these currently still in service, the number of manufacturers that continue to make them has I believe dwindled to just one (*www.LouisvilleLadder.com*).

TRIGONOMETRY— Most lighting calculations involve trigonometry, whether this has been set up on a computer by someone else or whether the lighting designer does the math himself on a pocket calculator. There are compelling reasons why the lighting designer should know how to do the calculations himself. See LIGHTING CALCULATIONS for a more detailed discussion.

TRIM HEIGHT— This refers to the working height of all pipes in a proscenium house. It is set from front to back by sitting in the first row and first setting the height of the teaser, followed by every subsequent pipe. Once the trim height of a masking border has been set, the light pipe behind it cannot come down any lower than what can be seen by the first row audience. Trim heights are crucially important to the lighting designer, and he must insure that the concealed light pipe can light the areas it is supposed to without hitting scenery. If not, then the trim height of the masking borders should be reset to the position that will mask the light pipes, but this is not always possible if they must also mask the scenery in its storage position.

TRIP— This is what circuit breakers do when they are overloaded, and once they have tripped, they need to be *reset*.

TRIPLEX CABLE— A cable composed of three insulated conductors. This is not a term that is heard much anymore.

TROMBONE HANDLE— This refers to a focusing adjustment on a followspot or zoom ellipsoidal that varies the distance between the two lenses of the optical train, thus changing the size of the beam of light.

TROUBLESHOOTING— This usually means that a light won't come on when its channel is brought up. When this happens during the run of a show, it is almost always the lamp.

When it happens during a changeover period, one can't be so sure. There is a four-step process that works every time.

(1) Is there power at the place where the light plugs in? The instrument should be unplugged and a neon tester plugged in instead. In the absence of a neon tester, a neighboring instrument that has already been proved to work could be temporarily plugged in instead. If it lights, then there is power coming to this location, which means that (2) the circuit breaker isn't blown and (3) that the softpatch is correct and (4) there is nothing wrong with the conduit wire.

Most technicians would change the lamp in the instrument at this point and plug it in again. Most of the time, this works.

If it fails, then the problem is either in the wiring of the connector, the wiring of the socket or in the way the socket makes contact with the lamp or the wire. Remove the new lamp and plug in the instrument again and put the test contacts of the neon tester on the two lamp contact points. If there is no light, then the problem is not in the way the lamp contacts connect to the lamp.

Connectors with transparent covers can provide a good indication of whether the problem is within the connector or not. The problem is almost never in the wire itself, which leaves only the socket wiring as the most likely source of the problem.

TROUBLESHOOTING SESSION— After the lights are hung in position, they need to be tested to see that they all work on their assigned channels. While this theoretically could be done as part of the hanging session, it usually isn't. Usually the master electrician and possibly one assistant do this at some subsequent time, often while the carpenters have primary use of the stage. The guiding principal here is that there is no point in keeping a whole crew waiting while two people check out one light. The point is to make sure that all the lights are working for the focusing session.

TROUGH LIGHTS— This refers to the older style of borderlights that were not made up

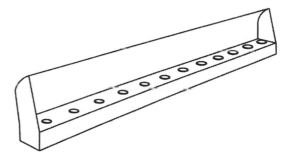

Trough-type borderlight

of modular units but rather were troughs approximately as wide as the stage. While these could be compartmented and have reflectors, the use of the term *trough light* suggests the older uncompartmented troughs that were painted white inside and that used household light bulbs.

TRUNNION— Originally an artillery term referring to the two projections on the sides of cannon, on which it pivots. In the context of a striplight positioned on the floor, the trunnion is the sidepiece that holds the unit slightly above the floor and provides the pivot point. It usually has a bottom plate that can be bolted or screwed to the floor.

TRUSS— This is usually a three or four-pipe composite beam that often incorporates its own plugging positions and is designed to span long distances. Typically the instruments are hung and plugged into this in advance and then it is hoisted into position by chain motors (or other means) onstage.

TUBE LIGHTS— Also called *rope lights*, these are small lights about an inch apart inside what looks like a 3/8" shower hose. They usually come in 12–18' lengths and can be hooked together end to end. They are waterproof and can be walked on and the tube comes in colors (red, blue, green, yellow and clear being the most common). They can be used to mark aisles or walkways and can be used to write with light (and are better for this purpose than miniature Christmas lights that are typically a foot apart and harder to work with).

TUNGSTEN-HALOGEN (Abbr. TH)— This refers to a lamp that has a tungsten filament and the glass envelope is filled with a halogen-type gas to prevent the blackening of the lamp. They are now considered the standard of the industry.

TWIN CABLE— A cable made up of two individually insulated conductors. This is not a term that is heard much anymore, and there aren't many uses for cables that only have two conductors, but it might be encountered in an older book.

TWIST-LOCK CONNECTORS— Special connectors that are supposed to resist disconnecting because they "twist-to-lock." See CONNECTORS, KINDS OF for a more detailed discussion.

TWO-FERS and THREE-FERS— This is a system to attach two or three instruments to the same circuit outlet. There used to be a commercially available stagepin multiple connector that would accept up to three males, but it was expensive, so it became more practical to create two-fers and three-fers in the field (often from wiring kits). There are two different styles:

Spoke-Style: Connects all wire sets to the male connector and attaches a single female to all the 18–36" spokes. If the plug-in point is halfway between the two instruments to be plugged, this is an ideal arrangement. In a situation where three 750-watt instruments are connected to a single 20-amp circuit, each spoke will carry 750 watts and it is only the male connector of the three-fer that has to carry the full 2250-watt load, but by code all the cabling will be 12 gauge and rated for the full load anyway.

Daisy-Chain Style: Connects a male and a female connector to the first wire set and the second wire set connects the second female to the first. If there were a third female, it would connect to the second, and so forth. This is most useful in situations where the first instrument is close to the plug-in point and the second and subsequent points are further away. In a situation where three 750-

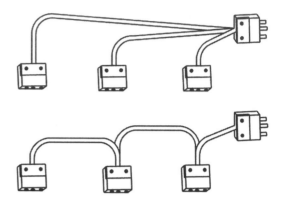

Top: Spoke-style three-fer; *bottom:* Daisy-chain style three-fer

watt instruments are connected to a 20-amp circuit, the last female carries 750 watts, the middle one carries 1500 and the first one carries the full 2250-watt load, but since all the cabling will be 12 gauge and rated for the full load, this won't make a difference.

TYPE (of cue)— In the context of a computer lightboard, this is a command and frequently the name of a button that sets the kind of cue, i.e. crossfade, effect, blocking etc. See LIGHTING CONTROL/Computer Memory Lightboards for a more detailed discussion.

ULTRAVIOLET LIGHT— Also called *black light*, it is electromagnetic energy of wavelengths shorter than can be perceived by the human eye. When it is aimed at certain surfaces, the non-visible ultraviolet light is absorbed and a visible light is reflected, much in the same way that short wave light radiation can enter through a car windshield and can be transformed into long wave heat radiation that cannot escape back through the glass, thus making the car 150 degrees when the outside temperature is only 90 degrees (greenhouse effect). Incandescent sources typically produce very little blue light and as a result do not do as well producing ultraviolet light as do fluorescent (mercury vapor) lights which have a much higher blue content. Sources of ultraviolet for the theatre are typically unable to filter out all the visible light, and as a result the light appears to be a deep blue-purple rather than invisible.

UNDERHUNG— In reference to a lighting instrument, the yoke forks point downward and the instrument does not defy gravity. Unless otherwise specified on a Light Plot, all instruments are assumed to be underhung. See YOKING for a more detailed discussion.

UNDERWRITERS' LABORATORY— This is an independent testing organization that tests electrical components. Most local codes require that all devices used onstage be UL approved, which effectively eliminates any homemade lighting equipment, which once used to be permitted but now isn't.

UNION (labor)— Mostly this refers to IATSE, the International Association of Theatre and Scenic Employees. Actors and stage managers are covered under the Actors Equity Association. Designers are covered by the United Scenic Artists, and directors are covered under the Society of Stage Directors and Choreographers.

UNIPLUG— Where this term is used, it usually refers to a patch panel connector that only has one conductor.

UNISTRUT— This is a tradename for a kind of c-shaped steel extrusion that looks very much like a traveler track. It has special fittings that allowed objects like lighting instruments to be hung along its length. At one time it was thought by some that this system or something very similar, would replace instruments hanging on round pipes, but this has not happened.

UNITED STATES INSTITUTE OF TECHNICAL THEATRE (USITT)— A national organization devoted to providing national and international standards in stagecraft, they publish a quarterly journal for their members, *Theatre Design and Technology*. They host an exposition each year somewhere in North America, which most major manufacturers attend and display their wares. Around the time of the exposition (early spring), their website will list the web addresses or a means of contacting all exhibitors. They also have created a library of common lighting instrument symbols. Their web site also provides links to many other organizations and businesses. They are one of the best places to find current manufacturers or suppliers. (*www.usitt.org*), the other source being *Lighting Dimensions* magazine (*www.etecnyc.net*).

UNITS (lighting)— A term usually reserved for something that produces light that is neither a practical nor an instrument. Disco effects used to project shafts or sparkles of light across a dance floor would fall into this category, as would a moonbox or a lighted sign or a laser (or other device) used to create a Tinkerbell effect.

UNIVERSAL JOINT— Cliplights have universal joints. A universal joint is any joint that allows movement in four directions: up/down and left/right, and it usually involves some kind of ball moving against friction in a cup-like clamp.

UPDATE— In the context of a computer lightboard, this is a command and frequently a button name that records changes to one particular cue or input source in the event that there is a pile-on situation. See LIGHTING CONTROL/Computer Memory Lightboards for a more detailed discussion.

UPLIGHT— Any light from below that is pointed upward. It is the opposite of *downlight*, but it is much more rare to have lights from below, as it is not as naturally occurring an angle for light.

UPSTAGING— This refers to an actor who is not supposed to be the focus of the scene doing something which draws focus away from where it was intended to be. It is not looked upon favorably, and either the director or the stage manager or another actor will usually tell the offender to quit doing it. It is often used to illustrate that the stage lighting has very little to do with where the audience will look because otherwise upstaging would have ceased to exist long ago, but upstaging does still exist and the lighting is completely powerless to control where the audience will look when its attention is being drawn away from the stage action by something distracting happening somewhere else.

UPTIME— This is a computer lightboard term that refers to the time it takes those channels that are increasing in a transition to reach their new levels. In most cues, uptime and downtime will be the same.

USITT— Abbreviation for the UNITED STATES INSTITUTE OF TECHNICAL THEATRE.

UV LIGHT— See ULTRAVIOLET LIGHT.

VALUE— One of the three perceivable properties of color, this refers to the darkness of a color as it is compared to a grayscale. See COLOR for a more detailed discussion.

VARIABLE-FOCUS— See LIGHTING INSTRUMENTS/Lensed Instruments/Zoom Ellipsoidals.

VARIABLES OF LIGHT— Also called the *properties of light*. Basically the question is how many ways can the light produced by two instruments be different from each other. It could be a different color, come from a different place, be in hard focus or soft-focus and so forth.

There are actually eight variables. ACID TESS is an acronym for remembering them all.

A stands for *angle* and refers to the direction at which the light hits the subject. This is usually described in terms of one of the 26 ideal hanging positions. See HANGING POSITIONS, IDEAL for a more detailed discussion.

C stands for *color*. See COLOR for a more detailed discussion.

I stands for *intensity*, meaning brightness. See BRIGHTNESS for a more detailed discussion.

D stands for *distance*, meaning the throw distance. Distance is often ignored because once the architect has decided upon ceiling heights and located the hanging positions it is often not a variable for the individual lighting designers. None the less, lights that are hung far away produce a very soft light that is very different from (and that can't be duplicated by) lights hung close. See DISTANCE for a more detailed discussion.

T stands for *texture*, which refers to something created by a gobo pattern or a really bad lens system as on a PAR lamp. See TEXTURE for a more detailed discussion.

E stands for *edge-quality and evenness*, which refers to hard or soft focus and the way in which the light is distributed across the pool of light (which includes cosine distribution and its opposite which has no name but involves a hot center spot). See EDGE-QUALITY for a more detailed discussion.

SS refers to *size* and *shape* of the light. The light size is fixed on a standard ellipsoidal, but adjustable on a fresnel or zoom ellipsoidal. The shape of the light produced can be changed by the barndoors on a fresnel and by the framing shutters or gobo on an ellipsoidal. See SIZE and SHAPE for a more detailed discussion.

These last four (texture, edge quality & evenness, size and shape) are often lumped together and referred to as *choice of instrument* or *distribution*, but neither term really conjures up specifically what is actually going to be different.

Whenever there is a light cue, one or more of these variables will change. Although lightboards mostly control only the intensity of a light or a group of lights (we're ignoring intelligent lights for the moment), by replacing one group of lights with another complete set that are a different color or have a different focus or whatever, it is possible to achieve the effect of having changed any one of the other variables. Sometimes this *movement* of light resulting from a light cue is mistakenly considered to be a variable also, but it is not a variable in the context described here which is to say a difference between two static lights.

VEEING PROBLEM— Also called *scalloping.* When borderlights or cyc footlights are placed close to the surface (like the sky cloth) that they will light, they often don't have enough space for the cones of light to have met and blended yet. As a result, there is a visible "vee" coming from each compartment. Both Louis Hartmann and Stanley McCandless talk about this problem. There is no problem with borderlights that are used as acting area downlights because they typically have plenty of distance in which to blend.

The solution to this problem would be obvious if the problem were presented in a slightly different way. Let us say the plan is to use individual floodlights instead of a striplight and let's say these individual floodlights have been placed on the floor at 30" intervals. There will, of course, be veeing. Ask any first year student how to fix this, and he will tell you that the floods need to be moved closer together. When striplights are used at close range like this, all three circuits should obviously be the same color. If more colors are needed, then more lines of striplights are needed. There is little point in using a three-color system if none of the colors looks acceptable, used alone or in any combination.

VERTICAL ANGLE— More commonly called the THROW ANGLE.

VERTICAL ELEVATION— The distance between the nose plane and the source of light. The source of light is usually assumed to emanate from a foot below the pipe for underhung instruments and a foot above for overhung instruments. The nose plane is the height of the actors' noses, which is taken to be 5'6" for adults and is the aim point for the lights.

VIEWING AN EVENT (mechanics of)— This is a discussion of the various factors involved in making it possible for the audience members to see over the heads of other audience members. The choices that are made in this regard have a profound effect on the ability to then light the performers.

Everyone is familiar with raised stages and raised audience seating but few people actually understand how it works, much less understand the subtle differences intrinsic to viewing different kinds of events.

There are two important factors to be considered: the eye-level of the performers in relation to the first row of audience and the height that succeeding rows of audience would need to be raised to see over these heads in front of them (i.e. the height from eyeballs to top of head—usually taken to be 4–6"), but as will be explained below this will vary or, at least, should vary based on the eyelevel height.

The general rule is that either the performers should be raised or the audience but not both, as raising both just recreates the current situation at a slightly higher altitude. The raising can be by means of steps or ramps, and both have been used at various times in history for both audience and performers. Current practice is to use steps out in the house (movie theatres use ramps out in the house).

Fact 1: When the audience is seated, their heads tend to be more nearly at the same height compared to when they are standing. Look at any posed photographic portrait if you doubt this, and you will see the heads of those seated in front are more-or-less evenly aligned while those standing behind will be at greater, varying heights. In Shakespeare's day, the *groundlings* stood. They would have been able to see better had they been seated. In a modern theatre that has *standing room,* it is traditional for it to be only one row deep, and this is one of the reasons why.

Fact 2: When the rows of audience are staggered, one can look between the shoulders of the people in front rather than attempting to see over their heads. When people crowd around something, they instinctively, or by habit, are looking for a gap between heads through which to look. In a standing crowd, if the first row changes their body position to see something better, then the row behind them has to readjust, as does every other row behind as they all try to find a new gap between heads. In a seated crowd where the seats are in a fixed and staggered position, no one will be able (or need) to change position

Fact 3: The more the audience is looking down on an event, the higher their row has to be in relation to the row in front. Conversely, the more the audience is looking up at the event, the less the seating has to be raked. In a movie theater, where the screen starts at about 8–12 feet off the floor, it is not uncommon for the first 15 or 20 rows to be on flat (or nearly-flat) floor because everyone is looking up and the heads in front are not at all in the line-of-sight. As the rows progress toward the back, the rake has to become steeper as the audience eye-level becomes more nearly level with the screen, because the audience members increasingly need to see over the heads in front. In a movie theater where everyone is looking up at the action, increasing the height of each row by 4" is often more than enough. In a live theatre where the first row of audience tends to be more nearly level with the performers, the rows need to be raised at least 6–8" and sometimes more. It is not at all uncommon in a balcony situation for the feet of one row to be more-or-less at the shoulder height of the row in front as they all look downward. Another factor that affects this is the legroom or distance between rows. When the audience is squeezed together with about the same legroom as a Greyhound bus, then less height is needed to see over the heads in front because the heads are closer together, and with expanded legroom the reverse is true.

Fact 4: Given a choice between raising the stage or raising the audience, raising the audience is generally more effective for events that occur in depth. Boxing and wrestling matches can raise the stage because the area is small and confined. Baseball, football, basketball, hockey and live theatre occur over too great an area for a raised playing area to be effective. The movie theater looking-up configuration only worked because the movie was a completely flat, two-dimensional event

that had no depth. If one were to put a live actor on an 8–12 foot high stage, he would vanish from view almost instantly as he moved upstage because the front row's view would be cut off by the front edge of the stage. Also, anyone standing upstage would be blocked by the objects and actors in front of them. It is possible to have platforms on the stage that get higher as they go back (raking the stage), which would in part solve this problem, but this would only work if the audience viewed the action from the front only, which producers are reluctant to do nowadays as it decreases the potential number of patrons that can be seated for any one performance.

The most common solution is to put the feet of the first row audience at same height as the stage floor and install a *modesty wall* in-between, or raise the stage just enough to create a sense of separation that does not invite audience members to stretch their legs onto the stage, which in either case puts the first row eye-level at the same height as a seated actor and about 2 feet below that of a standing actor. From a producer's point of view, more audience can be seated if their knees are hard up against the edge of the stage and if the first row is as low as possible in relation to the stage as this creates more rows that look up which reduces the amount of rake and overall height at the back of the house.

This from a lighting standpoint is the worst possible scenario as it almost certainly ensures that the first several rows of audience will be lit as brightly or almost as brightly as the stage itself. It would benefit the lighting designer enormously if there were a generous 4 or 5 foot wide walkway between audience and stage with the first audience row raised up some 8 or 9 inches, creating a light moat to catch spill light and thus keep it out of the house. Some theatres are set up this way. Most are not.

In live theatre situations the audience will mostly be looking either levelly, or down, on the action, which allows them to see forward and back movement on the stage floor. Obviously, the more one looks down on the action, the more one sees the tops of heads rather than the fronts of faces, which is why balcony seats are typically cheaper.

Fact 5: The human eye can only make out facial features up to about 50 feet away. See VISIBILITY and OPERA GLASSES TEST for a more detailed discussion. In any event the quality of the view degrades, as the audience gets further away.

Fact 6: If visibility drops off at about 50 feet, more audience can be crowd into good seats by allowing the audience to more nearly encircle the playing area, as would be the typical arrangement at a sporting event. See the Introduction for a more detailed discussion of the various configurations of theatres that seat audience on more than just one side.

Lest there be any confusion, the lighting designer is expected to keep light out of the house (*audience separation*). This is often the second most important thing expected after lighting the action on the stage so the audience can see it. There will be times, however, when it won't be possible to do both. Experienced lighting designers, as one of their first orders of business, before they meet with the director for the first time, usually want to examine in detail any new theatre they have not worked in before (*measuring the stage*) so that they can discuss potential lighting problems. In addition to looking at all the light hanging locations they are particularly interested in *how far back from the stage* and *how high* the first row of seating is in relation to the stage because this is a good indicator of how hard it will be to keep spill out of the house.

Also when the lighting designer finally gets a chance to view his lighting from various parts of the house, he needs to know where to spend his valuable, but limited, time. The show as seen from the balcony usually looks great because the audience is looking down on something lit from above, and while they may only be able to see tops of heads, the heads will be spectacularly well lit. The first rows of the orchestra are a completely different situation because the audience is now looking up at something lit from above, and the lack of any light coming from their viewing direction causes the actors to appear to have raccoon eyes, which is to say black holes where their eyes should be because the light from above is not getting into the eye sockets.

VISIBILITY— This is the primary, some would say the only, function of stage lighting. Light is the catalyst for human vision and vision cannot exist without it, but light is not the only necessary component. Visibility has four essential components, the absence of any one of which will cause vision to fail. Three of these are related to lighting; one is not.

The first component is **distance**. Let's assume that someone is waving good-bye to you as you drive away. There will be a point at which you won't be able to tell if they are still there anymore. There will have been an earlier point at which you weren't able to tell which of your friends, man or woman, it might have been who was waving, and there would have been a still earlier point at which your view of their face had degraded to the point where you couldn't tell if they were happy or sad to see you go. It is this last point that we are interested in for theatrical purposes. The last row of audience should not be further away than this. For most people this occurs at about 50 feet away, and this is the distance at which the vast majority of normally sighted people can make out print that is an inch high. There are people who think this distance should be closer to 30 feet, and others who think perhaps 100 feet is closer to the ideal. Everyone (certainly anyone hoping to work as a lighting designer) needs to do this test for themselves and reach their own conclusion. It is especially critical that the lighting designer know if he is normally sighted or not, because he will be designing for a normally sighted audience. Having arrived at a determination of where the last row should be, it will become evident that there are many theatres and opera houses, especially, where this distance has been exceeded. If you have heard of opera glasses and wondered how they got their name, you have but to sit in the back of one of these large theatres and you will instantly understand both their purpose and their popularity. The lighting designer is not responsible for audience members who can't see because they have been seated too far away for visual acuity. There is a direct correlation between how far away one is and how well one will see. The closer one is to the action, the better one will see, and this is completely unrelated to the lighting.

The second component is that there must be **enough light present to see by**. Considering that one can read by candlelight and that candlelight was for hundreds of years the standard for indoor lighting, this is a condition easily met at levels well below 5 footcandles (Stanley McCandless' minimum). Using the example of 1" print that we know can be read at distances up to 50 feet, were you to stand a foot away from a print sample in a darkened theatre with a candle in your hand, you would easily be able to read it in the approximate 1 fc of light present. If you were then to move a foot back from it, it would be only a quarter as bright (inverse square law). At another foot back it would be only a sixteenth of a footcandle bright, and you probably could not read it anymore because of lack of light. So the threshold of visibility would occur for you (and other normally-sighted people) at a fraction of a footcandle. Were you to set the candle a foot from the 1" print, you should be able to back up all the way to 50 feet and still be able to read the print, as it is the distance between the light and the object that makes the difference, not the distance from the object to the audience member, which is discussed in more detail in relationship to the EYE.

The human eye can see in conditions that are 10,000 times brighter than a single candle (noon on the equator on the brightest day of the year) and in conditions that are 10,000 times dimmer (starlight on an exceptionally dark night) but a single candle is the midrange of our vision. It is also the point at which we lose color perception and also the point at which the stage becomes too dark to play a scene in. When the scientists say that we can see in conditions 10,000 times dimmer than candlelight, they mean that we can "see movement" at these levels. In very dark conditions, the pupils of our eyes are opened to their widest extent. At about 20 fc, they begin to close and this continues up until 10,000 fc when they are as closed down as they can get.

We have an idiom in the language to the effect that, "If you want to see better you need to put more light on the subject." There is a brief period after the threshold of visibility has been reached where putting more light on the subject allows us to see better, then there is a long middle period where increasing levels simply mean our eyes have to adjust more to compensate, and finally at a level that is thunderingly bright, adding more light will have the reverse effect, and it will make the thing that needs to be seen, more difficult. Do remember that sunglasses were invented to help people see better by limiting the amount of the incoming light.

How much light is too much? Certainly by the time that sunglasses are being talked about, we are far advanced into the "too much" range. Some would say that as soon as the eyes begin to close down it is because there has been too much light. There are however two things that need to be said at this point. First, we expect the amount of light in the scene (scene level) to reflect the time, place and situation of the scene. There is no point in arguing that one can read the labels on the cans in 10 fc of light if this is supposed to be taking place in the sunlight. On the plus side, we have a very poor ability to recall the actual look of a sunlit day, so while a real sunlit day might really be 5000 fc bright, we are prepared to accept as credible a 70 fc substitute. Second, there are many theatrical problems that are lessened when the light levels can be kept low. Chief among these are the Bounce Light Problem, the Glare Problem, the White Color Problem and Raccoon Eyes Problem.

The third component of visibility is commonly called **plasticity,** which means that objects will look three-dimensional. This is achieved by the direction and color of the light or lights. Let's suppose one is 30 feet away from the subject, and the light level is 20 fc but coming from behind. The distance is within range, and there is an adequate quantity of light, but the face can't be seen because the light is coming from the wrong angle (behind). Having the light come from the front won't be that much of an improvement. The human face has hills and valleys. In order to be seen from a distance, the hills have to look different from the valleys. In real life, they look different because some are in direct light and others are in a dimmer reflected light. In the theatre as well as in painting, the shade or valleys will be in a different color. This idea that the hills have to be a different color from the valleys is both the guiding principle of stage make-up and stage lighting, and this can either be done in a realistic way or it can be exaggerated, as is the case when psychedelic colors are used. Adolphe Appia called it *plasticity* and everyone else has either used his word or explained that three-dimensional objects need, through the use of shade and shadow, to appear to be three-dimensional.

The fourth and last component of visibility is **contrast.** While the human eye can see in a wide range of brightness levels, it can only see at one eye adjustment setting if the contrast remains in the range of about 20:1. The pupil always adjusts to the brightest light present in order to protect the sensitive retina of the eye from damage. Actually, the pupil only has about a 16:1 adjustment factor, so it is simply the first (and most recognizable) of a series of internal sensitivity changes made by the rods and cones. Also, the 20:1 contrast range varies and is closer to 10:1 at the extreme low end and closer to 1000:1 at extreme top end of the visual range, but neither extreme is likely to be encountered in the theatre, so for our purposes 20:1 is sufficiently accurate.

When one encounters an oncoming car at night on a country road, its headlights will cause a sensation of glare and will seem exceptionally bright because the eyes have been adjusted for nighttime driving. Were one to encounter a line of cars with their headlights on during the daytime, it might go unnoticed because at that point the eyes would be adjusted for the brighter conditions of daytime driving. The actual light from the oncoming headlights would still be equally as bright and aimed the same way, but it would be experienced differently.

In situations where visibility is a problem, it is usually a contrast problem where taking down the level of certain lights will improve it and where bringing up the level of the scene as a whole is almost certain to make it worse. The idiom that ought to be in the language, but won't ever be, is that if you want to see better, you need to turn down the lights.

I once saw a scene that had been lit by a single metal halide fixture placed top-dead-center, more-or-less like the sun at noon lighting the earth. We all reached for our sunglasses. The actor was within visual range, the amount of light present was certainly many times more than enough, the plasticity requirement was fulfilled by the presence of an incredible amount of bounce light and because of the bounce there weren't any contrast problems. Had the lighting designer achieved visibility? He resoundingly had. Unfortunately in the theatre, we are not merely striving for visibility alone. We are striving for something that is commonly called "selective visibility," which is discussed next.

VISIBILITY, SELECTIVE— In theatrical situations, it is seldom desirable to light everything to a single uniform brightness, as might be the objective when lighting the workstations on a factory floor. Some objects may be rendered fully visible (one would be able to read printed words as described previously), other objects would be rendered partially visible, and still others would be kept in relative darkness. This is relative to the general level of the scene. It is clearly more possible to leave things in darkness in dark scenes than it is where the scene level is higher as in daytime scenes. Full visibility in absolute terms is often achieved at levels below 10 fc. At levels higher than this the pupil in the eye often simply closes down to admit less light, which provides the same level of visibility.

It is comparatively easy to throw enough light at the stage to cross the threshold of visibility, but it requires extraordinary skill to be able to light one actor while keeping the person next to him in darkness. The art of stage lighting lies in this ability to place light only in those places where it is wanted. Of the places that are intended to remain in darkness, the house where the audience sits is usually at the top of the list. Whenever the audience sees a scene that seems partially obscured, it is usually the result of a deliberate choice.

If the scene were set in the middle of a vast ocean, vast desert or vast anything, then evenness of lighting might be just the way to best present the monotony of the circumstances. For most theatrical situations, just the reverse is what is typically called for. The sun streams in through the windows making one side of the room brighter and a slightly different color. When the fireplace is lit, the actors get dimmer as they move away from it. This is commonly called *dramatic interest*, and it refers to the ability of the lighting to make one big stage look like a lot of smaller related areas. It accentuates the movement of the actors. One of the reasons why fluorescent lights for home use failed so miserably (when first introduced at the New York Exhibition in 1938) was because of the evenness of their light that washed out the pockets of interest created by table and floor lamps.

Stanley McCandless said that the imagination was more completely awakened by the mere suggestion of dimly lit forms, and Louis Hartmann compared flooding the stage with light to the idea that if a spoonful of medicine was good, then taking the whole bottle

would be even better. Both understood the dangers of using too much light.

After a half century of having followspots follow the speaking actors around the stage, it suddenly became possible with theatre spotlights to light the stage both better and more brightly. The point of the followspots had not been to direct the eye of the audience to what they should be looking at, as some have suggested, but to put the only adequate light available on the action so that the audience could see. When the practice ceased and the followspots got packed away, it became traditional to then reduce the amount of lighting in unused parts of the stage. The unused areas would still look lit but just not as brightly lit, and this is another reason why the stage is selectively lit.

VISORS— One of several lighting add-on accessories. See ACCESSORIES for a more detailed discussion.

VISUAL CUE— A cue that is triggered by something visual happening rather than something heard, like an actor turning on light switch. In situations where the visual cue is as visible to the lightboard operator as it is to the stage manager, the board operator may be allowed to take the cue by himself. Although the stage manager will typically give a warning and stand-by, he will either not say "go" at all, or he will give a "go" with the understanding that it is just to make sure that the cue was executed.

VOLT— A measure of electromotive force, named after the Italian scientist, Count Alessandro Volta (1745–1827).

VOLTAGE DROP— The ability of electric wire to carry current depends on the temperature and on the cross-section of the wire and on the length of the wire. In normal circumstances, the temperature and the length of the wire are ignored and only the gauge is taken into account. In situations where the cable runs are long (as to the front-of-house), then larger wire may have to be used to prevent a drop in voltage, which would cause the lights to be dimmer. Both the electrical code and most simplified wiring books contain tables indicating the maximum permissible length for various gauge wires loaded to various capacities.

VOLTMETER— Another name for a *multimeter*. See ELECTRICAL TESTERS for a more detailed discussion.

VOM— Abbreviation for a volt, ohm, meter, commonly called a *multimeter*. See ELECTRICAL TESTERS for a more detailed discussion.

WAIT TIME— Sometimes called *delay*, it refers to a situation where two cues (or two parts of the same cue) are launched by a single push of the go button. A wait delays the launch of the second cue by a fixed amount of time. When applied to the uptime and downtime of a single cue, the wait time can often be applied to either part, so that one could have either an uptime wait or a downtime wait.

WALKERS— These are production assistants brought in on dry tech night or during a level-setting session to stand where the actors would normally stand, and thus, for at least one night, they fulfill Gordan Craig's dream of replacing actors on the stage with *Übermarionettes*. The problem is that no one ever remembers exactly where all the actors usually stand in any given scene. There are almost never enough walkers for there to be one for every actor onstage, so the overall look of the stage cannot successfully be evaluated. They have different facial coloring, they aren't wearing costumes, they are slow, they have short attention spans and using them can add hours to an otherwise short rehearsal. Time spent lighting them is almost always wasted, and since most lighting designers know this, they are mostly used at the request of the director.

WALKPATH— This refers to where the actors' feet would need to be to keep his face in the light.

WALL BRACKET— A metal angle iron designed to provide a hanging position for an instrument on a wall. This was a vintage method of securing a single instrument to a wall that was typically sheathed in wood. Now it is more common to have walls sheathed in plasterboard. It would be more common now to put horizontal 1x3 straps on the wall or a rectangle of plywood that could span from stud-to-stud and to which a carriage bolt had been added to provide a way to hang the instrument.

WALL COVES— A recess in the sidewalls of the house to accommodate a lighting boom.

WALL POCKET— A recessed receptacle in the wall. See POCKET for a more detailed discussion.

WARM COLOR— Warm colors are those found in flames or embers (i.e. red, orange, yellow). The cool colors are the opposite and include greens and blues and some violets. When a green color becomes too yellow, it becomes a warm color. The same thing happens when a violet color (shortest wavelength spectral color which by definition has no red in it) gets enough red in it to look like magenta. Whether a color is warm or cool is to some degree a matter of personal judgment, but it is affected by what other colors it is seen next to. Surprise Pink is usually used as an example of this ability to change from warm to cool (or visa versa) because it appears warm when seen along with blue colors and appears cool when seen with reds and oranges.

WARMING-THE-FILAMENTS— If the filaments in the lamps are cold, then when current is first applied, there will be a noticeable lag before any light becomes visible. When the filaments are kept warm, the response time is almost instantaneous. In the days of manual lightboards, it was common at the start of a cue to bump the master up to a level of about 4 and as the filaments warmed up, the light onstage would appear to dim up, and as that happened the operator would then continue the fade manually. With preset boards, it was possible to very slowly begin sneaking in the lights for the new scene so that when the cue was called, the filaments would already be warm. On a computer board, this is typically done by partially piling-on the next cue on top of the present cue until the new cue readings just start to show (usually at levels below 05). This composite is then re-recorded as the present cue. Some lightboards can do a variation of this semi-automatically, but whereas most stage lights can be set at 01 or 02 and show no light, this is often not true for practical lights that will often appear to ghost at 01 or 02, so it is not possible for this to be done entirely automatically.

WARNING— This is the first announcement of an upcoming cue. It is followed by a *standby* and a *go*. See CUES, CALLING OF for a more detailed discussion.

WASH OUT—(1) The effect of strong colors are washed out (lessened) by the addition of neutral colored lights that have the appearance of white light. (2) Shadows are washed out (lessened) by applying direct lighting to the surface. Most stage instruments produce shadows, which are clearly visible when the instrument is seen alone. When the shadows are seen in the context of all the other stage lights, all shadows tend to get washed out.

WASHES (color)— One or more instruments of the same color used to cover either the whole stage or a portion of the stage. The instruments typically all come from the same direction and are of the same type. In open staging situations, "from the center outward" and "from the perimeter inward" are considered to be directions for the purposes of this discussion. Each color wash is also considered to be a *system* of lights.

WATER EFFECT— See EFFECTS, KINDS OF.

WATT— A unit of power, named after James Watt, a Scottish scientist (1736–1819).

WAVELENGTH— In the context of color, the wavelength (or dominant wavelength) determines the color. Each spectral color has been found to have a wavelength range.

WEST VIRGINIA FORMULA— Another name for the *power formula*. See ELECTRICITY.

WHEELS— In the context of a computer lightboard, this refers to a method of setting levels by rolling a wheel up or down. By imagining a handle attached to the wheel, it is easy to see that *up* means rolling the wheel away from the operator and *down* means rolling toward the operator. A wheel is uniquely useful for capturing all the channels onstage and rolling them upward until something touches full. This creates the brightest possible version of the original cue, and it would not be uncommon to record this as both a *sub* and a *group* and use it as a building block for cue setting purposes, as it has great flexibility.

WHIPPING or WHIPPING TAPE— Whipping refers to treating the ends of ropes or cordage so that they will not unravel. This used to be done with whipping cord, which was wound around the end, but it is now more common to use plastic tape like electrical tape (sometimes masking or gaffer's tape) for this purpose.

WHITE COLOR PROBLEM— This is a problem that relates to making the actors' faces the most brightly lit object on stage. The problem is this: when the faces are seen against a background of white or any color that is lighter than the skin tones, then the white (or lighter color) reflects more light and appears to be brighter. When more light is applied, the face gets brighter and so does the background, so it becomes a problem, which, once it has started, cannot be fixed by the lighting designer. White shirts or costumes around the face are particularly troublesome. Often the addition of a vest or shawl can cut the expanse of white enough to prevent it being objectionable.

A huge white stucco wall or the sail of a ship would be of concern. If there is a balcony that looks down on the action, then a light colored floor will be the background against which they see faces.

Often times, the whites can be grayed down by dyeing, but there are dramatic situations where white is simply called for and cannot be avoided. Wedding dresses, doctors and nurses, scenes that take place in the snow are all examples where the color white has to be used, but in all cases it makes the faces significantly harder to see. If the background color approaches skin tone color, then the scenery is said to have *eaten* the faces, and from a distance it can truly look as if the faces are a moving part of the background wall or floor. See SKIN TONES, LIGHTING OF for a more detailed discussion.

WHITE LIGHT— Any light that, like the sun, appears to be colorless.

WHITE LIGHTERS— A colloquial term to describe anyone who believes that light in the theatre should be absolutely colorless white light. Bertolt Brecht is usually credited with being the first to espouse this idea. In plays lit only by white light, scenes have to be differentiated by brightness and plasticity has to be provided by level differences, which makes most scenes look amazingly alike, and it puts some of the audience members on the shady side of the action, where they are rarely happy.

Frequently, this is an over-reaction to a previous experience where the lighting designer used overly strong colors, which called attention to the lighting and distracted the audience from the action of the play. The use of tints in the lights, allows most of the advantages of using color without losing the sense of the light being colorless, which is often the objective in realistic plays. See APPEARANCE OF WHITE LIGHT for a more detailed discussion.

WHITE WIRE— A normal female connector has three slots or holes, each connected to a different color of wire. The hole connected to the white wire is the neutral wire, and not the one that will produce a potentially life-ending shock. For stagepin connectors, it will be the hole closest to the center prong. In terms of either parallel-

blade-ground or twist lock, when looking at the male with the grounding prong on the bottom, it will be the one on the right and visa-versa for the female. Often they will make this easier by making the male prong silver-colored or wider or both.

WIGGLIES or WIGGLY LIGHTS— Colloquial for moving lights in general and specifically for the newer moving head types. See INTELLIGENT LIGHTS.

WINDOW BACKING, LIGHTING OF— See LIGHTING SPECIAL PROBLEMS/Window Backings.

WING ENTRY, LIGHTING OF— See LIGHTING SPECIAL PROBLEMS/Wing Entries.

WING WASHES— Also called *leg washes*, these are lights directed at the vertical scenic legs. If the wing pieces are painted as they often are, these lights will both illuminate the wing pieces themselves and the area directly in front, which is often an actor entrance. Where the legs are simply nondescript masking, the leg washes are really wing entry lighting and would be handled slightly differently. See LIGHTING SPECIAL PROBLEMS/Wing Washes and Wing Entries.

WIRE— An insulated conductor designed to conduct electrical energy.

WIRE SIZES— See AMERICAN WIRE GAUGE.

WIRENUTS— Plastic caps that are internally threaded and are twisted onto electrical conductors to establish electrical contact between them. They come in color-coded sizes and are the common way to "splice" two wires together. Except for low voltage lines, they are not allowed outside of electrical boxes.

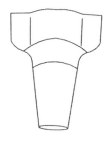

Wirenut

WIREWAY (electrical)— This is an electrical-code word that refers to a non-circular container of conduit wires. In other words, it's not conduit or a conduit variant like EMT but is instead some kind of rectangular metal channel (one side of which usually screws on or off for access). It may also be called an electrical gutter or a raceway. In stage lighting applications, it usually has either female connectors flush mounted on its surface or female connectors on pigtails hanging out one side and would more commonly be called a *plugging channel* or *plug chan* for short.

WIRING DIAGRAM—Any drawing or sketch that assists a technician in wiring up an electrical circuit. There are usually two kinds. A *schematic* drawing is a simplified drawing that uses electrical symbols and is designed to make it easy to understand the current paths. A *component* diagram shows the electrical components with their electrical contact points and is laid out to mimic the actual locations of the components, which makes it easier to do things like count how many conductors have to be run to each location. While the *schematic* is more suited to the design of the circuit, the *component* format is generally easier for the electrician who will wire up the devices.

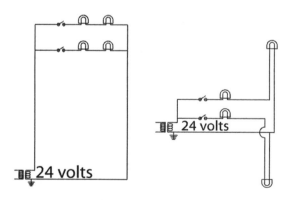

Left: Cuelight schematic; *right:* Cuelight component diagram

WORKING HEIGHT—This refers to the height at which pipes are set for any particular show and is synonymous with *trim height*.

WORKLIGHT—A set of light fixtures used to light the stage during rehearsals or work calls when the stage instruments are not required. They are typically tungsten-halogen floodlights of some type that are operated from the booth and usually several backstage locations by means of on/off (or dimmer) switches. Yardlights or a close relative are commonly used.

WRAP—Short for BLACK WRAP™, which is heavy weight black aluminum foil used for masking light leaks, making mats, etc.

WRENCHES (lighting)—The most common attachment method for instruments is the c-clamp, which has three different sizes of bolts plus whatever is on the yoke of the instrument (hopefully hand knobs or wheels). There are a number of different kinds of wrenches that have been used at one time or another.

8" Crescent Wrench: Sometimes called a *c-wrench*. This is the most commonly used tool because it can be adjusted to fit any size bolt. Sometimes the original c-clamp bolts become lost or bent and are replaced by something almost as good that came from the local hardware store but that has different sized heads. The crescent wrench can adjust to these. However, if it is not adjusted properly, it can slip off the bolt head and cause banged knuckles and perhaps lost balance.

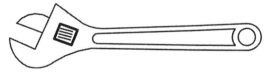

Crescent wrench

Special Lighting Wrenches: There are several lighting wrenches that are supposed to simplify the process. They typically cost less than $10 a piece and typically have a hole corresponding to each size of bolt (making them in effect closed-end wrenches), which eliminates most of the slipping-off-the-bolt problem. If they are very small, they may lack the leverage necessary to loosen a really stub-

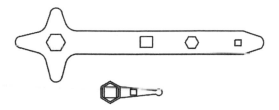

Lighting wrenches

born bolt. If they are more the size of a crescent wrench, the cutout at each end will be the easiest ones to use.

Speed Wrenches: These are closed-end box wrenches that have a ratcheting mechanism at each end. One end typically works on the big bolt on the c-clamp (yoke attaching bolt) and the other end works on the bolt that attaches the c-clamp to the pipe (pipe-attaching bolt). A different speed wrench (or a crescent wrench) would be needed for the small ¼" shaft locking bolt, but this bolt is often deliberately tightened down hard, so that it won't be used.

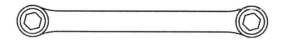

Speed wrench

Alligator Socket™: This is sometimes mentioned as a possible lighting tool. It is a deep socket with a set of 30 or 40 spring-loaded pins inside. When it is pressed against the head of a bolt, some of the pins depress and the rest are left to grip the side of the bolt head — in other words it works on all sizes of

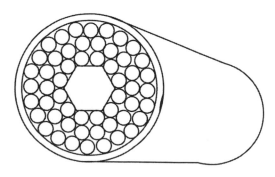

Alligator socket

bolts (¼–¾). It doesn't slip on the bolt heads, and it ratchets using the existing reverse button on a standard socket handle, which is usually easier to work than the speed-wrench system where the wrench has to be flipped over or turned around. It is hard to center it on the square pipe-attaching bolt, even though it works even when not centered, and depending on how the instrument is angled it may be hard to get the deep socket onto the yoke-attaching bolt. Its real problem, however, is that it is a heavy and unbalanced tool and, therefore, tiring to use and carry around. The safety cord is going to attach on the end of the socket handle, but that's the end that it is the most logical end to want to put in one's pocket. There is also no easy way to secure the socket to the handle, short of drilling a hole and inserting a pin. None of that would be insurmountable if the tool actually worked better than say a speed wrench, but it doesn't.

WRITE—(1) In the context of manual or preset lightboards, after a cue had been set or modified, the operator would be told to write it, and there would be a longish wait during which the whole rehearsal would stop while the operator wrote notes to himself about how to recreate the present setting. (2) In the context of a computer lightboard, the machine records cues at the push of a *record* button and *write* refers to *saving* the entire contents of the machine's internal memories onto a disk (or other storage media).

WYE CONNECTION—This is the most common connection method for a three-phase, four-wire system used for an electrical service that provides 208 volts between any two hot legs and produces 120 volts between any of the hot legs and neutral. The alternate method is called a *delta connection* in which the voltage between any two of the hot legs is 240 and the voltage between

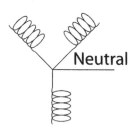

Wye connection

two of the hot legs and neutral is 120 volts, but the voltage between the third hot leg and the neutral is 180–190.

X-RAY— A brand name of early striplight circa 1897 that used silvered glass reflectors. It's name may have been related to the diagonal cross (or "x") of wire that ran across the gel frame to help keep the gel from falling out. The name was used generically for a while to describe any borderlight on the first electric pipe. Now the term is mostly only encountered in vintage books.

YARDLIGHTS— A compact tungsten-halogen floodlight used by homeowners to illuminate their driveways and yards. They are

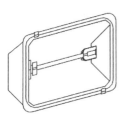

Yardlight

typically about 10" square with a high-temperature removable glass cover and are in the 150–500 watt range. They usually are hardwired to a standard electrical box and can be panned and tilted to point where they are needed. In the theatre, they are typically mounted on a handy box, which is either hooked directly onto a pipe by means of a c-clamp or the handy box is mounted on a short piece of 1 · 3 that is screwed to a wall or a piece of scenery.

YOKE (Brit *trunnion*)— A c-shaped metal strap (part of the instrument housing) that connects at its centerpoint to the c-clamp and at its ends to the cylindrical barrel of the lighting instrument. It permits the instrument to move up and down (*tilt*), and it permits the instrument to swing from side-to-side (*pan*).

YOKE ATTACHMENT BOLT— This is the ½–13 hex head bolt (usually an inch long) that attaches the c-clamp to the yoke of the instrument.

YOKE CLAMP— This was a vintage method of attaching the instrument yoke to a pipe. It was a two-part, two-bolt device that

required that the electrician support the weight of the instrument for a longer period of time, whereas a modern c-clamp transfers the weight as soon as the instrument is hooked onto the pipe.

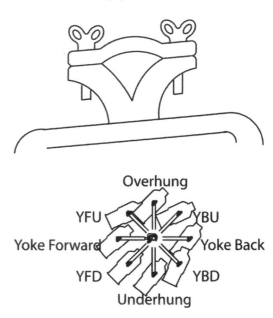

Top: Yoke clamp; *bottom:* Yoking

YOKING— Having very little to do with the yoke at all, it controls the way the c-clamp is attached to the pipe in those situations where the light pipe is fixed in place and will not rotate (i.e. grids, box-booms and such). The normal or default position (the one that gravity favors) is called *underhung* (UH). When the instrument is instead hung above the pipe (yoke points up), this is called *overhung* (OH). Where the instrument yoke points forward, it is called *yoke forward* (YF) and where the instrument yoke points backwards (away from the aim-point), it is called *yoke back* (YB). The intermediate points are usually called YFU (*yoke forward up* 45 degrees), YFD (*yoke forward down* 45 degrees), and YBU (*yoke back up* 45 degrees) and YBD (*yoke back down* 45 degrees). This makes a total of eight possible positions for discussion purposes, although it is obvious that there are in fact many possible steps in-between. One thing that should be noted is that when using the yoke back positions, one has to be careful that the light does not hit the support pipe and cause a shadow of it to appear onstage.

The reason for needing to yoke is usually described as getting more (or less) distance or getting a better angle. Neither of these is usually a significant factor as the distance gained or lost is usually less than 2 feet and the angle gained or loss is usually well below 4 degrees. Yoking is most commonly done to get light over a scenery piece that has been tied tightly against the grid, to miss some obstruction in the light path or to put up to four instruments in the same 6–8" location on the pipe, as the c-clamps are only about 1.5 inches wide and by rotating the lights at least four of them can essentially be located in the same place. On double-decker sets, where the actors' heads may be within a few feet of the lighting instruments, the instruments are typically overhung so that their lenses are above the grid, which makes the headroom look more spacious.

Yoking is a two-handed activity where one hand has to support the weight of the instrument as the other hand tightens the pipe-attaching bolt. Usually the pipe-attaching bolt is already finger tight, so even if one hand were to slip, the instrument would not slip off the support pipe.

Yoking is not possible on light pipes and trapezes that are suspended on rope or wirerope. Sometimes sidearms are attached to the support pipe and lashed to the support ropes in an attempt to prevent the pipe from rotating. This usually works only in the sense that it reduces the amount of rotation, but even a little rotation is unacceptable because it will throw off the focus of every instrument on the pipe. As a general rule, when working with suspended pipes, all the instrument accessories (barndoors, tophats, etc) are put in place loosely and the instruments are pointed in the correct general direction (pre-focused) and all the cabling is put in place (everything done that might affect the center of gravity of the pipe) before the c-clamps are locked down tightly.

Line-sets in a proscenium house are typically a foot apart. If the instruments stick out upstage or downstage as they often do, then they may very well disable adjacent line-sets. If a different hanging angle is needed, a much better plan would be to use the next closest line-sets front or back at a lower or higher trim height and underhang all the instruments. If the two additional line-sets have no circuits of their own (they usually won't), then instruments hung on them would need to plug-into the circuits that are on the main electric pipe, and then all two or three pipes would need to be lowered or raised (when that was necessary) as a group. If other line-sets are not available, one could suspend trapezes below the existing light pipe or one could (with somewhat more effort) attach an additional pipe above the existing light pipe (attached to the support ropes or wires) all raised and lowered by the same line-set. Trapezes are obviously easier, but the plugging channels are typically above the pipe, so putting another pipe above the plugging channel allows direct plugging without the need for additional jumper cables, and this is sometimes the smartest method to use.

ZEBRA CORD (BRITISH: *banded cable*)— A bundle of cords or cables taped together at intervals of about 12" usually by white masking tape (hence the name). A zebra cord is typically run to the tech table in the house containing all the necessary wires to hook up the lightboard, headsets, supply AC power, and so forth. When the bundle is not needed anymore, it can be easily pulled apart and cleaned of tape. There are now some commercially made products designed for computer users to bundle and hide their cords that involve split plastic tubing or plastic spirals that could be used to achieve the same objective.

ZERO COUNT— In the context of executing a light cue, it means as fast as possible. When this relates to a blackout, it replaces the older term *switch out*, and a zero count blackout on a computer lightboard approximates the old-time practice of pulling open the knife switch.

ZERO TOLERANCE METHOD (of integrating the lights)— A method of integrating the lights into the show that involves stopping every time they are not the way they should be. See INTEGRATING THE LIGHTS for a more detailed discussion.

ZIP CORD— A colloquial name for LAMP CORD commonly used on household appliances. In the theatre, it is commonly used for low voltage cuelights or as speaker wire.

ZONES— Another name for ROWS (of areas).

ZOOM or ZOOM LENS INSTRUMENTS— See LIGHTING INSTRUMENTS/Lensed Instruments/Zoom Ellipsoidals.

BIBLIOGRAPHY

Belasco, David. *The Theatre Through Its Stage Door*. New York: Harper & Brothers Publishers, 1919.

Bellman, Willard F. *Lighting the Stage: Art and Practice* (2nd ed.). New York: Harper and Row, 1974.

Bentham, Frederick. *The Art of Stage Lighting* (2nd ed.). New York: Theatre Arts Books, 1976.

Bergman, Gosta M. *Lighting in the Theatre*. Stockholm: Almqvist & Wiksell Intl., 1977. This is a history of stage lighting from medieval times up until about 1950. It is almost 400 pages long and its author drew upon original material written in Italian, French, German, English and Swedish. Almost all historical material that can be found elsewhere is mentioned here.

Bongar, Emmet. *The Theatre Student: Practical Stage Lighting*. New York: Richard Rosen Press Inc, 1971.

Boulanger, Norman C. and Warren C. Lounsbury. *Theatre Lighting from A–Z*. Seattle: University of Washington Press, 1992.

Bowman, Wayne. *Modern Theatre Lighting*. New York: Harper & Brothers, 1957.

Carpenter, Mark. *Basic Stage Lighting*. Sydney: University of New South Wales, 1996.

Corry, P. *Lighting the Stage*. London: Pitman Publishing Corporation, 1954.

Cunningham, Glen. *Stage Lighting Revealed*. Cincinnati: Betterway Books, 1993.

Essig, Linda. *Lighting and the Design Idea*. Harcourt Brace College Publishers, 1997.

Fitt, Brian. *A–Z of Lighting Terms*. Focal Press, 1999.

Frazer, Neil. *Lighting and Sound*. New York: Schirmer Books, 1989.

Fuchs, Theodore. *Stage Lighting*. Benjamin Blom Inc., 1963.

General Electric Company. *Light and Color*. GE Bulletin, TP-119, General Electric Company, 1978.

Gillette, J. Michael. *Designing with Light* (2nd ed.). Mountain View, CA: Mayfield Publishing Company, 1989.

Hartmann, Louis. *Theatre Lighting*. New York: Drama Book Specialists, 1970.

Hays, David. *Light on the Subject* (3rd ed.). New York: Limelight Editions, 1992.

Hood, W. Edmund. *Practical Handbook of Stage Lighting and Sound*. Tab Books Inc. 1981.

Illuminating Engineering Society. *IES Lighting Handbook*. New York, 1947.

Illuminating Engineering Society. *History of Stage Lighting* with foreword by John H. Kliegl, January 1956.

Luckiesh, Matthew. *Color and Its Application*. New York: D. Van Nostrand Company Inc., 1927.

McCandless, Stanley. *A Method of Lighting the Stage* (3rd ed.). New York: Theatre Arts Books, 1953.

McCandless, Stanley. *A Syllabus of Stage Lighting*. New Haven, 1953.

Miller, James Hull. *Stage Lighting in the Boondocks*. Arthur Meriwether Inc., 1981.

Morgan, Nigel H. *Stage Lighting for Theatre Designers*. Heinemann, 1995.

Mumm, Robert C. *Photometrics Handbook* (2nd ed.). Louisville: Broadway Press, 1997.

Newberry, W. G. *Handbook for Riggers* (rev. ed.). Canada: Newberry Investments, 1977.

Ost, Geoffrey. *Stage Lighting*. London: Herbert Jenkins, 1954.

Palmer, Richard H. *The Lighting Art, The Aesthetics of Stage Lighting Design*. New Jersey: Prentice-Hall Inc., 1985. Very authoritative on the workings of the eye and optical and color effects. He demonstrates how to compose a lighting score that will express the meaning of the play complete with examples.

Parker, W. Oren and Harvey K. Smith. *Scene Design and Stage Lighting* (3rd ed.). New York: Holt Rinehart and Winston Inc., 1974.

Pilbrow, Richard. *Stage Lighting* (rev. ed.). New York: Drama Book Publishers, 1991.

Rainwater, Clarence. *Light and Color*. Racine, WA: Western Publishing Company, 1971.

Reid, Francis. *The Stage Lighting Handbook* (4th ed.). New York: Theatre Arts Books/Routledge, 1992.

Ridge, Harold C. and F. S. Aldred. *Stage Lighting, Principles and Practice*. London: Sir Isaac Pitman & Sons Ltd., 1945.

Rubin, Joel E. and Leland H. Watson. *Theatrical Lighting Practice*. New York: Theatre Arts Books, 1966.

Seldon, Samuel and Hunton D. Sellman. *Stage Scenery and Lighting*. New York: F. S. Crofts & Co, 1934.

Sellman, Hunton D. *Essentials of Stage Lighting*. New Jersey: Prentice-Hall Inc., 1972.

Shelley, Steven Louis. *A Practical Guide to Stage Lighting*. Focal Press, 1999.

Sobel, Michael I. *Color*. Chicago, IL: University of Chicago Press, 1987.

Strand Electric. *A Completely New Glossary of Technical Theatrical Terms*. London: Strand Electric and Engineering Co. Ltd., 1947.

Streader, Tim and John A. Williams. *Create Your Own Stage Lighting*. Prentice-Hall Inc., 1985.

Sylvania, *Lighting Handbook*.

Vasey, John. *Concert Sound and Lighting Systems*. Boston: Focal Press, 1989.

Walters, Graham. *Stage Lighting Step-by-Step*. Betterway Books, 1997.

Wehlburg, Albert F. *Theatre Lighting: An Illustrated Glossary*. New York: Drama Book Specialists 1975.

ENCYCLOPEDIA OF
STAGE LIGHTING